O'NEILL

LIFE WITH MONTE CRISTO

ARTHUR AND BARBARA GELB

O'Neill (left) in his first produced play, *Bound East for Cardiff*, presented in Provincetown, Massachusetts, July 28, 1916.

O'NEILL

LIFE WITH MONTE CRISTO

ARTHUR AND BARBARA GELB

APPLAUSE
NEW YORK • LONDON

An APPLAUSE Original

O'NEILL: LIFE WITH MONTE CRISTO

Copyright © 2000 by Arthur and Barbara Gelb
All rights reserved

Publisher and Editor:	Glenn Young
Line Editor:	Glenn Young
Interior Design:	Greg Collins
Indexer:	Shelby Coleman
Production Director:	Paul Sugarman
Publicity Director:	Kay Radtke

Library of Congress Cataloging-in-Publication Data
Library of Congress Card Number: 00-102548

British Library Cataloging-in-Publication Data
A catalogue record for this book is available from the British Library.

ISBN: US & Canada: 0-399-14609-1

This APPLAUSE title is distributed to the trade by Penguin Putnam Inc:
1-800-847-5515

For all other APPLAUSE titles, please contact:
1-800-524-4425

APPLAUSE BOOKS
1841 Broadway
Suite 1100
New York, NY 10023
ph: 212-765-7880
fax: 212-765-7875

To the memory of Fannie and Daniel Gelb
who made the writing of our book possible

CONTENTS

INTRODUCTION
O'NEILL REVISITED

Stephen Spender, the British poet, critic and novelist, expressed astonishment when we told him we were rewriting from beginning to end our biography of Eugene O'Neill, which had been in print for thirty-two years. "No biographer ever does that," pronounced Sir Stephen, at a small dinner party in his honor on October 25, 1994 at the New York Public Library. "That would be tantamount to admitting he didn't get it right the first time; it would be acknowledging that the original biography was less than the final word on the subject." (Amending his remark, he said he did know of one — only one — such author, Michael Holroyd, who rewrote his biography of Lytton Strachey.)

Somewhat ruefully, we had to admit that we did not, in fact, get it absolutely right the first time, and we explained why we felt fortunate to be able to take another crack at it — this time as a three-volume work.

There were reasons aplenty:

In 1956 when we embarked on our original research a scant three years after O'Neill's death, we were both barely out of our twenties. Although we had been passionate theatergoers and ardent admirers of O'Neill since adolescence, and had written extensively about the theater for The New York Times and other publications, we were too young, really, to tackle such a complex subject.

But the just-published, posthumous *Long Day's Journey Into Night* promised to be a fascinating window on the author's life and we simply couldn't resist. We were particularly struck by the fact that O'Neill was that exceptional biographical anomaly, a major literary figure whose life — despite his stature as America's only Nobel Prize-winning playwright — had never been comprehensively documented.

We marvel now at the artless audacity with which we undertook our search, innocent of what the biographer, Justin Kaplan, had to say about writing biography: " . . . you need ox-like endurance, resignation to the swift passing of time without much to show for it, and the capacity to feed on your own blood when other sources run dry . . . The work doesn't get easier as you go along from book to book. You may have acquired narrative and stylistic skills, a little bit of confidence, and some understanding of what makes people and biographies tick, but at the same time your standards go up and you demand more and more of yourself."

All too true, as we have come to realize. As biographers, we now have a different sensibility than when we began our seminal research. We have changed, along with the world. And we do, unquestionably, demand more of ourselves. Furthermore, a giant of the theater like O'Neill, whose plays are revived constantly, deserves to be reexamined and reevaluated in the light of the ever-changing cultural climate.

As the parents of grown children (not to mention grandparents of four), we are now more in sympathy with the concerns of O'Neill's own parents. While conducting our original research between 1956 and 1962 we tended to identify with the rebellious O'Neill and his "misunderstood" older brother, Jamie, and were sometimes impatient with what we believed to be James and Ella O'Neill's insensitivity toward their sons.

Over the years, attending the many revivals and reinterpretations of O'Neill's plays, and tracking the emergence of previously unknown details of his life and work, we found ourselves viewing him with what we hope is a more mature balance.

Because O'Neill was such an intensely personal writer, a biographer can go on endlessly probing the sources of his imagination, trying to unravel the process of his creativity, discovering in his plays new clues to his character — and discovering in his character new clues to his plays.

While we now have a clearer idea of the O'Neill family dynamics, we are still haunted, even these many years later, by at least one fundamental question: Was O'Neill a wounded and melancholy figure because of his parents? Or did he use and exaggerate his parents' difficulties to explain (not to say justify) his tragic view of life?

Of course, had O'Neill not been the ruthless, prolific innovator whose vision gave birth to the modern American theater, our fascination with him would long since have flagged. His great power as a writer lies in his unflinching honesty; exposure to his conjured world is a personal catharsis, for he has the often disquieting genius to reveal you to yourself. Even after studying him for so many years, we still find him to be full of significant surprises — one of the rewards of this revisit.

Our early start did give us unprecedented access to an essential source — O'Neill's widow, Carlotta Monterey, at that time in her late sixties and still in rude health — as well as to some five hundred relatives and friends. A number who were acquainted with O'Neill's famous actor-father, his shy and aloof mother and his alcoholic older brother were in their seventies and eighties, and even beyond. Almost all of these elderly interview subjects were to expire within the next few years, some within weeks of our talking with them.

Among them was a 90-year-old O'Neill cousin, Lillian Brennan, institutionalized in Connecticut with senile dementia and out of touch with the present, but able to relive scenes from the late 1800's and early 1900's, in which she evoked vivid images of O'Neill's mother.

Another was Joseph McCarthy, whom we tracked down in the Veterans Hospital in upstate Bath, New York. Although still alert at 72, he was suffering from the after effects of tuberculosis and a paralyzing stroke that ended his life not long after our interview. McCarthy had been Eugene's roommate for two years at the Catholic boarding school where Eugene was sent at the age of seven.

At yet another hospital in New York we found a former seaman, James Joseph Martin, nicknamed "Slim," who, it turned out, knew a side of O'Neill few others did. Slim, once an itinerant construction worker, sometimes helped build sets for the experimental theater that presented O'Neill's early one-acters on its tiny Greenwich Village stage. It was their shared seafaring experiences that had endeared Slim to O'Neill.

Before we could interview Slim — who, like McCarthy, was recovering from tuberculosis — we had to spring him from the locked psychiatric ward where he was confined because he was considered "violently alcoholic." When we found him, he was sober, perfectly tractable and bored. After we arranged to have his eyeglasses returned to him, he agreed to set down his well-remembered conversations with O'Neill, which we collected on visits to him over a period of months.

As with Slim, we encouraged all our interview subjects to hold forth with little or no prompting. We believe that the basis of good biography is exhaustive research and, as experienced journalists, we knew how easy it was to lead interviewees into supporting preconceived conclusions of one's own. Memory is tricky enough as it is; most recollections about past events are subjective and have to be evaluated as such.

"How can you know history?" asked Mark Helprin in his novel, *Memoir from Antproof Case.* "You can only imagine it. Anchored though you may be in fact and document, to write a history is to write a novel with checkpoints, for you must subject the real and absolute truth, too wide and varied for any but God to comprehend, to the idiosyncratic constraints of your own understanding.

"A 'definitive' history," Helprin observed, "is only one in which someone has succeeded not in recreating the past but in casting it according to his own lights, in *defining* it. Even the most vivid portrayal must be full of sorrow, for it illuminates the darkness of memory with mere flashes and sparks, and what the past begs for is not a few bright pictures but complete reconstitution. Short of that, you can only follow the golden threads, and they are always magnificently tangled."

Part of the tangle for a biographer is that several witnesses to the same event will each provide a different slant, in some cases furnishing "facts" that are exaggerated or even invented. We found one such example in the dramatically differing accounts of how O'Neill was "discovered" by the Provincetown Players in the summer of 1916. In our new work, we can do no more than give all the versions, which we are now able to enhance with our extended research.

The downside of our early start in 1956 was that we could gain only limited access to much of the archival material we knew existed. Although able for our earlier biography to draw upon hundreds of letters held by various individuals and by universities, many others were unavailable, as were texts of O'Neill's abandoned plays, his work diaries, notes and scenarios, and Carlotta Monterey O'Neill's diary.

Much of this material, deposited at Yale University's Beinecke Library, was kept strictly under wraps on orders from Mrs. O'Neill, and Yale did not begin lifting its restrictions until after her death in 1970 (eight years after our original biography was published).

As her husband's heir and literary executor, she was possessive and fiercely protective of his, as well as her own, legends — and not always entirely rational in her management decisions. It was only through the good graces of Brooks Atkinson, one of the few critics O'Neill respected, and who continued to befriend Carlotta after O'Neill's death, that she agreed to talk to us. Over a period of five years, she told us, often with amazing candor, about her life with O'Neill. But she was capricious — to put it mildly — about what we could and could not see at Yale.

We were at a disadvantage also in having to tiptoe around aspects of O'Neill's relationships with a number of people still living — not only his contentious widow, but also his two previous wives. We could not, for instance, present as forthrightly as we would have wished the circumstances of the out-of-wedlock pregnancy of Kathleen Jenkins, whom he married reluctantly.

When we interviewed her during the conservative — not to say restrictive — social climate of the 1950's, this discreet, twice-married elderly woman was concerned about being ostracized by her proper neighbors in the small Long Island suburb where she had settled. It was at Kathleen's urgent request that we agreed to "protect" her reputation by tempering our account.

While we did, on the other hand, write at some length about O'Neill's vitriolic divorce from his second wife, Agnes Boulton, we were not in possession of the details we have now amassed (including his accusation that she stole and sold some of his papers).

Moreover, we did not have the complete picture of Carlotta's bold betrayal of O'Neill's wishes in releasing *Long Day's Journey Into Night* three years after his death — rather than withholding it for the twenty-five years that O'Neill specified.

Although Carlotta told us — giving various contradictory reasons — that O'Neill had lifted the interdiction not long before his death, we have found nothing to support her claim. On the contrary, the new evidence indicates that he never changed his mind. The full documentation to support the chain of events that led to Carlotta's action was not, however, available to researchers at the time.

O'Neill's publisher, Bennett Cerf, of Random House, was skittish about giving us the full details during Carlotta's lifetime. But Cerf's widow, Phyllis, has now given us access to the complete Cerf correspondence file. And with the availability of O'Neill's work diary and Carlotta's own diary, we have at last been able to fully document the story.

All three wives are now gone, as are O'Neill's three children, as well as the close friends who gave us their confidential recollections;

some of these friends, fearing Carlotta's vengeance, asked that certain pieces of information be withheld until some future time. That time has now come, and much of this material has been incorporated into our new biography. In several instances, following publication of our first book, friends of O'Neill sent us memories that had been jogged by anecdotes in the original book. One such account, by a member of the family O'Neill boarded with while attending a playwriting class at Harvard, vividly described his unpredictable behavior during his months at Cambridge.

One research source that was most tantalizingly dangled out of our reach was a notable cache of sixty love letters and thirty poems written by O'Neill between July 22, 1914 and July 25, 1916 to the 20-year-old Beatrice Ashe, with whom he began a headlong love affair in New London that continued throughout his Harvard stay.

We interviewed Beatrice during the summer we spent in New London in 1957, where we had taken a house with our young children to seek out the local people who had known the O'Neill family during the more than thirty summers they had spent there. But she would do no more than hint at the extent of the passionate vows she exchanged with O'Neill, and would not show us the letters she had kept, and presumably treasured, for more than forty years. She was planning, she said, to write her own book about the relationship. She never did; and it was not until shortly before her death in 1974 that she sold the letters and poems to the New York Public Library.

A biography of O'Neill that fails to document comprehensively this frenzied love affair is incomplete, for these letters flesh out O'Neill, the Olympian observer of human frailty and blundering passion, casting him as an all-too-human victim of his own needy, uncontrollable and often adolescent emotions. O'Neill's relations with Beatrice, as well as with the women who succeeded her in his affections, reflect his conflicted feelings for his mother, as, indeed, do the depictions in his plays of the female psyche — a concept that these letters now allow us to reinterpret and enlarge upon.

Although the New York Public Library is one among many institutions that contain collections of O'Neill documents and other relevant material, it is the Beinecke Library that has provided the richest lode. In this long-restricted material we have found revealing aspects of O'Neill's progression in his major works, from original concept to final draft.

It was astonishing to discover, for example, that O'Neill's early list of the characters who inhabit Harry Hope's saloon, in which *The*

Iceman Cometh is set — most of them based on people he had known in his days of drunken dereliction — did not include the salesman, Hickey. The play's pivotal role appears to have been something of an afterthought.

In his early notes, O'Neill attributed parts of Hickey's messianic message to the play's daytime bartender, who evolved as Chuck Morello. At that point O'Neill was calling the bartender by his real name, John Bull, and he listed the saloon's proprietor as the real-life saloon keeper, Tom Wallace (renaming him Harry Hope in the final version). After noting that Wallace "has never left the place since wife's funeral," O'Neill wrote that it is Bull who encourages him "to get out of house."

Similarly — Hickey not yet having been conceived — it is Bull who, in this incipient concept of the play, prods the down-and-out former war correspondent, nicknamed Jimmy Tomorrow, to prove to himself he can "make Tomorrow come true."

And then there are the work notes and the early drafts of O'Neill's changing attitudes toward the members of the Tyrone family in *Long Day's Journey Into Night*. In his first draft, for instance, he depicted a family far more embittered, vituperative and denunciatory of each other than in the final version.

Also made available, too late for our original biography, is the so-called "Work Diary" kept by O'Neill from January 1, 1924 — the day he "Got idea for *Desire Under the Elms*" — through May 4, 1943, when he noted the 33rd birthday of his oldest son, Eugene Jr. He made an entry, sometimes consisting of only two or three words, almost every day during those nineteen years, noting not only the precise moment he conceived of a play idea and the progress (or lack thereof) he was making on each act, but how he viewed productions of his plays, the state of his physical and emotional health, and all manner of routine activity in his daily life.

In one entry, for example, he curtly but significantly chronicled the struggle he made toward the end of 1925 to give up drinking. On December 28, when living with his second wife on a wooded estate in Ridgefield, Connecticut, he wrote: "Worked in woods — read — tapering off — 5 [drinks] today."

Two days later he had only one drink and wrote, "Feel much better but nerves shot all to hell." Adding that he had to go to New York for rehearsals of his new play, *The Great God Brown*, he wrote, "Must get in shape." On December 31, he noted: "On wagon. Good'bye — without regret — 1925 . . . " And on January 1, his entry read:

"Welcome to a new dawn, I pray!"

He did not, in fact, succeed until 1929 in conquering the alcoholism that had nearly killed him in his twenties. This struggle is an aspect of his life we have examined in considerably greater detail in our new biography; we simply did not have the analytic acumen forty years ago to delve into the pervasive significance of alcohol in O'Neill's life (or for that matter in the lives of an astonishing number of American writers, whose careers were affected by alcohol).

An invaluable item that we were unable to include in our 1962 biography is an extraordinary, one-page self-analysis, handwritten in a minute script that O'Neill obviously hoped would be all but indecipherable to an outside eye (which it is). The document was found among the papers of O'Neill's second wife after her death on November 25, 1968.

Although undated, it was probably written when O'Neill was 38 and undergoing an abbreviated psychoanalysis. In a series of stream-of-consciousness phrases, he described his shifting emotions — from infancy through early childhood — toward his parents: the dominating, poverty-fearing matinee-idol father, whose theater of melodrama and bombast Eugene was bent on overturning; and his lovely, defeated, morphine-addicted mother, whose neglect of him he tried to understand but could never fully forgive.

In this raw, compressed and highly charged outpouring can be discerned the germ of an outline for *Long Day's Journey Into Night* (which he was not to write until thirteen years later). While we are not the first to draw upon the document, we believe we are the first to weave its various revelations meaningfully into the narrative, thus supporting some of our prior suppositions and conclusions about O'Neill's family relationships.

Inevitably, during the last forty years or so, countless studies of O'Neill's plays have been published, along with chronicles of his life and times. Many used our early biography as a guide, and some surpassed segments of our own research, elaborated on our early discoveries and caught us in errors. We are pleased to have pointed the way for them (and not displeased now to correct *their* errors).

Essential to our new research are the additional letters that have surfaced over the years (such as those to Beatrice Ashe), crammed with personal revelation. These include letters from O'Neill to all three of his children: Eugene O'Neill Jr., the son from his forced marriage to his first wife, as well as to Shane and Oona, the offspring of his second marriage. Although initially concerned and loving, this group of letters serves to underscore O'Neill's ultimate callousness toward his children.

The letters are among those caringly collected by Travis Bogard and Jackson Bryer for *Selected Letters of Eugene O'Neill*, a volume greedily combed by successive O'Neill scholars. Not published until 1988, these 560 letters were culled from the more than 3,000 written during a fifty-year period (a number of them contributed by us and kindly acknowledged by Bogard and Bryer in their work). Not having had access to the complete (or nearly complete) file of letters was a decided obstacle to our early start in 1956.

Included with the previously unknown letters are those that document a brief romance with Marion Welch, an 18-year-old from Hartford, who visited New London in the summer of 1905 when Eugene was 17. It is clear from this innocent and poignant correspondence that Marion served as a part-model for the adolescent Muriel McComber in *Ah, Wilderness!* — a connection unsuspected by O'Neill scholars before 1988.

We had always been well aware that the tragic seeds of O'Neill's most powerfully realized work were sown years before his birth, in the family history that began in Ireland and that culminated in the family's exodus following the Great Famine. But we did not initially have the resources to explore that history fully.

For this rewritten biography, we have managed to discover James O'Neill's birthplace in the obscure rural townland of Tinneranny in Kilkenny, Ireland. Digging more deeply into census reports and with the help of genealogical researchers in Buffalo and Cincinnati, we have accumulated a comprehensive agglomeration of new material that bears directly on the traumatizing early poverty of O'Neill's father. This deprivation profoundly affected James's personal and career decisions and, in turn, influenced the personality and creativity of his son, Eugene.

O'Neill's own most compelling statement of the family tragedy, *Long Day's Journey Into Night*, is permeated with references to James's early life. And yet, not even Eugene himself, profoundly Irish in temperament as he always boasted of being, and fascinated as he was with his own Gaelic history, knew all the facts of his father's family relationships.

If he was aware of his father's actual birthplace (mistakenly believed by earlier chroniclers to have been Thomastown, also in

Kilkenny), he never mentioned it; we had considerable difficulty in pinning it down — which we finally did with the help of dedicated Kilkenny historians, who searched obscure and scattered records dating back to the early 1840's, including church archives, land maps, local newspapers and shipping data.

We were also able to examine, among other details, the coroner's reports filed after the suspicious death in Tinneranny of Eugene's grandfather, Edmund (or Edward) O'Neill, who deserted his family to return to Ireland several years after their arrival in Buffalo, an incident referred to circuitously in *Long Day's Journey*.

Another new discovery was Army pension papers showing that a brother of James O'Neill was fatally wounded in the Civil War; these records enabled us to trace other members of the family, and establish that an Army pension helped to support James's mother, Mary, supplementing what James could provide out of his wages as a young actor.

Of even greater importance, we have come to grasp more clearly the character of O'Neill's mother, Ella Quinlan O'Neill. She has traditionally been portrayed (by us as well as others) as being withdrawn, indifferent and, indeed, outright hostile to her husband's professional life, almost from the moment she married the gregarious and hard-drinking James. This depiction evolved largely because Eugene O'Neill himself viewed her in that light.

But he, of course, did not know her in the early years of her marriage and we have found that Ella's character was far more nuanced. The fact is that she did not really begin to fall apart until after the death of her infant second son, for which she never forgave herself.

At the Fales Library of New York University, a collection of letters and diary entries by an exceptionally astute young actress in James's company, Elizabeth Robins, with whom Ella formed a warm friendship eight years prior to Eugene's birth in 1888, reveal Ella as an affectionate, often spirited friend. Robins depicted her as very much interested in James's business dealings and his backstage life, disclosing that she sometimes served as her husband's dresser, and frequently made casting suggestions; and at least during the first eight years of her marriage, Ella was in some ways more outgoing and eager for social contacts than James.

Other new details are based on extended research in New London, where we found documents that established the actual circumstances and date — given erroneously in previous narratives (including our own) — when the O'Neills moved into the cottage that served as the model for the settings of both *Long Day's Journey Into Night* and *Ah, Wilderness!*

We have newly examined (or reexamined) unpublished material — for example, a memoir by Louise Bryant, wife of John Reed (who wrote *Ten Days That Shook the World*) and with whom O'Neill had a brief but ardent affair shortly before he married Agnes Boulton in 1918.

For this volume we have also revisited our own collection at the University of Texas in Austin to recover bits of conversations with interviewees whose significance had earlier escaped us. And after the publication of our first book, we held further conversations with one of our major sources for O'Neill's life in New London, Arthur McGinley (on whose family O'Neill partly based the Millers of *Ah, Wilderness!*). We recently had the additional assistance of McGinley's nephew, Morgan McGinley, editor of the editorial page of the New London Day, who helped us trace in detail the amusing story of O'Neill's attempt to dodge the draft during World War I.

While we noted much of the source material for our original biography in the text itself, we did not think it necessary to use end notes; we were chided for this omission in academic circles, and we have come to believe the complaint justified. We have more than compensated in this volume.

Still another important reason for our reexamination is that O'Neill's universe has been steadily expanding over the years. New generations, drawn to the honesty, humanity and dramatic boldness of his work, are eagerly attending revivals not only of his final masterworks but of the powerful, experimental plays that made him the most successful (if often controversial) dramatist of the 1920's and 30's. Even from the beginning, he was hailed abroad — from Sweden to the Soviet Union — as a master dramatist of tragedy. Since his death, he has been studied and produced in countries as diverse as Egypt and China. Nanking University has a full-fledged O'Neill curriculum, using his texts translated into Chinese.

In 1971, two of O'Neill's homes became registered national landmarks — one in New London, where he wrote his first plays, and another in Danville, California, where he wrote his final ones. Cared for lovingly, both serve as museums and active centers for O'Neill scholars and drama students. To track the latest O'Neill scholarship there are The Eugene O'Neill Review and The Eugene O'Neill Society.

It has been a special pleasure to participate in both panel and informal discussions with the directors and casts who have staged O'Neill's work. No one was as spiritually in tune with O'Neill's vision as José Quintero, the playwright's preeminent interpreter — with whom we began exchanging thoughts soon after his watershed off-Broadway revival of *The Iceman Cometh* in 1956 and his presentation that same year of the Broadway première of *Long Day's Journey Into Night*.

As recently as the summer of 1998, a few months before Quintero's death, we attended his lecture to students at New York University, in which — still contagiously passionate about his subject — he greatly enhanced our understanding of O'Neill's use of religious symbolism in *A Moon for the Misbegotten*. Perhaps only a lapsed Catholic like himself could so clearly have analyzed the contradictions inherent in O'Neill's anticlericalism and the enduring cultural grip of his Catholic heritage.

We are indebted to Quintero, too, for being the first to crystalize for us how fallacious are the often leveled charges against O'Neill's "unnecessary" use of repetition in his plays. As Quintero pointed out, O'Neill "knew that life is repetitious, but he did not merely echo this fact; he employed repetition to reveal progressively more of his characters and situations. There is a different mood with each repetition, giving it a new meaning, orchestrated as music is orchestrated."

As an illustration, he cited the line in *The Iceman Cometh*, "The kick has gone out of this booze," repeated a half-dozen times, which "moves from exposing the reality of a simple drink to the reality of a life lost." O'Neill, Quintero added, "was too dedicated an artist with too great a sense of purity to use anything, including repetition, as a meaningless, mechanical device."

Some of the fine actors who have appeared in O'Neill's plays have enriched our psychological understanding as well. Most prominent among them is, of course, Jason Robards, the unforgettable Hickey of the 1956 revival of *Iceman*, and the equally memorable originator of the role of the drunk and deteriorating Jamie Tyrone in *Long Day's Journey*. Robards, who went on to star in most of O'Neill's major plays, is as serious a scholar of O'Neill as any academic. He is intimately knowledgeable and articulate about all the roles he has played, and has acutely interpreted the character of Jamie, who, he maintains, "is the kind of drunk I understand."

"He uses drinking to be more drunk than he actually is — he's a two-purpose drunk — the kind who, when he really wants to say something, says it and then covers up as a drunk. He switches back and forth. That's the way I used to drink during the seven years I was in the Navy, and for a while after I got out — when I was 25 and living started getting complicated."

We have discussed at length the character of Mary Tyrone with a number of actresses who have interpreted her. Both Geraldine Fitzgerald and Zoe Caldwell, for example, believed that she was not the helpless victim portrayed by Florence Eldridge (the actress who originated the character on Broadway), but, rather, a manipulative and sometimes vindictive woman well able to hold her own.

At even greater length, we discussed aspects of Josie Hogan's character in *A Moon for the Misbegotten* with our cherished friend, Colleen Dewhurst, the role's quintessential interpreter. And early in 1999, we met with Kevin Spacey, at the time rehearsing the role of Hickey for Broadway, who was eager to exchange analyses of the deluded salesman. Spacey, like Robards before him, had become a tireless O'Neill scholar.

Just as the performances of these actors — inspired and memorable as they have been — will doubtless be matched and perhaps even surpassed in time, we realize that this new evaluation of O'Neill, the man and the artist, comprehensive as we have tried to make it, will not be the final word. O'Neill's ghost is relentless and demanding.

PART ONE

THE PAST IS THE PRESENT

"None of us can help the things
that life has done to us."—

— MARY TYRONE,
*Long Day's Journey
Into Night*

Chapter ONE

In the late spring of 1939, Eugene O'Neill and his wife, Carlotta Monterey, were living in a Chinese-style, white concrete-block house on a 158-acre estate in California. Built on the side of a mountain thirty-five miles east of San Francisco, reachable only by a private road and guarded by electrically-operated gates, it was designed as an ideal, secluded haven where O'Neill planned to spend the balance of his creative life. He and Carlotta had moved in a year and a half earlier.

In his study O'Neill, with habitual precision, had arranged his outlines, scenarios and drafts, as well as the notebooks that accompanied him wherever he lived — the sort he had been cramming with ideas for the future since 1912 when he first began writing plays at the age of twenty-four.

At fifty, O'Neill was at the peak of his artistic power. Despite recent bouts of ill health, he managed to draw on the intellectual resources and physical determination that had sustained him throughout an astoundingly fertile career, and he was at work on a vastly complicated cycle of eleven plays, depicting the 175-year history of an Irish-American family. It was his most ambitious project to date and he expected that it would take several more years to complete. As always, his pencil could scarcely scribble fast enough the epic ideas churning in his mind.

By early June, however, his West Coast Eden was no longer serene. His physical condition — diagnosed some months earlier as Parkinson's disease — was worsening; a gradual breakdown of brain cells caused faulty coordination between nerves and muscles.

While retaining his mental clarity, O'Neill, at ever-more frequent intervals, would lose control of his arms and legs. Reaching for a sheet of paper, his hand flew upward. Attempting to walk forward, he stumbled backward. Trying to clear his throat before speaking, his tongue clove to his palate, his voice emerging as a croak, his words unformed.

He never knew when he would be ambushed. His symptoms varied in intensity, possibly aggravated by emotional stress. Even as a young man his hands had trembled slightly, a trait he believed he had inherited from his mother and which doubtless was exacerbated by the excesses of a derelict, alcoholic youth.

Now his hands had begun to shake severely. He could not set down a creative thought except by pencil, and the tremor made writing difficult. He found it impossible to dictate or to use a typewriter and, to help control the shaking and conserve energy, he formed ever smaller letters. His calligraphy became so cramped that he found himself squeezing a thousand words onto a sheet of paper he had once filled with two hundred. Much of his writing had to be deciphered under a magnifying lens.

Abruptly persuaded that he was running out of time, that crippling illness would forestall his ability to write at all, he set aside the cycle in favor of work that held a compelling personal meaning for him. As he wrote to a friend, he felt "a sudden necessity to write plays I'd wanted to write for a long time that I knew *could be finished*."

On June 6, he noted in his work diary the ideas for two plays. One was *The Iceman Cometh*, a soulful meditation on the most destructive period of his youth, which he completed in December, 1939. The other was the play that would bare the dark family secrets that had shaped his tragic vision: his deeply troubled relationship with his famous actor-father gripped since childhood by a terror of poverty; with his morphine-addicted mother and with his cynical, alcoholic older brother.

O'Neill was wrenchingly aware that in reimagining his family's devastating interaction — husband embattled with wife, mother and father both in bitter conflict with their two sons, brother challenging brother — he had the makings of his greatest work, the play that was to take its place as the monumental American tragedy of the century, *Long Day's Journey Into Night*.

O'Neill believed he had achieved a compassionate detachment that would allow him to expiate the demons of his youth while writing of his parents and brother with understanding and forgiveness. And yet he was uneasy in setting out to betray his family's heretofore hidden life. But there was really no way he could *not* put the story on stage, to portray — as he believed they really were — his parents, brother and himself trapped in an unrelenting dance of death.

His wife, Carlotta, a maternal, protective presence for the past ten years, was helpless to soothe his pain. A dedicated diarist, she noted on June 21, 1939: "Gene talks to me for hours about a play (in his mind) of his mother, his father, his brother and himself (in his early 20's) in New London! (Autobiography). A hot, close, sleepless night — An ache in our hearts for things we can't escape!"

O'Neill had, in fact, been writing disguised versions of his family mythology since the beginning of a career that began off Broadway in 1916 with the one-act sea play, *Bound East for Cardiff* — a career that was firmly launched four years later. It was in 1920, when the commercial American theater was awash in a sea of trivial melodrama and farce, that his *Beyond the Horizon* was staged on Broadway and was instantly hailed by critics as the first authentic American tragedy.

The play won him his first Pulitzer Prize and it was only a year later that The New York Tribune acknowledged the thirty-two-year-old dramatist's rising stature by publishing, under a two-column headline, "Eugene O'Neill's Credo and His Reasons for His Faith," a doctrine that was to govern the whole of his career, and that expressed his view that "the tragic alone" had "that significant beauty which is truth"; it was, he declared, "the meaning of life — and the hope." O'Neill scorned the artificial glibness and hypocrisy that defined traditional Broadway melodrama, in which stick-figure men and women confronted each other with superficial problems and resolved them with equally superficial denouements. These were the sort of plays calculated by commercial producers to send audiences home feeling reassured and smug about their own lives.

O'Neill wanted no part of it. "Most modern plays are concerned with the relation between man and man, but that does not interest me at all," he once said. "I am only interested in the relation between man and God."

He was determined to substitute honest emotions and attitudes as he saw them. He wanted to demonstrate that ordinary men and women, often alienated and inarticulate, ensnared in lethal passions and striving for redemption, could be ennobled by their struggle with destiny. He exhorted audiences to confront a new native genre, defined by realistic plots and naturalistic characters in the grip of mystical forces they could not escape. Hewing to this philosophy, O'Neill went on to revolutionize the American stage. Year after year, he presented plays in which his characters met life head-on, in which they wrestled with societal constrictions and confronted their illusions — usually to succumb to forces they were powerless to control.

He made it his mission to compel the American theater to grow up, to demonstrate that the stage could be as valid and powerful a literary medium as the most revealing of contemporary novels. And under his fierce and unflagging tutelage, the American theater did indeed continue to mature year by year.

As he once explained, he himself did not love life because it was pretty: "Prettiness is only clothes-deep. I am a truer lover than that. I love it naked. There is beauty to me even in its ugliness. In fact, I deny the ugliness entirely, for its vices are often nobler than its virtues, and nearly always closer to a revelation."

Unafraid to grapple with the consequences of incest, uxoricide, matricide, fratricide, infanticide and suicide, he also experimented with masks, wrote serious roles for black actors in an essentially segregated theater, audaciously borrowed the technique of Shakespearean ghosts and asides and even dared to write at Shakespearean length.

Then, in a startling turnaround — after such well-received tragedies as *The Emperor Jones* (1920), *"Anna Christie"* (1921), *The Hairy Ape*, (1922) *Desire Under the Elms*, (1924) *Strange Interlude* (1928) and *Mourning Becomes Electra* (1931) — he ventured into nostalgic comedy with *Ah, Wilderness!*, an homage to the carefree boyhood he wished had been his, and an instant hit on Broadway in 1933.

By that time, he had earned two more Pulitzer Prizes — one for *"Anna Christie"* (the only title he enclosed in quotation marks, presumably because the heroine's real name is Anna Christopherson) and another for *Strange Interlude*. Three years later, he became the first American playwright to achieve the Nobel Prize for Literature and was embraced as Broadway's promethean emblem. His prominence was such that the Marx Brothers were inspired to parody his style in their film, *Animal Crackers*, and Cole Porter to celebrate him in the lyrics of "You're the Top" (along with Toscanini, Fred Astaire and Mickey Mouse).

In 1934, however, O'Neill's *Days Without End* was dismissed by the critics as bleak and sanctimonious. It was in fact an earnest if high-flown and overly-solemn re-evaluation of the Catholic faith that had never ceased to hound him, and O'Neill thought the critics had utterly missed the point; he was stunned and aggrieved by what he called "the barrage of idiotic reviews."

O'Neill and his wife, Carlotta Monterey, in Danville, California, 1940. O'Neill was two years into the writing of *Long Day's Journey Into Night*, completed the following year.

O'Neill and Carlotta at the Martin Beck Theater during a rehearsal for *The Iceman Cometh*, 1946.

Scene from the Broadway première of *Long Day's Journey Into Night*, 1956.
Florence Eldridge and Fredric March (seated) as Mary and James Tyrone. Jason
Robards (right) as Jamie, and Bradford Dillman, as Edmund.

Concluding that audiences were simply "not interested in the modern theater," he jeered at Broadway as "showshop." Deciding to distance himself from the Broadway he had for fourteen years bent to his will, he vowed to withhold production of all future work. It was then that he shut himself away with his wife, evading interviewers eager to learn what might come next. At the time he began writing *The Iceman Cometh* and *Long Day's Journey Into Night*, no new play of O'Neill's had been produced in New York for five and a half years and his reputation as America's titan of the drama was in limbo.

O'Neill at fifty looked ten years older. His dark hair was streaked with white and deeply-cut lines were etched into a lofty forehead. A sparse, gray triangular mustache roofed a mouth at whose corners lurked the hint of an ironic smile. His cheekbones, under the sagging skin, were high and strong. His jaw was still firm, his chin chiseled from granite. He smiled rarely, but when he did it was like the sudden lifting of a fog.

His eyes, set wide apart under heavy brows, illuminated his face. Large, dark, immeasurably deep, they were neither critical nor disconcerting; his gaze was one of profound and gentle searching. An artist who sketched him on two separate occasions described his eyes as "circles of intense darkness" that "one sees in the faded daguerreotypes of Poe." Like Poe, too, the artist observed, "he looks as if he were surrounded by an aura of mysterious sorrow." Nothing shocked him. "To me," he once declared, "there are no good people or bad people but just people."

The California house in which O'Neill had chosen to seclude himself was staffed (until the end of 1941 when America entered World War II) by efficient servants, but the O'Neills saw few people. It was Carlotta's declared avocation to maintain an atmosphere conducive to O'Neill's work. "Orders were," she said, "not even if the house is on fire, he is never to be disturbed."

O'Neill labored on *Long Day's Journey Into Night* every morning, many afternoons, and sometimes in the evenings. Often he wept as he wrote. He slept fitfully, in a room adjoining his study, in a bed converted from a Chinese opium table of carved teak. It was one he had fancied and that Carlotta had bought in San Francisco to accommodate his six-foot frame. Occasionally in the night, he would go to Carlotta's room and talk of the play and of his suffering.

In interviews following her husband's death, she tried to convey

his creative struggle. After eating his breakfast on a tray in his bedroom at 7:30, he shut himself into his study to work until one o'clock.
"He would come out of his study looking gaunt, his eyes red from
weeping. Sometimes he looked ten years older than when he went in
in the morning. For a while he tried to have lunch downstairs with
me.

"But it was very bad, because he would sit there and I knew his
whole mind was on his play — acts, lines, ideas — and he couldn't
talk. I would have to sit there perfectly dumb. I didn't even want to
make a sound with the chair that might disturb him. It made me very
nervous and it made him nervous seeing me sitting there like that.
We decided it would be best for him to have his lunch on a tray,
alone."

O'Neill napped during the early afternoon and then, if the weather was mild, he swam in his pool, from which he had a soothing view
of the valley below. Later in the day he and Carlotta sometimes
walked about the grounds and looked in on the chickens he kept as a
hobby (a wistful recreation of a brief childhood effort at poultry-rais-
ing).

On some days he went back to work until dinner time. In the
evenings he and Carlotta usually sat before their outsize fireplace,
O'Neill reading aloud, most often from Yeats, while his Dalmatian,
Blemie, lay at his feet.

"If he felt gay, he would act something out," Carlotta recalled.
"He could be the worst ham you ever met. But if he was sick, he
would be silent and just sit and think. Sometimes he wouldn't talk all
day long."

O'Neill explained to Carlotta that he had to write the play
because he had "to forgive his family and himself." He held a bone-
deep, biblical belief that the sins of the father were laid upon the children, a concept nowhere articulated with more force than in *Long
Day's Journey Into Night*.

O'Neill's focus for the play was the eventful summer of 1912
when, about to turn twenty-four, he was pulled up short by a frightening (if short-lived) attack of tuberculosis. It also marked a crucial
stage in his mother's chronic morphine addiction and a time when
his father was forced to confront the fading career that had soared
during the late 19th century.

James O'Neill, in his son's view, was a man crippled by the fear
of the poorhouse that had been implanted in childhood by the Irish
famine. This fear had not only fatally obstructed his artistic develop-

ment but had stunted him as husband and parent.

O'Neill viewed his convent-educated and seemingly fragile, drug-dependent mother as crushed by life's calamities but nevertheless a woman both manipulative and formidable in her helplessness.

As for his often malicious older brother, James Jr. (or Jamie as he was known), O'Neill saw him as emotionally hobbled by his parents' blunders, an irredeemable failure at thirty-four, ruthlessly drinking himself to death.

O'Neill was equally unsparing of himself, acknowledging that he had been resentful and alienated, wrecking his health with defiant juvenile adventuring and taking refuge in the nihilism of Nietzsche.

Long Day's Journey Into Night, while not literal autobiography, in many ways does mirror the characters and events of that vividly recalled summer of 1912. It is, in fact, set in a replica of the living room of his parents' vacation home in New London, Connecticut. To heighten the tragedy, O'Neill condensed the action to a single day in August.

Steeped in Gaelic history, O'Neill named the family Tyrone, after a county in Ulster once ruled by the great O'Neill clan. He chose not to disguise the given names of his father and brother, but naming the mother proved more complex. Christened Mary Ellen Quinlan, but known since her marriage as Ella Quinlan O'Neill, in the play she is called Mary Cavan Tyrone (Cavan being another county in Ulster).

He bestowed on himself the name Edmund, the most symbolic in the play, borrowed from a brother who had died in infancy before O'Neill was born. Destined to be always "a little in love with death," O'Neill morbidly designated the dead infant as Eugene.

All four Tyrones are skilled (as were the O'Neills) in the perverse game of love-hate, with its cycles of punishment and forgiveness: the husband alternately excoriating and pardoning his wife for her addiction; the wife taunting him for his Irish-peasant parsimony and barroom carousing, then wearily forgiving him with the lament, "None of us can help the things that life has done to us."

The game is perpetuated by the sons in a sometimes vicious sibling rivalry that inevitably subsides into lachrymose reconciliation. Their father, after repeatedly berating them for ingratitude, re-embraces them with the rueful acknowledgment, "a poor thing, but mine own."

In revealing what he held to be the truth, the artistic, if not in every detail the precise truth, about his own heritage, O'Neill was, in effect, justifying himself to the world for being the son of his father.

"Facts are facts," he emphasized early in his career, "but the truth is beyond and outside them."

A year into the writing of the play, O'Neill summed up his satisfaction with what he had variously thought of calling *A Long Day's Journey, Diary Of A Day's Journey* and *The Long Day's Journey*: " . . . a day in which things occur which evoke the whole past of the family and reveal every aspect of its interrelationships. A deeply tragic play, but without any violent dramatic action. At the final curtain, there they still are, trapped within each other by the past, each guilty and at the same time innocent, scorning, loving, pitying each other, understanding and yet not understanding at all, forgiving but still doomed never to be able to forget."

What O'Neill did not mention was that by play's end no member of the household is sober. James and his two sons have been drinking all day while Mary has been poisoning herself with morphine. Even the housemaid, the fifth member of the cast, has imbibed enough to loosen her tongue (and the offstage cook has been plied with whiskey, as well). An inspired O'Neill has been dosing his characters with the truth serum that will force them to reveal both their strangled love and their naked hostility.

In fact, in one of his notes he referred to the play's progressively "shifting alliances in battle" among the father, mother and sons and even thought of giving it a bellicose title: *The Long Day's Insurrection*. It is hard to imagine a family more furiously embattled, more avid to wound, than the four Tyrones. But in his first draft, O'Neill presented a family even more embittered, vituperative and denunciatory of each other.

From this draft, as well as from his work notes and early scenario, it is apparent that as he continued to revise the play he achieved a perspective that had at first eluded him. In addition to deleting some of the more openly vicious accusations, he tempered the dialogue to soften the characterizations. In some instances, no doubt, he made the changes purely for dramatic balance. But he appears to have made others as he gradually came to a more compassionate understanding of his family's fated torment.

It was not until March 30, 1941 that O'Neill finished "going over" the typescript of what he described as "second & I think final draft." On that date, he noted, " — like this play better than any I have ever written — does most with the least — a quiet play! — and a great one,

I believe." He appears to have made one final addition two days later: a revelatory speech for James Tyrone in Act IV.

By then, all but spent from the effort, he told Carlotta, "Well, thank God, that's finished." In his inscription of the typescript he gave Carlotta on their twelfth wedding anniversary that July, he wrote it was her love that had enabled him to face his dead at last and write the play "with deep pity and understanding and forgiveness for all the four haunted Tyrones."

Although sublimely confident of the play's sweep and power, O'Neill knew he did not want it presented during his lifetime nor did he inform his long-time Broadway producers, the Theater Guild, of its existence.

"There are good reasons in the play itself," O'Neill wrote to his friend, the critic, George Jean Nathan, "why I'm keeping this one very much to myself, as you will appreciate when you read it." Two weeks later he confided to Nathan, "I'm not even having it copyrighted so it won't be on record anywhere."

On November 29, 1945, O'Neill consigned the sealed manuscript to his publisher's safe at Random House, stipulating it be kept from the public until twenty-five years after his death. A second sealed manuscript was sent to the O'Neill collection at Yale.

While O'Neill's true reason for insisting that the play be withheld will probably never be known, one possible explanation is the overarching egotism of the artist: a fear that the play, if released without distance, would be judged as mere confessional autobiography, rather than a pure work of art.

O'Neill completed only two more works after *Long Day's Journey Into Night* — the one-act *Hughie* in 1942 and *A Moon for the Misbegotten*, finished in 1943. By then, at fifty-five, illness had robbed him utterly of the ability to work.

"The worst part . . . in the bad spells," he explained to Lawrence Langner, a co-director of the Theater Guild, "is the inner shakes which are so much harder to take than the outer — when you feel it inside all over your body until even your brain seems to do the shimmy."

O'Neill had become a semi-invalid. In despair over all the work he would never finish, he began to vent his frustration on Carlotta, and she fought back. They battled with increasing intensity.

Early in 1946, the Theater Guild was still unaware of the existence of *Long Day's Journey Into Night*. Knowing, however, that O'Neill had completed other new works, the Guild began coaxing him to release them. With the war ended, the Guild believed it was the right time to reestablish O'Neill's voice on Broadway.

At first O'Neill refused. A Broadway production would not only again risk his reputation in the "showshop" but would further erode his precarious health. Finally, however, he was persuaded to release one play — *The Iceman Cometh*. With profound misgivings, he left California for New York, accompanied by an equally apprehensive Carlotta, to oversee casting and rehearsals.

Because *The Iceman Cometh* marked the first production in a dozen years of a new O'Neill play, let alone the reemergence into public view of its reclusive author, newspapers and magazines made much of the event, gleefully quoting O'Neill on his generally pessimistic world view.

During rehearsals O'Neill, as was his wont, strenuously resisted the Guild's appeals to cut the play; and he found fault with some members of the cast, as well as with the director.

The Iceman Cometh opened on Broadway October 9, 1946 to mostly respectful and, in some cases, laudatory reviews, but many of the critics, even those who praised it, complained that it was excessively long and repetitious; like his earlier *Strange Interlude* and *Mourning Becomes Electra*, the production required a dinner intermission. The play had an unspectacular run of 136 performances, partly attributable to the fact that in an atmosphere of postwar optimism Broadway audiences were not in a mood for literary tragedy.

O'Neill was stung by the failure of his once-loyal public to respond to the power of what he knew was a masterful work. And when, early the following year, the Theater Guild's flawed production of his final play, *A Moon for the Misbegotten*, closed during its out-of-town tryout, he felt himself to have been mortally wounded.

Only another writer of O'Neill's stature could have understood the severity of the blow. Experiencing a similar period of rejection, Tennessee Williams told an interviewer in 1981: "I'm very conscious of my decline in popularity, but I don't permit it to stop me because I have the example of so many playwrights before me. I know the dreadful notices Ibsen got. And O'Neill — he had to *die* to make *Moon* successful." It is true that *A Moon for the Misbegotten* remained grievously undervalued for more than twenty years after O'Neill's death, until it underwent a resurrection on Broadway that wrung from it every last tragic, cathartic drop and finally garnered its merited acclaim as a major work of the American theater.

Suffering under his twin disappointments, O'Neill foresaw the final withering of his reputation. Gloomily, he fled New York with Carlotta, as he had in 1934 after the failure of *Days Without End*. This time, however, it was to await his death in a seclusion that was almost absolute, on the rocky coast of Marblehead in Massachusetts.

By now, Carlotta was herself ailing. She could no longer summon the boundless resilience with which she had dedicated her life to O'Neill's nurture and comfort; her nerves tattered, she had lost the vitality to focus on his needs or sympathize with his temperament. Their self-imposed exile, unsurprisingly, was anything but tranquil. Dejected over his progressive frailty and unable to release the torrents of his imagination through writing, O'Neill seemed bent on wrenching what drama he could from his domestic life.

The suicide of his older son, Eugene Jr., in September of 1950, plunged him into an even deeper gloom, and he and Carlotta fell into an ever-more destructive ritual of punishment and forgiveness that seemed almost consciously to mimic the scenes of battle between James and Mary Tyrone. It was not long before the discord between O'Neill and Carlotta erupted into a humiliating public episode of marital warfare, during which O'Neill attempted to have Carlotta certified as "an insane person" and have her consigned to the care of a legal guardian. She countered with a petition for separate maintenance, charging O'Neill with "cruel and abusive treatment."

Both actions were eventually dropped, but while they were pending, O'Neill's friends, including his publisher and producers, tried to remove him from what they considered Carlotta's suffocating, if not malevolent, control (thereby invoking her eternal hatred). In the end, however, O'Neill made it clear he wanted no one but his wife to attend him. After negotiating a wary peace, he submitted himself to her stern protectiveness, clinging to her with the last of his feeble endurance.

Shortly before his death, he presented Carlotta with yet another typescript of *Long Day's Journey Into Night*. He addressed it to his "beloved wife" and, in handwriting that had grown infinitesimal, he wrote: " . . . wife, friend, helper & lover . . . I have loved you for 23 years now, Darling, and now that I am old and can work no more, I love you more than ever!"

In a hotel suite in Boston, Carlotta nursed her husband during the grueling final months of his illness, a martyrdom O'Neill rewarded by willing to her the sole control of his estate.

Carlotta Monterey O'Neill, after her husband's death on November 27, 1953, took stock of her situation as the widow and heir of America's only Nobel Prize dramatist. Depleted and brimming with self-pity, she spent the next two years poring over (and editing) the daily diaries she had kept since her elopement with O'Neill in 1928, reacquainting herself with the dozens of manuscripts O'Neill had devotedly inscribed to her, and rereading the ardent love letters and poems he had written to her.

It was in the early spring of 1955, that Carlotta made up her mind to publish *Long Day's Journey Into Night*. As is all too often the case with the literary departed, O'Neill's mandate was cavalierly disregarded and the play was published and produced in 1956, a scant three years after he died.

Carlotta told anyone who asked that O'Neill had initially stipulated that publication be withheld to spare the feelings of his cherished older son, who would not have wished to see the secrets of his grandparents' troubled marriage laid bare. Eugene Jr. was one of the trusted few to whom O'Neill had shown the manuscript; in an entry in his work diary he wrote that his son was "greatly moved, which pleases me a lot."

With Eugene Jr.'s suicide in 1950, however, Carlotta insisted that the reason for withholding the play had ceased to exist. In this instance, her argument is negated by a letter dictated by O'Neill to his publisher, Bennett Cerf, at Random House, nine months *after* Eugene Jr.'s death, in which he thanked Cerf for returning various manuscripts and notes he had requested, and emphatically reiterated his earlier instructions to the firm:

"No, I do not want *Long Day's Journey Into Night*," he wrote. "That, as you know, is to be published twenty-five years after my death — but never produced as a play."

There is evidence that O'Neill, at a much earlier date and before he made his stipulation, briefly did consider the possibility of a production; he left notes in which he speculated about the running time of a four-act version as against a five-act version. The fact remains, however, that there is no evidence O'Neill, having once imposed his twenty-five-year interdiction, ever lifted the ban.

In her eagerness to justify her release of the play, Carlotta further claimed that O'Neill, not long before his final illness, had made a point of assuring her she need not fear running out of money after his death, for she was to regard *Long Day's Journey Into Night* as her "nest egg."

True or not, it is a typically O'Neillian irony that he might well have remained all but forgotten in his own country if his instructions to withhold the play had been honored. For it was the play's premature release that revived, with full glory, O'Neill's stature. And all because his willful widow chose to contravene his wishes.

In April of 1954, Carlotta had asked Donald C. Gallup, curator of the Collection of American Literature at Yale's Beinecke Library, which housed the bulk of O'Neill's papers, to return the original typescript of *Long Day's Journey Into Night*. "We had been holding [it] sealed, among the materials restricted for twenty-five years," Gallup said.

It was then that Carlotta, having made up her mind to publish the play, approached Random House. After consulting her lawyer, she wrote in her diary on June 20, 1954 that she "rang up Cerf in regard to *L.D.J.I.N.* & sent him a letter of permission to read it! (As if he hadn't done it before! He must think me a most gullible person.)"

Carlotta worried, however, about Cerf's reaction to her instructions to break the seal. And indeed he let her know promptly that he disapproved.

On July 2, Carlotta noted that Cerf had phoned: "He is 'horrified' over *Long Day's Journey Into Night*!? What an uncultured brain for a supposed adult [?] publisher, no wonder his book 'list' is so poor. A harmless person but has not 'grown up' — just the 'punster'!"

Although Cerf had said nothing about wanting to publish the play, she chose to assume that that was what he had in mind. Her diary entry for July 4 read: "I can't allow Random House to publish *Long Day's Journey Into Night* — they haven't the *understanding* or the *feeling* for such a book!"

According to Cerf's account, Carlotta asked him to come to her suite at the Ritz-Carlton in Boston to discuss the publication, but he decided to write to her instead, expressing his dismay:

"Ever since I spoke to you on the phone over the weekend, I have been pacing up and down worrying about *Long Day's Journey Into Night*. Before I come to see you, I think it would be helpful for both you and myself to get my own thoughts down on paper."

Allowing that the play had "some of Gene's most magnificent writing in it," Cerf nevertheless found the portraits of his parents and brother "simply horrifying," and said he could well understand the provision O'Neill had made to withhold publication until twenty-five years after his death.

What purpose, he asked, would be served by this premature publication? The secret morphine addiction of O'Neill's mother, he said, would now be flaunted "to all the world." Even worse, the portrayal of O'Neill's father was, in Cerf's opinion, "so awful" that it would prompt "thousands of people" to say "'How could any man write that way about his own father?'"

Cerf conceded that Carlotta had the legal right to have the play published and said that if she felt "strongly enough" about it he would set aside his own objections and accommodate her — with certain provisos "for the protection of our Random House name."

He then proceeded to list them, surely aware they would infuriate Carlotta: an "explicit statement" setting forth her precise reasons for overruling the twenty-five year stipulation "set down by Gene himself"; authorization "not only to give the statement to the newspapers, but to include it in the edition of the book itself."

Mercilessly pressing his point, Cerf went on to say that while Carlotta might be indifferent to how her action was viewed, he "would resent very strongly any possible insinuation that we had published this play now either for purposes of getting publicity or making a profit on the project." Cerf ended with a half-hearted apology for sounding "harsh and uncompromising."

Needless to say, Carlotta — having recently told Cerf, "I am O'Neill" — did not accede to his terms. On July 9, she wrote in her diary: "Receive the most astounding letter from Cerf! Write him in reply — & then think better of it!" Instead, she sent Cerf's letter, together with her unmailed reply, to her lawyer, Robert Meserve. "Cerf will *have* to give up L.D.J.I.N.," she wrote.

A month later, she took a sly slap at him in a letter to Brooks Atkinson, the drama critic of The New York Times, whom O'Neill had admired. While complaining to Atkinson that Random House had allowed its set of O'Neill's plays to go out of print, she inadvertently confirmed Cerf's implication that profit was at least partly her motive for wishing to publish Long Day's Journey Into Night.

The unavailability of O'Neill's plays, she told Atkinson, had curtailed her income because if the books were not to be had in the stores, "the would-be purchaser gives up his effort of owning O'Neill's works — and *Mrs.* O'Neill eats less — so to speak!"

Late in 1955 Carlotta left Boston and moved to the Lowell, a serene, elegant hotel on New York's upper East Side, where she and O'Neill had stayed briefly many years earlier. On November 27, she again wrote to Atkinson: "Two years ago today — at this hour — Gene was dying! Will I ever be able to free myself from this man —

and the love I felt for him!"

Spiritual captive though she declared herself to be, Carlotta felt sufficiently empowered to give the manuscript of *Long Day's Journey Into Night* to the Yale University Press, which, evincing none of the qualms voiced by Cerf, published the play in February of 1956; it became the best-selling book in its history. (Carlotta deeded the income from American and Canadian publication to the Yale Library for upkeep of its Eugene O'Neill Collection and for scholarships at the Yale Drama School.)

Even before publication, however, Carlotta had decided to test the waters by granting permission for an initial staging of the play in Stockholm by Sweden's Royal Dramatic Theater, which had a long history of popular O'Neill productions (including *The Iceman Cometh* in 1947). In June of 1955, Carlotta had written to Karl Ragnar Gierow, the theater's director: "A few weeks before my husband died he dictated a long list of things he *wanted* done and *not* done. But, under *no* circumstances was [*Long Day's Journey*] to be produced in the theater in this country. And he gave me the reason why." (Carlotta in her letter did not specify "the reason why.")

The Royal Dramatic Theater presented the world première of *Long Day's Journey Into Night* (as translated into Swedish) on February 10, 1956 (which, coincidentally, was the same month it was published in the United States) and word of its triumph in Stockholm was not long in reaching New York.

In 1956, the off-Broadway theater was in the early fervor of a renaissance. A new wave of quixotic novices descended on Greenwich Village in search of any cheap space that could serve as an experimental arena — much as had been the case forty years earlier when a newly-formed off-Broadway group called the Provincetown Players provided the young Eugene O'Neill with his first crude stage off Washington Square.

Radically departing from the slick productions of Broadway, the downtown idealists of the 1950's made do with sketchy sets and costumes, concentrating on the often tentative work of untested writers, and also on re-imagined revivals of plays they believed had never been produced with their authors' intended vision.

Many of the actors, as in the days of the Provincetown Players, were singular but as yet undiscovered talents. The audiences, themselves mostly young, were stalwart theatergoers willing to sit on unpadded chairs or backless benches. Anyone who participated in those fledgling days of off-Broadway understood that here was truly a case of the play's the thing.

Centered in this creative cauldron was the Circle in the Square at 5 Sheridan Square, with only 199 seats ranged along three sides of a small, open stage. Audiences felt an intimacy with the action and, if an actor stumbled, he could literally fall into the lap of a viewer in the front row. Actors quickly realized they could not hide behind the sort of tricks and mannerisms possible on a proscenium stage and, if they wanted to survive, they were forced to develop a style of absolute honesty.

Indeed, they could have done no less under their relatively inexperienced but intuitive director, José Quintero. With an equally unseasoned but stagestruck business manager, Theodore Mann, the Circle had begun presenting plays on a shoestring in 1952. Following the productions of several works that failed, Quintero was inspired to reexamine Tennessee Williams's *Summer and Smoke* and the delicacy of his approach gained the rapturous attention of Brooks Atkinson. The revival, which opened on May 24, 1952, enjoyed a long run and made a star of the luminous Geraldine Page.

Early in 1956, Quintero sought Carlotta's permission to revive *The Iceman Cometh*. The fact that it had vanished from Broadway after a relatively short run ten years earlier was a reason in itself. And the realistically bleak setting that belied the play's complexities of theme and action were challenges that the 32-year-old Quintero was eager to confront on the minimally adorned, open stage of the Circle in the Square.

Quintero, in view of his achievement with the Williams revival, did not doubt that he could obtain the rights to *The Iceman Cometh*. He was by now aware through news reports of both the published *Long Day's Journey Into Night* and the acclaimed Swedish production, but it did not occur to him, neophyte that he was, to put himself forward as that play's American director.

After seeking Brooks Atkinson's advice, Carlotta invited Quintero to visit her on March 15 and, according to both their accounts, they hit it off at once. Quintero was dazzled by her.

Much courted and thrice-married before she met O'Neill, Carlotta had been accustomed to adulation and luxury. A former actress renowned for her glamour, she was, at sixty-eight, still vital and magnetic, if decidedly mercurial.

Her hair, now steel-gray, was thick and silky and brushed straight back. Her face, pale and nearly unlined, was devoid of makeup, and she habitually wore tinted glasses that concealed the deep shadows under her eyes. While little trace remained of her once-famous beauty, she had not lost her supremely regal bearing. Her voice was theatrical and magnificently self-assured. Always known for her immaculate grooming, she now dressed only in black — the expensively-tailored, dramatic black of resolute and wealthy widowhood.

Carlotta, for her part, was charmed by Quintero and it is easy to understand why. Despite his Panamanian heritage and Spanish accent, he bore an uncanny resemblance to the moody and intense Irishman whom Carlotta had married. Like O'Neill, Quintero was slim, dark and handsome and his piercing, deep-brown eyes reminded Carlotta of her husband's.

Quintero was also hypersensitive, recklessly self-dramatizing and as volatile as Carlotta herself. She astonished Quintero by almost at once regaling him with intimate details of her life with O'Neill, to which he responded with awed empathy. Their meeting concluded with Carlotta giving Quintero the rights to *Iceman*. "I trust you. I like you," she said.

Daringly casting against type, Quintero chose an unknown, 35-year old actor named Jason Robards Jr. for the pivotal role of the 50-year-old Hickey. Quintero recalled many years later the cataclysm engendered by Robards's audition: "Suddenly, my understanding of the depths of the play began to emerge. He knew more about O'Neill than I did. He added texture and I could almost feel it in my hands. I could certainly feel it resonating inside me. Not since *Crime and Punishment* had guilt been so tangible to me."

Robards as Hickey proved to be nothing less than magisterial; his horrifying transformation from manic salesman to fanatical purveyor of death left audiences awestruck.

The unorthodox open staging created an intimacy not only with Hickey but with all of the play's disintegrating barroom characters. The audience was so close to the stage that a patron in the front row once reached out and touched Robards. "I guess he wanted to make sure I was real," the actor recalled. O'Neill's tragic intent was at last fully realized. The play's underlying message, that hope, however forlorn, is the essence of survival proved to be timelier and far more intelligible than had been the case with the stiff proscenium staging of the original in 1946. As Quintero later noted, "Passion for life is what makes man invent the pipe dreams that keep him from dying." What was at last clear to audiences, Quintero said, was that through "the dark journey" of O'Neill's plays, "there is the echo of celebration."

Critics extolled O'Neill, Quintero and Robards, and *The Iceman Cometh* became the surprising off-Broadway success of the season, its author's faith in the play belatedly vindicated. The revival of *Iceman* opened May 8, 1956 and ran for 565 performances, an unusually long engagement for off-Broadway at that time.

Carlotta could feel well-satisfied with the way she had so far manipulated O'Neill's posthumous career (which had, in effect, become her career): within just one year, she had overseen the successful American publication and the overseas triumph of a new O'Neill play, as well as the galvanizing off-Broadway revival of an all-but-forgotten one. As a result, Carlotta was besieged by requests from Broadway producers who were eager to mount the American première of *Long Day's Journey Into Night.*

Among these producers was Alexander H. Cohen, whose offer Carlotta peremptorily (not to say speciously) rejected.

"I regret to have to tell you *Long Day's Journey Into Night* is *not* available for production in this country," she wrote to Cohen on April 7, 1956. "I am carrying out O'Neill's wishes to the letter. He wished me to *publish* this play but *not* allow it to be *produced* by *anyone* under *any* conditions!"

Cohen, of course, knew the play had been produced in Stockholm, and was baffled by the phrase *"anyone* under *any* conditions!" Actually, Carlotta's stated reasons for her high-handed (if admittedly astute) management of the play were many and varied — not to say contradictory. And she soon found that, despite her denial to Cohen, there *were*, after all, conditions under which the play *could* be produced in America — one of those conditions being the opportunity to further enhance her own aura and bank account. Although she lived comfortably, she constantly feared running out of money.

Gratified by the victorious revival of *The Iceman Cometh* and acknowledging Quintero's affinity for O'Neill, she decided to entrust him with the Broadway première of *Long Day's Journey Into Night.* She was confident that, despite the brevity of his career as a director, he somehow could illuminate the magic of O'Neill's demanding tragedy. She gave him O'Neill's wedding ring as a symbol of her faith in him.

Once again, her intuition proved sound. The play, which opened on November 7, 1956, left many of the first-nighters in tears; when the final curtain fell, a stunned silence of nearly a minute seized the audience, as the actors, themselves emotionally drained, paused before returning for their curtain calls. And then — in a day when standing ovations were a rarity — the playgoers sprang to their feet, hailing play and players with thunderous bravos. Still wildly applauding, the audience, as if drawn by a magnet, began to surge down the aisles, pressing against the stage apron, seemingly unable to sever themselves from the overwhelming experience through which they had just lived.

The notices were, in the main, ecstatic. Brooks Atkinson, who led the chorus of cheering drama critics, wrote that with the presentation of *Long Day's Journey Into Night*, the American theater had acquired "size and stature." The size, he said, referred to O'Neill's "conception of theater as a form of epic literature." He described the play as "a saga of the damned" that was "horrifying and devastating in a classic tradition."

In his second-thought Sunday column, Atkinson noted the play's distinctively autobiographical derivation, and asked rhetorically how much of an audience's response was governed by this knowledge; his answer was, "Not much, probably," adding that the play stood "on its own feet as an inquiry into pain." While the material was subjective, Atkinson concluded, the method was objective. Nothing O'Neill wrote, said Atkinson, had the "size, perspective, patience and mercy" of *Long Day's Journey Into Night*.

Along with the other New York critics, Atkinson singled out Quintero's insightful direction and the electrifying performances of Fredric March and Jason Robards, as James Tyrone and Jamie; the production certified the Broadway stardom of Robards. Arguably the greatest play written by an American, *Long Day's Journey Into Night* became the unforgettable theater event of the season and brought O'Neill, posthumously, his fourth Pulitzer Prize.

With *Long Day's Journey Into Night* instantly recognized as a universal tragedy, Carlotta found herself not only amply nourished but restored to a role she had foresworn when she assumed that of O'Neill's protector.

She fell into step with her new life, exchanging the reclusiveness in which she had dwelt with her husband for twenty-four years for the flattering attention of directors, producers and actors. But while basking in the glory of O'Neill's resurrection, she seemed burdened with his despair as well. When she talked to friends about O'Neill's torment in writing *Long Day's Journey Into Night*, she appeared to experience no little torment herself. Compulsively twisting her fingers, her eyes would cloud over in pain. In some mystical sense she had, indeed, *become* O'Neill.

More than any other of his works, *Long Day's Journey Into Night* defines O'Neill as a man and an artist. While its premature release violated his wishes, it was a blessing for theater historians. In 1956 O'Neill's hidden family life was still traceable through the recollections of numerous surviving contemporaries. Had the play been buried until 1978 (the specified twenty-five years after O'Neill's death), few would have been alive, and vital information that shed light on the roots of O'Neill's genius would have been forever lost, as would the ultimate key to his tragic outlook in life and in art.

As he himself surely became aware during the creation of this "play of old sorrow, written in tears and blood," it was, after all, his family's legacy that gave him the soul-wrenching vision that inspired him to blaze forth as the greatest of American dramatists.

Chapter
TWO

T HE O'NEILL AND QUINLAN FAMILIES, ALONG WITH MORE
than a million of their countrymen, fled Ireland in the wake of the
potato famine that crested in 1847, wreaking starvation, disease and
death.

The O'Neills settled in Buffalo, a city of thriving commerce in
upstate New York, the Quinlans in the less pressured environs of
New Haven, Connecticut. It was not long before both families
pushed west to the Ohio frontier which beckoned so many in quest
of a better life. Beyond their shared Irish Catholic roots, however,
James O'Neill and Mary Ellen Quinlan grew up with little in common.

James was self-made and proud of it. His wretched, early poverty coupled with an unquestioning faith in his Catholicism, taught
him to be self-reliant, adaptable and pragmatic. He had an ingrained
sense of Irish pride, tested and strengthened in childhood, when he
was obliged to defend himself against American-born Protestants
who despised the immigrant Irish as a threat to their established way
of life.

With no more than a brief sampling of grammar school, yet hun-
gry for knowledge, James, in defiance of the immigrant stereotype,
immersed himself in Irish legend, poetry and drama. Blessed with
arresting good looks and a sunny charm, he bore himself with an air
of confidence. It is not surprising he should have been drawn to and
embraced by the stage, although he later claimed he had become an
actor by pure chance.

Mary Ellen was the pampered daughter of parents who aspired
to middle-class status. Her doting father oversaw her conventionally
strict Catholic upbringing, but also provided her with a higher education and a taste of culture.

Decorous and pious, she leaned toward a spiritual view of life. Unlike James, she was vulnerable and shy, but she could be stubborn when she wanted her own way. Her apparent diffidence was often misconstrued as hauteur and she did not make friends easily.

Mary Ellen was born on Grand Avenue in New Haven on August 13, 1857, not long after her parents, Thomas Joseph and Bridget Lundigan Quinlan, arrived from Tipperary. Thomas was twenty-four and Bridget at least one year older.

Confronting the ever-growing prejudice against the Irish tide that overwhelmed American cities for the fifteen years following the famine, Quinlan struggled to establish himself as a general store-keeper. He found the going difficult, for the country was in the grip of a financial panic. It was soon after the birth of his daughter that he moved his family, including an older son, William Joseph, to Ohio.

While many of their countrymen were streaming to the Far West in pursuit of gold, the Quinlans were attracted to Cleveland, which seemed to offer more immediate opportunities. Although not yet recovered from a state-wide wave of bank failures, Cleveland was a beautiful, lake-port city that promised quick financial recovery. Only a few years earlier, it had been joined by railroad (largely through the labor of Irish immigrants) to Cincinnati, then the largest city in the Midwest.

In Cleveland, Thomas Quinlan became a news dealer and, thanks to the business boom provided by the Civil War, his shop at 204 Superior Avenue began to thrive. By 1867, when Mary Ellen was ten, Quinlan had expanded his business to carry books, stationery, bread, cakes, candies and "fancy goods." During the next few years, through judicious investment in real estate and increased patronage of his shop, he became a man of substance and an upstanding member of Saint Bridget's Parish. He consistently encouraged his children's religious commitment in an era when "keeping the faith" was an unimpeachable parental doctrine and rigorously enforced by parish priests and nuns.

Quinlan enrolled Mary Ellen at the Ursuline Academy on Euclid Avenue near her home, a convent school with exacting religious and academic standards. There the symbols of her faith were a daily presence, none more potent than the statue of the Virgin Mary confronting her each morning in her classroom.

By the time Mary Ellen was thirteen, her father had acquired a partner and had again expanded his business, this time to include the sale of wine, liquor and tobacco. The Quinlan family, now solidly middle-class, moved to an even more respectable, Irish Catholic neighborhood at 208 Woodland Avenue, on the prospering east side of the city.

Quinlan began to accumulate a library and, discovering that Mary Ellen was musically gifted, he purchased a grand piano and arranged lessons for her. He was enlightened enough to give his son and daughter, along with their religious training, all the cultural advantages a newly affluent businessman and devoted father could provide. He wanted them to be independent — William Joseph to succeed him in his business and Mary Ellen to one day supplement her inheritance by playing concerts or perhaps teaching.

As regards Mary Ellen, this might have been wishful thinking. Despite an occasional show of willfulness she seemed ill-equipped to make her own way in life. No trace of the rugged adaptability that had brought her parents from Ireland could be found in her pliant personality or delicate features.

Slender and tall for her generation — five feet six inches — she had pale, smooth skin, large dark-brown eyes, a wide, tremulous mouth, a high forehead and long hair which she often wore knotted on the nape of her neck. In *Long Day's Journey Into Night* her stand-in, Mary Tyrone, laments her once-beautiful hair: "It was a rare shade of reddish brown and so long it came down below my knees."

Mary Ellen, with her quick, shy laugh, her low-pitched voice and her refined tastes, seemed destined to take her place in Cleveland's well-bred Catholic world, probably as the wife of a dependable businessman much like her own father.

Thomas Quinlan made the acquaintance of James O'Neill toward the end of 1871. Quinlan's shop, on Superior Avenue in the heart of Cleveland's business district, was just a block and a half from the city's celebrated Academy of Music, where James was engaged as leading man.

Actors often patronized the shop for cigars and liquor and it was there that Quinlan and James, both gregarious, both fond of their drop, struck up a friendship based on their common Irish heritage, which included their hailing from neighboring counties: Quinlan from Tipperary, James from Kilkenny.

Quinlan, a dedicated theatergoer, relished James's stories of backstage life. Although actors for the most part were outside genteel society it was not unusual for local businessmen to befriend prominent touring stars. Some, like James O'Neill, could boast of patrons in every city, who entertained and occasionally even housed them.

As a girl of fourteen, Mary Ellen met James, then twenty-six, in her father's home. Not long after, she was taken to see James on the stage. She had been to the theater with her father before at discreet intervals and, like her friends, was beguiled by the dashing, itinerant leading men. The handsome James O'Neill, however, fired her imagination as had no other.

Bridget Quinlan, straightlaced and far less genial than her husband, primly disapproved of his friendship with an actor. In *Long Day's Journey Into Night* she is characterized, in Mary Tyrone's words, as "very pious and strict," and that was doubtless why Mary Ellen favored her pampering father. As is true of many mother-daughter relationships, Bridget was jealous of Mary Ellen, and Mary Ellen knew it.

Their conflict forever figured in Ella O'Neill's inventory of complaints, a fact made clear in *Long Day's Journey* when Mary Tyrone irritably parrots her mother's diatribe to her father: "'You've spoiled that girl so, I pity her husband if she ever marries. She'll expect him to give her the moon. She'll never make a good wife.'"

In his notes for the play, O'Neill wrote that Mary felt she "ought to have admired, loved" her mother, "but really held [her] in contempt." James Tyrone shared his wife's feelings, according to an early draft of the play, in which he dismisses his mother-in-law as "an ordinary, common-sense little Irish woman."

Bridget Quinlan was annoyed by her daughter's schoolgirl crush on James, and could only hope it would dissipate when Mary Ellen went off to boarding school.

In early September, 1872, Mary Ellen, at fifteen, was enrolled by her father at St. Mary's Academy, a convent school just west of Notre Dame at South Bend, Indiana. Carrying her dreams with her, she confided to her school friends her thrilling acquaintance with the matinee idol.

Mary Ellen's arrival at St. Mary's coincided with James's departure from Cleveland for McVicker's Stock Company in Chicago. While Mary Ellen may have chattered about him, even imagined herself as his bride, James, if he thought of her at all, could only have remembered her as the sheltered, demure schoolgirl she was. James spent the next four years mostly in Chicago and San Francisco, flitting from one love affair to another.

St. Mary's Academy, founded in 1844 by four valiant French Sisters of the Holy Cross as a frontier school for girls in Michigan, was later moved to the site near the boy's school that was to become Notre Dame. Mary Ellen's father chose the academy in part because of its recently-established music conservatory. Only very well-off families provided their daughters with a higher education, but Quinlan was determined to give both his children every advantage. In 1872, board and basic tuition cost $115 plus an extra $35 for piano instruction.

Less than two months after his daughter arrived at St. Mary's, Quinlan, in failing health at thirty-nine, specified his wishes for his family in an explicit will.

He bequeathed to his wife all his property on condition that she remain unmarried "during the period of her natural life"; to his son, William, he left his "Library of Printed Books" and to Mary Ellen his "One Piano Forte." (Some years after her marriage, she moved this heirloom to her house in New London; it figures as an offstage prop when Mary Tyrone attempts to play it in the climactic scene of *Long Day's Journey Into Night*.)

Quinlan took pains to secure his children's' future in a codicil to his will, which reflected a certain lack of confidence in Bridget: "I devise that my children . . . shall receive at the hands of my wife the same opportunities for education and self improvement, and be supported and clothed and treated as my wife knows and believes they would be treated by me and are treated by me now."

Quinlan concluded with a vigorous admonition that his children "shall use the talents which they possess and the education which they may acquire to earn for themselves, when they arrive at an age proper for them to do so, an honest, honorable and independent livelihood, not relying upon their mother nor upon such share of the property as may descend to each after her demise nor before then." John Brennan, the husband of Bridget's older sister, Elizabeth, to whom she was very close, was listed as the administrator of the estate.

Mary Ellen was registered at St. Mary's as Ella Quinlan, but her classmates and teachers called her Ellen — the Sisters having insisted upon what they deemed the more dignified designation.

She went by the name Ellen until her marriage (as indicated on her marriage certificate), but shortly thereafter she reverted to Ella, the name on her will and most other documents. "Ella" is engraved on her tombstone in St. Mary's Cemetery in New London.

Eugene O'Neill, in giving the mother the name Mary in *Long Day's Journey Into Night* — his own mother's baptismal name — might not have done so for biographical accuracy, as was the case with the names of his father and brother. Presumably, had he wished to identify his mother unequivocally, he would have called the fictitious mother Ella, by which name his own mother was known after her marriage.

Psychiatrists who study literary creativity have speculated that O'Neill, in calling the mother Mary, wished to link his real mother to the Virgin Mary, attempting, perhaps unconsciously, to stress her frustrated desire to have become a nun.

While it did not become an accredited college until 1906, St. Mary's Academy took pride in providing instruction at the college level, and attracted not only Catholic girls but a number of Protestant and Jewish students as well. For her day and background, and despite the secluded environment, Ellen was exposed to an unusual diversity of cultural currents.

One of eleven girls who lived in a spotlessly-maintained, red-brick dormitory, Ellen, eager to please her indulgent father, applied herself to her studies: church history, dogma and catechism, along with English, ethics, rhetoric, philosophy, astronomy, French and courses in the theory and composition of music as well as piano technique.

In *Long Day's Journey Into Night*, Mary Tyrone's contention that she could have become an accomplished pianist is scoffed at by her husband: "The piano playing and her dream of becoming a concert pianist. That was put in her head by the nuns flattering her. She was their pet. They loved her for being so devout. They're innocent women . . . when it comes to the world . . . "

This is a puzzling passage, if read as autobiography. In reality, the nun who taught Ellen Quinlan piano was far from the unworldly woman James Tyrone describes in the play. Her name (alluded to by Mary Tyrone) was Mother Elizabeth Lilly. A convert who did not join the Sisters of the Holy Cross until after she became a widow, Mother Elizabeth was a descendant of Dr. George Arnold, the organist at Winchester Cathedral during the reign of Queen Elizabeth.

Herself a gifted pianist, Mother Elizabeth was educated in Europe and was worldly enough to set the foundation in the early 1850's for the music department at St. Mary's, still in existence more than a hundred years later.

Perhaps, in his fictionalized portrait of his father, O'Neill wished to subtly convey a sense of guilt on the part of James because the touring life he and his wife lived deprived her of the pleasure of playing the piano except at rare intervals.

At school, Ellen practiced faithfully and, in Mother Elizabeth's judgment, was exceptionally talented. Mother Elizabeth also was astute enough to recognize Ellen's tendency toward self-dramatization.

When Ellen declared a wish to become a nun, Mother Elizabeth instinctively knew this was more daydream than conviction and advised her to postpone her decision. Ellen's feelings were hurt but Mother Elizabeth's intuition proved sound. Ellen was married just two years after her graduation.

Toward the end of the second year of Ellen's three-year course of study, on May 25, 1874, she suffered the first trauma of her young life. Her father, only forty-one but weakened by a drinking problem, succumbed to tuberculosis, the condition that had prompted him two years earlier to write his will.

Still grieving for her father, Ellen returned that fall for her final year at St. Mary's. Both her mother and brother attended her graduation in June, 1875, at which, wearing the required white dress with sash, she played Chopin's Polonaise, Op. 22.

Mother Elizabeth, who selected the piece, must have felt supremely confident of Ellen's musical virtuosity, for the polonaise is one of Chopin's most complicated and rarely-performed. It requires a great sense of calm and poise to convey the elegant simplicity of its first part, and calls for superior technical dexterity during the second.

Ellen's recital capped her earlier achievements in music, for which she was awarded a gold medal. She earned additional honors for politeness, neatness, order, amiability and correct observance of the academic rules.

After graduation, and with her father gone, life in Cleveland seemed pallid. Ellen reminded her mother of her father's wishes and Bridget agreed to take her to New York, where she could enroll for advanced studies in music. Bridget was not motivated entirely by maternal indulgence. In New York she would be a two-hour train ride from her only sibling, Elizabeth, who lived with her husband in New London, Connecticut.

Mother and daughter reached Manhattan early in 1876, funded by substantial checks drawn on Quinlan's estate. Ellen had been in New York with her mother for six months when James O'Neill arrived that fall to fill an acting engagement.

Eager to renew her acquaintance with her idol, she persuaded her uncle, John Brennan, to take her to the theater and, afterward, backstage. At nineteen, she still clung to her schoolgirl's daydreams and was already half in love.

"He was handsomer than my wildest dream," Mary Tyrone rhapsodizes in *Long Day's Journey Into Night*, about the meeting that changed her life. "I couldn't take my eyes off him ... "

Almost pedantically precise in most of the play's realistic detail, O'Neill took dramatic license in creating the first meeting between the two lovers. The expository dialogue indicates that the play's Mary was introduced by her father to her future husband during the spring vacation of her senior year at St. Mary's, when she was nearly seventeen.

This of course was not the case in real life, since the future Ella O'Neill had actually met James for the first time in Cleveland when she was fourteen; by the time she was seventeen her father had been dead for a year.

O'Neill appears to have melded his mother's memories of her first girlish encounter with James in Cleveland (at the age of fourteen and in the company of her father) with the second, more meaningful meeting five years later in New York (in the company of her uncle). The emotions expressed by Mary Tyrone in recalling the meeting sound more like those of a marriageable young woman than of a sheltered schoolgirl:

"My father had said we'd go backstage to his dressing room right after the play, and so we did. I was so bashful, all I could do was stammer and blush like a little fool ... I fell in love right then ... I forgot all about becoming a nun or a concert pianist. All I wanted was to be his wife."

In any case, the sparks ignited by the backstage meeting when it did take place, were as transforming as the play's speech conveys. James, now thirty and somewhat jaded in love, was enchanted to see that the schoolgirl he had met five years earlier had grown into an exquisite young woman. He found himself genuinely smitten.

"Your mother was one of the most beautiful girls you could ever see," James Tyrone tells his younger son in *Long Day's Journey Into Night*. "She knew it, too. She was a bit of a rogue and a coquette ... She was bursting with health and high spirits and the love of loving."

Unquestionably, James was captivated by Ellen's beauty and innocence. Winning her represented yet another break with his squalid early background. By the social standards of the day, Ellen should have been unattainable for James, a fact that made the conquest seem even sweeter to his ambitious spirit.

There was, too, the incentive of Ellen's modest financial independence. Her inheritance was almost certainly not a deciding factor, but James was aware of the extent to which it could help smooth their way until he had arrived at the top of his profession.

CHAPTER
THREE

AT THE TIME JAMES O'NEILL FELL IN LOVE WITH ELLEN
Quinlan in 1876, he was regarded by theater cognoscenti as a likely
successor to Edwin Booth, universally acclaimed as the country's
greatest actor.

Beneath James's affable manner lay a single-minded resolve to
rise to the pinnacle of his profession. While none who knew him
would have called him ruthless, he was, nonetheless, capable of
sweeping aside any impediments to his career, real or imagined. He
belonged first and foremost to the theater and devoted himself entirely to wooing his audience.

If there was intoxication in the mass worship he inspired, there
was an emptiness in his personal life. To fill this void he sought the
conviviality of barrooms and kept a bottle in his dressing room, often
draining it in a day.

The drinking, which had little visible effect beyond evoking a
brilliant sparkle in his eyes, never seemed to detract from his performance. On rare occasions he did overindulge, but such episodes grew
fewer as he matured.

To the end of his life, James maintained the noble bearing
acquired during his early days in the theater. At five-feet-eight inches, he was only slightly taller than the willowy Ellen Quinlan, but his
stature was enhanced by an impeccably upright carriage as well as by
the high-heeled boots he wore on stage.

Depicting his father in the guise of James Tyrone, Eugene O'Neill
described "a soldierly quality of head up, chest out, stomach in,
shoulders squared . . . He is by nature and preference a simple, unpretentious man . . . But the actor shows in all his unconscious habits of
speech, movement and gesture."

James O'Neill's black hair curled over a high forehead; his melting, deep-set eyes, brown and intense, regarded the world with candor and could burn with passion. His nose and chin followed classically molded lines; his even white teeth under a black mustache gleamed against a ruddy complexion, and his lilting voice was a caress.

He was self-conscious about his sketchy schooling, a shortcoming shared by most actors of his day. However, his career had obliged him, as it had all the best of his colleagues, to study Shakespeare in depth. His need to understand each passage inside and out — to convey its poetic subtleties and nuances — led to a rich education in itself.

Living on intimate terms with the wit and wisdom of his revered Shakespeare, James could instantly produce offstage the appropriate quotation to suit any occasion. "He quoted Shakespeare like a deacon quotes the Bible," Eugene O'Neill once said. His father constantly recited poetry. "Instead of singing in the bathtub," O'Neill added, "he'd break out into Shakespeare."

James was further broadened by his cross-country touring, which brought him into contact with regional cultures. During his travels he encountered the great stars, about whom he accumulated a repertoire of lively stories. In the Irish tradition of storytelling, he became an entertaining raconteur, bursting with arcane bits of actors' lore and mimicry and invariably attracting an appreciative entourage.

For the stage James taught himself to stride with a buoyant step just short of a swagger, and to gesture with the grandeur required to project to the furthermost reaches of the cavernous playhouses on his itinerary. These attributes, along with the expertise he acquired with a rapier, perfectly suited the extravagant melodramas as well as the Shakespearean productions for which the public evinced an endless appetite.

James also had begun to train his mellifluous voice to resonate in a theater's last rows. He jocularly referred to his voice as "my instrument," having learned the trick of increasing its volume while raising its pitch by only two or three notes.

In this way he could convey fervid emotion without shouting, and set himself apart from those actors who resorted to ranting. His voice, in the years of his ascendancy, was described by one critic as "the best on the American stage," possessing "the gamut and quality of the lower notes of an organ."

Higher than any critic's praise was that of his fellow actors; David Perkins, who became a member of James's company in 1899, spoke of his vocal dexterity with awe: "When he whispered, his voice carried to the last rows of the balcony."

As James himself once described his voice, "It was a tenor at the beginning. I was my own instructor. I worked it out in my room, never had a lesson in vocal culture in my life."

The theater then equaled in popularity that of motion pictures of the 1930's and 1940's (before the advent of television). There was scarcely an American city that did not support a stock company (a resident repertory ensemble), with the larger cities sustaining two or more.

These companies developed their own favorite performers, and in the major cities, most notably New York, San Francisco and Chicago, such actors often attained local star status. Custom dictated that these provincial stars drop temporarily into supporting roles whenever nationally recognized performers such as Edwin Booth arrived for heralded limited engagements.

At a time when stock-company stars ruled public emotions, James was sighed over and gossiped about. "Chicago adored James O'Neill," read a typical newspaper account. "Girls built romances about his private life, some with substantial foundation . . . One was that the leading lady of McVicker's Stock Company was hopelessly in love with the dashing James and that it grieved him sore not to be able to return her purple passion. Droves of girls went every week just to see the heroine droop and wilt when Jimmy kissed her." In the same vein, Mary Tyrone reminisces in *Long Day's Journey Into Night*, "Women used to wait at the stage door just to see him come out."

James was a boon to stock-company managers, whose prime object was to wrest waves of emotion from their audiences. Attempting to measure the response, some managers sat in the upper boxes and faced the house during a play's initial performances to test what they called the "shock waves" passing from viewer to stage; the play would then be doctored accordingly.

If at last all went as programmed, bursts of applause and cheers would be wrung from the engrossed playgoers. A highly-charged scene often elicited applause so prolonged that the stars had to stop and take repeated bows.

With the promise of a radiant future, James had grown a long way from the buffeted five-year-old who emigrated with his destitute parents from Ireland to Buffalo in the spring of 1851. He was then still wearing the red flannel "skirties" in which Irish peasant women dressed their small children, to prevent them from being abducted by malevolent fairies; and, like the rest of his family, he spoke with an unvarnished Kilkenny brogue. The O'Neills were what F. Scott Fitzgerald, referring to his own forebears, once mockingly described as "strictly potato-famine Irish." James, however, never publicly acknowledged the famine's devastation, preferring to present a romanticized account of his beginnings: "It was Kilkenny — smiling Kilkenny . . . where I was born one opal-tinted day in October, 1847," he wrote for a theater magazine three years before his death in 1920.

Confusion has long reigned over James O'Neill's birthdate, with three different years cited in various interviews, articles and records.

Eugene O'Neill maintained that his father was actually born in 1846. In a 1940 letter correcting a monograph being written about his father, he said that "like all actors he cut his age for publication. Only one year, however."

While this date is supported by a census in Buffalo conducted four years after James's arrival, the accurate date is doubtless the one on his baptismal record in the Roman Catholic church in the district of Rosbercon, County Kilkenny: October 14, 1845. This was also the date provided by his wife on his death certificate in New London.

Of far greater significance than James's two-year slurring of his birthdate, was his failure to note that on the "opal-tinted day" he commemorated, potato fields throughout the south of Ireland had blackened from a wind-born fungus that devastated the countryside with fever and famine. On James's actual birthdate, according to the Kilkenny Journal of October 15, 1845, the disease had already begun to kill the potato crop in Kilkenny.

James O'Neill was often vague about his early history. As he gained fame and became a much-interviewed public figure, he began to embroider and conceal — from all but his immediate family — the harsh facts about the poverty of his formative years.

"My father kept few records of his family or career," Eugene O'Neill wrote to the author of the monograph being written about James, "and most of what he had kept was lost after his death. Nor did he ever go in for much reminiscing about the past."

It was odd that O'Neill should make this comment, considering he had by that time (in June, 1939) outlined the autobiographical details of the play he was then calling The Long Days Journey. His reticence was an indication that he had already determined to guard the play's personal derivation.

On the other hand, some of the information he did reveal to the author of the monograph was inaccurate — that his father was eight, rather than five, upon his arrival in the United States, and that his father had only three sisters, when in fact he had six. The errors were probably not subterfuge, however; either his father did not always inform him correctly about his early life, or O'Neill's memory of what his father did confide had faded.

Outside of his family, James was inclined to imbue life with the gallant optimism and orthodox pride that invariably earned him love and respect.

"I beg leave to think," he ruminated in the same article in which he had trimmed two years from his birth date, "that were I permitted to chose a birthplace for any Irishman's child . . . 'twould be that same little town in old Leinster" (the eastern province of Ireland that includes County Kilkenny). He went on to describe his birth in "the shadow of Strongbow's castle," where he "tumbled and played and crowed lustily with the babes" of his time.

Earl Strongbow was the ruler of Leinster and his clan erected castles throughout the region. Two castle sites associated with Strongbow were situated near James's birthplace in the county's rural townland of Tinneranny (in the district of Rosbercon), on the banks of the Nore River.

James might have been referring to a small tower castle two miles down river, formally known as Mountgarrett. Built on a lofty hill and commanding a panoramic view of two river valleys, the Nore and the Barrow, it was a magnet for local children.

Nearby was also the site of MacMurrough Castle, long fallen into ruin, but still the subject of local lore, for it was thought by historians to have been the home of Strongbow himself and his wife, Aoife, in 1171.

It was in Rosbercon, a valley rich not only in potatoes but also wheat, barley and oats, where James's father, in the years before the blight, toiled as a tenant farmer. He was known as Edmond or Ned (and was sometimes identified in documents as Edmund). His surname was listed in various official records as Neill, Neil or Neile, although the original name had been O'Neill. The practice of omitting the prefix "O'" originally attached to a surname (and standing for "descendant of") was not uncommon in that period.

One theory holds that civil-service bureaucrats, part of the country's Anglo-Irish Protestant establishment, automatically dropped the "O'" when listing names to make them conform to English nomenclature. A second theory is that some Catholics themselves dropped the "O'" to gain the respect of the ruling class and improve their circumstances.

James's father had married his cousin, Mary Neil, who was at least seventeen years his junior and whose parents' farm was believed to be less than a mile away. Intermarriage was not uncommon in that small, insulated area dominated by the O'Neill clan.

Edmond and a relative named William Neill, presumably his brother, shared the operation of a farm they leased from a wealthy Protestant landowner, Lord Richard Tottenham. While the bulk of the crops from local farms were shipped to England and other parts of Europe by the Anglo-Irish landlords under the watchful eye of their agents, the O'Neills managed to keep some produce for themselves and enhanced their diet with salmon from the Nore. They supplemented their income by drawing silt to be used as fertilizer from the bed of the Nore, periodically traveling up and down the river in a small barge, supplying the silt to other farmers.

Like farmers everywhere, Edmond worked long hours in Tinneranny to provide for his family. The hardships he and his neighbors endured were offset, however, by evenings of music and dance and, most particularly, of storytelling. The storytellers were adept in their art, which descended from father to son and was rooted in Homeric tradition.

The tales, recounted around a nocturnal fire, ranged from escapades of ancient Gaelic heroes to cautionary fables about outwitting the Devil and thwarting evil spirits. Not always entirely laudatory, the stories sometimes slyly depicted their protagonists' flaws. Often epic in scope, the narratives could continue for two nights, and the listeners, even when familiar with the oft-told tales, were held rapt by the narrator's skill at conveying emotion and depicting character.

In rural Kilkenny the dancing was often spirited but sometimes, as preferred by the parish priests, it was restrained, with partners holding their arms rigidly to their sides. Bent on suppressing any glimmer of sexuality before marriage, local priests sternly warned that public touching would lead to an "occasion of sin." The Irish mother, perhaps unconsciously extending this proscription and forever mindful of her precarious immortal soul, appeared to have reined in a tendency to be demonstrative with her children.

Irish Catholic children, denied the formal education available to their Protestant counterparts, grew up with scant knowledge of the outside world, save what they learned from small, informal classes in the basic three R's. Ignorant but shrewd, the children learned to rely on their native wit.

Drink was present at most social gatherings, held in the kitchen, which was the largest room of the house. It was the custom to place in the center of the table a large bowl filled with a homemade brew of water, sugar and a powerful potato distillation called poítin, always stored in sufficient supply — and so strong that Kilkennymen were apt to remark that two or three swallows would "knock you into the middle of next week."

With the potato blight, life for much of the Irish peasantry, already harsh, became desperate. Husbands and fathers, themselves beginning to starve and no longer able to feed their families, watched their wives and children, crowded together in barren hovels, fall ill of malnutrition and fever.

Already conditioned by English contempt to think of themselves as inadequate, the famished Irish felt even more worthless as hunger overtook them. Instead of receiving compassion, they were savagely derided by the English, who sneered at them as indolent, diseased and barbaric, and caricatured them in newspapers and pamphlets as brutish and ape-like. Alcoholism proliferated and it is not surprising that those who could scrape up a few shillings escaped into the she-beens, where they could forget their woes in drink — "hiding in the bottle."

With conditions in Kilkenny steadily worsening, Edmond and his family, though better off than many, found it ever more difficult to coax a living from the land. One problem was that part of Edmond's farm was marshland and when the river overflowed during the heavy October rains, soaking the tillable land under three or four feet of water, his crop was wiped out. Helpless in the face of this sort of calamity, Edmond and his fellow farmers could do little more than lament, "The land is cursed!" While life was hard enough for farmers like Edmond, for the thousands who subsisted on potatoes alone the blight was proving deadly.

"They who were in the south of Ireland during the winter of 1846-47 will not readily forget the agony of that period," wrote Anthony Trollope in his 1860 novel, *Castle Richmond*. "For many, many years preceding and up to that time, the increasing swarms of the country had been fed upon the potato, and upon the potato only; and now all at once the potato failed them, and the greater part of eight million human beings were left without food." Trollope did not mention that many tried to survive by eating dogs and rats.

According to one Kilkenny historian, "Hundreds of unemployed had paraded in Kilkenny with placards calling for work or bread. Starvation in 1847 bred violence: that year there were robbery and murder in the county. The Kilkenny Work House, a notoriously bad one, was packed. Typhus, dysentery and cholera took their toll. In 1851 there were four thousand people in the work house."

While the potato had become inedible, such commodities as butter, cheese and bacon produced on the larger farms were designated for export to England and elsewhere. Cartloads of food were callously routed under guard through the very villages where people were starving.

Somehow, Edmond and his family managed to weather the next few years of famine, but finally, in 1851, they felt compelled to join the swelling migration. This was not an easy decision.

By then Edmond was sixty-one and Mary forty-four, the parents of eight children — five girls and three boys — approximately ranging in age from nineteen to three. Between the eldest, a girl named Mary, and the baby, Stasia, were Richard, fifteen; Josephine, fourteen; Anna, thirteen; Adelia, ten; Edward, eight; and James (Eugene O'Neill's father), not yet six.

The prospect of such a tortuous journey with a brood of that size, including four small children, must have caused both Edmond and Mary grave misgivings. While it seems likely the O'Neills, like most of their compatriots, wanted to settle in the United States, they set sail for Canada because it was a British Dominion and the passage cost a third or so less.

In some cases the English underwrote the fare, so eager were they to prevent the wretched Irish — a growing embarrassment if not a burden to the government — from flooding into the mother country. Those who survived the ocean voyage to Canada found comparatively little difficulty in making their way to the United States.

According to descendants of the O'Neills in America, Edmond and his family sailed on a ship they recalled as the "Great India." A three-masted clipper ship named the India did embark from the port of New Ross, just across the river from Tinneranny, in early spring of 1851. Edmond most likely had been lured by an advertisement in the March 19 Kilkenny Journal, which announced that the India, "the splendid and very fast sailing ship," would leave for Quebec on April

1 (although it actually sailed four days later).

"Owing to the few number of persons who landed at Quebec last year," the advertisement continued, "it is expected that Tradesmen and Labourers landing there this Spring will find good demand for their services."

The advertisement's promise of jobs was misleading as, almost certainly, was its boast of ample supplies of "water, breadstuffs and groceries," and the claim that the India would have on board "experienced Surgeons." Conditions on nearly all the vessels — widely known as coffin ships — that transported the hundreds of thousands fleeing starvation were notoriously brutal.

Many passengers slept on the floor in the hold. Neither food nor water lasted the journey, which took an average thirty-five days, depending on weather conditions. Sanitary facilities were non-existent and the stench of excrement was pervasive.

Often, by the time the ship reached port — "Experienced Surgeons" notwithstanding — as many as half the passengers were sick with typhus, or had already died and been heaved overboard. Many more succumbed in the makeshift, overcrowded, understaffed hospitals that awaited them ashore.

Had Edmond known of an account, published the year before in New York, of an 1847 calamitous voyage made by the India, he might not have chanced the crossing. The account detailed an eight-week passage between Liverpool and New York with three-hundred passengers in steerage.

Battered by one vicious storm after another and beset by thirst, hunger and disease, twenty-six aboard, including the captain, were buried at sea. One hundred twenty-three were taken to the hospital, many in a dying state, when the ship docked in New York.

There is no account of the crossing undergone by Edmond's family but it is known that the ship carried four hundred and twenty passengers, twice as many as it was supposed to. The voyage must have been a protracted nightmare that no child could ever forget.

Arriving in Quebec on May 11, the family followed a common route for Irish emigrants: sailing down the St. Lawrence River into Lake Ontario, then crossing into the United States via the Welland Canal and finally arriving in Buffalo. It seems a near-miracle that all ten members of the family survived the odyssey.

In the early 1850's, more than half of Buffalo's Irish lived in the First and Eighth Wards. It was in the Eighth, a little north of the Niagara River, leading into Lake Erie, that Edmond and Mary Neil arrived with their children. Not long after, Edmond became known as Edward, the "O'" was restored to his surname and (arbitrarily, it would seem) a second "l" was added.

The newly designated O'Neills found themselves amidst an impoverished immigrant colony where conditions were scarcely an improvement over life in the old country. Whatever their dreams might have been for a better life, they were quickly dashed. Prejudice followed them to the new world. The Irish in Buffalo were at the bottom of the social ladder, and held the poorest-paying jobs. Many employers tacked up signs candidly announcing, "No Irish need apply." Unsurprisingly, only one in four Irish families owned their own dwelling.

Edward, with no qualifications except as a farmer, worked on the docks, unloading grain from the Lake freighters for shipment to eastern cities by rail. It was the only work available and the pay was meager.

In winter, when the river froze, there was no work at all for the men and Mary, together with those of her daughters who were older than ten, became the family's breadwinners, taking in laundry and mending, and serving as domestics in the houses of Buffalo's wealthy. Before long the O'Neill's had yet another mouth to feed: a sixth girl was born in 1852, bringing the number of children to nine.

The poverty experienced by James O'Neill as a child scarred him unforgettably. Throughout his life he was a victim of this terror, which infected not only his career and his relations with his family but influenced the artistic outlook and career of his son, Eugene.

Families like the O'Neills squeezed their proliferating broods into one-room shanties, which in winter they sometimes shared with chickens and pigs. The animals were their only source of food and, if not brought inside, would have frozen. The men often left their families to seek work elsewhere. In their defeat, they were frequently given to drink and violence. James never forgave the scorn with which the Irish were regarded, not only by the Protestant establishment but by the German Catholic population that had by now achieved relative economic stability.

After five years of struggle, the oldest O'Neill son, Richard, died at twenty. In the midst of the family's grief, Edward, apparently in response to an ethereal summons from his Celtic ancestors, deserted his family and returned to Ireland to live with his twin sister.

How he managed to scrape up money for his passage and whether he planned ever to return to America is a riddle. He was not alone, however, among the recent immigrants to give up on America.

"The Irish Emigrants to America Returning to Ireland," read the headline over a letter published in the Kilkenny Journal in 1857.

"Alas! where can the poor persecuted Irish find a resting place from their sorrows," sighed the letter-writer, a Dr. Cahill, pointing out that within the last month "ships crowded with hundreds of the Irish were about to sail [in this instance from New York], preferring the poverty of their native land and the Irish Poorhouse, and the Irish grave, to the misery felt at this moment in the States of America."

He cautioned his countrymen "that every new draft of adventurers from Ireland will share the fate of their unhappy countrymen there — namely, when their little means are exhausted and their hopes blasted, they must return on the same voyage of grief to the former scenes of their national despair."

When Edward left Buffalo, it fell upon James's surviving brother, Edward Jr., then eleven, and James himself, aged ten, to provide the major support for the family. Young Edward worked in a furniture factory and James in a machine shop.

In *Long Day's Journey Into Night*, James Tyrone states the case differently. Speaking of the period immediately following his father's desertion, he says it fell upon him to support the family: " . . . My two older brothers had moved to other parts. They couldn't help. They were hard put to keep themselves alive."

It is possible that James O'Neill had misinformed his son about Edward Jr. remaining at home following their father's desertion and, for whatever reason, suppressed the fact of Richard's death. It is equally likely, however, that O'Neill chose to twist the facts — as he had in the case of Mary Tyrone's description of her marriage — to heighten the dramatic effect of James's travail as "the man of the family" at such a tender age.

James's father died in Ireland without ever again seeing his wife and children. His "sudden death" in Tinneranny six years later, on July 18, 1862, was held to be "suspicious" and the following day the police requested a coroner be brought in to conduct a postmortem.

He was found to have ingested a "large quantity of arsenic." An inquest held by two magistrates concluded that Edmond, whom they characterized as "a sickly old man," had been "poisoned by eating soda bread" baked by his sister or another member of the household.

The investigators reported they were "perfectly satisfied there was no criminality in the case, as the whole family partook of the bread and were ill." Nevertheless, suspicions lingered and the case was not officially closed until April of the following year.

How and when Mary learned of her husband's death is not known, but in the legal pension document she filed three years later, she stated that her husband died "on or about June 7, 1862."

The bizarre circumstances of his paternal grandfather's death were noted by Eugene O'Neill in a private soul-searching, tightly condensed summary of what he knew (or surmised) of his family background. This singular, self-analytical document, of more than 800 words, written in pencil and crammed onto one side of a sheet of standard typewriter paper, was discovered after O'Neill's death.

Although undated, it may be assumed he wrote it when, at thirty-eight, he underwent an intensive, albeit brief, series of sessions with a psychoanalyst, Dr. Gilbert V. Hamilton.

The summary included the following parenthetical (and somewhat inaccurate) reference to his grandfather: "(He died of poison taken by mistake although there is suspicion of suicide here in fit of insane depression — guilty conscience for desertion [?])"

According to O'Neill's self-analytical document, James himself referred to his father's abandonment. When depressed in his later years, James sometimes spoke "of doing as father did, deserting family, going back to Ireland to die."

O'Neill again referred to this episode when he caused a somewhat inebriated James Tyrone in *Long Day's Journey Into Night* to recall the trauma of his father's desertion. "I hope he's roasting in hell," Tyrone growls to his younger son. "He mistook rat poison for flour, or sugar, or something . . . "

It was after his father's departure that ten-year-old James was seized by a terror of the poorhouse, the demon that was to plague him for the rest of his life. During the seven or eight years that James was growing up in Buffalo, half of the city's poorhouse population was Irish, preponderantly women. Week after week, James saw his mother's friends and neighbors reduced to such abject loss that the poorhouse was their only recourse, and the poorhouse, as often as not, was a sentence of death.

In later years James often reminisced privately about the unspeakable bleakness of his boyhood, attempting to defend himself against his sons' snide attacks on his penury. Eugene remembered his father's efforts at self defense during the writing of *Long Day's Journey Into Night*.

He told Carlotta he had reproduced his father's words almost verbatim in the play:

"It was at home I first learned . . . the fear of the poorhouse . . . Twice we were evicted from the miserable hovel we called home . . . I cried . . . though I tried hard not to, because I was the man of the family. At ten years old! There was no more school for me. I worked twelve hours a day in a machine shop, learning to make files. A dirty barn of a place where rain dripped through the roof, where you roasted in summer, and there was no stove in winter, and your hands got numb with cold, where the only light came through two small filthy windows. And what do you think I got for it? Fifty cents a week! And my poor mother washed and scrubbed for the Yanks by day and my older sister sewed . . . We never had clothes enough to wear, nor enough food to eat."

Publicly, however, James chose to recall his Buffalo childhood with no hint of rancor. "I tried many kinds of work after my father died," he once told an interviewer. "I was a newsboy for one day." He had been hoodwinked into buying a stack of newspapers, only to discover they were a day old; he barely escaped being turned over to a policeman by his first customer. (James professed to find this funny.)

The miserable drudgery in the machine shop described by James Tyrone in *Long Day's Journey Into Night* was casually dismissed by James O'Neill as an "apprenticeship to a machinist."

Waxing positively lyrical, he wrote: "Somehow the clank of iron, the ring of the hammer, the heavy glow of the forge seemed unattuned to the romance of Kilkenny's mossy towers where walked the shadowy ghosts of Congreve, and Bishop Berkeley, of Dean Swift and Farquhar — Irishmen all, who wore their college gowns in and out of the grassy quadrangle of the venerable seat of learning that is Kilkenny's boast."

It is true that not long after Edward O'Neill's desertion the family's fortunes improved somewhat, largely due to the resourcefulness of James's elder sister, Josephine. While still in her early teens she seems to have determined to better herself. Very much her own woman, she became well-read, swiftly shed her brogue and married a well-to-do saloon keeper who lived in Cincinnati.

A four-hour train ride from Cleveland — where the Quinlan family had settled not long since — Cincinnati was the undisputed industrial center of the West. A tradition-bound and somewhat prudish city as well, it did not tolerate red-light districts and prided itself on its temperance movement. The city's refusal to license saloons was the reason Josephine's husband kept his establishment in Covington, Kentucky, just across the Ohio River, also the place where Cincinnatians sought their fleshly pleasures.

Personable enough to have captured five husbands by the time of her death in 1933 at the age of ninety-five, Josephine was also sufficiently strong-minded to become a Methodist (to the horror of her mother). Despite the plethora of husbands, she remained childless, and appears to have taken James temporarily under her wing. Sometime in the late 1850's Josephine sent for her mother and the rest of her siblings.

"And so," continued James in his rosy account of his boyhood, "three or four years went along, careless young years, when spare evenings were spent poring over a Shakespeare given me by an elder sister, or losing myself in the land of romance at the theater where I was an established gallery god."

In 1861, shortly after the beginning of the Civil War, Josephine moved to Norfolk, Virginia, taking with her James, now sixteen. Her husband evidently had changed his trade from saloon keeper to shopkeeper and James found a brother-in-law, doing a brisk business in military uniforms, willing not only to provide him a decent salary but a tutor.

"For three years I worked in the store all day and studied with my tutor in the evening," James recalled. "He was a man of liberal tastes, and, liking the theater, he took me with him twice a week to see the plays. It was then that I formed my taste for the theater. When the war was over my brother-in-law sold out his business and moved back to Cincinnati, and I went with him."

James, now twenty, moved in with his mother, who had been in mourning for Edward Jr. since his recent death in the Civil War on July 18, 1865.

Edward, in August of 1862, had enlisted at eighteen in the 10th Regiment of the Ohio Infantry Volunteers. His mother's main support, he had turned over to her his savings of ninety dollars and sent her his monthly pay. After only two months, he was shot in the upper right arm during the Battle of Perryville (Kentucky) and was discharged with a monthly pension of eight dollars.

In 1864 he re-enlisted, this time giving his mother his savings of three hundred and fifty dollars. A year later he fell in the rain down a slippery hill near his camp at Greensboro, North Carolina, seriously reinjuring his arm, which had to be amputated, and he died four days later at the Post Hospital. His mother was awarded his monthly pension of eight dollars.

James undoubtedly also contributed to her support when he could. "Having saved a little money I tried to go into several small businesses, but was not successful," he recalled. "I found my money going and wondered what I should do."

This was a relatively sober account; some years later he reverted to the sort of creatively colored history he preferred: "I believe I had a subconscious assurance — the promise of a sublime — possibly a ridiculous faith — that I should be an actor one day, although no possibility seemed more remote. However, what's an Irish lad without his dream? And so I carried mine along with me, cherishing it . . . "

Many years earlier, however, in writing to A. M. Palmer, a New York theater manager, James prosaically informed him that he had "drifted to the Stage without interest."

"I was fond enough of the play-house," he wrote, "and had the curiosity, common among boys, to have a peep behind the scenes, so that I took an opportunity to go on as one of the lads in the last act of *The Colleen Bawn*, which was being played at the National."

At that time Cincinnati, known as the "Queen of the West," hummed with musical and theatrical activity. "I began the thing as a lark," James continued, "but the Stage Manager prevailed on me to remain."

That was on October 17, 1867, when James was twenty-two and still living with his mother. One evening, he was playing billiards with a friend next door to the theater when, an hour before curtain time, the man in charge of the numerous walk-on parts, known as supers, rushed into the room.

"What's the matter, Cooper?" asked James's friend. "Confound it," sputtered Cooper, "my supers have gone on strike and there are no guests for the ball in *Colleen Bawn*." "I'll go if you'll go," James and his friend challenged each other in one breath.

James recalled that Cooper eagerly accepted their offer, directed them to find the wardrobe man, and rushed off to find other guests for the scene.

The Colleen Bawn (subtitled *The Brides of Garryowen*), was a comedy written in 1860 by Dion Boucicault and, constantly revived, had made him a millionaire within two years. He had begun spinning broad comedies, as well as swashbuckling melodramas, when only nineteen; himself an Irish immigrant, he aimed his humor at the Irish masses, who found his caricatures of old-country bumpkins and social climbers hilarious.

Boucicault was a principal exponent of the melodramatic theater of the day: lurid, artificial plots in which the heroes inevitably triumphed, virtue was always rewarded and life was portrayed as either a cartoon or an unmitigated idyll.

At his death in 1890, Boucicault left more than 120 plays. He could piece together a script as readily as a carpenter could mend a broken table leg and, in fact, once declared that "playmaking" was "a trade like carpentering." Dismissing the concept of originality, he claimed it was "a quality that never existed," adding (sensibly enough) that "an author cannot exist without progenitors any more than a child can."

Boucicault's hubris was such that he bragged of being "an emperor," stating that in the interest of what he thought "best for Art" he would not hesitate to help himself to the plots or themes of anyone else's novel or play.

"I despoil genius to make the mob worship it," he grandly summed up. And his spoils were, in truth, warmly applauded not only by the Irish but by English and American audiences (if not by critics).

James and his friends were well-acquainted with Boucicault's plays from boyhood, especially his early triumph, *The Corsican Brothers*, adapted in 1852 from the Dumas novel. The Irish in James must have leaped at the chance to participate in any vehicle by the Dublin-born playwright.

James's debut, about which he later gave differing versions, required him to wear a velvet suit with lace ruffles at his wrists. "I did not have a line to say," he recalled thirty-seven years later in a newspaper story that appeared under his own byline, "but there was a scene in which I was the central figure for the moment, though nothing was expected of me except to look the part." In the scene, the leading lady was rejected by the man she loved.

"I had my own ideas of chivalry," said James, "and possibly my high regard and respect for the weaker sex caused me to jump into the breach. Having forgotten for a moment where I was, I said to her: 'I'll take you! He's no good anyway!'" While "the audience howled in sheer joy," the actors were appalled and, as James confessed, "I realized then that I had made a fool of myself."

If, before this event, James had been only halfheartedly interested in a theatrical career, there is little doubt that his first sniff of greasepaint, however foolish his behavior, exhilarated him. From that day on, acting was the only career he could envision.

James stayed on at the National where he was paid twenty-five cents nightly. Soon after he was promoted to captain of the supers and general utility man, and his rising fortunes enabled him to add to his mother's support. It was not long before he achieved a small speaking role, that of The Flying Messenger, in a melodrama called *Metamora*.

The play starred the great Edwin Forrest, the first of the three American actors who — along with Joseph Jefferson and the much younger Edwin Booth — achieved international recognition during the 19th century. Forrest had a powerful physique, a voice like a trumpet, a violent temper and a monumental ego.

His scandalous divorce from the actress, Catherine Sinclair, also helped make Forrest one of the most gossiped-about figures of the American stage. Sinclair brought suit for "cruel and licentious conduct" and won; Forrest countersued for adultery and lost.

For forty years audiences filled theaters to cheer him in Shakespearean roles until, in 1857, rheumatism forced him into semi-retirement. Three years later, though still afflicted, he reemerged briefly, feeling threatened by the ascendancy of Edwin Booth, then only twenty-seven. Booth's father, the volatile and demonstrably deranged actor, Junius Brutus Booth, had been a friend (and sometime rival) of Forrest, and had named Edwin in his honor.

Edwin Booth was now winning acclaim in the same Shakespearean roles that Forrest had long since stamped as his own. With dwindling success, Forrest challenged Booth's climb. Whereas Forrest had once won over audiences with his dazzling bombast, Booth, slight of stature, was now impressing them with an artfully modulated voice and a comparatively restrained, intellectual elegance.

In 1865 Forrest became partly paralyzed, but was advised by his physicians to continue acting in order not to allow the machinery to rust. Sixty years old when James first met him in Cincinnati, Forrest held the stage with the ferocity of a wounded lion.

Metamora, whose hero was a swaggering Indian chief, had been in Forrest's repertory for thirty-six years. Written for him in 1829 by a novice named John Augustus Stone and shrewdly bought by the actor outright, the play earned Forrest a fortune. Still imposing despite his years and infirmity, Forrest was warmly received at the National. James was somewhat overawed at finding himself for the first time supporting so great a star. He strode on stage and promptly forgot his lines.

"It was my first experience in stage fright and my last," he later recalled. He somehow survived this embarrassing lapse and moved on to bigger, if not always better, things. For the next three years he served his apprenticeship, traveling to St. Louis, back to Cincinnati, then to Baltimore, Augusta and Washington. He soon found himself playing such roles as Hotspur and Macbeth — with the incongruous brogue that no one had yet thought to call to his attention.

"My brogue was rich and unadulterated and unadorned," James once remarked. "I played James, King of Scotland to the Queen Elizabeth of Jane Larned, in a play called 'Queen Elizabeth.' A newspaper spoke most pleasantly about me, yet they crushed me with a concluding sentence, 'But young Mr. O'Neill must be reminded that King James was not an Irishman.' Oh, that brogue."

When James again played with Forrest, it was in *Virginius* by Sheridan Knowles, a staple of the road since 1808 and almost as favored a vehicle of the reigning stars as the tragedies of Shakespeare. Set in ancient Rome and written in blank verse, it was regarded as a classic in its day, and had long been in Forrest's repertory.

After a disappointing reception in San Francisco, Forrest, now at the very end of his career, was avoiding the larger cities where he knew he could no longer draw audiences. Heretofore jealous of any actor who displayed genuine talent, as James evidently did in the role of Icilius, Forrest now realized he was hopelessly out of the running and could finally afford to be magnanimous.

He made a comment to his dresser, repeated to James, that made more of an impact than that of any critic:

"That fellow O'Neill will make a capital actor if he ever gets rid of that — brogue." Finally brought up short, James set to work in earnest on the offending dialect.

It was with a stock company in Washington in 1869 that James supported the second of the three great American actors, Joseph Jefferson.

The forty-year-old Jefferson, who had been performing since he was three, brought *Rip Van Winkle* to the capital, and James was cast in the substantial role of the young sailor, Heinrich. Jefferson had made his own dramatization of Washington Irving's story in 1859, but had asked Boucicault to redraft it. It was that version that turned out to be a staple of the road almost up to the time of the actor's death in 1905, forever identified with Jefferson as he was with it.

When Jefferson sent for James at the close of the first performance, the young actor was panic-stricken, certain he was about to be picked apart. However, Jefferson, with a genial smile, waved James to a chair in his dressing room.

"My boy," he said, "you got six rounds of applause tonight, and that is good. Very good. But there are eight rounds in the part and we must get them."

Then the man James later described as "the kindest and finest of men and of actors" listed the places where applause might be elicited, and painstakingly analyzed why it had not been forthcoming. "A lesson in acting money could not have bought," James recalled.

At the next performance, James tried to follow Jefferson's advice, but nervousness caused him to stumble and he received only seven rounds of applause.

"Better, my boy, better," said Jefferson. In subsequent performances, James garnered the full eight.

At the conclusion of Jefferson's engagement, he praised James's acting and encouraged him to study. James was emboldened to request a list of books that would help improve his technique.

"Shakespeare first, for breadth and depth and height of thought and fancy," said Jefferson, "and for insight into human nature read all the standard old comedies."

Although James had already devoted considerable time to Shakespeare and knew some of the plays by heart, Jefferson's advice "unlocked the treasures" of classical drama for him: "Congreve and Farquhar (Kilkenny bred, both) and along down the line to those other Irishmen Goldsmith and his brilliant young disciple Richard Brinsley Sheridan — I devoured them all —and Dion Boucicault too — together with every French and German comedy I could find."

James had been performing for three years when, in September of 1870, he was invited to be leading man at John Ellsler's Academy of Music in Cleveland, then at the height of its fame. At nearly twenty-five, James, in the words of an anonymous critic, had become "The patron saint of the matinee girls."

Acknowledging James's magnetic personality, Ellsler cast him in a variety of romantic roles. Himself a prominent actor, Ellsler had coached Jefferson in the dialect for *Rip Van Winkle*. The Academy, like many theaters of the day, was manorial in its architecture: a three-story, white-brick-and-stone edifice, equipped with a vast stage hung with red plush curtains.

Gas footlights provided the stage lighting, while a massive chandelier illuminated the auditorium; its hundreds of candles were laboriously lit with a long taper every evening from one of the theater's boxes. Many reigning stars made the Academy a regular stop and the Ellslers did a brisk business, charging the customary admission of one dollar for orchestra seats and twenty-five cents for the gallery.

James was now accustomed to play not only the romantic heroes of the era, but every Shakespearean role that was offered. During his first season with the Ellslers he again supported Joseph Jefferson in *Rip Van Winkle*.

In those days, an actor was scorned by his peers if his repertory consisted of fewer than fifty parts; he was expected to be letter-perfect in most of Shakespeare, as well as in numerous contemporary melodramas and farces.

James by now had committed the requisite number to memory, including Othello, Iago, Macbeth, Hamlet, Lear, Romeo, Julius Caesar, Mark Anthony and Richard III. He also had learned to suppress the thicker part of his brogue, although it still tended to escape during impassioned scenes.

His rosy reputation had spread as far west as Chicago, where J. H. McVicker operated his renowned theater, outranked only by Mrs. Drew's Arch Street Theater in Philadelphia and Wallack's in New York. Chicago was still recovering from its great fire of 1871, which had destroyed a third of the city, and the fever of reconstruction served as a stimulus to theatrical activity.

In the fall of 1872 James, with some trepidation, accepted McVicker's proposal to join his stock company. "I was terribly frightened at the idea of being leading man to the great stars of that day," James said. " . . . I told Mr. McVicker my fears and wanted to back out. He insisted on my staying, however, for he said if he could stand the risk surely I ought to be able to."

During the next two years, James shared the stage at McVicker's with a succession of touring stars and had his first taste of being one himself.

CHAPTER
FOUR

THE MOST MEMORABLE EVENT OF JAMES O'NEILL'S CAREER
was the arrival of Edwin Booth at McVicker's early in 1873. Now that
the great Forrest no longer dominated the American stage, Booth had
the field to himself. Forrest had died two years earlier, following a
superhuman farewell tour during which — despite near-crippling
bouts of gout and rheumatism — he traveled seven thousand miles
to play fifty-two cities.

At forty, Booth had become an unparalleled stage presence, the
most exalted American interpreter of Shakespeare. He had assumed
the mantle of not only Forrest, but of his own father, Junius. Slightly
built, Booth wore his dark hair long and his glowing charcoal eyes
shone from a thin, sensitive face. "Booth as a young man was the
handsomest actor I have ever seen on the stage," James in his later
years would tell younger actors. Almost as an invocation, he would
recite the same phrases in praise of his idol: "Booth was the picture of
manly beauty . . . Not only all women, but men, as well, were enthusiastic over his personal charm."

As a boy, Booth was obliged to serve as his father's guardian during his national tours; for while Booth *père* was prodigiously gifted,
he was alcoholic, and his son often had to restrain him during calami-
tously unstable episodes onstage and off.

Shy and taciturn, Edwin found his only friends backstage —
friends all too willing to school him in the bohemian life. He gradually learned, however, to reject what he came to recognize as second-
rate in both plays and players. Venerating Shakespeare as his father
had, he also emulated his parent in his craving for alcohol.

"Before I was eighteen I was a drunkard, at twenty a libertine,"
Booth confessed at twenty-six to his nineteen-year-old bride, Mary
Devlin. "I knew no better. I was born good, I do believe, for there are

sparks of goodness constantly flashing out from among the cinders
. . . I was neglected in my childhood and thrown (really, it now seems
almost purposely) into all sorts of temptations and evil society I
was allowed to roam at large, and at an early age and in a wild and
almost barbarous country, where boys become old men in vice."

Mary Devlin, herself an actress, had been introduced to Booth by
Joseph Jefferson, who with his wife acted as her guardians. At sixteen, while playing Juliet to Booth's Romeo, Mary fell in love with
him, despite his undiminished drinking. After their marriage Mary
quit the stage at Booth's request. When she was only twenty-three in
1864 she was stricken with pneumonia while Booth was on tour.
Unable to sober up in time to reach her deathbed, he was devoured
by guilt and at last gave up drinking. It was in the following year that
his younger brother, John Wilkes, whom he dearly loved, shot
Lincoln, sending Edwin into a year's seclusion.

When he returned to the stage, Booth put all his savings into
building a showcase for himself in New York — the Booth Theater, at
Twenty-third Street and Sixth Avenue — where he could perform
Shakespeare under his own management. He opened the theater on
February 3, 1869, with *Romeo and Juliet*, choosing as his Juliet the nine-
teen-year-old daughter of one of his benefactors, J. H. McVicker, the
Chicago stock-company impressario.

Mary McVicker, delicate and high-strung, had been a student, like
Ellen Quinlan, at St. Mary's Academy, albeit six years earlier. Mary
was cruelly derided by the critics for her portrayal of Juliet but,
despite her evident lack of talent and a burgeoning neurosis that
Booth was slow to detect, he married her four months later. Mary, a
petite woman, gave birth the following year to a ten-pound baby,
which had to be delivered by forceps. Its skull was crushed and it
lived only a few hours.

There were disasters yet to come. Booth was a negligent businessman and soon found himself in financial peril, forced to make up
his losses by again accepting short bookings with stock companies in
other cities. Always welcomed as a guest star in Chicago at his father-
in-law's theater, he chanced to be at McVicker's in early March of
1873 during James O'Neill's first season there. With his habitual mag-
nanimity toward younger actors, Booth invited James to play
Macduff to his Macbeth. James rose to the opportunity and was duly
extolled by the critics.

A playgoer's letter to a Chicago newspaper in the early 1900's —
and preserved by James in a scrapbook — illustrates the power he

could wield over audiences:

"The house was packed to the doors, and when Macduff announced the foul murder the curtain went down on a wave of applause, which continued until Mr. Booth stepped before the curtain, when all at once the applause ceased. Mr. Booth walked across the stage from left to right and disappeared. Then the applause was renewed in tones of thunder, men and women stood up waving their handkerchiefs and crying 'O'Neill, O'Neill, O'Neill!'

"This applause and shouting were deafening. O'Neill came before the footlights blushing like a boy. The audience had no desire to say to Mr. Booth by their applause that they did not appreciate his great acting, but they did want Mr. O'Neill to know that his fine acting had highly registered. The writer of this letter has witnessed the performances of all the best actors, from Edwin Booth to the greatest actors of the present day. But never has he witnessed better acting than James O'Neill's, on the occasion herein mentioned."

Later the same month James was again applauded when, as Laertes, he supported Booth in *Hamlet* and when he appeared alternately as Brutus and Marc Antony in support of Booth in *Julius Caesar*. For James, after sharing the stage with the great Booth, all was anticlimax — even the arrival at McVicker's in early April of the fabled English actress, Adelaide Neilson, of whom Henry Wadsworth Longfellow once wrote, "I have never in my life seen intellectual and poetical feeling more exquisitely combined."

At twenty-six, Neilson was preceded by her reputation as the loveliest Juliet on either side of the Atlantic, as well as by tales of a somewhat mysterious past. From the little that was known it appeared that she, like James, had endured an impoverished and painful childhood. Also like James, she had been deserted by her father (whose name she never knew) and had been forced to leave school to work in a factory.

For both, the discovery of the stage had been their salvation. Clever and quick, she had, like James, relied on Shakespeare for her education, and had taught herself to discard a regional accent — in her case that of her native Yorkshire. And like James, she had taken to investing in real estate; among her holdings was a lot on Manhattan's upper West Side at Broadway and Eighty-first Street. Yet another trait she had in common with James was a reputation for generosity and amiability and a nature free of petty backstage jealousies.

Cast as Romeo, James was impressed but not overawed by the

privilege of playing opposite so exquisite an actress. One night, on a playful impulse, instead of letting his head sink to his chest in the death scene, thereby screening his face from the audience, he threw his head back. With his face in full view, he knew that Neilson could not fake her kiss. Flustered, she was obliged to give him, as he put it, "a kiss of the sterling variety."

When the curtain fell she fixed James with her limpid eyes. "How could you? How could you?" she cried.

"How could I what?" asked James, trying to suppress his glee.

"How, how — how could Romeo throw his head back after he was dead?" Neilson asked lamely.

James was never at a loss for a chivalrous riposte: "Miss Neilson," he said, "your Juliet was the cause of it. It would make anyone come back to life."

The Chicago Tribune, hailing Neilson as "a phenomenal Juliet," declared that she was "fortunate in so excellent a Romeo as Mr. O'Neill." And while the critic quibbled that James was "lacking in that extraordinary and somewhat uncommon degree of fervor and warmth which should be ennobled by such a Juliet," he conceded that James looked and read the part "with admirable taste."

Neilson herself had no reservations about James's performance. At the close of her engagement she begged him to accompany her on the rest of her tour, which, James recalled laconically, "I did not do."

In England some years later, Neilson was asked to name her finest Romeo. A list of distinguished actors was rejected. "The greatest Romeo I ever played with," she finally said, "was a little curly-haired Irishman. When I played with other Romeos, I thought they would climb up the trellis to the balcony; but when I played with Jimmy O'Neill, I wanted to climb down the trellis, into his arms."

Having conquered Neilson, along with much of Chicago, James basked in popular as well as critical acclaim. One Chicago newspaper focused on his remarkable resemblance to his idol: "Most of all did he become the pattern of Edwin Booth. So keenly did he study Booth that he copied even his defects in mannerisms. He dressed like him, posed like him, and finally came to speak like him."

The writer offered a few words of caution, urging James to develop his own style and not carry imitation too far. Allowing that "after the study of a single year he is the equal of some stars, and the superior of many more," he warned that James's work was "only beginning" and that "this year will determine whether he is to become an artist or an egotist." That October, James also managed to hold his own when playing Macbeth opposite Charlotte Cushman, a Valkyrie of a woman, who had begun her career as an opera singer, and whose Lady Macbeth was lauded above any other. The deep-voiced Cushman, equally at home in the roles of Hamlet, Romeo and Shylock, rarely concealed her disdain of men; but she was so charmed by James that she took the trouble to coach him, predicting a brilliant future. She too, according to James, admonished him to "work, work, work!"

Toward the close of James's first season at McVicker's, the Chicago Daily Times described him as "One of the best of the few good leading men in the country."

Edwin Booth returned to McVicker's during James's second season in 1874. Booth now found it necessary to tour regularly, as he had been forced into bankruptcy during the panic of 1873 and lost his New York theater. This time, he accepted his father-in-law's invitation to stay at McVicker's for at least two months. His wife, still distraught over the loss of her baby, had also grown bitter over the failure of her acting career. Indeed, there were signs that her mental health was disintegrating, and Booth finally had to accept that he no longer had a marriage.

James was as much taken with Booth's personal dignity in the face of calamity as with his acting genius. "Booth was not only the greatest actor without a doubt the world has ever seen, but the noblest man the stage has produced," James declared, acknowledging his mentor's fortitude. "It is hard to tell how lovable he was personally, how high minded and lofty was his purpose and how pure his character, but we who knew him intimately will always reverence him above all other men we ever met in life."

In their second season, Booth invited James to alternate with him in *Othello*. It was an extraordinary offer, for this was a ritual only followed, as a rule, when two stars of equal fame appeared on the same stage together. For more than a week, beginning on February 24, James alternated with Booth in the roles of Iago and Othello.

James, later in his career, was moved to contrast Booth's demeanor with that of other actors he characterized as "so-called stars." Their overbearing, not to say tyrannical, behavior made young actors "feel that instead of confrères they are servants, which conduct would make the blood of Edwin Booth boil."

Eugene O'Neill, in *Long Day's Journey Into Night*, recorded in accurate detail his father's account of the occasion on which he and Booth alternated roles:

" . . . The first night I played Othello, he said to our manager, 'That young man is playing Othello better than I ever did!' That from Booth, the greatest actor of his day or any other! And it was true! And I was only twenty-seven years old! As I look back on it now, that night was the high spot in my career."

Booth had not, in fact, intended to play Othello at all. He felt challenged, however, by the Chicago press, which had predicted he would not dare portray the Moor in the wake of the Italian tragedian, Tommaso Salvini, who had acted Othello just a week before.

It was Salvini's most famous role, electrifying both American and English audiences with its ferocity. Salvini had so steeped himself in the role that it became an inseparable part of his persona. His Desdemonas lived in terror of his realism during the strangling scene.

Unable to overlook the challenge, Booth had promptly announced *Othello* for his first week. Rivalry among stars — especially British and American — was the fabric of theatrical tradition, and it could reach destructive heights. Many still recalled New York's Astor Place riot of 1849, the worst in theater history.

The uproar resulted from a feud between Edwin Forrest, who symbolized the virile, pioneer spirit of America, and William Charles Macready, who represented the arrogant British aristocracy. Their animosity evolved into something of a class struggle.

Forrest had been hissed during a performance of *Macbeth* in England. Blaming Macready's fans for the insult, he retaliated by hissing his rival during a performance of *Hamlet*. Not too long after, when Macready brought his *Hamlet* to New York's Astor Place Opera House, a mob of ten thousand outraged adherents of both stars surrounded the theater. Despite the efforts of the militia to contain them, they fought a bloody battle in the streets, hurling paving stones and bricks. Forrest was held morally responsible for the twenty-two dead and one hundred wounded.

By 1874 the theater had grown somewhat more civilized, and Booth adopted a more peaceful means of putting Salvini in his place.

"He could not only play the part of Othello as well as Salvini," James later told a Boston journalist, "but he could do something which Salvini would never attempt — he could play Iago." While Booth's Iago, along with his Hamlet, was in truth among the greatest ever seen, his Othello, according to critics of the day, was over-intellectualized and lacking in fervor.

James, however, was loyal to his idol: "And so after one performance in the title role, Mr. Booth determined to appear the next night
in the latter character, and I was cast for Othello. I was in a quandary.
I knew that everyone who would be in the house that night would
know me; that nearly all of them would have seen Salvini and Booth,
and that they would expect me to fail. To imitate either one or the
other of the well-known actors too closely would be bad policy; yet
how to introduce something original puzzled me. It came like a flash
at the last rehearsal."

James said nothing to the other members of the cast about the fil-
lip he planned for that evening's performance. Actors in leading roles
seldom did bother with such formalities, for there was no such person as a director to orchestrate the production.

Rehearsals were casual, the star withholding anything resembling a performance until he or she actually appeared before a paid
audience. If they were of great enough stature and were so inclined,
the stars might "direct" other members of the cast, but normally they
were too preoccupied to bother, being more concerned with their
own strategy for achieving a tour de force.

Customarily, performers would strike a pose and declaim their
speeches, oblivious to all others on stage. How they gestured, how
they moved, how they intoned were set by them alone. Since each
supporting player also followed his or her own agenda, the result,
not surprisingly, was somewhat anarchic. Audiences, however, were
indifferent to any such concept as ensemble interpretation. What they
came to see was their idols go through their familiar paces.

No more in harmony were the scenery and costumes. If a backdrop was sufficiently ornate, it drew good notices — never mind if it
furthered the mood of the play, or even if it was appropriate to its
period. The costumes were a matter of individual taste, with each
actor providing his or her own, without regard for coordination of
design or historical accuracy.

In the case of the fanciful melodramas that alternated with the
classics in stock-company repertories, the reverse was often true.
These action-packed productions, foreshadowing motion-picture
thrillers, relied on intricate stagecraft: shipwrecks and near-drown-
ings in ocean waves (lumpy canvas groundcloths manipulated from
below); raging fires (strips of red and yellow cloth fanned from the
wings); and howling snowstorms (confetti by the barrelful loosed
from the flies).

In these extravaganzas a stage manager supervised the action. In productions of the classics, however, the players were free to declaim their lines as they saw fit, just as long as they drowned, scorched and shivered on cue.

James was merely following established procedure when, on his own, he conceived the novel bit of business that was to distinguish his Othello. The cast was running through the third scene of the third act on the afternoon before the performance.

"Of course, this is your scene, O'Neill," Booth said. "I will be at the side here whenever you want me. And, by the way, O'Neill, I wouldn't wear the sword in that scene if I were you. You will find that it is in your way and that it hampers your movements, while at the same time you will not need it."

The sword in question was an ancient scimitar James had picked up during his early barnstorming days, and he had never had occasion to draw it from its ornamented scabbard. Offstage, he tried to pull it out; it came only halfway and then clanged back, as he had anticipated. Deciding the effect suited his purpose — and ignoring Booth's counsel — he wore the sword. Sidling across the stage toward Booth, he uttered his lines:

> If thou dost slander her and torture me,
> Never pray more; abandon all remorse;
> On horror's head horrors accumulate;
> Do deeds to make heaven weep, all earth amaz'd;
> For nothing canst thou to damnation add
> Greater than that.

James approached Booth, his sword half drawn. When Booth had spoken his response, James sprang his surprise.

"Nay, stay: — thou shouldst be honest," James said menacingly, and let go of the sword hilt. The sound reverberated throughout the huge hushed theater. The audience, so knowledgeable that it could be enchanted by even such a minute innovation, nearly fell out of its seats in its effort to applaud James. Booth called James back on stage to take extra bows.

"The scene is yours," said Booth. "You couldn't have done it better." To James's relief, Booth never mentioned the brazen disregard of his advice.

Tricks like these were not, of course, the sole basis on which James won the hearts of Chicago audiences. He had a genuine flair for

Shakespeare that earned their respect. Reviewing a performance of
Othello in which James played the title role and Booth played Iago, a
critic wrote: "It is not often that a star is as well supported . . . by the
actor playing Othello as Mr. Booth was last evening."

The "passion, jealousy and suspicion" expressed by James as
Iago, the critic added, were "admirably rendered and bring down a
round or two of applause in the middle of the scene."

Years later, James appreciatively recalled the tribute.

"I think I laid the foundation in those two years I put in at
McVicker's. Chicago people took very kindly to me."

As a result of his triumphs at McVicker's, James received an offer
from Richard Hooley, who operated a respected rival theater in
Chicago. Hooley, who had a reputation for benevolence and was
known by actors as "Uncle Dick," offered James a larger salary and
the opportunity to form his own company. They would present adap-
tations of French melodramas during the week but on Saturday
nights, Hooley promised James, he could play Hamlet, Othello,
Shylock, Romeo and other Shakespearean roles.

James assembled a troupe that included Louise Hawthorne, who
was beautiful on stage but required heavy makeup to conceal a vivid
scar that ran from her temple to her chin. Though married to an actor
in the company named George Morton, she evidently had more than
a platonic interest in James and he, respectful of her talent, did not
rebuff her. She played Juliet to his Romeo in October of 1874, and not
long after, Ophelia to his Hamlet.

His growing success was not without its accompanying burdens.
James had been trying for some time to disentangle himself from a
relationship formed four years earlier with a woman named Nettie
Walsh who, jealous of Louise and furious at being spurned, was now
seeking revenge by telling James's colleagues and friends that she
was his abandoned wife and that he was the father of her three-year-
old son.

James had met Nettie in Cleveland in 1871 when he was starting
out with Ellsler's company. Nettie, only fifteen, had dark red hair,
snapping eyes and was, by her own later account, "wholly inexperienced in the ways of the world."

James was, in fact, living with Nettie during the very time he was
cultivating Thomas Quinlan's friendship in Cleveland, although
Quinlan almost certainly had no inkling that his engaging new

acquaintance was keeping a mistress only a year older than Quinlan's own precious Mary Ellen.

James evidently supplied Nettie Walsh with worldly experience (and financial support) in both Cleveland and Chicago, before dropping her in favor of Louise Hawthorne (and conceivably others); he was, after all, a handsome, debonair bachelor, increasingly in the limelight, at whom women tended to throw themselves. And he had reason to believe that Nettie, clearly mature for her age, was exploring multiple amatory interests of her own.

At any rate, he seemed surprised that Nettie refused to acknowledge that their intimacy was at an end, and was now threatening to sue him.

James was prepared to swear under oath that he had never married Nettie and that the child was not his. Nevertheless, he made cautious inquiries about his possible legal responsibility. Persuaded she had no claim, he chose to brush aside her allegations, believing himself safe against any proof of paternity.

Nonetheless, he was glad to leave Chicago for San Francisco in early May of 1875, where Hooley's troupe was to fulfill its next engagement. James invited Louise to accompany him and she joyfully accepted, evidently as unconcerned about leaving her husband behind as James was happy to escape the wrathful Nettie.

San Francisco was as exuberant a theatrical center as New York. The Comstock Lode, miraculously rich in silver, had been discovered in nearby Nevada some years before, and San Franciscans felt a sense of participation, however illusory. Theaters reflected the inflationary times and Hooley's troupe had a profitable run, with audiences taking James to their hearts in an assortment of trivial romances of which *On the Rhine* and *Van the Virginian* were typical.

At last, early in 1876, James's long-held dream was realized: he received an offer to join New York's ranking stock company, A. M. Palmer's Union Square Theater, the following season. Louise Hawthorne was not included in the invitation, nor did James tender her a personal one, and she made her last appearance with him in a play called *Ultimo*, in March.

Two months later, a "Grand Farewell Benefit" was held in James's honor. Without such benefits, actors were hard-put to keep up their stage wardrobes, let alone appearances. Salaries frequently were paid on an irregular basis, dependent upon how honorable the theater manager happened to be and on how much money was left in the box office after the star had collected his piratical guarantee.

James, well-versed in frugality and ever mindful of the periods of impoverishment that were a hazard of his profession, needed a benefit less than most of his fellow actors. Still, he did not decline either the honor or the cash.

Before James left San Francisco, A. M. Palmer requested him to join his touring stock company in Chicago prior to its arrival in New York. James was obliged to accept, even though he feared Nettie Walsh was lying in wait there. He opened in Chicago on June 28 in an adaptation of the French melodrama, *The Two Orphans*, which had already earned Palmer a fortune; it was with a new production of this play that Palmer intended to begin his New York season in October.

Louise Hawthorne's husband was expecting her to rejoin him in New York. Unwilling, however, to part from James just yet, she decided to accompany him to Chicago, hoping he would wish her to linger there a while.

After attending James's opening performance, Louise went back to her hotel, the Tremont House, where James was also staying. Shortly after, as reported the next day in all the local newspapers, she fell or jumped from a sixth-floor window and was instantly killed. The coroner's report characterized her death as accidental, but according to local gossip she had killed herself over unrequited love for James O'Neill.

With Louise's death on his conscience, with Nettie's fury hovering, James was more than ready to turn his back on Chicago and hurry toward the glittering promise of his first starring New York season.

Chapter
FIVE

PROSPERING AFTER THE CIVIL WAR, NEW YORK REVELED in the glitter of its theater district, now the liveliest and most densely-populated entertainment center in the nation.

Situated in and around Union Square, the district had established its roots in 1854 when the 4,600-seat Academy of Music opened on Fourteenth Street to present grand opera. Creeping northward, the district, by the mid-1870's, flaunted some twenty playhouses; among the three sturdiest were Lester Wallack's, at Broadway and Thirteenth Street, A. M. Palmer's Union Square Theater abutting Wallack's and Augustin Daly's, at Broadway and Twenty-eighth Street.

Wallack, Palmer and Daly had arrived on the scene by disparate routes. Wallack, the son of an English actor-manager and himself an actor, played amorous light-comedy roles in his own stock company. Daly, a critic turned playwright, resuscitated old standards and developed a knack for creating stars. Palmer, enticed by the glamour of the stage, abandoned a career as a librarian in 1872 to take over the Union Square Theater, turning it from a variety house into a legitimate playhouse. He made his reputation by raising the standards of professionalism, immediately imposing disciplined rehearsals — a rarity in the theater of his day. A generous man, he helped organize the Actors Fund and was regarded throughout the district as the mayor of Union Square.

Palmer's theater, on the ground floor of a hotel congenial to actors, could seat 1,200. Operated as a stock-company, it was the city's most influential playhouse when James, in September of 1876, arrived with his wardrobe trunk to rehearse for the revival of *The Two Orphans*.

Two years earlier, when Palmer had first mounted the Parisian success, the critics dismissed it as mawkish and trivial. But audiences took it to their hearts and word of mouth turned the play into the biggest money-maker of Palmer's career.

Palmer had assigned James the role of Pierre Frochard, the cripple, in support of the company's leading man, Charles Thorne Jr., who was to play Chevalier. Tall, slim, handsome (and seven years James's senior), Thorne was the darling of New York theatergoers. Under Palmer's tutelage and Booth's influence, he had acquired an understated, courtly style that critics hailed as refreshing.

It was rare for any production to run more than a few weeks. The quick turnover resulted from the public's ever-increasing thirst for variety and was reflected in the low caliber of the plays, many of them pirated versions of European melodramas and farces, or scripts stolen from the stock company across the street and brazenly re-titled and doctored to suit the particular talents of a reigning star. The more enterprising companies supported "house playwrights," among whom Dion Boucicault was sui generis.

Since New Yorkers of all social levels, however catholic their tastes, were voracious theatergoers, double bills were common. Audiences sat spellbound through four, or even five, acts and thought nothing of arriving at seven and lingering until the curtain fell at midnight, or sometimes even later.

An item in The Times on October 2, 1876 noted that the revival of The Two Orphans would "introduce, as Pierre, Mr. James O'Neill, a fresh candidate for metropolitan honors." The production, in four acts, included scenes of an illuminated garden near Paris, a prison courtyard, a boathouse on the banks of the Seine and a snowstorm. The story, about two cruelly victimized orphan girls, piled villainy upon villainy until, at last, honor and chivalry won the day.

Word of James's success in Chicago and San Francisco had reached New York's Irish community, which was well-represented in the gallery on opening night. The Tribune critic found James's performance satisfactory, but The Times, while lauding Charles Thorne and his leading lady, Kate Claxton, dismissed James with one sentence: "Mr. O'Neill is altogether too robust as Pierre."

Audiences, however, took to James and The Two Orphans ran until November 20, when Palmer moved it to the Brooklyn Theater with its cast intact — except for James. Palmer wanted him to stay at the Union Square Theater for his next production, Miss Multon, and, by plucking him from the Orphan company, Palmer possibly saved his life. The actor who replaced James, Harry Murdoch, was one of several hundred who died when the Brooklyn Theater was destroyed by fire on December 5.

In *Miss Multon* — a French adaptation of the wildly popular *East Lynne*, readapted into English — James was cast as a Parisian advocate, Maurice de Latour. His leading lady, Clara Morris, famed for her emoting, had risen to stardom three years earlier as a scar-faced madwoman in *Article 47*, adapted for her by Augustin Daly. *Miss Multon* marked Clara Morris's first New York engagement in two years and her return, greeted by a clamorous audience, overshadowed James's appearance.

The Times again declined to be charmed by him: "Mr. James O'Neill, as Maurice, occasionally appeared more astonished at his presence on the stage than *au fait* of the proceedings he was supposed to be engaged in."

James must have found it hard to understand why the New York critics failed to respond to, or even mention, "his handsome face, his luminous eyes, his fine presence and magnetic personality" — attributes that the San Francisco Chronicle had cited as reasons for his "rapid rise to stellar eminence."

He should have been forewarned that the New York critics were a notoriously jaded, savagely opinionated and often overworked clique. Required to judge a new production almost every night, they had little tolerance and less reverence for even the most sacred of stage icons. They thought nothing of tearing apart a Booth or a Forrest if their performances were in any way wanting.

James O'Neill's next appearance, as Count Vladimir in yet another French melodrama, this one set in Moscow and called *The Danicheffs*, again drew a sour comment from The Times: "We do not admire Mr. O'Neill's Vladimir — a hard and artificial portrayal." To be sure, the anonymous critic did not care much for Charles Thorne's performance either; his portrayal of the serf, Osip, was dismissed as "deficient in pathos."

Despite his inability to win over the critics, James was building a loyal following. Although the city's economy was in a periodic reversal, the Union Square Theater drew full houses and James enriched his bank account. If he was bewildered by his failure to please the critics, he continued to present an affable, unruffled surface to the cronies with whom he dined, drank and exchanged shop talk in the saloons of Union Square.

James undoubtedly felt very much at home in the New York of 1876, which prided itself on having attained a population of just over one million and was bursting with immigrant energy. As yet the city had nothing resembling a skyline. But its populace could marvel at the visionary Brooklyn Bridge, in the midst of its thirteen-year construction. New hotels in the theater and business districts accommodated booming numbers of tourists, while row upon row of four-story brownstones dominated the area from City Hall to Fourteenth Street. Somewhat further uptown, skirting the expanse of Central Park, private residences and small hotels were gradually replacing the wilderness of rocks and crude vegetable gardens inhabited by squatters and capering goats.

If he pleased to leave the theater district, James could ride the horsecars that jogged along dusty cobblestones (or, to save time, join the hurried businessmen who rode the Pullman cars of the steam-engined Third and Ninth Avenue elevated railroads). There was little reason, though, for him to venture out of Union Square.

Crammed with theatrical agencies, publishing offices, costume and gift shops, bookstores, piano showrooms and photography studios, the district had lured some of the best restaurants, among them a branch of Delmonico's, the epicurean palace that introduced New Yorkers to haute cuisine; its eleven-page menu listing forty-seven veal dishes and fifty fish dishes featured a specialty known as *agneau farci à la* Walter Scott.

Here, in this center of bustle and conviviality, James continued to court Ellen Quinlan, doubtless praying no word of his entanglement with Nettie Walsh would travel eastward. When he was not himself performing, he accompanied Ellen to the theater. Edwin Booth was in town, as were a number of lesser luminaries with whom James was on easy terms, among them Adelaide Neilson.

Neilson had opened in a Shakespearean repertory at Daly's on May 8, 1877, three days after *The Danicheffs* closed, and it is likely that James took Ellen to see her perform. Ellen, secure as she was in James's love, appears to have felt a twinge of jealousy toward such actresses as Neilson. In *Long Day's Journey Into Night*, O'Neill may have been referring to his mother's sentiments when he caused Mary Tyrone to reminisce: "I thought to myself . . . 'You're just as pretty as any actress he's ever met, and you don't have to use paint.'"

While Ellen was spellbound by James's aura, her mother was not overjoyed at the prospect of welcoming him as a son-in-law. The fact that James appeared to be an upright Irishman and an observant Catholic did not mitigate Bridget's concern. Although it was considered permissible for respectable families to lionize prominent actors, as Thomas Quinlan had done in Cleveland, they were not held to be sound matrimonial prospects for pampered daughters.

Even the best-established actors led nomadic lives, rattling by rail from town to town, more often than not for one-night stands. Like James, the younger ones often lived hand-to-mouth. First-class hotels seldom accepted them because they were known to jump their rent when their shows closed unexpectedly. Then, too, actors were reputed to be philanderers and drunkards, and newspapers boosted circulation by exposing the scandals in their lives.

Bridget Quinlan doubted that Ellen, with her gentle upbringing and refined tastes, could accommodate herself to the mercurial world of the actor. But bewitched by her matinee idol, Ellen summoned all her resolve to override her mother's warnings of potential hazards.

As for James, nothing seemed beyond his powers. He was as determined as Ellen to marry, and just as confident that they were blissfully suited. That he could have deluded himself into believing that Ellen, coddled as she was, would make him an appropriate wife, is even more of a puzzle than Ellen's naive faith. James, after all, was under no illusions about the hardships of a touring actor's life, and it must have occurred to him that Ellen might not cheerfully adapt to it.

Her tenacity fortified by infatuation, Ellen more than likely badgered her mother to agree to a wedding date. James suggested June, during a pause in his acting commitments, and Bridget finally yielded. New York was chosen for the wedding to fit James's schedule.

Throughout May, Ellen passed enchanted hours along the Ladies' Mile, an area stretching from Union Square to Madison Square and from Broadway to Sixth Avenue, where she opened charge accounts at Lord and Taylor, Arnold Constable and James McCreery. (Tiffany's, at Union Square and Fourteenth Street, was conveniently close to Palmer's theater, and a likely place for James to buy Ellen's wedding ring.)

Bridget drew a thousand dollars from her Cleveland bank to pay for her daughter's trousseau; Ellen, who always dressed stylishly, was apt to spend as much as one hundred dollars on a dress, an exorbitant price in 1877. The costly simplicity of her wardrobe was, in later years, recalled with precision by relatives and friends.

James and Ellen were married on June 14, 1877, at the new St. Ann's Church on East Twelfth Street, a few blocks from the Union Square Theater. Designated by the press as the "beau monde parish," it was the locale for most of New York's chic Catholic weddings.

Eugene O'Neill, with his sense of foreboding, probably would have endorsed nature's choice of the weather for his parents' wedding day. According to The New York Times, the day dawned under a "somber pall of clouds that, every lapsing moment, grew deeper and darker . . . The whole scene was weird beyond description and silently menacing."

The nuptial ceremony was small and quiet. Bridget Quinlan was her daughter's matron of honor and attendant relatives included Bridget's older sister, Elizabeth Brennan, as well as Ellen's brother, William, who had established himself as a grocer in Cleveland.

No member of James's large, scattered family was present. He appears to have lost touch with most of them, once he became an actor. He did, however, remain close to his mother, who was to die of asthma a year later. According to a nephew of James, Frank A. Kunckel, he had married "a Cleveland Society Girl" and that was why no one in the family ever saw him. "As far as an uncle us poor kids might just as well hadn't had an uncle," he once complained.

The marriage was not publicly announced. James wanted his fans to continue thinking of him as a romantic bachelor. And then, too, he doubtless feared that news of his marriage would provoke Nettie Walsh into action against him.

Gossip about Nettie's claim, however, had already begun to infiltrate New York theater circles, and before long newspaper items hinted about James's recent marriage. Reports of the wedding soon spread to San Francisco, where James's popularity was still intact. Two weeks after the wedding, the San Francisco Evening Post stated, "Mr. O'Neill had not let even his most intimate friends know of the event."

As in the case of Mary Tyrone's initial meeting with her future husband in Long Day's Journey Into Night, O'Neill chose to reinvent at least one aspect of the real-life wedding on which the play's action is based — once again invoking the ghost of Ellen's father, Thomas Quinlan.

Although Quinlan had been dead three years at the time of his daughter's marriage, there are references in the play to the participation of Mary's father in her marriage to James Tyrone. The father's presence is underscored by the allusion to his purchase of an elaborate wedding dress:

"My father told me to buy anything I wanted and never mind the cost," Mary Tyrone joyously recalls. "The best is none too good, he said. I'm afraid he spoiled me dreadfully . . . [He] even let me have duchesse lace on my white satin slippers, and lace with the orange blossoms in my veil . . . "

Yet with this one exception, all the details of the wedding as recounted in the play are based by O'Neill almost literally upon the actual facts, as conveyed to him by his mother over the years (and confirmed by family members). What, then, was the inspiration for this affecting passage?

One possibility is that Ellen Quinlan, still devastated at the time of her marriage by her beloved father's demise three years earlier, herself constructed the fantasy; in that way she could view herself as an even more poignant victim: a fragile young bride thrust into her husband's harum-scarum world *directly* from the sheltering home of her father. In time, she might have come to believe in this myth and recounted it as fact to her son.

Some support for this theory can be found embedded in the play itself, wherein O'Neill signaled his awareness of his mother's tendency toward self-dramatization (and his father's parallel inclination to deprecate her theatrics). Cautioning his son to take his mother's memories "with a grain of salt," James Tyrone elaborates: "Her father wasn't the great, generous, noble Irish gentleman she makes out . . . He was prosperous enough . . . an able man. But he had his weakness . . . He became a steady champagne drinker, the worst kind . . . Well, it finished him quick — that and the consumption — ."

Even more likely, however, is that O'Neill, always the dramatist, concocted the story of the father's presence during the wedding preparations, to provide dramatic tension. Causing Mary Tyrone to enter her husband's precarious world directly from her father's protective home clearly does serve to heighten the play's tragedy.

In actuality, James and Ellen were helplessly in love long before either realized how rudely their outlooks clashed. Unknowingly, they were destined to become victims of a destructive misalliance. She could not forgive James for enclosing her within the precarious and isolating world of the touring 19th-century actor, while he writhed under her disdain for that world.

Ultimately laying bare the accumulated wounds of his parents' marriage, Eugene O'Neill in *Long Day's Journey Into Night* hammers at the thwarted dreams of both husband and wife, the bitter accusations, the guilty withdrawals and the thwarted attempts at mutual understanding.

In the play, James and Mary Tyrone are shown to be deeply in love, although irrevocably embattled. Mary, unreconciled to having married beneath her out of defenseless passion, despises James's penny-pinching, even though she understands that his terror of poverty stems from his hard early life. She also blames him for having separated her from her former friends and deprived her of a regulated life. Her frustration has driven her to morphine addiction, and she is given to wrenchingly self-pitying monologues.

James, for his part, adores her but squirms under her censure and withdrawal, which he blames on an overindulged childhood and weakness of character. In the end he has to resign himself to caring for her as one would a child, hoping to salvage the fragments of their marriage.

In a much earlier play, *All God's Chillun Got Wings* (written in 1923), O'Neill portrayed an analogous relationship between a married couple, in which he called the wife Ella (the name his mother permanently adopted after her marriage) and called the husband Jim (his father's actual nickname). Like James and Mary in *Long Day's Journey Into Night*, Jim and Ella marry out of desperate need and cling to each other, though neither is able to give the other happiness, let alone tranquility.

Ella regards herself as Jim's superior by birth and background and Jim is forced to concede her superiority. Ella resents Jim's inability to overcome the burden of his heritage. She is furious at being dependent on him, and is incapable of accepting his self-sacrifice and devotion; and he cannot follow her behind the locked door of her disillusionment.

Jim and Ella are fused in conflict but they cannot let each other go. In the end, Ella is reduced to a childlike state; Jim's hope of rising above the petty cruelties of his life is crushed, and he resigns himself to being Ella's nurse.

"I can't leave her. She can't leave me," says Jim to his sister, who has asked why they do not separate. "And there's a million little reasons combining to make one big reason why we can't. For her sake — if it'd do her good — I'd go — I'd leave — I'd do anything — because I love her . . . but that'd only make matters worse for her. I'm all she's got in the world! Yes, that isn't bragging or fooling myself. I know that for a fact! Don't you know that's true?"

It was a truth O'Neill could eloquently expound upon, and he did not bother in *All God's Chillun Got Wings* to disguise the true names of his parents for two reasons: first, they were both recently dead; second, Jim was black and Ella white, and the play on its surface appeared to focus on miscegenation — in itself a daring theme for its day. O'Neill was confident that no one would dream of identifying the leading characters with his parents.

Throughout his career O'Neill continued to portray his mother and father — in many guises — as lovers communicating in code, neither able to find the other's key. It was clear that he attributed his own profound sense of alienation to the inability of his parents to make sustained, meaningful contact, either with each other or with him.

A heartfelt expression of this tragic malaise is given voice in *The Great God Brown*, which O'Neill wrote two years after *All God's Chillun*. The play's protagonist, Dion Anthony, inspired by O'Neill's own character, tries after the death of his parents to comprehend their estrangement and the injury it inflicted on him:

"What aliens we were to each other! When [my father] lay dead, his face looked so familiar that I wondered where I had met that man before. Only at the second of my conception. After that, we grew hostile with concealed shame. And my mother? I remember a sweet, strange girl, with affectionate, bewildered eyes as if God had locked her in a dark closet without any explanation."

In his notion of the mother locked in a dark closet, O'Neill plainly was influenced by Strindberg's *The Ghost Sonata*. In that terrifying drama by one of O'Neill's early literary heroes, a woman referred to as the Mummy does, in fact, live in a closet and talks to her family in parrot-like jargon. "Most of my life I've spent in the closet," says the Mummy, "so that I won't have to see — or be seen."

Shortly after his own mother's death in 1922, O'Neill confided to an intimate friend that there had been intervals during which she kept to a room from which she seldom ventured — that she was, in a way, like Strindberg's Mummy.

Among James O'Neill's many friends interviewed for this biography, there were none who could say they really knew Ella. As for Ella's own surviving relatives in New London, where she and her family spent their summers for thirty-six years, none claimed to have been intimate with her.

The circumstances of his parents' marriage preoccupied O'Neill throughout his career as he struggled to reconcile his ambivalent feelings. In the private, soul-searching document that O'Neill wrote while undergoing his brief psychoanalysis, he strove to evaluate the nature and motivations of his parents and the effect he believed their behavior had upon him and his older brother.

The notations are difficult to decipher without a magnifying glass and were obviously meant for no one else's eyes. Underscoring the secrecy, O'Neill used no proper names, referring to his father as "husband" and in some cases using initials — "M" denoting his mother, for example, and "E" referring to himself.

It appears likely that he might have been encouraged to draft this document by his psychoanalyst as an attempt to better understand his own psyche. And these insightful notes, in turn, could have led to the idea for what he described in early 1927 as "series of plays based on autobiographical material," to be called *The Sea-Mother's Son*.

He pursued the idea the following year when, at forty, he outlined a scenario in which a forty-year-old man, lying in a hospital "at the point of death," examines his past life "from the beginnings of his childhood": does his life have "any meaning that he should wish to continue it — peace is at hand, why shouldn't he accept it — there is a strong death wish in him which instinctively he fights against."

According to the scenario, the play ends when, "accepting all the suffering he has been through, he is able to say yes to his life . . . to conquer his death wish, give up the comfort of the return to Mother Death." While he dropped that particular idea, as he did a multitude of others, the scenario seems to presage a play closely based on his life, foreshadowing in surprising detail many of the elements he later wove into *Long Day's Journey Into Night*.

When making his psychoanalytical notations, O'Neill appears to have been immersed in his mother's viewpoint and to be evaluating his family history with a passionate bias through her eyes — and to be judging his father with implacable harshness. This is in marked contrast to the portraits he drew in *Long Day's Journey Into Night* thirteen years later, in which both parents, despite the exposure of their hapless failings, are viewed with a balanced and almost Olympian blend of compassion.

Intensely subjective though they are, the notations provide the only record in O'Neill's own voice of his intimate family history. Of his mother, for example, he wrote: "Spoiled before marriage (husband friend of father's — father his great admirer — drinking companion) — fashionable convent girl — religious & naive — talent for music — physical beauty . . . "

O'Neill went on to explain that his mother's father was "her idol" who "spoiled her with generous gifts," and then noted: "M always a bit of snob in reaction to world which finally becomes altogether her husband's world since she has little contact with reality except through him."

James O'Neill's adoring bride briefly basked in a state of innocent euphoria. Not yet twenty and blooming with tranquil beauty, she began calling herself Ella (finally opting for what she thought the more glamorous name). Soon, though, she found herself confronting the weightier problems predicted by her mother.

After a three-week honeymoon in the mountains, James accepted an engagement to join the Union Square company, again on tour prior to its regular New York season. James was certain Nettie Walsh would be awaiting his arrival, but he could not avoid Chicago without hindering his career. He braced himself for the worst.

His initial vehicle was *Forbidden Fruit*, yet another vapid melodrama. It was this engagement that gave Ella her first taste of the alien life she was often to confront during the next forty years. She soon discovered there was less glamour and more tedium than she had anticipated as the wife of a sought-after actor.

Worse, James devoted nearly all his time to rehearsals and business connected with the theater. Such free moments as he had were frequently spent with fellow-actors, managers and agents. Before her children were born, Ella was often left alone in hotel rooms, without even the consolation of her piano.

James did try to bring Ella into his backstage life, at times successfully. While she never entirely overcame her sense of being an outsider, she at times expressed an interest in such matters as the casting of James's vehicles and the mechanics of his costume changes.

If Ella's genteel tastes often translated into disdain of her husband's fellow-actors of both sexes, she did form several friendships with young actresses whose backgrounds and deportment met her standards of gentility. Eugene O'Neill's observation that his mother "had rather an aversion for the atmosphere and people of the stage in general" was something of an exaggeration — as, indeed, was the complaint he attributed to Mary Tyrone in *Long Day's Journey Into Night*:

"Even though Mr. Tyrone has made me go with him on all his tours," she says to her housemaid, "I've had little to do with the people in his company, or with anyone on the stage . . . Their life is not my life."

Ella did tend to be defensive with her girlhood friends, convinced they looked down on her because of her marriage to an actor. Mary Tyrone's complaint that after her marriage "All my old friends either pitied me or cut me dead" was not literally the case. A classmate of Ella's at St. Mary's, Loretta Ritchie, of Pinckneyville, Illinois, kept up a correspondence with Ella for many years. One of several such early friends, she preserved a letter in which Ella wrote of bringing up her children in hotels, and sometimes cradling them as infants in dresser drawers. Another classmate during part of Ella's stay at St. Mary's, Ella Nirdlinger, spoke of her as a beautiful pious girl to her son, George Jean Nathan, later to become one of the first critics to recognize Eugene O'Neill's talent.

Because she was deeply in love, Ella tried to make the best of a life that was not easy. Marriage to a touring star required a resilience that could take in its stride such daily hardships as jolting, unventilated trains and shabby hotel rooms with the pervasive presence of whiskey.

She was helpless in her attempts to improvise temporary domestic arrangements and, in later years, bemoaned her confinement to hotels. That James's acting commitments prevented her from having a permanent home became, in one way, something of a boon, serving to camouflage her housekeeping deficiencies. Even in the New London summer home she later occupied, she could not cope with household arrangements and the engagement of efficient servants defeated her.

In O'Neill's self-analytical document of 1927, he compressed his thoughts about his mother's state of mind as a bride, presumably based on sentiments she had conveyed to him. He made note of her "ostracism after marriage" and her "lonely life," emphasizing that she had "no contact with husband's friends — husband man's man — heavy drinker — out with men until small hours every night — slept late — little time with her . . . "

Heaped upon her other disappointments, the discovery of James's steady drinking was a severe jolt for Ella. In *Long Day's Journey Into Night* O'Neill elaborated on his mother's resentment (perhaps exaggerated) of her husband's behavior early in their marriage:

"I remember the first night your barroom friends had to help you up to the door of our hotel room and knocked and then ran away before I came to the door . . . ," Mary Tyrone laments. "I had waited . . . hour after hour . . . I imagined all sorts of horrible accidents. I got on my knees and prayed that nothing had happened to you . . . I didn't know how often that was to happen in the years to come . . . "

And now, as a bride of less than three months, an even ruder shock awaited Ella, one that might have unnerved a far worldlier woman.

That September in Chicago, Nettie Walsh, apprised of James's marriage, finally decided to act. She brought a suit for divorce, sparing none of the details of her relationship with James. She claimed to have married him in Cleveland on August 1, 1871, and to have lived with him as his wife until the spring of 1875, when he left her. She formally charged him with fathering her son, Alfred — now three years old — and of having committed adultery both in Chicago and San Francisco with Louise Hawthorne.

On September 8, 1877, a headline on Page 5 of The New York Times read (misspelling James's name): "James O'Neil In Court In Chicago To Answer For Deserting His Wife, Nettie O'Neil — Adultery With A Deceased Actress Also Charged."

In noting that James had acquired a bride in New York, Nettie Walsh implied he was a bigamist, although her list of grievances did not specify this fact. She did, however, point out that her "husband" was a prominent actor, earning $195 a week, and that for the past five years he had been earning between $3,000 and $5,000 a year, so that now, being "parsimonious in his habits and disposition," he must be worth at least $15,000. She concluded the recital of her wrongs by requesting a divorce, the care and custody of her child, and suitable alimony.

Since there had been no marriage, according to James, and since he was not eager to acquire custody of the child — whose paternity he steadfastly disavowed — the crucial point was the alimony. James was disinclined to provide it. The scandal titillated Chicago and, on the day Nettie Walsh filed her suit reporters crowded backstage when James arrived for his evening performance in a play appropriately called *Forbidden Fruit*.

Reacting with unaccustomed anger to their shouted questions, James denounced Nettie's statement as "false from first to last." While he acknowledged that he knew she had a child she attributed to him, he declared that the whole thing was a piece of blackmail and an old story that had been pursuing him ever since he acquired prominence. Moreover, he saw no reason why he should have to make any public explanation.

At one point during the interrogation James's eyes filled with tears.

"There is only one woman in the world that I ever asked to become a wife to me," he said in a choked voice.

The reporters were back at the theater the following day, mercilessly pressing for details about his relations with Nettie and demanding that he be "open" about the facts.

By now, James had regained his composure and wit. He said that if the reporters wanted him to be "open," they were welcome to come to the Clifton House at six and watch him having his supper. "I shall open my mouth there," he quipped. The Clifton House was where he and Ella were staying, and where Ella was trying valiantly to cope with the humiliating situation in which she found herself.

A week later, with Chicago still buzzing about the scandal, James did make a public answer through his lawyer, Frank Crane. Crane filed a paper on September 16 in which James alleged he had become acquainted with Nettie Walsh in Cleveland on August 1, 1871, but that she, so far as he knew, had adopted his name simply for the purpose of the suit and had no legal right to it. He denied marrying her in Cleveland or anywhere else, adding that their acquaintance after he left Cleveland for Chicago in 1872 had "continued at wide intervals of time up to the present."

James further declared, through his lawyer, that Nettie was "under the influence of sundry designing persons" who sought "to ruin" his professional prospects and that it was they who had advised her to "set forth a pretended and bogus marriage with that end in view." At the beginning of their acquaintance, James averred, Nettie Walsh "was not a chaste and virtuous woman." He said he had no way of knowing whether he was the father of her child and challenged her "to make a proof, as she may deem most beneficial to her cause," as to his paternity.

The countersuit ended with James's allegation that he had considered the relationship "extinguished" in 1875, when he went to San Francisco. Since that time, he added, Nettie Walsh had been "the recipient of improper attentions from divers men," whose names he did not know. He claimed she was currently living with one of these men, who was not her husband but who provided for her and enjoyed "the marital relations of a husband."

Evidently James was referring to an older actor named Alfred Hamilton Seaman, known by the nickname, "Pop," who had befriended him when he first went on the stage. When James's career quickly outstripped Seaman's, the older actor grew jealous, and he spitefully encouraged Nettie Walsh to claim James as the father of her child (whose actual name was Alfred Hamilton, and who might just as probably have been Seaman's child).

By way of establishing his own probity, James pointed to his recent marriage to Ella Quinlan, which had been "solemnized according to the forms of law and sealed with the obligations of religion in the church." Ever since his marriage, he said, he had endeavored to support himself and his wife "in a just and lawful and honorable way." Moreover, he refuted Nettie Walsh's charge of his affluence. He was not worth $15,000, and offered to make an exhibit to the court of all his property — though he also maintained Nettie had no right whatever to call for such a statement, nor had she any claim upon his property.

Begging the question of his relationship with Louise Hawthorne, James denied that he was "addicted to vicious and obscene habits." He said he was "living a laborious life and making provisions for the future." He summed up by rejecting every one of Nettie's "outrageous charges," declaring them to be "without substance or in fact."

In spite of James's spirited defense, Ella was mortified, aware that Nettie Walsh's action had drawn prurient press notice not only in Chicago, but in New York and San Francisco, as well as her home town of Cleveland — wherever, in fact, James was known. Eugene O'Neill indicated the depth of the wound by having Mary Tyrone hark back accusingly to the episode in *Long Day's Journey Into Night*: " . . . right after we were married, there was the scandal of that woman who had been your mistress suing you."

Ella learned to take comfort from James's fidelity after their marriage. As Mary (in a morphine-induced talking binge) observes in the play to her housemaid, "There has never been a breath of scandal about him. I mean, with any other woman. Never since he met me. That has made me very happy . . . It has made me forgive so many other things."

Despite Ella's distress and despite the ongoing scandal, James missed no performances and, in fact, garnered excellent notices for his appearance in *Othello* with the Shakespearean star, Lawrence Barrett.

On October 23, five months after James's marriage and three weeks before he was due to open in his New York engagement, the case designated "Nettie O'Neill against James O'Neill" was heard in Superior Court in Chicago.

Judge Erastus W. Williams listened patiently to depositions of witnesses representing both sides. Alfred Hamilton ("Pop") Seaman,

James's former friend and current nemesis, testified that James and Nettie Walsh had been "clandestinely" married in Cleveland and a woman named Mrs. James Eyster stated that Nettie had lived with her in 1875 and that she "had often urged Nettie to demand recognition as the wife of O'Neill and support from him as such." Nettie Walsh's lawyer avowed his client was "suffering from poverty, while the defendant was in good circumstances," but offered no further argument.

In all, support of Nettie's claim was less than compelling. James, in rebuttal, simply offered an affidavit denying the marriage. He was supported by sworn statements from two friends, Henry Pratt and John O'Neill (who later became Eugene O'Neill's godfather). James's lawyer also introduced as witnesses two women — Sarah Howard and a Mrs. Brockman — who alleged Nettie had told them she was not the wife of James O'Neill, but that she intended to "make money out of him."

Judge Williams ruled that the evidence before him was insufficient to prove the marriage, but that, pending a hearing on November 26, he would allow Nettie Walsh $100 for attorney's fees and $50 a month for her support.

By November 13, James was back in New York, appearing at the Union Square in a play called *The Mother's Secret*. The Chicago hearing was conducted, after a postponement, on December 6, without James's presence. The court held that Nettie Walsh "was not and never has been married" to James O'Neill and that she "has not been and is not now" the wife of James O'Neill. The bill for divorce was dismissed.

Ella could not bring herself to accept graciously the well-meant sympathy of James's colleagues and she shrank from what she perceived as the scorn and pity of her own few friends. One such, a former St. Mary's schoolmate named Lillie West, recalled thirty-two years later how she had been rebuffed by Ella. Writing in a Chicago newspaper under the pseudonym, Amy Leslie, she reported having asked Ella (none too tactfully, to be sure), "Oh, Ella, what on earth can you do about this woman?" Ella, according to West/Leslie, loftily responded, "What woman, honey?"

As the year 1877 drew to a close, Ella, not yet twenty-one and a bride of only six months, resigned herself to the insecure life that seemed to stretch before her, aware she had nothing to cling to but the ardent love she and James felt for each other. She devoutly hoped that would suffice.

CHAPTER
SIX

Eが早ARLY IN 1878, JAMES AND ELLA SET OUT BY TRAIN WITH the Union Square company for San Francisco. Nearing the city, their coach was coupled to a train filled with soldiers returning home after quelling an Indian uprising. A wildly festive greeting awaited both soldiers and actors, especially James, still fondly remembered as a matinee idol with Richard Hooley's company two years earlier.

Due to the recent scandals of Louise Hawthorne's death and Nettie Walsh's lawsuit, he was also an object of facetious fascination. "Mr. James O'Neill, your black-mustached Adonis, had . . . stood in the foremost rank in New York, been claimed in Chicago by three or four wives, and finally comes back to us as handsome, as talented and as well-mustached as ever," wrote a local journalist upon his arrival.

San Francisco was trying to regain its poise after a financial panic. The new society was still attempting to rival the East in its embrace of popular culture and castles continued to sprout on Nob Hill. While the theaters were in a temporary slump, James was optimistic about the city's recovery and his own chances of success.

He knew San Francisco was renowned for its wildly seesawing economy and took happily to the city's swirling currents. Infected by the fever of speculation, he soon began investing in real estate and mining operations. When the company settled in at the Baldwin Theater, ensconced in a lavish new edifice that contained a hotel and shops, James confidently occupied the star's dressing room.

That March, he learned, no doubt to his delight, that Ella was pregnant. As she anticipated motherhood, her pain over the Nettie Walsh scandal slowly receded. She had further cause to rejoice when James, wishing to give her a sense of stability during her pregnancy and early motherhood, decided to stay put in San Francisco for an indefinite period.

When the Union Square company, having fulfilled its commitment, returned to New York, James took the opportunity to join the Baldwin's highly-respected resident stock company. Ella, having already endured trauma enough to daunt any young bride, could now, at least for a time, look forward to a settled life.

James had a secondary reason to pause in San Francisco: he wished to be close to his investments. Although he eventually lost money on most of his real-estate deals, he never lost faith in his judgment as an investor. Throughout his life he continued to sink a portion of his earnings into various land schemes.

Shortly after James's death in 1920, an old friend wrote to Eugene O'Neill, remarking that his father's "queer investments were a continual source of worry" to his friends. At the same time, the friend said, "there was a pathetically humorous side to it all."

"He was nearly always 'done' by an Irishman!," the letter continued. "Such a lover of his own people was he that any plausible swindler had simply to possess an Irish name in order to get his ear, and if he happened to have an O' in front of it, all the king's men couldn't hold the dear fellow back . . . "

As Eugene himself was later to point out, his father was "an easy mark for anyone with a spare gold mine, zinc mine, coal mine, silver mine, pieces of real estate, etc. — and he rarely guessed right." But at least, he added, "he never went into anything so heavily it could ruin him."

It was not that James enjoyed gambling. On the contrary, he invested because of his pathological fear of poverty and thought he was securing his future. As James Tyrone rationalizes in *Long Day's Journey Into Night*, "Banks fail, and your money's gone, but you think you can keep land beneath your feet."

His closest friend in the west, Nate Salsbury, a thriving theatrical manager, was responsible for one of James's more successful investments. Salsbury, who had been an actor with the troupe assembled by James for "Uncle Dick" Hooley in Chicago in 1874, later became a partner of Buffalo Bill Cody in his touring "Wild West" show.

He persuaded James to invest in a Montana cattle ranch, known as the Milner Cattle Co., of which Salsbury was a principal owner. Long after James's death, the ranch was still yielding dividends. As late as 1932, O'Neill received a stipend from the ranch, which he passed on to his older son, Eugene Jr., then twelve. " . . . I am enclosing a dividend check endorsed over to you," he wrote. " . . . A grand surprise to me, this one was! It represents a small share in a cattle ranch in Montana your romantically-investing Grandfather left me. I thought those cows had all perished of hoof-and-mouth disease long ago!"

The same instinct that drove James O'Neill to invest also made him miserly in his personal expenditures (about that, Nettie Walsh had been correct). In the self-analytical notes Eugene O'Neill made in 1927, he attempted to understand James's parsimony, describing his father as " . . . stingy about money due to his childhood experience with grinding poverty after his father deserted large family to return to Ireland . . . "

Oddly, James's frugality in family matters was complicated by an opposing desire to appear generous in the eyes of his colleagues. He economized on lodgings that were sometimes minimally comfortable and he wore his clothes until they were threadbare. Yet, in the bar-room, he could always be counted upon to stand his friends to drinks. Thus, while his family regarded him as miserly, his peers saw him in quite another light.

Not an actor, manager or agent ever had anything but glowing praise for James's generosity — remarkable in a profession where petty jealousies and vindictive gossip throve. The esteem accorded him was accurately summed up by a contemporary San Francisco journalist:

"Among his fellow actors [James O'Neill] is much respected . . . He is noted for his kindness to young actors, and if called on will readily advise them about the business of their parts. Although holding the leading position in the theater, he . . . is generous in allowing anyone in scenes with himself to make a point when they can, and this is the secret of how he gains so many friends behind the scenes. He is charitable to the deserving, and is always ready to help those who are in need of his assistance."

James O'Neill Jr. was born at the home of a friend on September 10, 1878. His parents seemed, to their acquaintances, to be calm and secure. Ella, transfigured by motherhood, devoted herself to her baby, whom she called Jimmie (the same nickname by which his father was known). For the first time since her marriage, she found purposeful occupation. Doubtless, she could even read with amusement the publicity given to James's love scenes in Bronson Howard's *Saratoga*. Young men in the audience organized betting pools on the number of kisses James would exchange each night with his leading lady, Nina Varian.

In his self-analytical notes, Eugene O'Neill emphasized this period of tranquility during which Ella rejoiced in her motherhood: " . . . Birth of first son 1 year after marriage. Father's life in profession more stable then — in stock — for long periods in one city — more sense of home than in later years when constantly touring — M physically healthy then . . . "

Despite occasional negative reviews, James's popularity with audiences continued undiminished. The Baldwin was operated by a tempestuous pair, Tom McGuire and Elias Jackson Baldwin. McGuire, an expatriate New York saloon keeper, became San Francisco's leading impresario and called himself the "Napoleon of the San Francisco theatre." Baldwin was known in theater circles as "Lucky," because he had made a fortune in Nevada mines and in stock gambles.

Some time before James's arrival, the management of the Baldwin had acquired the services of a young actor-cum-stage manager who was also a self-proclaimed playwright of remarkable nimbleness. One of his feats was an "adaptation" of Bronson Howard's New York success, *The Banker's Daughter*; the "adaptation" consisted in changing the play's title to *The Millionaire's Daughter*, deleting Bronson Howard's name, and substituting his own, which happened to be David Belasco.

Although this play and others of commensurate banality kept James profitably occupied until early 1879, he yearned to distinguish himself in a loftier vehicle. His prayers were answered with an unconventional, but to him irresistible, offer: the role of Jesus Christ in an adaptation of *The Passion*. The production, which required an inordinately deep stage, was booked into the Grand Opera House.

Clearly, James's vision of himself in the role of Jesus was so strong, he was blind to the tawdriness of the script. It had been concocted by an egregiously untalented writer named Salmi Morse (succinctly taken to task by a local newspaper for being "not nice in his syntax").

Morse, who dressed in black, had flowing gray hair, a drooping mustache, an abbreviated beard, mournful eyes and the general demeanor of a religious fanatic, was regarded as outlandish even in San Francisco, where eccentrics were as common as telegraph poles.

His dramatization of the life of Christ was, he claimed, the result of twenty years of research in the Holy Land. In his possession were

yellowed parchment documents to prove the authenticity of his find-
ings. The fact that Morse, who was a Jew, proposed to produce what
amounted to a Christian religious service, did not disturb James any
more than the fact that he himself, an Irish Catholic, should be called
upon to depict the Nazarene.

Neither of these details, however, escaped the acid observation of
San Francisco's journalists. Long before the play was unveiled, angry
protest was registered by the newspapers, prodded by a contingent
of Protestant ministers. Salmi Morse averred that California's
Catholic bishop had expressed approval of the script, but no church
official spoke out publicly either for or against the production.

Despite the objections, James and his cast plunged into rehearsals
at the Grand Opera House, staging *The Passion* in a grandiose, pseu-
do-biblical style that anticipated, by four decades, the silent film
sagas of Cecil B. De Mille.

Young Belasco, ecstatic over the opportunity that had come his
way, chased about the city in search of one hundred nursing mothers
to appear in a tableau entitled "The Massacre of the Innocents." He
then proceeded to round up a flock of sheep and engage two hundred singers and four hundred supers. He visited the Mechanics
Mercantile Library, where he stood lost in scholarly study before two
biblical canvases that he proposed to replicate on stage.

James, meanwhile, had determined that in justice to his role he
must embrace the life of an ascetic. He gave up drinking, tobacco and
other worldly pleasures. He forbade the members of his company to
use rough language or to engage in any backstage frivolity.

He conducted solemn rehearsals, after which he retired to his
dressing room for contemplation. His fans were astonished and
impressed to read of his new personality, and his fellow actors, finding his pious approach contagious, began to walk and speak softly.
Belasco, quick to take his cue, carried about a Bible and, though
Jewish, murmured of plans to enter a monastery.

Secure in his devotion, James had persuaded himself that *The
Passion* was both elegiac and elevating, and he was baffled by the pre-
opening rumbles in the press, which criticized him for a misguided
attempt to mix religion with commercialism.

Ella became increasingly alarmed as the protests mounted and
she implored James to cancel the project. Despite her pleas and the
threats of irate citizens to take legal action, *The Passion* opened on the
night of March 3, 1879.

"I was uncertain up to ten minutes before I went to the theater [on opening night] whether I should not give up the whole thing," James later told his friend, Nate Salsbury. "My wife threw herself upon her knees at my feet, and pleaded with me to send word that I would not go on. She said the people would kill me."

Pandemonium greeted the opening. When James appeared onstage with a halo floating above his head, women in the audience, consisting largely of San Francisco's parochial Irish, fell to their knees in prayer. And when James was crowned with thorns, some fainted. As the play ended, a number of patrons, inflamed by the portrayal of Christ's suffering, rushed into the streets to assault Jews and vandalize pawnshops and other Jewish-owned establishments.

Newspaper critics were hostile, one of them calling the play "an absurd and irreverent money-making spectacle." The editorial pages rang with protest, the Protestant clergy redoubled its denunciation — and at first it looked as though the publicity alone would create a box-office bonanza.

After only eight days, Tom McGuire, the self-styled "Napoleon" of the theater, who had financed *The Passion*, decided to close it; he had received letters threatening his life and was unwilling to risk continuing, even for the sake of assured profits.

Members of the company returned to the Baldwin, where they hastily dragged a potboiler out of stock, this one called *The Miner's Daughter*. When audiences failed to respond, McGuire had second thoughts. Swallowing his fears, he revived *The Passion* on April 15, even though a newly passed city ordinance made its presentation illegal and its cast subject to prosecution.

"It shall be unlawful for any person," the ordinance stated, "to exhibit . . . in any theater, or other place where money is charged for admission, any play or performance displaying . . . the life or death of Jesus Christ, or any play . . . intending to debase or degrade religion."

Although some of the actors withdrew from the company, James supported the decision to challenge the ordinance. The attempt at defiance was short-lived. Toward the end of the performance, which drew a full house, two policemen served James and seven of his fellow-actors with warrants and led them to jail, still in costume and makeup.

Belasco preferred not to share in their martyrdom and foiled arrest by hiding in the cellar. James and his colleagues were released on bail provided by Lucky Baldwin and the next day were found guilty of violating the ordinance.

The San Francisco Newsletter indignantly took up arms on James's behalf, commenting in a sarcastic editorial that the restrictive legal action taken by "wicked, reckless, dashing San Francisco, and her Board of Supervisors" was shocking. "It is not decorous England or puritan Boston that convicts Mr. O'Neill," said the editorial, "nor is it some obscure, little village board, which might well be pardoned for narrow-mindedness . . . . We expect next to hear of an ordinance for the burning of all old women who keep cats or have a mole on their noses."

The mortifying episode was closed three days later, after an appeal to the Superior Court, which upheld the Lower Court decision and ordered James to pay a fifty-dollar fine. The others in the company payed penalties of five dollars each.

James never wavered from his conviction that *The Passion* was in the nature of a religious service, nor did he concede there was anything disrespectful about his performance. "I experienced not the slightest irreverence in giving expression to the actions reproduced from the life of Our Saviour," he later remarked.

Following this fiasco, however, James resigned himself to more traditional impersonations and San Francisco soon forgave him. At the same time, San Franciscans ignored Lester Wallack, who had arrived from New York to open an engagement at the rival California Theater. Wallack was so indifferently received that he was forced to pack up. He was unable to contain his spleen, however.

"Sir," he told a reporter, just before leaving the city, "you can judge what I think of average San Franciscans when I state my opinion that if Jesus Christ himself came down from Heaven they would give O'Neill the preference in the character."

Toward the end of October, 1880, James concluded the time had come to take his place among the brightest stars in the east. He knew it would mean resuming the rigorous touring of former years, but he had, after all, provided Ella with nearly three years of stability and she was obliged to concede that two-year-old Jimmie was big enough to travel with them.

A rising producer named Henry E. Abbey (later to become director of the Metropolitan Opera) had just proposed bringing James to New York's Booth Theater, which had come under his management. Abbey wanted James to star in — of all things — Salmi Morse's *The Passion*. James leaped at the chance, agreeing with Abbey that cosmopolitan New Yorkers would view the production with more understanding than parochial San Franciscans. *The Passion* was announced for December 6, scheduled to follow Sarah Bernhardt in a rare and raucously heralded four-week engagement.

James had misjudged yet again. Led by New York's press and clergy, the outcry against Abbey's production was even more clamorous than in San Francisco. Abbey refused to yield. Perhaps most mortifying for James was the contempt voiced by his idol, Edwin Booth, not only for the production but for James himself. "Abbey is mad & will regret his obstinacy in this matter," Booth complained in a letter to his friend, William Winter, the Tribune's critic, on November 23. "I hope you'll let the people know that though the theater bears my name I have no connection or authority — if I had I'd put a stop to the profanation. I am surprised that all the actors (except Jim O'Neil [sic]) do not refuse to take part in it."

Abbey was cowed at last into withdrawing the play, and James, in his bewilderment, had to concede it was "stark blasphemy" to American audiences. "Of course after such a setback," he said, "I firmly believed myself at the end of all success as an actor." He was wrong as it turned out. Abbey at once substituted *A Celebrated Case,* an acclaimed vehicle in James's repertoire, in which he was well-received.

During the months that followed, James, Ella and Jimmie occupied rooms in a genteel, moderately priced boarding house at 39 West Twenty-fourth Street, just a block from Booth's Theater. It was at this boarding house where, late in 1881, they met a nineteen-year-old woman named Elizabeth Robins, set on making her mark on the stage. The O'Neills formed an affectionate relationship with her that lasted several years. She later achieved considerable success not only as a novelist and playwright, but as an actress-manager in London, where she was befriended by George Bernard Shaw.

James, always on the lookout for friends for his shy and aloof wife, quickly perceived that Elizabeth was refined as well as intelligent. Only five years younger than Ella and mature beyond her years, Elizabeth might have reminded Ella of her own youthful self, newly arrived in New York to study music, brimming with dreams of a brilliant future. The two women were quickly drawn to each other, and James, eager to keep Elizabeth nearby for Ella's sake, was much inclined to assist her career.

At the time she met the O'Neills she was already a perceptive diarist and letter-writer and she left a rare portrait of James and Ella as a companionable, if occasionally hard-pressed, young married couple.

In James she found a gracious although sometimes autocratic mentor. In Ella she discovered a gentle, considerate and often high-spirited confidante. She quickly came to understand and empathize with Ella's self-sacrificing role as a stage wife. "What a life," she wrote in her diary some months after making Ella's acquaintance, "traveling about with actor-husbands, no occupation but to watch them."

Born in Louisville, Kentucky, on August 6, 1862, Elizabeth was the daughter of a southern gentlewoman and a self-made business-man from the north, who were first cousins. Her mother suffered a nervous breakdown after losing two of her children in infancy, as well as an adolescent stepson, and Elizabeth, at ten, was taken to live with her paternal grandmother in Zaneville, Ohio. No one in her family had ever had any connection with the stage, and they were baffled by her longing to be an actress.

Her father wanted her to attend college, but Elizabeth, after accompanying him on a business trip to New York, became more than ever stagestruck. She reluctantly returned to Ohio, but could not tolerate her humdrum life and struck out on her own for New York, although she had little money and no idea how she would support herself.

Moreover, she was not beautiful in any conventional sense; her hair was dark and curly and her features strongly defined in an oval face with a square chin. Her gray eyes, deepset and dreamy, were probably her best feature. It was her buoyant personality that was attractive, together with a ready wit, ample self-confidence and an iron will.

After meeting James on the morning of November 29 at his room-ing house, she wrote excitedly to her grandmother, explaining he was "a stock actor who has played with Booth [and] is a man of estab-lished reputation."

He "was extremely polite," Elizabeth reported, and promised to "speak to the manager of Booth's Theater & see if he can get me a foothold there."

James did take her to Booth's, where he was starring in yet anoth-er revival of *The Two Orphans*, with the prominent leading lady, Kate Claxton. He contrived to find Elizabeth a small role in which she appeared until the end of the run two weeks later.

Writing to her father on January 2, 1882, Elizabeth praised James's kindness, coming, as she put it, "from a popular star to an unknown, way down at the foot of the ladder." Her father evidently expressed a concern that James's interest was not completely platonic, and she hastened to assure him James had been "a *good friend & perfect gentleman*" but that "his wife likes me better, that is thinks more about me than he does; & often prompts his kindness."

During 1882 James continued to make appearances in New York in old standbys and also took them on tour, managing always to find small roles for Elizabeth, who with the impatience of youth pressed James to cast her in larger and better roles. By now, she and Ella had become dear friends, although, conforming to convention, she referred to her as "Mrs. O'Neill" or "Mrs. O"; Elizabeth, on the other hand, was "Bess" or "Bessie" to Ella.

It seems clear from Elizabeth's comments in her diaries and letters that Ella took a lively interest in James's career and kept herself well informed about the day-to-day details of his professional life. While keeping her distance from most of his associates, she did not hesitate to offer advice both to him and to those few members of his company, such as Elizabeth, to whom she felt close. Nor was she, during the early years of her marriage, the constantly brooding creature depicted by her son in *Long Day's Journey Into Night*.

In the years before Eugene's birth, she enjoyed her share of conventional socializing with selected acquaintants — a feature of her early married life she evidently failed to convey to her son, or that he simply chose to ignore. In fact, it was James who at times shrank from formal social visiting, preferring to relax among his peers in the less restrained atmosphere of the barroom or the club — an aspect of the O'Neill marriage his son conveyed accurately in *Long Day's Journey*.

One piquant example of the different attitudes held by James and Ella was described by Elizabeth in her diary. Having noted an invitation to a cousin's reception, Elizabeth wrote that Ella " . . . says she will come 'if James will.'" James, however, when handed the invitation, said he had an engagement for that evening. Then, according to the diary, James "confesses he is dreadfully opposed to meeting strangers and never feels at home in a parlor."

"You see," he tells Elizabeth, "they come to see me act & then expect me to be a hero & all that sort of thing off the stage & the strain is too great, I can't keep it up." Ella, disappointed, takes revenge by chiding James for having gone the previous evening to a place called "The Drum" — where, she explains to Elizabeth, "all the 'queer' theatrical people go."

Thrown together as they were, Elizabeth and Ella grew ever closer. During performances, when she was not on stage, Elizabeth often sat with Ella in James's dressing room. Between performances, Elizabeth spent much time with Ella and Jimmie in their hotel. When Elizabeth fell ill, Ella nursed her and when Ella felt unwell Elizabeth was all devoted attention.

Elizabeth's diary and letters are punctuated with comments about the conditions that existed on the trains and in the hotels during her tours with the O'Neills. In one entry, she described a train that had no sleeping cars, with everyone having to "spend night in common car pregnant with odors of whiskey & bad tobacco."

Writing to her grandmother on May 10, she described (with considerable understatement) "a rather uncomfortable trip to St. Louis" with James, Ella, three-year-old Jimmie and his nurse, Annie, during which the entire company fell ill.

"The motion of the cars, the heat and dirt made us all wretched & I could not touch a mouthful," she wrote. An actress in the company "had one of her terrible attacks, lay for 8 hours in a dead faint, & after dreadful convulsions finally came to."

Ella regarded the younger woman with such trust that she began confiding in her. "Mrs. O. makes me lie on her bed and talks of the past," wrote Elizabeth in her diary, "tells me all the particulars of the Chicago affair, the Nettie Walsh case & I admire her for standing by her husband."

Evidently Nettie had resurfaced. She did not bring any further public action against James, having decided instead to try private pressure, and when James, that July, brought his repertory to Chicago, she began hounding him.

On July 5, Elizabeth noted in her diary, "Go & see Mrs. O. Find her depressed, calls me in close & tells me about 'that woman & the child' who are following Mr. O . . . Latter keeps appointment with this woman at backdoor of Hooley's. [She] calls him 'James,' brings child too, wants child supported and educated yet retains possession of him. Mrs. O. sleepless & wretched."

And yet, five days later, as Elizabeth wrote in her diary, an arrangement had evidently been made about Nettie Walsh's eight-year-old son. "[Mrs. O] says they will stay till they get custody of 'the child' & will take him with them on their way to N.Y. & leave him at school in Detroit." By July 15 the custody plan appears to have fallen through and the O'Neills departed Chicago — without "the child."

The new episode with Nettie Walsh had frayed Ella's nerves and

in the waiting room of the railroad station she complained to
Elizabeth about "the recent trouble." James, too, was in an irritable
mood, and Elizabeth described the sort of spat and its reconciliation
as not untypical:

"Mr. O. finds Jimmie & says next year he will not pay expenses of
a nurse, a wife might do something to help a husband, & taking a
nurse about the [country] was a terrible expense, etc. He says some
sharp things, she is not far behind him. Later they sit together &
talk . . . "

James's sudden determination to save the expense of a nursemaid
for his legitimate son, after having just offered to pay for the education of his illegitimate one, was yet another example of his irrational
attitude about money.

James, by this time, had regained sufficient confidence to proceed
with his plan to catapult himself to national fame. Emulating
Jefferson and Forrest, he searched for a vehicle in which to tour under
his own exclusive management. At first he thought of buying outright *A Celebrated Case*, but ultimately decided to commission a new
play tailored just for him.

He sought out a writer named Charles T. Dazey, who had written
a script grandiosely entitled *An American King*. Its convoluted plot
turned on the character of a California gold miner, Nat Ruggles, who
becomes a millionaire and is treacherously brought to ruin by his
friends. James added the play to his repertoire and, though it fell
short of becoming the audience-pleaser he had envisioned, he continued to perform it through the end of the year.

The play provided Elizabeth Robins with a new role, albeit the
least important of all the female roles and one she hated for its triteness — that of the spinster, Prudence Holdfast. She felt so embarrassed that she adopted the stage name, Claire Raimond, for the
play's run. Elizabeth was growing impatient with the slow progress
of her career and resented James's insistence that she must be patient.
At times she was openly huffy with him.

She also complained that her salary, twenty-five dollars a week,
was "wholly inadequate to defray" her expenses to lodge at the
decent hotels where the O'Neills stayed (when such accommodations
were available). "Living as we do we must spend money or leave the
good company in our party to consort with the rag-tag & bob-tail."

Then, describing a most uncharacteristic stance taken by James,

Roots

Eugene O'Neill attributed his profound sense of alienation to his parents' inability to communicate meaningfully with each other or with him. His father, James O'Neill (above), as a young actor.

Eugene's mother, Ellen Quinlan, as a pious school girl at St. Mary's Academy, early 1870's.

James's older sister, Josephine Sears, who rescued him from poverty in Buffalo, New York.

Advertisement in the Kilkenny Journal, March 19, 1851, that probably prompted James's father to sail from Ireland with his wife and children.

EMIGRATION FROM NEW-ROSS

TO QUEBEC.

The Splendid and Very Fast Sailing Ship.
"INDIA,"
1400 TONS BURTHEN,
JOHN WILLIS, Commander,
On the 1st APRIL, Next.

The Remarkably Fine and Fast Ship
"GLENLYON"
1700 TONS,
On the 15th of APRIL Next.

I. Population. CENSUS of the Inhabitants in the *Eight* Election District of the *Ward* City *Buffalo* in the County of *Erie* taken by me on the *Twenty fifth* day of June, 1855.

Edward O'Neill	65	M W		Ireland	
753 Mary O "	48 F W	wife	"	
Mary O "	22 F W	Dght	"	
Richard "	19 M W	Son	"	
Ann "	17 F W	Dght	"	
Johanna "	16 " "	"	"	
Bridget "	12 " "	"	"	
Edward "	10 M W	Son	"	
James "	8 " "	Son	"	
Ellen "	6 F W	Daugh	"	
Margaret "	3 F W	"	"	

Buffalo census, 1855, listing James O'Neill and his parents and siblings.

The south side of Superior Avenue in Cleveland, circa 1860, where Ellen's father, Thomas Quinlan, had a shop.

Dion Boucicault, the prolific playwright, in whose *The Colleen Bawn* James O'Neill made his stage debut.

Richard Hooley (standing) invited James to star in his Chicago stock company in 1874. James acted in French melodramas during the week and performed Shakespeare Saturday night.

Edwin Forrest (top), and Joseph Jefferson, two of the reigning American stars James supported early in his career.

Adelaide Neilson, the English actress renowned on two continents for her portrayal of Juliet. She hailed James as the best Romeo with whom she ever performed.

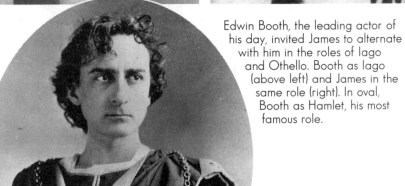

Edwin Booth, the leading actor of his day, invited James to alternate with him in the roles of Iago and Othello. Booth as Iago (above left) and James in the same role (right). In oval, Booth as Hamlet, his most famous role.

The Union Square Theatre, where James made his New York debut in *The Two Orphans* in October, 1876.

James as the crippled Pierre Frochard in *The Two Orphans.*

James as Count Vladimir in *The Danicheffs* at the Union Square. It was during Ellen Quinlan's backstage visit that James fell in love with her.

Ellen Quinlan at about the time of her marriage. Soon after, she changed her name to Ella.

James O'Neill (below) as Christ in *The Passion* at San Francisco's Grand Opera House, March 1879. He and Ella had been married less than two years.

James O'Neill Jr., nicknamed Jamie, at about six. He was born September 10, 1878.

Ella O'Neill, circa 1880's.
James O'Neill (right) as Edmond
Dantes, the Count of Monte
Cristo, and as Dantes after his
escape from the Chateau D'If.

Elizabeth Robins (below) toured
as a member of James O'Neill's
company, and became an
intimate friend of Ella O'Neill.

she wrote, "Mr. O'Neill argues you have only one life, the world owes you a living, get the best you can. Go to the first class hotels, the best is none too good for you, besides it is false economy to eat bad food & sleep in poor rooms etc, etc, so I keep with the best portion of the company & live well while I have the chance."

Evidently Elizabeth was beginning to comprehend the contradictory traits in James's character, traits familiar to his wife and, later, painfully to his sons. She described him as "a strange genius I can liken only to quicksilver, unstable in purpose, changeable in opinion, highly gifted, a good-hearted and *just* man."

At the end of January, 1883, James, having completed a recent run in Toronto and upstate New York, received an unexpected offer from the Boston-born impressario, John Stetson, who had taken over the lease of the Booth Theater in New York. Stetson had built a lucrative career arranging tours for such stars as Salvini, Lily Langtree and Madame Helena Modjeska, had produced minstrel and variety shows and had operated gambling houses, cafés and pawnshops.

Charles Thorne Jr. had opened at the Booth on January 8 in *The Corsican Brothers*. Two nights later, he was stricken with an ailment diagnosed as "rheumatic gout" and had to be hastily replaced.

When it became clear he would not recover in time to star in the next attraction — as Edmond Dantes in *The Count of Monte Cristo* — Stetson offered James the role at the respectable salary of $600 a week. A dramatization of Alexandre Dumas's novel by the admired actor, Charles Fechter, Monte Cristo was one of the period's most durable romances. (Fechter had died four years earlier after touring in the play for several seasons.)

Conceivably, it was Charles Thorne himself who suggested James for the role of Dantes, recalling James's popular appeal when they played together at the Union Square Theater. Having toyed with the idea of dropping *An American King* from his repertoire, James eagerly took up Stetson's offer, little guessing it was to be his ticket to the superstardom that had so far eluded him.

On February 11, New Yorkers learned Charles Thorne had died of internal hemorrhages. His funeral was held the next day and, that night, the cast engaged to support him in *The Count of Monte Cristo* supported James O'Neill instead.

At thirty-seven, James was still slender enough to look rakish in tight velvet breeches and a close-fitting doublet. (According to Elizabeth Robins he looked "half a dozen years younger" than his age.) He had honed a persona (largely in emulation of Edwin Booth) that was swashbuckling, but without the grandiose swagger and excessive gestures and vocal tricks so beloved of stars of the era.

There were gasps from the opening-night audience when, after escaping from his unjust imprisonment in the Chateau d'If by leaping into the sea, James emerged with blazing eyes from the churning waves, his breast heaving with the triumph of his daring. The waves, a blue ground-cloth manipulated from below by hard-breathing stagehands, seemed to have assumed a newly menacing wetness.

And when the liberated Dantes cried out, in a voice that penetrated to the last row of the gallery, "The world is mine!" the audience, thrilled to find the tired old vehicle infused with new life, gave James an accolade that seemed to prove the truth of his statement. Dantes, the wronged, avenging and ultimately victorious Count, suited James to perfection; in his hands the role became the be-all and end-all of the glorious, make-believe French nobleman.

The critics, however, disagreed with the enraptured first-nighters. The crusty theatrical journal, Spirit of the Times, for example, stated that "the revival of Monte Cristo was a failure and . . . it deserved to fail . . . Mr. O'Neill is an actor with an Irish name and an Irish accent but without any Irish sympathy, passion or magnetism."

To the critic of The New York Times, the Irish accent was undetectable and the magnetism was at least moderately in evidence. However, he found the production itself "tedious and awkward."

"The chief actors in the cast," he complained, "seemed unfamiliar with their parts. The cast was, however, respectable and may become, after a few evenings, effective. Mr. O'Neill failed to make an impression of strength because he applied to broad and dashing romantic acting the restrained method of realism. His intensity at the closing scenes of the play was, nevertheless, dramatic and somewhat magnetic." The Tribune was even tarter, dismissing the production as "mechanical" and "tiresome."

James admitted, many years later, that he had given a poor performance on opening night because of insufficient rehearsal time. "When Mr. Stetson had billed the play and myself," he explained, "I begged him to postpone the opening for a week, but he said he couldn't. 'I know all the newspaper boys, and will tell them that you had only three rehearsals,' he promised. 'They will understand and overlook crudities.' But on the opening night he was busy and forgot. The next morning the papers were severe.

"The critics were right that time. I was bad. I knew it. But I got at the play with hammer and tongs. I rehearsed all day in my rooms. By the end of the week the play was going well. The public saved the life of the play."

Evidently, the suddenness with which James had stepped into the cast of *The Count of Monte Cristo* had put all thought of Elizabeth Robins and her career out of his mind. She attempted to strike out on her own professionally when she returned to New York in January. She moved into a rooming house on the same block as the O'Neills and maintained close contact with Ella, who, as she wrote to her grandmother on February 23, was "as sisterly as ever." James, however, had grown unapproachable, preoccupied as he was with his new production. She did not consult him about her plans, informing him only after the fact that she had turned down a proffered role.

"Mr. O'Neill tells me I should not have declined without consulting him," she commented acerbically to her grandmother, "seems piqued that I acted so independently of him, says had I come to him a week ago he could and would have secured me a position but my incomprehensible reticence and independence have operated against me. Mr. O was so wrapped up in his own business in fact, he forgot me & now is indignant because I was too proud to remind him of broken promises."

She could not take the time to go into details, she said, but indicated she and James were again on friendly terms and that he had promised to "do all in his power" to help find her an engagement. However, she added, "there could not be a worse time to try. The city is overbooked with professionals out of employment." Nonetheless, James found a small role for Elizabeth in *The Count of Monte Cristo*.

When the play closed at the Booth on St. Patrick's Day to go on tour, Elizabeth left the company, convinced she could speed her career under different auspices, and for a time she was out of touch with the O'Neills.

On tour, *The Count of Monte Cristo* pulled in audiences, and John Stetson, realizing he had a solid moneymaker, signed James to a new contract that guaranteed him $1,000 a week plus a box-office percentage — more than James had ever commanded.

Ella and her son, now five, continued to travel with the company. The closeness of mother and son was unusually intense; without a settled home, without familiar playmates, the child depended largely on his mother (and to a lesser degree on his nurse) for daily, even hourly, companionship.

Within the often cramped confines of hotel rooms, week after week, month after month, mother and son were forced into overdependency. The little boy had now been given the pet name Jamie, because his father had tired of hearing his own nickname, Jimmie, called out by his son's nurse.

Pregnant again, Ella found traveling more difficult than ever. But she had no more wish to be separated from her husband than he from her, and she continued on the road, only returning to New York in time to give birth on September 16, 1883 to a second boy at an apartment-hotel at 22 East Forty-ninth Street.

The baby was christened Edmund Burke O'Neill in honor of the Dublin-born English orator — a curious choice in view of James's bitterness against his father, who had gone by the name Edmund in Ireland; evidently James's admiration for Edmund Burke outweighed his anger against his father.

While it is commonplace for a child to resent the intrusion of a new sibling, to five-year-old Jamie it was as though the ground beneath him had cracked open. Over-attached as he was to his mother, and taking it for granted he was and always would be the focus of her daily tenderness and love, he could barely comprehend the altered circumstances caused by the arrival of an infant brother. Slowly and sadly, he learned he was now expected to share his mother's love.

Edmund's birth was noted by Elizabeth Robins, who, while touring on her own, reestablished contact with James when he brought *Monte Cristo* to Boston's Globe Theater in early October. According to her diary, he told her that Ella was in New York and had "a little son 3 wks old."

Wherever James appeared, most often playing one-night stands, audiences crowded to see him. But Stetson, convinced that a single season of touring would exhaust the play's popularity, decided to sell it to James for $2,500, in what turned out to be one of Stetson's less astute deals. James on the other hand had for once guessed right. ("My good bad luck," James Tyrone ruefully reflects in *Long Day's Journey Into Night*.) Under James O'Neill's management, the play began to bring in more money than James had ever dreamed he would earn.

Newspapers tracked his itinerary, somewhat baffled by the play's success; sixteen months after the New York opening, a probing critique was published in the San Francisco News Letter:

Monte Cristo . . . is exciting and interesting in spite of its many absurdities of detail . . . Dantes in prison protrudes his head through a hole within a few inches from the top of the parapet, and at the same time he goes on mining for his freedom; an order is given to double the guard for the purpose of shooting Dantes as he escapes, and the guard is then withdrawn. In the ballroom scene Monte Cristo transacts business in the presence of the hostess and guests and bandies vulgar and insulting words with a bystander. Danglars writes a letter with his left hand at the rate of 199 words a minute. Nortier shouts good-night from his room in the inn, and ten seconds afterwards, by the watch, his would-be murderess announces that he is asleep.

The waves in the Chateau d'If scene are simply dreadful. The apotheosis of all this absurdity is the scene where Dantes, standing on a two-by-four rock in the midst of bobbing chunks of wood and canvas, receives a shower of salt. That this play, with all these supremely ridiculous details . . . should still excite and amuse, is a proof of its strong romantic interest and powerful dramatic force. It is bound to draw for some time.

The prediction, as it turned out, was far too modest.

CHAPTER SEVEN

DESPITE CRITICAL CARPING, THE DEMAND FOR *MONTE Cristo* was inexhaustible. With all its foolish flaws and inconsistencies, this marvel of the 19th century stage encapsulated a mix of romance, heightened action, pathos and bravado that no other melodrama of the era could duplicate. Together with James's singular suitability for the role of Dantes — his good looks, agility, melodious voice and patent sincerity — the play touched a response in both young and old that sent them back to see it over and over.

Newly-laid railroad track made touring easier, and for a thirty-week season he was soon earning close to thirty thousand dollars. At last, he felt almost free of the threat of the poorhouse — although he never could liberate himself from the compulsion to pinch pennies.

With a growing family and an expanding income, James and Ella decided they could afford a modest vacation home during their summer hiatus from touring. They chose the small Connecticut town of New London, within reasonable reach of New York by train or boat. Built on a succession of low hills with breathtaking views and cooled by breezes from the Thames River and Long Island Sound, it was to be the wandering O'Neill family's only permanent home.

Ella's mother, Bridget, already had taken up residence in New London to be near her sister and brother-in-law, Elizabeth and John Brennan. James also had a friend in New London, John McGinley, who was as eager to see him settle there as Bridget was to have her daughter and grandchildren nearby.

McGinley had worked in New York in the white-goods business and James, chancing to meet him in the barroom of the Union Square Hotel and learning that McGinley's grandfather had arrived from Ireland in the late 18th century, felt an immediate kinship. McGinley's grandfather had settled in New London, which in the

mid-1800's boasted the second largest whaling port in the world, surpassed only by New Bedford. McGinley had proceeded to spin tales
of New London's recent history, and of his father, known as Strong
Arm Jack, a whaling captain.

John McGinley gave up his New York business in 1881 and
returned to New London to raise a family and change careers, becoming the first (and at that time the only) reporter on the fledgling newspaper, the New London Day. He was thus engaged when James and
Ella arrived in 1884.

A narrow strip of land, the town measured only three quarters of
a mile at its widest point; three miles long, it encircled a large, deep-
water harbor. The mouth of the Thames opened into the Sound, providing an ideal anchorage not only for steamers but for the square-
riggers and windjammers that still sailed the seas.

The town's mainstay was small industry related to shipping, tex-
tiles and the tag end of the whaling business, commemorated by
three stately, white Greek Revival houses built in the 1840's by prosperous whaling captains. The houses, with their embellishment of
Corinthian columns, stood on Huntington Street — "Whale Oil Row"
— in the center of town. These dwellings, in vogue during the first
half of the 19th century, inspired the setting in part for the New
England house in *Mourning Becomes Electra*, whose facade is a "white
Grecian temple portico" with "six tall columns."

New London's possibilities as a yachting and swimming haven,
on a par with Rhode Island's Newport and Narragansett Pier, had
already been recognized by the socially prominent of New York,
Boston and Philadelphia, a fact that did not escape James's business
eye.

James and Ella, with young Jamie and the infant Edmund, spent
at least part of the summer of 1884 in New London. Anecdotal information suggests that they rented a small house on Vauxhall Street, in
a fashionable section of town. From there, James looked around for
property to buy. It was not long before he acquired two tracts of land
on Pequot Avenue, an area that intermingled greengrocers, farm
houses and barns with the grand residences of wealthy new arrivals
in search of the picturesque.

Once paved with crushed clamshells and called Harbor Road,
Pequot Avenue, renamed as a salute to the Pequot tribes that
camped along the Thames in the 17th century, stretched from the
edge of town for about a mile along the banks of the river to a curve
of land where a slender white lighthouse marked the beginning of

the Sound.

James paid two thousand dollars for the two tracts, on one of which, Number 134 Pequot Avenue, stood a house, and on the other, Number 136, were a store and a barn. Number 134 was a two-story, gable-roofed structure with three second-floor dormer windows facing the Thames.

Painted pink and known to neighbors as "the Pink House," it was unpretentious compared to the large summer estates that lined Pequot Avenue and its side streets. Built in the early 1700's, it did have the distinction of being the oldest dwelling on Pequot. As yet, no houses had sprung up across the avenue along the river bank, and the Pink House, perched on a knoll with a wide sloping front lawn, had an unobstructed view of the Thames.

Although dwarfed by those nearby mansions, the house was adequate for a family of four. Two front parlors with a fireplace in each faced east toward the river and were bathed in morning sunshine. Behind the parlors was a room running the length of the house, also with a fireplace, whose windows overlooked a shady garden.

While the rooms were low-ceilinged, they were high enough to accommodate James's five-foot-eight-inch frame. The two front bedrooms, one designated for James and Ella and the other for Jamie, were small; the two rear bedrooms, one of them for Edmund, were even smaller.

Before leaving their rented Vauxhall Street cottage in the fall of 1884 to begin his new season of touring, James ordered some repairs to the Pink House to render it habitable for the following summer: modernizing the kitchen, covering the pine boards in the parlors with hardwood floors and installing an upstairs bathroom. Once moved in, he planned to supervise the conversion of the adjacent store at Number 136 into a rental property.

Back in New York, Ella moved with her children into The Richfield, a small, well-run apartment-hotel, on Forty-third Street between Broadway and Eighth Avenue. Both she and James were tormented by the prospect of separation but it was Ella who suffered the greater conflict.

She did not think she could bear the pain of being parted from her sons, particularly the baby, who was only a year old. Yet she dreaded the thought of scrambling with two young children across the country on one-night stands. With deep reluctance she decided to postpone accompanying her husband.

Ella missed James as much as he missed her. From various stops on his tour, James pleaded with her to join him, insisting the children could be adequately looked after by Bridget. As the new year arrived in 1885, Ella at last yielded, albeit with misgivings, and placed her children in her mother's care at The Richfield. Jealousy may have played a part in her decision. James, at thirty-nine, was increasingly the object of female attention, and Ella must have realized that long separations were risky, even though she appears to have been secure in her husband's devotion.

Jamie, now nearly seven, was still not resigned to his baby brother's presence nor to the attention his mother lavished on him; but he had learned the hard way to keep his feelings under control.

According to Eugene O'Neill's self-analytical notations, Jamie was "strictly brought up" and was not unaccustomed to being "punished physically by whipping." O'Neill did not say who administered the punishment, but it was not an uncommon practice; fathers of that day were all too apt to apply a trouser belt to a misbehaving child's bottom.

Ella explained to her seemingly tractable older son that she was going to visit his father, and instructed him to help his grandmother Bridget, now fifty-eight and not in robust health, to care for the baby.

In later years Ella came to believe that James had coerced her into joining him on tour. Eugene O'Neill seems to have accepted his mother's one-sided version of the harshness of the choice she had to make. In his self-analytical notes he ignored his mother's eagerness to be with her husband, writing: "While still infant, M is forced to leave [Edmund] to travel with her husband who is morbidly jealous of her, even her affection for children."

Ella joined James on his western tour early in 1885, where she was pleased to resume her friendship with Elizabeth Robins, now playing Mercedes in *The Count of Monte Cristo*. The reunion was short-lived.

In mid-February, she received word from New York that Jamie was ill with measles. Though concerned, she was apparently reassured by Bridget's ability to manage until, a few days later, on February 27, she was informed that Edmund also had contracted the illness. All too aware that measles in an infant could be fatal, Ella prepared to leave on the next train.

James, who had booked rooms in the Windsor Hotel in Denver for March 1, preparatory to his appearance at the sold-out Tabor Opera House, could not abandon the *Monte Cristo* company, which was entirely dependent on him; without James the tour would have had to be suspended, leaving the actors stranded and unpaid. And so Ella embarked on the long, anxious trip back to New York alone.

At 4 o'clock on the morning of March 4 — the day James was to appear at the Opera House and Ella was still entrained miles from New York — Edmund died.

James, despite his shock, led his cast in their scheduled performance of *Monte Cristo* that night. The Denver Republican expressed (with heartfelt, if excessive, sentiment) the turmoil he had stoically quelled onstage the previous evening:

> The inexorable demands which an actor's life imposes were never better or more painfully exemplified than at last night's performance of *Monte Cristo*. The vast audience did not know that poor Jim O'Neill, who lived as Monte Cristo, was heartbroken. It did not know that at that moment his little child lay dead in far distant New York, and that the agonized mother had just taken a tearful farewell of him to attend the burial of the dear little one. It laughed and clapped its hands and gave no thought but to the actor's genius and dreamed not of the inward weeping that was drowning his heart. But actors are actors and they must strut upon the stage though their hearts break. God pity them; their lot is a hard one.

Years later, in his self-analytical notes, O'Neill attempted to understand the frenzied aftershock of Edmund's death. He wrote that Ella, "prostrated by grief," turned in fury first on her mother for her "carelessness" in allowing Jamie into the baby's room, then on her husband "for keeping her away" from home — and finally on Jamie.

Indeed, Ella was convinced Jamie had effectually killed his brother, and O'Neill in his notes wondered if Jamie had done so "unconsciously." Later, in a draft of *Long Day's Journey Into Night*, he caused Jamie, under the influence of alcohol, to make an extraordinary confession. Jamie tells his younger brother he "hated" the baby and purposely went into his room, hoping to give him measles.

"I was glad when he died," Jamie blurts out. Whether or not Jamie O'Neill uttered these words in real life, O'Neill crossed them out in the play's final version, evidently believing they placed Jamie Tyrone in too villainous a light. In any case, the real Jamie, though he apparently repressed his own misery for a time, was ultimately destroyed by the guilty conviction that the mother he worshiped believed he had killed the baby and could not forgive him.

Ella's anger at her husband was of a different sort. As indicated by her alter ego, Mary Tyrone, she tried at times to suppress her wrath against James. In an early delineation of Mary, O'Neill noted that while she blamed her husband for her baby's death, she recognized that it was his love for her and his jealousy that "made him selfish." But this awareness, O'Neill wrote, threw her into a state of "bewilderment [and] bafflement" that compelled her to "escape backward via dope."

In an early draft of *Long Day's Journey Into Night*, Mary, in a torrent of spite, accuses her husband of unmitigated callousness following their baby's death: "I remember now you showed hardly any sign of grief! But you were just as guilty of his death as I was! More! I didn't want to leave him! You used my love for you as an excuse! You made me leave him!"

O'Neill substituted a somewhat softened version of this bitter speech in his final typescript, presenting Mary as a more sympathetic character. In an even more crushing line, also ultimately dropped, Mary cries out, " . . . if I could have foreseen I would have cut my heart out rather than loved — love is so horrible — ."

Despite the deletions in his scenario and early script, O'Neill's final version of *Long Day's Journey Into Night* contains quite enough evidence of Mary Tyrone's obsessive fury and guilt to indicate that — in O'Neill's mind at least — the death of the baby came to be the defining event of his family's tragedy. (Even earlier, in *All God's Chillun Got Wings* and *Desire Under the Elms*, he portrayed women whose neuroses stemmed at least in part from having lost infant children.)

Ella's anger festered like a gangrenous wound and in the end she appears most of all to have blamed herself. Never able to fully recover, she spent much of the rest of her life in guilt-ridden grief. She began to question her Catholic faith, giving herself up more and more to periods of melancholic introspection, her moods alternating between resentment of her husband and son and loving concern for their welfare.

As for James — having stoically survived a childhood of almost inconceivable deprivation, pain and terror with both his sanity and his love of life intact — he alone seemed to rally from the blow of Edmund's death.

Edmund's body was kept in the vault of Calvary Cemetery in the Woodside section of Queens until James completed his tour in early April of 1885. Then he and Ella buried the baby in New London.

In the midst of their mourning, they were obliged to debate the future of Jamie, who was now of school age. James, resorting to the solution commonly employed by other well-off touring stars, decided to send his son to boarding school. Ella at first balked, but was overruled. In his self-analytical notes, Eugene O'Neill cited his parents' conflict over the fate of seven-year-old Jamie, who was "sent to school at husband's command, despite M's protests as to his youth . . . "

Ella realized that unless she gave up traveling with her husband to stay at home with Jamie, a solution neither she nor James was willing to consider, there was no other way to ensure an adequate education for the boy.

Notre Dame boarding school was chosen by James for its highly rated classical curriculum and Ella consoled herself with the knowledge that the school was close to St. Mary's Academy, her fondly remembered alma mater. Furthermore, her son would be looked after by the same caring nuns of the Holy Cross who had taught her as a girl.

In early December, nine months after Edmund's death, Ella took Jamie to South Bend, Indiana, formally registering him as a minim (or elementary) student on December 7, 1885. He was to remain at the school for the next nine years.

If being sent away struck Jamie as banishment for his part in his brother's death, it did not seem to embitter him, for he strove to be in every way an exemplary student. He had inherited his father's open, sunny personality, his ready wit and humor and his quick intelligence. He endeared himself to his teachers by earning high grades and winning one award after another in such subjects as Christian doctrine, rhetoric, elocution and oratory.

James, Ella and Jamie spent part of the summer of 1886 in New London. While there was much she disliked about the town, Ella could not escape the fact it was now and forever her home; if for no other reason, she was anchored there by Edmund's grave.

The Pink House was still undergoing renovations. James, seeking to ease Ella's bereavement, had engaged an architectural firm to undertake a complete modernization. Since the house would not be ready until the following spring, the O'Neills stayed in the Pequot

House, a block-long resort hotel, whose guests could relax on the sandy riverbank and bathe in the Thames. Ella might well have been among "the fine ladies with parasols over their heads," recalled by a little girl who lived across the avenue and delighted in watching people arriving at the hotel in their carriages.

In the fall, with her son settled at school, Ella was back on the road with James. She missed the companionship of Elizabeth Robins, who had left the company for good at the end of the previous season. The two women continued to correspond until Elizabeth moved permanently to London in 1888. On January 29, 1887, Ella, in a period of relative equanimity, wrote to her from Montgomery, Alabama: "I am here all by myself trying to get a little rest. The traveling has been something — (There is not a word strong enough to express it) & I am completely worn out." James, she said, had gone on to Columbus.

She informed Elizabeth that on the preceding Wednesday night in Mobile, "Mr. O' produced *Hamlet* . . . & I think [it] was a success — as I was his dresser on that particular night, I did not get the chance to see any of the performance. Am delighted he has 'at last' made a break from *Monte Cristo* & I am sure you will agree with me that it is about time. My only regret is that you were not the 'Fair Ophelia.'"

An actress in the company, describing James's Hamlet, said "he looked it to perfection, he wore a reddish blond wig that was very becoming to his face, his costume was purple and black and made him look very slim and tall; not a day over twenty! . . . Although he was very nervous his work though not always original was at times *great*! And his beautiful voice was never heard to better advantage." Nevertheless, James soon felt obliged to abandon *Hamlet* in favor of the infinitely more lucrative *Monte Cristo*.

In her letter to Elizabeth, Ella, aware of her friend's fondness for Jamie, wrote with evident amusement of the boy's latest prank: "Jamie has become quite a little terror at school. He has been playing tricks on his teacher . . . The last I heard was when asked (in the classroom) where his little playmate was, he yelled at the top of his loud voice, 'He is in his skin' — can you imagine he would say such a thing . . . He writes he would like to stay at Notre Dame forever."

While sounding cheerful enough in her letter, Ella was in fact growing ever more melancholy with the approach of March 4, the second anniversary of Edmund's death. James decided that a trip abroad might cheer her. When his tour ended in the spring of 1887, instead of moving his family into the now-completed Pink House, he leased it to an acquaintance.

Having made provisions for Jamie's care, James and Ella sailed for England on June 9. For James, the highlights of the trip were visits to two places that held a particular poignancy. One was the Chateau d'If, the castle near Marseilles on which Dumas based the scenes of Monte Cristo's incarceration and escape. The other was Oberammergau in Bavaria, the original site of the *Passion Play*, where James could once more indulge his fantasy of bringing Jesus to the American stage.

While still abroad, Ella received news of her mother's death in New London on July 28. Bridget Quinlan, who was sixty, had suffered from a severe bone ailment for three years. Ella did not return to New London for the funeral, which was arranged by her mother's relatives.

James and Ella arrived back in New York on August 23, where Ella was met and comforted by the actress Grace Raven, who had replaced Elizabeth Robins as Mercedes in James's company. A friend of Elizabeth, Grace idolized Ella. She was a well-bred woman who, like Ella, had been convent-educated (and who later left the stage to become a nun).

Although not as clever or perceptive as Elizabeth Robins, Grace was welcomed to intimacy with the O'Neills, and Ella singled her out, as she had Elizabeth, for special kindnesses. "If angels are on the earth, she certainly is one," Grace wrote of Ella to Elizabeth, adding, "she has the most lovely refined patient disposition I have ever met."

Grace was shocked by Ella's appearance on her return from Europe. "I know you will feel sorry for poor little Mrs. O'Neill when I tell you that she has lost her Mother," she wrote to Elizabeth. "When I saw her she looked very very sad and ill."

Toward summer's end, James and Ella returned to New London to take possession of the Pink House. While it was little more than a small farmhouse, typical of its time and place, James took pride in its possession.

Not only did the house have the advantage of fronting on the Thames, but it was only a mile from the neighboring town of Waterford, the locale of two of the area's grandest mansions — one owned by Edward Crowninshield Hammond, the railroad tycoon, the other by Edward Stephen Harkness, an heir to the Standard Oil fortune. James's house, no less than theirs, commanded a view of the Sound. If he thought back to his impoverished Kilkenny roots, he could hardly be faulted for reveling in the good Irish luck that had thrown this sterling property his way.

He was no less pleased with himself for recently having expanded his holdings on Pequot Avenue. In addition to the Pink House at Number 134, and the abandoned store and barn next door at 136, he had purchased (on October 4, 1886 for $2,500) an adjacent third tract of land at Number 138. On it stood a two-story structure dating from about 1840 that at one time had been a store with living quarters above; the property also held a dilapidated barn and an additional building that had once been the Harbor District schoolhouse.

This third site (eventually renumbered 325) became, some years later, the O'Neills' final summer home. And it was this house that was to serve as the setting for both the torments of *Long Day's Journey Into Night* and the happier moments of *Ah, Wilderness!*

Number 138, with its clapboard exterior and gingerbread trim, was as much in need of extensive repair as had been the Pink House. It was James's plan to remodel it, as well as the store and barn next door, and turn them into rental properties.

Accompanied by Ella, James resumed touring in Hartford on September 5, 1887. Ella was enjoying "better health than she has for a long time past," wrote Grace Raven to Elizabeth Robins from New Orleans on November 28, adding that Ella attributed it "to the trip abroad." She even appeared to take in stride one especially rigorous run of sixteen consecutive one-night stands.

By the end of 1887, after more than four years of virtually non-stop touring as Monte Cristo, James was beginning to lose the jaunty swagger he had originally brought to the role. While his fans seemed not to care that his performances were often listless, the critics took notice. He was severely reprimanded by one San Francisco reviewer, for example, who wrote that *The Count of Monte Cristo* had "degenerated into an extravagant melodrama."

The critic went on to gripe that the play had "become a bit of coarse theatricalism, that pleases only the more ignorant of theatergoers." James O'Neill, he said, "is reaping the pecuniary profit of his business sagacity, but it is at the cost of art.

"If the actor concerned had no previous claim upon critical consideration the matter would not deserve so much comment, but James O'Neill has done admirable work — artistic work — in the past, and it is a cause of regret that he should have abandoned his better abilities."

James was neither the first nor the last gifted actor to be rebuked by critics for selling out. Though stung by the adverse reaction, he must in his heart have felt it was justified. He needed no one to tell him what he already knew: that he was further than ever from attaining the stature once predicted by Booth, Forrest and Jefferson.

It doubtless occurred to him that his achievement in *The Count of Monte Cristo,* instead of marking a step on the way up, had become a trap from which it was too late to escape. James also needed no one to tell him that Dantes was not Hamlet. He was forced to face the painful truth that easy popularity in shallow roles had blurred his early dreams.

Ella, evidently sharing her husband's misgivings, could not sustain the buoyancy described by Grace Raven, and her own spirits sank lower. In his private self-analysis, Eugene O'Neill wrote, "Husband now 'on his own' touring nine months place to place, one-nights mostly, no chances to form contacts except for brief summers in N.L. which M hates. Her feeling [of] superiority to people there. Her poor relatives who live there make this hard. She feels they are obstacles to her socially, make that town impossible. Her husband prefers barroom companions to whom he is rich hero." He noted that since her mother's death she was "absolutely alone, except for husband & a brother, no good & shiftless, whom she despises and never sees, feels no affection for."

O'Neill's view of his mother's isolation during this period — not to mention his father's implied neglect of her — was, as always, somewhat exaggerated. Her son did not, after all, know her as she was during the early years of her marriage.

It was true, however, that Ella felt she was looked down upon by New London's elite, who relegated Irish Catholics to the lower rungs of the social ladder. It was a mind-set Ella felt helpless to combat. Gently bred, educated, traveled, elegant in her dress, she was herself inclined to snub some of her mother's provincial relatives. Certainly it was clear from their somewhat resentful recollections that they thought she had patronized them.

The self-pitying mother O'Neill described in his private notations was the only mother he knew: a woman who had retreated into drug addiction after his birth, and who regaled him with overwrought accounts of the difficulties of her life. But even during those later years, when she suffered from severe depression, there were periods of remission (however brief) when his mother was tranquil and to all appearances contented with her lot.

While O'Neill accurately noted that Ella never had a stable social life — any more than any other touring actor's wife of that period — her friendship with both Elizabeth Robins and Grace Raven had given her many moments of pleasant intimacy and even joy. In addition, she did have the care of a young son, whose welfare occupied her even though he was away at school much of the year. She took pride in Jamie's academic progress and looked after him attentively during his vacations.

Most importantly, she had long since learned to accommodate herself to the eccentricities of her husband's social behavior. James had always been the center of her universe, and she continued to involve herself in his career, empathizing with his growing concern over his artistic decline.

PART TWO
A VAGABOND CHILDHOOD

"I was born in a theatrical hotel and my mother put me in a bureau drawer on two pillows for my cradle. I was fed and dressed and put to sleep in hotel rooms. I can't see that a theatrical life on the road is such a marvelous thing."

— EUGENE O'NEILL, to a friend

CHAPTER
EIGHT

Ella had determined not to have another child
and was dismayed in early 1888 to find herself pregnant. Her guilt
over Edmund's death, O'Neill noted in his private self-analysis, was
evidently why she shunned the "idea of another child," even though
her husband had expressed a wish for a large family. But she was
convinced that James's "stinginess" would make the raising of additional children "difficult for her."

O'Neill went on to reveal the startling fact (no where else documented) that, despite her piety, his mother had aborted several earlier pregnancies. He pondered possible motivations for her "series of
brought-on abortions." Were they due to "defiance" of her husband?
And how could she "justify" this behavior with her religious beliefs?
Most crucially, did her actions mark the "beginning of break with
religion which was to leave her eventually entirely without solace?"
Tentatively, he concluded that the child she was bearing was not
wanted "at first (?)" but that then it became "desire on both parents'
parts it should be girl."

This wish was evidently known to at least one of Ella's relatives.
A cousin, Claire Brennan Sherman, remembered that Ella said to her
mother, "Oh, if only I could adopt a daughter!" And according to
O'Neill's second wife, Agnes Boulton, Ella communicated this forlorn wish to her soon after they first met. "You know," Ella told
Agnes, "I always wanted a little girl so much — and then I had three
boys."

O'Neill endlessly assessed the nuances of his mother's conflict in
Long Day's Journey Into Night. At one climactic point, Mary Tyrone
blurts out her guilt about bearing a child to take the place of her dead
infant. "You thought that would make me forget his death," she
accuses her husband, and goes on to castigate herself, adding that she

"wasn't worthy to have another baby," and that she knew God would punish her if she did.

In late August of 1888, James settled his wife, by then eight months pregnant, at the Barrett House in New York. Built five years earlier to the imposing height of eight stories, it was situated in the area known as Longacre Square, where, owing to the recent introduction of the iron skeletal frame and the elevator, structures were growing ever taller. A family hotel, it stood on the northeast corner of Forty-third Street and Broadway, on the same street as (and less than a block west of) The Richfield, where Edmund had died.

From their windows, James and Ella could look out on a cobblestoned Broadway, where green streetcars drawn by horses passed at a leisurely pace. The Barrett House, in an area of brownstones, was in the center of the carriage-building industry and the rich kept their horses and carriages in stables scattered along the quiet side streets; a store on West Forty-second Street sold oats and hay. The Barrett House clock, set into a gabled tower, was a neighborhood landmark.

In a brisk ten-minute walk, James could reach the theater district, still centered in Union Square but already pushing uptown to Thirty-fourth Street and beginning to take root in Longacre Square (renamed Times Square in 1904). James's old mentor, Joseph Jefferson, taking a brief vacation from *Rip Van Winkle*, was announced to appear with John Gilbert and Mrs. John Drew in *The Rivals*, and Gilbert and Sullivan's *The Yeomen of the Guard* was having its American première.

While electricity had been installed in parts of the city, many street lamps continued to be lit by oil-tipped torches and most theaters still were illuminated by gas. That New Year's Eve, Edwin Booth opened his residence in Gramercy Square as an actors' club called The Players, with James among its founding members.

Missing from the scene was the Union Square Theater, where James had made his New York debut; eight months earlier, a four-hour fire had destroyed it.

The Times, in its front page story, noted that "Every actor in town whose business didn't compel him to be elsewhere was on 'the Rialto' to witness the destruction of the playhouse. It was like a meeting of the Actors Fund in the Union Square Hotel lobby. There must have been 100 actresses all wearing sealskin wraps and diamond earrings who had words of sympathy for the actresses who lost their wardrobes." Ellen Terry, fearful for the safety of the Star, the neighboring theater at which she was appearing, arrived in a cab but quickly left on being assured that the Star was in no danger. The

Times noted that a stagehand saved the theater's mascot, a large cat named Jim, along with its wicker cradle, a gift from Mme. Modjeska.

Leaving Ella at the Barrett House to prepare for their baby's arrival, James took *The Count of Monte Cristo* to New Jersey the week of September 3, followed by one-night and two-night stands in Massachusetts, Maine and New Hampshire. He played without a break through Saturday, October 13, in Worcester, Massachusetts, and returned to New York on Sunday to spend his forty-third birthday with Ella, who had been alone since Jamie's departure for boarding school.

Ella had turned thirty-one a month earlier. Her beauty was undiminished, although her anxiety during the final months of her pregnancy left her at times pale and drawn. As for James, he was as ever trim and dapper and, despite his private self-doubts, continued to present to the world an unruffled and smiling exterior, endlessly milking the only role that ensured him a good living.

On the Monday after his birthday, James played in Brockton, Massachusetts. It may be assumed that he returned to the Barrett House in time to be at Ella's side the next day, when she gave birth. Had he been absent, Ella would surely have made this fact known to her sons in later life and O'Neill doubtless would have included it in Mary Tyrone's litany of marital grievances in *Long Day's Journey Into Night*.

"**Y**ou were born afraid. Because I was so afraid to bring you into the world . . . " While these plaintive words of Mary Tyrone in *Long Day's Journey Into Night*, spoken to her third-born son, may not have been the literal words of his mother, it seems clear that Eugene O'Neill believed, from his youth, that they conveyed his mother's true feeling of apprehension over his birth. Further supporting his conviction, Mary Tyrone decries the event to her husband: "I should never have borne him. It would have been better for his sake."

Eugene was forced to bear the burden of being the unwelcome, substitute child whom James had cajoled Ella into conceiving. "Dead son becomes only child she loved — because living sons cause too much pain" was how O'Neill phrased it in early notes for *Long Day's Journey Into Night*.

O'Neill pursued this concept in several other early notes and bits of dialogue that he later dropped from the play. In his early scenario, for example, he attributed to Mary the line that if only her second child had lived, she and James "might have had one son we could be proud of."

Somewhat later, in a typescript, he softened Mary's sentiments, although not in a manner likely to reassure an already insecure son. She loved him "so much," she declares, because he was both himself and his dead brother. "I wanted you to take his place," she says.

There is other evidence of the distress his mother's rejection caused him, most notably in *More Stately Mansions*, the raw, ungainly manuscript draft of a never-completed play he abruptly set aside (in 1939) to write *Long Day's Journey Into Night*. The tragic, half-mad Deborah Harford of *Mansions* is a highly fanciful and symbolic version of the naturalistically depicted Mary Tyrone.

Nearing the end of his creative strength when increasingly in the grip of illness, O'Neill conceivably concluded he had already drawn one too many veiled portraits of his mother and decided to confront her at last head-on in the person of Mary Tyrone. Having made his decision, he proceeded to mine the abandoned draft of *More Stately Mansions* to explicate his later characterization of Mary Tyrone in *Long Day's Journey Into Night*.

While *Mansions* is set in and near Boston in the 1830's and 40's, and while Deborah Harford is nine years younger than Mary Tyrone, the resemblance between the two is unmistakable: Deborah's youthful face is "framed by a mass of wavy white hair." Her mouth is "full-lipped," her "beautiful eyes" are "black, deep-set" and "look enormous in her small face" and her fingers are "thin, strong, tapering."

Compare this description with that of Mary Tyrone, whose mouth is "wide with full, sensitive lips . . . Her high forehead is framed by thick, pure white hair . . . her dark brown eyes appear black" and are "unusually large and beautiful." She has "long, tapering fingers." Beneath Deborah's "well-bred manner" lies "a nervous tension and restlessness," while Mary is described as gripped by "extreme nervousness."

Deborah frequently withdraws into the seclusion of a "summer house" on the grounds of her estate, where she indulges in romantic daydreams of being Napoleon's mistress — a symbolic version of Mary's withdrawal into morphine-induced reveries of her romanticized past life.

What makes it obvious that O'Neill used the unfinished *Mansions* script as at least a partial scenario for *Long Day's Journey* is the way he lifted lines almost intact from one to the other, most notably in speeches that convey the mother's dismay over the birth of a son.

"I never even wanted him to be conceived — " Deborah protests, referring (in his presence) to her younger son, Simon. And, a little later, she vengefully tells Simon's wife, "I have forgotten him several times before in my life. Completely as if he had never been born." Still later (this time to Simon's face), she spits out: "Ah, how I hated you! How I cursed the night you were conceived, the morning you were born! How I prayed that you would die . . . "

Interestingly, while Deborah is forty-five at the beginning of the *Mansions* scenario, she is fifty-four, the same age as Mary Tyrone, at its end. O'Neill must have felt he needed the nine years to depict Deborah's decline into madness, whereas — having at last brought himself to identify narcotics as the true cause of his mother's derangement — he was able to push Mary Tyrone over the edge within the span of a single day.

Obviously for dramatic effect in *Long Day's Journey Into Night*, he chose to emphasize the dark side of his mother's character by understating her gentler maternal side, of which he was perfectly aware. In his self-analytical notes he grappled with the paradox of his mother, submerged in guilt over his birth and struggling to subdue her demons with morphine — and yet unable to deny her maternal instincts.

She had, for instance, breast-fed him. Moreover, she was "fierce" in her "concentration of affection" on him as an infant. He was, O'Neill wrote, "spoiled from birth" because his mother, "in her loneliness," concentrated all of her love on him.

Further evidence of Ella's tender feelings for Eugene as an infant — however much these feelings might have been at war with her anxiety over his birth — was the way she herself recalled the occasion in later years.

By then, free of her addiction, her torment had been replaced by a serenity of which there is no hint in *Long Day's Journey*. Receiving news of the birth of Eugene's second son, Shane, on October 30, 1919, Ella wrote a letter in language differing diametrically from Mary Tyrone's:

"I am one of the happiest old ladies in New York tonight," she told Eugene, "to know I have such a wonderful grandson but no more wonderful than you were when you were born and weighed *eleven pounds* . . . " She enclosed a picture of Eugene at three months and added, "Hope your *boy* will be as good *looking* . . . "

While growing up, Eugene was indoctrinated by his mother to believe his father had chosen a minimally qualified physician to

attend her. It was his father's eagerness to save on medical bills that
had prompted his casual choice of the hotel doctor, whom he had met
in the barroom. That Eugene was undeniably an outsized infant
apparently contributed to Ella's difficult and prolonged labor, and it
does seem certain the doctor ordered morphine, not an uncommon
remedy of the time, to ease her pains.

In *Long Day's Journey Into Night*, Mary Tyrone harps on the memory of " . . . that ignorant quack of a cheap doctor — All he knew was
I was in pain. It was easy for him to stop the pain." Ella seems to have
spared her son none of the agonizing details of his birth. As he later
recalled in his private self-analytical notations, it was at this point
that his mother started "treatment with Doc, which eventually winds
up in start of nervousness" — and that in turn led to her morphine
addiction.

Actually, *Long Day's Journey Into Night* is not the only play in
which O'Neill brooded about his unwanted birth. He had agonized
over the subject many years earlier when writing *The Great God
Brown*, albeit in a far more fanciful and allusive manner.

"There is so much of the secret me in it," he wrote to Carlotta
Monterey at the start of their love affair in 1926. In the play, written a
year earlier, his autobiographical hero, Dion Anthony, muses upon
the futility of his existence:

"Why am I afraid to live, I who love life and the beauty of flesh
and the living colors of earth and sky and sea? Why am I afraid of
love? Why am I afraid, I who am not afraid? . . . Why must I live in a
cage like a criminal, defying and hating, I who love peace and friendship? Why was I born without a skin, O God, that I must wear armor
in order to touch or to be touched? . . . Or rather, Old Graybeard, why
the devil was I born at all?"

The self-lamented birth of Eugene O'Neill took place on a Tuesday
afternoon, October 16, 1888. An intermittent light rain turned the day
gray and dreary — not an omen of hope for a mother already in the
grip of gloom. While O'Neill accepted his mother's foreboding about
his birth, he inherited her inconsistent nature and could, like her,
abruptly shift gears and wax sentimental.

Thus, he cherished all memorabilia pertaining to his early years,
especially a photograph of himself as an infant in his mother's arms.
He was sentimental even about family mementos predating his birth,
such as the document certifying his parents' marriage.

"Their wedding certificate," he once said, "is one of the few records of my parents in their early days that I possess." He was unshakably nostalgic about his neighborhood and all his life was half-humorously resentful of any changes.

Two years after his birth, the Barrett House merged with an adjoining structure and was renamed the Cadillac. "Every time I go past," O'Neill said in his late thirties, "I look up because the room was on the fourth floor, third window from Broadway on the Forty-third Street side. I can remember my father pointing it out to me."

In at least one instance, he impetuously hustled a friend up to Room 236, knocked on the door, explained his mission to the startled occupants, and was granted permission to look around.

In 1940 the hotel was torn down to make way for a two-story structure housing a group of stores, topped by a towering electric sign advertising Kleenex. He complained it was "a dirty trick" to have torn down the hotel where he was born. "There is only empty air now where I came into this world," he told an interviewer in 1946, a few days before his fifty-eighth birthday, after a long absence from the city.

Back in New York to prepare for the production of *The Iceman Cometh*, O'Neill bemoaned the fate of the entire area. "The green horse cars we used to take when we went to see friends who lived at Seventy-seventh Street had vanished," he said, adding sadly that above Fifty-ninth Street, a shady lane once known as the Boulevard had become Broadway."

Only five years before his death in 1953, O'Neill was gratified to receive from an old friend, who shared his Irish heritage, a photograph of the Barrett House as it looked when O'Neill was born. "I know of no gift which could have pleased me more," O'Neill responded, facetiously adding that the figure in the picture leaning against the lamppost outside the hotel obviously "had a bun on."

"I remember seeing him there the day after I was born," he quipped. "You forget there were men in those days and when they decided it was fitting they should go on a drunk, *they went on a drunk*! Not like the weaklings of today, who after ten days of weak mixed drinks have to have an animal trainer bed them down in Bellevue and gently subdue their menagerie visions! In the old days when I was born, a man — especially one from Kilkenny — went on a five year drunk and finished by licking four cops, and then went home to raise hell because dinner was late."

The Kilkenny reference was, of course, to his father, who began to instill in him, almost from the moment of his birth, a pride in his pure Irish lineage, traceable to the O'Neills who ruled Ulster until vanquished by the armies of Elizabeth I and Oliver Cromwell.

According to ancient legend, an early O'Neill forbear was in a struggle over land with another Gaelic warrior. The rivals agreed to race for the coast of Ulster, with the first one touching shore gaining title to the land. The O'Neill forbear, seeing he was about to lose the race, resourcefully cut off his right hand and threw it onto the shore, claiming victory.

The Red Hand of O'Neill eventually became the emblem of Ulster, a fact well known to Eugene O'Neill, who referred to his own immediate family as "this branch of the Red-Handed O'Neills."

It is likely that James named Eugene in honor of the noble 17th-century Tyrone, Eoghan Ruadh Niall (or Owen Roe O'Neill); while Owen is the more generally accepted Anglicization of Eoghan, it was also commonly translated in Ireland as Eugene. His middle name, Ruadh, means red, which was the color of Eoghan Ruadh Niall's hair. (The name, Owen Roe, appears in the unfinished *More Stately Mansions*. In the draft of the play — which was to have been a sequel to *A Touch of the Poet* — Sara Harford, nee Melody, tells her mother that if the child she is expecting is a boy, it will be called Owen Roe.)

For his son's middle name James chose Gladstone (which O'Neill later dropped) in salute to the Liberal English prime minister, who promoted the social causes of Ireland's poor and who, only two years earlier, had championed Irish home rule during an impassioned debate in Parliament.

Taking to heart his father's stories about his heroic forbears, told over and over with theatrical flourishes, Eugene could not fail to absorb James's strutting Irish pride. "One thing that explains more than anything about me is the fact that I'm Irish," he confided years later to his older son, Eugene Jr. "And, strangely enough, it is something that all the writers who have attempted to explain me and my work have overlooked."

Despite the powerful tug of his Irish roots, O'Neill never visited Ireland. He told an interviewer in 1923 he had "always wanted to go," then confessed he had once "started to study Gaelic" but had found it "too difficult" and gave it up.

Over the years he came to temper somewhat this unqualified veneration of all things Irish. Answering a letter in 1943 from a fellow writer, James T. Farrell, who had sent him a copy of an essay about James Joyce, O'Neill noted that critics "seem to understand so little

. . . of the Irish past in Joyce." He recommended a recent book called *The Great O'Neill*, by Sean O'Faoláin, a history of Hugh O'Neill, Earl of Tyrone and the last of the great Gaelic chieftains.

"I learned from it a lot of Irish past I had mislearned before," wrote O'Neill. "You know what most Irish histories are like — benign Catholic benediction-and-blather tracts, or blind Jingo glorifications of peerless fighting heroes, in the old bardic fashion."

Hugh O'Neill, he said, was "no pure and pious archangel of Erin, but a fascinatingly complicated character, strong, proud and noble, ignoble, shameless and base, loyal and treacherous, a cunning politician, a courageous soldier, an inspiring leader, but at times so weakly neurotic he could burst openly into tears (even when sober!) and whine pitiably that no one understood him. In short, Shakespeare might have written a play about him." (As, indeed, might Eugene O'Neill, who surely recognized the traits he and Hugh held in common).

The Irish in Eugene, far from reflecting his father's cheery outlook, manifested itself in darker tones. Eugene fitted the somewhat mythologized designation of "Black Irishman" that is vaguely based on looks, temperament and adherence to the church. The looks are dark (arguably the result of intermingling with Spaniards who reached the shores of Ireland after the defeat of the Armada in 1588); the temperament is reputed to range from moody to morose (with alcohol often a factor); and Faith has lapsed.

In his self-analytical notes, O'Neill cited the fact that his birth made his father "very proud." And in his single lapse into the first-person he added that his father's pleasure had been "confirmed by stories told to me."

James permitted himself to bask in his new fatherhood for only two days. Obliged to resume his travels in *Monte Cristo*, he left Ella with a baby nurse in New York. Eugene was baptized on November 1 at the Holy Innocence Church on Thirty-seventh Street just off Broadway, six blocks from the Barrett House. Because it abutted the theater district, it was known as the "Actor's Church."

Thirty years after his christening, when he was beginning to gain public attention, O'Neill was enchanted to receive a letter from a seventy-two-year-old woman, Elizabeth Murray, who reminded him she was the nurse at his birth.

"I have thought of you many times during the last thirty years," she wrote, "and wondered how you and your dear mother were getting along. I carried you in my arms to the church the day you were christened, a beautiful baby."

It was not long before Ella once again joined her husband on tour. Determined not to be separated from either James or her baby, no matter what the difficulties might be of traveling with an infant, she engaged a nursemaid willing to deal with the hardships of the road. Bolstered by this support, she also counted on her new medicine to help smooth the way.

In early January of 1889, Ella took her three-month-old baby to Notre Dame to be inspected by his brother. "Master Eugene Gladstone O'Neill . . . is a beautiful child, and promises to do honor to his name," reported the Notre Dame Scholastic on January 12. According to Carlotta, her husband treasured the clipping and occasionally showed it to friends commenting it was his "first publicity."

Jamie could not have been sanguine about this new intruder who, like Edmund, had effectually replaced him with his adored mother. Older and wiser now, however, he tried to appear pleased with the baby. It was a little easier to suppress his jealousy, for he now had a life and friends apart from his parents. He no longer felt compelled to vie for his mother's daily attention, although he yearned for her visits.

Whenever James and Ella arrived at Notre Dame, they were fussed over by faculty and students. On an earlier occasion, James traded recitations with Jamie's classmates and donated a gold medal at commencement "to the Minim who shall have distinguished himself more than the others for good conduct and proficiency in study."

While the students were enraptured by James, his son had begun to harbor feelings of resentment toward his overpowering father. These feelings were soon to surface but, for the moment, Jamie was clever enough to keep them to himself.

He continued to do well at school, distinguishing himself, at twelve, as something of an ecclesiastical poet. His tribute to the school's president, in seven stanzas, with devout references to God's Eternal Light, the Holy Cross and the Good and the True, was featured on the cover of the school magazine.

If O'Neill's early scenario for *A Moon for the Misbegotten* may be taken literally, Jamie, as a schoolboy steeped in his catechism, drew profound solace from his religious belief. "There was once a boy who loved . . . purity and God with a great quiet passion inside him," reads a line describing Jamie, who says he had actually contemplated giving up "self & the world to worship of God . . . "

Jamie's religious fervor did not prevent him from engaging actively in the school's other activities. Far from being a bookworm and a teacher's pet, he was popular with his fellow-students, finding time to appear in dramatic productions and to play shortstop on the baseball team. No one who knew this bright, ingratiating, high-achieving boy would have predicted anything but the rosiest of futures.

Having introduced Eugene to his brother, James and Ella resumed the *Monte Cristo* tour. George Tyler, engaged by James as his advance publicity man, assumed the obligation to "scramble round and do things" for Ella, who with her baby was often sent ahead of the company to rest from the grind of one-night stands.

When Tyler took on the job, James advised him, with the Irish chauvinism so ingrained in his character, that if ever he needed a special favor or "inside information" in an unfamiliar town, to find someone whose name began with an O'. "We stick together, we O's," James declared, though his two most trusted business associates — William F. Connor, his business manager, and Tyler himself — failed to fit the category.

Tyler, who later became a prominent producer, once received a frantic summons to Ella's hotel room in Chicago, where she awaited the arrival of James and his company. Tyler found Eugene "sort of black in the face and gasping and raising Cain." He ran for a doctor, who, after a hasty examination, told the terrified Ella that the baby's condition was nothing more serious than colic.

Now ten years older than when she had toured with the infant Jamie, she evidently was finding travel more arduous. She could not alleviate her discomfort even by attendance at mass or by escape into sedated fantasies.

It was many months before James realized Ella had become addicted to morphine. According to a cousin of the O'Neills, Claire Brennan Sherman, James had no suspicion of Ella's habit until he overheard her sending an elevator attendant to the apothecary one day to replenish the patent medicine she had been taking for "nervousness." James was on the point of going out himself and told the attendant he would pick up the medicine.

The druggist, a conscientious man, asked James if he knew the medicine could become habit-forming. James, after further inquiry, began to suspect the truth, as was later confirmed by Claire Sherman, who was among the few surviving relatives and friends not unduly surprised by the revelation of the mother's morphine habit in *Long Day's Journey Into Night*. She learned these facts as a lively-minded, inquisitive teenager when eavesdropping on a conversation among her elders.

The words O'Neill gave James Tyrone in the play seem to bear out the facts. Answering his son's accusations of neglect in failing to recognize the seriousness of his wife's addiction — and of miserliness in not employing specialists to attempt a cure in the early stage — James protests: "What did I know of morphine? It was years before I discovered what was wrong. I thought she'd never got over her [childbirth] sickness, that's all."

James probably was justified in failing to comprehend the seriousness of Ella's problem. In those days, morphine (a derivative of opium) was available without prescription, and was an ingredient in many patent medicines, such as cough syrup. Morphine was listed in the catalogues of mail-order houses, and was advertised in newspapers as a remedy for jangled nerves. It was not until 1914 that a Federal law restricted the sale of opium and its derivatives. Codeine, a milder drug, succeeded morphine in many patent remedies.

Morphine not only dulls physical pain but blurs the edges of reality, removing fears and worries and relegating the user to what O'Neill once described, in speaking of his mother, as "a kind of twilight zone."

According to medical evidence, underlying mental problems — particularly a tendency toward depression — are apt to increase a person's vulnerability to the habit-forming drug, and the family history strongly suggests Ella O'Neill had been suffering for some time from depression, doubtless brought on by Edmund's death.

While it is true that a "quack" hotel doctor introduced her to the drug, Ella apparently was only too willing to seize upon a means of escape from a life that baffled and disappointed her. The drug offered her an illusional world in which she could hide. It dawned on her only gradually that she could not do without it. Quite possibly as well, Ella, in her distraught condition, considered her use of morphine a just response to James's drinking.

Bedeviled since his early teens by the conviction that he had been unwanted, Eugene was convinced it was his birth that led to his mother's addiction. In *Long Day's Journey Into Night* he pitilessly reiterates his mother's accusations. Her speeches throughout four acts stress the fact that she was "so healthy" before the birth of her third son, that she never had a gray hair or a nerve in her body before he was born. Bearing her third son was "the last straw," says Mary Tyrone, adding, "I was so sick afterwards."

During the seven years Eugene toured with his parents, his companions, apart from an English nanny, consisted mainly of railroad conductors and hotel porters. Attempts were made to befriend him by members of his father's company, however.

After a matinee one day, he accompanied his mother to the dressing room of Margaret Anglin, at that time a relatively obscure ingenue. Eugene hung back bashfully in the doorway. "Come in, little boy," coaxed Anglin. "Don't be afraid. I won't kiss you." Eugene did not budge. "You might," he said.

"Usually a child has a regular fixed home, but you might say I started in as a trouper," O'Neill once told an interviewer. "I knew only actors and the stage. My mother nursed me in the wings and dressing rooms."

In retrospect, he deplored the vagabond life thrust upon him. He was quick to disparage the concept, flaunted by the offspring of some theatrical families, that a nomadic life was a romantic one for an infant.

"John Barrymore, like a lot of dizzy actors, boasts about having been born in a trunk," O'Neill once sneered to a friend. "As if that were something wonderful. I was born in a theatrical hotel and my mother put me in a bureau drawer on two pillows for my cradle. I was fed and dressed and put to sleep in hotel rooms. I can't see that a theatrical life on the road is such a marvelous thing."

In a typically toilsome route followed by James's *Monte Cristo* one November, the company played (in sequence) Scranton, Pennsylvania; Albany, New York.; North Adams, Northampton and Westfield (all in Massachusetts); Hartford and Middletown, Connecticut; Worcester, Massachusetts.; Woonsocket, Rhode Island.; New Bedford, Massachusetts; Newport, Rhode Island; Fall River and Boston, Massachusetts.; and Providence, Rhode Island.

All but four of these stops were for one night and only two were for full-week engagements. The zigzagging did not abate throughout the theatrical season, and only their New London summers provided the family with a respite.

Ella's sense of isolation during the tour turned to panic on one occasion when, as O'Neill wrote in his self-analytical notes, he nearly died from typhoid fever at the age of two (never mentioning that this was the age at which Edmund had died of measles).

Many years later, O'Neill reminisced about getting to know a group of Indian chiefs who periodically came to sit around his bed during the four-weeks illness. It had chanced that Buffalo Bill's company and James's troupe had crossed trails in Chicago, and Nate Salsbury, Buffalo Bill's partner and James's close friend, had dispatched the chiefs; Salsbury assured Eugene that one of the Indians was Sitting Bull, who sometimes traveled with Buffalo Bill's "Wild West" show.

Eugene remembered that they arrived in blankets and feathered headdresses, but he could not recall what words they spoke, if any. The experience, as he once told a writer acquaintance, left him with an "acute sympathy" for the plight of the Indian.

He expressed more than sympathy while in New York during rehearsals of *The Iceman Cometh* in 1946. In an era of postwar optimism and elation over America's victorious emergence as the leading world power, O'Neill was, as always, outspoken, chastising the American government for its "treachery against the Indians" (among others).

"The great battle in American history was the Battle of Little Big Horn," he said. "The Indians wiped out the whitemen, scalped them. That was a victory in American history. It should be featured in all our school books as the greatest victory in American history."

While convalescing, Eugene also picked up some gossip that surely would have gone over the heads of most toddlers. He learned, as he told his writer friend, that "Salsbury was riding herd on Buffalo Bill lest he go on a toot with a blonde." Eugene, the writer noted, "was wise to many of the underground dark phases of life during his wild adolescence and early youth," but few realized that as an infant, "he knew all about Indians and blondes."

When Eugene recovered, the O'Neills resumed their tour, his mother sharing him "reluctantly" with his nurse, a fact on which he elaborated in a handwritten, free-associative diagram. Somewhat enigmatic, this diagram supplemented the self-analytical document written when he underwent his brief psychoanalysis at thirty-eight. Like the document, it was possibly constructed at the analyst's suggestion, for it was evidently intended to chart the cataclysmic turning-points in his life from birth to adolescence.

Emphasizing his guilt over having been born, he headed the diagram with the word, "Nirvana," implying that this state of bliss had existed only before his birth and was never again to be attained. He immediately followed "Nirvana" by the word, "birth," and went on to reinforce his acute awareness of his mother's equivocal attachment to him, indicating that "nurse love" began to compete with "mother love" as a "protecting influence" soon after "weaning."

As he elaborated in his self-analytical notes, his mother made a "friend and confidant out of nurse to further compensate for loneliness." He acknowledged that his mother did have a handful of "loyal friends scattered over the country," but pointed out that they were "resented as social superiors" by his father (a statement for which there is scant supporting evidence).

In a few crucial lines of the self-analytical document, O'Neill reached the heart of his parents' marital tug of war, citing his mother's pleas "for home in N.Y." and his father's refusal. One of his mother's "bitterest resentments" against his father "all her life" was that "she never had home."

O'Neill was detached enough to conjecture that his mother was quite capable of retaliating for the distress her husband caused her: "M gets rid of one nurse at end of year or so (Irish woman) and gets English woman. (Husband hates English intensely. Always hostile to nurse secretly and she to him. Was M actuated by revenge motives on husband in this choice — to get reliable ally in war with husband [?].)"

The English nurse employed by Ella, Sarah Jane Bucknell Sandy, was a formative presence during Eugene's early years. Thirty-four when Ella engaged her, Sarah was the eldest of four children in a struggling Episcopalian family.

At sixteen, she had come to America from Cornwall, under instructions to send money home. She had, ever since, borne her parents a grudge for coercing her into service to help educate her younger siblings and bring them to America.

Rotund and only five feet tall, with gray-blue eyes and dark blond hair, Sarah was, apart from her fast-held resentment against her parents, a goodhearted woman. For the next several years she devoted herself to Eugene, often substituting for his aberrant mother.

Sarah did her best to compensate for Eugene's lack of a settled life and playmates. She sometimes took him to stay with her own relatives and, both in New York and on the road, zealously sought out aquariums, zoos and circuses. Years later, O'Neill responded to a letter from his eight-year-old son, Shane, who had written to tell him of his own similar outings with his nurse, whom he called "Gaga":

"It must have been great fun when you went to the Aquarium

and the Museum of Natural History and the Zoo. I used to have a nurse like Gaga when I was a boy and . . . she used to take me to every one of those places . . . "

O'Neill's earliest memory, however, as he once told an interviewer, was of feeding squirrels in a park in Memphis. A chubby infant, he was dressed for his outings in Little Lord Fauntleroy suits with lace collars.

In a photograph of him at five, Eugene wears his light brown hair in straight bangs over a high forehead, but cut short in back, revealing prominent ears. His rounded cheeks and fleshy chin contrast oddly with the dreamy sadness of his wide-set eyes and the wistful downturn of his mouth.

Sarah had a passion for Dickens and Edgar Allan Poe and, in blithe disregard of their impropriety as nourishment for an infant mind, read both authors aloud to the mesmerized Eugene, often supplementing them with horror tales of her own invention. She further sought to entertain her young charge with the sordid details of contemporary murders, enlarging on this information with visits to museums displaying wax effigies of criminals and the malformed.

In New York, in addition to shepherding him to the Museum of Natural History and the zoo, Sarah took Eugene to the Horror Chamber of the Eden Musée, which featured, for a twenty-five-cent admission, "a world of wax" and Hungarian gypsy music. Eugene, always attentive even when terrified, was the perfect captive audience for his ill-advised if well-meaning nurse, who doubtless felt as isolated and unbelonging as Eugene.

The reference in *Long Day's Journey Into Night* to Edmund/Eugene's "continually having nightmares as a child," although not related to his nurse, was obviously factual and probably traceable, at least in part, to the imaginative Sarah. Her lurid tales, if terrifying to Eugene, very likely stimulated the sense of drama that was later to hold audiences spellbound.

His childhood fear of the "world of reality," O'Neill noted in his free-associative diagram, was "emphasized by nurse's murder stories." James had his own remedy for the nightmares caused by his son's "terror of dark." He fed him "whiskey & water."

According to a scribbled comment enclosed in one of the balloons with which the diagram was embellished, the palliative whiskey was connected with "the drink of hero father," not yet perceived by his son as a "dangerous rival."

In *Long Day's Journey Into Night*, Mary Tyrone reviles her husband's "people" as "the most ignorant kind of poverty-stricken Irish," who "honestly believed whiskey is the healthiest medicine for a child who is sick or frightened."

While Ella O'Neill could excoriate her husband for his "ignorant" belief in the efficacy of whiskey, she evidently was not above resorting to it herself, along with morphine, as an occasional remedy for anxiety. It is something of a shock to learn from O'Neill's self-analytical notations that his mother's "nervousness" following his difficult birth eventually wound up in "drinking & drug-addiction." He emphasized there had been "No signs of these before."

In an ensuing note he referred once again to his mother's drinking, this time with reference to Sarah Sandy, who, he revealed, "later becomes companion in beer & stout drinking — later still (after E is in school) in whiskey drinking and probably messenger for obtaining drugs (?)"

The references are particularly arresting, since it is the only documentation that Ella had a tendency for "drinking." (In *Long Day's Journey Into Night* there is no suggestion of it — unless James Tyrone's halfhearted accusation in Act Three may be read as such. Tyrone, returning home from town, finds his bottle of whiskey watered and he turns on his wife in momentary suspicion: "I hope to God you haven't taken to drink on top of — " Edmund, guessing his mother has "treated" the housemaid and the cook to drinks, quickly disabuses him.)

If Sarah Sandy drank, she must have had a good head for alcohol, for no one recalled ever seeing her inebriated. She seemed to thrive under the trying conditions of touring, and she found herself, along with Eugene, picking up a firsthand backstage education. Sarah was fond of declaring that she had seen *The Count of Monte Cristo* so many times she could go on stage and play any part at a moment's notice.

As for Eugene, one of his early memories (by his own later account) was of his father dripping with salt and sawdust, climbing on a stool behind the swinging profile of dashing waves.

"It was then," he recalled, "that the calcium lights in the gallery played on his long beard and tattered clothes, as with arms outstretched he declared that the world was his. This was a signal for the house to burst into a deafening applause that overwhelmed the noise of the storm manufactured backstage.

"It was an artificial age, an age ashamed of its own feelings, and the theater reflected its thoughts. Virtue always triumphed and vice always got its just desserts. It accepted nothing half-way; a man was either a hero or a villain, and a woman was either virtuous or vile."

Eugene, amid bouts of horror with Sarah, awed glimpses of his "hero father" on stage and the alternating neglect and coddling by his mother, found early and pleasurable release in solitary reading. Even as a child he felt alienated, preferring to escape into an imaginary realm where he could not be hurt by an often remote mother or an overwhelming father.

Twin photographs taken of him at six in New London — acknowledged by O'Neill in later years to be "amusing and characteristic" — show him seated alone on a rock. In one pose he is hunched over a book, in the other he gazes dreamily out to sea.

He is fetchingly dressed in a dark jacket, short pants, an Eton cap, long dark stockings and high-laced boots. It was his habit to sit for hours among the smooth yellow rocks that lined the harbor road, reading, sketching trees and ships, contemplating the circling sea gulls.

According to relatives, he was moody, oversensitive and "delicate." Though he had no more than his fair share of the usual childhood diseases, including measles (which must have terrified his mother even more than his bout with typhoid), he was plagued by colds, tonsillitis and respiratory infections and was often pale.

" . . . I can remember when I was a boy, my Mother, whenever she would see me thoughtful, would ask suspiciously 'What are you doing, Eugene?'" he once reminisced. "'Thinking,' I would say portentously. 'What is the matter with you — do you feel sick?' she would ask with a naive maternal solicitude that used to exasperate me."

CHAPTER
NINE

DURING THE FIRST FEW YEARS OF HIS LIFE, EUGENE WAS painstakingly shielded from his mother's drug-induced lapses by both Sarah Sandy and his father. It was otherwise with his brother, who was ten before his mother began relying on morphine. He was old enough to notice her erratic conduct during his school vacations — her abrupt withdrawals, her vaporous spells, her swings from tranquility to melancholia, her episodes of insomnia, her recurrent, prolonged silences followed by surges of compulsive, excited chatter.

In his early teens, he was stunned to discover the truth. "Caught her in the act with a hypo," Jamie Tyrone tells his younger brother in *Long Day's Journey Into Night*. "Christ, I'd never dreamed before that any women but whores took dope!"

James made an effort to account to Jamie for Ella's addiction. It was not her fault, she had tried many times to overcome it and, while no remedy so far had lasted, he was optimistic that one day a cure would be found.

Doting as he did on his mother, Jamie at first laid the blame on his father. Next, he sought to attach blame (as Ella did) to the birth of Eugene. In his heart, however, he also blamed himself for the lasting grief caused by Edmund's death. With so heavy an emotional burden, he could turn to no one but his father, despite his mistrust. Father and son were bound by shared misery over Ella's affliction.

When Jamie returned to school in the fall of 1892, he was given to periodic outbursts of outrageous conduct. But after being punished, he was always forgiven because of his exemplary school grades and the charm and wit with which he had learned to apologize.

Jamie knew how to be resourceful outside of school as well. During one vacation in New York, when his father had denied him permission to attend a circus matinee, he decided to find the price of admission on his own. Wandering about the neighborhood of Madison Square Garden, then situated on the northeast corner of the Square, he spotted a "Boy Wanted" sign in a luggage shop window. He approached the proprietor, who was absorbed in his bookkeeping, and brashly announced, "I want that job."

"You do, do you?" the proprietor growled. "Well, go outside and walk down the block and if I call you back, I'll hire you. If I don't, you just keep walking."

"Thank you, sir," said Jamie, and turned to go. In front of the store was a display of trunks and suitcases with price tags attached. Without breaking stride, Jamie picked up the most expensive bag he could carry and started down the street.

The proprietor, who had been watching to see the effect of his maneuver, shouted: "Here, you, come back!" Jamie trotted back and the proprietor, outmaneuvered, hired him. After working a few hours, Jamie fast-talked his boss into giving him not only a small advance on his salary — enough to pay for the forbidden circus ticket — but also the afternoon off.

This type of prank was easier for James O'Neill to overlook than the sort of misbehavior that, he feared, might lead to disciplinary action at Notre Dame. Self-conscious as he was about his own lack of formal schooling, James was determined Jamie should receive a sound education and conform to all the institutional regulations.

And then the news came from Notre Dame: Jamie was in trouble — for smoking on campus and other infractions. James tried to find ways of punishing him, but guiltily sensing his son's behavior might be related to anxiety about his mother's condition, he tried to find excuses for him.

During a brief winter vacation Jamie joined his father in Chicago, and for the first time displayed open disrespect. James attempted to reason with him, but to no avail. On January 9, 1893, shortly after his son's visit ended, James voiced his concern in a letter to the Reverend Thomas E. Walsh, Notre Dame's president, addressing him as "Dear Friend."

" . . . I trust Jamie reached Notre Dame in good spirits after his pleasant stay in Chicago. I gave him a stern lecture on the result of smoking those vile *Fire Crackers* and he promised he would not smoke anymore of them. Still I think he will bear watching. If he can be kept well in hand for the next two years I am sure he will make a good man."

Momentarily dropping his guard, James added despondently

(and prophetically): "On the other hand there is a possible chance of his going to the dogs. During my conversation with him in Chicago I found I was no longer talking to a child. He has some very old ideas of *Life* and not the best by any means. I suppose he has picked these ideas up from the older boys with whom he comes in contact in his department. I shall watch his progress anxiously. During the next few years I shall write him often, doing all I can to keep him at his work and in the right path."

James ended on an almost pleading note: "The satisfaction of knowing you have always looked upon him with a friendly eye will be a lasting comfort to his Mother and Your friend, James O'Neill."

Only a few weeks later, evidently confirming James's surmise as to the bad influences of the "older boys" on his son, an editor wrote in the school paper: "They fill all space with air-y screeches and yelps." And, zeroing in on one particular individual who may well have been Jamie, the editor described a student who, locking himself into his room as a precaution, "imagines himself to be King Lear, or Shylock, and he rants and roars until his very voice gives out."

Then, again generalizing (and perhaps including Jamie), the editor went on to depict "the would-be tough": "His clothes hang carelessly about him. His face wears a natural jeer heightened by a contemptible smile. A cigarette always decorates his mouth, and he walks with a genuine Bowery swagger."

Despite his sporadic misbehavior, Jamie sailed through the first half of the school year 1893-94 creditably enough, being listed on the Carroll Hall Roll of Honor that January. By term's end, however, he was no longer on the honor roll and he informed his father he did not want to continue at Notre Dame.

That summer, James patiently endured Jamie's new habit of taunting him at every opportunity, and tried to salvage what he could of his difficult son's reputation. On August 27, he wrote to the Reverend Andrew Morrissey, the new president of Notre Dame, and complained of his growing disenchantment with Jamie, now just a month short of his sixteenth birthday:

" . . . I regret to state that after many Fatherly chats with [Jamie] I have discovered that he is dissatisfied not with Notre Dame but with the result of his last year's work. He seems to have lost heart [and] appears devoid of ambition and we all know his great fault is lack of application. I have talked this matter over with his Mother and after due consideration we have come to the conclusion that a change is absolutely necessary. He needs a 'spur to prick the sides of his intent.'

On the other hand Mrs. O'Neill's health may not permit her to go west with me. She will likely spend most of the winter in New York. Under these circumstances we have decided to send James to Georgetown where his mother can run over to see him frequently, doing all in her power to keep him on his mettle."

James's reference to Ella running over to Georgetown (presumably from New York) may seem somewhat puzzling. To reach the preparatory school, which was on the campus of Washington's Georgetown University, would have entailed a trip of more than six hours each way, as there was no direct train service between Manhattan and Washington at that time. Ella would have had to board a Pullman car at a terminal in lower Manhattan, which was loaded onto a barge-like craft called a lighter and floated across the Hudson to New Jersey; there it was coupled to an engine that drew it to Washington (stopping several times for coal). Ella, conditioned to the tedium of travel, would doubtless have been unfazed by the prospect of a monthly six-hour trip between New York and Washington.

A "new institution, new teachers, strange faces," continued James in his letter to the Reverend Morrissey, "may have the desired effect. I need not state that this is a great disappointment to me as I have always esteemed Notre Dame highly and looked forward with pleasure to his finishing brilliantly at your College."

James ended with an appeal to the Reverend Morrissey to say anything he could to further Jamie's interests "and give him his proper standing at Georgetown."

Jamie entered Georgetown on September 13, 1894. Oddly, he registered as James Henry O'Neill. It seems likely he bestowed the middle name, that of a 15th century prince of Tyrone, upon himself, at the same time dropping the "Jr." The most obvious explanation was a wish to distance himself from his father.

His board and tuition for the year was $168.50 and his first expenditure was $4.05 for books that included a volume of Cicero and a Latin grammar. James allowed him fifty cents a week "pocket money."

The expense of private school was of no small concern to James, for the country was suffering a devastating depression. The stock market had crashed that spring, unemployment was soaring and real estate values plummeting. The Panic of 1893, which lasted four years, brought to an abrupt end the Gilded Age — a twenty-year period of booming industry across the country.

For someone with James's pathological fear of poverty, maintaining two children in fine private schools must have been a serious worry. Eugene was now nearing school age and there was as ever the expense of treatment for a chronically ill wife.

Jamie's "new institution" did not have the desired effect. Though he began with his accustomed academic brilliance, earning, during September and October, two consecutive 95's in geometry, a 96 and a 95 in French, and an 80 and a 79 in classics, by November his grade in classics had slipped to 63 and his geometry mark to 87. By the end of January, his mark in geometry was a disastrous 25, French 43, and classics 30.

Clearly he had undergone some sort of emotional stress, probably during the Christmas vacation. The following marking period, under the name, James Henry O'Neill, there was only the notation, "Gone," with the explanation, "Left college February 24, 1895." His stay at the school had lasted five months. The final notation in the ledger was an outlay of $27.50, for "trip to Atlanta." No reason was given for the trip, but it is likely James was performing in the vicinity and had sent for him.

With Jamie out of school, James and Ella had a serious problem on their hands. Their headquarters in New York was still the Barrett House, where Ella, six-year-old Eugene and Sarah Sandy stayed, when not touring with James. It was not the sort of household that could comfortably contain a rebellious and rudderless sixteen-year-old. James and Ella, confounded by Jamie's waywardness, searched for a new school.

By the time the family moved back into the Pink House in June of 1895, their summer home for the past eight years, they had found a school, St. John's Prep, that agreed to take Jamie the following fall. Meanwhile, Jamie continued to voice his indifference, if not his contempt, for his father's well-meant advice.

He had not yet acquired the insolence with which he later treated James. Even when angry, he continued to address his father as "Papa" and sometimes as "Governor," although he was soon to adopt a more sneering manner, addressing him as "Pater" and, behind his back, as "the Old Man."

Both James and Ella were tormented by the uncertainty of whether their son, now approaching his seventeenth birthday, would stay put at St. John's. With his undoubtedly brilliant mind, he was capable of shining at any school. But his anger and resentment toward both his parents was so intense, it was hard to predict what course he would take.

While holding their breath about Jamie, his parents found it necessary to turn their thoughts to the change they were planning in Eugene's life. Having reached school age, he could no longer live a gypsy road existence. They had decided to send him, as Jamie had been sent at the same age, to a Catholic boarding school.

It was not easy to persuade their shy, nervous, illness-prone child to accept this planned upheaval. Even though the loneliness and isolation of his first seven years marked him with a permanent sense of rootlessness, the prospect of going off by himself to an alien environment, to sunder himself not only from his parents but his beloved Sarah Sandy, terrified him. According to those who knew Sarah, she was Eugene's "great attachment in life."

His exile to boarding school signaled the beginning of his "resentment & hatred of father," as he later wrote in his free-associative diagram. Like Jamie at the same age, he blamed his father for what he characterized as "break with mother."

Eugene was not comforted by his parents' assurances that the school, in the Bronx, was no great distance from the Barrett House, nor was he propitiated by his mother's promise of frequent visits. He pleaded not to be sent away.

Amidst these pending and worrisome rearrangements in their children's' lives, James and Ella made plans to move back to the Barrett House to await the start of the school year and James's coming tour of *Monte Cristo*. Toward summer's end, James's business manager, William F. Connor, arrived in New London to discuss the new season.

With Jamie, they went off one evening to New London's Lyceum Theater to see James J. Corbett in a show featuring his championship boxing technique. Deciding to take a shortcut into town, they walked along the elevated railroad tracks, which for some distance followed the banks of the Thames.

Crossing a culvert, James missed his footing and fell twenty feet to the street, spraining his ankle, among other injuries. Connor and Jamie managed to help him home, where Ella, alarmed by his bruises, put him to bed. Despite James's protests, she sent for a doctor and the pastor of James's church, Mary's Star of the Sea. The doctor treated the sprain and bruises and left. The priest, Father Thomas P. Joynt, an old friend, lingered.

"Well, James," Father Joynt said good-humoredly, "God was with you this time."

"I wish He'd been with me a minute earlier," James drily replied. He was obliged to use crutches and then a cane. Connor had to postpone by three weeks James's theater dates for the new season. It is easy to imagine that Ella, worried about and fussing over her husband, had little time to soothe Eugene.

Most likely the self-centered actor in James gave less thought to Eugene than to the consequences of his disrupted season. If he spared any thought for his children, it was probably concern over the unpredictable Jamie's reaction to his new school. As usual, Eugene doubtless found his solace in the devotion of Sarah Sandy.

On October 18, 1895, two days after his seventh birthday, Eugene entered St. Aloysius Academy for Boys in the northern Bronx, on the grounds of a school for girls called Mount St. Vincent that closely resembled Ella's alma mater, St. Mary's Academy.

Established in 1847 by the Catholic Sisters of Charity in Manhattan, Mount St. Vincent had moved uptown to a perch upon a hill overlooking the Hudson River. The boys' adjunct, set up primarily to accommodate the younger brothers of Mount St. Vincent girls, approximated the curriculum of second through sixth grades.

While the sisters made every effort to put the boys at ease, Eugene was unresponsive. The five years he spent at St. Aloysius only heightened his sense of not belonging.

"O'Neill has acute memories of the outbursts of hysterical loneliness that overtook him on every return to his rigid Christian exile," wrote Elizabeth Shepley Sergeant, the journalist and biographer who became his friend after interviewing him in 1926 (which happened to coincide with the time of his psychoanalysis). "Gazing afar upon a stage where a heroic figure strutted, towards a lovely distant mother to whom he stretched his arms in vain, he conceived the world in which he was at mercy of his affections as disastrous."

In his free-associative diagram, O'Neill charted these feelings in shorthand: "Reality faced & fled from in fear — life of fantasy & religion in school — inability to belong to reality." He elaborated on this state of unreality to his second wife, Agnes Boulton, according to the memoir she published after his death.

Describing a recurrent childhood fantasy, he told her, "It was a dream of my childhood — when I had to dream that I was not alone.

There was me and one other in this dream. I dreamed it often — and during the day sometimes this other seemed to be with me and then I was a happy little boy. But this *other* in my dream, this other I never quite saw. It was a presence felt that made me complete. In my dream I wanted nothing else — I would not have anyone else!"

Eugene desperately missed Sarah Sandy. Although she wrote to him and sent him birthday and Christmas gifts and occasionally visited him in New York on holidays, she was gone from his daily life. It was perhaps a blow more cruel than being parted from his mother. Sarah, whatever her shortcomings, had provided him with the protective warmth he craved — and he had never had to share her love with anyone.

Jamie, meanwhile, matriculated at St. John's Preparatory School, which, like Eugene's St. Aloysius, was in the Bronx, on the site of what later became Fordham University in the then village of Fordham. He was now registered as James H. O'Neill. Up until his senior year at college, he played games with his name, sometimes signing himself James H. O'Neill, other times James O'Neill, and sometimes reverting to his baptismal James O'Neill Jr.

While his name-switching was whimsical, the sudden improvement in his behavior seemed unaccountable. The concerned lecturing by his father over the past months may have had an effect at last; or it is possible that Ella's addiction had been in abeyance during the summer, giving Jamie hope for her recovery. At any rate, his earlier, self-destructive behavior evaporated.

James and Ella once again began to receive glowing reports of Jamie's academic achievement. He earned one award after another in Greek, Latin and Elocution, among other subjects, and won first prize in English composition. His grades held consistently in the high nineties. And, as during his early years at Notre Dame, he shone as a debater. It was a truly remarkable comeback.

Relieved of day-to-day responsibility for her children, Ella could visualize the two respectable institutions in the rural Bronx where Jamie and Eugene — at a safe distance — were being properly educated and presumably well cared for. With both her sons away, she no longer had to worry about concealing her morphine habit. Nor did she have to account for her periodic absences for rehabilitation at one or another sanatorium.

But Ella did miss seven-year-old Eugene.

According to O'Neill's self-analytical notes, his mother experienced his departure more keenly than Jamie's at the same age. The reason, O'Neill concluded, was that she had been able to leave Jamie at Notre Dame in the care of "some nuns who had known her as a girl" and in a place that gave her a "feeling of home."

If St. Mary's at South Bend had felt like home to Ella, St. Aloysius on the grounds of Mount St. Vincent pleased James for its association with his early stage mentor, Edwin Forrest. The school's fifty-five acres along the Hudson had originally been owned by Forrest, who had christened the estate Fonthill.

The estate included a turreted, gray-stone, pseudo-Norman-Gothic castle, its foundation hewn from bedrock. Forrest had designed Fonthill for himself and his wife, but never lived in the castle because the marriage ended before the construction did. On the property, which he sold to the Sisters of Charity in 1856 for the Forrest-like sum of $100,000, stood a small, gracefully designed, two-story stone cottage in which Eugene was to spend his next five years.

Eugene was never happy at Mount St. Vincent. Its lovely wooded paths and rolling farmlands in the surrounding wilderness of the Bronx, the insistent cries of sea gulls circling above the Hudson and the solicitous attention of the Sisters only increased his sense of deprivation and loneliness. He was remembered by the Sisters as a "refined and quiet boy," who preferred to spend his free time with books, rather than in play with his companions. Though usually solemn, he had a heart-melting smile.

The foreman of the farm, who cut the grass and always invited the boys to pile the hay and roll in it, remembered Eugene as the only pupil who habitually declined the invitation. Sometimes Eugene would stroll down to the river alone to watch with dreamy yearning the boats sail by.

What he longed for most was his dog. He and a New London cousin both had acquired odoriferous hounds, bestowing on each the name, Perfumery. Eugene had been obliged to leave his Perfumery behind, in the care of an older cousin, Josephine Brennan.

Eugene pleaded with his teachers to let him send for the dog and finally a sympathetic priest agreed to have a doghouse built on the grounds. Eugene, elated, wrote Josephine to prepare Perfumery for shipment. On the day before the letter reached her, Perfumery ran under the wheels of a carriage and was killed. It was two years before Eugene would speak to Josephine. After they were reconciled, Josephine remained a favorite relative until her death in her nineties.

The stone cottage in which Eugene lived, ate and studied housed only fifteen boys, ranging in age from seven to twelve. On the top floor were the students' bedrooms, only six in all and on the ground floor were two classrooms and a dining room.

The boys were neither overindulged nor deprived. Their freezing nocturnal trips through the snow to a privy were compensated for by generous morning meals of oatmeal drenched in farm butter and fresh milk, prepared in the main building and conveyed to the cottage, nearly a mile away.

Cherry trees abounded and Eugene feasted on the crop, when the birds did not beat him to it. In the late spring, a section of the Hudson was fenced off as a pool and it was here that he had his first formal swimming lessons. His father, an accomplished swimmer, had taught him the rudiments in New London, and swimming became the only sport in which Eugene excelled. In his pastoral surroundings he developed an affinity for nature, which was later reflected in his plays.

A contemporary glimpse of Eugene and his schoolmates has been preserved in a quaint volume, *A Famous Convent School*, written by Marion J. Brunowe and published in 1897. Brunowe's encounter with the academy boys occurred in October, 1896, when Eugene was eight. In spite of his reluctance to join in the recreational activities of his companions, he was obliged to take a certain amount of outdoor exercise, and it may be assumed he was among the youngsters immortalized by the author:

"Shouts of clear, high laughter . . . proceed from a group of lads just issuing from yonder picturesque stone cottage . . . They are all little fellows, but they make a big noise. Here they come, the jolly little chaps, in ones, in twos, in groups, running, skipping, jumping, laughing in unrestrained glee, a glee which is not so wild, however, that good breeding is forgotten.

"No, with the sight of visitors, off go caps; each, to be sure, in the peculiar method of the wearer, from the tiny lad who clutches his head covering quite in the middle of the top, to the small, punctilious Cuban youth of ten, who removes his cap with a grace worthy of his Spanish ancestors. This duty once performed, however, the small men grow supremely indifferent to any presence save their own, and that of the young religious who superintends their sports, and looks as if she might perhaps not be averse to joining in a game now and then herself."

Although Eugene may have been a part of this group physically, he seems to have been detached from it spiritually. His roommate for two years, Joseph McCarthy, who was three years older, recalled

Eugene as always remote.

"He talked very little," McCarthy said years later, "and he didn't have much to say to me, either, although he seemed to be fond of me and considered me a sort of protector. Once, I punched another boy in the nose for calling Gene a sissy."

McCarthy could still, at seventy-two, enjoy reminiscing about his former roommate. He was a diffident, frail man, suffering from the after effects of tuberculosis and a paralyzing stroke, but his eyes crinkled with humor as he recalled a nun who used to jab the students with her elbows and rap their heads to impress them with the salient points of a lesson. ("Do you ever think of Sister Martha who used to knuckle us on the bean? and Sister Gonzaga? They often come back to me," O'Neill wrote to McCarthy in 1930.)

"Gene had an aura of sophistication that endeared him to the Sisters — even to Sister Martha, in spite of her jabs and punches," McCarthy recalled. "Most of the boys liked him, too, though they considered him a little queer. He read Kipling — he used to call me 'Mowgli' — and other authors way beyond his years." Among those authors, McCarthy remembered, was Anatole France, who had not yet been sentenced to the Catholic Index of forbidden books.

Eugene also devoured the wildly popular books of the "Wolfville" series, which he began reading at ten. Authentic, humorous tales of frontier mining and cattle-raising life during the late 1800's, they were written between 1897 and 1908 by Alfred Henry Lewis, who temporarily gave up the practice of law and journalism to spend several carefree years in the Southwest as a cowboy.

Using the pseudonym, Dan Quin, Lewis narrated the stories in the voice of "Old Cattleman," who lived in the fictitious town of Wolfville, Arizona, and spoke a Southwestern range jargon. Appealing to adults as well as boys, the stories featured such odd characters as Dead Shot Baker, Black Jack, Curly Ben, Texas, Moon, and Cynthiana. Eugene developed a lifelong attachment to the six books in the series. "During his years with me," Carlotta Monterey once said, "whenever he was fed-up with writing plays, the business of living, or was not well — he would re-read the 'Wolfville' stories over, & over & over again!"

At Mount St. Vincent, Eugene insisted that Joe McCarthy read everything he read, but declined to discuss the books with him.

"He was mediocre in his studies, and not really interested in anything except his reading," McCarthy said. "He did talk once in a while about wanting to go to sea. I don't know if it was his own idea or his mother's, but he used to wear a sort of sailor blouse and short pants most of the time. And I remember he wrote to his brother, of whom he was very fond."

McCarthy was not surprised that Eugene willingly took part in plays in preference to other after-class activities, for he knew Eugene was the son of a popular actor. In common with his classmates, he had been taken more than once to see *The Count of Monte Cristo*. But McCarthy found Eugene blasé when the other boys displayed admiration for James O'Neill's fencing prowess.

One classmate, Stephen Philbin, recalled that the boys would engage in animated discussions about James's swordsmanship and, with sticks, imitate his dueling scenes.

The boys' most heated discussions centered on the Spanish-American War. There were a number of Cubans at St. Aloysius, and the blowing up of the Maine prompted comradely patriotism in the student body. The nationwide chorus, "Remember the Maine," was echoed at St. Aloysius and reinforced by picture-postcard novelties depicting the battleship that, when touched by a match, exploded into flame.

From what both McCarthy and Philbin have remembered about the school routine, it would seem Eugene had ample time to pursue his reading. The boys arose at six-thirty and received classroom instruction from eight until three-thirty. From then until bedtime at nine, they were more or less on their own.

Sunday Mass in the Chapel of the Immaculate Conception was, of course, obligatory, as was daily classroom drilling in the Catechism, the doctrinal questions and answers that point the way to the final goal of eternal salvation. The volume in use was the children's adaptation of the Baltimore Catechism of 1884.

Parochial schools were increasingly coming under the domination of religiously conservative, strictly moralistic, Irish-descended priests and nuns. Forged by the stern Catholicism of the old country, they demanded unwavering adherence from their charges.

This rigid indoctrination had its predictable effect on the heart and mind of young Eugene who, in later years, was apt to remark, "Once a Catholic always a Catholic." No matter how far behind he left the instruction of his youth, he always believed literally in the sin and redemption he had learned from his Catechism.

"Revulsion," he once said, "drives a man to tell others of his sin . . . It is the Furies within us that seek to destroy us. In all my plays sin is punished and redemption takes place."

The "age of reason," as defined by the Catholic Church, had not yet been lowered to seven (decreed in the early 1900's). Consequently, Eugene did not receive his first Holy Communion until nearly twelve and, by that time, he was steeped in the Creed, the Commandments and the Sacraments. Prior to being administered the Holy Eucharist, he was required to make "fervent acts of faith, hope, love and contrition" and to promise he would continue to study the Catechism and remain committed to the rituals and commands of the church.

Catholicism clearly was an integral part of his daily being, but its practice had taken on a meaning more imperious than that of his first seven years. Ella, who remained an observant Catholic throughout much of her long struggle with addiction, conveyed to Eugene her gentle religious devotion; and he learned to perceive her God as "One of Infinite Love — a very human lovable God Who became man for love of men and gave His life that they might be saved from themselves."

At Mount St. Vincent, he evidently encountered a more demanding Deity and he began to chafe under the unyielding requirements of the church. McCarthy, who had a less questioning mind than Eugene's, never forgot a comment of his roommate's.

"Religion is so cold," pronounced the nine-year-old Eugene.

Even while conforming unhappily to the religious rituals of Mount St. Vincent, Eugene often harked back to the time when his Catholic sensibility was intimately entwined with his mother's. Listening to her wistful descriptions of her own girlhood indoctrination at St. Mary's, he could evoke parallel images of the girls at Mount St. Vincent.

In fact, in his mind he transposed his mother as a schoolgirl to his own campus — a trick of imagination illustrated by his reference in *Long Day's Journey Into Night* to the "shrine of Our Lady of Lourdes, on the little island in the lake," which Mary Tyrone recalls from her senior year at school.

No such shrine existed on the campus of St. Mary's Academy when Ella was a student there. The shrine was at Mount St. Vincent. Built as a replica of the grotto in France, where Bernadette reported her visitation from the Virgin Mary, the shrine stood on an island in a tiny lake, spanned by wooden bridges.

Ella did look in at Mount St. Vincent's grotto when she visited Eugene. The walk to her son's dormitory from the Mount St. Vincent station, a stop of the New York Central Railroad, led past the lake where the grotto stood.

If anything could have called to Ella's wavering faith it would have been the sight of the young girls worshipping at the statue of Mary, whose mystically healing grace Ella often sought for redemption.

In addition to visiting both Eugene and Jamie from time to time, occasionally accompanied by one of the New London relatives she had deigned to patronize, Ella also saw her sons during school recesses. Despite her emotional stress, she offered no objections when Eugene suggested inviting Joe McCarthy to New London during Easter vacation in 1897.

McCarthy always wondered why Eugene had invited him. The eight-and-a-half-year-old Eugene, after offering Joe free run of his father's library in the Pink House, left him to do as he pleased. Eugene made no effort to entertain Joe in any way, never suggesting they leave the house or see any friends; nor did Ella offer suggestions for the boys' diversion. According to McCarthy, an orphan, she behaved pleasantly and normally. McCarthy could not remember seeing James, who, he assumed, was on tour.

Eugene spent the week reading in his room or on the porch. As he once told Elizabeth Shepley Sergeant, his father's library in New London stoked the fire of his early literary imagination. He could not have survived his loneliness without it, for his agonizing shyness and fear of being misunderstood rendered him ill at ease with acquaintances and even with most of his relatives.

According to Sergeant, he read and reread "the fifty volumes of Dumas, the complete works of Victor Hugo and Charles Lever, the Irish romancer." She added that "To the pleasure of James O'Neill, who used to harp on the glorious deeds of Shane the Proud and the other O'Neills, he was also an avid reader of Irish history. The romantic poetry of Scott he loved at a very early age and was — this seems important — 'a fiend on Byron,' reciting 'Childe Harold' interminably. He absorbed Dickens and Kipling."

Vacation over, Eugene and Joe returned in friendly silence to St. Aloysius, which Joe was to leave at the end of term, and although they had a brief exchange of letters in later years they never saw each other again.

CHAPTER
TEN

AT BOARDING SCHOOL, EUGENE WAS SHIELDED FROM THE ongoing stress of his parents' lives. In early March of 1897, their tensions were heightened when a long-buried scandal suddenly resurfaced.

In a Dickensian twist of plot, Nettie Walsh's son, now twenty-three, took it upon himself to revive his mother's court claim of twenty years earlier. James had just ended a run at McVicker's and was still in Chicago when Nettie's son, who called himself Alfred Hamilton O'Neill, filed a bill on March 9. He alleged that his mother had lost her suit for divorce in 1877 because she had been "misled by designing people."

The bill stated there had been "a series of false and plausible promises" as well as "threats of various sorts" against his mother's good name. These proceedings, the bill charged, had perpetrated "the most outrageous fraud upon the court," enabling James O'Neill to procure a decree "finding that no marriage ever existed between the mother of said Alfred O'Neill and the defendant, James O'Neill."

Alfred Hamilton O'Neill, who worked for the D. M. Davis Soap Company, protested that since his own legitimacy was in question, he intended to remove the blemish as well as reestablish the good name of his mother. He asked that James be restrained from leaving the state and that a receiver be appointed for his property. In a separate suit, he demanded $20,000 in damages. Discomfited on Ella's behalf and grumbling about the nuisance and the expense, James once again put his politically connected lawyers to work.

The case inevitably was reported in the press, and Jamie, now eighteen, soon was in possession of all the squalid details. The shocking discovery of a prior claimant to his birthright only served to harden his cynical view of his father.

Although the son's suit was no more successful than the mother's in establishing the marriage, it dragged on for three years before being resolved in 1900. Evidently James was persuaded by his lawyers to offer Alfred Hamilton O'Neill a modest settlement. (It enabled Alfred, before long, to go into business for himself as a soap manufacturer's agent.)

Presumably because Ella was embarrassed by news accounts of the scandal's revival, the O'Neills did not occupy the Pink House in the summer of 1897, instead renting a cottage on Staten Island.

Returning from school to join his family for their summer vacation, eight-year-old Eugene grew ever more aware of his family's disquietude, and was perplexed, as Jamie had been at his age, by his mother's spells of remoteness. He sought revenge in childish pranks, at one time writing his own name in his father's books and, on another occasion, pouring a can of green paint over a box of shiny, metal statuettes of James as Edmond Dantes. The paint hardened, permanently cloaking the figures in sickly green, before the crime was discovered.

Eugene's resentment of his father was reinforced by Jamie's own naked antagonism. Hero-worshipping his older brother, Eugene felt Jamie could do no wrong. Jamie had completed his freshman year at St. John's College and James was obliged to commend his academic progress, squirm as he might under his older son's ever-hardening animosity.

Jamie had won awards in six subjects and had been elected class historian. (In his junior year, he was to distinguished himself once again as a debater, and became an editor and contributor to the literary magazine, the Fordham Monthly.)

Even while upholding his superior academic record, Jamie found a way to take a backhanded slap at his long-suffering father. In December, 1898, he wrote an essay for the Fordham Monthly, "The Drama in America," surely aimed, at least obliquely, at James (and that uncannily foreshadowed the view Eugene was to adopt as a playwright).

Citing "public taste" as the cause of the current-day "decadence of the drama," Jamie declared: "It is the light and frivolous taste, which at present characterizes the American people, that causes the neglect of Shakespeare and the flooding of the country with inane society plays, risqué farce comedies, costly extravaganzas, and light, plotless, comic operas . . . "

Expressing his reverence for Shakespeare (and, at the same time,

implicitly relegating his father to oblivion), Jamie bewailed the passing away of "the actor giants." He also noted the sad fact that
"Shakespeare, who can so exquisitely 'set to music' all the varied
moods of the human heart, has been banished to one-night stands,
and is mangled and done to death by the clumsy hands of the bombastic ranter.

"Things have indeed come to a pretty pass," he continued, "when
in the great city of New York, with its two millions of inhabitants,
there is not a single play-house devoted to tragedy."

His disparaging analysis was not only apt but prescient. Less to
his credit was his view that it was "the Jews who own or have leased
all the theaters in the big cities throughout the United States." Rather
than being "impelled by enthusiasm for art or any such nonsense as
that," he maintained, they were "after the spoils" and were impelled
to "serve up to the people only what will tickle their degenerate
palates."

In 1898, such outspoken bigotry was generally accepted even in
academic circles. The essay won first prize in that year's literary competition and Jamie became editor-in-chief of the magazine at the start
of his senior year in September of 1899; he was listed in the masthead
as James H. O'Neill.

Although Jamie had continued to maintain high grades the previous year, he had already begun to cut classes to visit Manhattan's
gaudier places of entertainment and to drink recklessly. His behavior
on campus had become noticeably erratic. As manager of the baseball
team, for example, he failed on one occasion to meet his players at the
railroad station; with the train tickets in his pocket, he went off to a
saloon, where he was discovered drunk after the train's departure by
a stranded team member.

The drunker Jamie became, the meaner he grew — especially
toward his father — and, after a while, it became habitual for him to
deride James to friends and acquaintances (shocking and embarrassing them) as "the old skinflint," "the old miser," and even "the old
bastard."

Less than two months into his senior year, Jamie was already in
the decline from which he never sprang back. Infractions of college
seniors were routinely winked at by the faculty, and Jamie continued
to be pardoned for similar episodes. But his behavior culminated in a
gesture of defiance too outrageous to be overlooked.

On a bet, in late November of 1899, six months before graduation,
Jamie brought a prostitute to the St. John's campus and tried to pass

her off as his sister. He was asked to leave the college and did so on December 3 — "withdrawn by request," as the record stated.

Once again, the hopes of James and Ella were rudely dashed. After having endured Jamie's heartbreaking failures at Notre Dame and Georgetown, they had allowed themselves, during the previous three and a half years, to bask in his truly spectacular academic turn-around at St. John's.

They had confidently expected him to go on to a successful career in law school. Instead, Jamie, at twenty, was already on his way to becoming the blighted alcoholic his younger brother was to depict in *Long Day's Journey Into Night* and *A Moon for the Misbegotten*. Dumbfounded by his son's expulsion, James felt particularly humiliated, for he could not help but regard Jamie's behavior as a direct attack upon himself.

Eugene, now eleven and in his final year at Mount St. Vincent, never forgot the impact that Jamie's expulsion made on his family. Forty-four years later, the episode with the prostitute was still alive in his mind. He recreated it (with the wry humor of distance) in *A Moon for the Misbegotten*, which he set in 1923, the year of Jamie's death from alcoholism at forty-six.

O'Neill described Jamie's expulsion from college in a bantering scene between Jim Tyrone and an Irish farmer who had been a tenant of his father's. O'Neill transcribed the story as he heard it from his brother on more than one occasion:

"There had been a slight misunderstanding just before I was to graduate . . . I made a bet with another Senior I could get a tart from the Haymarket to visit me, introduce her to the Jebs as my sister — and get away with it . . . It was a memorable day in the halls of learning. All the students were wise and I had them rolling in the aisles as I showed Sister around the grounds, accompanied by one of the Jebs. He was a bit suspicious at first, but Dutch Maisie — her professional name — had no make-up on, and was dressed in black, and had eaten a pound of Sen-Sen to kill the gin on her breath, and seemed such a devout girl that he forgot his suspicions . . . Yes, all would have been well, but she was a mischievous minx, and had her own ideas of improving on my joke. When she was saying good-bye to Father Fuller, she added innocently: 'Christ, Father, it's nice and quiet out here away from the damned Sixth Avenue El. I wish to hell I could stay here!' . . . But she didn't, and neither did I."

Eugene watched in consternation as his father and brother conducted their baleful battle of wits. Jamie would taunt, disappoint or outrage James and then, by some brash, engaging trick, win his for-giveness and yet another reprieve. Longing for reassurance, Eugene, once back at school, sought comfort in his religion. He was able to find it, probably for the last time, in his first Holy Communion, which he received on May 24, 1899.

Four years after his death, a sweet-faced, elderly nun at Mount St. Vincent, Mother Mary Fuller, led the authors of this biography to the altar at which the earnest young boy, having fasted and confessed and made fervent acts of faith, hope, love and contrition, solemnly accepted the Holy Eucharist. Eugene believed literally he had achieved union with God, had been granted an increase of grace, and would be preserved from mortal sin.

Mother Mary, who had not herself known Eugene, had neverthe-less interested herself in his career and questioned Sisters who remembered him, and she understood that he had ultimately lost his faith. "Doesn't it break your heart to think of the poor little fellow?" she asked.

The century's turn was not auspicious for any of the O'Neills. After leaving college toward the end of 1899, Jamie looked for work. A good job would, of course, have been easier to come by had he received his degree. Even without it, Jamie, with his genuinely fine intellect and ingratiating manners, might have found a respectable career in New York, for this was a time of great opportunity. Only a year before, Brooklyn and Queens, along with Staten Island, had con-solidated with Manhattan and the Bronx to form the nation's largest and most influential metropolis, with a population approaching three and a half million. Advancement in a career would have been easy for Jamie. But he had lost heart.

His father, in perpetual conflict about how much help to offer, never could summon the courage to force Jamie's independence from him. Years of accumulated guilt was certainly part of the reason: the early trauma suffered by Jamie at Edmund's death, the anxiety caused by his mother's addiction, and, most recently, the humiliation of Alfred Hamilton "O'Neill's" claim as first-born son.

At one point Jamie, trading on his college literary success, attempted to become a newspaper reporter. But he discovered it was a poorer-paying and less glamorous occupation than he had antici-pated. He tried other jobs, including that of traveling salesman for a lumber company. It was not long before he succumbed to what seemed the easiest way out, and grudgingly allowed his father to launch him on an acting career.

As a youth, Jamie had taken walk-on roles in his father's company, but he had never contemplated earning his living on the stage. In view of his recent attack on the quality of the American theater, he must have shuddered at the prospect.

Indeed, as he continued to grow ever more cynical, his contempt intensified for the theater in general and for his father's abilities in particular. However, he had to concede he was suited for nothing else. And since he had his father's looks, if somewhat coarsened, and glimmerings of his father's Irish wit and charm, the stage did seem to suit him.

Jamie had, moreover, his father's fondness for quoting Shakespeare and a fair echo of the resonant paternal voice. Eugene O'Neill, humorously recalling his brother's vocal capacity, once wrote to his young son, Shane:

"My brother, your Uncle Jim, . . . used to be able to make a noise just like a lion roaring and for a joke he used to go out to the Zoo and go up close to the lion's cage when the lion was asleep, and when the keeper wasn't looking your Uncle Jim would lean over close to the lion's ear and make the roaring imitation and the lion would wake up startled and jump to his feet mad as the dickens and wanting to fight and he'd start roaring, and then all the other lions and tigers and leopards would get mad too and start roaring, and the keeper would come running to see what was the matter but Uncle Jim would walk away as if he hadn't done anything and he'd be laughing to himself because he thought he'd played a great joke!"

Jamie began his reluctant stage career as an understudy in *The Musketeers*, an adaptation by Sydney Grundy of the Dumas novel. The play was one more in a series of his father's futile attempts to separate himself from *The Count of Monte Cristo*.

A few years earlier, in 1890, James had appeared in *The Dead Heart*, all but a carbon copy of *Monte Cristo*. It was an immediate failure. The following year he opened in a lurid melodrama, *The Envoy*, which New York critics dismissed as preposterous. It ran less than two weeks.

Not long after, in a rare outburst of public anger and frustration, James complained: "New York does not seem to want good plays or good acting . . . New Yorkers want buffoonery, so I shall not play again in New York . . . New York is the town of towns for fads, skits, and horse-play."

For the next ten years, James tried a dozen or so new plays and revivals, including, from time to time, some Shakespeare. He did, of course, return many times to New York. But in his effort to turn his career back onto a worthier path, he could not seem to make the right choice. Even when he did win mild critical approval for some new production, audiences did not storm the box office. He was forced to fall back, for a part of almost every season, upon *Monte Cristo*, always a sure-fire money-maker.

Struggle as he might to escape the snare of *Monte Cristo*, James wound up playing Edmond Dantes well over five thousand times. He earned what was a fortune for that day — close to a million dollars — as he hustled the Count across the country for more than a quarter of a century.

James was past sixty before he managed to slip from Dantes' grip and that of the $50,000 net profit a year *Monte Cristo* by then was bringing him. Although he became an idol to two generations of easily pleased playgoing masses, he was remembered by discriminating audiences merely as a one-character actor.

Instead of achieving the sublime stature of Edwin Booth, he followed in the shallower footsteps of Joseph Jefferson, who had also contented himself with a reputation as a one-character actor. The felicity of Jefferson's prolonged run as Rip Van Winkle remained unquestioned for he had the good luck not to spawn a playwright son who dissected his father's career and pronounced it an artistic failure.

While James's production of the *The Count of Monte Cristo* left no lasting mark, it did in its way become a milestone of the American theater, for it helped shape the strange genius of Eugene O'Neill.

When O'Neill began writing, he brooded endlessly about what he saw as the tragedy of his father's misstep. In letters and in conversations recalled by friends, he spoke of his father's own wretched awareness of this blunder. "That God-damned play I bought for a song and made such a great success in — a great money success — it ruined me with its promise of an easy fortune," says James Tyrone in *Long Day's Journey Into Night*.

In 1927, seven years after his father's death, O'Neill expressed his contempt for an actress who seemed to him about to make a similar error (she had turned down his *Strange Interlude*). He told Brooks Atkinson that the rising actress, Katharine Cornell, planned to secure her reputation by playing shallow modern drama, and only then devoting herself to great art. Undoubtedly with his father in mind, O'Neill predicted she would have accumulated so many facile mannerisms by that time that she would be lost to the ways of genius.

However much O'Neill derided the commercialism of his father's theater, he owed it an eternal debt. His intimate knowledge of its bombastic hollowness enabled him to understand what had to be overthrown by something grander.

"My early experience with the theater through my father really made me revolt against it," he once recalled. "As a boy I saw so much of the old, ranting, artificial, romantic stage stuff that I always had a sort of contempt for the theater." While he insisted that the first seven years of touring with his father gave him a thorough dislike of the theater's conventions, he conceded those years injected the theater permanently into his blood. Gradually, he came to understand not only what was wrong with American drama, but what was right with it — what he could borrow and remold to his own vision. It was necessary to be immersed as he was in the grandiloquence of 19th century theater, to conceive of creating a monumental drama of his own. As he came to believe, "Only those who know the theater thoroughly are entitled to break the rules now and then."

James still had hopes of ridding himself of Edmond Dantes when the newly booming Liebler and Company, founded by Theodore Liebler, George C. Tyler, and James's business manager, William Connor, offered him *The Musketeers*. Like a number of producers during the late 1800's and early 1900's, Theodore Liebler had begun on little more than high hopes, nerve, a few hundred dollars in cash and precarious credit. His rapid rise as a theatrical manager was typical of the era.

The son of a German artist, he opened a lithographic shop specializing in theatrical posters. He grew interested in show business when managers, in lieu of paying their bills, gave him a percentage of their productions. This sort of payment proved profitable and by 1890 Liebler found himself the proprietor of a thriving establishment in New York's Park Place. On Saturday, August 22, 1891, an explosion in the basement's paint shop toppled the five-story building, killing sixty-one people. Liebler, whose loss was not covered by insurance, was forced to abandon his business. He had, however, managed to salvage a small amount of cash and, deciding to become a producer, he began looking around for someone who had a play.

He found George Tyler, James O'Neill's one-time advance man, who coincidentally was seeking a backer for *The Royal Box*, a Charles Coghlan vehicle the actor himself had written based on the life of the English tragedian, Edmund Kean. The once-brilliant Coghlan was now addicted to champagne and deeply in debt.

Tyler himself was in bad repute for his recent overblown presentation of *As You Like It* in Asbury Park, New Jersey. His opening-night box-office receipts had been insufficient to pay his all-star cast and he had only recently dared to come out of hiding.

Liebler persuaded the manager of the Fifth Avenue Theater, recently abandoned by the show's star, to book *The Royal Box* as a temporary bill. It was thus that Liebler and Company came into existence. *The Royal Box* was a great success from the moment it opened. Liebler and Tyler followed that play with another triumph called *The Christian*, and it was soon after these two hits that they invited James O'Neill to star in *The Musketeers*.

They offered him $500 a week, ten percent of the gross profits, and an all-star cast that included Blanche Bates, Margaret Anglin and Wilton Lackaye. James was willing to throw in with Liebler and Tyler if it meant a chance to get away from *The Count of Monte Cristo* without financial risk.

Meanwhile, another preeminent manager, Daniel Frohman, announced a rival production of the same Dumas novel, this one called *The King's Musketeers* — a new version by Henry Hamilton, and starring E. H. Sothern. Sothern opened at the Knickerbocker on Thirty-eighth Street at the end of February, 1899. James opened at the Broadway on Forty-first Street on March 13, several days later than originally scheduled, his voice still hoarse from the after-effects of a severe cold. Illness was such a rare occurrence in his fifty-year career that his younger son felt he could take the license, in *Long Day's Journey Into Night*, of having James Tyrone twice boast that he had "never missed a performance" in his life.

Both *Musketeer* productions ran until mid-April of that year and the competition brightened the Broadway season, with critics and playgoers debating the acting ability of the two d'Artagnans. Although James was thirteen years older than Sothern, he still possessed, at fifty-three, more agility than many actors half his age. Night after night he dominated the stage in a series of ten tableaux that lasted almost four hours. He had explained how he kept fit to an interviewer three years earlier: "I have lived simply and taken good care of myself. I eat only plain food; sweets I never touch . . . After hard work I have rested and I exercise as much as possible off the stage."

In the interest of fitness he did without a dresser, he said, making even the most complicated costume changes by himself. "I keep my muscles fairly hard and fat cannot accumulate upon me, while I do all the work in my dressing room," he explained.

According to a young member of James's company, David F. Perkins, who played one of numerous combatants, James sought actors "who could put up a good fight," and had chosen Perkins for his skill as a swordsman.

"Those dueling scenes weren't faked much," Perkins recalled. "We used rapiers with only slightly blunted points; they were genuine displays of fencing skill, except, of course, that the right man had to end up winning."

Perkins was the designated loser in a scene requiring much leaping about in a bedchamber and on the bed itself. "I used to have bruises on my knuckles from O'Neill's sword thrusts," he remembered with satisfaction. But James was no more exempt from harm than Perkins.

During one performance, in a scene where three men attacked him at once, the swordplay became frenzied and James was stabbed through his leather doublet, inches from the heart. "Watch yourself, or you'll have a dead man on your hands," he cautioned his overzealous adversaries backstage. But he said it with a smile.

Although James as D'Artagnan had effected his escape from Edmond Dantes, at least for the moment, he soon realized he had not managed to flee very far, for the two roles were vexatiously similar. The similarity, however, did not in the least vex Liebler or Tyler. At the turn of the century (as Jamie had accurately pointed out in his college essay), managers (Jewish or not), had eyes only for box-office receipts, not for artistic departures.

There were, to be sure, some timorous exceptions. Ibsen's *The Master Builder* was presented for one performance in January, 1900, and in that same year Richard Mansfield added Shaw's *The Devil's Disciple* to his repertory. The most potent critic of the time, William Winter, of the New York Tribune, did his influential best, however, to dismiss the realism of Ibsen and Shaw, among other major European playwrights. In so doing, he was merely reflecting the public's craving for popular romance and melodrama. And managers continued to pay high prices for proven vehicles (not unlike Hollywood later in the new century).

The Musketeers, despite James's own well-received performance, was not a financial success in New York, but Liebler and Company hoped to recoup its money with a road tour. Early that summer, during rehearsals, James sat for a detailed interview, in which he expressed some unusually thoughtful opinions about the theater. From the tone of the interview, it seems certain that a number of his remarks referred to Jamie's disparaging college essay written only six months earlier.

The interviewer began by asking James why, with his early training and his success in Shakespeare, he had abandoned the classics for melodrama. James explained that in the days when he and other stars like Booth and Forrest were at their height as Shakespearean actors, productions cost very little to mount because the public did not expect lavish scenery and costumes. "They came to see acting," he said, emphasizing that he had not given up hope of appearing in some "big" productions of the classics in the future.

Explaining that tragedy was more difficult to play than melodrama, James declared: "Tragedy deals with the passions in their highest and grandest moods; it carries the actor completely out of himself; transports him as it were to scenes beyond the ken of ordinary minds."

Citing "the exhaustion that follows a performance of 'King Lear,' 'Othello' and 'Macbeth,'" James cautioned that "lest the utmost care is observed tragic acting soon wears out the machine."

Asked what was "the secret of acting," James offered his idiosyncratic view: "What is the secret of poetry? What is the secret of music, painting, or any of the other arts? You might as well ask me what is genius. In my opinion acting is altogether due to soul. The man who feels, who aspires, who wanders in thought from this world and mingles with the higher intelligences has a soul that lends itself to artistic effort; in short, he is a genius. He may be a poet, a painter or an actor, and I am proud to say that in my profession there have been many geniuses . . . "

Evidently conceding Jamie's point about the passing away of "the actor giants," James acknowledged that the geniuses of his profession were "growing smaller in number year by year, for the sensation monger has supplanted the poet, and the sycophantic counter jumper has usurped the place of the real actor."

The interviewer, perhaps hoping to ingratiate himself, interjected: "By the way, it has often been stated that your countrymen are especially endowed for the dramatic calling." James did not speak "for a few moments," very likely thinking of Jamie's bigoted comment in his Fordham Monthly article.

"I am not much of a believer in national characteristics," James finally responded, "though I must admit that the history of the stage contains many illustrious Irish names, both as dramatists and as actors, but I don't wish to be provincial, and a man of genius is equally dear to me, no matter what country he come from, be it Judea or Ireland. We all come from a common source, no matter where we were born, and when God gives man or woman genius He has little regard for the geographical place of their birth."

The liberal sensibility expressed by James was as rare in the society of that day as the prejudice of his older son was commonplace. But then, the theater was always a world unto itself, its disciples traditionally tolerant and forbearing.

When the road tour of *The Musketeers* failed to bring in the anticipated profits, Liebler and Company somewhat desperately decided to assemble yet another revival of *The Count of Monte Cristo*, this one to be newly grand and glossy, and featuring as its scenic centerpiece an enormous staircase. As George Tyler later reminisced, the device was "certainly good judgment because the royal grace with which James O'Neill could walk down a staircase was practically a guarantee for any production."

James appreciated Liebler's considerate treatment and, according to Theodore Liebler Jr., who ultimately became general manager of the company, his father and James O'Neill became close friends.

"As soon as the new firm of Liebler and Company was established, O'Neill became 'one of the family,' so to speak," Liebler said, adding that both his parents visited the O'Neills in New London from time to time. He recalled in particular a visit "when young Eugene was a happy, lively, little youngster, wildly jubilant over a new model railway which his father had just given him." Liebler also recalled that James gave Eugene some chickens, encouraging him to sell their eggs. Eugene did — at inflated prices.

Theodore Liebler Jr. was among those who responded wrathfully to the revelations of *Long Day's Journey Into Night*, when it was published in 1956, and sought to refute what he called the "horrible implication that Mrs. O'Neill was addicted to narcotics." He indignantly noted that if the addiction "had any basis in fact, it was never suspected by those nearest the couple."

That was just the point. Like others who regarded themselves as close friends, the Lieblers were kept absolutely in the dark about the O'Neill family problems. There were many times, of course, when Ella was in a period of remission and when family problems were in abeyance.

If, for example, the Lieblers had walked in on the Tyrones in the opening scene of Long Day's Journey, they would have found themselves in the company of a normal-seeming (if slightly jittery) family. Indeed, O'Neill emphasizes in the dialogue that life had been serene for at least several weeks. What the Lieblers were permitted to see, in common with others, was this side only.

"In 1912," Liebler continued, attempting to reinforce his own conviction, "O'Neill played for us in Joseph and His Brethren and for the following two seasons Mrs. O'Neill accompanied her husband when this production went on the road. I can refer you to several former members of this company who came to know the unfailing kindness of this elderly couple and who are all indignant at what they feel to be a despicable slur on Mrs. O'Neill's memory."

PART THREE

FALTERING FAITH

"So the poor fool prayed and vowed his life to piety and good works! But he began to make a condition now — *if* his mother were spared to him! . . . He abased and humbled himself before the Cross — and, in reward for his sickening humiliation, saw that no miracle would happen."

— *Days Without End*

CHAPTER
ELEVEN

IT WAS DURING THE SUMMER OF 1900 THAT JAMES AND Ella decided they had outgrown the Pink House (at 134 Pequot Avenue). With twenty-one-year-old Jamie and eleven-year-old Eugene, they moved to Number 138, the more substantial house James had owned and rented out since 1886 (and that was to serve as the setting for both *Long Day's Journey Into Night* and *Ah, Wilderness!*).

In none of the innumerable studies of Eugene O'Neill has any notice been taken of the fact that his first eleven summers were spent in the Pink House. Contemporaries of the O'Neills evidently viewed the two houses, separated by only a narrow lot, as interchangeable. Each, in turn, was known as the Monte Cristo Cottage.

The O'Neills' new home at Number 138 had been extensively, if somewhat eccentrically, refurbished by 1900. Street addresses were systematically revised by the city of New London in 1905, when Number 134, the Pink House, became 313 Pequot Avenue, and Number 138, the ultimate Monte Cristo Cottage and the setting for *Long Day's Journey*, became 325 Pequot Avenue.

James had begun to improve Number 138 soon after buying it. One of his first changes was to convert the former store on the property into a living room and join it to the main dwelling. Frugal as always, James had the adjunct propped up with a large tree trunk, in lieu of a properly installed foundation.

Other improvements soon followed, often contrived in the thriftiest possible way. He remodeled the three small upstairs bedrooms so they gave onto a narrow hallway. He ordered the installation of a bathroom, as in the Pink House, to replace the outhouse. And he rebuilt the staircase between the first and second floors, but saved money by shortening the rails between baluster and steps.

When completed, the ground floor held a small entry hall domi-

nated by the new staircase; a front parlor, reserved for company; the
dining room; a windowless back parlor and a lean-to kitchen. Family
life revolved around the living room, depicted virtually down to its
last detail not only in the set description of *Long Day's Journey Into
Night* but in *Ah, Wilderness!*, as well as in two negligible earlier efforts,
Bread and Butter and *The First Man*.

James had also spruced up the grounds and by this time the
smoothly kept front lawn sloped down to a neatly trimmed privet
hedge that afforded privacy from the road. Near the house were
planted hydrangeas, hostas, bleeding hearts and phlox. In the rear
was a spacious lawn, bounded by a typical Connecticut wall of low-
piled stones. The rear garden, unfortunately, was darkened by several huge, weeping elms that appeared to hug the house (and that died
of old age in the 1980's). These ancient anthropomorphic trees were
transposed by O'Neill to his setting for *Desire Under the Elms* (1924):

"They brood oppressively over the house," O'Neill wrote in his
stage directions. "They are like exhausted women resting their sagging breasts and hands and hair on its roof, and when it rains their
tears trickle down monotonously and rot on the shingles."

O'Neill also transposed to that play, in a speech by the hard-bit-
ten old farmer, Ephraim Cabot, the stone fence that marked the property's rear boundary. "God's hard, not easy!," Cabot expostulates.
"God's in the stones! . . . Stones. I picked 'em up an' piled 'em into
walls. Ye kin read the years o' my life in them walls. Every day a heft-
ed stone . . . fencin' in the field that was mine."

Some further improvements James made to the cottage over the
years were touchingly fanciful, suggesting he had anticipated a time
when he would himself occupy it. He ordered the addition of a covered porch, reached by twelve broad steps, to wrap halfway around
the house, and installed two French doors to open onto the porch
from the front parlor. For each of the doors he designed a transom
window with rose-colored glass that bathed the parlor in a cheerful
glow when the sun rose over the river.

In the entrance hall, the front parlor and the dining room, he had
the ceilings lifted to eleven feet seven inches, a trick of stagecraft
designed to give the entire house a sense of airiness the Pink House
lacked.

He had the exterior of the house painted a pale gray and hung a
turret with a "witch's hat" roof to the side of the second story bedrooms. Turrets, normally installed atop a house as a purely decorative
element, were popular symbols of a homeowner's wealth. James,

however — captive as he was to his own sense of thrift — managed to have his cake and eat it by turning his ornamental turret into a useful fourth bedroom.

When James and Ella moved in with their two sons, they occupied the bedroom overlooking the back garden, while Jamie and Eugene slept in the two front bedrooms looking out on Pequot Avenue and the river. The upstairs also held two tiny rooms built over the lean-to kitchen, one used as a maid's room, the other as a storage attic. A narrow back staircase ran between the first and second floors.

Still spending extravagantly with one hand and pinching pennies with the other, James installed costly parquet floors, but saved expense by piecing together a half-dozen different kinds of cheap wood for the paneling in the living room and then, to give it a unified texture, covering the patched-together wood in orange shellac. "It was wrong from the start," Mary Tyrone complains in *Long Day's Journey Into Night*. "Everything was done in the cheapest way."

On chilly days the house could be heated by three fireplaces on the ground floor — those in the back parlor and dining room of serviceable red-brick. But James framed the fireplace in the front parlor with pink-tinted tiles. In this room, the showiest in the house, painted a dark, ivy green, Ella installed her father's piano.

One aspect of life unchanged from the Pink House was the waterfront fog and the mournful lowing emitted by the lighthouse at the end of Pequot Avenue, both as familiar to New Londoners as the ceaseless shrieking of sea gulls. The lighthouse horn is heard at rhythmic intervals throughout the action of *Long Day's Journey Into Night*, and both Mary and Edmund welcome the fog's power of concealment. According to an early note for the play, Mary "exults" in the fog — "it is in her."

After having undergone all of James's solid improvements and whimsical frills, the cottage, while comfortable enough, made no claim to elegance. In James's view it was not a home to be ashamed of, decidedly better-situated than the homes of Ella's relatives. At the same time, he knew that compared with the houses of some of his Protestant neighbors, Monte Cristo Cottage was modest, even humble.

Ella complained that James would not spend the money to furnish their new home invitingly, but had it been really important to her she surely could have persuaded him to do so. It seems evident that Ella had no inclination to keep house or to entertain in a town that was hateful to her. She herself had never learned to cook, nor did she seem able to adequately supervise the summer help she sometimes employed; for the most part, the O'Neills preferred to board with families in the neighborhood.

To promote the new Liebler and Company revival of *The Count of Monte Cristo*, James agreed to an interview for a Boston newspaper in early September, not long before shutting down Monte Cristo Cottage. He also consented to pose for two photographs with both his sons, yielding the only known portraits of the three together.

In one of the photos, a not-quite-twelve-year-old Eugene is seated in a rocking chair on the porch of the family home, seemingly oblivious to the camera. His chin on his chest, he is, as usual, immersed in a book. Jamie, twenty-two, wears a jaunty straw boater and stares cockily into the camera lens. And James, approaching fifty-four and still handsome, if tending toward corpulence, regards the photographer with a benevolent half-smile, his chair tilted back, wholly at ease, his own straw boater on the floor by his chair.

Only Ella is missing. Conceivably she was away, undergoing yet another of her periodic "cures." In any case, she seems to have been almost pathologically camera-shy. There are no known photographs of her with James or either of the children, and only four head shots of her alone (two of them slight variations of the same pose), none of which do justice to the beauty invariably ascribed to her by her friends.

O'Neill periodically sought photographs of his mother after her death. In 1931, he received a letter from a family friend, offering to send him early photographs of his father, brother and himself. Responding with gratitude, O'Neill asked: "Have you one of my mother, by any lucky chance? She had so few taken in her life and I have only one."

With rare exceptions, the O'Neills always closed 138 Pequot Avenue, as they had the Pink House, when the weather turned cool and returned to New York. Before resuming his touring, James would install his family in one or another small residential hotel on Manhattan's West Side, pending the time when Ella felt ready to join him on the road. This year was different.

James would be spending more time in New York than usual, for he anticipated that the new production of *Monte Cristo* would enjoy a long Broadway run beginning in October. With Tyler's approval,

James, always hopeful, had promoted Jamie from understudy in *The Musketeers* to a small speaking role in *Monte Cristo* at a salary of $20 a week (generous for a minor role by the day's standards).

All the circumstances seemed to provide an ideal opportunity for the four O'Neills to ensconce themselves in the city as a family, actually keeping house together for the first time in years, and James and Ella had decided to enroll Eugene in the De La Salle Institute in Manhattan as a day student, living at home throughout the school year.

While *Long Day's Journey Into Night* amplifies the misery that enveloped the Tyrone family like an impregnable fog, the reality was that the year 1900 promised to be one of those intervals when Ella was temporarily free of morphine and the O'Neill family was able to enjoy a period of relative peace and harmony. James found a commodious, floor-through, furnished service flat in a well-maintained, six-story apartment house at 9 West Sixty-eighth Street, called the Vera, a few doors from Central Park West and only a half-mile walk to Eugene's new school at Fifty-ninth Street and Sixth Avenue.

Liebler and Company's new revival of *The Count of Monte Cristo* opened for a tryout at the Boston Theater the week of September 24, 1900, prior to Broadway. Despite his father's coaching and his efforts to bolster Jamie's confidence in himself as an actor, Jamie made an awkward debut that was not kindly noted by the critics. In an interview some years later, Jamie recalled he had been so nervous he had inadvertently slammed into a curtain, which collapsed and ruined the scene.

On October 24, the new production of *The Count of Monte Cristo* settled into New York's Academy of Music. No production of the vehicle had ever been so elaborately mounted. In addition to the grandiose staircase, it depicted a ship in full sail gliding into the port of Marseilles. The reviews were generally favorable, even for Jamie.

Eugene, so long deprived of family living, relished his new routine. It was a delight to return home from school every day to be greeted by his mother and exchange occasional banter with his father and brother. It was a treat to go with his mother for walks in Central Park and on visits to museums. He also accompanied her to the theater, dropping in now and then to visit his father and brother backstage.

Jamie regaled him with wild and funny stories but, whenever the two brothers huddled together in laughter, James was convinced he was the target of their humor. The truth was that James was essentially incapable of dealing with Jamie's insolent assaults, just as he was helpless in coping with Ella's cyclical withdrawals.

In choosing the highly rated De La Salle Institute for Eugene, James once again contravened his reputation for parsimony, demonstrating, as he had with Jamie, that he was prepared to invest whatever it took to provide his children with a first-rate education.

The Christian Brothers, in need of larger quarters, had taken over the building that had once housed the Charlier Institute, one of New York's most exclusive schools for the sons of the rich.

The Brothers were a humble order dedicated to education, and their surroundings must have seemed somewhat anomalous, for the building was ornately, not to say ostentatiously, furnished with mahogany and rosewood. Its block-long entry hall flaunted a marble floor and its reception rooms held fireplaces with carved mantels. The building also housed a pipe organ and a shooting range, and light poured in through the enormous French windows facing Central Park.

Despite all this grandeur, the Christian Brothers did not coddle their students. Eugene entered on October 16, his twelfth birthday, and soon found his new school not only insisted on academic achievement but physical prowess. This had not been the case with the Sisters of Charity at Mount St. Vincent, where Eugene, who never believed himself quite good enough for competitive sports, devoted himself to reading.

The school, with an enrollment of one hundred and eleven, was attended, as was Mount St. Vincent, by scions of wealthy Catholic families from both the United States and abroad. The preponderance of the sons of prominent actors inspired one of Eugene's teachers, Brother Basil, to arrange contests in reading and declamation, attended by the proud professional parents, among whom James was soon to find himself.

The O'Neills' well-intentioned attempt at family unity was short-lived. One day, toward the end of his first year at school, Eugene returned unexpectedly to his apartment and, like Jamie years earlier, came upon his mother with a hypodermic needle in her hand. Neither his father nor brother was home. Eugene, in his innocence, ventured to question his mother and was baffled when she accused him of spying. Uncomprehending, he numbly bore her tirade.

He later made several attempts to learn from his father and brother what ailed his mother. They were evasive, believing him too young to be told the full truth. They said only that his mother was subject to periods of ill health. To Eugene, this vagueness seemed shifty and, coupled with Ella's often-erratic behavior, it merely increased his concern for her. He was not to learn the truth until more than two years later, when he was nearly fifteen.

Both James and Ella decided it was best Eugene should not live at home, where he would be constantly watching his mother with wounded and suspicious eyes. When he returned to De La Salle on October 4, 1901, for his second year, it was as a boarding student. In *Long Day's Journey Into Night*, the mother defends herself against her younger son's accusation that she seemed never to care about his absences from home: "You might have guessed, dear, that after I knew you knew — about me — I had to be glad whenever you were where you couldn't see me." Away from his mother, as he later told his wife, Carlotta, his fear for her health became an obsession. He correctly suspected some terrible truth was being concealed from him. He began frantically to pray for his mother's cure, challenging God to prove Himself by restoring his mother to health. This was undoubtedly the first serious crack in his faith.

He thinly disguised this personal crisis in *Days Without End* (subtitled "A Modern Miracle Play"). Apart from his later revelations to Carlotta, the play provides the only detailed (if coded) glimpses into the young O'Neill's soul-searing confrontation with his mother's addiction, later described in *Long Day's Journey Into Night* with the resignation of the mature dramatist.

The protagonist, John Loving, is represented by two characters — John and Loving — to convey the man's morbidly warring, dual nature. Speaking of himself in the third person, John describes his youthful disappointment with the climate of Catholicism and the God "of Infinite Love": " . . . Later, at school, he learned of the God of Punishment, and he wondered . . . Afterward . . . he saw his God as deaf and blind and merciless — a Deity Who returned hate for love and revenged Himself upon those who trusted Him!"

John/Loving's mother is depicted as a widow "worn out by nursing his father and by her grief" during her husband's fatal siege of flu. The well-intentioned John, recounting his boyhood experience in the third person, says, "Then his mother . . . was taken ill. And the horrible fear came to him that she might die, too."

Loving, more gruffly, picks up the narrative: "It drove the young idiot into a panic of superstitious remorse. He imagined her sickness was a terrible warning to him, a punishment for the doubt inspired in him by his father's death. His God of Love was beginning to show Himself as a God of Vengeance . . . "

The milder John continues: "But he still trusted in His Love. Surely He would not take his mother from him, too."

Loving jeeringly interjects: "So the poor fool prayed and vowed his life to piety and good works! But he began to make a condition now — *if* his mother were spared to him! . . . He abased and humbled himself before the Cross — and, in reward for his sickening humiliation, saw that no miracle would happen." "Something snapped in him then," says John. And "in a tone of bitter hatred," Loving continues, "He saw his God as deaf and blind and merciless — a Deity Who returned hate for love and revenged Himself upon those who trusted Him!"

"His mother died," says John. "And, in a frenzy of insane grief — . . . "

"No!," Loving interrupts, with "malignant bitterness," declaring that "In his awakened pride he cursed his God and denied Him, and, in revenge, promised his soul to the Devil — on his knees, when everyone thought he was praying!"

This overwrought fictional session of prayer and revolt mirrored Eugene's own religious crisis during his second (and final) year at De La Salle, according to Carlotta, with whom O'Neill discussed *Days Without End* scene by scene, line by line, and to whom he dedicated the play.

Young Eugene, like John Loving, "vowed his life to piety and good works," applying himself with unprecedented zeal to his studies. He did particularly well in religious studies, steadfastly attending Mass at school, as well as on Sundays at St. Patrick's Cathedral.

Under a strict grading system, he stood seventh in a class of twenty-two. In religion he tied with two others for fifth place, achieving an average of 84. In English, he was third highest, with an average of 87. (The two students who surpassed him averaged 88.) His highest grade was 88, in history; his lowest was 57, in geometry and algebra, subjects he consistently resisted.

Eugene's life was not by any means pure martyrdom; few children of that age, however buffeted by family difficulties, fail to enjoy lighter moments. He took part, for example, in what was his first documented stage appearance, a school variety program. He and another student, Henry Francis Elias, performed a number called "O Tell Us Merry Birds."

At the beginning of the new term, Eugene embarked upon his lifelong habit of letter-writing. He once recalled a precocious correspondence with the daughter of friends of his parents, who had visited him when, at the age of five, he was sick in bed in San Francisco. The young woman, Anita, made "an extraordinary impression" and he "promptly fell in love." He also remembered, he said, "how kind she was later when I had gone to school and she used to let me write her letters and answer them so promptly."

While these early missives have vanished, his whimsical side is illustrated by his first extant letter, sent from De La Salle to his New London cousin, Lillian Brennan. It exemplifies the chatty, colloquial and usually ingratiating epistolary style still evident fifty years later.

"I was very glad to hear from you that Teddy is doing nicely," he wrote, referring to a pet dog that presumably had replaced the defunct Perfumery. "I wonder would he remember me but I suppose he has forgotten all about me . . . I think . . . I will take Teddy back to school with me as the Director of this place says I may. He would have a nice large yard to play in and another dog for company."

In the same letter, Eugene wrote proudly of Jamie's recent debut in the important supporting role of Edmond Dantes' son, Albert de Morcerf. "Jamie has made a big hit . . . and there are big notices about him in all the papers wherever they go." He ended with the complaint that he had had a bad cold and, worse, had "to take bitter tasting coff medicine."

Eugene's fraternal pride was justified. James's company was enjoying a highly profitable repertory season, alternating *Monte Cristo* and *The Musketeers*, and Jamie's salary was raised to $50 a week. When he appeared at McVicker's in Chicago, the scene of his father's earlier triumphs, he drew enthusiastic applause.

"Last evening's entertainment," wrote one critic, "was made particularly charming by the debut of James O'Neill Jr., who by his unusual resemblance to his father promises another generation of Monte Cristo . . . He acts extremely well too."

In what may have been Jamie's first formal interview, he dissembled glibly about his recent background and his embrace of a theatrical career, claiming to have graduated from Fordham College and implying it had been his considered choice to pursue an acting career, rather than attend law school.

"I found a number of lawyers among my college chums," Jamie told the interviewer, "and all of them were starving. They had offices and knowledge, but no clients." After trying the lumber business, the interviewer reported, Jamie, "at a propitious moment," told his father "there was only one profession that he believed he could follow with success, and that was the stage."

James, despite the triumph of his tour (and Jamie's momentary docility), was turning bitter about the state of the theater, for which he blamed both audiences and critics. While his company was in Detroit he gave an interview far more acerbic than was his custom, declaring that the stage had "never been in such a diabolical condition."

"Anybody can go to New York and become a star, regardless of merit," James sighed. "New York managers keep a would-be star in New York for a run, losing money every day, and then they send the star out to get money from the 'gawks,' as they call the Western people.

"People of the present day know nothing about acting. I have special reference to the younger generation of critics. Ye gods! The highest priced theater in New York to-day is Webber & Fields's. Can you ask for any better corroboration of my statements?

"Of course, if Sir Henry Irving opens up in New York, society will go, not because it will revel in the drama with such a superb exponent as Sir Henry, but because it is the society fad, and society goes there to see society, not to see Sir Henry."

Eugene had by now begun to dramatize himself. He embraced the misery of his mother's illness and of his father's inexplicable recalcitrance. He decided he had finally hit upon the root cause of all his adolescent anxieties and, most particularly, the justification for his faltering faith.

Toward the end of his final year at De La Salle, Eugene confronted his parents with a bold ultimatum: He demanded to be allowed to enter a nonsectarian preparatory school, declaring he would no longer submit to the yoke of Catholic indoctrination.

Years later, he tried to explain his rebellion, comparing his father's attempts to impose his standards on him to what he called "the oppression of the Jesuits." He said his father's despotism reminded him of "the saying, 'Give me a child until he is seven and then you can have him.' They meant, of course, that he would be true to the faith."

James saw his son's defiance as rank ingratitude. He could not help reminding Eugene of the privileged life bestowed upon him and of how he had had to give up his schooling at ten to toil in a machine shop.

Eugene, with a determination startling in that Victorian era for a boy not yet fourteen, held his ground against all of James's and Ella's arguments. The rebellion had only just begun.

CHAPTER
TWELVE

FLOUTING RELIGIOUS RITUAL, EUGENE FOR THE FIRST TIME
entered a nonsectarian school in the fall of 1902, shortly before his
fourteenth birthday. Influenced by his ravenous reading, his mutiny
only hardened during his four years at Betts Academy in Stamford,
Connecticut.

He began to challenge every tenet of his rejected faith, setting out
in quest of an alternative. As Elizabeth Sergeant later wrote (with his
approval) he was gradually to evolve into "an agnostic in search of
redemption." But no matter how far behind he left his Catholic ortho-
doxy, and however anticlerical his stance, he never lost his awe of
religious mystery, as demonstrated by the spirituality of his plays.

Betts Academy was among the preeminent preparatory schools in
the East, noted for its practical and liberal grounding in the classics
and sciences. Because its enrollment was limited to sixty, it could
offer a ratio of one teacher to every six pupils. Betts aimed to sur-
round its pupils with a relaxed "home atmosphere," to concentrate
on their individual needs and abilities and to encourage "each to proceed at his own rate, and to cultivate in them sound habits of observation and research."

The school emphasized the importance of sharpening its pupils'
powers of observation. "The first task of the student," according to its
brochure, "is the inspection of things that are constantly before him,
such as plants, animals, the stars, etc. He is thus taught first to *see* and
then to *tell* what he *sees* going on around him in nature and in practical life, and is required to record his observations in well-systematized notebooks."

It was an admirable approach, one particularly well calculated to
provide basic training for an incipient dramatist. Eugene's acute eye
and ear for the "things" that were "constantly before him" became a

principal facet of his talent. From the time he began to write, he kept the sort of voluminous "well-systematized notebooks" that served as the outlines for his plays, and that he first learned to use at Betts.

James and Ella were at considerable pains always to provide their sons with surroundings that were physically harmonious as well as academically challenging. About an hour's train ride from Manhattan, Betts was built in 1838 on an elevation called Strawberry Hill, in Stamford's finest residential enclave.

The grounds included a four-acre lawn with football and baseball fields and a tennis court; in winter a depressed section of lawn was flooded for ice skating. Two rambling, yellow wooden buildings afforded comfortable living quarters for students and staff (until they burned to the ground in 1908, ending the school's seventy-year existence).

Eugene had his own sunny room in the three-story main building, furnished with a high dresser, an iron-frame bed, desk, chair and throw rug — all stiffly Victorian, yet not un-homey. Here in Stamford, water formed part of Eugene's background, as it had at Mount St. Vincent. From his window, on clear days, he could see his familiar Long Island Sound; it was seventy-five miles up the coast to his New London home. The annual cost for this atmospheric and academic inspiration was five hundred dollars.

Presiding over the school was William Betts, known behind his back as "Billy." A squat, middle-aged man with a handlebar mustache, Betts took an indulgent stand on boyish pranks, but was strict in his academic demands. As one of Eugene's schoolmates has recalled, "Billy knew Latin and Greek backwards and was a stern taskmaster; anyone who stayed the course at Betts had to come out with a thorough classical education and was, invariably, accepted by a top college." Betts was an acknowledged preparatory school for Yale, of which William Betts was himself a proud alumnus.

Eugene was a fair student in French, a good student in natural history, and an excellent one in English and Latin. He also did well in Greek and Roman history, which Betts accentuated as a background for classical languages and which helped spark Eugene's subsequent fascination with Greek drama.

Writing, many years later, to his older son, a Greek scholar on the Yale faculty, O'Neill said, somewhat defensively, "I really liked Latin in Prep school, especially Cicero, and was good at it — used to be able to reel off parts of his *Cataline* by heart. This liking Latin was regarded as a startling mental defect by one and all of my fellow students."

Math, however, was another matter. One of Eugene's teachers, Arthur G. Walter (called "Algie" by the boys), waged a four-year battle with Eugene on the fields of algebra and geometry. It was never entirely clear, in the end, who had won. Eugene would sulkily ask, "What's the good of studying that stuff?" and Walter would patiently attempt to explain. When Walter told James O'Neill, during one of his visits, that Eugene had failed in algebra, James agreed to support whatever disciplinary measures the school saw fit to impose.

At fourteen, Eugene had grown into a strikingly attractive youth, tall, lean, with darkening brown hair and uncannily luminous eyes. He had inherited the best features of both his parents: his mother's sensitive mouth, his father's profile with its strong jaw and prominent nose. His graceful hands, with their long, delicate fingers, were characteristic of both parents.

His teachers at Betts, like those at Mount St. Vincent, remembered Eugene as a dreamer, who liked to go off on solitary walks. A number of classmates recalled he was popular, if not gregarious.

He took the normal teenager's pleasure in opposing authority and one evening he placed an egg in the headmaster's bed. Another time, he and several friends gathered all the chamber pots in the dormitory to build a tower atop the stairs outside their rooms. They tied a rope to the bottom pot and, as soon as all the teachers were asleep, they pulled the rope and produced a horrifying clatter.

Billy Betts was unable to isolate the ringleader, as all the boys had taken an oath of silence, but he was inclined to favor Eugene as a chief culprit. In his frustration he predicted Eugene was destined for the electric chair. Eugene told classmates he was flattered.

Eugene was also among those who crept from the dormitory and raced for town the night the Town Hall burned down. At other times he participated in the game of knotting sheets together and escaping from a dormitory window after lights-out at nine. When they reached town, about a mile's walk along a dirt road, the boys headed for a saloon owned by the former prizefighting champion, Bob Fitzsimmons, who kept a lion cub as a pet. Fitzsimmons looked the other way while his bartender slipped a beer, or even something stronger, to his underage patrons. When in an expansive mood, he regaled the boys, to their immeasurable delight, with tales of his victories in the ring. Occasionally the boys would find their headmaster grimly confronting them upon their return from town, and they were penalized with canceled weekend leaves.

Every so often, Fitzsimmons, sporting a tall silk hat and holding his lion on a leash, turned up on the Betts baseball field to root for the home team. Athletics, especially football and baseball, were emphasized. (The son of Richard Croker, the Tammany Hall boss, was on the football team.) Eugene, as far as his teachers and classmates could recall, declined to participate in sports, as he had at De La Salle. Only now and then did he languidly swing a golf club or a tennis racquet.

Eugene, however, implied he had played football during at least part of his time at Betts, and that he was a runner, as well. "I am not playing football this year but run two or three miles every day in preparation for track," he wrote to a teenage girl, of whom he was briefly enamored in 1905.

But there is no doubt that he had a boundless, lifelong admiration for athletes. Friends with whom he attended sporting events in later years attributed his exuberance to the fact that he was himself not robust and was awed by physical endurance in others. He often sought the acquaintance of athletes, among them Jack Dempsey, Gene Tunney, Ted Williams and a legion of six-day bicyclists and circus acrobats.

According to Algie Walter, Eugene smoked in his room in defiance of a school rule. "His room was across the hall from mine," recalled Walter, who was in charge of Eugene's dormitory. "I often invited Gene to drop into my room for a chat, but he never accepted."

Another way to come by a smoke was to visit the town lunch wagon, stationed during the day in an alleyway near the firehouse. It was the only place within walking distance of Betts where the boys could eat out. In the evening a horse towed the lunch wagon to the center of town, where it was transformed into a dinner wagon.

The bill of fare was inferior to that of the Betts dining room, where second helpings of nutritious food were always provided. Nevertheless, the boys enjoyed the wagon's specialty, listed ambiguously on the menu as "tenderloin"; it cost fifteen cents and was actually a chunk of pork pounded into a flat slab and fried brown.

Although James O'Neill was a frequent visitor at Betts, Ella rarely accompanied him during Eugene's first two years. Her addiction had worsened, with predictably invidious effects on her family. During school vacation in the summer of 1903, Ella, according to her Sheridan relatives in New London, fell into a protracted depression. Monte Cristo Cottage had become less a haven of togetherness than a pressure cooker in which the four O'Neills fed upon each other's neuroses.

It was during this summer that Eugene finally discovered the precise nature of his mother's long-term "illness." "You never knew what was really wrong until you were in prep school," Jamie says to his younger brother in Act Two of *Long Day's Journey Into Night.* "Papa and I kept it from you. But I was wise ten years or more before we had to tell you."

The revelation was precipitated when Ella, having run out of morphine one summer night, rushed from the house in her nightdress and tried to throw herself off the family's dock. In the play, O'Neill's alter ego, Edmund, in an accusatory speech to his mother, recalls that "It was right after that Papa and Jamie decided they couldn't hide it from me any more."

In later years, O'Neill confided not only in his wife and Elizabeth Sergeant, but also in a sympathetic doctor, Robert Lee Patterson — who treated him when he was gravely ill — that the discovery of his mother's addiction had marked the spiritual turning point in his life. But it was Sergeant who, in her probing and sympathetic interviews, extracted from O'Neill the essence of his outlook.

Having agreed not to write about the closely-held secret of his mother's addiction, Sergeant phrased her evaluation of O'Neill's family tragedy somewhat cryptically: "O'Neill started with a twist — the twist of revenge. Life had made him glowing promises. Life failed to keep them. He would pay it back in its own coin for its betrayals."

For the first time, Eugene began to comprehend fully how his mother's illness had affected every member of the family. In his own words under the heading, "Adolescence," he noted in his free-associative diagram: "Discovery of Mother's Inadequacy." When he finally absorbed the implications of her failing, he felt no pangs at giving up even the small semblance of religious conformity he had accorded his parents. Eugene decided the time had come to stop attending church.

One Sunday morning James, watching his son descend the stairs of their New London cottage, told him to get ready. Eugene informed his father of his decision. James took a few steps up the staircase to confront Eugene and the two began shouting. James grabbed his son, attempting to shake sense into him. Eugene twisted and pulled under his grip. Grappling and arguing, they reached the ground floor and glared at each other. James was rigid with frustration, but Eugene would not budge. James went off to church alone.

Jeering at his parents' pleas, Eugene pointed out that religion had proved of little use to them; why insist on it for him? And in truth, his parents' arguments were weakened by Ella's own struggle to hold on to her faith. She had, by now, stopped attending church herself. ("She hasn't denied her faith, but she's forgotten it, until now there's no strength of the spirit left in her to fight her curse," James Tyrone says in his wife's defense in *Long Day's Journey Into Night*.)

Then again, Ella and James were unlike most of their Catholic contemporaries, and certainly unlike Ella's New London relatives, in that they rarely made any overt display of their faith. In his meticulously described set for *Long Day's Journey Into Night*, detailed down to the titles of books in two glass-fronted bookcases and a picture of Shakespeare on the wall, there is no mention of a religious artifact of any kind.

It was not until thirty years later that Eugene O'Neill, in *Days Without End*, expounded upon the loss of his faith and conceded his yearning to confess and receive forgiveness. (The very title of the play, in fact, echoes one of the first prayers he learned: "Glory be to the Father, and to the Son, and to the Holy Ghost. As it was in the beginning, is now, and ever shall be, *world without end*.")

Since her attempted suicide and her own struggle to hold on to her faith, Ella had continued to seek help in various sanatoriums. In September, 1904, she was in New York, evidently well enough to help Eugene prepare for his return to Betts for his third year.

On September 17, Eugene wrote to a former teacher at De La Salle from the Belleclaire, on Broadway and Seventy-seventh Street, the current West Side family hotel housing the O'Neills: "Mama is here in the hotel with me . . . [She] is very well and wishes to be remembered to all her old friends especially Sister Aloysius." His father and brother had opened their season in Boston, he continued, bemoaning his own fate at having soon to "go back to work" at Betts.

By the time he returned to Betts, Eugene had grown so scornful of his Catholicism he would request permission at school to attend Mass simply as an excuse to get off the grounds for a smoke. "Permission was always granted whenever he asked," Algie Walter recalled. "We had a few Roman Catholics in school besides Gene, but he never went to Mass with any of them."

Eugene's adolescent rebellion, much as James deplored it, was but a passing bother compared with the ongoing problems presented by his wife and Jamie. Nonetheless, with his soldierly hardiness, he had taken to the road yet again, this time with an all-star revival of *The Two Orphans,* in which he had made his New York debut in 1876. The play had been laboriously updated, and James had enjoined his cast to be "quiet and natural" and to eschew all "ranting." In an interview before the opening, he attempted to defend his choice of the creaky vehicle:

"You ask me why such plays as *The Two Orphans, Uncle Tom's Cabin,* etc., continue like Tennyson's brook, to 'go on forever'? For the simple reason that they have in them human nature. They have a heart interest. They are natural. They appeal not to the classes but to the masses."

The nineteen-week tour of one-night stands in the south and southwest, followed by more than a month of longer runs in big cities, was Jamie's real introduction to the rigors of the road. He did not stand it well. An actress in the cast, Bijou Fernandez, recalled the tour with horror, nor was she unduly surprised when Jamie buckled under the strain.

"We almost died doing it," she said. "I don't know where they found all those cities." Herself a novice at touring, she was helped to survive the frenzied itinerary by James's avuncular advice: Ignore the official timetable for each morning's train departure and, instead, after the evening's performance, ask the hotel clerk to call your room in the morning with the train's actual time of departure. She was thus often saved hours of waiting on station platforms.

No amount of well-meant advice had any effect on Jamie. His acting career had turned erratic. His humor had grown malevolent and he was becoming a mortification to his father. Drunk after every performance, he was often so late the next morning that the train had to be held for him.

In a New Orleans hotel, he nearly succeeded in cremating himself when his cigarette set fire to his mattress. An actor in the company, Tom Meighan, tried briefly to reform him. He would take him out for a snack after the show, then deposit him at his hotel with instructions to go to bed. Meighan gave up when he discovered Jamie would sneak away to a bar as soon as his back was turned.

The Two Orphans tour consolidated Jamie's flagrant defiance of his father. As always, however, after taunting James, he wheedled his way back into James's good graces by some brazen prank. The contentious father-son relationship was exemplified in a story widely circulated in the theater community:

One August day in 1902, father and son arrived at the offices of

Liebler and Company to discuss the details of the coming season with William F. Connor.

Bantering with Jamie, Connor declared that he soon would be as big as his father. Jamie slyly turned the comment into an opportunity for a free drink. Pretending to believe Connor was talking about chest and not box-office measurements, he bet his father drinks for the office staff that his own chest measurement was already the greater.

Priding himself upon his robust physique, James took the bait, as he invariably did. Now almost fifty-seven, he could still boast he had been sick scarcely a day in his life. A tape measure duly demonstrated James's chest measured forty-four and a quarter inches, while Jamie's measured only forty.

Smiling triumphantly, James told his son to lead the way across the street to a saloon called the Normandie and Jamie, affecting chagrin, complied. He ordered drinks for his putative guests and thirstily downed his own. When the bill for $6.90 was handed to him, he pointed to his father and, in a carrying voice, told the bartender:

"Present this bill with my compliments to the elderly, gray-haired gentleman . . . He has a wallet filled with banknotes sewed to the inside of his shirt that increases his chest measurement exactly five inches." After James paid the bill, Jamie said, "Pater, I hate to give you away, but six-ninety . . . is too much for a poor young actor!"

In his heart James must have realized Jamie would always rely on him for support and, while he often deplored Jamie's dependence, a part of him derived bittersweet pleasure from his son's abject reliance.

Jamie took pleasure in running down the production of *The Two Orphans*, calling it slovenly. He made self-disparaging jokes about his own drinking, justifying his behavior by reiterating that it had not been his choice to become an actor. No doubt accurately, Jamie Tyrone reflects Jamie O'Neill's sentiments when he tells his father, "I never wanted to be an actor, you forced me on the stage."

James reacted with what dignity he could muster. Always the perfectionist in his demands on other members of his company as well as on himself, he found his son's flouting of professional standards especially galling. He knew of course that no other manager would have sanctioned Jamie's wanton behavior, and that he alone could keep his son afloat.

Concerned about dwindling box-office receipts, James wearily switched in mid-tour to *The Count of Monte Cristo*. While he must have realized Jamie would surely let him down, he nonetheless reinstated him in the role of Albert. Despising the part, Jamie turned it into caricature.

He wore buckskin tights that he knew would draw the eyes of women in the audience. James did not mind that, but he did mind the prostitutes whom Jamie invited to sit in the boxes and cheer him on. He was also distressed by his son's lascivious poses at the stage apron, flagrant enough to elicit the critics' ridicule.

James was even more offended by a bit of sly stage business Jamie introduced during a scene in which he kneeled to receive a blessing. Jamie concealed a strip of muslin in his hand and, as he knelt, ripped it in two, creating the effect of his tights splitting. His father's face flushed red through his makeup. "Someday it's really going to happen to you," James fumed offstage.

Jamie also doubled in the small part of an old man, making his entrance in a frowsy gray wig he never combed, plus the black eyebrows of the youthful Albert. "Horrible, horrible," James would mutter. He knew, and was aware that his company knew, that any other actor would have been dismissed for such effrontery.

On New Year's Eve, when the company arrived in San Francisco, Jamie and a friend closeted themselves in a furnished room and drank through the night. In their stupor they smashed the china basin, windows and furniture. Shortly before the New Year's Day matinee, Jamie's landlady presented herself at the theater, demanding payment. John Hewitt, who doubled as stage manager and actor, remembered taking the landlady's message to James.

"Governor," said Hewitt, employing the honorific by which everyone in the company addressed James, "I have some very unpleasant news for you on New Year's Day."

"Well, out with it, lad."

"Your son . . . "

"Ah, my son of the Golden West?" asked James with heavy sarcasm, in a reference to Jamie's San Francisco birthplace. Hewitt presented the landlady's bill for $80. James wrote a check. "Case dismissed," he said, smiling ruefully.

Jamie, pale and numb, arrived soon after, barely in time for the curtain. "My son of the Golden West!" was James's greeting, punctuated by what sounded like a raspberry. And yet, at the end of Jamie's shaky and mechanical performance, James asked him, with genuine solicitude, "How are you feeling, laddie?"

Jamie was even more dependent on whiskey than his mother on

morphine. By contrast with Ella, who had frequent periods of remission, he was rarely sober and never traveled without a bottle in his suitcase. On long train trips he always packed two or three.

Once, when the company was about to cross the Rockies from Denver to Salt Lake City, the conductor was asked to delay departure to wait for Jamie. A few minutes later he arrived on the run. As Hewitt gave him a hand up the platform, his suitcase sprang open and two bottles smashed to the ground. Jamie, according to Hewitt, was almost in tears.

In the small towns on their tour, the actors often fell asleep to the sound of Jamie's boisterous singing in the hotel bar or adjacent tavern. Jamie had one peculiar saving grace even at his most inebriated: he could rarely be goaded into a barroom brawl. As soon as he realized a situation was slipping from his control, he invariably held up his hand, palm outward, like a policeman halting traffic. "What ho!" he would say, in a frozen voice, turning his back and lurching away with a pathetic attempt at dignity.

If there was a town prostitute, Jamie could always find her. In the larger towns he was often greeted at the stage door by the leading madam, who would triumphantly bear him away in her carriage. At the end of a run in St. Louis he sent word to Hewitt he was not leaving with the company. He had chanced upon a pretty, twenty-year-old brunette in the town's best bordello, where Hewitt found him. He said he had fallen in love, but Hewitt managed to tear him away.

Ella, still making the longer stops on James's itinerary, appeared backstage from time to time and, according to actors in the company, gravely disapproved of her son's behavior. She was also distressed at James's tolerance of Jamie's drunken antics.

"You brought him up to be a boozer," Mary Tyrone accuses her husband in *Long Day's Journey Into Night*. "Always a bottle on the bureau in the cheap hotel rooms! And if he had a nightmare when he was little, or a stomach-ache, your remedy was to give him a teaspoonful of whiskey to quiet him."

Eugene accompanied his mother during vacations from Betts and, to members of the company, she appeared especially attentive to him, while keeping a cool distance from Jamie. Some in the cast thought Ella's partiality toward Eugene obliged James to compensate by favoring their older son, thereby fanning all the edgy O'Neill tempers into new flame.

When Eugene visited backstage, he queried Hewitt about the scenery and the props. Hewitt remembered showing him how hoof-beats were simulated: coconut shells, tapped on a piece of marble covered with chamois cloth. Whenever Eugene watched a performance from the wings, Jamie clowned and strutted for his kid brother. Jamie also bragged to him about his offstage exploits and, little by little, Eugene was drawn into what James perceived as a filial conspiracy to undermine him.

Eugene could not help but be aware of the intensifying antagonism between his father and brother. The two constantly complained about each other and Eugene's sympathies had at first been divided. Now, approaching his middle teens, he was inclined to take Jamie's part.

With growing maturity Eugene sensed the torment of his brother's self-hatred, which Jamie took pains to conceal from the world. Eugene was also struck with his brother's pitiable defenselessness against their overbearing father and he recognized Jamie's despair over the mother he adored.

Even when inebriated, Jamie took pains to dress impeccably. Friends found it difficult to reconcile the raging-drunk, furniture-smashing, obscenity-shouting Jamie with the partially-drunk, stiffly-polite, grandly-aloof Jamie. He was actually both men, and the change from one to the other was merely a question of a little more or a little less whiskey.

Even his casual acquaintances retained an image of Jamie in a derby hat, spotless white shirt, brightly shined shoes and, on occasion, yellow spats. When rain threatened he was apt to carry a furled umbrella and a well-pressed coat over his arm. When mildly drunk, the fact could be detected only by a heightened color that spread like rouge over his cheekbones. His father was as familiar with that sign as he was with the drug-induced vacancy in Ella's eyes.

Jamie's drinking progressively worsened, and with it his venom toward James. Sobering up after the most vicious attacks on his father, he was apt to apologize with the excuse that it had been "the booze talking." Always, that was the rationale for the cutting things all four O'Neills said to each other — that and a similar catchall phrase: "It's the poison talking."

Chapter
THIRTEEN

W ELL BEFORE HIS SENIOR YEAR, EUGENE LOST NOT ONLY the last shreds of his religious faith but much of his innocence. He was abetted in this by Jamie's affectionate if mocking tutelage. While not yet mature enough to fathom the depth of his brother's cynicism, he was beginning to understand Jamie's devil-may-care attitude — largely a facade to conceal his truly terrifying insecurity.

It was several years before Eugene sensed his brother was drinking himself to death. Clinging to his literary indoctrination and insouciantly spouting nihilistic poetry, Jamie managed much of the time to fool his adolescent brother into accepting his pose as the embodiment of self-possessed worldliness and social ease. For the time being, Eugene could not help but admire and envy him. "We were very close, my brother and I," O'Neill once said, understating the ties that bound them. "We were a very close family — perhaps too close."

Their fraternal symbiosis is most graphically encapsulated in the words of Jamie Tyrone to his younger brother in *Long Day's Journey Into Night*: " . . . You reflect credit on me. I've had more to do with bringing you up than anyone. I wised you up about women . . . And who steered you on to reading poetry first? Swinburne, for example? I did! And because I once wanted to write, I planted it in your mind that someday you'd write! Hell, you're more than my brother. I made you! You're my Frankenstein!"

In an even more explicit allusion to the relationship, Jamie, in a line O'Neill deleted from the typescript, declares: "You're more my son, in a way, than Mama's or Papa's . . . . You're me. I'm inside you!"

Jamie's overwhelming presence in his brother's life is emphasized over and over in the plays, many of which contain actual or symbolic brothers in conflict. In some cases, such as *Beyond the*

Horizon, they are rivals for the same girl. In others, such as the expressionistic *The Great God Brown* and *Days Without End*, they represent dual aspects of the same person. Largely because of Jamie, O'Neill was constantly mulling over "the eternal struggle of the duality in the soul of the individual."

More than anyone, Eugene grew to understand his brother's alienation, echoed by Eugene's own sense of unbelonging.

In a highly fanciful characterization of Jamie Tyrone as an alien in an early scenario for *A Moon for the Misbegotten* (later dropped), he wrote that when Jamie was born, the first thing he did was "look around at the round earth and realize" he had "been sent to the wrong planet and God had double-crossed him and so he began to curse . . . and he reached for a bottle of whiskey and said to himself, By God, I'll show you! Try and catch me now. And so he lived on cursing & drinking, being slapped on the back and no one ever caught him . . . "

The most cynical lesson Jamie tried to teach the younger brother who tagged along on New York weekends was that women were treacherous. While Eugene was impressionable enough to believe much of Jamie's instruction, not all of it quite took. Eugene was unwilling, for example, to make more than a halfhearted effort to replace his own fast-held dream of a pure and ethereal mother with Jamie's substitute of the compassionate whore. Jamie was chronically sardonic, whereas Eugene — his skepticism usually overcome by his innate idealism — was in fact an unswerving romantic; it was a trait that surfaced whenever Eugene found himself attracted to a girl he believed to be pure and innocent.

The recollections of Eugene's classmates at Betts illustrate this inner conflict. Some remembered instances when Eugene seemed to be awkwardly imitating his brother's pose as a cavalier "ladies' man," while others recalled Eugene's sporadic interest in girls regarded as "nice." Once, uncertain how to entertain a nice Stamford girl, he asked a Betts boy named Sawyer Robinson how much he ought to spend on her.

Jamie liked to brag to his cronies about having taught his kid brother the ropes. "Gene learned sin more easily than other people," he said. "I made it easy for him."

Eugene, however, confided to his wife Carlotta, that his first sexual encounter under Jamie's tutelage was anything but agreeable. He might have been recalling the experience in the opening scene of *Strange Interlude*, through the partially autobiographical character of

Charles Marsden. In the first of the stream-of-consciousness asides
that infuse all the characters' speeches in this psychoanalytically
inspired, nine-act play, Marsden quickly gets to the point:

"Ugh! — always that memory! — why can't I ever forget? — as
sickeningly clear as if it were yesterday — prep school — Easter vacation . . . that house of cheap vice — one dollar! — why did I go? —
Jack, the dead-game sport — how I admired him! — afraid of his
taunts — he pointed to the Italian girl — 'Take her!' — daring me —
I went — miserably frightened — what a pig she was! — pretty
vicious face under caked powder and rouge — surly and contemptuous — lumpy body — short legs and thick ankles . . . 'What you
gawkin' about? Git a move on, kid' — kid! I was only a kid! — sixteen — test of manhood — ashamed to face Jack again unless . . . oh,
stupid kid! — back at the hotel I waited till they were asleep — then
sobbed — thinking of Mother — feeling I had defiled her — and
myself — forever!"

Marsden, like O'Neill, is a writer, with the eyes of "a dreamy self-
analyst, his thin lips ironical and a bit sad." He has "long fragile
hands . . . and has always been regarded as of delicate constitution."

Eugene's idealism is tellingly revealed by a tender encounter in
New London during the summer of 1905 with a teenaged girl named
Marion Welch — his first documented romance. His decorous handling of the infatuation is in bewildering contrast to Jamie's style of
sex education.

Ephemeral as it was, the episode was poignantly recalled by
O'Neill more than a quarter century later, when he wrote his nostalgic comedy, *Ah, Wilderness!* (set in 1906), and based the character of
the adolescent Muriel McComber — at least in part — on Marion
Welch.

Marion lived in Hartford, Connecticut, where her father was an
insurance doctor. Eugene met her when she came to visit a friend
who lived near the O'Neills. He taught her to row on the Thames and
they took snapshots of each other. On the basis of this flimsy intimacy they struck up a flirtatious correspondence when she returned to
Hartford at the end of July, that lasted a little over four months.

Eighteen and a recent high school graduate, Marion was a pretty,
sweet-faced girl with smiling eyes and, while demure, she was evidently susceptible. Eugene, although not quite seventeen, managed
to convey an air of sophistication beyond his years. During the three
years he had been at Betts he had made what he evidently regarded
as triumphant progress in French. In his first letter, he addressed

Marion as *"Ma chère 'Boutade'"* (literally "whim" or "fancy").

"I cannot say how much I missed and still miss you," he wrote, beseeching her "for the millionth time" to send him a photo of herself. "Please! Ah! Please! I think you're the meanest girl I ever knew." He signed himself "Your eternal slave."

Early in August, again to *"Ma chère Boutade,"* he praised her for having learned by heart Poe's "Annabel Lee," remarking flirtatiously, "Some of the lines express my feeling exactly, especially the following:

"'And neither the angels in heaven above/Nor the demons down under the sea/Can ever dissever my soul from the soul/Of the beautiful Annabel Lee.'

"Except her name is not Annabel Lee but M . . . W . . . "

In subsequent letters, Eugene advised Marion what to read, at one point recommending Thomas Moore. "He has written some 'peaches' and I never tire reading them and have learned a few," he confided. He also recommended Dumas the elder. "I could read every book in the world and no heroes could ever replace 'D'Artagnan, Athos, Porthos and Aramis,' 'Monte Cristo,' 'Bussy,' in my estimation."

Eugene went on to inform her that he and his brother "swam the river this morning"; but he complained about the boredom of New London life:

"It makes the famous 'Simple Life' look like 'The Pace That Kills.'" The latter phrase was the title of a popular novel by the prolific writer, Edgar Saltus, about a high-living scoundrel who comes to an untimely end. The youthful Eugene was not only an insatiable reader, but an eclectic one; along with his dedication to the classics, modern poetry and radical philosophy, he avidly read contemporary, and sometimes trashy, fiction.

In the nostalgic mood that engendered *Ah, Wilderness!* nearly thirty years later, O'Neill incorporated the Saltus title into the play's dedication to a friend who shared his memories of boyhood escapades: "To George Jean Nathan *who also, once upon a time, in peg-top trousers went the pace that kills along the road to ruin."* O'Neill also referred to the phrase when the play's adolescent Richard Miller, describing his misery over his girlfriend's putative faithlessness, tells her: " . . . I thought, what difference does it make what I do now? I might as well forget her and lead the pace that kills, and drown my sorrows!"

"The pace that kills" was also a sporting adage of the era, sometimes applied to the racetrack. While Eugene complained regularly to

Marion about his boredom in New London, he could not refrain from swaggering about a trip to Saratoga, evidently with Jamie. "I visited the race track," he told her "and won some money on the 'ponies.'"

Eugene had a precocious love of the track, was a knowledgeable reader of the racing forms and prided himself on his ability to handicap. After attending the Saratoga races, as he informed Marion, he went on to Canfield's Saratoga Club, which he described as one of the most "fashionable and notorious" of the world's "gambling joints," where he "watched the rich boys throw away coin on roulette and faro."

"Having acquired a fever for gambling," he continued, "I went back to the Hotel and 'rustled my pile' on the slot machines." He lost. Eugene told Marion he was reading Victor Hugo's *The Laughing Man*, and closed with a debonair effusion: "*Au revoir ma chérie je vous aimerai toujours et je vous baisserai en pensée.*"

In early September, Eugene and his family left New London by boat, arriving in New York after a stormy passage, during which, he wrote Marion, "the fog horn kept me awake all night." From New York, Eugene made a brief visit to a farm in Zion, New Jersey (a town not far from Princeton), owned by his father and rented to a breeder of racehorses. Only occasionally visited by the O'Neills, the small farm had been taken over in payment of an uncollected debt.

"There is nothing to do but ride horseback and dream — of you," he wrote to Marion.

It was from the racehorse breeder in Zion that Eugene had learned to handicap; additional instruction had been provided by his father's New London coachman, who himself owned a few undistinguished trotters that he raced at country fairs. The coachman once took Eugene to the races at Sheepshead Bay, where he met an old friend, the prominent trainer, Al Weston.

"They started to talk," O'Neill recalled many years later, "and the minute they'd mention a horse I'd break in and say, 'Oh, yes; Laddie Z by Buzzfuzz out of Guinevere; ran second at Morris Park, June 16th; fourth at Sheepshead, July 10th.' I knew them all; I couldn't help it. After half an hour of this, Weston gave me a hard look and said, 'Kid, either you'll be a jockey or you'll get yourself killed.'"

By the end of September, Eugene was back at Betts, "poring over Vergil, Trig, etc." rather than figuring the odds at the track. Although in his senior year, he still engaged in schoolboy pranks, describing to Marion "a fine 'rough house' here a few weeks ago," reminiscent of the earlier episode with the chamber pots. His gleeful letter revealed just how much of an adolescent he still was:

"It consisted, in the main, of wet towels and pillows and soap and pails and waste-baskets, thrown with intent to injure the visages of the Herr Professor on our floor or of any one else in the way . . ." Eugene merrily went on to report that Billy Betts "does not know who were engaged in the adventure nor is he liable to find out."

Early that December, in what was apparently his final letter to Marion, Eugene responded to her report of having seen *The Count of Monte Cristo*. While the play might "be all right for those who have never seen it before," he declared, it was "worm eaten." He went on to brag about his own playgoing during Thanksgiving vacation: "I saw six plays . . . and we only had five days. They were all musical comedies. (I always confessed to degraded tastes.)"

Eugene enjoyed taking school friends with him to Broadway shows, which he could attend free of charge, thanks to a practice called "professional courtesies." In those days anyone connected with the theater could identify himself at the box office and, if there were available seats, would be allowed in. "I don't know if it made me an expert on the drama," O'Neill once recalled, "but it made me an awful lot of girl friends."

Another school friend had access to free tickets, although limited to the Majestic Theater. He was Hans Schleip, whose father ran Papst's Café, next door to the Majestic, where a musical based on *The Wizard of Oz* was having a long run. The Betts boys were happy to settle for repeated attendance there, since the student body was collectively in love with the golden-haired ingenue, Anna Laughlin.

Eugene could maintain a lofty attitude about this mass unrequited love, for he was personally acquainted, through Jamie, with the musical's star, Lotta Faust. Almost twenty-five years later he still remembered her beautiful legs, and reminisced about her with another fan, George Jean Nathan.

"There, my boy, was a love-apple," Nathan claimed that O'Neill once told him, "and who said anything about acting?" Nathan had a tendency to attribute his own brash locutions to his friends, and the O'Neillian dialogue he quoted in this and other instances was apt to be at least fifty percent Nathan's own. O'Neill was amused by Nathan's inclination to garnish, and rarely challenged him. In one instance that was one-hundred-percent O'Neill, the playwright said, "While other boys were shivering themselves into a fit of embarrassment at the mere thought of a show girl, I really was a wise guy."

Eugene graduated from Betts in the spring of 1906. Nearing eighteen, he was exceedingly well-mannered, despite the eruptions of juvenile mischief that contrasted so oddly with the worldly-wise, off-campus romps with Jamie. He dressed nattily in imitation of his brother, the Broadway fashion plate. On school days he wore knickers and pullovers and, on weekends and holidays, white flannels with dark jackets.

Yet in spite of his sartorial conformity, Eugene was distinctly non-conformist in his outlook. Unlike most (if not all) of his peers, he had by this time swallowed large doses of Tolstoy and Dostoevsky, as well as the modern French writers, and had embraced (under Jamie's tutelage) the misogynistic poetry of Swinburne, Dowson, Baudelaire and Wilde. He was also fascinated by Conrad and London and dreamed of going to sea. But he had no serious plans for his future.

James urged his son to apply for admission to college, knowing this meant four years of support at an Ivy League school — and once again demonstrating he could suppress his instinctive penury when it came to educating his sons. With little enthusiasm (and less gratitude) Eugene agreed, but instead of Yale, where virtually all his classmates were bound, he perversely chose Princeton.

That same spring, James, exhausted from touring and concerned once again about his wife's emotional state, informed his sons that he and Ella planned to go abroad in June and made provisions for them to live at the Monte Cristo Cottage. Ella was relieved to be free of New London even if just for a month and James threw himself into the spirit of a real holiday, which was to include a visit to his native Kilkenny.

The O'Neills arrived in London in time to attend a benefit for Ellen Terry at the Drury Lane on June 12, after which they vacationed in Ireland. From there, James corresponded with a young New York writer, James Slevin, who had completed a play about John the Baptist called *The Voice of the Mighty*. James, still lusting for stardom in a Biblical spectacle, planned to produce it the following season.

"When in London I attended a revival of Oscar Wilde's *Salomé*, and in a way I can say I enjoyed it," James wrote to Slevin from Dublin, adding, "Though you have written your play on the same subject, you have taken an entirely different view. Your choice of situations is not the same and your handling is quite the opposite. He tells his story in most picturesque language, delicate figures and subtle conceptions, but very little action. You, on the other hand, have presented your play in a series of strong dramatic actions and incidents, painted your pictures with a broader brush and with a more virile hand. His pleases the student — yours will please the people."

In his letter, James also confided he had been "down to the old home," where he found little change in familiar places, but where "strange faces greet me on every side."

"I sat for hours on the old porch last night," he wrote, "thinking of the dear ones departed." He made no reference to his less-than-dearly remembered father, who had deserted him in Buffalo. But he could not resist a half wistful, half sardonic comment on his homeland:

"Ireland is the most peculiar place in the world. Prolific in its benefits to all other countries, it never seems to benefit itself. There is not a nation that cannot boast of some great man, soldier, statesmen or poet, originally from this quaint little place. And here it is, as quiet and unassuming as though it had never been the mother of half the great men in the world."

James and Ella returned to the United States in late July, rejoining Eugene and Jamie in New London. James was bursting with a new repertoire of Irish stories, the kind he loved to tell in barrooms and, when he could gain his family's attention, in his own living room. Eugene, as he was growing up, absorbed the racy flavor and earthy wit of his father's tales. They became, along with the fruits of his comprehensive reading, an ineradicable part of his literary heritage — as he was later to demonstrate in such plays as *A Moon for the Misbegotten* and *A Touch of the Poet*.

Eugene doubtless was amused, for instance, by his father's sketch of the typical Irish railway porter, who, said James, "simply can't help being funny."

"On one of my trips through the Emerald Isle," James recounted, "I got into a third-class car by mistake with a first-class ticket; a zealous porter wrathfully pulled me out of the car and told me 'I was chating the Kumpany.' After I was comfortably seated in the first-class compartment, he put his head in and asked: 'Is there anyone there for here?' But even this genius was eclipsed by the conductor of the train who, before the train departed, fiercely rang a bell and bellowed in gloomy warning: 'This train shtops nowhere at all!'"

Jamie, as always, considered it obligatory to deprecate their father's facile gift of mimicry. Once when James reminded his sons of how hard he had to work as an actor, Jamie sneered, "You call that work?"

James, of course, meant it was hard to be a good actor and, as always, he was both stung and challenged by Jamie's disparagement.

But Jamie's memory was, in fact, almost as good as his father's and, now and then, he condescended to learn the subsidiary roles in James's touring repertory so that he could take over for any actor who defected or was indisposed.

Jamie liked to boast how easy it was to memorize lines and once bet his father ten dollars he could learn Goldsmith's *The Deserted Village* in a week. He even persuaded Eugene to make a similar bet that he could learn the role of Macbeth in the same period. This episode was recalled by O'Neill in *Long Day's Journey Into Night* (but transposed to 1912, with the bet reduced by half).

James happened to have played Macbeth only a few months earlier at the Metropolitan Opera House in New York, as a testimonial for Madame Modjeska, in which he appeared opposite the Polish star. (He had, on that occasion, caused a bit of a backstage stir when it was discovered, just before the murder scene, that he had somehow forgotten to provide himself with a costume. He went on stage in an ancient dressing gown, wearing it with such aplomb that none in the audience dreamed of questioning its suitability.)

Since neither Eugene nor Jamie could afford to lose the bet, they both applied themselves to the task of memorization. At week's end Jamie recited *The Deserted Village* for his father and collected his money, proving nothing more than that he could work harder in a petty cause than in a worthy one.

Eugene, as he began his own recitation, must have been nervous. He was all too familiar with his father's dismaying habit of whacking him on the shoulder and crying, "Get that hump off your back! Straighten up there! Open your mouth and let the words come out!"

As he recalled many years later, he was letter-perfect; but before he had gone very far, James closed the book and fixed Eugene with his penetrating gaze: "You certainly have a good memory, and I see you've worked hard, but never go on the stage."

Eugene could not help laughing. Nothing was further from his mind.

CHAPTER
FOURTEEN

I T IS CLEAR FROM EUGENE O'NEILL'S ONLY FULL-LENGTH comedy, *Ah, Wilderness!*, that the summer of 1906 was an all-too-brief, bittersweet New London interlude he could later evoke with pleasure. In a prefatory note to the first draft (later deleted), he wrote: "A Nostalgic Comedy Of the Sentimental Days when Youth Was Young, and Right Was Right, and Life Was a Wicked Opportunity."

His nostalgia for that period sprang from a confluence of factors, among them his mother's refreshed and relaxed mood upon her return from Europe. Set in July of 1906 in a "large-small town in Connecticut" plainly recognizable as New London, *Ah, Wilderness!* centers on Richard Miller, a boy "going on seventeen, just out of high school" and ready to enter Yale in the fall. Eugene, in the summer of 1906, while just out of preparatory school, was actually "going on" eighteen, but, like Richard, he was readying himself for college in the fall, albeit Princeton rather than Yale.

Twenty-seven years later, the summer came back to him in a dream. "I woke up one morning with this play fully in mind — never had even a hint of an idea about it before — title and all . . . It simply gushed out of me," he informed his editor, Saxe Commins. "Wrote the whole damn thing in the month of Sept."

When the play was produced on Broadway in 1933, there was considerable speculation as to its autobiographical derivation. But O'Neill insisted the actual resemblance between Richard Miller's life and his own was trifling. *Ah Wilderness!*, he explained, was what he wished his adolescence might have been.

"The idea that Richard in the play resembles me at his age is absurd," he once wrote. "I was the exact opposite." The truth, he later amended, "is that I had no youth." Later still, he said, "It was a sort of wishing out loud."

While averring Richard was not based on himself, he wanted it understood the play did reflect the intimately recollected period of his lost youth.

"The people in the play," as he stressed to Commins, "are of the class . . . which I really know better than any other — my whole background of New London childhood, boyhood, young manhood — the nearest approach to home I ever knew — relatives, friends of family, etc. all being just this class of people."

A few days later he confided to his older son (somewhat tortuously) that *Ah, Wilderness!* reflected "the spirit of a time that is dead now with all its ideals and manners & codes . . . a memory of the time of my youth — not of *my* youth but of the youth in which my generation spent youth — "

He did not, however, want the play's director, Philip Moeller, to take the New London locale literally, underlining that the the play's overall theme was universal:

"Don't think of this play as a New England play!!! It isn't, you know, in any essential respect . . . It could be laid in the Middle or Far West with hardly the change of a word. There are no colloquialisms in it, I think, that aren't general American small town . . . I happened to have my old home town of New London in mind when I wrote — couldn't help it — but New London, even in those days was pretty well divorced from its N. E. heritage . . . with New York the strongest influence."

In some respects, according to O'Neill, *Ah, Wilderness!* was a morality play. Its "mood of emotion of a past time," he said, was something "we badly need today to steady us." What he wanted was to recreate the impact on his youthful contemporaries of the "new radical literature of that day" — "(Shaw, Ibsen, Wilde, Omar Khayyam, etc)."

O'Neill also sought to evoke the era's spirit of youthful rebellion, influenced by anarchists such as Emma Goldman. Thus, in *Ah, Wilderness!* Richard Miller spouts the outrageous jargon Eugene himself was apt to employ in his naive embrace of all things radical. Richard's father, Nat, at one point admonishes him (as James no doubt admonished the adolescent Eugene), "Son, if I didn't know it was you talking, I'd think we had Emma Goldman with us."

One of O'Neill's chief concerns about the play was that, if taken as a portrait of his family (rather than of generic Americans), he himself would be viewed as the product of a benign — rather than a tragic — environment. (How he actually viewed his younger self and his family did not, of course, emerge until twenty-three years later, when *Long Day's Journey Into Night*, set in the New London of 1912, appeared in print.)

Nonetheless, *Ah Wilderness!* and *Long Day's Journey Into Night* can be regarded as two sides of a coin — one a genial glimpse of what the O'Neill family, at its best, aspired to be, and the other, a balefully heightened picture of his family at its worst.

The jarring disparities in mood and character reflected in *Ah, Wilderness!*, written in 1932, and *Long Day's Journey Into Night*, written in 1941, may be understood in terms of the epic changes in O'Neill's life during that nine-year span.

When he wrote *Ah, Wilderness!* he was a still-vigorous forty-four, happily remarried and at the height of his success; when he embarked on *Long Day's Journey* he was depressed, not only over his own failing health, but over the critical disparagement that had followed the 1934 production of *Days Without End*, as well as over the onslaught of fascism and the onset of World War II.

Yet, in the disparate outlooks of the two plays, there are striking likenesses — even such a minor one as the presence in both plays of a raw, young Irish maid, or "second girl." In *Ah, Wilderness!* her name is Norah, but she speaks in the same brogue-larded phrases and is the same thorn-in-the-side to her mistress as Cathleen in *Long Day's Journey Into Night*.

The two plays are set in an almost exact copy of the living room of the O'Neill home at 138 (later 325) Pequot Avenue. If the resemblance between the two settings is not readily evident, it is because in *Ah Wilderness!* the living room is seen through rose-colored lenses, while in *Long Day's Journey Into Night* it is viewed through a glass darkly. Nevertheless, if executed literally for the stage, the two sets as described by O'Neill could, with the shifting of only a few minor details, substitute for each other.

Both the Miller "sitting room" and the Tyrone "living room" are first seen empty, with early-morning sunshine streaming through the windows. Porch, doorways, bookcases and windows are almost identically situated.

In the center of the Tyrone family's living room is "a round table with a green-shaded reading lamp, the cord plugged in one of the four sockets in the chandelier above." In the center of the Miller family's living room is "a big, round table with a green-shaded reading lamp, the cord of the lamp running up to one of five sockets in the chandelier above." In the Millers' sitting room "a medium-priced, inoffensive rug covers most of the floor" and in the Tyrones' living room "the hardwood floor is nearly covered by a rug, inoffensive in design and color."

Undoubtedly the room was etched in O'Neill's brain as a symbol of small-town domesticity. He first described such a setting as early as 1914 in *Bread and Butter*: the "sitting-room of Edward Brown's home in Bridgetown, Conn.," featuring a "large, sober-colored rug which covers all but the edge of the hard-wood floor," as well as "an electric lamp wired from the chandelier above."

While the Millers of *Ah, Wilderness!* find their home cheerful and pleasant, the Tyrones of *Long Day's Journey* (with the exception of James, who has grown indifferent) regard their home as little better than a hovel.

These opposing viewpoints were indeed attested to by contemporary New Londoners who, depending upon their social status, saw the house one way or the other. James's Irish friends and his in-laws thought it comfortable, attractive and more than adequate for the four O'Neills. Members of the town's more pretentious families considered it ordinary, if not shabby.

There is evidence to bolster the *Long Day's Journey* (or gloomy) view — especially when, in later years, the house suffered from neglect. But the *Ah, Wilderness!* (or sunny) view has support as well. The cottage survived years of later abuse and was still standing long after Eugene O'Neill's death (ultimately restored as a landmark and museum). Its beautiful old wooden staircase, solid door and window frames, heavy sliding doors, tiled fireplaces and fine, hardwood floors were virtually intact; even its pale, gray-shingle exterior and the Victorian gingerbread trimming of the porch eaves, while something less than architectural gems, were robust enough to withstand decades of waterfront weather.

Unable to take pride in her home despite James's well-meant improvements, Ella continued to nag her husband about the house being ill-constructed, haphazardly furnished and cheaply maintained. As Mary Tyrone grumbles in *Long Day's Journey Into Night*, "I never felt it was my home."

James believed he had triumphed in coming as far as he had from his Irish peasant beginnings, and stoically endured his family's accusations of frugality. However, it must have taken the resolve of a martyr to bear his wife's incessant carping about their home.

It is evident Ella expressed her frustration with the relentlessness of water torture, for in *Long Day's Journey Into Night* it is a recurrent theme. Mary Tyrone not only berates her husband, but complains about her deprivation to her sons:

"Your father could afford to keep on buying property but never to give me a home," she tells her younger son. And to both sons she laments (perhaps with unconscious humor) that their father "doesn't understand a home. He doesn't feel at home in it . . . "

Endlessly resourceful in her indictment, as only the obsessed can be, she conjures up one rationalization after another to justify her anger. At intervals throughout the play's four acts she accuses James:

"You never wanted a home. You should have remained a bachelor."

"In a real home one is never lonely. You forget I know from experience what a home is like. I gave up one to marry you — my father's home."

"Oh, I'm so sick and tired of pretending this is a home!"

"I know you can't help thinking it's a home."

And the most devastating accusation of all: "Children should have homes to be born in, if they are to be good children, and women need homes, if they are to be good mothers."

Inevitably, Mary's lamentations about her home lead to the more ingrained complaint of her husband's stinginess. In early notes, O'Neill set the play on the Tyrones' wedding anniversary, apparently to allow Mary to vent her anger.

With a venom O'Neill diluted in the final version, Mary complains how often her husband "has forgotten — or remembering, pretended to forget, hoping I had forgotten — so there need be no present . . . " In a later scenario, in lines also deleted from the final script, Mary tells the cook her husband dislikes anniversaries because they "cost money" and they remind him he is "getting old."

Nothing akin to the Tyrones' accumulated resentment is depicted in *Ah, Wilderness!* Although O'Neill did, to some degree, base the play on an idealized vision of his own family, it was the family of his friend, Arthur ("Art") McGinley, that served as his principal model. Art was the son of John McGinley, who in 1883 had prevailed upon James and Ella to buy a house in New London.

O'Neill was self-pityingly given to contrasting his own boyhood summers in New London with jovial times spent by Art McGinley and other New London youths, whose parents devoted themselves with apparent artlessness to each other and their children.

In addition to the McGinleys, O'Neill particularly admired the family of Frederick Palmer Latimer, a judge of the Probate Court in nearby Groton, who was soon to become the editor of the New London Telegraph. O'Neill wove elements of both Latimer and John McGinley, who had left the New London Day to become the city's postmaster, into the character of Nat Miller. He rounded out the character with some of James O'Neill's benevolent attributes.

Like Nat Miller, John McGinley was the head of a large family. He had seven sons and a daughter and James as well as Eugene regarded with awe the family's sanguine domesticity.

Once when visiting the McGinleys and observing their easy, close-knit camaraderie, James wistfully confessed to his friend, "I may have made some money and achieved some fame, but you're the man I envy." Whenever James appeared as Monte Cristo in New London, he reserved a box at the Lyceum Theater for the McGinley clan. The children would show up for the event scrubbed, shining and eager. Arthur McGinley saw the play no less than nine times.

In *Ah, Wilderness!* O'Neill characteristically used actual names, or close approximations, of people connected with the era and locale. He named characters Arthur, Tom and "Wint," and a boy named Lawrence is mentioned (but does not appear); all four names belonged to the McGinley boys.

John McGinley's wife, Evelyn Essex, became Essie, and the daughter, Mildred, took her name from a girl O'Neill knew in that period; her nickname, in the play and in life, was "Mid" and O'Neill also contrived to work her last name, Culver, into the text.

Nat Miller's spinster sister, Lily, drew her name and part of her character from O'Neill's spinster cousin, Lillian Brennan, nicknamed Lil (the same cousin to whom the thirteen-year-old Eugene had written so affectionately from school in 1901).

It was Lil who often protested to Ella and James that Eugene's precocious and iconoclastic reading ought to be censored. She also objected to his lack of respect for her family's Catholic tradition. But in other matters she was inclined to take Eugene's part against his father. She saw, for example, that James had made Jamie (and was making Eugene) overdependent on him, and felt it unreasonable for James to expect his sons to have a sense of responsibility unless he changed his methods.

However deeply the youthful Eugene suffered from a lack of domestic equilibrium, the adult Eugene, yielding to an iron bond of affection beneath his resentment of his father, endowed the character of Nat Miller with at least two of James's amusing traits.

One was James's conviction that "a peculiar oil in bluefish" had a poisonous effect on his digestion; it was a family joke that Ella served him bluefish at dinner under the guise of weakfish. The other trait was James's tendency to reprise familiar stories of his youth, illustrated in *Ah, Wilderness!* by a rare nontheatrical reminiscence about how he once rescued a boyhood friend from drowning.

Responding to a researcher's query a few years after the play's production, O'Neill said Miller was like his father "in some aspects, but totally unlike him in others," volunteering that his own father "had many extraordinary contradictory sides to his character."

The character of the mother in the play, Essie Miller, bears little resemblance to Ella O'Neill and, in fact, is much like Evelyn McGinley, who looked a bit like Queen Victoria and possessed the maternal, bustling, good-natured officiousness Eugene missed (or told himself he missed) in his own mother. Essie was partly modeled as well on a warm-hearted, cheery mother of seven, named Maude Rippin, in whose New London home Eugene boarded contentedly during the winter of 1913-1914.

The play's older brother, Arthur, is of course a far cry from Jamie O'Neill. Two years Richard Miller's senior, Arthur is a Yale undergraduate and almost as innocent as Richard himself — whereas Eugene's older brother was by now a chronic alcoholic, a favorite in the New London brothels, and a man who could be maliciously informative about the least savory aspects of the reigning Broadway soubrettes. If Jamie is present in *Ah, Wilderness!*, he is there in aspects of the character of Essie's bachelor brother, Sid Miller, an intractable drunkard.

As for Richard (despite O'Neill's disavowal), there are indeed strands of young Eugene in his makeup, though bits of his personality were borrowed from a contemporary named Charles Hutchinson ("Hutch") Collins. When *Ah, Wilderness!* was produced, Arthur McGinley wrote O'Neill that he recognized his own family in the play. O'Neill, fearing he might have embarrassed his friend, protested that no one had been taken from life.

"They are general types true for any large-small town," he wrote. "But the boy does spout the poetry I and Hutch Collins once used to." There was more, however. Hutch shared with Eugene (and Richard) a passion for the works of such scandalous writers as Wilde and Swinburne, and both boys could recite long passages from *The Rubáiyát of Omar Khayyam*, the source of the play's title. O'Neill substituted "Ah" for "Oh" because, he once explained, he thought the former conveyed a stronger sense of nostalgia.

Like Richard, the two teenage boys believed Oscar Wilde had been imprisoned for bigamy. It was Eugene who guided Hutch's early reading, but he did not have to guide his taste in clothes. Hutch sported a snap-brim hat with a London label that drew both envy and scorn from friends, all of whose parents referred to him as "Jerry Collins's damn fool." Both Eugene and Hutch, often seen leaving the New London library hugging stacks of books, elicited the bewildered respect of their less studious peers. One such friend declared definitively, "That Gene O'Neill — he reads deep stuff!"

Many years later — but long before writing *Ah, Wilderness!* — O'Neill described the kinship he had felt for Hutch: "He possessed . . . such a pronounced delight in living, in the sheer physical joy of breathing and moving about, of feeling so consciously alive. That eternal boy in him which exulted in his own bodily prowess and was so full of admiration for the muscular deeds of others was one of his greatest charms."

The Hutch of New London, said O'Neill, was "an athlete brimming over with animal strength; always in a bathing suit in summer, whooping, diving, swimming, rowing, canoeing, sailing; in winter plowing through a blizzard in flannel pants and T shirt, bare headed, for the pure satisfaction of his defiant health." They became intimate because they supported each other's eccentricities, frowned on in the narrow-minded New London environment. They were, as he put it, "twin disreputables in the village gossip," which bound them "hilariously together."

Despite Eugene's contempt for New London's stuffiness, he savored its Fourth of July rituals, later recreating them in *Ah, Wilderness!* The setting off of fireworks began at midnight on July 3 and lasted until midnight of the Fourth. True, Eugene celebrated with his friends, rather than his family, for his mother, even when in good health, could seldom rise to the cheerful give-and-take of the McGinley (and the Miller) clans.

Eugene also enjoyed attending the Yale-Harvard boat races on the Thames, a frenetic spectacle that opened the summer season and drew as many as fifty thousand. He later recreated the event in *Strange Interlude* (although transposing the setting to New York's Hudson River).

The competing crews and their relatives and friends crowded the hotels of New London, and Eugene was an eager participant in the

carnival spirit, accentuated by the barroom music of the day. He also
reveled in popular player-piano tunes, some of which turned up in
Ah, Wilderness!, among them "Waiting at the Church" and "Bedelia."

O'Neill attributed his love of music, which included chanteys,
jazz, show tunes (especially Irving Berlin's) and an indiscriminate
smattering of the classical, to his mother's musicianship. He boasted
that she had once been "a fine pianist — exceptionally fine, I believe";
and, until rheumatism affected her hands, had liked to play her
father's old "pianoforte" in their New London home.

In later life O'Neill acquired a sizable record collection and professed to be partial to Beethoven, Schubert and César Franck; but
nothing could send him into quite the same raptures as the tinny
sound of a player piano rendering the tunes of the early 1900's. He
humorously confessed as much in an early poem he called "Ballard
of the Modern Music Lover," of which these lines are illustrative:

> I have tried to fall for the stuff of Mozart
> Handel, Haydn — a dozen or more
> But I guess my ear isn't framed for "beaux arts"
> For I found them all a terrible bore . . .

> . . . The long-haired high-brows call me "vulgarian"
> When the "Great Big Beautiful Doll" I croon
> For I'm strong for the music that's real American
> And the joy of my heart is a rag time tune . . .

> . . . High-brows, whom classic music quickeneth,
> Heed well the burden of my vulgar rune,
> Your lofty tumbling wearies me to death,
> The joy of my heart is a rag time tune.

Evidence of music's pull on O'Neill's emotions appears in many
works besides *Ah, Wilderness!*, in which songs underline mood, evoke
atmosphere or convey character — such plays as *The Hairy Ape, The
Great God Brown, Mourning Becomes Electra, All God's Chillun Got
Wings* and *The Iceman Cometh.*

Travis Bogard, the O'Neill scholar who collected and annotated
the music for *The Eugene O'Neill Songbook*, speculated that O'Neill
"used song to enhance the action of his plays more than any dramatist since Shakespeare." Bogard pointed out that somebody sings or
plays an instrument in thirty-one of O'Neill's works, including two
unfinished scripts, *More Stately Mansions* and *The Calms of Capricorn.*

No matter what other activities occupied him in the summer of 1906, Eugene devoted himself to reading, often in the apartment of a dashing New London doctor, Joseph Ganey. Ten years Eugene's senior, Ganey had been a butcher and a coal dealer before deciding to become a physician. Shortly after settling down to medical practice in an office on Main Street, above which he lived, "Doc" Ganey made an impetuous trip around the world, during which he collected a number of first editions.

It was only after he had exhausted the classics in his own home that Eugene approached Doc Ganey's more sophisticated shelves. Ganey tolerated Eugene even though he thought him sullen and difficult and something of an adolescent poseur. While denying Eugene permission to take home any of his precious volumes, Ganey allowed him to read as much as he pleased in the apartment. He would often return at three in the morning from a night on the town to find Eugene poring over Wilde, Zola or Schopenhauer.

Doc Ganey's "Second Story Club" was a raffish, preponderantly Irish assemblage that would have stood Richard Miller's hair on end. Across the street was a dressmaking establishment employing young Italian women, among them Aida Rovetti. She recalled being warned by her mother to have nothing to do with Eugene and "the rest of the riffraff," who "would whistle, make remarks and generally carry on for the benefit of the seamstresses."

The club's members, who gathered to talk, drink and play cards, were looked at askance by the town's respectable citizens. Art McGinley, viewed mistrustfully by some of his friends as "a left-footed Irishman" because his family was Episcopalian, said, in recalling Doc Ganey, "We ate his food, drank his liquor, wore out his carpets, read his books and got free medical attention."

Unlike Richard Miller, who is shocked by his encounter with a prostitute in a shady hotel and resists her efforts to entice him to an upstairs room, Eugene by now was beginning to feel at home with the ladies of Bradley Street, a narrow avenue at the northern end of town that encompassed the flourishing red-light district.

It might have been there that Jamie took his brother for the unsavory assignation chronicled in *Strange Interlude*. In any case, by the summer of 1906, Eugene evidently had put aside his qualms, and joined the members of the Second Story Club on visits to Bradley Street.

The brothels, about a dozen in all, were housed in rickety wooden structures flanking the police station; the proximity facilitated periodic raids and abetted the convenient arrangement between the anointed upholders of the law and the merry purveyors of vice. While awaiting customers, the girls would lean out the windows to exchange small talk with policemen. When a house was raided, the prostitutes were marched to court. "Occupation?" the judge would ask matter-of-factly. "Seamstress," was the matter-of-fact reply.

O'Neill accurately described the interior of a Bradley Street brothel in *The Great God Brown* (written in 1925) and it was recognized with delight by some of his old comrades in sin:

"An automatic, nickel-in-the-slot player piano is at center, rear. On its right is a dirty gilt second-hand sofa. At the left is a bald-spotted crimson plush chair. The backdrop for the rear wall is a cheap wallpaper of a dull yellow-brown, resembling a blurred impression of a fallow field in early spring. There is a cheap alarm clock on top of the piano."

Reference to the whores of Bradley Street is also made in *Long Day's Journey Into Night*, when Jamie Tyrone tells his brother of a recent visit to the brothel of "Mamie Burns." "Guess which one of Mamie's charmers I picked to bless me with her woman's love," asks Jamie. "It'll hand you a laugh, Kid. I picked Fat Violet." According to Art McGinley, one of the brothels did indeed house a good-hearted, piano-playing prostitute named Violet, a woman of generous dimensions.

"Here comes the kindergarten," the "seamstresses" would call out when Eugene and his friends showed up. For reasons of economy the "kindergarten" usually arrived en masse; a round of beer cost one dollar, regardless of how many were in the group.

Eugene's predilection (at not quite eighteen) for rowdy behavior was beginning to earn him an ominous reputation among the mothers of New London. Even though he himself was not yet a heavy drinker, he was tainted by his brother's notoriety. James, believing it his moral duty, took it upon himself to warn some of the parents of impressionable daughters to keep them away from his profligate sons. As for Ella, she considered none of the New London girls good enough for either Jamie or Eugene.

Eugene and Richard Miller were dissimilar in other ways. There is nothing, for example, in Richard's character that suggests Eugene's profound love of the water and of ships; nor does *Ah, Wilderness!* more than hint at a tradition of sea history in the town. Eugene rarely missed watching the arrival or departure of the square-riggers that still, in the early 1900's, glided with breathtaking grace into New London harbor — a harbor that held (in addition to Navy craft and a training vessel for Coast Guard cadets) the floating palaces of millionaires.

Eugene, however, was interested only in the schooners under full sail. Dazzled by the novels of Joseph Conrad and Jack London, whose writings featured struggles for survival in rough corners of the world, he spent long hours talking to the captains and crews of the anchored sailing ships.

Perhaps he hoped to coax from them sea tales similar to Conrad's and London's; both had shipped out in their teens — Conrad as a gunrunner, London as an oyster-bed pirate.

Ella disapproved of Eugene's familiarity with the old salts who hung about the harbor, just as she deplored the fact that both Eugene and Jamie — and James, too, for that matter — seemed to prefer almost any environment to their home.

She scarcely even took pleasure in James's purchase of the first Packard in town in a year when there were fewer than eighty thousand automobiles in the entire country. Twice in *Long Day's Journey Into Night* Mary Tyrone disparages the car as "secondhand." If the car was indeed secondhand, it did not appear to diminish Eugene's pleasure. Fondly recalling the Packard shortly before he conceived *Ah, Wilderness!*, O'Neill wrote:

"My father . . . always got me the classiest rowboat to be had, and we sported the first Packard car in our section of Conn., way back in the duster-goggles era." He went on to describe himself as "an A One snob when it came to cars and boats, which must have speed, line & class or 'we are not amused.' This snootiness dates back to early boyhood days."

The sort of carefree, duster-and-goggles outings indulged in by the Millers in *Ah, Wilderness!* were simply beyond the O'Neill family, and Ella was usually chauffeured on drives alone. Eugene and Jamie, when feeling devilish, appropriated the car for themselves. The brothers once got the car "up to a mite over 40. A great day — from which the car never fully recovered!"

In spite of James's uncharacteristic largess in the matter of cars and boats and good clothes, the seventeen-year-old Eugene had virtually no pocket money and often had to borrow a nickel from a friend for trolley fare.

Evidently too arrogant, or lethargic, to take on a menial summer job while awaiting his grand entrance into Princeton, Eugene had no source of income but what he could earn from his father for trimming the hedge that surrounded Monte Cristo Cottage: fifty cents for a good day's work that was supposed to teach him the value of money.

Neither Jamie nor Eugene could comprehend their father's satisfaction in doing his own work about the grounds. James stoutly maintained he found it relaxing to tend his own lawn and shrubbery and that no "lazy loafer" he could hire would do it half as well. His sons accused him of trying to save money on help. Similarly, James's refusal to avail himself of the city's water supply (because, he claimed, it was not pure enough) in favor of an old well on his property, was mocked by his sons as a niggardly reluctance to pay water taxes.

Although his cash was restricted, Eugene managed to pay his way at the Montauk Inn, the prototype for the tavern in *Ah, Wilderness!* as well as the offstage barroom in *A Moon for the Misbegotten*. Other teenagers who accompanied him to the inn, which had upstairs rooms, later recalled it as an inelegant establishment on the corner of Montauk Avenue at the fringe of New London's stylish residential district, and a brisk walk from Monte Cristo Cottage.

A player piano provided tinny background music for the coachmen and farmers, and the occasional prostitute, like Belle in *Ah, Wilderness!*, who was partial to sloe gin. Behind the bar hung a pair of boxing gloves the proprietor vowed had been worn by John L. Sullivan when he won his final, seventy-five-round bout with Jake Kilrain in 1889 — oblivious of Sullivan's use of bare knuckles.

One of the inn's regular customers was a salty Irish immigrant known as John ("Dirty") Dolan, on whom O'Neill based a major character, Phil Hogan, in *A Moon for the Misbegotten*, set in 1923. Hogan's uproarious encounter with a millionaire estate owner, in the play called T. Stedman Harder, was drawn from an account O'Neill heard at first hand in the inn in 1912.

T. Stedman Harder confronts Phil Hogan to complain his pigs have infringed on the estate's ice pond (from which, in the winter, blocks of ice were sawed and stored in silos to last through the warm weather). Harder, it seems, does not care for the taste of pork in his drinking water. Hogan attempts to turn the tables by accusing Harder of knocking down his own fences to lure the pigs into his ice pond to give them pneumonia. The same episode also occurs in *Long Day's Journey Into Night*, but as exposition, and with Hogan's name altered to "Shaughnessy" and Harder's to "Harker."

The disreputable Irish farmer who so delighted Eugene with his impudence was a tenant of James O'Neill. Having settled in New London in the late 1880's, "Dirty" Dolan had worked as a coachman before switching to pig farming, with garbage collecting as a sideline.

In 1912 he settled on an unkempt parcel of land off Niles Hill Road that straddled the border of New London and the adjoining town of Waterford, for which he paid James thirty-five dollars a month. A combination of pasture and swamp flanked a ramshackle house and an outbuilding or two. The tract had been bought by James in 1909 as one of his real estate investments. Living in a style not much different from that of James's own family upon their arrival in Buffalo fifty years earlier, Dolan shared his house with his second wife, two daughters and two sons, along with several pigs and a brood of chickens.

Short, thickset and round-shouldered, he shaved only occasionally and wore filthy overalls and a tattered brown hat. He had a lust for the bottle and, though he could not write his name, he had a quick wit, delivered in a thick brogue, that was the joy of his drinking companions. He chose to be followed wherever he went by a worshipful Saint Bernard.

In creating Dolan's millionaire adversary, T. Stedman Harder, O'Neill drew on the backgrounds of two Waterford estate owners whom he held in almost equal contempt. One was Edward Stephen Harkness, whose father had joined John D. Rockefeller in founding the Standard Oil Company, the most powerful and despotic monopoly of its day.

The Harkness property, known as "Eolia," consisted of 235 acres, a forty-two-room mansion, formal gardens and assorted barns, greenhouses, caretakers' cottages and stables. It was run by twenty indoor servants, including three butlers, and an additional staff of forty groundskeepers, including vegetable and flower gardeners, chauffeurs, dairymen and watchmen.

But the real-life owner of the ice pond invaded by the real-life Dolan's pigs was a railroad tycoon named Edward Crowninshield Hammond. His own estate, Walnut Grove Farm, while somewhat less imposing than Eolia, also fronted on Long Island Sound. Hammond had created his ice pond by damming a brook that ran through his own property and the land farmed by Dolan.

The moody Eugene, in his youthful radicalism, held a grudge against Standard Oil and millionaires in general, and the thought of grubby old Dolan standing up to, and actually routing, a Yankee millionaire, was enough to send him into gales of laughter that echoed in his mind for years.

O'Neill forever dwelled on the landmarks — both physical and emotional — of his New London youth, just as he often pointed out to friends his birthplace in New York. Despite his often-asserted insistence that he resented New London's small-town narrow-mindedness —"It wasn't a friendly town," he once remarked — he was far from wishing to forget it.

CHAPTER
FIFTEEN

Even WHEN EUGENE'S MOTHER WAS BETWEEN CURES AND free of morphine, as she was during the summer of 1906, she shrank from social contacts, was loath to entertain at home and rarely ventured out. James, having accustomed himself to her wish for seclusion, continued to seek companionship in his clubs and in hotel barrooms, where he invariably exuded good cheer.

Every now and then, however, when Ella felt up to it, she would join James in a stroll along Pequot Avenue. At other times, accompanied by Jamie, she called on her Brennan and Sheridan relatives, all children or grandchildren of her mother's sister, long since deceased. But not even they were permitted close enough to penetrate the enigmatic web of Ella's illness. That was a secret world inhabited only by the four O'Neills.

"My family's quarrels and tragedy were within," O'Neill confided to his older son, Eugene Jr., four years after completing *Long Day's Journey Into Night*. "To the outer world we maintained an indomitably united front and lied and lied for each other. A typical pure Irish family. The same loyalty occurs, of course, in all kinds of families, but there is, I think, among Irish still close to, or born in Ireland, a strange mixture of fight and hate and forgive, a clannish pride before the world, that is peculiarly its own."

This "clannish pride" was at its fiercest when concealing the shame of Ella's addiction. And while Eugene and Jamie were steadfast in their loyalty to one another, the "indomitably united front" did sometimes slip with regard to the father and his sons. James was known to grumble outside the home about Jamie's heavy drinking and Eugene's defiance of convention, and both boys griped to friends about their father's tightfistedness.

A few of Ella's younger relatives, who lived to witness the publication of *Long Day's Journey Into Night*, found themselves in the uncomfortable position of having to defend, out of that very loyalty and family pride, a situation they had barely guessed existed. Nor did they relish coming to Ella's defense, for they resented her having held them at arm's length. Even so, they indignantly disputed the portrait of Ella in the play.

Two granddaughters of Elizabeth Brennan, contemporaries of Eugene and Jamie, denied, for instance, that Ella would ever have permitted her husband or sons to keep a whiskey bottle on a living-room table, as is the case in *Long Day's Journey Into Night*. Most of Ella's relatives preferred James to his wife and were vocal in his defense, insisting in particular that he was never stingy to his sons.

"The boys wore only tailor-made suits," Bessie Sheridan pointed out. "And the O'Neills had a chauffeur and, before that, a coachman." She added that she had "always liked Gene — he was a fine boy, simple and good — until he wrote this disgraceful book [*Long Day's Journey Into Night*]." Her married sister, Irene Moran, expressed similar indignation.

In 1914, when Eugene published a collection of one-act plays under the title, *Thirst*, an aunt of the Sheridan sisters, Josephine Brennan, threw the book into the furnace. "I like a clean taste in my mouth," she declared. O'Neill expressed his contempt for the relatives of an idealistic man in a 1921 play, *The First Man*. They were depicted as capable of judging others only by the standards of their own limited experience, and bound by petty pride and stultifying conventionality.

The recollections of another of Elizabeth Brennan's granddaughters, who was ten years younger than Ella, are more poignantly revealing. Lillian Brennan, who served as part-model for Lily in *Ah, Wilderness!*, having fallen victim to senile dementia, was confined to a nursing home in Norwich, Connecticut, not far from New London.

In 1957 her doctor agreed to allow the authors of this biography to visit her, but cautioned she was in no condition to be "interviewed." The meeting would probably prove futile, he said, for Lillian, at eighty-nine, was out of touch with reality. Much of the time she alternated between periods of blank withdrawal and delusional babble. It was true that every so often she would lapse into a dreamlike state to relive scenes from her earlier life, but those intervals were rare.

The visitors upon entering her room found Lillian seated in a chair, in animated conversation with someone visible only to her. She was graphically reliving the late 1800's and early 1900's, believing herself to be in her thirties. She spoke of what she thought were recent events and of people she believed were still alive.

With the doctor's concurrence, her visitors interjected a gentle question about Ella O'Neill and were rewarded with a vividly authoritative tintype of Ella as a young matron, already troubled by the demands of her unsettled life.

"Mama always says, 'Be nice to Ella, she has a difficult life,'" Lillian declared. "Mama never can see any wrong in anyone, but Ella O'Neill keeps to herself; she passes me in the street and doesn't even notice me."

With childish malice she added, "She's stuck-up, that's what she is, stuck-up! And she touches up her hair! When I go back to New York next week, I'm going to tell Agnes what she said to me."

The period she recalled was 1907 and Agnes was her sister who had died at eighty. They had lived in New York City for a while, Agnes studying the piano and Lillian trying to establish herself as a milliner. She thought if she could persuade Ella to become her customer she could use this prestige to attract other fashionable women. "Do you know what Ella said when I asked her to buy some hats from me? She said she bought her hats at Bendel, but she'd give me her old ones to make over and sell. I was never so insulted!"

Only someone as young and naive as Lillian would have expected Ella O'Neill to buy homemade hats. Ella's hats, like her dresses, were the last word in expensive good taste. She rarely went outdoors without a veil as well. Her relatives believed she wore it to protect her smooth, white complexion against sun and wind, but she might have had another reason: to hide the morphine-induced brightness of her eyes.

These same relatives gossiped about Ella's vanity in wearing fifty-dollar French corsets. Ella did not aspire to a sylphlike figure, striving rather to emulate the buxom and corseted Lillian Russell, the era's model for young matrons. But Ella once cautioned the mother of Bessie and Irene Sheridan, "Don't ever let yourself weigh over a hundred and forty-five pounds."

The awe Ella inspired in her relatives did not compensate for the snubbing she endured from the elite of New London, who persisted in regarding the O'Neills as beneath their notice.

"I've always hated this town and everyone in it," says Mary Tyrone in *Long Day's Journey Into Night*. And in a scenario for the earlier *Mourning Becomes Electra*, in which O'Neill identified the setting as New London, he wrote of Christine Mannon (the disguised representation of Ella O'Neill): "Christine has always hated the town of N.L. and felt a superior disdain for its inhabitants."

The condescension of New London's upper crust was based partly on James's peasant-Irish background, partly on what they regarded as his unsavory career as a "road" actor and, finally, on his unpretentious mode of living.

The same families that shunned the O'Neills eagerly socialized with Richard Mansfield and his wife. But Mansfield, ten years James's junior, had become a star of considerably greater stature soon after his arrival from England. He had, like James — but six years later — made his New York debut under the auspices of A. M. Palmer in a French melodrama at the Union Square Theater and become an overnight star.

Holding himself to the highest standards, Mansfield went on to play classical roles; he not only had made a great success in Rostand's *Cyrano de Bergerac,* but he had summoned the courage to perform both Shaw and Ibsen — knowing he would be lambasted by New York's preeminent critic, William Winter, who had nothing but contempt for their work.

Mansfield was, moreover, as arrogant as any of New London's first families. Demonstrating he knew how to live well, he occupied not one but two elaborate estates diagonally across Ocean Avenue from each other, one called Seven Acres and the other the Grange, where he held his formal dinner parties. He created a coat of arms for himself, displaying it prominently above the mantlepiece — clasped hands over the word, *Maintenant,* with its double meaning of "Now" and "Main Tenant." He often affected a monocle and a cape, and in his twin roles as lionized leading man and country squire, he, too, looked down on the O'Neills.

Other local families who snubbed the O'Neills included the Chappells, whose prominence derived from coal and lumber. Eugene O'Neill never forgave the Chappells for snubbing his mother, although he did not bother, in any play, to subject them to the sneering, full-dress treatment he reserved for the Harknesses and the Hammonds, symbols for him of the robber barons who exploited the working class.

In *Long Day's Journey Into Night* the Chappells (disguised as the Chatfields) are casually referred to by Mary Tyrone as "big frogs in a small puddle." The reference was ruefully acknowledged years later by one of the younger members of the Chappell family, in recalling New London parochialism in the early 1900's.

Edith Chappell Sheffield told of a time when her mother, returning in her Victoria from a drive that took her past the O'Neill house, remarked, "My, I certainly had a sweeping bow from James O'Neill." But, she added, her mother would not have dreamed of calling upon Ella.

"We considered the O'Neills shanty Irish," Edith Sheffield confessed, "and we associated the Irish, almost automatically, with the servant class. As a matter of fact, I remember being very upset when I first started going to church — my father became a Catholic convert — and I recognized only servants in the church. 'Why do we go to the Irish church?' I remember asking my mother, to her embarrassment. We were among the few Catholic families considered acceptable."

When O'Neill, some years after achieving fame as a dramatist, visited Doc Ganey in New London to reminisce about the days of the Second Story Club, he revealed a fantasy of revenge harbored since boyhood: "You know, I always wanted to make money. My motive was to be able, someday, to hire a tally-ho and fill it full of painted whores, load each whore with a bushel of dimes and let them throw the money to the rabble on a Saturday afternoon; we'd ride down State Street and toss money to people like the Chappells. Now that I've made as much as I need, I've lost interest."

This professed indifference was later belied in his work. His venom for elite New Londoners was aimed not only at his contemporaries (as in *Long Day's Journey Into Night* and *A Moon for the Misbegotten*) but at their early 19th century forebears, the "Yankee skinflints" (as in *A Touch of the Poet*), who rebuffed the prideful Irish protagonist, Cornelius Melody.

Despite New London society's ostracism of the O'Neills, James, somewhat surprisingly, was accepted as a member of the selective Thames Club, founded by New London's leading businessmen. Mansfield, of course, was a member, as were most of the town's prominent male residents. Aside from James, however, only a handful of Irish gained admittance.

James did not disgrace his nationality and, within the club's dignified chambers, was treated with respect. During the summer he visited the club two or three times a week, sometimes bringing an actor friend.

The club's Irish bartender, Jim Shay, recalled that James habitually ordered bourbon and milk, and that he often bought drinks for any other members who happened to be at the bar. His manner was courtly and genial and he invariably raised his glass in the same toast. "Sunny days and starry nights," he would say, in his deep, lilting voice, flashing the dazzling O'Neill smile. He confined himself to only two or three drinks at the club. His serious drinking took place in the less formal atmosphere of hotel barrooms, where he was always boisterously welcomed.

A particular favorite with the town's Irish, James had been asked more than once to run for mayor. He declined on the ground that his career would leave him insufficient time to discharge his mayoral duties. One reason he was championed was his conviction that the town could become a major terminal for transatlantic traffic — a port city second only to New York and Boston in wealth and prestige. There were, in fact, grounds for this belief. For one thing, the town's three-mile-long harbor was large and deep enough to accommodate ocean liners.

The Boston Sunday Journal reported it was "doubtful if there is another citizen in New London who is more enthusiastic about the city than is Mr. O'Neill." The newspaper explained he had invested "a great deal in real estate about the town and has watched its growth carefully during the last ten years." Even to business heads more level than James's, New London seemed destined for a great future.

James could not foresee the opposition that was to arise from a group of influential estate owners determined to keep New London a noncommercial, exclusive playground. Although several attempts were made by business tycoons — J. P. Morgan was one — to realize New London's commercial potential, they came to nothing, as did many of James's local investments.

While his sons accused him of scrimping on the family's needs, James seemed always to have ready cash to buy property, and was likely to describe himself, not without pride, as "land poor."

Eugene O'Neill's portrait of his father as a miser in *Long Day's Journey Into Night* has been disputed not only by relatives but by many of James's old New London friends, and O'Neill knew this would be the case. Indeed, he took it into consideration in his final play, *A Moon for the Misbegotten*, as part of an exchange between Jim Tyrone and Hogan's daughter, Josie, who contests Jim's disparagement of his father as "an old bastard."

> JOSIE: He wasn't! He was one of the finest, kindest gentlemen ever lived.
> JIM TYRONE (*sneeringly*): Outside the family, sure. Inside, he was a lousy, tightwad bastard.

Of all the bars in town, the Crocker House was James's favorite. A bustling and convivial hotel on State Street, the Crocker House was always packed during the summer months with the town's eminent businessmen, millionaires off their yachts, and Coast Guard cadets. William Randolph Hearst could be found there on occasion, along with various Morgans off their yacht, Corsair. The Whitney and Astor yachts sometimes dropped anchor in the Thames and their passengers, too, were likely to patronize the Crocker House bar.

James held court there in the afternoons and often on into the evenings. One of his loyal cronies was Captain Nathaniel (Nat) Keeney, a Yankee sailor with a weathered face, a spicy vocabulary and an endless repertory of improbable stories. He, too, turns up in *Long Day's Journey Into Night* — as Captain Turner and (under his own name) as Captain Keeney, in O'Neill's early one-act play, "Ile."

James, whose own language was restrained, and who would not have dreamed of swearing before a lady, relished Captain Keeney's uninhibited speech. Nearly everyone, in fact, tolerated his lapses.

One story was told of Keeney's neighbor, a prudish spinster, who complained to him that a shopkeeper had insulted her by shouting, "Keep your shirt on." Keeney listened sympathetically, then said, "Did that goddam sonofabitch say that to you?" "Yes, he did, Captain Keeney," replied the spinster, not turning a hair.

Captain Keeney and his wife lived at 347 Pequot Avenue only two doors south of the O'Neills. On their front lawn they displayed a bed of foliage shaped into a large anchor. The small Keeney grandchildren were frequent visitors and one of them, Frances, retained vivid memories of James and Ella O'Neill.

As she later wrote in an informal essay, she and her younger brother used to "see Mr. and Mrs. O'Neill coming down the avenue, arm in arm." James, she noted, wore a dark suit and she remembered Ella dressed "in pink chiffon," her bearing "queenly." Although her hair was white, wrote Frances, "no queen could satisfy a little girl better."

Frances went on to write: "We get the signal from Grandpa that we may run down . . . to meet them." James could always be counted on to clown a bit. Ella "does not speak, but as she sees our glee, there is her lovely smile, all in modest fashion, typical of that quiet beauty of hers." Keeney's granddaughter did not date this long-ago summer, but it was clearly in the early 1900's during a period when Ella was relatively calm.

Captain Keeney, to whom James presented a sword he said he

had brandished as Edmond Dantes, was only one among James's local boon companions. Another was a portly, white-haired, frock-coated, silk-hatted, cane-carrying Irishman named Thomas F. Dorsey.

Eugene, once observing him devour two steaks at a sitting, told his friend, Art McGinley, that Dorsey should be between the covers of a book — and later put him there, calling him McGuire, in *Long Day's Journey Into Night*. Dorsey was a lawyer and real-estate promoter with a reputation as a wag.

In spite of his local fame, however, Dorsey could not gain admission to the Thames Club and James regularly met him at the Crocker House. Their relationship was not purely social. It was Dorsey who sold James the bulk of his New London real estate — often plots or buildings on which James lost money. The consummation of these deals (referred to in *Long Day's Journey*) was necessarily accompanied by endless talk and consumption of liquor (for which James habitually paid).

If, as often happened, they had not finished when the bars closed at eleven, James availed himself of a special arrangement he had with the Crocker House night clerk, a tall, thin young man named Alexander Campbell, who happened to be a friend of Eugene's and a member of the Second Story Club. James could usually persuade Campbell to set out a bottle for him and Dorsey in one of the hotel's offices.

Dorsey had a wonderful time selling James property and James never held it against him that the purchases seldom showed a profit. Eugene and his brother, however, resented it and Jamie often asked Dorsey, albeit in an offhand, contemptuous manner, to stop selling land to his gullible father.

While Jamie had his own coterie at the Crocker House, he did not inspire anything like the devotion shown to his father, but he could make people laugh when he was in the mood. He particularly relished gallows humor and seized on the murder in Manhattan of the architect, Stanford White, the dominant topic during the summer of 1906.

Jamie boasted that he knew Evelyn Nesbit, the flamboyant showgirl married to Harry K. Thaw, who in a jealous rage shot White on June 25 at Madison Square Garden. Professing to have inside knowledge of the affair, Jamie held his barroom cronies spellbound. Private testimony not yet published, he told them, revealed that Evelyn Nesbit, while unconscious, had been ravished seven times by Stanford White.

His eager listeners wondered how, if she had been unconscious, such an explicit count could have been established. Jamie, talking out of the side of his mouth as he often did for effect, replied with deliberate vulgarity that Nesbit had a taxi meter affixed to a specific part of her anatomy.

Jamie never learned to stand his liquor as well as his father, who still drank a daily quart without showing it, and boasted that whiskey never caused him to miss a performance. Jamie, with his more compulsive craving, was constantly battling his father on the subject. Although James at times had recourse to a shot or two before breakfast, he saw no reason why Jamie should emulate him.

He fought a losing fight, however, to limit Jamie's consumption. A New London relative who was Eugene's age, Phil Sheridan, brother of Irene and Bessie, was a witness to this contest. Close to the O'Neills since his boyhood, Sheridan remembered passing Monte Cristo Cottage one day when James, out cutting the hedge, invited him in for a drink.

"Jamie eyed the bottle with his tongue hanging out, while the Old Man poured me a drink," recalled Sheridan. But Jamie (as depicted by his brother in *Long Day's Journey Into Night*) often managed to help himself, behind his father's back, to the bottle on the sideboard, afterward watering the depleted whiskey.

Finally, according to Sheridan, James put all his liquor under lock and key in the cellar — a gesture that is mocked, in the play, by the mother, as well as by the two sons. James, however, could often be wheedled into giving both Jamie and Eugene a drink or two.

"He always came through handsomely," O'Neill once said, in this case referring to the times when the family regrouped in New London for the summer. "He'd ask us a few questions we couldn't answer, and then assure us of our general unworthiness and invariably end by saying, 'Well, I suppose you want a drink?'"

It was one of the paradoxes of the O'Neill family dynamics that they simultaneously deplored each other's abuse of alcohol, yet constantly encouraged each other to imbibe. In *Long Day's Journey Into Night*, for example, both James and Jamie Tyrone try — at one moment — to prevent the tubercular Edmund from drinking and — in the next moment — declare a few drinks won't harm him.

Even Mary Tyrone, though she admonishes her husband and sons for their drinking, is secretly pleased when they go off to get drunk, leaving her to escape into her own mode of oblivion.

CHAPTER SIXTEEN

THE CAVALIER ATTITUDE THAT EUGENE BROUGHT TO Princeton was a guarantee of failure. He arrived in September, 1906, with the idea, as he later acknowledged, of "getting through with the smallest possible amount of work." Brilliantly advanced as he was in his reading, he regarded himself as already educated well beyond the tame, ritualized Ivy League agenda.

Eugene's thinking had grown ever more nonconformist, what with Jamie's misanthropic literary guidance, Doc Ganey's esoteric library, and the iconoclastic authors Eugene had discovered on his own. Not long into his first Princeton semester, he grew convinced the lectures he attended were of little value, emanating from a world of stale conventions.

Contemptuous of the prescribed freshman reading lists, he was far more interested in what George Bernard Shaw had to teach him in *The Quintessence of Ibsenism*, a volume he stumbled upon in a New York bookstore toward the end of his final semester at Betts.

Shaw's appraisal of Ibsen as a social reformer opened Eugene's eyes to what the theater could be in the hands of an uncompromising visionary. Even more importantly, it taught him that the artist must be prepared to endure opprobrium for challenging the tenets of state and church.

Shaw articulated the difference between the brave innovator and the stultified, commercially driven conformist who follows the easy road to popular success. His concepts no doubt heightened Eugene's awareness of the contrast between his father as materialist and himself as poetic dreamer. *The Quintessence of Ibsenism* planted in Eugene the seeds of independent, creative thinking and inspired in him the courage an artist needs to believe in himself.

In Ibsen's truth-speaking world (as interpreted by Shaw), Eugene perceived characters who confronted each other with the reality of their cramped and crippled lives, giving the lie to pious doctrines imposed by society. Shaw argued that "masks" concealed the false lives led by those deluded into believing they were content in their rote concession to convention.

Shaw's dissertation, which included synopses of everything Ibsen had written up to that time (including *Hedda Gabler*), was as much a statement of his own dissident philosophy as Ibsen's, and it bolstered Eugene's view of a sanctimonious world.

Alienated as he was, he understood the pain of hiding his own mutinous feelings behind a mask. Although not yet quite eighteen, Eugene had grasped the closely argued, intellectually lofty thesis set forth in the 170-page volume — an expansion of a paper Shaw had presented to the Fabian Society in 1890. Eugene savored the book as a more conventional youth might have relished *Tom Sawyer*. By the time he entered Princeton, *The Quintessence of Ibsenism* had become gospel.

As he began to question the validity of his required courses, Eugene discovered a more relevant substitute syllabus far removed from Ivy League academia. His guide to this unorthodox fount of enlightenment was an exuberant youth his own age named Louis Holladay. Although not himself an undergraduate, Holladay knew several of Eugene's classmates and, recognizing a fellow-rebel in Eugene, took an instant liking to him.

Sandy-haired, with a football player's build, Holladay aspired to be a writer and, like Eugene, read incessantly. He lived on handouts from his mother, Adele, and an older sister, Polly, who had recently opened a cramped, homey cellar café in Greenwich Village that drew writers and artists.

Unlike Eugene, Holladay was a bohemian by birth. His mother was one of the pioneering free spirits of the Village, who had felt herself a misfit amid the proper society of her hometown of Evanston, Illinois. Voluptuous, self-centered and unstable, Adele Holladay had a voracious sexual appetite and flitted from one man to another. There was little affection between her and her son and even less between her and Polly, whom she scorned for her lack of beauty but envied for her madonna-like composure.

Years later, far removed from youthful radical ties, O'Neill often spoke of Holladay, dead by then, as having been his "only real friend." (He was considerably less admiring of Holladay's mother and her "poisonous tongue.")

Holladay vastly expanded Eugene's knowledge of the era's revolutionary ferment by introducing him to the Unique Book Shop on Sixth Avenue near Thirtieth Street. A cluttered establishment, owned by a philosophical anarchist, Benjamin R. Tucker, it was headquarters for New York's radical intellectual life during the blossoming of the socialist idea in America.

In his early fifties then, Tucker was an icon of dissent. A New Englander of Colonial and Quaker ancestry, he had received his calling as a self-styled agitator at eighteen, influenced by the transcendental philosophy of Ralph Waldo Emerson.

Tucker longed to see the State abolished and "all the affairs of men" managed by "individuals or voluntary associations." He espoused "the right of the drunkard, the gambler, the rake and the harlot to live their lives until they shall freely abandon them."

Anarchists of his persuasion, wrote Tucker, "look forward to a time when every individual, whether man or woman, shall be self-supporting . . . when the love relations between these independent individuals shall be as varied as are individual inclinations and attractions; and when the children born of these relations shall belong exclusively to the mothers until old enough to belong to themselves."

Although Tucker proffered no plan for providing equal liberty for all, Eugene was stirred by his utopian credo. He was impressed by the way Tucker put his theories into practice at least for himself — a considerable feat of social defiance in that Victorian era. Tucker rejected religion as well as the formalities of marriage and divorce and lived with a woman by whom he had a child, but never married.

Tucker was the leading spokesman for an American individualist-anarchist movement that advocated attacking the establishment with words. The communist-anarchist movement, led by Prince Peter Kropotkin (who had renounced his title for the cause), espoused the use of force, such as bomb-throwing. Tucker's advocacy of non-violent resistance did not stem from moral scruples; rather, he believed force to be "utterly useless," insisting it was "by means of education that anarchism must grow."

"If, however," he said, "the present perverted order of things could be overthrown by a stroke, and a new and proper order established, I and the anarchists who believe as I do would not oppose such a stroke."

As described in a contemporary newspaper account, Tucker was a "large, fine-looking man" — the "last man one would pick out in a crowd as an anarchist." He was, in fact, "all that is conventional" and "would fit better in the chair of a bank president or the office of a prosperous broker than in a narrow book stall from which is dispensed more anarchist literature than from any other one place in the United States."

With his own limited funds and at no profit, Tucker published European works not previously translated into English, among them *What is Property?* by the French anarchist Pierre Joseph Proudhon, who denounced ownership as "robbery." Eugene studied Proudhon's theory that the ideal republic was "a positive anarchy ... free from all shackles, superstitions, prejudices, sophistries, usury, authority"; this form of anarchy, Proudhon proclaimed, was "reciprocal liberty, and not limited liberty; liberty not the Daughter but the Mother of Order."

Eugene was even more awed by another Tucker publication, *The Ego and His Own*, by the German anarchist, Max Stirner, who undertook to revile every accepted standard of social and ethical behavior.

"A fig for good and evil!" sneered Stirner. "I am I, and I am neither good nor evil. Neither has any meaning for me. The godly is the affair of God, and the human that of humanity. My concern is neither the Godly nor the Human, is not the True, the Good, the Right, The Free, etc., but simply my own self, and it is not general, it is individual, as I myself am individual. For me there is nothing above myself." Stirner's tome, according to Tucker, was "the greatest work of political philosophy and ethics ever written."

Tucker achieved early renown in cultural as well as political circles when, in 1891 in Boston, he became the first American publisher of *The Quintessence of Ibsenism*, issued in London the same year. Tucker also translated and published such controversial European works as Zola's *Money and Modern Marriage*; Mirabeau's *A Chambermaid's Diary*; and Tolstoy's *Kreutzer Sonata*.

Eugene was particularly pleased to learn that Tucker was also the American publisher of Wilde's *The Ballad of Reading Gaol*, for he had long been entranced by *The Picture of Dorian Gray*. Here, again, was the theme of the mask — the debauched inner man represented by a hidden portrait, while outwardly enjoying the benign appearance of an angel. *Dorian Gray*, O'Neill told an early interviewer, "made an indelible impression" and was the result of "responding logically" to the authors he had discovered on his own — authors not part of the college curriculum.

In his spare time, Tucker edited a magazine, Liberty, that Eugene and Holladay read with the zeal of disciples. In its first issue, the magazine declared: "Monopoly and privilege must be destroyed, opportunity afforded, and competition encouraged. This is Liberty's work, and 'Down with Authority' her war cry."

For a time, The Unique Book Shop became Eugene's alternative classroom and Tucker his mentor. He and Holladay found that most of Tucker's patrons were, like themselves, young men who enjoyed browsing for hours among the books and pamphlets crowding the shelves and listening to Tucker expound on arcane points of his philosophy. These devotees were described in a contemporary newspaper account as "well dressed, seemingly well educated . . . whose mental processes have led them into out of the way or unconventional intellectual channels."

From his browsing Eugene learned how Tucker first defined his stand, at the time of the Homestead Strike in 1892. In protest against the strike, Alexander Berkman, a militant-anarchist armed with an arsenal of revolver, dynamite and poisoned dagger, shot and stabbed (but failed to kill) the steel magnate, Henry Clay Frick.

Tucker declined to defend Berkman's act or to protest his imprisonment, thereby infuriating Berkman's lover and champion, Emma Goldman, the fiery labor organizer who had herself served a year in prison for inciting to riot.

"The hope of humanity," Tucker wrote at the time, "lies in the avoidance of that revolution by force which the Berkmans are trying to precipitate. No pity for Frick, no praise for Berkman — such is the attitude of Liberty in the present crisis."

Berkman's release after a fourteen-year imprisonment revived the debate in the fractured anarchist world. Tempestuous and long-suffering, the ardent revolutionist Emma Goldman considered Tucker heartless. How could anyone calling himself a believer in anarchy fail to endorse Berkman's high-minded and selfless attempt to remove a villain like Frick? In her fervid and humorless autobiography, she described Berkman's botched assassination attempt on Frick as an "heroic deed."

Goldman's fury was aroused, not by Berkman's failure to finish off Frick with three bullets and a stab wound to the thigh, but by the fact that Berkman had been "pounded into unconsciousness" by Frick's rescuers. She grew even more indignant when her former mentor, Johann Most, a prominent anarchist leader, dismissed Berkman's deed as not noteworthy and suggested that he had used a toy gun.

Eugene evidently did not share Tucker's contempt for either

Berkman or Goldman and sympathized with their courage. He became a faithful reader of Goldman's magazine, Mother Earth, first published in March, 1906, and was entranced by Goldman's letterhead slogan:

"The philosophy of a new social order based on liberty unrestricted by man-made law; the theory that all forms of government rest on violence, and are therefore wrong and harmful, as well as unnecessary."

Long after the anarchist movement in America had withered, O'Neill could still respond graciously to the old cause. In 1928, he agreed to contribute to the Emma Goldman Fund established by friends to enable her to write her memoirs. A year earlier, O'Neill had granted Berkman permission to translate his play, *Lazarus Laughed*, into Russian. Reminiscing about their first meeting in a Greenwich Village restaurant (probably around 1916), O'Neill wrote with the generosity he could always summon for the downtrodden:

"Yes, it is a long time since that night at Romany Marie's! But I am quite sure that you do not remember me better than I do you . . . I had had a very deep admiration for you for years, and that meeting was sort of an unexpected wish fulfillment. As for my fame, (God help us!) and your infame, I would be willing to exchange a good deal of mine for a bit of yours. It is not so hard to write what one feels as truth. It is damned hard to live it!"

Further evidence that violent anarchism was less repugnant to O'Neill than to Tucker can be found in the early play, *The Personal Equation* (1915). In it, O'Neill, not unsympathetically, examines the forces that drove the early militant labor movement, along with Tucker's nonviolent anarchism. The play, later disavowed by O'Neill, is an undigested mash of Ibsenism and Tuckerism, as well as melodramatic devices from the theater of James O'Neill.

More successfully, O'Neill used elements from his early anarchist education in *The Hairy Ape* to create the ship's stoker, the victim of a materialistic world. It was not until O'Neill wrote *The Iceman Cometh* in 1939, however, that he succeeded in humanizing the abstract anarchist philosophy he had absorbed from Tucker in 1906 and 1907. (During rehearsals for the 1946 Broadway production, O'Neill quipped, "I am a philosophical anarchist, which means, 'Go to it, but leave me out of it.'")

Tucker's most pivotal contribution to Eugene's education was to focus him (for better or worse) on Friedrich Nietzsche's *Thus Spake Zarathustra*. When nearly forty and established as America's leading dramatist, O'Neill wrote to a friend that *Zarathustra* had influenced him "more than any book" he had ever read.

"I ran into it," he said, "through the book shop of Benjamin Tucker, the old philosophical anarchist . . . and I've always possessed a copy since then and every year or so I reread it and am never disappointed, which is more than I can say of almost any other book." He admitted, however, that while he had always admired *Zarathustra* "as a work of art," there were "aspects of its teaching I no longer concede."

The son and grandson of Lutheran pastors, Nietzsche — who died in 1900 — underwent a loss of faith at eighteen comparable to Eugene's and became a devastating critic of Christianity and its ideals. The youthful Eugene was inclined to swallow whole Nietzsche's impious teaching, adopting it as his new Catechism.

Instead of the Catechism's "What is man? Man is a creature made up of a rational soul and an organic body," Eugene embraced Nietzsche's "Man is a rope stretched between the animal and the Superman — a rope over an abyss." Instead of "What is a rational soul? A rational soul is a spiritual substance, endowed with intellect and free will, and immortal," Eugene seized upon *Zarathustra*'s: "'Body am I, and soul'— so saith the child. And why should one not speak like children? . . . the awakened one, the knowing one, saith: 'Body am I entirely, and nothing more; and soul is only the name of something in the body.'"

For the Golden Rule's "Love thy neighbor as thyself," Eugene substituted Nietzsche's enjoinder: "Do I advise you to neighbor-love? Rather do I advise you to neighbor-flight and to furthest love! Higher than love to your neighbor is love to the furthest and future ones; higher still than love to men, is love to things and phantoms . . . My brethren, I advise you not to neighbor-love — I advise you to furthest love!"

Having already rejected the "life-denying spirit of Christianity" — as he was to characterize it in his 1925 play, *The Great God Brown* — Eugene eagerly substituted the laughing, life-affirming Nietzschean deity and committed passages of *Zarathustra* to memory.

Indeed, Eugene's life eerily began to mirror the German philosopher's: first in such small ways as the drooping black mustache he affected in his twenties, then in the solitude of his most creative years and the prodigious demands he made upon himself.

Finally, like Nietzsche, he appeared to take somber pride in being misunderstood, ending his life in emotional and physical collapse.

CHAPTER
SEVENTEEN

AFTER GULPING LARGE DOSES OF BENJAMIN TUCKER'S philosophical brew, it is hardly surprising that Eugene found Princeton bland if not irrelevant. While he had nothing personal against Woodrow Wilson, then Princeton's president, he concluded that the university was inordinately tradition-bound and self-consciously superior.

There is little doubt Eugene had matriculated to please (or at least propitiate) his father. But he also had no idea what else to do with his life. Unlike Jamie, who had been devoted to his college studies — if not to the rules of decorum — Eugene was both unstudious and indecorous during his brief stay at Princeton.

For the first time, he had to cope with an unstructured academic environment, unlike his earlier experiences at Betts Academy and the Catholic schools that had watched over him since the age of seven. He was now presumed to possess the maturity to impose his own scholastic discipline. The presumption was unfounded. Despite his intellectual worldliness, he appeared to be less stable emotionally than the average Princeton freshman.

Eugene arrived on campus September 20, 1906, and left the following June. He had the grace to confess, seven years later, that he was not proud of his record: "I succeeded in paying so little attention to the laws regarding attendance, etc. that I was 'flunked out' at the end of Freshman year for over-cutting."

He tried to articulate his dissatisfaction with the curriculum some years later — after he had wandered the world and achieved his first Broadway success. At Princeton, he explained, he felt "instinctively" that he and his fellow students "were not in touch with life or on the trail of the real things." Perhaps, he added, "I was merely lazy. Who knows just what is going on inside of him?"

Eugene found Princeton not only dull but clannish. While he grudgingly wore the black beanie and black tie required of all 350 freshmen, he refrained from any word or deed that might be misinterpreted as school spirit. Instead, he did his best to establish that his soul flew free.

To this end, he once engaged in an hallucinatory experiment inspired by Marie Corelli's torrid novel, *Wormwood, A Drama of Paris*. In the story, the son of a French banker falls victim to "absinthemania," a common addiction at the time of the book's publication in London in 1890.

Having refused to accompany two friends into town, Eugene, cradling a bottle of absinthe, shut himself into his dormitory suite one flight up at University Hall, where he had been allotted a sparsely furnished study and small bedroom with an iron cot.

According to a reminiscence by two of his classmates, Warren H. Hastings and Richard F. Weeks, the absinthe, prohibited by Federal law, was brought from Greenwich Village by Louis Holladay, who had been invited by Eugene to spend the weekend.

Eugene lit some incense, covered a light bulb in red paper and began to drink. "It was around 4 o'clock in the afternoon," wrote Hastings and Weeks, "when Holladay, in great agitation, hunted up O'Neill's particular friends" and led them to his room. "O'Neill had gone berserk. The room was found in a shambles with O'Neill glassy-eyed and still in a frenzy so great it took three to pin him to the floor when he shortly collapsed and was put to bed."

Attempting to throw a chair out the large window in his study, Eugene had shattered it against the window frame. "Retrieving a chair leg," wrote Hastings and Weeks, "he had gone to his bedroom and smashed his washbowl, pitcher and jar. He had pulled out every drawer of his bureau and tossed their contents about the room."

While the episode, according to Hastings and Weeks, "never leaked to the University," it unnerved his classmates, as did subsequent bouts of heavy drinking.

Convinced that most Princetonians were far too straight-laced to comprehend his rebellious nature, Eugene never went out of his way to make friends. But in three freshmen he discovered sparks of an adventurous spirit, and to them he deigned to be offhandedly charming. The three were often in his company throughout his abbreviated stay at Princeton, despite the disapproval of their peers and even though they themselves tended to be flabbergasted by his behavior and opinions.

The three — Ralph Horton, Tom Welsh and Al Zimmermann — were roommates and, by their own accounts, had enjoyed conventional boyhoods. None would have dreamed of questioning the orthodoxies of university life.

"Princeton was a difficult place to get along in with only three or four friends," said Horton in recalling Eugene's willful isolation. "Gene wasn't popular. He wouldn't put himself out to make friends, and as a result he didn't have many."

Horton, Welsh and Zimmermann encountered understandable obstacles in trying to get Eugene accepted by their eating club. At that time, freshmen ate in "The Commons," on the ground floor of University Hall. It was customary for groups of twenty to fifty kindred freshmen to organize themselves into a club, so that members could regularly dine together on well-prepared food in a room off "The Commons."

Clubs were distinguished by the color of the hats worn by their members, who were permitted to discard their black beanies at the end of February. Non-club members were relegated to a non-convivial communal area with an indifferent institutional menu. Horton, Welsh and Zimmermann joined the elite White Hat club and, after making friends with Eugene, proposed him for membership.

Eugene was promptly blackballed.

His three friends suspected the reason was partly his reputation as a radical and partly his pose of aloofness. But principally, his peers were wary of him because of his wild drinking (although never again in his dormitory room after the absinthe episode).

Despite the rebuff from the White Hats, Eugene's friends remained loyal. They continued to propose him for membership on successive Monday election nights, invariably with negative results.

Welsh, the club's president and a popular freshman football player, at last found a way. He appointed Horton and Zimmermann as tellers and, when Eugene's name was resubmitted, they simply ignored the negative votes and pronounced him elected. Those who had voted against him were puzzled but chose not to make an issue of the fraud. For the rest of the semester Eugene dined wearing a white hat.

Eugene's dormitory room was a magnet for Horton, Welsh and Zimmermann, as well as for Weeks and Hastings, on whom Eugene consented to smile darkly. With bravado fueled by alcohol, he was apt to hold forth by the hour, quoting poetry and philosophy with supreme self-assurance and gesturing largely.

He sometimes climbed upon a table to expound on religion, literature and politics. His words were didactic, rendered more impressive by a halting delivery that had become characteristic.

He spoke, as Elizabeth Sergeant once observed, "rather in pauses than in sentences." With cheeks flushed and dark eyes flashing, he seemed to his five rapt disciples the embodiment of the smoldering Black Irishman, whose unleashed dreams they barely comprehended.

In one typical harangue, Eugene proclaimed himself an atheist. "If there is a God," he bellowed, "let Him strike me dead!" His audience could not suppress shudders. "I was eighteen at the time," Weeks recalled, "and I was afraid that God would heed him."

On another occasion, Eugene announced he was not, after all, an atheist but rather an agnostic. With more fervor than originality, he explained that the human mind was incapable of comprehending infinity and there had to be something beyond the human mind — and that something might be God. But despite his expressions of scorn, he was obliged to make a formal concession to religion. Attendance at chapel was compulsory every other Sunday and twice during the week. Each student was obliged to hand a signed card to the clergyman as a check on his obedience.

"Sometimes we'd try to slip Saint Peter, as we called the clergyman, two cards — one to cover up for an absent friend," Horton recalled. But there were times when the ruse failed, and Eugene had to sit through a number of sermons by Dr. Henry Van Dyke, who in 1900 had left his Presbyterian pastorate in New York to become a professor of English literature.

Van Dyke did not impress Eugene then or later. Twenty-five years after leaving Princeton, O'Neill wrote to a friend: "I hold Van Dyke in grudging memory because his sermons were so irritatingly stupid that they prevented me from sleeping."

While he was forced to attend chapel, Eugene flouted every college rule he could. "Gene was lawless, as far as the university was concerned," Weeks said. "He would take books out of the library and never return them. One time I got a book out for him and after he left Princeton — with the book — the library got after me. I wrote Gene and he sent back the book — to my surprise."

Weeks was amazed by Eugene's reckless class cutting and persistent barroom carousing. Free for the first time to drink when he pleased, he discovered what Jamie had learned long since: alcohol brought oblivion from the ever-present pain of childhood. At

Princeton he established a pattern of binge drinking that evolved into the pervasive alcoholism that hounded him until he was past forty.

While his classmates patronized a traditional college-town bar on Nassau Street called "Doc" Boyce's, Eugene preferred a shabby working-class tavern on Alexander Street, described by Hastings and Weeks as a "dump." When, on occasion, he was accompanied by classmates to the bars of Trenton, he shocked them by drinking hard liquor. They adhered to table wine or beer, holding that "only bums drank the other stuff."

One night in a Trenton barroom, Eugene attempted to demonstrate his prowess as a boozer to Horton and Weeks. Waving off his customary Old-Fashioneds, he told the bartender, "I want something to knock the top of my head off."

The bartender obliged with a libation called a Yale Punch. Horton and Weeks ordered the same and, although neither ever discovered its ingredients, it had the desired effect. A less potent drink (for lean days) was English stone ale. It came in tall stone bottles and, as Horton and Weeks remembered, it approximated the kick of four beers.

In one extended absence from the campus, Eugene and a classmate (who in an interview for this biography requested anonymity) headed for New York. When they returned a week later, they boasted to Weeks and Horton about their self-bestowed holiday with two whores in a brownstone in the upper Twenties. Eugene sometimes returned from New York with licentious tales of his brother's escapades, once captivating his friends with details of how Jamie and a fellow actor conducted a weekend orgy with two popular actresses.

On another New York excursion, accompanied by Horton, Eugene pointed with pride to a two-dollar house, where, he said, lived an "older woman" who was in love with him. He gloated about other conquests — a married woman in New London and several accommodating women in Trenton. One was known to campus sophisticates as the Widow of Nassau Hall; Eugene was apt to take offense if anyone spoke of her slightingly.

"He had a pessimistic attitude toward the female species," wrote Hastings and Weeks. "He would shock his friends by declaiming that 'there is not such a thing as a virgin after the age of fourteen.' His friends' reaction was readily understandable. It was the era of chaperones, when a girl invited to a football game was usually accompanied by a young married friend."

Now and then, Eugene took Horton with him to New York's

Hotel Lucerne, yet another residential West Side hotel, at Seventy-ninth Street and Amsterdam Avenue, and where his parents were now making their winter home. Eugene introduced Horton to the Lucerne's bar, which had the best free lunch in town, featuring a lobster salad.

For the most part, Eugene's New York excursions were solo, notably when he visited Tucker's bookstore or attended the theater, for he regarded his fellow freshmen as intellectually naive. He did not, for example, share with them a memorable interlude in New York during the early spring of 1907 when he saw *Hedda Gabler*, the first Ibsen play he attended.

Familiar as he was with the text, he was nonetheless stunned by the stark honesty of the production's emotional confrontations. This kind of realism, in which good did not always triumph, was virtually absent from the American stage.

Eugene was also impressed by the play's electrifying Russian star, Alla Nazimova, as Hedda, who brings ruin on all who have befriended her before destroying herself. Nazimova was the pride of the Moscow Art Theater's Konstantin Stanislavsky, whose mission it was to obliterate the false pathos and artificiality of conventional acting.

In 1920, after he himself was already being lauded as an innovative playwright, O'Neill saluted *Hedda Gabler*'s creator: "I needed no professor to tell me that Ibsen as dramatist knew whereof he spoke. I found him myself outside college grounds and hours . . . If I had met him inside I might still be a stranger to Ibsen."

Years later, responding to a request by the editor of an American-Norwegian newspaper to send a tribute on the 110th anniversary of Ibsen's birth, O'Neill wrote that he remembered well the impact of seeing *Hedda Gabler* "at the old Bijou Theater in New York." He added that he "then went again and again for ten successive nights."

"That experience discovered an entire new world of the drama for me," he said. "It gave me my first conception of a modern theater where truth might live." He had recently reread all of Ibsen's plays, he said, and that "as dramas revealing the souls of men and women they are as great today as they will be a hundred years from now."

James O'Neill, capricious as always about money matters, seems to have provided his son with a generous allowance, probably unaware of his illicit trips off campus. Eugene had ample money to dress well and, according to his classmates, was seldom troubled by lack of ready cash. But he seemed chronically unable or unwilling to buy his own cigarettes. He cadged them from Weeks, who finally found a way to discourage him by offering Sweet Caporals, a cheap brand he knew Eugene detested.

When on occasion he did run out of cash, Eugene told his friends he was thinking of "putting the bite on the Old Man." While some forty percent of Princeton's undergraduates, according to college records, were earning part or all of their way through school, Eugene was not required to lift a finger toward his support.

His freshman expenses, including pocket money, came to fourteen hundred dollars. Eugene evidently appreciated his father's unexpected generosity, for he spoke of James with tolerant humor to Horton and other friends. He even went so far as to put in a good word for *The Count of Monte Cristo*, which he defended as the only American play to have withstood the test of time.

Between drinking and women, not to mention his self-assigned reading, Eugene had little time for required courses. At mid-term in February, however, he did manage to pass French, English and Latin — mainly because of the solid grounding provided by Betts Academy. But as at Betts, math proved his nemesis. He barely passed spherical trigonometry and failed algebra and physics, which he was obliged to repeat in the second semester.

He seemed for some reason to have misplaced the enthusiasm for spectator sports he had manifested at Betts. He was so repelled by what he perceived as the callow, herd-instinct called college spirit that he refused to attend football or baseball games and, indeed, avoided all extracurricular activities. He viewed with profound sarcasm the rowdy parade and bonfire celebrating a Princeton baseball victory over Yale in the spring of his freshman year.

He expressed his impatience with college sports in an early one-act play, *Abortion*, in which he mocked his protagonist, a campus baseball star, Jack Townsend. Set in "a dormitory in a large eastern university in the United States," the play centers on Jack's dilemma over a girl he has "got in trouble"; but O'Neill digresses to depict his hero's mindless immersion in a typical campus sports revel.

The writing of *Abortion* (in the spring of 1914) evidently purged his bias against college sports. Less than six months after copyrighting the play, when enrolled in a playwriting workshop at Harvard, he attended the Harvard-Princeton game and went so far as to lament that Harvard had "smeared up my dear almost-Alma Mater something dreadful."

Although Eugene's Princeton career was, by his own later admission, a self-willed failure, the circumstances of his departure were not as picturesque as George Jean Nathan's version, which for a time was accepted as fact.

After many years of friendship, Nathan felt impelled to "reveal" the lighter side of a nature that O'Neill's public generally regarded as somber. He did not, therefore, shrink from invention to establish that O'Neill had a devilish sense of fun. With his knack for comic improvisation, Nathan created the legend that O'Neill had been thrown out of Princeton for an act of vandalism against the university's august president. Nathan even invented dialogue for O'Neill:

"Princeton . . . [kicked] my tail out of the place as an undergraduate because I was too accurate a shot with an Anheuser-Busch beer bottle and hit a window in Woodrow Wilson's house right where he lived." Not above spinning contradictory versions of an anecdote himself, O'Neill did not allow Nathan's fiction to ruffle their friendship. But he did periodically feel impelled to disavow this particular story about the man who was to become America's twenty-eighth president.

"I *liked* Woodrow Wilson," he told an interviewer in 1948. "I wouldn't have done a thing like that if I had been swimming around in a lake of vodka." To another interviewer two years earlier, he confided that Wilson was "the last politician I ever had any respect for."

Eugene did incur disciplinary action in April, shortly before the end of the term — but not for throwing beer bottles. He and Weeks and another undergraduate (whose name Weeks withheld) got drunk in Trenton one Monday night in early spring. They missed the last trolley back to Princeton and took the 1 A.M. train to Princeton Junction, three miles from the campus. From there they had to walk and, as they were passing the stationmaster's house, a dog barked.

"There's a dog barking at us, Gene," Weeks grumbled. "I don't think we should tolerate that."

The three hurled roadbed stones in the general direction of the barking — which happened to be in the direction of the stationmaster's front porch. One stone broke a window. Exhilarated by their vandalism, they climbed onto the porch, where Eugene proceeded to kick over the furniture. The stationmaster suddenly appeared at his front door and shouted threats. The three made for the railroad tracks, which they followed home, satisfied with an evening well spent.

The next day the stationmaster lodged a complaint with

Princeton authorities and, after an investigation, Eugene, Weeks and their companion were summoned for questioning. Faced by their accuser, they confessed. The following Saturday all but Eugene appeared before the Discipline Committee. Eugene was punished in absentia, receiving, along with Weeks and the other undergraduate, a two-week suspension from April 25 to May 8.

The dean wrote to all three fathers, and Eugene hurried home to intercept the letter to James, in a wretched attempt to forestall the distress he was about to cause. But the truth could not be long suppressed. He did not bother to return for his final examinations and, at the end of June, was dropped by the Committee on Examinations and Standings for "poor scholastic standing."

Eugene's two friends returned to Princeton the following fall, but Eugene by then knew college was not what he wanted. He was persistent in his disdain for the clubby college-bred American youth. Not only in *Abortion* but in later plays as well he held this collegiate type up to ridicule, contrasting it with the sensitive, artist-dreamer (himself). The character of Stedman Harder, in *A Moon for the Misbegotten*, is one example of the despised species:

"No matter how long he lives, his four undergraduate years will always be for him the most significant in his life, and the moment of his highest achievement the time he was tapped for an exclusive Senior Society at the Ivy university to which his father had given millions. Since that day he has felt no need for further aspiring, no urge to do anything except settle down on his estate and live the life of a country gentleman."

Sam Evans, in *Strange Interlude*, is another member of the breed:

"Although he is twenty-five and has been out of college three years, he still wears the latest in collegiate clothes and as he looks younger than he is, he is always mistaken for an undergraduate and likes to be. It keeps him placed in life for himself."

Eugene was very clear about wanting no Ivy-stamped niche in life. He was, more than ever, convinced he could learn more out of college than in and, in common with Shaw and O'Casey — two dramatists he held in lifelong admiration — he ultimately demonstrated that a college education was not essential to the writing of great plays. What was essential, he often said, was "life experience."

In a letter to his prep school headmaster, William Betts, in 1923, when he was already an established playwright, O'Neill compared the satisfying four years he had spent at Betts (calling it his "Alma Mater") with the empty year he had spent at college.

"Princeton," he said, "was all play and no work — so much so that the Dean decided I had, by enormous application, crowded four years play into one, and he graduated me as a Master Player at the end of that year." When pressed by an interviewer seven years later to explain his dismissal, he shrugged it off as "general hell raising."

As the Princeton year faded further into the past, however, O'Neill's flippancy was replaced by nostalgia. Writing to his older son in 1942 of his decision to give certain manuscripts to Princeton, he said, "I can never get over my affection for Old Nassau. It's a neurosis!"

PART FOUR

ADRIFT ON LAND AND SEA

"I landed in Buenos Aires a gentleman so-called, and wound up a bum on the docks . . . "

— O'NEILL, to an interviewer

CHAPTER EIGHTEEN

Eugene's post-Princeton drifting was viewed, in that era of the Protestant work ethic, as the height of self-indulgence. The more than six years it took him to come to grips with reality were stigmatized by his father as loafing.

James could not help but bewail the family's second academic failure. He believed that Eugene's literary heroes were at least partly responsible, and suspected, not without some justification, that his son was drawn to these writers as much by their sordid personal lives as by their unorthodox ideas. In *Long Day's Journey into Night*, James Tyrone vilifies his younger son's "damned library." "Atheists, fools and madmen!" he rants. "And your poets! This Dowson and this Baudelaire, and Swinburne and Oscar Wilde and Whitman and Poe! Whoremongers and degenerates!"

It was James's lifelong optimism that finally tempered his anger. With a forbearance few fathers would have displayed, he not only absolved Eugene for failing to stay in college, but allowed him an idle New London summer. He did, of course, repeatedly remind Eugene that he had thrown away his chance of a superior education, and prodded him to think about what sort of job he might find at summer's end.

Since Eugene had no ideas of his own on the subject, James cast about — as with Jamie after his expulsion from St. John's — to find a suitable business concern in which Eugene might work his way up.

James appealed to a friend, Henry Brittain, who owned a small costume-jewelry firm in which Ella had a minor investment. The New York-Chicago Supply Company, on lower Broadway near Fulton Street, did most of its business by mail order, but also gave prizes of a cheap phonograph and record to children who peddled a quota of tawdry rings and pins to neighbors and relatives.

James suggested to Brittain that Eugene's literary background might be useful in handling the firm's correspondence. Eugene was hired as secretary at twenty-five dollars a week, the job to begin in October. He was not happy about it, but felt he had little choice.

The O'Neills left New London earlier than usual, returning in August to the Lucerne, so that James and Jamie could begin rehearsing for a repertory production alternating *Julius Caesar* with *Virginius* — the vehicle in which James, years earlier, had supported Edwin Forrest. It was the play he had always regarded as "a poetic masterpiece," almost "on a level with the tragedies of Shakespeare."

The two plays were scheduled to open at the Lyric Theater in mid-September and then be taken on the road. Eugene was pleased to have this chance to loaf in New York for an additional two months before starting his job.

Meanwhile, he subsisted on his father's dole of a dollar a day, the prevailing wage of an unskilled laborer. He found the sum niggardly, but ultimately came to appreciate his father's forbearance. "More than I should do in the same circumstances," he confessed years later when he himself had become a parent.

Because of Jamie's presence in the cast, Eugene attended rehearsals of *Virginius* and *Julius Caesar*, and soon struck up a friendship with his father's new press agent, James Findlater-Byth. As he did with anyone who would listen, Byth regaled Eugene with details of an astonishing past.

Findlater-Byth had been born, so he said, into a privileged family on an estate in Scotland, had graduated from Edinburgh University and subsequently covered the Boer War as a Reuter's correspondent. An unusually appealing figure, he so impressed Eugene that he not only wrote a short story about him, entitled "Tomorrow," but based a major character in *The Iceman Cometh* on him — the onetime Boer War correspondent, James Cameron ("Jimmy Tomorrow").

Eugene was not alone in suspecting that Findlater-Byth's background and career were pure invention. But Eugene was willing to pretend he believed him. "A fairy tale like that is no great matter to hold against a man," he wrote in "Tomorrow."

Even the hyphenated name was a press agent's hyperbole. He was born, un-hyphenated James Findlater Bythe, on March 19, 1866, the son of George Bythe, an upholsterer, in Church Town, Illogan, a working-class district of Cornwall, England, and later added the hyphen and subtracted the final "e." He arrived in America sometime before 1892, and found work as a theatrical advance man and press agent.

Byth's expertise on the Boer War, in fact, was derived from research he undertook as a press agent for a theatrical spectacular that opened at the St. Louis World's Fair on April 30, 1904.

The pageant, according to local accounts, was a gigantic reenactment of two battles of the War, staged "in daring realism" on twelve acres of the fairgrounds. The cast included "one thousand Boer and British heroes of the Transvaal," headed by the fearless General Piet Cronje, "the Lion of South Africa."

Byth mastered an authoritative spiel about the heroics of General Cronje, as well as the exploits of two other Boer War commanders, Christian Rudolph DeWet and Ben Viljoen. Byth's florid dissertations on the heroes and villains who participated in Boer War skirmishes stuck in O'Neill's mind and suggested two characters in *The Iceman Cometh*: the Boer general, Piet Wetjoen, whose cowardice forfeited a crucial battle; and Captain Cecil Lewis, who was forced to leave his native England after misappropriating regimental funds.

If Findlater-Byth's background was an invention, it seemed immaterial, for he was incontestably brilliant, witty, wondrously resourceful and entirely persuasive — if often drunk. Some years later he was to play a crucial if transitory role in Eugene's life.

At the end of Act Three on the opening night of *Virginius* on September 16, 1907, James, moved by the audience's warm response, made a touching speech. He could scarcely have forgotten the many past occasions on which New York playgoers had spurned him, but there was no bitterness when he thanked them for their generous appreciation that night.

"Though for the last thirty years I have occupied a somewhat conspicuous position on the stage," he said, "I have seldom visited New York. I am sure I don't know why. I am no worse than other actors. Tonight's greeting encourages me to say that I intend to be back among you every year of the few years that are still left to me, playing something of this sort, and when I depart for that bourn from which no traveller returns I trust you may be able to say of me: 'Ah, well, he could do something else than act dear old Monte Cristo.'"

The following day's notices for James's acting were indeed enthusiastic and, briefly, his star shone once more in New York. "His was a dignified performance, the performance of an actor who had personality and volume, conscientiousness and ability," wrote one critic, while another commented, "Mr. O'Neill has forgotten more about acting than some of our favorites will ever know."

But the reviewers, though kind to James, disparaged the vehicle. One pointed out that not even James could "lift the dead weight of this long ago play." Audiences did not flock to *Virginius* and a worried James put off the opening of *Julius Caesar*, resignedly substituting a revival of *Monte Cristo*. He explained to the press that *Julius Caesar* would be added later as the third play in the repertory.

When James and Jamie left for their road tour in October, Ella stayed behind to be with Eugene at the Lucerne, presumably to look after him when he began his mail-order job. For whatever reason, however, neither mother nor son availed themselves of this rare opportunity for intimacy.

Ella, like her husband, often seemed less at ease with her own children than with their contemporaries. When she felt up to socializing, she, like James, was inclined to befriend talented young people she considered in need of encouragement. That fall, she took under her wing a second cousin, Agnes Brennan (the sister of Lillian, whose hats she had declined to buy). Agnes endeared herself to Ella by showing promise as a pianist.

Ella's patronage included Agnes's friend, Sadie Koenig, whose struggle to pay for music lessons earned Ella's admiration. Ella went out of her way to be kind to Sadie. Unable to afford the five-cent fare for the horsecar, Sadie often had to walk from her rooming house on Seventh Street to her school on Twenty-third Street. Ella coaxed Sadie and Agnes (who was being supported by her family) to visit her often at the Lucerne, where she served them coffee and cake while inquiring about their progress.

"Mrs. O'Neill was a wonderful woman," Sadie recalled. "She gave me help and advice when I really needed it." In spite of her gratitude and admiration, however, Sadie could not help noticing that Ella behaved strangely at times, appearing drowsy, incoherent, repeating herself or trailing off into vague silences. Sadie had no idea what was wrong, but she did suspect that Eugene pained and disappointed her.

Eugene predictably detested his job with the mail-order firm and spent most of his office hours reading. He spent much of his salary on the town, often in the company of Louis Holladay, who continued to guide Eugene through the byways of Greenwich Village bohemia.

According to Sadie, Eugene occasionally showed up at the Lucerne in the late afternoon or early evening, presumably after

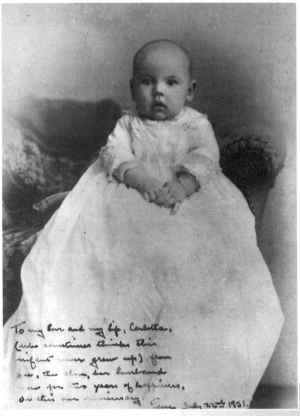

The Early Years

Eugene's first seven years of touring across the country with his parents gave him a permanent sense of rootlessness. Later exiled to boarding school, he found his only tenuous security in his family's summer home in New London, Connecticut.

O'Neill presented this photograph to his third wife, saluting her as "my love and my life, Carlotta, (who sometimes thinks this infant never grew up) . . ."

The Barrett House, the family hotel where O'Neill was born on October 16, 1888. "Every time I go past," he once said, "I look up because the room was on the fourth floor, third window from Broadway on the Forty-third Street side. I can remember my father pointing it out to me."

Eugene, at three or four
(below); at five (right)
and aged six (above).
He later said the photo
on the rock was
"amusing and character-
istic." It was his habit to
gaze wistfully out across
the New London har-
bor, contemplating the
circling sea gulls,
reading and sketching
trees and ships.

Sarah Sandy, the
Englishwoman who
was Eugene's nurse
until he was sent to
boarding school. He
was more attached
to her than to his
mother

Eugene, as always slumped over a book, with his older brother, Jamie, and his father, in 1900 on the front porch of the New London house that was to serve as the setting for *Ah, Wilderness!* and *Long Day's Journey Into Night.* Eugene, a debonair sixteen, flirted in New London with eighteen-year-old Marion Welch, on whom he partly modeled Muriel McComber in *Ah, Wilderness!*

Above, The O'Neill summer home on Pequot Avenue in New London that was known as Monte Cristo Cottage, in tribute to James's most famous role. Right, the so-called Pink House, where the family spent their New London summers from 1885 to 1900.

The McGinley family, circa 1912, on whom O'Neill partly modeled the Miller family of *Ah, Wilderness!* Standing (left to right): Laurence, Arthur (O'Neill's closest New London friend), Thomas, Stephen and Evelyn; (front row), the McGinley matriarch, Evelyn Essex, Morgan, John, Winthrop E. and father, John, who was James O'Neill's old friend.

James O'Neill (right) in one of the realistic dueling scenes in *The Count of Monte Cristo*.

George C. Tyler (above left) at eighteen, looking like a precocious entrepreneur. He became James's producer and, later, Eugene's. Jamie O'Neill (above) in his debut as Albert, Monte Cristo's son, in his father's company. Right, James in *Virginius*, a role in which he hoped to escape his subjugation to *The Count of Monte Cristo*, a vehicle so lucrative he could not give it up.

Ed Keefe (left), O'Neill's New London friend, and the artist, George Bellows, with whom O'Neill shared a studio after dropping out of Princeton at the end of his freshman year.

The celebrated Russian actress, Nazimova. O'Neill found her performance inspiring as Hedda Gabler in 1907 and in 1931 cast her as Lavinia in *Mourning Becomes Electra*. Left, Benjamin Tucker, the erudite anarchist, who influenced O'Neill's radical thinking in his late teens.

George Bellows painted the ramshackle farm-house and its rustic surroundings, owned by James O'Neill in Zion, New Jersey, where he, O'Neill and Keefe spent a winter interlude in 1909.

O'Neill's first wife, Kathleen Jenkins, whom he married in 1909 because she was pregnant. He never lived with her, and did not see the son he had fathered until he was eleven. At right, their marriage certificate.

Jamie O'Neill (center) in
The Travelling Salesman, in
which he toured during his
brother's absence

O'Neill (below) on his twenty-first birthday aboard a
banana boat bound for Honduras, with Earl Stevens,
a mining engineer. James, unaware his son had
married Kathleen, sent him off on a gold-mining
expedition to remove him from her influence. Above,
in Honduras with Mrs. Stevens and a Spanish priest.

work, drunk and argumentative. He seemed, to the innocent Sadie, to be "a kind of bum." He would fling himself onto a bed, and Ella would ask, in the presence of the two young women, "Are you at it again?" And Eugene would shout from the bedroom, "You'd be better off if you'd sleep a little more."

Once, in front of Eugene, Ella told Sadie, "I hope you'll be a success someday. Study hard so you won't have to struggle later." Eugene then put his arms around Sadie and mocked, "Now, you work hard, and don't touch any liquor." Because of her family connection, Agnes was somewhat more inured to the O'Neills' unconventional behavior and tried to make light of it. But Sadie was baffled and upset.

While the out-of-town reviews were more sympathetic than New York's, James's tour, even with *Monte Cristo* added to the repertory, was not the success he had expected. Not until the company settled in at McVicker's in February, 1908, did any of the three productions receive enthusiastic reviews.

The Chicago Record Herald wrote that *Virginius* "now nearly a hundred years old, does in truth wonderfully survive . . . it impresses upon [people] certain heroic and elemental ideals." The same reviewer found "The chief charm" of James's portrayal to be "the rare beauty of perfect enunciation and pronunciation of the English language."

The critic for the Chicago Journal also liked James's portrayal of Virginius, but preferred him as Marc Antony in *Julius Caesar*, writing that he "greatly strengthened his claim upon public attention" in the role. The reviewer found James's Antony "soldierly, eloquent, firm and subtle," a performance "alive with feeling," that stirred his audiences "as they had not been stirred in a long time."

Jamie, cast as Trebonius, had been receiving lukewarm notices, when noticed at all, and in this instance was listed in the general praise for what the Chicago Journal called "very good support." In *Virginius*, in the role of Lucius, Jamie drew generally poor reviews, although one critic commented that he "gave good promise." It was now eight years since his "promising" debut as Albert in *Monte Cristo*.

James's inherent graciousness, coupled with his sheer longevity, had earned him the sympathy of many regional journalists. Aware of the pathos in James's confinement to the role of Edmond Dantes, they had long since ceased to chide him.

No one, however, had ever brought to an interview with James quite the reach and depth, let alone the wit, of a reporter for the Chicago Record Herald named Richard H. Little. His article captured all the drama and sentiment of the sixty-two-year-old actor's career — and, incidentally, took humorous note of James's irreverent press agent, none other than James Findlater-Byth.

"Haunted by the Ghost of Monte Cristo," read the headline in two-inch-high letters over Little's story, which ran on January 9, 1908.

"James O'Neill has been the Count of Monte Cristo 5,678 times," Little began. "I went over to McVicker's last week to ask him why, and fell among press agents. I first asked the man in the box office why James O'Neill had played Monte Cristo 5,678 times." "How the 'ell do I know? Stand back, I'm checking the line," was the answer.

"Then appeared on the scene one J. Findlater-Byth," wrote Little. He asked the press agent the same question. Findlater-Byth instantly invited Little to join him in a drink. After this reinforcement, Findlater-Byth disappeared, to return a few minutes later with James's general manager and his general representative.

Little again asked his question and Findlater-Byth suggested that "before proceeding to the discussion of the main question, all hands be piped forward to splice the main brace" — a common nautical reference to the practice of serving grog to a ship's crew as reward for strenuous labor. The main brace was duly spliced and Little waited patiently while Findlater-Byth held forth about his own background.

Little put his question yet again and after some discussion it was resolved to repair to the "Governor" himself for an answer. The group trooped backstage.

"I don't know," said the manager, "whether it is because he has played Monte Cristo so many times — next week, you know, will be the twenty-fifth anniversary of his appearance as Edmond Dantes — or whether it is because he so identifies himself with the part that has caused the public to clamor for it when, if he had his way, he would long ago have put it on the shelf.

"But when he is Edmond Dantes on the stage he is Edmond Dantes back in the wings until we shake him and bring him back to himself. I always make it a point to be back of stage myself or have someone else here ready to seize him when he comes off the stage in *Monte Cristo* and take him back to his dressing room. Otherwise he would blunder around here for I don't know how long before he got himself out of the part."

Finally, Little found himself face to face with James O'Neill in his dressing room.

"Why have you played Monte Cristo 5,678 times?" asked Little.

"Why?" mused James, looking dejected. "Well, because I cannot get rid of the cursed thing."

"Oh, you love your art, Governor," hastily interposed Findlater-Byth. "And the artistic possibilities of *Monte Cristo* are so great that you feel it would be an imposition on the public to put aside a play that so appealed to the emotions and has such a great influence on so many."

"Do I, Jimmy?" mused James. "Thanks. But I would like to bury Edmond Dantes so deep that he would never come to life again. Edmond Dantes is the old man of the sea around my neck. I have carried him twenty-five years but he won't let go. I can't break his hold. I want to play Virginius and Julius Caesar . . . But I can't shake this Nemesis, this nightmare, this spectral shape of Monte Cristo. It haunts me and I can't escape it."

"You're sick, Governor" said his press agent, unnerved by James's candor.

"No," said James, "I'm not sick. I was never sick in my life . . . Every year I start out with the fixed determination that I am done with Edmond Dantes forever, and before I know it he has me by the throat and I am climbing the rock once more and shouting: 'Mine the treasure of Monte Cristo; the world is mine.' No, when I play Monte Cristo they pack the house. When I play Virginius — well, they give me good audiences, but they don't take me as I want them to take me."

James left to go on stage and Findlater-Byth called Little's attention to the fact that it was thirteen minutes past ten. It was his invariable custom, at thirteen minutes past ten, to take a gentle stimulant.

After Findlater-Byth's stimulant, he escorted Little back to the box office to observe the large number of elderly persons buying tickets. Little stopped one and got as articulate an answer to his question as any reporter could hope for:

"I suppose it's a habit with me," said the ticket-buyer. "I saw O'Neill play Monte Cristo twenty-five years ago. I've seen him since whenever it was possible. I suppose I've seen that piece forty or fifty times, and I never get tired of it. I suppose it belongs to the old days, but if they only put plays over nowadays that gripped me like *Monte Cristo* does I'd be for them, but they don't.

"Say, honest, in all this riot over musical comedy and broilers and show girls and vaudeville that they have nowadays do they give you anything that makes the chills shoot up and down your spine like *Monte Cristo*? Say, when O'Neill climbs up there out of the sea with the salt water dripping off his clothes and waves his knife and yells, 'The world is mine,' I want to stand up on a chair and holler. I don't suppose it affects young people that way. They're spoiled by the class of plays they see nowadays. I took my granddaughter to see O'Neill down in New York a short time ago and she was much disappointed because he only *said* 'The world is mine.' She wanted to know why he didn't stay up there on the rock and *sing* it. I told her that it wasn't a song, that it was a line in the piece.

"'Oh, no, Grandpa,' she said, 'it's a song, "Love me and the world is mine."' Well, maybe it is, but I would just as lief that O'Neill didn't sing it. *Monte Cristo* is human. I don't care how impossible they say it is. At least it always seems to make a direct appeal to me and I hope O'Neill goes on playing it for another twenty-five years. He may think that Shakespeare is greater, but what is greater than to feel that you have touched the heart, whether you do it in a classic or in a melodrama? I've bought seats for three nights next week and I'm only sorry I can't come every night."

Little was impressed. He went backstage to say good-by to James and found him still pondering the question.

"I am as much a prisoner of the Chateau d'If as Edmond Dantes ever was," said James. "The other day I saw in a Sunday illustrated paper a picture of a California redwood tree with the various events of the world's history pictured around it in the order they had occurred since the tree began to grow. When it was a little shoot, just appearing above the ground, Christ was born in Bethlehem. And so pictured out at various heights of the tree are drawings symbolic of the great episodes of the world. And, while these things were happening, away out in the California forests this redwood tree was growing.

"Do you know, I feel like that redwood tree. Twenty-five years, the time I have been playing Monte Cristo, is not long, and yet when I think back over that period I feel older than the California redwood. In that time I have seen great actors spring from obscurity to fame, flourish and die. I have seen careers built up and torn down. Children have been born and grown into men and women. Little towns where I once played one-night stands, or passed by entirely, have become flourishing cities. Inventions never thought of when I began playing Edmond Dantes have revolutionized everything. And all this time I have been climbing up on a rock, waving a knife, and announcing that the world was mine.

"Do you wonder I want to escape from it all? I want them to remember me as Virginius, but they won't. I suppose that I will be Edmond Dantes throughout the play and down to the final curtain."

CHAPTER
NINETEEN

APPROACHING HIS SIXTY-THIRD BIRTHDAY IN OCTOBER, 1908, James for the first time in his career was at liberty. Following his summer in New London, he had planned to begin a tour in New Jersey in a trifling new play called *Abbé Bonaparte*, partly because it provided a small role for Jamie. When it opened in Asbury Park on September 1, it was a categorical failure and the tour evaporated, leaving both James and Jamie jobless.

Adding to James's headaches, Eugene chose this moment to quit his own job, and James once more found himself with two grown sons to support. Eugene's excuse was that Henry Brittain's company had begun retrenching in the wake of the Panic of 1907. Not long after, it did in fact go bankrupt.

Not until January of 1909 was James able to maneuver a featured role for Jamie in the second company of *The Travelling Salesman*, a slight comedy by a writer named James Forbes. As for Eugene, he made no attempt to find a new job, perfectly willing to fall back on his father's dole. A dollar-a-day was, after all, sufficient for survival in an era when restaurants charged twenty cents for a portion of roast beef with mashed potatoes, a fresh egg cost one cent and a nickel bought three oranges or a tin of sardines.

Even thus rationed, Eugene continued his nocturnal carousing with Louis Holladay. They had recently been joined by Edward Keefe, who had arrived from New London in 1905 to study painting at the New York School of Art. Keefe had fished and swum with Eugene during New London summers and been a member of Doc Ganey's Second Story Club. He was tall and slim with dark good looks not dissimilar to Eugene's.

Keefe had left New London against the wishes of his father, who wanted him to be an architect like himself. Although he could sympathize, up to a point, with Eugene's rebellion against *his* father, Keefe, unlike the drifting Eugene, devoted himself to his painting. He shared a studio with a tall, bony fellow-student, George Bellows, soon to become a renowned exponent of the Ash Can School of realism.

Bellows and Keefe both loved basketball and, when not at their easels, played on the YMCA team. Their Studio 616, a sixth-floor walk-up with a northern skylight, was in the Lincoln Arcade Building at 1947 Broadway. It was here that Bellows painted the seamier side of city life.

To help pay the monthly rent of forty dollars, they took in a third roommate now and then, usually a friend of Bellows' from his hometown of Columbus, Ohio. Eugene was a frequent visitor, along with the artists, actors and writers who were welcome to meals of cheese and salami and to stay the night on one of the studio's narrow cots.

Eugene shared not only in this impromptu social life but was pleased to accompany Bellows and Keefe to the fights at Tom Sharkey's Athletic Club across the street. It was there that Bellows found the raw, sweaty realism of the ring he later captured on canvas — and where Eugene stoked his life-long enthusiasm for prizefighting.

Despite his attraction to the raffish world he painted, Bellows, unlike Eugene and Keefe, was a proper Victorian. Engaged to be married to a virtuous young woman, Emma Story, from the genteel New Jersey town of Upper Montclair, he frowned upon his friends' dissolute night life.

Keefe joined Eugene and Holladay in their forays to the Unique Book Shop to absorb Tucker's latest philosophical bulletins and samplings of new anarchist pamphlets. "I remember one book he made me buy: Max Stirner's *Ego and His Own*," Keefe later recalled. But they also browsed other book stores. "Gene introduced me to a lot of books — Oscar Wilde, Schopenhauer, Nietszche."

Their Saturday night ritual was marked by visits to shady establishments in the Tenderloin, an area including sections between Madison Square and Forty-eighth Street and between Fifth and Ninth Avenues. New York by the late 1800's had begun to strut its reputation as a wicked and gaudy city. White slavery and opium dens abounded and a corrupt Tammany Hall cleared hundreds of thousands of dollars a year in protection fees, bribes and percentages.

The Tenderloin served as the city's center of vice, with a red-light district, caves of gambling, illicitly operated saloons and hideouts for

gangsters. Known in some circles as Satan's Circus, the Tenderloin
had acquired its name when a police commander was transferred
there from a quiet residential area. He was pleased, he said, to avail
himself of tenderloin after years of making do with chuck steak.

Even with their severely limited funds, Eugene, Holladay and
Keefe managed to play a part in this exuberantly sordid life. They
generally began their Saturday nights at Mouquin's, a French restaurant on Sixth Avenue and Twenty-eighth Street, patronized by artists
and newspapermen. Housed in a wooden mansion, Mouquin's was
known for its excellent cuisine at moderate prices. According to
Keefe, it was here that they "ate dinner after a fashion."

Thus primed, they wandered to the Haymarket, a combined
restaurant, dance hall and variety stage, situated on Sixth Avenue,
just south of Thirtieth Street and close to Tucker's bookstore. The
ugly, yellow brick-and-frame building stood three stories high and
was a fruitful hunting ground for pickpockets, petty thieves and
prostitutes. Liquor was served all night long and Diamond Jim Brady
often could be found there, satisfying his enormous appetite while
entertaining out-of-town visitors. Its windows, shuttered by day,
blazed with light into the early morning.

The Haymarket had been built as a variety theater after the Civil
War and it retained the galleries and boxes that lined three of its walls
above the main floor. While the ground floor was reserved for dancing and drinking, the galleries had been fitted with cubicles where,
for a dollar, a customer could watch one of the girls do the kind of
dance popular at French peep shows. Here Eugene took several
strides forward in his rough-and-tumble self-education, setting down
(three years later) his impressions in a sonnet called "The
Haymarket":

> The music blares into a rag-time tune —
>   The dancers whirl around the polished floor;
> Each powdered face a set expression wore
>   Of dull satiety, and wan smiles swoon
> On rouged lips at sallies opportune
>   Of maudlin youths whose sodden spirits soar
> On drunken wings; while through the opening door
>   A chilly blast sweeps like the breath of doom.
>
> In sleek dress suit an old man sits and leers
>   With vulture mouth and blood-shot, beady eyes
> At the young girl beside him. Drunken tears

> Fall down her painted face, and choking sighs
> Shake her, as into his familiar ears
> She sobs her sad, sad history — and lies!

Similar young girls with painted faces and sad histories sidled into O'Neill's mind when he began writing plays. In addition to the memorably depicted Anna Christie, prostitutes ply their trade at intervals throughout O'Neill's canon.

Having rejected Jamie's view that whores were fascinating vampires, he professed to be concerned with their bruised souls, firm in his belief that most were women of arrested emotional development, condemned to a stubborn, childlike loyalty to anyone who showed them kindness. During that era of abject female dependency, Eugene frequently encountered women who confided their woeful stories of losing struggles to stay alive by respectable means.

O'Neill first took up their cause in a one-act play, The Web, written in 1913. The heroine, Rose Thomas, is helplessly bound to her pimp (identified only by the first name, Steve), who takes her money and mistreats her. Afflicted with advanced tuberculosis, Rose would probably have given up trying to stay alive if not for her baby, whom she protects in the squalid room where Steve keeps her.

A fleeing gangster, Tim Moran, tries to help her: "Why d'yuh stand fur him anyway? Why don't yuh take the kid and beat it away from him? . . . why don't yuh cut this life and be on the level . . . git a job some place?"

Rose explains that she has tried to do that, but her employer invariably discovers she has been on the street and fires her. "A year after I first hit this town I quit and tried to be on the level," she says. "I got a job at housework — workin' twelve hours a day for twenty-five dollars a month. And I worked like a dog, too, and never left the house, I was so scared of seein' someone who knew me."

Then one night a dinner guest recognized her and alerted her mistress. "There didn't seem to be no use. They — all the good people — they got me where I am and they're going to keep me there. Reform? Take it from me it can't be done. They won't let yuh do it, and that's Gawd's truth."

The more fully developed Swedish-American protagonist of "Anna Christie" — written seven years after The Web — expresses this same sense of entrapment. Confessing her past to her shaken father, Anna says:

"It was one of them cousins . . . the youngest son — Paul — that started me wrong. It wasn't none of my fault. I hated him worse'n hell and he knew it. But he was big and strong . . . That's what made me get a yob as a nurse girl . . . And you think that was a nice yob for a girl? . . . With all them nice . . . fellers just looking for a chance to marry me, I s'pose. What a chance! They wasn't looking for marrying . . . I was caged in . . . yust like in jail . . . lonesome as hell! So I gave up finally. What was the use? . . . men, God damn 'em! I hate 'em. Hate 'em!"

By the time O'Neill wrote *"Anna Christie"* his language had grown bolder but his maudlin sympathy for prostitutes was basically unchanged — and it never did change. When O'Neill was fifty-eight, shortly before *The Iceman Cometh* opened on Broadway, a reporter at a press conference asked if it was true that the play had a cast of fourteen men and "four tarts." The reporter had the wrong count (there are three, not four, self-styled tarts in the play) but O'Neill, intent on making a different point, ignored the error.

"Well, there are fourteen men and four — uh — *ladies,"* he answered.

That comment would not have surprised any of his friends. One of them once made a casual remark about an Army experience involving a "two-bit whore." He was staggered by O'Neill's reaction. He resented the slight, much in the same way that the "ladies" in *The Iceman Cometh* insist on the distinction between "tarts" — a calling they gladly own up to — and "whores," which they crossly insist they are not.

In 1907 few of Eugene's friends were interested in making such nice distinctions, and Ed Keefe, for his part, was content to characterize the women at the Haymarket (all of whom, he recalled, drank sloe gin fizz), as "pretty good."

"We were only living *at* the life, trying to be a part of it," Keefe recalled. "We didn't have the money to do it right." If they were careful, however, they did have enough to end their evenings at Jack's, an oyster house at Sixth Avenue and Forty-third Street. A hangout for writers and newspapermen, Jack's stayed open day and night and was famous for its Irish bacon and sea food and for its staff of conscientious waiter-bouncers.

Like the city in general, the theater colony continued its expansion uptown. The district, with its thirty playhouses, extended from Joe Weber's on Twenty-ninth Street to the Colonial, a vaudeville house on Sixty-second. Its center was now Eugene's birthplace, for the past four years known as Times Square.

Through his father's connections Eugene could still obtain complimentary tickets to almost any show, and there was a surfeit of glittering nonsense from which to choose. One of the season's triumphs was Somerset Maugham's *Lady Frederick*, starring Ethel Barrymore in a role rejected by both Mrs. Pat Campbell and Viola Allen because the mature heroine was required to play a scene at her dressing table without benefit of makeup.

The talk of Broadway, however, was *The Easiest Way*, by Eugene Walter, produced by James O'Neill's onetime stage manager, David Belasco, who had resurrected himself not long after the San Francisco fiasco of *The Passion*.

The play's heroine was an actress with a somewhat tarnished reputation named Laura Murdock. It boldly flouted happy-ending convention with a bitter conclusion. Her curtain line was repeated by playgoers with gleeful shock: "Dress up my body and paint my face. Yes, I'm going back to Rector's to make a hit and to hell with the rest!" Despite its florid and sentimental dialogue, the play was welcomed as a brave departure from the tepid fare of the period.

While Eugene was a regular theatergoer, he drew the line at *Monte Cristo* when his father brought it back to New York for a brief engagement later that year. Eugene obtained tickets for Keefe and Bellows but refused to accompany them. He met them instead after the final curtain. According to Keefe, he attended the twenty or so musicals produced during the 1908-09 season, including two by Victor Herbert and one by George M. Cohan.

Florenz Ziegfeld presented his first *Follies* in 1907 and his fabled showgirls reigned over Manhattan's nightlife. Eugene, who could not begin to afford them, was irked to see them courted by his nemeses, the invidious rich in their silk top hats. With Jamie's help, he did get to know the lower-ranked younger chorus girls.

"The girls in those days," he liked to recall, "were less ambitious and more fun." Once, expanding on this thought, he mused, "I can't imagine anything worse than having a date with one of the hardworking ballerinas they have nowadays instead of chorus girls."

Even as James grew ever more impatient with his younger son's evident lack of motivation, Eugene was spurred on to greater excesses. "I'm going to fix the old bastard," he told Keefe. He engaged a woman from a French bordello (with the allowance provided by his father). Her profession could not possibly have been mistaken by anyone and Eugene, perhaps recalling Jamie's prank of introducing a prostitute to his college campus, seated her next to him in a reserved box at the New York Theater, where Anna Held, the popular musical comedy star, was appearing in *Miss Innocence*.

He was reasonably sure he would be recognized by someone among his father's legion of acquaintances, who would give James a report. He was right. And James, finally losing patience, told Eugene to pack up and leave the Lucerne. Bearing a suitcase full of books, Eugene found Keefe at his studio and asked if he could sleep there. It chanced that a friend of Bellows's from Columbus, who had been staying at the studio, was planning to move out the following day. Keefe invited Eugene to take his place.

While Keefe and Bellows painted by day, Eugene scribbled poetry, although he claimed not to have had any ambition to be a writer at that time. "Everybody does that when he is young," he said dismissively some years later.

Bellows, listening askance to Eugene's tales of his sexual conquests, exhorted him to renounce his wild ways and settle down with a "nice girl," such as his own Emma. Bellows, himself passionately motivated and in love, was bewildered by Eugene's complete lack of direction. For his part, Eugene was baffled by Bellows's puritanical resistance to the charms of the city's nightlife.

Eugene and Keefe did at last tire of their prowling. Eugene, probably prompted by the more stable Bellows, apologized to his father for his recent offensive behavior, at the same time asking if he could take his two roommates to the farm James owned in Zion, New Jersey, for a few weeks' rest. James thought anything that would remove Eugene from the New York fleshpots was a good idea, but warned that the farmhouse had been long neglected and conditions there were primitive.

Eugene, Keefe and Bellows were undaunted. They arrived at the Zion station on the frosty afternoon of January 18, 1909, loaded down with canvasses, books and food supplies. A hired buggy drove them to the dilapidated farmhouse, which only youths as heedless as Eugene and his comrades could have regarded as habitable.

Situated at the bottom of a snow-covered hill, a stream and waterfall behind it, the house had been taken over by James in payment of an uncollected debt and had stood unoccupied for a number of years. To heat the three downstairs rooms Eugene and his friends had to tear out a false front concealing the fireplace and cut pine branches to clean the chimney.

The kitchen, in the middle of the house, contained an oil stove for their rudimentary cooking. Keefe, the only one able to cope with the stove, acted as chef. His specialty was dried-pea soup, but he occasionally varied the menu with bacon and eggs.

Eugene, incapable of cooking anything, chopped wood. The room containing the fireplace served as their sitting room. Another room, in which they discovered a broken-down bed and a sagging spring propped up on wooden boxes, became their bedroom.

The only feasible sleeping arrangement was for two of them to share the bed while the third slept on the spring. Since the bed arrangement promised to be the warmer, they tossed a coin to determine who would sleep in cold solitude. Bellows lost.

All three throve on camp life. Eugene took strolls during the day and worked on his poetry in the evening, sometimes reading it aloud to Keefe and Bellows. The poetry was highly derivative, as O'Neill himself came to realize, influenced not only by Nietzsche, but by Wilde, Baudelaire and Ernest Dowson among others. "I wrote a series of sonnets, bad imitations of Dante Gabriel Rosetti," he reminisced more than thirty years later.

Keefe and Bellows turned out forty paintings between them, a number reflecting the blue cold of their environment. Since there was no scenery but hills, they painted hills from morning till night. Since there was no reason to shave, they all grew beards. Shaving would have been difficult in any case; even washing was a problem. Water had to be pumped from a well and at times started freezing in the bucket on the run to the house.

An amusement to all, was the family privy, which had three toilets of graded sizes. It was the only spot from which the farmhouse could be conveniently painted, and Keefe often availed himself of this vantage point. James O'Neill, in a fit of generosity, sent some liquor and a box of cigars, and Louis Holladay was invited for a weekend to share the riches. Informed of this windfall, Bellows' fiancée addressed letters to him care of "Decadence Manor."

Except for James's gift, Eugene and his friends lived frugally. Their only expenditure beside basic provisions was replacing a pair of Keefe's shoes, burned to cinders when set by the fire to dry.

More than thirty years later, O'Neill wrote to his younger son about the five-week adventure on the farm: " . . . If you can call it a farm! I don't believe anyone ever raised much on it . . . Bellows and Keefe and I . . . damn near froze to death."

The three friends arrived back in New York toward the end of

February, heavily bearded, and bearing the results of their creativity.

Bellows was pleased with his finished canvasses, among them a significant painting called "In the Woods — Waterfall." Keefe, soon after, gave up his quest to be a painter and returned to New London, acceding to his father's wishes that he become an architect. His cot was almost immediately commandeered by another hometown friend of Bellows, a young illustrator named Edward (Ted) Ireland.

As for Eugene, he returned to New York with a sheaf of unpublishable poetry, and with still no sense of a future.

CHAPTER TWENTY

EUGENE FINALLY ACCEDED TO GEORGE BELLOWS'S urging that he curb his flagrant behavior. Bellows then asked Emma Story to introduce Eugene to some of her friends, but Emma, who considered him disreputable, refused.

At last, in the spring of 1909, Eugene met a pretty, spirited "nice girl" his own age — an encounter that began as a lighthearted romance, but soon collapsed into a misadventure that tilted both their lives.

An acquaintance of Louis Holladay, an advertising man named Frank Best, was courting a woman a bit less prudish than Emma, and she agreed — while Eugene was still in an acquiescent mood — to present him to her circle of friends.

Eugene and Kathleen Jenkins were both twenty when they met. The coddled daughter of a respectable family, she was accustomed to having her own way but was beginning to find life humdrum. Weary of eager suitors from her own environment, Kathleen was beguiled by the dark, handsome, remote young man whom Frank Best brought to one of her mother's parties.

While Kathleen, in her later years, retained only a dim memory of Best, her first meeting with Eugene left an indelible image. She recalled his impeccably tailored dark suit and soft, hesitant voice. Though both polite and reticent, he held an element of mysterious excitement. She found herself instantly responsive.

Tall for her generation at five-feet seven-inches, she typified the round-hipped, bosomy upper-class young women whom Charles Dana Gibson was idealizing in pen-and-ink sketches for popular magazines. She had big, blue eyes, her light-brown hair was piled high on her head, and she carried herself with studied grace. Kathleen's father, George E. Jenkins, traced his roots to pre-

Revolutionary America. He was for a time an appraiser with Tiffany and Company and served as commodore of the Larchmont Yacht Club. Kathleen's mother, Kate Shaw Camblos, was the daughter of Henry Shaw Camblos, who held a seat on the New York Stock Exchange and was a member of the elite Union League Club.

Henry Camblos's father had fought with Napoleon Bonaparte, and Kate had the volatile nature of her Corsican ancestry. Her parents had prevented her from marrying the young medical student with whom she fell in love at sixteen, and she had waited until thirty, in 1887, to wed the disappointing George Jenkins. Angry about her own life, she was determined to set her daughter on a better path.

Not long after Kathleen's birth, Jenkins began drinking. The family moved to Chicago in the hope he could pull himself together in a new environment. The drinking worsened and he was unable to support his wife and daughter.

Kate Camblos left her husband and, with assistance from her father, she and Kathleen moved into a modest cottage near where he lived in Larchmont. A few years later, Kate rented a spacious apartment for herself and her daughter at 551 West 113th Street near Broadway, a residential neighborhood close to Columbia University.

Kathleen was brought up, as were most of her frivolous friends, to believe that the best use she could make of her endowments was to give and go to parties and find a suitable husband. Her mother often arranged supper parties, as well as Sunday afternoon teas, that allowed Kathleen to shine. Worried that Kathleen might inherit the Jenkins failing, and believing that an early acquaintance with alcohol would forestall any such tendencies, Kate encouraged Kathleen to sip an occasional cocktail when she reached fifteen.

Eugene, always ill at ease in the presence of a genteel young woman, was emboldened by Kathleen's coquettish behavior upon their meeting and invited her on a date. According to Kathleen's account many years later, Eugene seemed to possess an aura of "strange romance." He lived in an unrestrained world she scarcely knew existed but which, in his depiction, appeared enticing. She found him appealingly "different."

She and Eugene took long walks in Riverside Park, a block and a half from her home. Two decades later, O'Neill fondly recalled the neighborhood as a place where the air was "healthy, carbon-monoxideless," adding "I used to be young up around the Drive many years ago and have never been there since."

During their walks, Eugene quoted Wilde, Ibsen, Swinburne and other writers of whom Kathleen had never heard and whose ideas she barely understood. While he shocked her with his radical attitudes about morality and the social order, he also read her his own tender, amorous poetry. Once, at a party in Bellows's studio, they danced and sang to the accompaniment of an upright piano and a victrola.

By now, Eugene's paradoxical nature was becoming more clearly defined. Given to mercurial reversals, he conveyed sharply different impressions of himself on different occasions — often with a childish and willful perversity. Vain and egotistical, he could at times appear touchingly helpless and in urgent need of mothering. Hard and bitter one instant, he could be shy and sentimental the next. Worldly in experience, he was emotionally immature and irresponsible — singularly so for a man his age.

Although he possessed uncanny insight and sensitivity, he often misunderstood (and disappointed) those who depended on him. He was a hero challenging fate, determined to live life to its fullest, to experience everything. At the same time, he was a victim of self-pity, subject to sudden black moods of hopelessness. These he attributed to his Irish heritage, coupled with the stress of his rootless early life. Whatever the cause, these fluctuating moods intensified as he grew older and were heightened when he drank.

Kathleen, however, saw only his sober, gentler side — or perhaps she closed her eyes to his darker side, since she was too immature herself to deal with so volatile a temperament.

That summer, Eugene remained in New York courting Kathleen. The New London cottage was closed, for James, not having worked all winter, had decided to tour in the spring with the Lambs Club All Star Gambol, a burlesque written and performed by the club's members and an annual tradition since 1888. By June, with Ella along, he was appearing for a two-month engagement at the Delmar Garden Summer Theater in St. Louis.

Kathleen immersed herself in her love for Eugene. He could never resist being loved and, inevitably, he took advantage of her infatuation. In her innocence, she believed his love was as earnest as her own.

Kathleen's mother liked Eugene and was gratified he was the son of a celebrated actor. Remembering her own thwarted love, she was determined to give Kathleen every chance to marry the man she wanted. There was, however, a gnawing problem: Eugene had no job, he was still supported by his father and he was evasive about his prospects.

In his own mind, Eugene did not regard the attachment as permanent. It never occurred to him, for instance, to introduce Kathleen to his parents. Kate Camblos may have been willing to accept a penurious son-in-law, but Eugene knew with certainty that James and Ella were not prepared to underwrite any such marriage.

In recalling her romance with Eugene nearly fifty years later (in the late 1950's), Kathleen Jenkins was careful to skirt any details that might impugn the unblemished reputation she had zealously guarded all her life. Widowed after a second marriage and then in her seventies, she was still imbued with the sensibility of her Victorian girlhood.

Indeed, she protested more than once that she had her "reputation" to protect in the decorous Long Island suburb where she then resided, and was reluctant to confirm that before either she or Eugene quite realized what was happening, she found herself pregnant.

Upper-class "nice girls" in Kathleen's day, of course, held their virginity sacred and a slip could never be acknowledged. It is, therefore, understandable that she dissembled about the details of her impetuous romance, including the fact that her pregnancy was out-of-wedlock.

There was another compelling reason for the elderly Kathleen to be reticent. After O'Neill's death, which preceded her own by twenty-nine years, his widow, Carlotta, continued the financial assistance O'Neill had been providing. Kathleen was not about to jeopardize this arrangement by ruffling Carlotta in any way. It might also have been the specter of Carlotta that impelled Kathleen to concede, so many years later, that she and Eugene were mismatched. "We could never have made a go of it," she said. "I'd be foolish to imagine that I could ever have given him the kind of understanding he needed."

As O'Neill later confided to Carlotta, he panicked when Kathleen told him she was pregnant. Not only had his passion cooled, but even had he loved her he did not see how he could marry her with no prospect of a job. On the other hand, he was distressed at the thought of hurting her.

Reverting to his little-boy dependency, Eugene was obliged to confess all to his father. James, always suspicious that any woman interested in his son was after *Monte Cristo* gold, told Eugene he would find a way to extricate him.

By then, James had been gratified to accept a supporting role in *The White Sister*, a new adaptation of a hugely successful novel by F. Marion Crawford, and planned for Broadway in late September by Liebler and Company. Although in rehearsals, he took time to come up with a scheme to remove Eugene from New York: he would send him on a mining expedition. Continuing his habit of speculation, James had invested some of Ella's money in a gold mine in Spanish Honduras. An engineer named Earl C. Stevens was about to travel there to investigate the holding.

James had met Stevens, a native of Eugene, Oregon, through other mining investments, and had formed a characteristically avuncular attachment to the appreciative, ambitious young engineer. He believed that Stevens, a Columbia University graduate and eleven years older than Eugene, would have a stabilizing effect on his son. James neglected to tell Stevens his real reason for sending Eugene along, stating only that he wanted to remove his son temporarily from "theatrical" influences.

The idea of searching for gold in Honduras appealed to Eugene. It sounded like an adventure out of Conrad, Kipling or London. With the date for his departure set, Eugene could now present himself to Kathleen as the helpless victim of an unyielding father determined to separate them.

Kathleen herself was beginning to suspect how little she and Eugene had in common, but she made it clear she expected him to marry her. In her view, any solution other than marriage was unthinkable, and she implored Eugene to legitimatize the relationship.

According to Kathleen, Eugene assured her that he wished to make her his wife before departing. All would turn out for the best, he told her, and she chose to believe him. They promised each other to keep the marriage a secret for the time being.

On October 2, 1909, a week before he was scheduled to sail for Honduras, Eugene furtively ushered Kathleen, now two months pregnant, onto a ferry to New Jersey. "We were married secretly in a civil ceremony," Kathleen told the authors of this biography in 1957, refusing to elaborate further. In fact, Eugene and Kathleen were married in Hoboken Trinity Church, where a Protestant minister named William G. Gilpin officiated. (On later documents, she always gave the date of her marriage as July 26, 1909.)

Although his twenty-first birthday was nearly two weeks away, Eugene entered his age on the marriage certificate as twenty-two. He listed his occupation as "engineer" and his residence as Zion, New Jersey, where he had recently shared the farmhouse with Keefe and Bellows. Kathleen (whose first name on the marriage license appears as "Katherine") listed her actual address.

Eugene was to sail for Central America from San Francisco. According to Kathleen, she went to say good-by at Grand Central Terminal — and there ran into James O'Neill. She knew Eugene had kept their marriage from him, but she did not know Eugene *had* told his father she was pregnant. Nor did she suspect, as she later claimed, that her pregnancy was the reason he was being shipped off to Honduras. The meeting must have been exceedingly uncomfortable for all three.

Kathleen, in her interviews, insisted that she never doubted Eugene would return to her after discovering his Honduran gold. She did confess to anxiety about what sort of married life she would face with her wayward husband. For the moment, however, her wedding certificate was her trophy, and she could now reveal her marriage and pregnancy to her mother.

Eugene, obediently following his father's instructions, did not intend to return to Kathleen. He had tentatively assuaged his guilt by marrying her, and was doing penance by allowing himself to be banished. He was content to let his father manage the problems that were bound to arise from the birth of his child.

True, he had not yet confessed the fact of his marriage, but he had full faith that "the Old Man" — after his initial rage — would find a way out when the time came.

CHAPTER
TWENTY-ONE

Eugene O'Neill's Voyage to Central America was his first venture into independence. While he spurned the protective support of his parents when nearby, he discovered how much he missed them as the distance widened. Although he strove for an insouciant air, he soon made it clear, in the pathetic letters he wrote home, that his expedition into the Honduran jungle was not the lark he had anticipated.

It began blithely enough. His twenty-first birthday, October 16, 1909, found him afloat on a banana boat in the Pacific Ocean off the coast of Mexico, an occasion he marked by having his picture snapped with Earl Stevens. In conformance with the fashion of the day, both men wore dark suits, shirts with high white collars and dark ties.

There was a self-conscious grin on Eugene's clean-shaven face and he pinched a cigarette between the thumb and forefinger of his right hand. He also posed with Stevens's wife, Ann, who had chosen to accompany him. A comely, slender woman not much older than Eugene, she too was dressed as for a city outing in a dotted shirt-waist and long skirt, her dark hair in a stylish upsweep.

Eugene had joined the Stevenses in San Francisco and the three sailed down the western coast of Central America, disembarking at El Salvador where they hired a native couple as guide and cook. During the next three days they traveled nearly a hundred miles on mule-back through the mountains, at last reaching the Spanish Honduran capital of Tegucigalpa.

After resting for two days, Eugene wrote to his "dear Father and Mother," complaining that the trip would have been "O.K. if it were not for the fleas that infest the native huts and eat you alive at night." He was, he said, "a mass of bites" and itched all over.

He went on to deplore the condition of the native villages where he and the Stevenses spent their nights: " . . . the most squalid and dirty it has ever been my misfortune to see. Pigs, buzzard, dogs, chickens and children all live in the same room and the sanitary conditions of the hut are beyond belief." It might well have occurred to James that the conditions described by his son were similar to those he and his family endured in Buffalo upon their arrival from Ireland.

The exhausting journey to the capital appeared to have erased for the moment Eugene's churlishness toward his parents. Mindful that his ordeal was, in a way, an atonement for the trouble his involvement with Kathleen had caused, he hastened to add a more cheerful note. The city of Tegucigalpa was "fine," and the climate was "wonderful." He described a band that played on the plaza at night, where no one was ever in a hurry, as in New York.

With more enthusiasm than he usually manifested, particularly in regard to any project initiated by his father, he expressed a liking for the country and the people and believed there was "every chance in the world for making good."

Unable to sustain his optimism, however, he added that he was plagued by "spells of dejection and the blues." But he assured his parents that because the Stevenses were so congenial "such fits generally do not last long."

Their party was to start for the mining site early the following morning but was not expected to arrive for about a week. The rainy season had made the trails rough. "So next week promises to be the hardest we will have to endure," Eugene wrote, adding piteously, "You probably will not hear from me for some time after this letter but do not worry about me for 'the devil takes care of his own.'"

On a more cheerful note, he bragged that he was "brown as a native" and was growing a mustache "in order to look absolutely as shiftless and dirty as the best of them." The mustache, his first, was to come and go until his late twenties, when it became a permanent adornment. "Well good-bye," he concluded. "Lots of love to both of you and please write and let me know the news . . . I must hurry to bed in order to snatch a few hours sleep before day light — if the fleas permit. Your loving son Eugene."

Eugene's unease increased as he and the Stevenses proceeded into the interior. His next letter to his parents, written on Christmas day, was a recitation of unmitigated woe:

"For you I hope it may be merry but speaking for myself it is the most dismal and depressing day I have ever passed." He had been ill for the past week with fever and what he called "an acute bilious attack" from the "rotten food, vilely cooked" that had been the only nourishment provided since he left the capital.

While he could hardly have expected an abundance of dairy products in a jungle outpost, he whined about the scarcity (or absence) of butter, bread, milk and eggs. He and the Stevenses were obliged to subsist on fried beans, rice and salt-dried meat "much tougher than leather" plus tortillas so heavy they would "poison the stomach of an ostrich."

"There is the limit of your bill-of-fare — breakfast, dinner and supper — day after day — week after week," he complained. Moreover, he was still being persecuted by fleas: "*I have never been free from bites one day since I arrived in this country.*" He had also been attacked by ticks that "burrow under your skin and form sores," as well as gnats and mosquitoes. Life in the jungle was "unbearable," and it was his "candid belief" that "God got his inspiration for Hell after creating Honduras."

Sounding like the most bigoted of Colonialists, he castigated the natives as "the lowest, laziest, most ignorant bunch of brainless bipeds that ever polluted a land and retarded its future . . . until the Universe shakes these human lice from its sides, Honduras has no future, no hopes of being anything but what it is at present — a Siberia of the tropics."

He told his parents he would "stick" for five more months, until the rainy season began on June 1, when the threat of malaria drove most Americans home.

The date also happened to be a month after Kathleen was expecting their child and, if he was keeping any kind of track, the event was surely on his mind, although he made no mention of it in his letter. He did express concern about whether Stevens was planning to pay him any salary, asking his parents to look into the matter. "It would sure be some shock to find out I was enduring all this for love," he wrote.

So far, they had found no gold, though they had heard about a number of possible sites. On the trail of one rumor, Eugene and Stevens, with some native guides, hired a dugout boat and floated down a large river called the Paducah, through unexplored country on the north coast. Ultimately they had to proceed on foot on a trail that proved too difficult.

As Eugene wrote, "the tropical jungle was so dense that cutting a trail would take months," and they were obliged to turn back. Their plan now was to establish a permanent camp on the Siale River and explore for gold from there. "The delays Stevens has had to put up with from the natives would have disheartened many a man," Eugene wrote, "and if he is longer in getting started than he expected it is no fault of his."

The promised gold remained maddeningly elusive. After telling his parents not to worry about a revolution then underway in Spanish Honduras — it was "of the comic opera variety" and had no effect on Americans except to delay their mail — he asked them to send his letter on to Jamie, still touring with *The Travelling Salesman*. Once again manifesting his homesickness — and expressing himself as the most consistently dutiful and affectionate of sons — he wrote:

"Cannot tell how I miss you both. I never realized how much home and Father & Mother meant until I got so far away from them. Lots of love to you both. Your loving son Eugene." He could not resist twisting their heartstrings with this postscript:

"Menu for Christmas Dinner
Beans
Tortillas
One egg
Tea made of lemon leaves"

In retrospect, O'Neill came to regard the Honduran adventure with considerably more humor than he had mustered while living it. It later amused him, for instance, to tell friends that in the jungle he looked like a "Preparedness Day Parade."

"I expected to do a lot of jungle shooting," he recalled in a typical account. "I wore a bandolier slung over my right shoulder and carried a .30-.30 Winchester and a machete . . . all I ever bagged was a lizard."

Significantly, he never reminisced publicly about the presence of Ann Stevens. His only recorded mention of her is in the November 9 letter to his parents, in which he wrote admiringly, "Mrs. Stevens is bearing up fine under all the hardships — which is more than one woman in a thousand could do."

It is a fair guess that Eugene developed a romantic attachment to her. A poem he wrote during the trip, dated January 11, 1910 and believed to be his first extant "literary" effort, might have reflected his jocular fantasy of a tropical love-affair.

"Ballade of the Two of Us" was signed "E.G.O." Evidently

regarding the acronym as both humorous and appropriate, he continued to use the initials for much of his poetry. A few sample lines convey the ditty's frivolous tone:

" . . . When the skies are blue,
　　And the clouds astray,
　　We shall laugh and play
As God's children do;
　　Put the world away,—
Just I and You . . .

I shall kneel and sue
　　And adore away.
I shall think up new
　　Sweet prayers to pray.
In a different way
I shall come to woo,
　　When we win our day; —
Just I and You.

Similarly, O'Neill's first play (written in 1913) doubtless reflects his earlier (and almost certainly unconsummated) yearnings for Earl Stevens's wife. A one-acter entitled *A Wife for a Life*, it is set in a gold-mining camp and deals with a young miner named Jack and his partner, an older man with whose beautiful and faithful wife Jack has fallen in love.

While O'Neill never attributed the idea for this labored effort to his Honduran adventure, he did acknowledge his jungle experience as the partial source for *The Emperor Jones*, one of his major experimental works (written in 1920). "The effect of the tropical forest on the human imagination was honestly come by," he once explained. "It was the result of my own experience while prospecting for gold in Spanish Honduras."

Specifically, the Honduran jungle was the inspiration for the "Little Formless Fears" — the hallucinations that obsess the superstitious protagonist of *The Emperor Jones*. In his stage directions, O'Neill described the forest as "a wall of darkness dividing the world" (probably how he remembered the impenetrable Honduran jungle):

"Only when the eye becomes accustomed to the gloom can the outlines of separate trunks of the nearest trees be made out, enormous pillars of deeper blackness. A somber monotone of wind lost in the leaves moans in the air. Yet this sound serves but to intensify the impression of the forest's relentless immobility, to form a background throwing into relief its brooding, implacable silence."

In mid-January, still with no sign of gold, Eugene longed to go home. His prayer was answered rudely when he was attacked by the malaria bug, whose annual invasion had not been expected until June. Almost every afternoon he suffered a bout of fever and, despite the steamy climate, was obliged to crouch beside a campfire to quiet his chattering teeth.

Leaving Stevens to pursue his slippery treasure, Eugene, led by an Indian guide, began the grueling return to Tegucigalpa. After ten days on muleback, frequently quaking with fever, he reached the capital, to find it in the midst of a fiesta and its one hotel completely booked. He sought out the American consul, who put him to bed in his own home and summoned a doctor.

Because of the town's high altitude, the nights were frigid. The consul, who could not supply enough blankets to keep Eugene warm, added layers of worn American flags. "I looked just like George M. Cohan," O'Neill quipped to an interviewer many years later. After three weeks, Eugene recovered. But before he was well enough to leave Honduras he received word that Stevens, too, had decided to call it quits.

Although still weak from his illness, Eugene headed for home in mid-February. Years later, providing notes of his early career for a theater historian, he summed up the failed expedition as "a chance to work off some of my latent romanticism," adding, "much hardship, little romance, no gold."

After O'Neill had achieved success as a playwright, Earl Stevens wrote to him, in the mistaken belief he had inherited his father's zest for speculation, to request financial backing in an Oregon mining venture. O'Neill, however, was disinclined. Softening his refusal with a jocular reference to their Honduran adventure, he told Stevens it was hard to imagine that it had really taken place. The image of himself "loaded down like an arsenal with ammunition, knives, and firearms," he added, would make "a first rate comedy hero of romance, especially if my faithful (?) mule could also play a part."

Stevens and O'Neill subsequently stayed out of touch until the winter of 1936, when O'Neill rented a house in Seattle in search of background material for a play. Hoping that Stevens still lived in the northwest, O'Neill initiated a search for him.

"O'Neill believes that Stevens is now operating a gold mine somewhere in Oregon," wrote Richard L. Neuberger, the reporter for The Sunday Oregonian who later became a United States senator. "If," said Neuberger, "Mr. Stevens should by any capricious chance read these words, and would communicate his address and whereabouts to the writer of this article, care The Oregonian, Mr. Eugene Gladstone O'Neill would be greatly appreciative."

In a remarkable switch of careers, Stevens had become a trumpet player with the Portland Symphony. He did read the words, and informed O'Neill of his whereabouts. O'Neill promptly invited Stevens and his wife to spend the night: "I look forward to seeing you both — although I shall feel a bit embarrassed, because as I remember myself in the Rio Siale days, I was a very obstreperous young Nut, and must have been a great trial to have around!"

Not long after their reunion on December 8, O'Neill moved to the milder climate of California, and the two never saw each other again. Stevens, who outlived O'Neill by three years, would gaze from time to time at the photographs of the two eager young men and the dauntless young woman who had shared a quixotic adventure.

On his return to New York in early March of 1910, Eugene telegraphed his father in St. Louis, where he was appearing in *The White Sister*, in which he had been touring since the previous November.

Eugene had by now confessed — to his parents' dismay — that he was married to Kathleen and James was distressed that Eugene had returned so soon. He regretted Eugene had not remained abroad until well past May, when Kathleen was expected to give birth.

James was fearful that if Kathleen and her mother knew Eugene was back from Honduras they would somehow cajole him into accepting his role as expectant father. And who but James would then have to assume the financial burden? It was expedient, James felt, to keep as much distance as possible between Eugene and his wife and he instructed his son to join him at once in St. Louis.

Submitting again to his father, Eugene arrived in St. Louis on March 15, and assumed the hastily improvised job of assistant company manager. James told Eugene the Jenkins family had been making life difficult. Kate Jenkins, once Kathleen had told her of her marriage and pregnancy, had attempted a rapprochement with the O'Neills in Eugene's absence.

She may not have realized at first how violently opposed James and Ella were to the match — and she was almost certainly unaware of Eugene's own resolve, prodded by his father, to foreswear his obligation. James sent word to Kate Jenkins that his wife's sudden illness precluded any discussion of the marriage. He was still hopeful that he could extricate his son from paternal responsibility, as he had long ago managed to free himself from his own entanglement with Nettie Walsh.

The difference was that by the standards of that day Kathleen — unlike Nettie — was a respectable woman and Eugene had no doubt he was the father of her child. Moreover, James miscalculated the extent to which the worldly and tenacious Kate Jenkins was prepared to do battle.

Ella O'Neill was traveling with *The White Sister* company (her "illness" this time apparently a delaying tactic) and Eugene's reunion with his parents was uneasy. He was evidently filled with guilt over the damage he had inflicted not only on Kathleen but on his own family. Ella later told her young friend, Sadie Konig, that Eugene had wept when they talked of his situation.

His involvement with Kathleen was still very much on his mind when he began writing plays. In *Servitude* (1913) and *Before Breakfast* (1916) he focused on men trapped into marriage by inadvertent pregnancies. In one of his last plays, *A Touch of the Poet*, he introduces the same theme.

Most emphatically, he expressed his sardonic awareness of the similarity between his entanglement with Kathleen and his father's affair with Nettie Walsh in the one-act play, *Abortion* (1913).

The hero, Jack Townsend, describing the "sweet, lovely girl" he does not love enough to marry, tells his father:

"Yes, yes, I know it, Dad. I have played the scoundrel all the way through. I realize that now. Why couldn't I have felt that way at the start? Then this would never have happened."

The father in *Abortion* is, like most of the fathers in O'Neill's plays, modeled at least in part on James O'Neill. He is a "kindly old man of sixty or so . . . erect, well-preserved, energetic, dressed immaculately but soberly" and he has himself been something of a rake in his youth — leading his son to expect a certain amount of understanding. In response to the father's "if you did not love this girl, why did you, — why, in the first place —?" the son replies:

"Why? Why? Who knows why or who, that does know, has the courage to confess it, even to himself. Be frank, Dad! Judging from several anecdotes which your friend . . . has let slip . . . you were no

St. Anthony. Turn your mind back to those days and then answer your own question." And further indicating his identification with his father's profligate youth, O'Neill called the girl in *Abortion* not quite "Nettie," but "Nellie."

Eugene's job as assistant manager for *The White Sister* did nothing to change his mind about the tawdriness of American drama. The play was yet another in a long list of mawkish melodramas with high-flown sentiments and dialogue — in this case actually underlined by flourishes of organ music. It was, if anything, a comedown from *Monte Cristo*. It was not much worse, however, than the other plays that had launched the Broadway season of 1909-10, among them *The Only Law* by Wilson Mizner and Bronson Howard; *Is Matrimony a Failure?* by Leo Ditrichstein; *The Melting Pot* by Israel Zangwill; *The Passing of the Third Floor Back* by Jerome K. Jerome; and *Springtime*, by Booth Tarkington.

Unquestionably the most original playwright of his day was Edward Sheldon. In 1908, when he was only twenty-two and fresh out of Professor George Pierce Baker's fabled playwriting course at Harvard, he had written *Salvation Nell*, a play admired for its unblinking realism. But even he could not free himself from the pre-dictable denouements audiences demanded.

The White Sister, adapted from a hugely successful novel by F. Marion Crawford, was the story of a pure-spirited woman who, believing her soldier-lover dead, renounces the world to become a nun. Five years later the man, having escaped from captivity, tries to persuade her to return to him. She resists. He shoots himself.

As was customary, the play was tailored to the talents of a partic-ular star, in this case Viola Allen. Tall and with shoulder-length dark hair, she was a commanding presence in controlled, romantic roles. As had once been true of James O'Neill, she could pack theaters wherever she toured. While the play had been received in New York with tempered enthusiasm, it was embraced by her regional fans.

While Viola Allen reaped most of the glory, the critics were kind to James. After forty-three years on the stage, he still had his fans. One critic said his role had "its good moments and to them all, Mr. O'Neill brings all the art that has marked his work for years."

At sixty-four, the once-firm line of his jaw sagged a bit and there was more than a suggestion of a double-chin. His hair was gray, his hairline receding, and there were tired lines under his eyes that makeup could no longer conceal. His eyes, however, still flashed with fire, and women who had swooned over him as a youthful leading man remained devoted to him as an aging character actor. "I am told that Mr. O'Neill is annoyed by women who gather at the stage door," a female reporter had written just a couple of seasons earlier, after lyrically describing James's "rose-petal hands."

Starring assignments were not easily come by at his age, and he had been grateful to his old friend George Tyler for the minor part of Monsignore Saracinesca (at a decent salary).

James's admirers were disappointed that his name did not appear with Viola Allen's over the play's title. At least one feature writer went so far as to inquire "why Liebler and Company paid such a large salary to have James O'Neill in the cast, when the part could be played perhaps not quite so well, but satisfactorily just the same, by some actor at one quarter the allowance."

The writer answered his own question: "The reason is very plain. When the firm embarked in the theatrical business . . . their chief asset was Mr. O'Neill in *Monte Cristo*. He gave the firm an opportunity to book some good routes and helped somewhat to bring the firm into the prominent position which it holds today. There is a certain amount of sentiment attached to the engagement and with George C. Tyler the salary is of no consideration. It is merely having the services of a man highly esteemed who was once the firm's mainstay."

Despite his own facile disparagement of James's career, Eugene thought it slighting that his father was now reduced to a supporting role in a play even more trivial than *Monte Cristo*. His resentment ripened in retrospect and in 1920, soon after his father's death, he confided in a letter to George Tyler — who was then producing one of Eugene O'Neill's own plays — that his father, because he had confined himself to *Monte Cristo*, "suffered as a retribution in his old age the humiliation of supporting such actor-yokels" as Viola Allen.

James was not displeased to have Eugene back with him, where he could monitor any possible problems arising from his entanglement with Kathleen. As James might have foreseen, his son functioned less than brilliantly in his makeshift job. "A courtesy title," Eugene explained years later. "I had to sit at the gallery door and see that the local ticket taker didn't let in any of his friends."

Unaware that Eugene was hiding out from an unwanted entanglement, members of *The White Sister* company thought he had come along just for the ride. According to Theodore Liebler Jr., son of the producer: "It didn't cost the company anything to have young

O'Neill travel along. In those days you could get a free baggage car on the railroad if you bought a block of twenty-five passenger tickets. Even with a company numbering around fifteen, it was the economical thing to do. *The White Sister* company was relatively small, so Eugene could travel in one of the paid-for empty seats."

As *The White Sister* continued on to Indianapolis, to Washington and then to Boston — where the company arrived the second week in April for a two-week run — Eugene grew increasingly bored. He was especially exasperated by having to wear a tuxedo to preside over the box office and he cast about for a way to change both his costume and his environment.

When *The White Sister* neared the end of its Boston run on April 23, 1910, Eugene yielded to a longing he had known since sitting on the rocks of New London's harbor as a boy, gazing out at the square-riggers. Drawn to Boston's Mystic Wharf, as he had been to the docks of New London, he lingered at the waterfront, entranced by the sight of the surviving clipper ships putting out to sea, talking with newly arrived crews and thirsting for the romance that beckoned.

Providing notes of his early career for a theater historian, O'Neill in 1922 tried to encapsulate the impetus that sent him to sea in the spring of 1910: "Had read Conrad's *Nigger of the Narcissus* some time before — also Jack London — got the urge for the sea, sailing ships."

He had given a more eloquent explanation two years earlier: "It happened quite naturally . . . as a consequence of what was really inside of me — what I really wanted, I suppose. I struck up one day by the wharf in Boston with a bunch of sailors, mostly Norwegians and Swedes. I wanted to ship with somebody and they took me that afternoon to the captain. Signed up and the next thing we were off."

Actually, it did not happen quite that expeditiously. In the first place, no captain was likely to "sign up" someone with no experience. And few of the commercial sailing vessels were willing to accommodate passengers. It took Eugene time to find a ship to his liking, and a captain who would agree to carry him as a passenger. Then, there was the fee for his passage, which would have to be provided by James.

After some preliminary talks with crew members of a bark called the Charles Racine, Eugene learned that the captain, Gustav Waage, occasionally took passengers. The ship was bound for Buenos Aires, to exchange a load of lumber for hides and salted meats to deliver to its home port of Stavanger, Norway.

Buenos Aires seemed an inviting destination. It was celebrating its centennial and enjoying a burst of economic prosperity that was drawing the young and venturesome from Europe and North America. Eugene asked his father to consider the idea. James was aware that Buenos Aires was a cosmopolitan city where American companies had begun to establish branches, and where there would be job opportunities.

James decided that a few weeks at sea living completely on his own would not only be healthy, but might teach Eugene responsibility. At any rate, that must have been how Eugene interpreted his father's motives, for in *Long Day's Journey Into Night* James Tyrone characterizes his younger son's seafaring episode as part of his "game of romance and adventure," his hankering to have "a bit of being homeless and penniless in a foreign land."

More importantly, the voyage would distance Eugene from Kathleen and perhaps at last convince Kate Jenkins that the O'Neills could never be reconciled to their son's marriage.

With the birth of Kathleen's baby imminent, Kate Jenkins had been putting increasing pressure on James to acknowledge his daughter-in-law. Not a woman to give up easily, Kate demanded to know when Eugene would be back from Spanish Honduras so she could personally appeal to him to be at his wife's side for the birth.

Not revealing that Eugene had, in fact, returned to the States, James once again declined (through his lawyer) to respond to her demands. Under the circumstances, James was more than ready to accompany Eugene to the wharf and meet the master of the Charles Racine. James was impressed with him.

Captain Waage, at fifty-six, stood six feet tall, had silver-gray hair, a walrus mustache, clear blue eyes and a warm smile. He was natty in a blue, double-breasted jacket, bow tie and black cap.

James felt sufficiently confident to pay him the then-sizeable fee of seventy-five dollars for Eugene's passage. More than ever determined to be a sailor, Eugene eagerly accepted the arrangement, which included a commitment to help with the ship's work.

"I wanted to be a two-fisted Jack London 'he-man' sailor, to knock 'em cold and eat 'em alive," he later recalled. He never mentioned, when discussing his voyage, his status as a paying passenger, preferring to give the impression he had sailed as an "ordinary seaman."

Although O'Neill over the years went into substantial detail in numerous letters and interviews about his adventures at sea, he was mystifyingly silent about one other noteworthy aspect of the voyage to Buenos Aires. He suppressed the fact that he was accompanied on the bark by another youth his own age, who also was taken on as a paying apprentice.

Captain Waage refers to this second youth in a letter to his employer, the Sigval Bergensen Line in Stavanger, Norway, written on June 7, 1910, the day after the Charles Racine's departure from Boston. Waage wrote of two paying passengers, " . . . boys whom I have been asked to take care of . . . "

It is fair to assume the other youth was a friend of Eugene's and that James paid for both boys to be looked after. Yet O'Neill never acknowledged publicly that a friend had joined him, nor did he refer to the mystery passenger's presence in Buenos Aires. Outspoken in later years about what he regarded as the most thrilling event of his life, he evidently felt its heroic aspect would be diminished if it were known he had embarked with a buddy at his side.

Eugene appears to have confided his name to only one person among the scores interviewed for this biography, a young woman named Nina Moise with whom he worked closely during his experimental theater days in Greenwich Village. She claimed O'Neill told her, during a long confessional evening, that it was Louis Holladay who had accompanied him to Buenos Aires.

According to Captain Waage's grandson, Gustav Adolf Waage, who heard stories about the voyage passed down from his father, Severin Waage, also a sea captain, sixty dollars for each young man was given into the captain's care. The money was to be handed to them on arrival in Buenos Aires for their first two or three weeks' living expenses, until they could find jobs.

With the details of the voyage settled, Eugene begged to be relieved from his pointless box-office duties. He promised his father he would lie low if allowed to go to New York to await the scheduled sailing on June 6. James, albeit with misgivings, agreed to the plan.

The White Sister company, scheduled to end its run in Philadelphia and then to reopen the following season, left Boston for its brief next-to-last stop in Portland, Maine. Eugene left for New York, where he took a room at a boardinghouse on 123 West Forty-seventh Street, to await his parents' stopover in early May.

He did not dare move into their suite at the Hotel Lucerne, for fear Kate Jenkins might find him. Kathleen's baby was due any day and Kate Jenkins was growing ever more demanding of James to produce Eugene.

James and Ella rejoined Eugene in New York on May 4, determined to keep him out of sight during the weeks remaining before the Charles Racine was to sail.

Chapter
TWENTY-TWO

HALLEY'S COMET WAS ALARMINGLY BRIGHT IN THE SKIES over Manhattan on May 4, 1910, when Eugene O'Neill Jr. was born. The comet's periodic advent had been frightening emperors, kings and popes out of their collective wits since 2616 B.C. and, on May 19 when the earth passed through its forty-six-million-mile-long tail, superstitious throngs fell to their knees, praying for deliverance.

Eugene Jr., when he grew old enough to understand the troubled circumstances of his birth, claimed the arrival of the comet for his personal omen of disaster. Only two days after his birth, misfortune descended.

On May 7, the New York World, seizing on a story juicy enough to feed any editor's appetite for scandal, announced, in a bold headline: "The Birth of a Boy Reveals Marriage Of 'Gene' O'Neill."

Taking Kate Jenkins's word for the details of her daughter's marriage, the story's subhead declared, "Son of Actor Was Wed Secretly Last July to Kathleen Jenkins, Who Was Sweetheart of His Childhood." Kate Jenkins had approached the World, hoping the twin revelations of the marriage and birth would force the O'Neills into publicly acknowledging their grandchild.

The baby, his maternal grandmother informed the newspaper, weighed a robust ten-and-a-half pounds, had black eyes, and was "the image of his dad."

"It was at the request of Mr. James O'Neill that my daughter's marriage was kept a secret," Kate Jenkins declared. "Mrs. O'Neill had been ill all winter and the announcement of her son's marriage, it was feared, would have grave consequences to her. She was only told recently. She seemed pleased when she learned of the baby's birth." (The World reporter, failing to reach Mrs. O'Neill at the Hotel Lucerne, was unable to confirm her pleasure.)

Making a propitiatory gesture toward the O'Neills, Kate Jenkins said, "My daughter told me that she had begged Eugene to be married by a priest, but he declined. But the child is to be baptized in the Catholic faith, as Kathleen feels it would be a sin not to do so . . . He will be named Eugene Gladstone O'Neill, 2nd."

Kathleen and her mother had no idea Eugene had returned to the United States and was back in New York. The World reported that "young 'Gene,' as he is familiarly known, does not know that he is a father, and will not know it for probably six weeks, as he is mining down in Honduras."

The World's story not only titillated its readers, but informed Eugene himself of his son's birth. When he chanced into a familiar Manhattan saloon on May 7, the bartender announced drinks were on the house. When Eugene questioned his generosity, the bartender, winking broadly, presented him with a copy of the World.

Baptized or not, James wanted no part of Eugene Gladstone O'Neill, 2nd. He reacted to the story with stony silence and his son's reaction was no less stolid.

Kate Camblos Jenkins, despite her inherited Corsican determination, soon came to realize that in James O'Neill she had met her Waterloo. In a follow-up story on May 10, the World published a two-column picture of a pensive Kathleen. "Mrs. O'Neill, Who Is a Mother, Does Not Know Husband Is in City," read the caption.

The reporter had traced Eugene to his West Forty-seventh Street boardinghouse, where he was told the missing husband had been in residence "for a week at least." At the nearby Green Room Club, a social center for actors, the enterprising reporter found an obliging clerk, who revealed Eugene and his father had dined there on May 4, one day before Eugene O'Neill Jr.'s birth.

"Gene also had been seen at Broadway restaurants in the last few days," the World added helpfully. "The young mother is still in ignorance of her husband's presence in this city. She believes him to be in a mine in Honduras, working to make a fortune for her and their infant son. Since O'Neill's return to New York he has not called upon his wife, according to her mother, Mrs. Kate C. Jenkins, at whose home Mrs. O'Neill is living. When Mrs. Jenkins was told yesterday that her son-in-law was here, she at first refused to believe it. She was so shocked she could say nothing for several minutes. Then, with tears of mortification filling her eyes, she exclaimed:

"'It seems impossible that Gene is in town and has remained away from his wife and their baby. There must be some mistake, but if there is not, Eugene's attitude is inexcusable. He knows how we all feel toward him and that he could have come to this house to live any time since his marriage to my daughter. There would have been no "Mother-in-law" about it, either, and he knew that. I felt toward him as if he were my own. If he is living in New York without coming to see his wife and baby, I am pretty certain who is responsible for his behavior. No, I will not say now who that person is.'"

James O'Neill knew whom she had in mind.

With the state of his marriage and fatherhood still unresolved at the beginning of June, and submissive to his father's instruction, Eugene returned to Boston. He shipped out on the Charles Racine on June 6 in a heavy fog. The moment he felt the deck of the square-rigger roll under his feet he knew he had found his natural element. For the first time in his life he felt he belonged, and at last he truly comprehended the religious ecstasy articulated in *The Nigger of the Narcissus*.

"The true peace of God," wrote Conrad, "begins at any spot a thousand miles from the nearest land; and when He sends there the messengers of His might it is not in terrible wrath against crime, presumption and folly, but paternally, to chasten the simple hearts — ignorant hearts that know nothing of life and beat undisturbed by envy or greed."

For the next thirty years, Eugene was to express similar feelings, and he made a groping start aboard the Charles Racine. Lounging on the deck one day after completing his chores, he began a poem called "Free," influenced by both Conrad and Masefield. "Actually written on a deep-sea bark in the days of Real Romance," he exulted when it was privately published:

> Weary am I of the tumult, sick of the staring crowd,
> Pining for wild sea places where the soul may think
> aloud.
> Fled is the glamour of cities, dead as the ghost of a
> dream,
> While I pine anew for the tint of blue on the breast of
> the old Gulf Stream.
> I have had my dance with Folly, nor do I shirk the
> blame;
> I have sipped the so-called Wine of Life and paid the
> price of shame;
> But I know that I shall find surcease, the rest my

spirit craves,

Where the rainbows play in the flying spray,
'Mid the keen salt kiss of the waves.

Then it's ho! for the plunging deck of a bark, the
hoarse song of the crew,
With never a thought of those we left or what we are
going to do;
Nor heed the old ship's burning, but break the shackles
of care
And at last be free, on the open sea, with the trade
wind in our hair.

It was in prose, however, that O'Neill was to proclaim with more genuine poetry and originality his passion for ships and the sea.

"Oh, there was fine, beautiful ships them days," says Paddy, the old Irish sailor, in *The Hairy Ape*, written eleven years later. " — clippers wid tall masts touching the sky . . . We'd be sailing out, bound down round the Horn maybe. We'd be making sail in the dawn, with a fair breeze, singing a chanty song wid no care to it. And astern the land would be sinking low and dying out, but we'd give it no heed but a laugh, and never look behind. For the day that was, was enough, for we was free men . . . Oh, to be scudding south again wid the power of the Trade Wind driving her on steady through the nights and the days! Full sail on her! . . . Nights when the foam of the wake would be flaming wid fire, when the sky'd be blazing and winking wid stars. Or the full of the moon maybe. Then you'd see her driving through the gray night, her sails stretching aloft all silver and white, not a sound on the deck, the lot of us dreaming dreams . . . 'Twas them days men belonged to ships, not now. 'Twas them days a ship was part of the sea, and a man was part of a ship, and the sea joined all together and made it one."

The Charles Racine was a steel bark, one of the last of the square-riggers to compete with the steamers gradually taking over the seas at the turn of the 19th century. Not in a class with the swift, slender clipper ships, she was — in the affectionate description Eugene picked up from his shipmates — an "old hooker."

Built in Sunderland, England, in 1892, the ship was exceedingly well-maintained. Captain Waage himself had supervised her construction, ordering her prow angled sharply for speed.

In ballast and under full sail she could drive at least twelve knots. To Eugene, sailing on such a ship seemed the only way to meet the sea. The Charles Racine became for him the kind of ship extolled by sailors as "a home."

The sea began to symbolize for Eugene both a source of life and an ecstatic freedom from life's burdens. This concept was partially embodied in the autobiographical play he never wrote, the play he thought of calling *The Sea-Mother's Son*; for it was only in the vast womb of the sea that he found Conrad's "true peace of God."

He differed in outlook from Conrad when he came to personify the simple-hearted sailors of the Charles Racine. He felt that when Conrad wrote about the sea he was detached and safe, looking down from the wheelhouse to describe the sailors on deck. O'Neill wanted to be on deck with the men.

He discovered he liked sailors better than men of his own kind. "They were sincere, loyal, generous. You have heard people use the expression: 'He would give away his shirt.' I've known men who actually did give away their shirts. I've seen them give their own clothes to stowaways.

"I hated a life ruled by the conventions and traditions of society. Sailors' lives, too, were ruled by conventions and traditions; but they were of a sort I liked and that had a meaning which appealed to me."

On another occasion he described the "simple people" he characterized in his sea plays as direct in action and utterance. "They have not been steeped in the evasions and superficialities which come with social life and intercourse," he said. "Their real selves are exposed. They are crude but honest. They are not handicapped by inhibitions. In many ways they are inarticulate. They cannot write of their own problems. So they must often suffer in silence. I like to interpret for them. Dramatize them and thus bring their hardships into the light . . .

"Life on the sea is ideal. The ship for a home. Sailors for friends. The sea for surroundings. Meals provided. A resting-place. No economic pressure . . . Tired of one ship he can sign up on another. I like the man of the sea. He is free of social hypocrisy."

On the Charles Racine, Eugene could blend in without fear of being misunderstood or hurt or — even more importantly — judged. The seamen wore no masks and among them Eugene needed none. He accepted them on their terms with no sense of condescension, and they returned the compliment.

Aspirations were simple and simply stated: a berth on a good ship, a girl and a drink in port, and back again to the sea; no room for petty social ambition. The men were concerned first with the basic law of the sea: One hand for yourself and one for the ship. No one begrudged the hand for the ship — especially not Eugene, who, as a paying passenger, was eager to prove his seaworthiness in a variety of chores — and the men welcomed his participation.

According to Rolf Skjoerestad, a sailor who reminisced about the voyage many years later from his home in Stavanger, Norway, Eugene had initially ingratiated himself by presenting each sailor with a corncob pipe from a supply he had brought aboard in his suitcase. Like the twenty other members of the crew, Eugene dressed in overalls or wool trousers with coarsely-knit cotton shirts; in tropical weather, he wore only trousers and often went barefoot.

He and the other paying passenger had been allotted a small cabin normally used as the sick bay. There, in his limited spare time, he patched his clothes and learned to tie intricate sailor's knots, or read the books he had brought along and that he shared with the crew.

Immersed in the lore of the sea through his reading and conversations with seamen he had met on land, he considered himself a natural sailor. And, indeed, he had no trouble learning to climb the rigging of the fore, main and mizzenmasts, and to furl and reef the Charles Racine's six types of sail.

In later years he loved to reminisce with a former sailor, James Joseph (Slim) Martin, about his days at sea. According to Slim, O'Neill would dwell ecstatically on the thrill — and hazards — of going aloft to the royal and gallant sails, with the mast sometimes swaying as much as 45 degrees, and pitching at the same time.

During the 4-to-8 o'clock morning watch, Eugene might be invited to follow a seaman up the ratlines to the highest yardarms — "the top floor" — and experience the dawn breaking over the ocean. "And here's a memory," O'Neill recalled for Dudley Nichols, who, in 1940, was writing the screenplay for one of O'Neill's early sea plays, *The Long Voyage Home*:

"When due for a crow's nest watch in a storm, the man about to relieve would wait in the door to the forecastle alleyway while a wave dashed over the forecastle head. Then as the wave receded down the deck, timing it just right, he would sprint for the ladder up the mainmast to the crow's nest — the idea being to get there and start climbing before the next sea came over and caught him."

Wherever he gazed, the sea met the sky in a vast circle around his ship. Approaching the end of his writing career a quarter of a century later, O'Neill relived the euphoria through his autobiographical protagonist, Edmund Tyrone:

"I lay on the bowsprit, facing astern, with the water foaming into spume under me, the masts with every sail white in the moonlight, towering high above me. I became drunk with the beauty and singing rhythm of it, and for a moment I lost myself — actually lost my life. I was set free! I dissolved in the sea, became white sails and flying spray, became beauty and rhythm, became moonlight and the ship and the high dim-starred sky! I belonged, without past or future, within peace and unity and a wild joy, within something greater than my own life, or the life of Man, to Life itself!"

As part of his agreement, Eugene was assigned to such humdrum occupations as holystoning — a Sunday ritual of scouring the deck with a porous sandstone fitted with a stick. The stone was called the "Bible" because it was about the size and weight of one. A smaller stone, hand-held to penetrate into corners, was the "Prayer Book."

Eugene volunteered for the duty of sluicing down the rigging with a rag soaked in a mixture of tallow and white lead, to prevent the cables that supported the masts from rotting. And he learned to bring the teak railing to snowy whiteness by scouring it with wet canvas dipped in sand.

While all this activity, in addition to the bracing sea air and the absence of alcohol, had a salutary effect, the rations did not. The food was only a slight improvement over the greasy beans and tortillas of Spanish Honduras: pea soup and salt pork one day, salt pork and pea soup the next.

It is true that at the beginning of the voyage the crew feasted on a supply of pigs, chickens and ducks slaughtered at sea, but this diet did not last long. The weekday fare was occasionally varied by dry salt-fish called stokfish, supplemented by potatoes cooked in sea water. On Sundays the men were treated to salt hash or Argentine canned beef.

Everyone received a daily dose of lime juice to prevent scurvy, but fresh water, even for drinking, was scarce; during a long rainless period the men were rationed to a pint a day. The water tank was in the hold, and buckets had to be filled by a suction pump. The ship's carpenter kept the pump locked in his quarters. The caskets containing the meat provisions were lashed to a rail above deck, where the captain could keep an eye on them. Every morning the cook would hack off a chunk of meat for the day's dinner.

"Good morning, Captain," he would say, as he approached the casket with his cleaver. If there was a fair wind, the captain would smile benevolently and allow the cook to cut as much as he wanted. If the weather was foul and the ship was making little headway, the captain was likely to snap, "Cook, you're taking too much. There's enough in that piece to feed an army."

The cook learned to accept the rebuke philosophically. He knew the captain was fuming over lost time and over the implacable opinion of the shipowners that "The wind is always on the side of a good sailor."

When the seas were calm, the men might try their luck at fishing, and the cook would serve their catch as a special treat. If meat was scarce, hardtack (or sea biscuit) was plentiful. Eugene learned to break open his allotment with a marlinespike, shake the worms out of the air holes and soften the biscuit in what he later described as "something called coffee."

Aboard the Charles Racine, Eugene conceived a love of sea chanteys as enduring as his affection for the popular show tunes and ballads of the early 1900's. Captain Waage believed music and singing were a healthy outlet. He himself played the flute and always signed on a few sailors who could perform in a miniature "orchestra." At least one had to be able to play the ship's small organ.

Long after his voyage, O'Neill was still apt to sing (and insert into his plays) the songs he had heard at sea. Among his favorites were "There Was a Maid from Amsterdam" and "No More I'll Go A-Roving" (to which he knew all the ribald words), "Blow the Man Down" (which he used in *The Moon of the Caribbees*), "Whiskey Johnny" (in *The Hairy Ape*) and "Shenandoah" (*Mourning Becomes Electra*).

In 1920 he asked Olin Downes, who was later to become music critic of The New York Times: "Did you ever hear chanteys sung on the sea? You never did? It's not surprising. There are even fewer sailing vessels now than there were ten short years ago when I pulled out for the open. They don't have to sing as they haul the ropes. They don't humor a privileged devil who has a fine voice and hell inside of him, as he chants that wonderful stuff and they pull to the rhythm of the song and the waves. Ah, but I wish you might hear that, and feel the roll of the ship, and I wish you might listen to an accordion going in the forecastle, through the soughing of winds and the wash of the sea."

The writer, Malcolm Cowley, recalled O'Neill's rendition of "Blow the Man Down," during which he paused to explain that the slow rise and fall of the refrain, "Way-o, blow the man down," was like the movement of a ship on an ocean swell; he illustrated his meaning with a wavelike gesture of his right hand.

Yarns spun by his shipmates also turned up with scant alteration in O'Neill's sea plays. One story he relished but for which he never found a place in any play, pertained to the ingenious captain whose hand-operated foghorn slid overboard during a storm. The captain, so the story went, hoisted a live pig aloft and tied a line to its tail; a tug on the line brought a squeal louder than the loudest foghorn.

Although Captain Waage was not a rigid churchgoer, he insisted on conducting informal Sunday services. According to his grandson, he had "a great respect for nature, especially the stars that guided his ship." He believed that since "no captain could control the forces of wind and sea, one must turn to a greater Force." He liked to say "I will be at sea as long as the wind blows."

According to the ship's log, the winds were favorable at the beginning of the voyage, but the weather turned foul after the ship crossed the equator in late June. Several times the winds reached gale force and all hands were required to work not only through their own watches but in unrelieved stretches of as long as twelve or sixteen hours.

At such times, Captain Waage was likely to reward his crew with the ritual of "splicing the main brace" — in this case a carefully measured ration of rum — undoubtedly reminding Eugene of his father's custom of doling out whiskey to him and Jamie. The captain would dispense the rations into each man's tin cup as he filed by on the poop deck.

Captain Waage, though a kindly man, insisted on strict obedience to the rules of the ship and the men for the most part labored willingly. As O'Neill later liked to point out: "'Discipline' on a sailing vessel was not a thing that was imposed on the crew by superior authority. It was essentially voluntary. The motive behind it was loyalty to the ship! Among seamen, at that time, this love of the ship was what really controlled them.

"Suppose, just as an example, that one of the yards was loose, hanging by a thread, so to speak. Suppose a gale was blowing and the captain or the mate ordered two men to go aloft to secure this loose spar. This might be a dangerous proceeding. The men could refuse to do it. And they would be entirely within their rights, because if any complaint was made of them or any punishment imposed, they could go before their consul at the next port and justify their refusal to obey.

"Now the motive of the captain, or of the mate, in giving the order, might be simply to save a spar which, if lost, would add an item of expense to the owners of the vessel. But the men who risked injury, or even death, by carrying out the order, would be impelled solely by their love of the ship. They wouldn't care about saving the owners a few dollars, nor about saving the captain's face. They would go simply because of their feeling that they owed the service to the ship itself."

If Eugene, inexperienced as he was, never took such risks himself, he did participate companionably in a pastime the Norwegian sailors called *Sjiste Faarnölse*, or Trunk Pleasure. Every sailor had a trunk, wide at the bottom and narrow at the top, that he kept by his bunk in the forecastle. In heavy seas, when the forecastle was awash, the trunks would float.

A sailor's most precious possession, the trunk held his letters, photographs, and such souvenirs and gifts as he had collected from or for his family and girlfriends. On the inside of the lid was usually painted a full-rigged ship.

During Trunk Pleasure the men sat by their chests with the lids up, each in turn displaying an item that recalled a personal experience, real or imagined. It was a point of honor to trust one's fellow sailors and leave the trunk unlocked. A locked trunk was resented as an insult, and each sailor would kick at it as he went by until, finally, the lock sprang open.

O'Neill drew on his memory of this custom for an early one-act play, *In the Zone* (1916), set during World War I. A seaman who conceals a locked metal box leads his shipmates to think him a German spy; they force open the box, only to find it filled with sad, intimate letters from his wife.

O'Neill became a devotee of nautical statistics, as well as of seamen's lore. Later in life he sometimes consulted reference books to compare the lengths and weights of the fastest windjammers of the clipper ship era. In the 1930's, he ordered models of some of these ships, including one called Lightning, from the New York studio of Donald Pace, a noted model builder. An illustration of O'Neill's near-obsessive preoccupation with authentic detail can be found in an inquiry to Pace:

"Are you sure you have the length-over-all, from knight-heads to taffrail, of this model correct to scale? . . . according to all three McKay, Cutler and Clark books she was 243 or 244 feet over-all — that is approximately two-and-a-half inches longer than your model is, as I have measured it. Whose figures did you work from on this model? Were they those of the museum (Webb, was it?) you told me about? Does this mean that the figures in the books are wrong? Are you sure the Museum is correct and the books incorrect?"

His nostalgia was still evident in 1946, when he told an interviewer, "the most beautiful things ever made in the United States were the clipper ships."

The Charles Racine, according to Captain Waage's log, anchored "in the roads of Buenos Aires" on August 4, after a voyage of fifty-seven days — the entire time out of sight of land. But when O'Neill spoke of the trip, he always said it had lasted sixty-five days — in his mind prolonging by an extra week the joyous and transforming experience.

Chapter
TWENTY-THREE

Still in flight but with hopes high, Eugene disembarked in a foreign port for the second time within ten months.

"Life then was simply a series of episodes flickering across my soul like the animated drawings one sees in the movies," he later recalled, "and I could not then see how the continuity of my own seeking flight ran through them as a sustained pattern."

It soon became clear that "the thrill of living" he had experienced at sea could not be sustained on land, where the familiar furies awaited him. This time he was truly on his own without even the protection that Earl Stevens, as surrogate-father, had provided in Spanish Honduras.

Once he had run through the sixty dollars intended to tide him over in Buenos Aires (roughly the equivalent of six times an ordinary seaman's pay) he discovered he was not ready for the responsibility thrust upon him. He ended up "on the beach," the sailors' term for down and out. "I landed in Buenos Aires a gentleman so-called," he later confessed, "and wound up a bum on the docks in fact."

After checking into the Continental, a reasonably priced tourist hotel, he sought out a congenial bar. His plan was to find a job, savor city life for a few months and then, once again, set himself "free, on the open sea" — this time as a wage-earning ordinary seaman.

Buenos Aires was enjoying an economic surge and many foreigners, including Americans, were lured by the promise of well-paid work. But Eugene quickly discovered he was unqualified for anything but an unskilled job — and there was no James O'Neill with contacts to hand him a sinecure.

One day, in the lobby of the Continental, it was Eugene's good fortune to meet an engineer named Frederick Hettman, who had arrived not long before from California to take a job as a surveyor in nearby Cordoba. Hettman was impressed to learn that Eugene was the son of his stage hero. "From that moment, we became friends," Hettman recalled. The two often went drinking together and Hettman suggested some places where Eugene might apply for work.

Eugene found a job with the recently established Buenos Aires branch of the Westinghouse Electric Company, presenting himself to the firm's American manager as a draftsman. After staring blankly at a T square and triangle, he was obliged to admit he had overstated his qualifications, and he was put to work tracing plans. He bore with the monotony for six weeks and then, predictably, quit. By this time the sixty dollars from his father was gone, as was most of his salary. No longer able to afford the Continental, he moved to a sailor's rooming house.

He found another humble job, this time as a temporary worker in the wool house of the Swift Packing Company in La Plata. The warehouse soon burned down, saving him the trouble of quitting. Meanwhile, he spent whatever he earned in brothels and in such infamous barrooms as the Paseo Colon and a notorious waterfront saloon called the Sailor's Opera, of which he had particularly vivid memories:

"It sure was a madhouse. But somehow a regular program was in progress. Every one present was expected to contribute something. If your voice cracked your head usually did, too. Some old sailor might get up and unroll a yarn, another might do a dance, or there would be a heated discussion between, say, Yankee and British sailors as to the respective prowess of their ships. And, if nothing else promised, 'a bit of a harmless fight' usually could be depended upon as the inevitable star feature to round out the evening's entertainment."

What Eugene's brother sailors regarded as an evening's entertainment made his rounds of New York's Tenderloin seem like a church social: "Pickled sailors, sure-thing race track touts, soused, boiled-white-shirt déclassé Englishmen, underlings in the Diplomatic Service, boys darting around tables leaving pink and yellow cards directing one to red-plush paradises, and entangled in the racket was the melody of some ancient turkey-trot banged out by a sober pianist."

He once attempted to convey to a friend the lurid details of his life in Buenos Aires. In describing the brothels, the available women in bars and hotels and how he resisted homosexual advances, he was obliged to use salacious language inimical to him.

The friend, a lawyer named Robert Rockmore, listened in astonishment to the profanity issuing from a man who seldom permitted himself more than an occasional "damn" or "hell."

"I'd never heard more colorful or fouler stories in my life," Rockmore said, "including when I was in the Marine Corps during World War I."

On another occasion, despite his usual discretion, O'Neill spoke of the pornographic films he watched in a Buenos Aires suburb.

"Those moving pictures in Barracas were mighty rough stuff," he said. "Nothing was left to the imagination. Every form of perversity was enacted and, of course, sailors flocked to them. But, save for the usual exceptions, they were not vicious men. They were in the main honest, good-natured, unheroically courageous men trying to pass the time pleasantly."

At the Sailor's Opera, Eugene met a young Englishman destined to become the character, Smitty, in three of his sea plays. In *Bound East for Cardiff*, Smitty is a minor figure; in *The Moon of the Caribbees* he is a sailor haunted by the memory of a shattered love affair and in *In the Zone* he is the owner of the locked sea chest filled with forlorn letters from his wife.

The real Smitty was the handsome, twenty-five-year-old younger son of a nobleman. He had had a traditional British education and been an officer in the Army. He had pale, delicate features and a blond mustache and was, in O'Neill's words, "almost too beautiful . . . very like Oscar Wilde's description of Dorian Gray."

When Smitty began to drink too much, his fiancée dismissed him. Miserable and disgraced, he had come to Buenos Aires, ostensibly to make a new career for himself. But instead of taking advantage of the letters of introduction he had brought from powerful Britons to equally influential South Americans, Smitty chose to go on an extended drunken spree.

Smitty had been in Buenos Aires ten months when Eugene arrived. His money was running out and he and Eugene roomed together for a time — while he tried, with little success, to pull himself together. "Between drinks, he'd drink to sober up," recalled O'Neill, who, by then, was doing his own best never to draw a sober breath.

Approaching his twenty-second birthday, Eugene decided to try one more respectable job. He found it with the Singer Sewing Machine Company — at a salary of two dollars a day. "The Singer people made about 575 different types of sewing machines at that time, and I was supposed to learn every detail of every one of them," he recalled. "I got about as far as Number Ten, I guess, before they gave me up as hopeless. I had spent a good deal of my time down on the waterfront when I should have been studying bobbins and needles."

Not at all unhappy to be fired, he returned to his loafing. He felt, he said, "like a boy let out of school."

At this juncture, Fred Hettman, who had been keeping a casual eye on Eugene, came to his rescue. "O'Neill didn't busy himself too much with work," Hettman said, chuckling at his own understatement. "He lived modestly in a pension and several times he couldn't pay his rent. Once, before leaving on a surveying trip to the interior, I decided to pay his rent in advance for several months so that he could live in peace. I then went on a business trip to Córdoba and when I returned to Buenos Aires I didn't find him there."

Eugene had taken to beachcombing, picking up an occasional odd job to pay for his whiskey. In later years he recalled those derelict months with a certain relish. He took pleasure, for instance, in describing a two-week interval of pickup work as a stevedore, when he helped load a German ship called the Timandra.

"That old bucko of a first mate was too tough; the kind that would drop a marling-spike on your skull from a yardarm," he said. The Timandra obviously was on his mind when he wrote *The Long Voyage Home*. The dreaded first mate in that play is referred to as a "Bluenose devil" on a ship thinly disguised as "Amindra," which is about to receive a sailor shanghaied from a shady waterfront saloon.

Out of funds and convinced he had exhausted the possibilities of working on land, Eugene longed to go back to sea. Unable to find a berth on a sailing ship as an ordinary seaman, he was driven to take a squalid job aboard a cattle-carrying steamship bound for Durban, South Africa. He was dismissively terse about this ignominious episode in later years, in marked contrast to his exuberantly detailed memories of his voyage on the Charles Racine.

In 1917 he first disclosed (in autobiographical notes) that he had " . . . worked on cattle ship, Buenos Aires to Durban, (South) Africa, and return." Two years later, he used almost the same laconic phrase: " . . . Followed another voyage at sea, tending mules in a cattle steamer, Buenos Aires to Durban, (South) Africa, and return." He was almost equally perfunctory in other interviews and letters, but added one small detail on two occasions — he had not been allowed ashore in Africa because he lacked the $100 required to enter the country.

The job as a cattle-tender was obviously undertaken in a last-ditch effort to keep himself alive — a brutally bitter experience he was eager to obliterate. In one interview he professed not even to recall the name of the ship.

Buenos Aires, less finicky than South Africa, permitted Eugene to come ashore, even though he was broke. He was worn out and profoundly dejected.

"In the months after his return O'Neill's health and good looks deteriorated," Hettman recalled. From early December of 1910 to May of 1911, Eugene not only gave up all pretense of working but did his best to hit bottom. He later described this interval as "a lengthy period of complete destitution."

There seemed nowhere Eugene could build a life. Optimistic at first about earning a living in Buenos Aires, he had found the work with Swift and Westinghouse and Singer even more repugnant than serving as a ticket-taker on the *White Sister* tour. And now, after his wretched journey to Durban, he was stranded back in Buenos Aires with not even the price of a flophouse.

It is unknown whether he communicated with his family during this period. In contrast to the letters he wrote to his parents from Honduras which they preserved, no letters from Buenos Aires to them — or to anyone else — have surfaced. And no other records exist to indicate whether Eugene asked his father to rescue him.

Although Eugene sought a berth as an ordinary seaman to work his way home, the few sailing ships that made port in Buenos Aires were not eager to hire someone with his limited experience. He continued to drift, inviting the fates to toss him where they pleased.

Like Nina Leeds, the heroine he created for *Strange Interlude*, Eugene sought the security that beckoned from the depths. In common with yet another of his self-destructive protagonists, Orin Mannon of *Mourning Becomes Electra*, he wallowed "so deep at the bottom of hell there is no lower you can sink and you rest there in peace!"

It was a hell he never forgot, an assault on his physical and mental health that ultimately shortened his life. In the last interview he ever gave he evoked the black despair of his situation in 1910:

"I was then twenty-two years old and a real-down-and-outer — sleeping on park benches, hanging around waterfront dives, and absolutely alone. I knew a fellow who used to work on a railroad down there and who had given up his job. One day, he suggested that we hold up one of those places where foreign money is exchanged.

Well, I have to admit that I gave the matter serious consideration. I finally decided not to do it, but since you aren't given to taking a very moral view of things when you are sleeping on park benches and haven't a dime to your name, I decided what I did because I felt that we were almost certain to be caught. A few nights later, the fellow who had propositioned me stuck the place up with somebody he'd got to take my place, and he was caught. He was sent to prison and, for all I know, he died there."

Asked by the playwright Robert Sherwood to autograph a volume of his plays for a library in Argentina, O'Neill, according to Sherwood, "expressed the doubt that there was a single park bench in Buenos Aires that had not, on occasion, served him as a bed."

When not sleeping in the park or evading the sadistic plain-clothes police known as *Vigilantes*, he slept in waterfront shacks made of sheets of galvanized metal that out-of-work sailors scavenged from discarded sections of storage sheds. For a time he shared one such hovel with a half-starved waif.

He begged for white rum and obtained food by following an old sailor custom: lowering a greasy rope, from which dangled an even greasier can, to the porthole of an anchored ship's galley.

The bonds among seamen obligated the ships' cooks to feed their penniless brothers, many of them "Wobblies" like themselves — members of the recently-organized Industrial Workers of the World.

Although in sympathy with their aim to overthrow capitalism and substitute a socialistic order, Eugene contributed little more to the cause than parroting the jargon he had heard in Benjamin Tucker's bookstore. As a brother in destitution, however, his tin can was filled with the best a ship had to offer (which was horrible enough).

While Eugene appeared indistinguishable from other outcasts along the waterfront, some instinct prodded him toward self-preservation. Time and again, after hovering at the edge of an abyss, he somehow found the will to pull himself up. He articulated this phenomenon in *The Iceman Cometh*, expressing the mysterious ability to survive as a belief in the "pipe dream." There was, he explained in an interview at the time, "always one dream left, one final dream, no matter how low you have fallen, down there at the bottom of the bottle. I know, because I saw it."

However debilitated he became, Eugene found the will to continue writing poetry, as he acknowledged to a young English reporter he met in a seaman's saloon. Charles Ashleigh, who free-lanced for the

Buenos Aires Herald, remembered Eugene as "rather morose," except when lauding Conrad and Keats. Ashleigh, too, wrote poetry, and he recalled how they each produced manuscripts from their pockets, "exchanged them across the sloppy table, read, discussed, criticized."

O'Neill himself attributed the stirring of his creative imagination to this otherwise dismal period. "My real start as a dramatist," he said, "was when I got out of an academy and among men on the sea."

At the back of his mind he already had an idea he might want to write some day and he began making notes of what he saw and heard. Less than two years after abandoning his life as a sailor he began drawing on his experiences at sea for his earliest plays.

After several muddled, long-forgotten efforts, he wrote (in 1914) the first of his memorable one-act sea plays, *Bound East for Cardiff* (originally called *Children of the Sea*). Through the eyes of the dying sailor, Yank, O'Neill distilled his days in Argentina, about which he had grown nostalgic with time:

"D'yuh remember the times we've had in Buenos Aires? The moving pictures in Barracas? Some class to them, d'yuh remember?

"And the days we used to sit on the park benches along the Paseo Colón with the *Vigilantes* lookin' hard at us? And the songs at the Sailor's Opera where the guy played ragtime — d'yuh remember them? . . . And La Plata — phew, the stink of the hides! I always liked Argentine — all except that booze, *caña*. How drunk we used to git on that, remember?"

Bound East for Cardiff was followed by three more one-act sea plays — *In the Zone*, *The Long Voyage Home* and *The Moon of the Caribbees* — all based on O'Neill's experiences at sea and written in 1917. The spell cast on O'Neill by his seafaring days continued to influence his writing to the end of his career. Of his fifty completed plays (including those he disowned or destroyed), no fewer than fifteen are set entirely or in part aboard ship, and in seven more the sea figures as an integral part.

The four most notable of the early, one-act sea plays (*Bound East for Cardiff*, *In the Zone*, *The Long Voyage Home*, and *The Moon of the Caribbees*), were eventually collected (and are usually revived) under the title, *S.S. Glencairn*.

Glencairn was the fictitious name for the S.S. Ikala, the freighter on which the twenty-two-year-old, world-weary Eugene — responding at long last to the inner voice urging him to live — found a berth for his own voyage home.

CHAPTER
TWENTY-FOUR

THE S.S. IKALA, A STURDY BUT CHARMLESS STEAM-powered freighter built in Glasgow, was a jarring contrast to the sleek square-rigger on which Eugene had set sail from Boston nine months earlier. The one thing the two ships had in common was that both were tramps with no fixed itinerary.

Picking up cargoes as she found them, the Ikala ran mostly between Atlantic and Indian Ocean ports, "God, what a dirty crate," O'Neill recalled, adding that when in ballast "she rolled like hell."

Eugene joined the Ikala's crew of thirty, most of them English and Scandinavian, on March 21, 1911. One of the few Americans to sign on, Eugene had managed to get his first berth as an ordinary seaman because the captain of a tramp like the Ikala could not be choosy. Living quarters were cramped, the work was hard and the pay was insultingly low. Consequently, Captain Robert Carruthers had to put up with a percentage of inexperienced men, or "scenery bums," who habitually jumped ship at the first port that beckoned.

Unlike the easygoing, clear-eyed crew of the Charles Racine, the deckhands of the Ikala, as Eugene soon realized, were not at one with the natural forces of wind and sea, nor were they possessed of that near-religious rapture known only to the hands on a sailing ship.

Forced to change from sail to steam, as desirable berths on wind-jammers became scarce, the men seemed joyless. As for the sweaty, begrimed coal passers and firemen, they appeared to smolder with profane anger at the pounding, foul-smelling engines imprisoning them below. Nevertheless, they provided Eugene with some of his saltiest and most original characters and expanded his knowledge of a vanishing seafaring era.

In the era before the maritime unions, a sailor's existence was both freer of restrictions and more hazardous. O'Neill lamented, long after his seafaring days, that labor leaders had "organized the sea-men" and "got them to thinking more about what is due *them* than what is due *from* them to the vessel." The "new type of sailor," he said, "wants his contract all down in black and white; such and such work, so many hours, for so many dollars."

While acknowledging that "probably some abuses have been cor-rected by this new order of things," he deplored the loss of "the old spirit."

This spirit, he explained, was more like that of "medieval guilds than anything that survives in this mechanistic age — the spirit of craftsmanship, of giving one's heart as well as one's hands to one's work, of doing it for the inner satisfaction of carrying out one's own ideals, not merely as obedience of orders."

Despite his status as an ordinary seaman, Eugene did not escape assignment to the same sort of menial chores he had drawn on the Charles Racine: scrubbing, painting and chipping. As for meals, he later recalled, "British food isn't too good even when it's good. They served something called 'preserved' potatoes. Preserved how, for God's sake; I never found out . . . . We lived on hardtack and mar-malade."

For all four *S.S. Glencairn* plays, O'Neill painted composites of the same basic crew — men he had met aboard both the Ikala and the Charles Racine, as well as some from the Buenos Aires waterfront, and others he was yet to meet.

The original Olson, for example, the model for the shanghaied sailor in *The Long Voyage Home* — described as "a stocky, middle-aged Swede with round, childish blue eyes" — was a Norwegian sailor on the Ikala, who had followed the sea since boyhood. Away from home for twenty years, he used to tell Eugene that the great sorrow of his life was having left the farm where he was born, to run away to sea.

"He was a bred-in-the-bone child of the sea if there ever was one," O'Neill recalled. "With his feet on the plunging deck he was planted like a natural growth in what was 'good clean earth' to him. If ever a man was in perfect harmony with his environment, a real part of it, this Norwegian was.

"Yet he cursed the sea and the life it had led him —affectionately. He loved to hold forth on what a fool he had been to leave the farm. There was the life for you, he used to tell the grumblers all in the fo'c'scle. A man on his own farm was his own boss. He didn't have to eat rotten grub, and battle bedbugs, and risk his life in storms on a rotten old 'limejuice' tramp. He didn't have to wait for the end of a long voyage for a payday and a good drunk.

"No, Sir, a man on his own farm could get drunk every Saturday night and stay drunk all day Sunday if he wanted to! (At this point the fo'c'scle to a man became converted to agriculture.) Then, too, a man could get married and have kids.

"Finally, the Norwegian, having got rid of his farm inhibitions for the time being, would grin resignedly, and take up his self-appointed burden of making a rope mat for some 'gel' in Barracas he had promised it to the next trip down."

Olson was a lesser character in *Bound East for Cardiff*, described as "a Swede with a drooping blond mustache," and a minor character in *The Moon of the Caribbees*. He also partly inspired the theme of *Beyond the Horizon*, dealing with two brothers; one leaves his home on a farm to seek adventure at sea, the other is trapped on the farm by a romantic attachment to his childhood sweetheart.

The voyage between New York and Buenos Aires, which had lasted nearly two months on the Charles Racine, took half the time for the steam-powered Ikala — including a week or so anchored off Trinidad for refueling and taking on a cargo of coconuts.

Three years later, Eugene tried to evoke the atmosphere of both voyages in a nine-stanza poem, "The Call." Inspired by Masefield's "Sea Fever," it foreshadowed Edmund's poetic speech about the sea in *Long Day's Journey Into Night*, as illustrated by this fragment:

> I have eaten my share of "stock fish"
>   On a steel Norwegian bark;
> With hands gripped hard to the royal yard
>   I have swung through the rain and the dark.
> I have hauled upon the braces
>   And bawled the chanty song,
> And the clutch of the wheel had a friendly feel,
>   And the Trade Wind's kiss was strong.
>
> So it's back to the sea, my brothers,
>   Back again to the sea.
> I'm keen to land on a foreign strand
>   Back again to the sea.
> I'm sick of the land and landsmen
>   And pining once more to roam,
> For me there is rest on the long wave's crest

Where the Red Gods make their home.
There's a star on the far horizon
    And a smell in the air that call,
And I cannot stay for I must obey
    So good-bye, good luck to you all!

So it's back to the sea, my brothers,
    Back again to the sea.
Hear the seagulls cry as the land lights die!
    Back again to the sea.

It was the layover off Trinidad, the ship anchored half a mile out because of the island's shallow harbor, that inspired *The Moon of the Caribbees*. The play's sailors reveal bits of their history and speak vaguely of their yearnings as they await a boatful of native women bearing smuggled whiskey. After an eruption into drunken brawling, the crew returns to its humdrum routine. The one-act mood piece was O'Neill's favorite sea play; its hero, he explained, was "the spirit of the sea — a big thing."

Eugene was not sorry to leave the Ikala when she docked in New York on April 15, but he was apprehensive about facing his father, after an absence of ten months, with no more concrete purpose in life than when he had left. True, he bore with him a bounty of experience for the makings of a future playwright. But if he himself did not yet grasp the significance of this nebulous treasure, how could he hope to convey to his father that the journey had been worthwhile?

"My father was worried about me," O'Neill later confessed. "He didn't know how to handle me, he didn't 'get' what I was trying to do; he only wanted me to settle down and make a living. He often used to think I was just crazy." And still later, he elaborated on their mutual misunderstanding: "There's no secret about my father and me. Whatever he wanted, I wouldn't touch with a ten-foot pole."

The returned voyager discovered that his father was about to conclude his second tour with *The White Sister* in New York and that both his parents were back in residence at the Hotel Lucerne. Jamie's two-and-a-half-year tour in *The Travelling Salesman* had recently ended and he, too, was in New York; despite his uncontrolled drinking, Jamie had received some good reviews in his role of Watts, the drummer.

Eugene put off visiting his parents, presumably unwilling to confront his father's disapproval. It is not known whether, in his state of despondency, he gave any thought to the wife and child he had abandoned. In all likelihood he did make contact with Jamie, although the brothers' paths had long since diverged. It is hard to imagine that they could even enjoy drinking together at this juncture. Jamie, alcoholic as he was, always maintained the facade of a dandy. He did his drinking in Broadway saloons in the company of other second-rate actors, small-time gamblers and out-of-work chorus girls. He would not have been caught dead in the sort of waterfront dive, populated by sailors and outcasts, where Eugene felt at home.

O'Neill once told Louis Kalonyme (who became a close friend after interviewing him about his life at sea), that on his return from Buenos Aires the one thing he needed was to go on a drunk. Regarding himself as truly one with his brother-sailors, he could not cut himself adrift from them. He tagged along with a couple of shipmates headed for a sailors' flophouse-saloon at 252 Fulton Street, facing the block-square Washington Market that teemed with trucks and wagons loading and unloading produce. Out of his meager pay from the Ikala, Eugene parted with three dollars for a month's rent.

The flophouse, known as Jimmy the Priest's, was half a block from West Street, which bordered on the Lackawanna Railroad tracks and the Hudson River. It was typical of the seedy saloons of the era known as "Raines Law" hotels. Under an 1896 state law, only hotels were permitted to serve liquor on Sundays and, to qualify as "hotels," such saloons rented out upstairs rooms.

"The house was almost coming down and the principal house-wreckers were vermin," Eugene later told Kalonyme. (The century-old building, with its faded, red-brick facade, was not quite as decrepit as O'Neill described. It survived, although not as Jimmy the Priest's, until 1966, when wrecking balls — not vermin — brought it down to accommodate the World Trade Center.)

Four-and-a-half stories tall, Jimmy the Priest's could accommodate twenty-two lodgers. Adjoining it, at Number 254, was a similar, equally scruffy, but larger establishment with beds for sixty. Sailors gravitated to the flophouses along the waterfront even though the American Seamen's Friends Society and other "reform" lodging houses offered clean, decent accommodations. (No doubt the prohibition of alcohol on the premises had something to do with this.)

Longshoremen and sailors made up the majority of lodgers, but there was a smattering of laborers, printers and even show-business folk, most of them alcoholic and down on their luck.

Cheap whiskey was the lure at Jimmy the Priest's. It was, in O'Neill's words, "a saloon of the lowest type of grog shop." Years later, O'Neill insisted that the grisly establishment's assorted down-and-outers were "the best friends" he had ever known. "Their weakness was not an evil." he said. "It is a weakness found in all men."

After fortifying himself with drink for a week or two, Eugene found the courage to meet briefly with his family. As he later confided to Kalonyme, his father berated him for his lack of direction, then once again cautioned him to stay away from Kathleen Jenkins.

In her initial interview with the authors of this biography, Kathleen declared that the first time O'Neill saw Eugene Jr. was when the boy was eleven. In a later interview, she contradicted herself, stating that O'Neill had, in fact, paid her a brief visit and had seen his son as an infant of ten months. But she was vague, claiming she did not remember any details. Later still, she gave differing versions of this putative visit to other interviewers. By then, it is likely she had become muddled about the facts of her early life — or decided to embroider on them. Given O'Neill's state of mind at the time — not to mention his fear of arousing his father's ire — it seems improbable that such a visit took place.

Soon after seeing his father, Eugene retreated to the succor of Jimmy the Priest's. The proprietor was a tall, wan man of fifty, known on the waterfront as a benefactor to luckless seamen. His real name was James J. Condon. He had earned his nickname because he looked more like an ascetic than a saloon keeper.

"With his pale, thin, clean-shaven face, mild blue eyes and white hair, a cassock would seem more suited to him than the apron he wears," O'Neill wrote, describing a character he called Johnny-the-Priest in *"Anna Christie."* "Neither his voice nor his general manner dispel this illusion which has made him a personage of the waterfront. They are soft and bland. But beneath all his mildness one senses the man behind the mask — cynical, callous, hard as nails."

The back room at Jimmy the Priest's was furnished with a round-bellied stove and anyone who could not afford a bed was welcome to sleep with his head on one of several wooden tables; all he needed for this privilege was a nickel to buy a schooner of beer or a shot of bad whiskey. "One couldn't go any lower," O'Neill said. "Gorky's *Night's Lodging* was an ice cream parlor in comparison."

Jimmy, who was always sober, followed a nightly ritual. Leaving his saloon in the care of his bartender, he went home to his wife in the respectable blue-collar neighborhood of East 102nd Street. During the day, however, he kept a sharp eye on his raffish clientele, who were well-warned that he did not permit fighting. Anyone who wanted to settle an argument had to step outside to a stretch of concrete known as "the Farm," where out-of-town farmers unloaded their market wagons. Jimmy did not mind if his patrons enticed the farmers into the bar, got them drunk and robbed them.

One of Jimmy's roomers, a broken-down telegrapher known as "the Lunger," who occupied the partitioned sleeping space upstairs next to Eugene's (and who eventually succumbed to tuberculosis), tried to teach him the International Code.

These lessons generally took place late at night when teacher and pupil were drunk, and the next day Eugene could not remember what he had been taught. He did remember enough of the Lunger's personality to dramatize him three years later as James Knapp in the one-act play, *Warnings*.

Knapp's affliction in the play is deafness, rather than consumption. And in the short story, "Tomorrow," set in "Tommy the Priest's," O'Neill appears to have been foreshadowing his own later bout with tuberculosis.

In the guise of the narrator, Art, O'Neill wrote of a night when "the Lunger" had "a violent attack of coughing which seemed to be tearing his chest to pieces . . . I thought of consumption, the danger of contagion and remembered that the window ought to be open. But it was too cold . . . "

The cubicle occupied by Eugene contained a rickety chair, a dilapidated chest of drawers and a narrow bed, covered with a threadbare blanket. The mattress, like all the others, was straw — easily disposed of when soiled by an insensibly drunken occupant — and usually writhed with bugs.

The cubicles were heated — inadequately — by a hallway stove and at night were dimly lighted by a kerosene lamp hung from the hall ceiling. Eugene's cubicle had one of the few upper-floor windows, leading to a precarious fire escape. Roomers at Jimmy the Priest's were entitled to a plate of free soup at noon, and Eugene lived on that and five-cent-a-shot whiskey. He managed to survive by spending scarcely any money on additional food, and by picking up an occasional job on a docked vessel. "The work was mostly cleaning ship; painting, washing the decks, and so on," he recalled.

When not sleeping off a drunk, swapping stories in the saloon or singing chanteys, he roamed the waterfront, walking the bluestone promenade along the Battery's edge or sunning himself on a bench overlooking the harbor in Battery Park.

In 1911, the Battery was the hub of international commerce, the world's busiest harbor, alive with ships and people. Every day, all day long, one ship followed another into its piers — ocean liners with horns blaring, tugboats, barges and ferries tooting their presence. Now and then a clipper ship in full sail glided through the Narrows. Watching the gulls wheel and shriek, Eugene must have been reminded of his often-stated wish to have been born a sea gull.

Immigration was surging and many of the eight hundred thousand souls, after being processed at Ellis Island, disembarked at the Battery that year. It was the one place that seemed to rouse Eugene every now and then from his alcoholic torpor. He could sit for hours watching the new arrivals who, like the O'Neill family six decades earlier, hurried off with transcendent optimism to begin their struggle for survival — not to waterfront shanties in Buffalo but to tenements on the Lower East Side and outlying areas.

Eugene may have convinced himself that his will to endure was all but extinguished. Embers of hope, however, must have flickered somewhere within, and he sensed a time would come when he would no longer desire to wallow "so deep at the bottom of hell there is no lower you can sink." Slowly, as he began to awaken from his stupor, he found himself again longing for the sea.

CHAPTER
TWENTY-FIVE

WITH CROSS-ATLANTIC TRAFFIC SPIRALING UPWARD, AN ordinary seaman's berth was not hard to find. Sufficiently sober to take himself to Pier 61, Eugene signed on the S.S. New York and carried his sea bag aboard on July 22, 1911. The basic pay for an ordinary seaman was $25 a month (shortly to be raised to $27.50).

Bound for Cherbourg, Plymouth and Southampton, the S.S. New York was an American Line passenger ship built in Scotland and, like her new recruit, was approaching her twenty-third year. After serving in the Spanish-American War as an auxiliary cruiser called the U.S.S. Harvard, she was remodeled with new boilers, two raked funnels (replacing her three old ones) and a covered promenade deck.

The S.S. New York and her sister ship, the S.S. Philadelphia, were the first twin-screw, express steamers to ply between New York and Europe. Fast for their day, they could do twenty knots, only three less than the unprecedented speed of the White Star liner, Titanic, when she plowed into an iceberg nine months later.

While the S.S. New York ensconced her passengers in luxury, she was anything but a soft berth for a seaman. Eugene again found himself performing such dreary chores as holystoning and "soogie-moogie" — scrubbing down outside bulkheads with hammock cloth soaked in a caustic solution that turned fingernails black. What he most detested was being patronized by the imperious passengers strolling the deck.

Helping to maintain the standing rigging was another task he resented. A seaman's life on a passenger liner, he said, was "an ugly, tedious job and no place for a man who wanted to call his soul his own." It was "hard work without any romance."

"There was about as much 'sea glamour' in working aboard a passenger steamship as there would have been in working in a summer hotel!" he said on another occasion. "I washed enough deck area to cover a good-sized town."

In later accounts he softened these sentiments, preferring to recall the only chores that gave him any satisfaction — making the ship's lines fast at her pier and, best of all, standing an occasional two-hour watch in the crow's nest. While writing *Long Day's Journey Into Night*, he chose to remember only the poetic moments, especially when he was "lookout on the crow's nest in the dawn watch."

"A calm sea that time," says Edmund Tyrone. "Only a lazy ground swell and a slow drowsy roll of the sea . . . Black smoke pouring from the funnels behind and beneath me. Dreaming, not keeping lookout, feeling alone, and above, and apart, watching the dawn creep like a painted dream over the sky and sea which slept together. Then the moment of ecstatic freedom came. The peace, the end of the quest, the last harbor, the joy of belonging to a fulfillment beyond men's lousy, pitiful, greedy fears and hopes and dreams! . . . "

The master of the New York was W. J. Roberts, called "Blackie" by the crew when out of earshot. Stout, kindhearted with a dark complexion, he looked more like an Italian than the Southampton Englishman he was.

Along with every crew member, Eugene was issued a navy-blue jersey with "American Line" stitched in white across its front, high-waisted blue pants, and a wool cap, all to be worn whenever leaving or entering port; during watches, he and the rest of the crew wore dungarees.

The seamen slept in the forecastle in three-tiered steel bunks. Mainly English, Swedes and Irish, with a few Americans, they were a tough lot. If a man came on board with a suitcase rather than a sea bag he was likely to be laughed off the ship; if he produced a toothbrush he was ridiculed.

Entitled to four quarts of water a day, the men also received the mandatory daily ration of lime or lemon juice (with sugar). Every Tuesday, Thursday and Saturday they were allotted one-and-a-quarter pounds of salt beef (called "salt horse"), and on Monday, Wednesday and Friday they were doled one pound of salt pork. On Friday they were also given one pound of fish (dry, preserved or fresh). On Sunday they feasted on a pound each of canned meat. The food, when not actually rotten, was often so badly prepared it was all but inedible. By now accustomed to even worse fare, Eugene no longer really cared what he ate.

The New York's first port of call was Queenstown (later renamed

Cobh) on the south shore of Great Island in Cork Harbor, only seventy-five miles from James O'Neill's birthplace in Kilkenny.

The crew was not allowed ashore, but the ship's pause in Queenstown was the closest Eugene had ever come to the land his father never ceased to glorify, and to which Eugene felt spiritually connected. (" . . . although I am all Irish on both sides of my family," he wrote to the wife of William Butler Yeats some fifteen years later, "I have never been nearer to Ireland than the harbor of Queenstown — when I used to be a sailor on transatlantic liners.")

The ship disembarked passengers first at Cherbourg and finally, at the end of July, at Southampton, where an often-violent and widely-reported sailors' and dock-workers' strike was in progress. The strike, begun in mid-June, was affecting all of England's ports and the New York was put into drydock for nearly three weeks of repairs.

Along with the rest of the crew, Eugene stayed aboard to work, but he had frequent shore leaves. Exploring the waterfronts of Southampton, London and Liverpool, he could not help but be aware of the strike's serious impact. In Liverpool, the police — wielding batons — and the strikers — responding with blackjacks — battled in the streets.

The deckhands and the firemen, traditionally contemptuous of each other, were for once united, and their militant opposition to the shipowners was achieving results. The crews of some passenger ships deserted, and their defiance, combined with the defection of dockworkers, prevented many sailings. Food was left to rot in the holds of cargo ships and on the quays.

While the British strikers were doomed to disappointment in their hope for an international uprising of transportation workers, they had nevertheless caused enough disruption by early July to force the shipowners to recognize their union and offer a rise in wages. Many of their other demands, however, went unmet.

Most of the strikers returned to work in London and other ports, but the Liverpool crewmen and dockworkers remained recalcitrant and the shipowners threatened to lock them out.

On August 15, with the lockout in effect, a strike was called of all transport workers in Liverpool and Birkenhead and military reinforcements were summoned. The following day, the press reported a "reign of terror" in Liverpool and a headline in the London Times declared, "Labor Agitation Gone Mad." The Railway Workers Union called on its men to strike, and in Liverpool the streetcar workers left their jobs.

Although O'Neill dwelt at length and with intense nostalgia on his voyage to England (as he did on other aspects of his seafaring days), he never spoke of the extended strike in interviews or letters.

The only evidence that he took any notice of it at all is the play, *The Personal Equation* (initially called *The Second Engineer*), written in 1915. The play was subsequently disavowed by him and not produced in his lifetime. It deals with plans to dynamite the engines of a ship called the S.S. San Francisco when she docks in Liverpool, with union leaders hoping the terrorist act will set off an international strike.

It is clear from the play that Eugene was less interested in the politics of the agitators than in the personal psychology and social habits of his fellow sailors. The only characters with any vitality are the sailors aboard the San Francisco — types he later portrayed in greater depth in the *S.S. Glencairn* cycle.

In the company of such sailors, Eugene explored the sprawling docks of Liverpool, Southampton and London, absorbing material for future plays — consciously or not — as he had during his earlier voyages. One exemplary sailor, Starbuck Perry, was remarkably articulate, possessed an awesome memory, and enriched Eugene's knowledge of a seaman's alienated life.

Starbuck then was fifty-eight, and had been putting out to sea for thirty-seven years. He was a mountain of a man who, in the words of a shipmate of Eugene's, "took nothing from no one." Describing himself as "a tough, rugged man" and "a hard drinker when ashore," Starbuck bragged that "every blanky blank bone" in his body had been broken and that he had a hole in his skull into which "you could put your thumb."

His left and right ribs had been smashed, he reported with evident glee. "My right arm has been broken. My right leg has been broken three times, my left leg once . . . Look at my right thumb! Out of joint in two places. Look at this finger! I had the tip slashed and cut off."

Starbuck, who wore an incongruous goatee and a handlebar mustache, had known Jack London and was not too modest to admit he had often held London spellbound with his tales. Among the stories in his repertoire to which Eugene was privy was the time he was shanghaied during his first sea passage at age twenty-one.

"I shipped as an able seaman on the barque, The Chieftain, in

1874," Starbuck said. "After we got paid off [in Liverpool] I went on a drunk, and the first thing I knew was when I woke up aboard of the Nova Scotia barque John Peacock, and found that I'd been 'shanghaied,' and was on my way to Rio de Janeiro . . . Some ships had a very bad name and had a hard time getting a crew. So the boarding-house masters used to fill up a few men with liquor and put them aboard a ship while they were drunk. By the time they came to, the vessel would be at anchor in mid-stream, or else towing out to sea."

Starbuck's tale partly suggested the episode in *The Long Voyage Home*, in which the hapless sailor, Olson, suffers a similar fate. But Eugene also saw at first hand the ugly treatment offered inebriated sailors. Considered fair game by the proprietors of disreputable boardinghouses and saloons, these newly landed sailors were lured to their establishments by street thugs and prostitutes, working on commission, with offers of free booze.

Any sailor who took the bait was likely to find himself not only relieved of his month's accumulated wages within a few days, but in debt to the boardinghouse proprietor — and often on board a ship he would not willingly have sailed in had he been sober.

The setting for *The Long Voyage Home*, "the bar of a low dive on the London waterfront — a squalid, dingy room dimly lighted by kerosene lamps," was a composite of a notorious saloon in London and a similar one in Liverpool; both were frequented by men like Starbuck and another seaman, James Francis Quigley, who was Eugene's age and, for a time, his shadow.

The proprietress of the Liverpool dive, which had sawdust on the floor and was patronized largely by ship's firemen, closed her eyes to the activities of a man called Shanghai Brown, who supplied her with customers, and who would have shipped his own father to China for a pound. Nick, the crimp, in *The Long Voyage Home*, could have been patterned on Shanghai Brown — "round shouldered . . . his face . . . pasty, his mouth weak, his eyes shifty and cruel . . . dressed in a shabby suit which must have once been cheaply flashy" and a man who pronounced Buenos Aires "Bewnezerry."

While Starbuck Perry himself is not a specifically identifiable character in any of O'Neill's plays, he was such a legendary and picturesque old salt that O'Neill could scarcely have avoided using bits of his personality and background in the composites he drew, or in the atmosphere he created aboard his fictional vessel, the Glencairn. Born in Brooklyn in 1853, as Henry Perry, he had endured just about every hazard a sailor could encounter on his voyages to every principal port of the world, and he knew just about everything there was to know about shipping out under sail or steam.

One of the hazards he survived was a fall, during a high wind, from the yardarm of an American windjammer bound from New York to London in 1879. "I struck my head on the edge of the pump, fracturing my skull and breaking my thigh," he recalled. "That's how I got this hole in my head."

When the ship reached London, Starbuck, unconscious, was taken to the hospital where, to the amazement of his doctors, he survived. "I got to drinking pretty heavily while I was still receiving hospital treatment," he said, "and the doctor advised me to move into the Sailors' Home, where there was no liquor and where the rules and regulations were more strict."

A few months later, he signed on another windjammer called the Tillie E. Starbuck, on which he made four long voyages around the Horn, and earned his nickname. His crew was a hardboiled lot and he had to be even tougher to control them — but, as he pointed out, he was never known as a bullying skipper.

"Some skippers and mates went to extremes and turned their ships into floating Hells," he recalled. "Many a sailor has been driven to desperation by being constantly picked on and bullied around by some mate that took a dislike to him; and many a victim of this kind of hazing has 'accidentally' dropped a marling-spike from aloft on to the head of a mate that was making his life miserable. And many a mate has 'fallen' over the ship's side on a dark night, and nobody has known how it happened when he came to be missed at the change of the watches . . . There used to be a saying: 'He that goes to sea for pleasure might as well go to Hell for pastime.'"

James Francis Quigley, who invariably joined Eugene during his Liverpool leaves, was a merry-eyed, wiry, boisterous sailor with almost as great a zest as Starbuck for the salty anecdote.

Still putting out to sea as a bosun in 1956, Quigley recalled how, in Liverpool, he and Eugene used to flirt with the "Mary Ellens," who, according to Quigley, were "good girls, ready to say hello to any friendly sailor — and they wore no pants." Quigley and Eugene dallied not only with the amateur Mary Ellens, but with the professional prostitutes frequenting the waterfront saloons. "Gene was so handsome," Quigley said, "that he didn't have to look for women. They'd come over to his table and ask for the privilege of sitting down with him."

Eugene was partial to a wide-hipped, languorous blonde who

wore a red rose in her bosom and laced her whiskey with bitters to stay sober. He called her Cecilia (though that was not her name). One evening Eugene confused and delighted Cecilia by fixing her with his dark eyes and murmuring: "My heart has dreamed dreams I might never have known — a beautiful whore!"

A few minutes later, when Quigley bent down to recover a dropped match, he could not resist fondling Cecilia's ankle under the table. She rebuffed him indignantly and returned to her dreamy contemplation of Eugene. Appreciative of her loyalty, Eugene poked fun at Quigley's clumsy attempt to steal his girl. One night, when a seaman made a slurring remark about Cecilia (and included Quigley's own girl in the insult), Eugene and Quigley started a free-for-all, from which they both emerged with black eyes.

In Liverpool, as well as in Southampton, Eugene and Quigley were sometimes accompanied by a coal stoker known only by his last name, Driscoll. Eugene had met Driscoll casually at Jimmy the Priest's, and was flattered that Driscoll was willing, in his case, to overlook the inbred animosity of the stoker for the deck sailor. It was not that either group regarded itself as superior, O'Neill once said, but that each had "a healthy contempt" for the other.

"I shouldn't have known the stokers," O'Neill once told an interviewer, "if I hadn't happened to scrape an acquaintance with one of our own furnace-room gang at Jimmy the Priest's. His name was Driscoll." And in a letter some years later he wrote that Driscoll "lived, when ashore, at the same waterfront dump — Jimmie [sic] the Priest's — that I did."

Driscoll had shipped as a stoker on the S.S. Philadelphia, and he and Eugene evidently cemented the tenuous friendship begun at Jimmy the Priest's — a detail confirmed in the short story, "Tomorrow." The story's autobiographical narrator says he and the stoker, Lyons (O'Neill's fictional name for Driscoll) "had become great friends through a chance adventure together ashore in Southampton."

Their relationship illustrated the sort of sympathy and protectiveness that Eugene seemed to inspire in older men who inevitably drew him into their idiosyncratic universe. Driscoll, ten years older than Eugene, was essentially uneducated. He possessed a lust for living that appealed to Eugene, who once characterized him as "a Liverpool Irishman," explaining that to sailors all over the world, "'Liverpool Irishman' is the synonym for a tough customer."

Driscoll had in fact been born in Ireland, not Liverpool, and became a citizen of the United States. But it was his powerful personality, not the details of his birth, that fascinated Eugene and inspired the ferocious portrait of the stoker, "Yank," in *The Hairy Ape*.

Driscoll began to appear in O'Neill's writing three years after the two met, turning up in all four of the *Glencairn* plays: in *Bound East for Cardiff* he is called by his real name, and described as "a brawny Irishman with the battered features of a prizefighter"; in *The Moon of the Caribbees*, also as Driscoll, he is described as "a powerfully built Irishman"; in *The Long Voyage Home*, he again appears as "a tall, powerful Irishman" and in *In the Zone*, identified merely as a seaman, he is given the same dialect as the Driscoll character in the other three plays.

In *Bound East for Cardiff* and *The Moon of the Caribbees*, O'Neill gave a character named Yank some of Driscoll's physical and personal attributes, splitting the character, as it were, with Driscoll.

A sort of offshoot (or mutation) of Driscoll appears in the *Glencairn* plays in the person of Paddy, a squat, ugly Liverpool Irishman. Paddy, incidentally, turns up again — this time as an old, wizened Irishman — in *The Hairy Ape* and, with the same characteristics, in "Tomorrow." In both the story and the play, Paddy is given to singing "Whiskey Johnny" "in a thin, nasal, doleful tone."

All of these miniature portrayals, though effective in their way, turned out to be preparatory sketches for O'Neill's full-scale portrait of Driscoll in *The Hairy Ape*, where he is described as "broader, fiercer, more truculent, more powerful, more sure of himself than the rest [of the crew]." A noteworthy foreshadowing of *The Hairy Ape* occurs in *The Moon of the Caribbees*, when one crew member insults another: "You ain't no bleedin' beauty prize . . . a 'airy ape, I calls yer."

"[Driscoll] was a giant of a man and absurdly strong," O'Neill told an interviewer not long after the successful production of *The Hairy Ape*. "He thought a whole lot of himself, was a determined individualist. He was very proud of his strength, his capacity for grueling work. It seemed to give him mental poise to be able to dominate the stokehole, do more work than any of his mates."

Eugene and Quigley were both broke by the time their leaves ended. This was often the way with sailors. According to Starbuck Perry, "Sailors were never very good hands at saving money, although some of course were more careful than others. I've known of men coming ashore after a long voyage, and having a payday of four or five hundred dollars; and then going through it all in two or three days, and not having the price of even a shirt or a pair of socks to show for all the hardships they had experienced at sea.

"Some men just threw their money away, squandered it; bought drinks for everyone in the house, round after round. Other men were more careful and had sense enough to rig themselves out with some good clothing before they started on a spree. The men who spent their money quickest were the first to go to sea again. If a fellow hadn't had sense enough to pay his boarding-master for a few weeks in advance before spending his voyage's earnings, he didn't stay ashore very long."

Eugene and Quigley were lucky enough to have inspired a sense of gratitude in the prostitute, Cecelia, and her friend, who, in return for having their honor defended, offered them money. Quigley never forgot Eugene's comment that only a whore would have displayed such generosity.

With the S.S. New York still laid up for repairs in mid-August, Eugene decided to transfer to the Philadelphia, on which Driscoll was about to return to New York. Eugene was advanced to the rank of Able-Bodied Seaman — an achievement he boasted about all his life — and he boarded the Philadelphia on August 19. It was this voyage that provided the background and atmosphere for *The Hairy Ape*.

Because they had certified their friendship in the saloons of Liverpool and Southampton, Driscoll permitted Eugene a rare glimpse into the environment he was later to dramatize. They had, in fact, become close enough to share their amusement over the eccentric ship's master, Captain A. R. Mills, a man of outsized girth who cultivated a walrus mustache and was rumored to drink a bottle of whiskey a day.

Hardboiled as Eugene had found the deckhands, he soon had a chance to confirm Driscoll's boast that there was no one tougher than a fireman in the stokehole. He saw for himself that firemen were truly a breed apart — endowed with inhuman endurance. One stoker groomed his hair with a scrubbing brush.

Stripped to the waist in the suffocatingly hot and airless pit that held the furnaces and boilers, the coal passers plunged their heavy shovels into bins piled high with coal, to replenish the mounds behind the firemen. It was the firemen who prodded open the furnace doors with their shovels, flung the coal into the flaming mouths and slammed the doors shut again.

Working at a murderous pace to feed furnaces that consumed

three hundred tons of coal a day, the men groaned about sweating "blood for steam," and this was almost literally true. Not infrequently an exhausted stoker thrust his head into the coal chute as a load came down from above, to be knocked out and laid up for a rest. Although such a tactic would doubtless have killed an ordinary man, it did not seem to give the stokers more than a bad headache. They had hard skulls, toughened by coal-shovel fights; the trademark of such a battering was a permanent bluish discoloration of the skin.

Even without this disfigurement, firemen and coal passers were a sight that shocked passengers who chanced to encounter them. In *The Hairy Ape*, O'Neill graphically illustrated such an encounter. A jaded young society woman who wants to see how "the other half" lives, persuades the second engineer to show her the stokehole. Confronted by Yank, she exclaims, "Oh, the filthy beast!" and faints.

Even ashore, as Eugene had already discerned, no amount of scrubbing could obliterate the embedded rings of black dust around a stoker's eyes and in the creases of his skin. In his stage directions for *The Hairy Ape*, O'Neill noted that the coal shovelers could not stand upright because "the ceiling crushes down" upon their heads, with "the resultant over-development of back and shoulder muscles."

He said they "should resemble those pictures in which the appearance of Neanderthal Man is guessed at. All are hairy-chested, with long arms of tremendous power, and low, receding brows above their small, fierce, resentful eyes." In acknowledgment of their superhuman labor, the stokers were doled a cup of rum following each watch, after which they collapsed into sleep on their narrow bunks. Four hours later they were back in their inferno, breathing flame and dust and sweating blood.

The S.S. Philadelphia reached New York on August 26, 1911, and Eugene collected his pay; less the amount he had spent in the canteen, it came to $14.84. He obtained his "Mutual Release" from the ship and, wearing his jersey with the "American Line" stitching and with his A.B. discharge certificate in his pocket, he headed back to Jimmy the Priest's. There, he recorded his mixed feelings about what was to be his last voyage as a seaman, in the poem called "Ballad of the Seamy Side."

Where is the lure of the life you sing?

Let us consider the seamy side:
The fo'c'stle bunks and the bed bugs' sting,
The food that no stomach could abide,
The crawling "salt horse" flung overside
And the biscuits hard as a cannon ball;
What fascination can such things hide?
"They're part of the game and I loved it all."

Think of the dives on the waterfront
And the drunken brutes in dungaree,
Of the low dance halls where the harpies hunt
And the maudlin seaman so carelessly
Squanders the wages of months at sea
And maybe is killed in a bar room brawl;
The spell of these things explain to me —
"They're part of the game and I loved it all."

Tell me the lure of "working mail"
With two hours sleep out of twenty four,
Hefting bags huge as a cotton bale
Weighing a hundred pounds or more,
Till your back is bent and your shoulders sore
And you heed not the bosun's profane call;
Such work, I should think, you must abhor!
"It's part of the game and I loved it all."

"I grant you the food is passing bad,
And the labor great, and the wages small,
That the ways of a sailor on shore are mad
But they're part of the game and I loved it all."

There is no doubt that Eugene, despite his complaints, did love it all. Yet, he never shipped out again, probably for a variety of reasons. First, the era of the clipper ship was over, and a sailor's work aboard a steamship was, as O'Neill pointed out, mainly drudgery. Second, there was very limited access to alcohol aboard ship and he could no longer live without it. Finally, he knew in some inner recess of his consciousness that he had got all the material he would need for possible future writing.

He never tired of recalling his "years" at sea though he spent no more than a total of some sixteen weeks actually aboard ship. His discharge certificate listing him as "E. G. O'Neill, A.B." was, he said in his fifties, among his "most treasured possessions . . . the only memento" of his sailor days "that didn't get lost, strayed, or stolen."

Every time he boarded a ship as a passenger in later years, his early ocean-going was instantly evoked. In 1926, for example, writing from a steamer en route to Bermuda, he told Carlotta Monterey, soon to be his wife: "She's starting to roll now, off the Hook. I remember in my sailor days what a thrill of living it gave me, that first feel of the great ground swell of ocean heaving under me."

"Gene's pride seemed to be in those years," Carlotta once said, trying to explain his exultant memories (but getting the details slightly confused).

"He used to talk about his sea years and his flat down on the waterfront, where he slept on the floor. And I said to him once, half-jokingly, 'I have dragged you about Europe. I have worked like anything to show you all the beautiful spots, and I have never heard you say once that you liked this or that or the other.' 'Well,' he said, 'I liked them, but they weren't very exciting.'"

Much as Eugene loved the romance of going to sea, and proud as he was of his A.B. rating, he knew he did not want a career as a sailor. But he could not summon the courage to commit himself to a writing career, although he continued to toy with the idea. His inertia, depression and lack of focus were undoubtedly traceable (as he himself believed) to the failings of his family. It is undeniable that he was also spoiled, egotistical and brimming with self-pity and, at twenty-two, still remarkably immature.

With money for whiskey in his pocket and despair in his soul, he had no plan beyond getting drunk at Jimmy the Priest's, the one place on land he had persuaded himself he belonged. His sense of being at one with the saloon's habitués is made clear in "Tomorrrow" — particularly in his delight at Driscoll's acceptance of him.

In the guise of the narrator, Art, O'Neill described a scene featuring Driscoll (called Lyons in the story) that took place at the rooming house not long after his final voyage:

" . . . there was a great tramping from the stairs outside. Our door was kicked open with a bang and Lyons, the stoker, and Paddy Mehan, the old deep-water sailor, came crowding into the room. Lyons was in the first jovial frenzy of drink . . . [he] patted me affectionately on the back . . . the jar of it nearly knocked me off my feet but I managed to smile. Lyons and I were old pals. I had once made a trip as sailor on the Philadelphia when he was in her stokehold . . . He stood grinning, swaying a bit in the lamplight, a great, hard bulk of a man, dwarfing the proportions of our little room . . . "

To an interviewer, O'Neill once elaborated: "The voyage after I quit going to sea, Driscoll shipped on again as usual. I stayed behind at 'Jimmy the Priest's' . . . When the ship returned to New York Driscoll was the first to swing the saloon doors open and bellow for a drink. We could usually calculate the time of the ship's docking from the moment of Driscoll's appearance."

The narrator in "Tomorrow" goes on to describe a typical night of drinking with Driscoll/Lyons, and later in the story he talks of walking with him down to the Battery. "We spent the afternoon there, lounging on one of the benches. It was as warm as a day in Spring and we sat blinking in the sunshine drowsily listening to each other's yarns about the sea and lazily watching the passing ships."

There is no hint that by the time O'Neill was recounting this fragmentary episode, Driscoll was dead. To his interviewer, however, he explained that after he had "drifted away" from Jimmy the Priest's, he learned Driscoll had come "to a strange end."

It was Quigley who had heard the story at sea: It began with Driscoll jumping overboard from an ocean liner. A passenger spotted him and called for help and Driscoll was pulled from the water.

Two voyages later, on August 12, 1915, at a spot two thirds of the way from New York to England and 700 miles north of the Azores, Driscoll managed a successful suicide plunge over the side of an American Line steamship, the St. Louis. According to his death certificate, he "jumped overboard and was picked up by ships [sic] boat, but life was extinct when brought on board."

Driscoll's suicide, O'Neill recalled, was a "bewilderment" to everyone who knew him. "Why?" O'Neill asked. "That's it. That's it. That's what I asked *myself*." After brooding a long time, he concluded that something must have shaken Driscoll's "hard-boiled poise," for he "wasn't the type who just gave up, and he loved life."

O'Neill believed it was Driscoll's sense of "belonging" that had been destroyed, and this became the thesis of *The Hairy Ape*: Yank falls apart when his faith in the importance of his superhuman endurance in the stokehole is shattered. "Anyway," O'Neill said, "it was [Driscoll's] death that inspired the idea for the Yank of *The Hairy Ape*."

After the unpleasant encounter with his father upon returning from Buenos Aires, Eugene felt more estranged than ever from his parents. He had, however, stayed tenuously in touch through James's producer and friend, George Tyler. James was still allowing Eugene a dollar a day (to be collected at his convenience from Tyler at the Liebler and Company office). While condemning Eugene's life-style and giving him up as all but hopeless, James still could not bring himself to abandon him, any more than he could cut away the sinking Jamie. It could have been Ella who interceded for Eugene, as she apparently did for Jamie. In a passage crossed out in an early typescript of *Long Day's Journey Into Night*, O'Neill attributes James's continued support of Jamie to their mother. In this draft, Mary Tyrone tells her older son: "If I hadn't taken your part against your father for years and years, he'd have thrown you out in the street. You know very well there have been times when I've even had to threaten I'd leave him, if he did. He'd let you sleep in the park and starve to teach you a lesson!"

Pacified by his father's dollar-a-day dole, Eugene felt absolved from any effort to find a suitable occupation, or even to ship out again. Instead, he slid by degrees into a state of mindless alcoholism.

CHAPTER
TWENTY-SIX

EUGENE O'NEILL'S PSYCHE WAS FOREVER ALTERED BY THE raw life he lived at Jimmy the Priest's. Harking back to the atmosphere of that waterfront saloon, on which he largely based *The Iceman Cometh*, a character in the play drunkenly remarks, "Don't you notice the beautiful calm in the atmosphere? That's because it's the last harbor. No one here has to worry about where they're going next, because there is no farther they can go."

The habitués of Jimmy the Priest's, O'Neill once recalled, "were a hard lot, at first glance, every type — sailors, on shore leave or stranded; longshoremen, waterfront riffraff, gangsters, down and outers, drifters from the ends of the earth."

It was at Jimmy the Priest's, he said, that he got to know them all and learned not to sit in judgment on people. "In some queer way," he said, "they carried on."

Filtering these outcasts through his artist's eye, O'Neill peopled a number of his plays with them, even prior to *The Iceman Cometh*. In 1919, for example, he portrayed a man he had met at Jimmy's in a play called *Chris Christophersen*, which he described as "a character study of an old Swede." The Swede, noted O'Neill, was "an old deepwater sailor," whose "end in real life was just one of many of the tragedies that punctuated Jimmy the Priest's."

O'Neill told friends at the time that his description of Chris in the play was exactly as he remembered him: "A short, squat, broadshouldered man of about fifty," with "a thick, drooping yellow mustache," and a "mop of grizzled blond hair." His light blue eyes "peer short-sightedly, twinkling with a simple good humor."

When the play failed in its out-of-town tryout, O'Neill rewrote it with the emphasis on old Chris's daughter, calling it *"Anna Christie"*. In this version, Chris's surname is spelled "Christopherson" (with a last-syllable "o"). Evidently O'Neill had discovered this was the Swedish form, whereas "Christophersen" (with an "e") was Norwegian or Danish — and he wanted his Chris, for whatever reason, to be Swedish.

O'Neill once explained that Chris, immortalized for his consuming hatred of "dat ole davil sea," had "sailed the sea until he was sick of the mention of it, but it was the only work he knew." At the time they lived together at Jimmy the Priest's, O'Neill said, Chris "was out of work, wouldn't go to sea and spent the time guzzling whiskey and razzing the sea. In time, he got a coal barge to captain. One Christmas Eve he got terribly drunk and tottered away about two o'clock in the morning for his barge."

In back-to-back interviews in late 1924, O'Neill described Chris's bizarre death in virtually the same words: " . . . next morning he was found frozen on a cake of ice between the piles and the dock. In trying to board the barge he stumbled on the plank and fell over."

O'Neill, however, reinvented the real Chris's life, in both *Chris Christophersen* and *"Anna Christie"*; instead of having him drown, he left Chris alive to ship out to sea once again. O'Neill seemed eager to point out to his interviewers the difference between the literal and the creatively imagined. Without actually saying so, he was implying that his decision to leave his Chris alive at the end of *"Anna Christie"* transmuted the mundane story into a work of art.

During the seven months he lived at Jimmy the Priest's, Eugene sometimes passed the day listening to confessions of maudlin dreams and regrets over dashed hopes. As a spiritual brother to these outcasts, and like them preoccupied with staying drunk, he had no ambition to change his surroundings. When his cash ran out, he ambled to the piers, where he earned a few dollars carrying mail sacks onto and off the ships. When possible, he availed himself of a less strenuous method of obtaining whiskey known as "lowering the boom on the live ones." This entailed watching the incoming ships and putting the touch on seamen he knew.

Insist as he might that he was one with the boarders at Jimmy the Priest's, he surely was aware of how dramatically he differed from them. He could not negate his privileged early education nor his inherited sensitivity. Moreover, he had a family to fall back on any time he chose to pull himself together — and he knew his daily dollar awaited him whenever he felt energetic enough to go uptown to collect it.

His own later claim that he had been a committed member of "the last harbor" was thus difficult to accept. It made a more romantic story to remember it that way, rendering his subsequent redemption more dramatic and delighting his sense of extremes.

It is highly doubtful, for instance, that any other member of the brotherhood at Jimmy's would have had the curiosity and motivation to make successive trips uptown to see the newly-arrived Irish Players in their stunning first New York repertory appearance. On behalf of Liebler and Company, George Tyler had brought the Players from Dublin's Abbey Theater for a five-month tour of thirty-one cities.

Headed by Sara Algood, Maire O'Neill, Cathleen Nesbitt, Arthur Sinclair and J. M. Kerrigan, the company arrived November 20, 1911 at Maxine Elliott's Theater on West Thirty-ninth Street. The repertory of sixteen plays by, among others, Yeats, Synge, Lady Gregory, Lennox Robinson and T. C. Murray, was an exhilarating event for true lovers of a literary theater, but to the working-class Irish it was a threat and a challenge.

Tyler was, of course, aware that the Abbey Players had run into trouble in Dublin with Synge's *The Playboy of the Western World*, in which the hero's swaggering was interpreted as an outrageous attack on the repressed Irish peasant character. Nonetheless, despite rumblings in the Irish press, Tyler hoped things might go more smoothly in New York.

On opening night, fifty plainclothes policemen mingled with the audience, which, Tyler noticed, included "a suspicious number of square-jawed lads and colleens." When the curtain rose they threw vegetables and stink bombs at the actors until the police hustled the agitators out of the theater. The performance was then resumed, with the first act repeated.

"Funny business that was," Tyler later wrote. "The play was written by an Irishman, the company was Irish, the rioters were Irish, the cops were Irish, and it was an Irish judge that fined them all for disorderly conduct." As for O'Neill, though he considered himself Irish to the core, he once told his fellow playwright, Sean O'Casey, apropos the rioting, "The Irish can't laugh at themselves."

The Players failed to draw large audiences during their scheduled six-week run. Eugene was among the minority that attended faithfully, using the entrée provided by his father's connections (in this case, the producer himself).

He was particularly responsive to Synge's one-act play, *Riders to the Sea*, which depicts an old peasant woman's desolation over the sequential drowning of her fisherman-husband and six sons. "They're all gone now, and there isn't anything more the sea can do to me," she keens, as the body of her sixth son is carried into her hut at the edge of the treacherous sea.

Another play in the repertory, T. C. Murray's *Birthright*, depicted two jealous, embattled brothers, the sons of a stern and ruthless farmer, which likely suggested aspects of O'Neill's first Broadway play, *Beyond the Horizon*, as well as the later *Desire Under the Elms*.

"It was seeing the Irish Players for the first time that gave me a glimpse of my opportunity," O'Neill later recalled — surely an indication that his state of mind at the time was not completely hopeless. " . . . I went to see everything they did. I thought then [in 1911] and I still think [in 1923] that they demonstrated the possibilities of naturalistic acting better than any other company."

It was not that he had forgotten the "entire new world of the drama" revealed to him in 1907 when he first saw the Moscow Art Theater's production of *Hedda Gabler*; but much as he had admired that production at the time, he later said the Moscow theater "could not hold a candle to the original Abbey Theater Company, which toured America."

Eugene's compulsion to rouse himself from his alcoholic apathy for the sake of traveling uptown day after day to see the Irish Players is mystifying. He must have been possessed of a half-conscious conviction even then — some eighteen months before he actually attempted to write a play — that he was destined to be a dramatist.

If that was the case, however, then his plunge back into a drunken and desolate existence at Jimmy the Priest's is equally bizarre. The explanation may lie in the fact that he was still trying to avoid taking responsibility for his life and for his entanglement with Kathleen Jenkins.

Kathleen herself, by this time, had agreed to be guided entirely by her mother, just as Eugene had submitted to his father. "My mother thought it was bad for my reputation to be a gay, grass widow," she recalled many years later. "I nursed the baby two weeks, but was very free after that because my mother had a French nurse and a maid. My mother felt I should either stop going out with men, or get divorced. When I agreed to the divorce, she said I mustn't ask for a cent of alimony, as she would support me and the baby."

Shortly before Christmas, 1911, Eugene received a letter from an attorney named James C. Warren, who stated Kathleen had decided to seek an uncontested divorce. She agreed not to ask for alimony or child support; all she wanted was custody of their son.

Warren explained that Eugene had to provide Kathleen with evidence of adultery, the only permissible grounds for a New York State divorce. For her part, Kathleen would quietly establish residence in the town of White Plains in Westchester County (at 17 Church Street), in an effort to avoid the sort of press coverage that the birth of Eugene Jr. had elicited.

Doubtless it was James who had provided the Jenkins attorney with Eugene's address. James was obviously delighted that no alimony was being sought and that the O'Neills were not being asked to take any responsibility for the baby. Now touring the vaudeville circuit in a condensed version of *Monte Cristo*, James was allowing Eugene to play out his derelict phase for as long as it took, but he could hardly pass up the chance to be rid, so cheaply, of the Jenkins encumbrance.

Eugene could have provided ample evidence of adultery, having frequently visited — among others — an acquiescent woman named Maude Williams on West Forty-seventh Street. Warren pointed out, however, that it was necessary for Eugene to be caught flagrante delicto by arranged witnesses, and Maude evidently was not quite that acquiescent.

The contrived business seemed not only embarrassing, but shabby and ignoble. If the sentiments O'Neill later expressed in his plays can be taken as a guide, he had the grace to feel sorrier for Kathleen than for himself. (As noted, the early *Servitude* and *Before Breakfast*, as well as one of the last plays, *A Touch of the Poet*, introduce the theme of men guiltily trapped into marriage by inadvertent pregnancies.)

Eugene realized, however, he had no choice. He discussed his dilemma with Ted Ireland, the illustrator who had replaced Ed Keefe at George Bellows's studio. Ireland, who occasionally accompanied Eugene on drinking sprees, volunteered to serve as one of the witnesses.

On December 29, 1911, Eugene, accompanied by Ireland, Warren and two other "witnesses," Frank Archibold and Edward Mullen, fortified themselves in a saloon called the Campus near Columbia University. While the group outlined strategy during several rounds of drinks, Ireland apparently decided he did not want to be involved in the court proceedings and left. The others continued their bar-hopping in the West Forties, ending at a brothel at 140

West Forty-fifth Street.

As prearranged, Eugene selected a girl and took her upstairs, while Warren and the others waited below. After two hours, Eugene sent a maid to summon Warren, Archibold and Mullen to his room, where, according to Warren's later court testimony, they "all had a couple of drinks," and where he "saw this Eugene O'Neill and this woman in bed together. O'Neill at the time was undressed," as was the woman. O'Neill, Warren said, "left there with me about six o'clock in the morning."

The grounds for divorce having been duly established, Eugene, in disgust, proceeded to drink himself insensible. A new year dawned but it evidently held no symbol of hope. On January 20 Eugene was served with the divorce papers.

Still numb with drink, he went uptown with a friend in search of escape. As he later told the story, he happened to find a five-dollar bill on the sidewalk and he and his friend decided to try their luck at a gambling casino on Forty-fourth Street east of Sixth Avenue.

Once owned by Dick Canfield, the establishment was the most famous in the country with private rooms set aside for high rollers. But Canfield had been forced out of business by the District Attorney in 1904, partly because of the fleecing of a member of the Vanderbilt family who lost a hundred thousand dollars in a single night's play.

Reopened by others but still called Canfield's, it remained a magnet for gamblers in 1912. O'Neill enjoyed recalling that he had gambled in a house just a block from the Hotel Metropole, the scene not quite seven months later of one of the era's most lurid underworld crimes.

Herman "Beansy" Rosenthal, who operated a gambling house of his own, was ambushed and shot to death in front of the Metropole by several gunmen — including Lefty Louie, Dago Frank, Gyp the Blood and Whitey Lewis — on the orders of a corrupt police lieutenant, Charles Becker. The lieutenant had taken offense when "Beansy" claimed publicly that Becker was his silent partner. Becker died in the electric chair.

A devoted follower of underworld news, Eugene worked the sensational crime into a poem he wrote for a New London newspaper a month afterwards, making reference to Becker, Gyp the Blood and Lefty Louie. Later, O'Neill tended to pepper his plays with the jargon of gangsters and the colloquialisms of the demimonde.

This obsolete slang, of which he had a fluent command, often turned up in his correspondence as well — frequently emphasized with the exclamation mark to which he was also inordinately devoted. "The old bean," "in the pink," "palship" and "the glad mitt" were among the expressions with which he felt at home long after they had become archaic.

One of his last plays, the long one-act called *Hughie*, written when he was fifty-three, is an amazing compilation of such argot. In O'Neill's mind it was less a play than a short story, about a petty gambler and a night clerk in a seedy Manhattan hotel.

Their dialogue consists of a wide range of jargon: sap, noggin, sucker, puss, moniker, hooked, bangtail, finn, babe, sawbuck, croaked, bum dope, old bones, raw babies, rubbed out, real jack, old turtle, round-heeled, in my book, the sticks, the Big Stem, run-out powder, fall guy, clam shut, hit the hay, crummy dump, the once-over, het up, beat the racket, poor boob, square shake, lap it up, put the bite on.

The story of what ensued at Canfield's after he found that lucky fiver became a significant part of O'Neill's personal mythology and was retold in various versions (some wildly inaccurate) after O'Neill became famous in the 1920's.

The most detailed account was confided to Norman Winston, a benefactor of the Provincetown Players, producers of O'Neill's early efforts. A wealthy builder and planner, Winston became a friend and drinking companion in 1927. O'Neill told Winston that within an hour of entering Canfield's, he found himself two hundred dollars ahead. By that time — since the gambling houses of the era served free champagne — Eugene and his friend were noisily drunk. They were thrown out, but allowed to keep their winnings. It was a cold night and, as O'Neill told Winston, the last thing he remembered before he "drew a blank," was wildly celebrating in a Broadway saloon and thinking, "I wish I was south in New Orleans."

Following his binge, he said, he awoke in the upper berth of a train pulling into New Orleans and, to his astonishment, saw a poster announcing the imminent opening of James O'Neill's vaudeville version of *The Count of Monte Cristo*.

Whenever he told the story, O'Neill stressed the coincidence of his turning up "by chance" in the same place as his father, after their protracted estrangement.

To a friend, for example, he wrote in 1931: "I was in New Orleans broke, on the tail end of a bust which terminated in that city," adding that his father had "happened to play there just as things were becoming desperate." In a version as late as 1946, he claimed that after "a bountiful champagne party at the old Astor bar," he awoke to find himself on a train headed for New Orleans "simply because somebody suggested it was a nice place to go."

It seems highly unlikely it was the coincidence O'Neill claimed. In frequent touch with the Liebler office, he could not have been unaware of his father's touring itinerary — anymore than his father was unaware of the recent steps to procure the divorce from Kathleen.

That Eugene knew his father was scheduled to appear in New Orleans is supported by an interview he gave just as he was coming into prominence early in 1920. Without mentioning the winning streak at Canfield's, he said that after returning from his voyage on an American Line ship, and living in a waterfront dive, he "finally went to New Orleans to join my father, who was playing a condensed *Monte Cristo* in vaudeville."

James, in fact, after fulfilling his *Monte Cristo* booking in Memphis, had just opened at the St. Charles Orpheum in New Orleans when Eugene's train pulled in. A review that appeared in the New Orleans Times Picayune on January 23, 1912, called his portrayal of Edmond Dantes "still a work of art, and one of the finest of stage pictures" and noted that he was given "a great ovation for his vaudeville classic."

Eugene O'Neill's simple statement in the 1920 interview — making no claim to coincidence — has the ring of truth. In later years, he might have been embarrassed to admit that after his long separation he hungered to return to the solace of paternal authority.

An article in The New London Day of September 2, 1911, seems to suggest that O'Neill had in fact made a brief overture to his parents much earlier — less than a week after his return on the S.S. Philadelphia, in fact. But the newspaper's evidence that such a visit took place is insubstantial at best. Obviously pieced together from hearsay, the article stated that Eugene was recently back after visiting the "majority of the countries of the world," where he had been "hobnobbing with Arabs, Chileans, Turks" and "in a few weeks . . . will be off on a tramp freighter."

This specious story (which spelled O'Neill's name with one "l") failed to quote Eugene or, indeed, any other source, and nothing in the article indicated Eugene had actually been in New London. More likely, his father or brother had mentioned to someone that Eugene had recently returned from a sea voyage, and the reporter fleshed out this story with local gossip.

O'Neill, in a letter to his former schoolmate, Joseph McCarthy, described the actual reunion he finally had with James. It took place in mid-January of 1912, at which point, O'Neill wrote (slightly exaggerating the elapsed time), " . . . I had not seen my father in about a year."

Chapter
TWENTY-SEVEN

EUGENE DID NOT SURRENDER TO HIS FATHER WITHOUT an inner struggle. Stepping off the train in New Orleans, he found himself unready for a confrontation. Ambivalent and panicky, clutching his seaman's papers, he headed for the waterfront. But, as he recalled, "no ships seemed to be taking on anyone — at least not ships bound for New York where I wanted to return." Instead, he found his escape in barrooms, where he discovered Sazerac cocktails at two-for-a-quarter, and spent what was left of his gambling bonanza.

When at last his money ran out, he "went around to put the bite on the old man for the fare back to New York," as he later recalled, "but he just waved a hand and said, 'Oh, no, you got here; you get yourself away.' Then he paused and said, 'I need a man in the act. Do you want it? Ten dollars.' Well, I was being overpaid, but it was experience."

Both James and Ella, who was along on the tour, were shocked to find Eugene looking so haggard. They thought it expedient to take advantage of his plight to keep him, at least temporarily, under supervision. James had evidently forgotten his fatherly advice a few years earlier never to go on the stage; but the proffered role was a minor one — an assistant jailer — replacing an actor who had abruptly quit.

"You'll go on with Charlie in Utah," James said, referring to Charles Webster. At nineteen, Webster had appeared in only one production before joining James's company and, despite his lack of experience, was playing Monte Cristo's son, Albert, a role Jamie was now too alcohol-ravaged to perform; he had been demoted to the minor role of Nortier.

"But I'm not an actor," Eugene objected.

"Do what I say," ordered James. "You'll have only one line and Charlie will tell you what to do."

Eugene's role, in fact, consisted of a mere two words, but he fretted about his debut all the way to Ogden, Utah, where the company arrived in mid-February.

"It was a case of work or walk home," Eugene remembered. "I acted for the rest of the tour over the Orpheum Circuit."

James had launched the tabloid version of *Monte Cristo* in the fall of 1911, determined to extract whatever profit might yet be wrung from the sputtering vehicle. On October 15, when the tour played Cincinnati, where James was still a favorite son, one critic greeted him as "most welcome." But it was a reception accorded a relic.

"James O'Neill has passed the meridian of the physical," lamented the critic. "His hairs are whitened, if his brow is unwrinkled, and there is scarcely that elasticity of tread that marked his graceful posings when he was the foremost romantic actor of our stage."

James, who had just turned sixty-seven, told an interviewer that Cincinnati inevitably evoked memories of the past. "I am not so inclined to look backward in other places," he said, "but when I stand before the old National I am carried to the beginning; getting back to the present my life passes in review . . . I was wondering where, had I not gone on the stage, I would be now; whether I would have been more, or less, successful; whether I would be here at all; whether I would be more happy or less happy. You can't help such thoughts, you know, at this time of life." Aware that the final curtain for Edmond Dantes was soon to fall, James was beset by a sense of failure and intimations of mortality.

Jamie, as ever, stood ready to trample on his father's feelings. Years later, members of the company recalled their embarrassment at having to witness the painful confrontations between father and son. When lectured by James, Jamie jeered, "Why worry about it? You're what I'll be twenty years from now." Jamie, even in his minor role, caused concern from performance to performance about whether he would be able to keep himself upright.

On the first night in Ogden, Webster, doubling as Chief Jailer, assisted the miserable, sweating Eugene into a bulky black coat with an attached cape, and helped him hook a flowing mustache into his nostrils. Eugene lurched on stage in Webster's wake for the scene in which the Abbé Faria dies in his cell.

Webster went through his business of unlocking the cell door with a monstrous bunch of keys, letting the light from his lantern fall on the body of the abbé. Webster knelt, put his ear to the abbé's chest and fixed a dark look on his assistant jailer. That was Eugene's cue. His line was: "Is he . . . ?" To which Webster replied, "Yes, he's dead."

Eugene's nervousness proved catching. Webster delivered the news of the abbé's demise in an overwrought falsetto. The blackout that followed, instead of eliciting suspense, provoked derisive laughter. Eugene and Webster exchanged stunned glances in the semi-darkness and bolted for the wings. As they fled, they could hear James's bewildered voice: "What happened? What happened? I'll kill those boys."

Webster and Eugene climbed to the flies and hid until James, still calling, "Where are they? I'll kill them," was obliged to take his place on stage for the next scene. According to Webster, when Eugene finally had to face his father, he tried to laugh off his discomfiture by commenting wryly, "A chip off the old block, eh?" Whereupon James returned, "Say, rather, a slice off the old ham." More seriously, and in private — according to Eugene's own later recollection — James scolded his son, "I am not satisfied with your performance, sir," to which Eugene fliply replied, "I am not satisfied with your play, sir."

When reporters came backstage after the performance, having heard that James O'Neill's younger son was making his debut, they found James poised and smiling.

"He's a very handsome boy, Mr. O'Neill," one of the reporters remarked. "He takes after his father."

"He's much better-looking than I ever was," replied James, with a fitting note of paternal pride.

Eugene was not his father's equal in gallantry. Years later he remarked of the tour: "That cut-down version was wonderful. Characters came on that didn't seem to belong there and did things that made no sense and said things that sounded insane. The old man had been playing Cristo so long he had almost forgotten it, so he ad-libbed and improvised and never gave anybody a cue. You knew when your turn came when he stopped talking." Eugene, however, was no less severe on his own performance, disparaging himself as "a punk actor."

It is true that *Monte Cristo*, condensed to a playing time of forty-five minutes, was a wonderfully botched affair. It is doubtful, however, that Eugene would have been any more cooperative in a respectable production. As he later gleefully admitted to a friend, "I am proud to say that I preserved my honor by never drawing a sober breath until the tour had terminated."

To another friend he confessed that "the alcoholic content was as high as the acting was low," adding that he was graduated from the Orpheum Circuit with the degree of "Lousy Cum Laude."

If the tour had lasted just a little longer, he said, he would also have won his "D.T." His only regret was that he was unable to forewarn audiences to get equally drunk before his performance. "Although I was only on the stage for minutes at a time, I imagine there are still people in this country who awake screaming in the night at the memory of it."

On yet another occasion he remarked that the "general frightfulness" of the production reached "a high spot in the formidable lousiness of my acting," adding, "I couldn't have been worse if I'd been playing Hamlet." In a typically paradoxical backward look, however, O'Neill took a measure of pride in the disastrous tour.

"So you used to be a vaudevillian, did you?" he once wrote to an acquaintance. "Well, so was I — for some months on the Orpheum circuit in 1912. So we're fellow White Rats!" (The White Rats was the vaudeville actors' union, "Rats" being "star" spelled backwards.)

It would be an understatement to say that James himself was dissatisfied with the tour. Although he tried to conceal his feelings from his company, he was humiliated at having to return, at sixty-seven, to the unbecomingly youthful and uncomfortably athletic Edmond Dantes. If that was not comedown enough, his vaudeville *Monte Cristo* was the second half of a bill presented twice a day, following a trained-horse act and a troupe of acrobats.

Not that vaudeville was not a perfectly respectable, if slightly lowbrow, medium. Motion pictures were in their silent infancy and many stars, to keep active and earn good money between regular stage appearances, took to the vaudeville circuit in one-act plays or condensed versions of longer plays.

Even the majestic Sarah Bernhardt made a vaudeville tour (stipulating she would not appear with animal acts or blackface comedians). Bernhardt, however, played the more lucrative Keith Circuit, whose Palace Theater, advertised as the "Valhalla of Vaudeville," opened its doors on Broadway the following year. The smaller Orpheum chain, which radiated out of Chicago and San Francisco, was popular mainly in the West.

James, however, did not take *Monte Cristo* to vaudeville as a novelty. As he grew older, his fear of the poorhouse loomed ever larger and, though he was now a relatively rich man, he felt compelled to amass additional capital. The vaudeville tour seemed to be his only remaining means of earning a living. He received $1,250 a week, out of which he paid the salaries of his company. While this was a size-able sum for its day, it did not compare with Bernhardt's $7,000. It appeared that audiences — after twenty-eight years — had finally tired of *Monte Cristo.*

James's continuing concern over money was understandable: his wife required constant medical care and he was the sole support of the thirty-three-year-old Jamie, by now blacklisted by managers throughout the country.

As for Eugene, James was convinced he had a long way to go before achieving financial independence (and likely suspected Eugene's turning up in New Orleans was not happenstance). Misunderstood and unappreciated by the three people to whom he was devoting his life, James nonetheless felt compelled to squeeze every last dollar from *Monte Cristo* to support them.

During his barely four weeks with the tour, Eugene did not, like his vengeful brother, set out to undermine his father. Not that he made any effort to please him either. He resented having been sand-bagged into performing (as he thought of it) and felt it served his father right if he chose to treat the tour as one long, drunken frolic.

Some of Eugene's antics were merely embarrassing to James per-sonally, but others struck at his professional pride and even threat-ened what was left of his career. According to Webster, James watched Eugene warily every night, worried that, like Jamie, he might arrive at the theater inebriated.

Eugene occasionally doubled in the part of a silent messenger and James never knew if, when he came on stage, he would remember to bring with him the "prop" message, or if he would frantically search in his costume for the paper and finally hand his father empty air — drawing snickers from the audience.

Even worse, Eugene at times was drunk enough to stagger on stage, confront another player (or even James himself) and say, "So there you are, Tim Sullivan!" — a reference to a New London police-man who later turned up in the dialogue of *Ah, Wilderness!* On anoth-er occasion, he and his brother bumped shoulders on stage and fell down while his father was delivering a speech.

Jamie's mischief was cruder. At one point, he campaigned to get young Webster to twist a line spoken by Albert: " . . . I thought it my duty to repress *calumny.*" Night after night, as Webster awaited his cue in the wings, Jamie stood next to him and muttered in his ear, "I thought it my duty to repress *calomel.*"

Finally, Webster did slip, substituting the name of the popular purgative. James was mortified. Later that night, when Jamie and another actor were threading their way through the dark alley leading from the stage door, they were drenched by a bucketful of water thrown from a dressing-room window; Jamie correctly suspected Webster.

For a time James tried to set his sons an example of moderation. After the evening performance, he took them to a bar, bought them one drink each, then pointedly wished them good night and left. It was a ritual "like going to Mass," O'Neill told a friend. But his sons knew James was retiring to a bottle of good liquor in his hotel room and the routine did not impress them; the free round was simply their start on a night's carousing.

By the time the company reached Denver in mid-February, their escapades were growing wilder and more resourceful. Webster recalled, for example, that one Saturday night, following the performance, Jamie sent Eugene to a bordello, having arranged with the madam to have him greeted by her six best girls. Eugene, determined to outdo Jamie, told the madam that she was his choice. She was flattered enough to spend the rest of the weekend with him.

At dawn on Monday, when Eugene slunk back to his hotel, he noticed the desk clerk staring at his legs. Several inches of flaming red satin hung out below the hem of his overcoat. He had forgotten to doff the madam's kimono before taking his leave. For the rest of the day he and Jamie celebrated Eugene's conquest.

As *Monte Cristo* continued on its western tour, James felt not only shamed by his sons, but crestfallen at the indifference of his audiences. He now found apathy where he had long been accustomed to ovations.

Adding to his burden was his wife's increasingly trancelike behavior. Fearful of leaving her alone in their hotel room, he brought her to the theater to sit in his dressing room during performances. According to Webster, she appeared oblivious to her surroundings, even ignoring her sons. Once she impulsively walked from James's dressing room during the scene in which Monte Cristo discovers that Albert is not the son of his enemy, Fernand, but is in fact his own son. Ella stood in the wings, as if hypnotized by the emotionally charged dialogue:

MONTE CRISTO [*who has forced Albert to his knees*]: Fernand, I hold thy heart in my hand.

MERCEDES [*the boy's mother, who had been married to Monte Cristo before his imprisonment and presumed death, and who later married Fernand*]: What will you do?

MONTE CRISTO: I will kill him.

MERCEDES: You dare not!

MONTE CRISTO: Why not?

MERCEDES: Because — he is your son!

MONTE CRISTO: My — !

At the point where James forced Webster to his knees, Ella shuddered and began moving like a sleepwalker toward the stage. James had been glaring down into Webster's face, but when he raised his eyes his startled gaze told Webster that Ella was in the wings. James feared she might reach the stage, but someone tapped her shoulder, waking her from whatever reverie the scene had inspired. Although members of the company believed Ella was an invalid suffering from arthritis and were uneasy about her, no one guessed she was addicted to morphine.

Between his wife's erratic actions, his sons' destructive drinking and the omens of his own faltering career, James found himself unable to keep up the sanguine facade that had distinguished his life on the stage.

The members of his company were disconcerted as he began to exhibit unprecedented irascibility. Forced to acknowledge he no longer had the strength to cope with a scene involving an elaborate change of costume and makeup, for instance, he transferred his lines in the scene to young Webster, then proceeded to question the actor's ability to deliver them.

It was utterly unlike James to taunt an inexperienced actor trying his best to juggle multiple roles. James's behavior left a lasting impression on Webster, who, even forty-five years later, squirmed when recalling the incident. The part James relinquished was that of Monte Cristo disguised as a Jewish peddler, and Webster had a bad time with the dialect.

Supposedly drenched from a storm, Webster delivered the line, "Vot vedder, vot vedder" (followed by other equally elevated

remarks). James summoned Webster to his dressing room and insisted on hearing the lines over and over. Webster believed James was
worried that the unskilled accent would be attributed to him.

"Go to the pawnshops and talk to the Jewish people and learn
their accent and mannerisms," James ordered.

Eugene undertook Webster's defense. "He's doing fine," he told
his father, "I don't know how he does it."

"Of course," Webster recalled, "what Gene admired was the fact
that I could memorize and play three roles; he had trouble getting his
one line down pat."

Despite the cumulative evidence of Eugene's disruptive activity
during the tour, a theory has been advanced by at least one scholar
that O'Neill *invented* the details of his drunken misbehavior.

Support for this theory is attributed to interviews with the same
Charles Webster who had earlier, in interviews with the authors of
this biography, provided many of the details to bolster O'Neill's version of his actions. The theory, otherwise unsupported, states that
O'Neill could not bring himself to acknowledge his humiliating inep-
titude as an actor, and therefore linked his sorry performance to fab-
ricated tales of a protracted, drunken revel.

True, Webster did remember one notable occasion in Denver
when both Eugene and Jamie were intimidated into relative sobriety.
James had been invited to dinner with his sons at Elitch's Gardens, a
long-established resort featuring a zoo and a theater. "For God's sake,
stay sober," James cautioned them.

Despite the warning, they brought a concealed flask and, by the
time dinner was announced, had managed to sneak a number of
drinks. James, observing their condition as they sat down opposite
him at the crowded table, pinned them with a look of such stern command that neither of them uttered a word during the meal.

This turned out to be but a small victory for James in light of the
defeat that followed. On February 14, 1912, Variety, the authoritative
show-business voice, carried the following item, datelined Denver:

"After next week James O'Neill will end his Orpheum Circuit
tour . . . The production and star have been favorably received, but
Mr. O'Neill's support brought adverse comment all along the line,
and the voluntary cancellation has followed. The sketch had still
about eighteen weeks of Orpheum time contracted for." James later
confided to Art McGinley in New London that "the only black mark"
in the theater against him was when he had to close down the vaudeville tour because "the boys were too drunk."

The production had survived as long as it had only because of James's own forceful personality. Eugene had the integrity to feel ashamed, as attested by his later admission to a friend. In 1942, when the behavior of one of his own children had embarrassed him, he recalled the difficulties he had created for the long-suffering James. "As my father often used to remark with feeling, 'God deliver me from my children!'"

The *Monte Cristo* company was snowbound in Denver for more than a week, during which time Eugene, according to Webster, soaked up all the alcohol he could absorb. Just before the company embarked on its final week in St. Paul, Eugene deserted, making his way back to New York — and Jimmy the Priest's.

Mournfully, James fulfilled his engagement in St. Paul, after which he and Ella also headed back to New York. Before entombing *Monte Cristo* forever, James made two gestures toward his rusty vehicle.

James appeared that May at the Manhattan Opera House with fellow old-time actors in a traditional all-star "Lamb's Gambol" for the benefit of the Lamb's Club, selecting a scene from *Monte Cristo* along with the forum scene from *Julius Caesar*. He repeated the two scenes in June at the Boston Opera House.

He also agreed to put *Monte Cristo* on film. Even though he was somewhat contemptuous of the infant motion picture form, he rather liked the idea of having a permanent record of the role that had won him his niche, however restricted, in theater history.

TWENTY-EIGHT

LIFE LOOKED SO BLEAK TO EUGENE IN THE SPRING OF 1912 that he longed for nothing more than "a brain-drowning drunk" to make him forget he was alive. Once, when he lacked even the price of a five-cent whiskey, he felt despondent enough to sample the camphor-flavored wood alcohol gulped down in lethal doses by waterfront outcasts at the end of their rope.

More than ever, he was convinced his life held no future. To begin with, he could envision no job he would not find stultifying. While he clung to the vague possibility of becoming a writer, he had so far attempted to write only poetry and had no illusions about earning a living as a poet.

Even while holding his father responsible for the family's antagonisms, and blaming him for the emotional gulf that had widened during the disastrous Orpheum tour, he was helplessly dependent on him. Then, too, he was still pricked by pangs of conscience over his abandonment of Kathleen and their son. And so he drank until he could no longer think or feel — and until even drinking could not blot out his pain.

Wondering if he ought not kill himself after all, he soon suited action to thought. He made the rounds of pharmacies to collect Veronal tablets, which could then be purchased in small quantities without a prescription. Returning to Jimmy the Priest's, he swallowed what he believed to be a lethal dose of the barbiturate and fell asleep in his room.

In *Long Day's Journey Into Night*, O'Neill makes a pointed reference to this episode. His alter ego, Edmund, tells his father he was not drunk when he swallowed the Veronal. Responding to the taunt that during his derelict days he was merely playing "a game of romance and adventure," Edmund says sarcastically: "Yes, particularly the time I tried to commit suicide at Jimmie [sic] the Priest's, and almost did . . . I was stone cold sober. That was the trouble. I'd stopped to think too long."

Fortunately for Eugene, two of Jimmy's roomers found him asleep, guessed his condition, walked him up and down and fed him coffee until he regained consciousness.

The story of his suicide attempt, like that of his forced departure from Princeton and the accounts of his turning up in New Orleans, ultimately sprouted many versions. He himself delighted in telling it over the years, embellishing it with ever more vivid details. In George Jean Nathan's widely circulated, but implausible version, an unconscious O'Neill was sped by ambulance to Bellevue Hospital; while he was worked over by two interns, his friends sought out James O'Neill and obtained fifty dollars from him to pay the hospital fee.

When they returned to Bellevue — having first spent most of the money getting drunk — they found Eugene conscious, and divided what was left of the money with him, whereupon he "rolled over, grinned satisfiedly, and went happily and peacefully to sleep."

O'Neill's second wife, Agnes Boulton, in the memoir she wrote more than thirty years after her marriage had ended, reported a version she said O'Neill had told her, quoting him in a lengthy monologue. She does not claim to have taken notes at the time, and her memory at that point in her life was cloudy (as attested to throughout the memoir), but the words do sound like O'Neill's. It can only be conjectured that they came from an account written by him, possibly in a letter to her that was later lost or destroyed.

According to Agnes's account, Eugene, after swallowing the Veronal, set the hook on his door and lay in his room in a semiconscious state for twenty-four hours or more, occasionally coming to and hearing a knocking.

"It didn't occur to me that I was alive — after all those pills . . . " he said (or wrote). "Then a horrible thought came to me — I was dead, of course, *and death was nothing but a continuation of life as it had been when one left it!* A wheel that turned endlessly round and round back to the same old situation! This was what purgatory was — or was it hell itself? My body was dead, but I was there too."

After more knocking, the door was finally pushed in, admitting his "old pals from below." They got him onto his feet and downstairs, where — while the old pals continued their drinking — Jimmy called Bellevue and was advised to bring him in to be looked over. " . . . we didn't get going for a couple of hours or more," O'Neill said, according to Agnes. "Jimmy would start to call a taxi, then put it off. At last we made it . . . [and] five of them climbed into the taxi along with me."

They stopped twice for drinks, inviting the taxi driver to join them, and by the time they reached the hospital O'Neill was the only one still sober. The taxi driver pulled up to the entrance of the emergency ward, where he forcibly ejected his drunken passengers.

"I was still in a sort of a daze when I heard the intern telling me he'd take care of them — they'd get the works and be all right in a few days . . . 'Tough job you had!' the intern said politely . . . I got into the taxi and drove back to Jimmy the Priest's and managed to get potted to the gills. We all thought it was the biggest joke in the whole damn world."

It seems clear from O'Neill's jocular recollection of his suicide attempt that he had been making more of a macabre gesture than a sincere effort. He told the New York doctor, Robert Lee Patterson, who attended him when he was in his fifties, that right after swallowing the Veronal he changed his mind about wanting to die.

Since there is no record of Eugene's admission to Bellevue — apparently because he was treated as an outpatient — the exact date of the suicide attempt cannot be ascertained. There is compelling evidence to suggest that it took place in the early spring of 1912, not long after his sheepish retreat from the aborted *Monte Cristo* vaudeville tour, and that it was triggered at least in part by guilt over his bad behavior. In *Long Day's Journey Into Night*, Eugene's prototype, Edmund, apologizes to his father for "all the rotten stuff I've pulled!" and adds, "I've treated you rottenly, in my way, more than once."

At the time of the attempted suicide it is more than likely that Eugene, not knowing how to apologize, seized on a circuitous method to gain his father's forgiveness. He waited to swallow the Veronal until he was certain James had returned to New York from his tour.

James's horror of suicide is reflected in *Long Day's Journey Into Night*. James Tyrone, even while cursing the father who abandoned him as a child, cannot bring himself, as a Catholic, to credit the gossip that his father might have died by his own hand.

The strongest indication of the timing of Eugene's suicide attempt is contained in the autobiographical one-act play, *Exorcism* (subtitled "A Play of Anti-Climax"), written seven years after the attempt and produced by the Provincetown Players on March 26, 1920. Following its brief run, O'Neill destroyed all copies of the script for reasons he never revealed — but possibly to placate his father, who some weeks earlier had suffered a stroke.

While no script exists, a notebook entry survives, in which O'Neill places the time of the action as "just after dark of a miserable foggy day *in the middle of March . . .* " The notebook further confirms the play's autobiographical derivation: the set of *Exorcism* (accompanied by a rough sketch) unmistakably evokes O'Neill's quarters at Jimmy the Priest's — "a squalid rooming house . . . near the downtown waterfront, New York City — the ground floor being a saloon of the lowest type of grog shop . . . "

O'Neill goes on to describe the protagonist's accommodations as a small, filthy cubicle; its "walls and low ceiling, white-washed in some distant past, are spotted with the greasy imprints of groping hands and fingers. The plaster has scaled off in spots, showing the lathes beneath. The floor is carpeted with an accumulation of old newspapers, cigarette butts, ashes, burnt matches, etc."

The notebook entry lists a cast of three, the first being Ned Malloy, obviously based on O'Neill himself. The second character in the notebook is Ned's roommate, Jimmy, presumably based on James O'Neill's one-time press agent, the convivial and bibulous James Findlater-Byth, now calling himself simply Jimmy Byth. The third character is listed as Major Andrews (based on another roomer at Jimmy the Priest's, Major Adams, an Englishman who had served in the Boer War).

Two additional characters were added at some point during rehearsals of *Exorcism*; they are listed in the Provincetown Players' program as Mr. Malloy, "Ned's father," and someone called Nordstrom.

While there is no record of the two men who accompanied Eugene to Bellevue after rousing him, one undoubtedly was Byth. After leaving James O'Neill's employ and sinking to the job of promoting a Coney Island fireworks show, he was now, at only forty-five, a down-and-out-drunk living at Jimmy the Priest's. It is not known under what circumstances Eugene renewed his acquaintance with Byth. Jamie might have run into him and told him Eugene was staying at Jimmy the Priest's. In any case, Eugene seems to have welcomed him as his roommate.

There is additional substantiation that the play was inspired by Eugene's inept attempt to end his life in 1912. During its brief run, it was reviewed by three New York newspapers, in which the plot was described in considerable detail. Alexander Woollcott in The Times, for example, described the protagonist as "a young man so full of contempt [for his family] that he has walked out head high and fallen into the gutter."

At the play's beginning, wrote Woollcott, "he is down to the dregs of existence . . . equally revolted by the character of his life and by the prospect of a surrendering, prodigal-son return . . . So he swallows poison . . . "

Characterizing *Exorcism* as "uncommonly good," Woollcott provided the most comprehensive account of its plot and consequently the clearest indication of how true it was to life. After describing the scene in which Ned Malloy takes poison and "curls up on his miserable bed," Woollcott continued:

"Twenty-four hours elapse and you find him stretched out under the delighted ministrations of two drunken friends, who are bibulously pleased with themselves for having yanked him back from the brink of the grave. You see him slowly reviving, only to find the ugly, inescapable world still closing in around him, with its intolerable tedium represented by the two souses, each still telling, over and over again, his favorite story.

"The suicide comes back to find everything wearisomely the same — everything except himself. Slowly he realizes that he is different — that the devils have gone out of him. Slowly it dawns on him that, when a fellow tries hard to kill himself and seems to fail, the effect is quite as though he had succeeded. The person revived is a new person, the life ahead is life in a new world."

This ending appears to confirm what actually happened. Eugene's attempted suicide elicited the desired remorse and forgiveness in James, and Eugene's inner rage was assuaged at least for a time. Not long after, he found the resolve to abandon Jimmy the Priest's. His brush with death had the effect of pointing him for the first time in a constructive direction. Gradually he even began to believe that there might be a future.

Exorcism was neither the beginning nor the end of O'Neill's literary preoccupation with death. The subject, like whores and the sea, recurs repeatedly in his plays, starting as early as 1913. A psychiatrist, Dr. Louis Bisch, after analyzing him for six weeks when he was in his early thirties, came to the fairly transparent conclusion that he had "a death wish."

Any layman can draw the same conclusion from an analysis of his work — most markedly *Long Day's Journey Into Night*, in which

O'Neill gave the character representing himself the name of his dead brother, Edmund, and named the dead brother Eugene.

Other evidence of the death wish may be found in numerous of his fifty completed plays in which a total of forty-one characters suffer violent or unnatural deaths. Of these, ten are suicides. Twenty-one of the poisoned, diseased, mangled, strangled, sliced, drowned, electrocuted, incinerated or bullet-riddled men, women and children meet their ends in full view of the audience.

O'Neill in a letter once playfully invoked "Shakespeare and the Greek dramatists" as his "illustrious masters in mass-murder and driving folks mad." For plays devoid of corpses, he provided dialogue containing the word "corpse," both in its literal and symbolic senses. Moreover, there is scarcely a play without the word "ghost" — usually in conjunction with the word "haunted." In three plays — *The Emperor Jones*, *The Fountain* and *Gold* — ghosts or spirits actually materialize on stage. In *Lazarus Laughed* (four acts, four violent deaths, two on-stage corpses) there are seventy-seven references to death in Act I alone.

In recovering his own hope, Eugene was more fortunate than Jimmy Byth, the subject of "Tomorrow"; and "Tomorrow" is a significant precursor of *The Iceman Cometh* (which, in fact, O'Neill first thought of calling "Tomorrow").

The story, written four years after Byth's death, features a character called Jimmy Anderson, roommate of the narrator, Art. O'Neill describes Anderson, not very prepossessingly, as having "wispy, grey hair combed over his bald spot, his jowly face scraped close and chalky with too much powder"; he has a "squat nose" and "wistful eyes," with "fleshy cheeks hanging down like dewlaps on either side of his weak mouth with its pale, thick lips." His possessions include a battered typewriter, piles of unread books shoved into a corner of the room, and, on the windowsill, a "dyspeptic geranium plant" that never blooms.

O'Neill attributed the Byth/Anderson character's "social decline" to "an appalling tragedy in his life," explaining, "The booze got him and he had reached the depths . . . But always, my friend — at least always when he had had several jolts of liquor — saw a turn in the road to-morrow."

To Art's astonishment, Jimmy goes on the wagon and presses Art to do the same. Jimmy lands a job on a newspaper, but when he returns from his first day's work he resumes drinking. He confesses to Art that he couldn't do the work.

"I'm done — burnt out — wasted!" he says. "It's time to dump the garbage. Nothing here."

At his most drunken, Jimmy tells Art a long story he has told many times before, about his brilliant early career; but this time he adds the details of how he discovered, ten years earlier, that his wife was deceiving him, and how this destroyed his faith in himself and life.

Finally, dead drunk, he collapses on his bed and Art, shaken, goes downstairs to join his cronies in the bar. Not long after, they hear a crash in the courtyard outside; Jimmy's geranium plant has fallen. Soon after, they hear another crash; this time it is Jimmy.

"We rushed into the hall and out to the yard," Art says at the story's conclusion. "There it was — a motionless, dark huddle of clothes, a splintered, protruding bone or two, a widening pool of blood black against the gray flags — Jimmy!

"The sky was pale with the light of dawn. Tomorrow had come."

Jimmy Byth's actual suicide occurred about a year after Eugene's own failed attempt, by which time Eugene was long gone from Jimmy the Priest's. Byth jumped from the window of his room and died of a fractured skull at New York Hospital on June 6 or 7, 1913. According to the obituary in Billboard, which O'Neill doubtless read, he had been deluding himself to the end, telling friends he was "lately engaged in writing motion-picture scenarios on subjects pertaining to the Bible."

In *The Iceman Cometh*, Jimmy Anderson evolved into James Cameron (nicknamed Jimmy Tomorrow), described (like Anderson) as having "folds of flesh hanging from each side of his mouth." While Cameron is ten years older than Anderson, he shares elements of James Byth's true history, as well as Byth's minutely detailed, if false, Boer War background. O'Neill also introduced into the play the war heroes Byth had meticulously researched and expounded upon to lend credence to his own purported history. For example, the names of Generals DeWet and Viljoen were combined in the character called General Wetjoen.

Some of the details of Byth's pseudo-history are transposed to a character called Captain Cecil Lewis, a name O'Neill borrowed from yet another actual Boer War commander. Most interestingly, Theodore Hickman (Hickey), the central character in *Iceman*, displays when sober the same self-righteous tendency as Jimmy Anderson in "Tomorrow" to lecture his drinking buddies on the virtues of abstinence (although Hickey's motivation proves far more sinister than Anderson's).

It was in "Tomorrow" that O'Neill first formulated his philosophy of the "pipe dream," two decades before crystallizing it in *The Iceman Cometh*. While the short story, as O'Neill himself realized, is not a successful literary effort, it illustrates his lifelong belief, first embraced during his recovery from tuberculosis in 1913, that a man must have his illusions to survive. Only if he can make himself believe he will resolve all his problems "tomorrow," can he endure another despairing today.

Thus, when Byth/Anderson can no longer lie to himself about the job he will find tomorrow, the job that will give him back his self-respect, his hopeless hope is shattered and there is nothing left but suicide. Even more potently, when Hickey's own ruined life stares him in the face, he murders his wife and then tries to enlist his drunken cronies into entering his own deluded world.

Despite its glum beginning, the summer of 1912 was a relatively sunny one for the O'Neill family. James, for the first time in many months, felt he had much to be grateful for. Ella had undergone yet another cure (as indicated at the start of *Long Day's Journey Into Night*) and James was once again encouraged to hope for her complete recovery.

Eugene had not only escaped death at his own hand, but seemed, at last, to be making a genuine effort to recover his balance. Not long after his suicide attempt he had the pleasure of seeing one of his poems appear in print for the first time. "Free," which he had written on the Charles Racine, was published in April in the Year Book of the Pleiades Club.

Although the publication was limited to five hundred copies and distributed mainly among club members, James took pride in knowing that his son's effort would be read by some of New York's artistic elite. The club held lunches at such places as the Hotel Brevoort in Greenwich Village, in the interest of what its members liked to call "Bohemian good fellowship," and Mark Twain was among those who accepted invitations to address them. Both James and Jamie occasionally participated in the club's festivities and it was through their contacts that Eugene's poem was published.

Also easing James's mind was the formal severing of Eugene's alliance with Kathleen — on terms he considered advantageous. James refused to acknowledge he was a grandfather, and only recently he had been infuriated by a confrontation thrust upon Ella.

She had been walking on Fifth Avenue with a friend, when a nursemaid, wheeling a beautiful infant, passed by. The friend, recognizing the nursemaid as an employee of Kathleen's mother, tactlessly — or perhaps spitefully — said, "Did you see that little boy? That's your grandson!" Ella returned home, badly shaken.

The divorce trial took place before Supreme Court Justice Joseph Morsehauser on June 10, 1912, in White Plains. Kathleen was represented in her suit by the New York law firm of Van Schaick and Brice, whose complaint alleged: "On the 29th day of December, 1911, at 140 West 45th Street . . . the defendant committed adultery with a woman whose name is unknown to the plaintiff," and that "at divers times during the months of June, July, August and September, 1911, the defendant committed adultery with a woman named Maude Williams of 123 West 47th Street, in the Borough of Manhattan."

Kathleen, precluded by law from giving testimony that would further the proof of adultery, testified only that she was married at Trinity Church on July 26, 1909 (as always setting the date back more than two months) and stated that the issue was a son.

Since the divorce was uncontested, Eugene was not required to appear, but Kate Jenkins was called as a witness to identify his photograph. Kathleen was awarded an interlocutory decree of divorce on July 5, 1912, giving her custody of the child.

Eugene was wistful about Kathleen. To the end of his life he spoke of her with respect, on one occasion remarking to his third wife, Carlotta: "The woman I gave the most trouble to has given me the least."

With the divorce trial over, James plunged into the motion-picture version of *The Count of Monte Cristo*, a five-reel (full-length) silent feature, for Daniel Frohman and Adolph Zukor, who had recently founded the Famous Players Film Company in New York.

James's misgivings about the upstart medium were somewhat mitigated by the aura of the company's first offering, *Queen Elizabeth*, starring Sarah Bernhardt, a four-reel film made in Paris. Shortly before the film opened at the Lyceum Theater on July 12, Frohman told the New York Herald he hoped to "have all the famous stars of the American stage before the moving picture camera soon."

James was pleased to accept a twenty percent share of the profits and, as part of the deal, even wheedled a role for Jamie. The film was shot in ten days in New York's Crystal studios and, as recalled by Eugene, was "one of the first twenty-five cent admission, Famous

Player feature films using a play and star from the legitimate stage."
He did not offer his opinion of it.

The preserved film is little more than a curiosity. Even allowing
for the primitive technique and the disjointed action, it conveys little
sense of James's magnetic stage presence. Well past his prime and
voiceless, he could be any aging stock company actor miscast as a
romantic hero in a second-rate vehicle.

The filming completed, James could concentrate on helping
Eugene rehabilitate himself. James proposed he spend the rest of the
summer in New London trying to write, while also helping support
himself with a job on one of the two local newspapers (following in
the footsteps of his friend, Art McGinley). This time, Eugene listened.

Chapter
TWENTY-NINE

THE NEW LONDON SUMMER OF 1912 THAT WAS TO BE immortalized as the family's long day's journey into night began in deceptive calm.

In late July, after all four O'Neills reassembled at Monte Cristo Cottage, James approached his old friend, Frederick P. Latimer, the former judge, now part-owner and editor of the New London Telegraph. Explaining that Eugene had written some poetry, he wondered whether there was a place for him as a cub reporter — or, as Eugene himself once put it, "a reporter of the common or garden variety."

A morning paper, published daily except Sunday, the Telegraph had been founded in 1885 and was nearly defunct by 1910, when Latimer energized it with his own brand of wit and flair. A generous man of high integrity and liberal principles, he agreed to give Eugene a tryout, even though, as he told James, his budget was limited and his staff already adequate.

Eugene soon discovered he was not cut out to be a first-rank reporter like Art McGinley, but he was determined to make a go of it and tried his best to fulfill his undemanding assignments. At the same time, he began to contemplate a writing career.

There is no indication in *Long Day's Journey Into Night* that he had already chosen his lifework, but a number of New Londoners who spent time with him that summer and fall recalled that he was making notes for plays and short stories. Indeed, he himself later confirmed this fact: "It was when I joined the staff of the New London Telegraph that I found I wanted to write for a living."

Acknowledging he was an inadequate gatherer of news, he was happy enough to participate in the camaraderie of a small-town newspaper and to observe the tribal customs. Reporters and editors on both New London papers ate and drank together and had intimate knowledge of each other's pursuits. Along with other colleagues, McGinley switched back and forth between the New London Day — the afternoon paper his father had helped launch in 1881 — and its rival, the Telegraph. What was not known in the journalistic community was that Latimer himself was leading a double life.

"During much of the time he ran the Telegraph," his son, T. H. Latimer recalled, "Dad wrote the editorials for the Day and had a grand time arguing with himself in print." A year later, Latimer actually sold his share of the Telegraph to resume his law practice and to write editorials exclusively for the Day.

It was rumored in the newsroom that, until Eugene proved himself, James was to provide his son's weekly salary of ten dollars. Not long after Eugene began work, he arrived in the newsroom late and slightly tipsy and was summarily fired by the city editor, Malcolm Mollan.

"Hell, you can't fire him," the Telegraph's business manager, Charles Hamilton Thompson, was reported to have said. "His father pays his salary." Whether this was fact or whether Mollan relented out of kindness, Eugene stayed on. But he was resentful when staff members joshed him about being the son of Monte Cristo. Somewhat self-righteously, considering he owed his job to his father, he once felt impelled to retort, "Someday I won't be known as his son. He will be known as my father."

The Telegraph's editors held lively and divergent views of foreign and political news, which gave the paper a more cosmopolitan outlook than its more reserved competitor. The Telegraph devoted considerable space to national news and, to Eugene's satisfaction, often focused on the intrigues of New York City's underworld.

Local events were covered by a small staff and, since the paper employed no copy editors, Eugene and the other reporters were required to write their own headlines. The most essential cog in the wheel was a printer's devil whom reporters sent to fetch pitchers of ale from the nearby Crocker House Bar.

The workplace was musty, loosely supervised and, in that day, exclusively male. The reporter's desk was his poker table, bar and bed — and at times where he wrote his stories.

Local news ranged from fires and the fainting on summer days of overweight women in the public square to the "classy scraps" (as they were sometimes labeled) that invariably erupted among sailors on Saturday nights. One such report was remarkable for the frenzy of its lead: "Brandishing a razor in one hand and a bedpan in the other, John Jones of no certain address ran amuck in the city hospital yesterday."

Staff members took their meals at an all-night hashery that featured a horseshoe bar flanked by mirrors. Jamie O'Neill made the bar a port of call at three in the morning and could be counted upon for an improvisational performance in front of the mirrors, highlighted by exaggerated gestures and grimaces.

Eugene found himself among friends at the Telegraph and was particularly encouraged by Latimer. "He's the first one," O'Neill once commented, "who really thought I had something to say, and believed I could say it." Latimer recalled that they used to argue their different philosophies: "I thought he was the most stubborn and irreconcilable social rebel I had ever met. We appreciated each other's sympathies, but to each, in the moralities and religious thought and political notions, the other was 'all wet.'"

As it happened, 1912 was a year of blossoming for the socialist idea. The illustrated radical monthly, The Masses, had been founded a year earlier in New York, and the millionaire Harry Payne Whitney bought the Metropolitan magazine and installed the British Fabian socialist, H. J. Wigham, as its editor.

Jack London, Lincoln Steffens and John Reed were holding court for the young radicals and visionary artists converging on Greenwich Village from all over the country and some, like Reed, went so far as to join the I.W.W. to protest working conditions. Only the year before, the Triangle Shirtwaist Factory fire off Washington Square had killed 146 women, becoming a cause célèbre for the socialist and anarchist movements.

It was the year Eugene's political consciousness was at its most acute, as he soon demonstrated in the poetry he wrote for the newspaper. Politics aside, Latimer was taken with his cub reporter's modesty, his good manners, and his unfettered literary style.

"It was evident at once that this was no ordinary boy," he recalled, "and I watched what he thought, wrote and did with extreme interest. From flashes in the quality of the stuff he gave the paper, and the poems and play-manuscripts he showed me, I was so struck that I told his father Eugene did not have merely talent, but a very high order of genius."

Latimer found Eugene "emphatically 'different,'" and admired his wit, his iconoclasm and his sympathy with the "victims of man-made distress." He recognized Eugene's imagination and appreciated the vigor of his convictions and his scorn for commercial value or conventional fame. "If he could only be in one of two places in a town — the church or the jail — I know where I would find him!" Latimer summed up.

Grateful for Latimer's tolerance of his rebellious views, O'Neill fondly incorporated Latimer's characteristics (along with John McGinley's) into the portrait of the scholarly, compassionate newspaper editor, Nat Miller, in *Ah, Wilderness!*

City Editor Mollan was more reluctant to recognize Eugene's "genius." Mollan, one of those who occasionally worked part-time on the Day as an editor to enhance his income, wore a silk hat and carried a cane. He cheerfully admitted that he conformed to the tradition of city editors who mercilessly took apart reporters' copy. Recalling Eugene's five-month stint on the Telegraph, Mollan wrote:

"Time was when . . . I used to bawl out, 'O'Neill!' and O'Neill would come to my desk and say, 'Yes, sir.'"

"This is a lovely story about that Bradley street cutting!" Mollan would say. "The smell of the rooms is made convincing; the amount of blood on the floor is precisely measured; you have drawn a nice picture of the squalor and stupidity and degradation of that household. But would you mind finding out the name of the gentleman who carved the lady and whether the lady is his wife or daughter or who? And phone the hospital for a hint as to whether she is dead or discharged or what. Then put the facts into a hundred and fifty words and send this literary batik to the picture framer's!"

The city editor remembered Eugene's abashed, puzzled look as he carried away his story, and the way he "pulled his hair about his eyes while he tried to do a conventional, phlegmatic news item in newspaper style."

Facts unadorned did not interest Eugene. According to Mollan, "It was what they signified, what led to them and what they in turn led to, their proportionate values in the great canvas of life, that intrigued his rapt attention.

"What difference did it make whether this particular brother of the ox, who had graven the proof of his upbringing on a woman's body, was called Stan Pujak or Jo Wojnik? What difference whether the knife found a vital or missed it by a hair? What O'Neill saw in the affair was just one more exhibit in the case of Humanity vs. the State of Things, another dab of evidence of the puzzling perversion of mankind, with its needless conflicts and distorted passions. He saw equally squalid bestiality usurping normal humanism in human beings. What he saw he wrote, that others might see. He had to."

Art McGinley, recalling Eugene's days at the newspaper, expressed a somewhat similar view: "He went off gaily on assignments riding his trusty bicycle, but rarely returned with a story. Eugene was living in a dream world — the plots of plays, some destined to be born later in his more mature years, others to die before even reaching the playwright's drawing board, and he could not be distracted by such prosaic things as fires, burglaries, a woman fainting in the public square, or the other items that go to make up the daily pattern in the life of a small town."

Eugene soon realized himself he was unfit for his job. "I was a bum reporter," he complacently confessed to friends and interviewers in later years (echoing his earlier disparagement of himself as a "punk actor" during the *Monte Cristo* vaudeville tour). Another time he described his newspaper work as "junk of the low order."

Some staff members of both the Telegraph and the Day would have gone even further. One, in fact, recorded his blunt opinion that Eugene was "The World's Worst Reporter." Under that headline, Robert A. Woodworth, a reporter at various times on both the Telegraph and the Day, recalled that Eugene would sit in a corner of the city room, smoking and dreaming. According to Woodworth, " . . . as far as any of the crowd can remember, he never typed a thing in the late lamented Morning Telegraph office which savored of genius."

It seems unlikely, however, that Eugene had much time to dream, for City Editor Mollan kept him running on a series of secondary spot stories and features. One story for which he did manage to collect the facts concerned the arrival in New London on August 17, 1912, of Theodore Roosevelt who, as the Progressive Party candidate, was in a tight race with the incumbent Republican President William Howard Taft and the ultimately victorious Democratic candidate, Woodrow Wilson. Eugene's own candidate was Eugene V. Debs, who headed the Socialist ticket and had received a paltry 96,000 votes when he first ran in 1900.

The story Eugene wrote is a good example of his flip and slangy newspaper style:

"Colonel Theodore Roosevelt, who is jocosely described by various pet names ranging from Bwana Tumbo to Chief Running Bull, passed through here on the east bound limited at 3:38 yesterday afternoon and his presence in a Pullman car at the Union Station drew a crowd of 150 people. The colonel was distinctly visible from the platform and he bowed de-e-e-lightedly to the onlookers. He did not offer to come to the car vestibule at first.

"Among the assembled throng was the rotund and genial Attorney Thomas F. Dorsey, who made the acquaintance of Colonel Roosevelt some years ago when his train passed through here. Teddy wasn't going to get away from New London without a handshake from somebody, not if Mr. Dorsey knew it. So the amicable disciple of Blackstone drew an engraved calling card from his pocket, carefully dusted it off and marched in with it to the hero of the jungle. The awestruck crowd without the portals watched the colonel accept the proffered pasteboard and give Mr. Dorsey the glad mitt.

"Then the engine bell sounded and the colonel accompanied Attorney Dorsey to the door of the car and waved a farewell to the spectators."

If Eugene did not exactly distinguish himself as a traditional reporter, he did earn something of a reputation as a poet with his sardonic contributions to an editorial page column entitled "Laconics." The column's form varied daily, sometimes consisting of a string of topical jokes or anecdotes and sometimes of caustic editorial comment.

Eugene's entries were invariably poetry, mainly parodies of — or homages to — such as Kipling, Longfellow, Masefield, Villon, Burns, Walt Mason, Robert W. Service. In the more than two dozen poems he submitted to Laconics, he played with free verse, allegories, ballads, villanelles and sonnets, and his subjects ranged from politics, the sea, mysticism and social problems to romantic love.

One poem, untitled ("with apologies to J. W. Riley"), appeared not long after Roosevelt's visit:

> Our Teddy opens wide his mouth,
>   N'runs around n'yells all day,
> N'calls some people naughty names,
>   N'says things that he shouldn't say.
> N'when he's nothing else to do
>   He swells up like he'd like to bust,
> N'pounds on something with his fist
>   N'tells us 'bout some wicked trust.
> I always wondered why that was —
>   I guess it's cause
>   Taft never does.

He tells the farmers how to sow
   N'shows the cav'lry how to ride,
N'if you try to say a word
   He's angry, n'he says you lied.
N'when it's quiet over here
   He goes way far acrost the seas
N'gets a great big gun n'shoots
   The elephants n'chimpanzees.
I always wondered why that was —
    I guess it's cause
    Taft never does.

Two earlier contributions concerned a major event that occupied New Londoners that summer, the national Waterways Convention scheduled for September 3 and 4, to be attended by President Taft and delegates from all over the country.

The town spent weeks sprucing up its streets and harbor in anticipation of the onslaught and Eugene, in addition to writing news stories about preparations, also jeered in verse at the disruptions caused by the conventioneers: they had "foundered all the taxis and they've swamped the trolley cars,/And you'll find them in the soda shops, and maybe in the bars."

In a second poem, Eugene snidely bewailed the convention's plans to create a bigger and more prosperous New London, plans that his father, because of his real-estate investments, heartily endorsed. Thankless son that he was, he mocked the prospect of an enhanced New London, at the same time showing off his familiarity with the evils of a big city like New York. The poem was called "The Waterways Convention, A Study in Prophecy (With apologies to Hiawatha)." Two stanzas provide the flavor of the whole:

Thirty-story office buildings
We will see the length of State street.
We will take the "tube" to Groton
And the subway clear to Noank,
Or the "L" to Oswagatchie.
We will gather at the new docks
To see off the Lusitania.
And our bay will be so crowded
We will have a traffic policeman
Rowing beats upon the waters.
And we'll have an adding expert
To keep track of the collisions.

A Stock Exchange will be on Main street
And the Capital we'll pilfer
From the puny grasp of Hartford.
We will then produce our great men.
Envy not New York its Becker
We will have a greater grafter.
We will have our bands of "gun men"
"Gyp the Bloods" and "Lefty Louies"
And mayhap — the gods propitious —
We will even have a Thaw trial.
Property will rise in value
Till we're all so rich, my brothers,
That our heirs will try to slip some
Cyanide into our porridge.

Eugene's hours on the Telegraph were from five in the afternoon to one in the morning and he worked on Sundays to help get out Monday's paper; Saturday was his day off. To save the five-cent trolley fare, he bicycled to work. (In one of his poems for "Laconics," after enumerating the pangs felt by Caesar, Joan of Arc and Napoleon in their various hours of trial, he noted: "I grant you their sorrows were great and real/But comparison makes them light/With the gloom I feel as I ride my wheel/To work on a Sunday night.")

After a few weeks, Latimer was sufficiently satisfied, principally with Eugene's poetic contributions, to end his trial period and raise his salary to $12 a week (presumably paid by the paper, not James). Eugene obviously preferred writing poetry for "Laconics" to chasing the news and he said as much in a spoof of the Telegraph's inner workings called "Hitting the Pipe," inspired by J. W. Riley. His editors were complacent enough to publish it on October 22:

When my dreams come true — when my dreams come
    true —
I'll be sitting in the office here with nothing else to do,
But to write a comic story or to spin a little rhyme,
I won't have to do rewriting, I'll have lots of leisure time
For to sit and chatter politics and dream the whole night
    through,
I will never cover socials when my dreams come true!

When my dreams come true I will never stoop to read
The proof of advertisements telling people what they need.

I will only write the stories that are sure to make a hit,
And the mighty city editor will never cut a bit,
But put them in just as they are and compliment me, too,
I'll be the star reporter when my dreams come true.

When my dreams come true there will not be a mistake
In a single line of copy that the linotypers make
I will never have to count the letters framing up a head
And every night at twelve o'clock will find me home in
  bed
I will shun the railroad station and the police station, too,
And only cover prize fights when my dreams come true.

When my dreams come true all my comments wise and
  sage
Will be featured double column on the editor's own page
Personals will be no object, I won't have to go and hunt
The history of the tug-boats that infest the water-front.
Fire alarms may go to blazes, suicides and murders too,
I'll be editing Laconics when my dreams come true.

If the mechanics of news gathering baffled him, Eugene had no trouble understanding the Telegraph's policy of defiant open-mindedness. The paper had guts — so much so it was doomed to failure in the stuffy local climate. (It folded in 1919, leaving the field to the more conformist Day.)

The Telegraph refused to be bullied by its advertisers and local potentates into any narrow channel of opinion, and in an editorial headed "Confidential" that appeared on October 5, 1912, it affirmed its independence:

"Some months ago the Editor received a postal from an anonymous person, expressing his appreciation of the usefulness of The Telegraph but inquiring rather pointedly, 'When in h—l will your paper make up its mind whether it is a republican or a democrat.'

"Happily or unhappily no such decision seems imminent. As long as we keep the words 'Independent Newspaper' at the head of the page we shall try as best we can to live up to the profession. If we ever take up a party affiliation we shall announce the fact with the boldest type in our fonts . . .

"The ownership of this newspaper is in the hands of a Democrat and two Republicans, each with different personal bias and political tendencies as between conservatism and progression. Among these three are the editor and the business manager.

"The city editor, who runs things while the rest of us are perforce in our beds, is a fierce Bull Moose. He divides his time between doing his work and cussing the owners.

"Our genial chief news-gatherer, Joseph Smith, 2nd, is a wildly enthusiastic Democrat. For a long time he said his prayers as often as not to Champ Clark, and his democracy is just as much a part of his religion as his ideas of marriage. There is a faint suspicion in some quarters that Mr. Smith attended the Democratic rally Thursday evening."

In an obvious reference to Eugene, the editorial continued:

"Another important staff official may be a mixed 'socialist and anarchist.' As far as possible we keep him off political assignments. But he writes satirical verse which is so really clever that we feel obliged to print it, albeit with the blue pencil in pretty constant use."

Eugene had by then contributed several additional satiric verses, including a stab (in the style of Rudyard Kipling's "Tommy") at one of his pet targets, Standard Oil, called "The Shut-eye Candidate." To Eugene's great satisfaction, only a year earlier the Supreme Court had decreed that the Standard Oil empire was in violation of the anti-trust laws and ordered it to be broken up.

Clearly, Eugene was not unappreciated at the Telegraph. He could not, however, convince Art McGinley, with whom he often drank on their days off or after work, to support Debs in the coming presidential election. Many times Eugene would go home with McGinley in the early morning hours and heedlessly wake McGinley's sister, who would obligingly move into a spare room so that Eugene could have her more comfortable bed. Or if no one happened to be at home in Eugene's house, McGinley would stay with him there.

Once when they were making a noisy night of it a neighbor telephoned James in New York and complained that Eugene and his friend had a "concubine" in the house. James called his son to find out what was going on and was only partially reassured on hearing the charge was untrue. It was episodes such as this that prevented James from thoroughly trusting and embracing Eugene, in spite of the newly visible signs of his reformation. McGinley, referring to those days, said, "Gene and I wanted to drink America dry. When we read somewhere that there were two thousand distilleries and four thousand breweries in the country, we realized we'd never make it." O'Neill borrowed some of McGinley's drunken speech patterns —

according to McGinley himself — for the character of Sid Davis, the inebriated newspaperman, in *Ah, Wilderness!*

Eugene and McGinley spent a good part of their salaries in such New London bars as McGarry and Neagle's, where Eugene enjoyed holding forth on anarchism, Irish kings and Irish independence. To McGinley, he also confided his ambition to be "a great writer," and he repeatedly recited his first attempt at a short story, written in his teens.

It was about a love-struck boy on his way to visit his girl. McGinley never forgot the opening sentences: "Jimmy Trevalyan walked up the winding path . . . It was early May and in the treetops the birds, drunk with the wine of spring, sang their roundelay."

Now and then Ed Keefe, his old new London friend and New York drinking companion, joined Eugene and Art and the three would head for the barroom in the rear of Holt's grocery store on Main Street. For Eugene, the chief attraction there was a bartender named Adam Scott, a powerfully built black man, six feet tall, with muscular arms, outsize hands and a round, bald pate. He tended bar during the week, and was an elder of the Shiloh Baptist Church on Sundays.

Before taking a drink himself, Scott always rubbed a drop or two of whiskey into his scalp; then, raising his glass, he exclaimed: "My best to every human being who breathes the breath of love." His rival for political leadership in New London's black community was Jim Lewis, headwaiter at the Crocker House. Eugene would tease Scott, pretending he had heard that Lewis was becoming a threat to Scott's supremacy.

"I'm a God-fearing man," Scott would say, "but someday I'm going to forget my Holy Ghost and slap the bejeezus out of that baby."

"How do you reconcile yourself, Adam," McGinley or Keefe might ask him, "to being religious and tending bar?"

"I'm a very religious man," Scott would reply, "but after Sunday, I lay my Jesus on the shelf."

Scott, who appointed himself unofficial bodyguard to Eugene and his friends, would tell them, "I gotta look after you boys. I gotta see nothing happens to you boys."

Scott's imperious personality so impressed O'Neill that he later borrowed it for *The Emperor Jones*. While the play was also derived from other sources, it was Scott's bravado, his superstition and his religious convictions that imbued the character of Brutus Jones.

According to McGinley and Keefe, O'Neill even reproduced some of Scott's figures of speech, as in these lines:

"Doesn't you know dey's got to deal wid a man was member in good standin' o' de Baptist Church? . . . [but] it don't git me nothin' to do missionary work for de Baptist Church. I'se after de coin, an' I lays my Jesus on de shelf for de time bein'."

Eugene centered his social life in Doc Ganey's Second Story Club and sometimes, instead of meeting in Doc's office-apartment, he and his friends repaired to Doc's cottage on the Niantic River in the neighboring town of Waterford.

There they took turns cooking — all except Eugene, who could no more share the amateur chef's enthusiasm for preparing food than for eating it. Doc was living with a woman named Kate, whom he and his cronies once disguised as a man and smuggled into the all-male crowd at a cockfight.

Eugene and Ed Keefe, though they did not smuggle women into cockfights, did attempt to recreate the roguish reputations they had earlier cultivated in New York. At least once, they carried their devil-try to an excess that made Keefe squirm years later in the retelling. According to Keefe, he and Eugene picked up two streetwalkers out-side New London and took them to a tawdry hotel near the railroad station.

"We were so polluted," Keefe acknowledged, "that we signed our real names on the hotel register. We each took a room. After half an hour Gene came into my room and said, 'Let's get out of here. I'm sick of these pigs.' That was a slur he'd picked up from his brother. We left the two girls in the rooms and walked out without paying the bill."

From all accounts, there was little discernible difference at times between the behavior of the nearly twenty-four-year-old Eugene of 1912 and the eighteen-year-old Eugene of 1906. In many respects he remained frozen in a state of adolescence. True, for the first time he held a paying job that did not bore him, and he did not have to depend on his father for handouts. But he clung to a childlike belief in his invulnerability, as well as a guileless disregard for the conse-quences of his savage drinking over the past six years. Signs of his debilitation had yet to set in. On the contrary, he was tanned and wiry, a tireless cyclist, an effortless swimmer and a familiar figure in his rowboat or canoe on the Thames.

His feat of swimming a mile across the river on July 22 was daring enough to be reported by the Day. As with Dorian Gray, the evidence of Eugene's debauchery lay hidden. To most of the world he was — if somewhat reticent and at times melancholy — a remarkably fit and handsome young man, intelligent, studious and well-mannered.

His slightly sinister reputation as a divorced man with a child was another matter. He endeavored that summer to avoid entanglements with the respectable young women of New London, unwilling to engage in their charade of conventional dating rituals, and wary of their rules of virtuous conduct. They sought him out, however.

His good looks, his boyish shyness and the gentleness he displayed when sober, together with his evident suffering from some unfathomable wound, were catnip for all but the very timorous — as irresistible to the nice girls of New London as they had been to Kathleen Jenkins. And New London could boast a number of distinctly untimorous maidens. Luckily for them, Eugene seemed to have absorbed at least one lesson from his marriage to Kathleen; from all accounts, his flirtations that summer were nothing if not chaste.

One young woman spending July in Groton, apparently sat glued to her window in the Griswold Hotel across the Thames from New London, watching for Eugene with field glasses. Every time he ventured out in his canoe, she sprang into her rented rowboat and met him more than halfway. When James learned of these watery trysts, he warned his son: "You just tell that young lady there's no money here."

Another sometime companion that summer, Mabel Ramage, worked in an elegant confectionery on State Street owned by Stavros Peterson, the Second Story Club's most affluent member.

Like a chemist mixing a formula, Peterson blended his own chocolate and came up with a syrup so thick and rich it would not flow through the fountain pump. It was poured, instead, from gleaming silver pitchers. His ice-cream sodas were served in delicate white goblets. No Du Pont, Morgan or Rockefeller would have thought of returning to his yacht without a supply of Peterson's marrons glacés.

Mabel, dark-haired, blue-eyed and fair-skinned, was one of fourteen young women who worked for Peterson as glorified waitresses, more decorative than utilitarian. Most were daughters of established New London families who wanted an unstrenuous taste of independence.

Eugene generally visited Peterson's on payday, to cash his salary check and order a chocolate ice-cream soda. It was there his eye fell on Mabel, in whom, as it happened, Peterson also was romantically interested.

Eugene would take Mabel on long walks. "My mother was adamantly against my going out with Gene," she remembered. "He called for me once or twice at my home and my mother was openly hostile. He didn't call there any more after that."

Instead, he met Mabel at the confectionery, to Peterson's irritation. Mabel saw Eugene only about a half dozen times in all, but he left a dramatic impression, as was the case with every young woman with whom he chose to trifle however briefly.

"I was fascinated with him," Mabel later said. "He seemed so different from other boys. I was flattered to be getting attention from a man like that."

Mabel could not reconcile Eugene's evil reputation with his gentle behavior.

"He never used bad language, and was always polite," she recalled. "He was the perfect gentleman. He never even tried to kiss me. He used to call me 'Queen Mab' and he wrote some poems for me, which I put inside a magazine to hide from my mother."

CHAPTER
THIRTY

TOWARD THE END OF SEPTEMBER, EUGENE MET A YOUNG woman who truly captivated him. Maibelle Scott was slender and tall with a dimpled, peaches-and-cream complexion and hair that Eugene, in the poems he wrote to her, described as "golden." Her wide-set eyes were blue in one kind of light, gray in another. Doc Ganey, who never forgot having once watched Maibelle stoop to make a graceful adjustment to her garter, was unreserved in his praise of her beauty.

Maibelle, who had more than her share of admirers, was quickly drawn to Eugene. What entranced the provincial, eighteen-year-old Maibelle (as it had the slightly older and more sophisticated Kathleen Jenkins) was Eugene's adventure-laced past. The actress, Lillian Gish, who became a friend of O'Neill's years later, once remarked that even she — though regarding herself as a worldly sizer-up of men — was amazed by "how fully he had lived at such an early age!"

As for Eugene, he did not at all mind being loved for the dangers he had passed. Maibelle, called "Scotty" by her friends, knew that Eugene had gone mining for gold in Honduras, sailed on a clipper ship and lived a dissolute life on the Buenos Aires and New York waterfronts — although she could scarcely conceive how dissolute. Doubtless, she would have been repelled, had she known the depths of his degradation.

Maibelle also had heard that Eugene sometimes allowed his drinking to get out of control. As had been the case with Kathleen, however, Eugene never permitted Maibelle to see the demonic ine-briate he could become in the company of male friends. Instead, he presented himself as sober, thoughtful and compassionate. The odd truth was that he actually did embody those conflicting qualities. Indeed, once he began to woo Maibelle, Eugene — except for sporadic outbreaks — seemed to abandon his dissolute ways.

Reading *Ah, Wilderness!* when it was first published in 1933, Maibelle thought she discerned (with something of a shock) that she was the model for Muriel McComber and that her brief intrigue with Eugene in the fall of 1912 had suggested the play's plot.

There were, of course, slight distortions of dates and ages, to accommodate echoes of Eugene's flirtation in 1905 with Marion Welch, the girl from Hartford, who was also a part-model for Muriel. For example, at the time of her romance with Eugene, Maibelle, like Marion, was three years older than the play's fifteen-year-old Muriel. Moreover, Eugene himself was by then eight years older than the play's sixteen-year-old Richard Miller. (There was to be a third model for Muriel McComber — a young woman named Beatrice Ashe, whom Eugene was yet to meet.)

Even though Maibelle and Eugene were older than Muriel and Richard, their tender interludes held very much the same breathless, innocent quality that imbued the fictional sweethearts of *Ah, Wilderness!*: the clandestine meetings, the parental disapproval, the exchange of notes through an intermediary and the earnest plans for marriage. It seems clear that Eugene's intense, if short-lived, courtship of Maibelle parallels more closely the romance in *Ah, Wilderness!* than does the earlier, briefer, and even more innocent dalliance with Marion Welch.

Maibelle's parents, who lived on Pequot Avenue not quite a block north of Monte Cristo Cottage, were an eminently respectable New London family and had been casually acquainted with the O'Neills for many years. Her grandfather was the retired, legendary Captain Thomas A. Scott, who weighed 300 pounds, had built two landmark lighthouses in Long Island Sound — Race Rock and Sarah's Ledge — and had founded a marine salvage company that overlooked the New London Harbor. In the years before his death in 1907, he had delighted the youthful Eugene with his tales of adventure.

Maibelle's father, John Scott, was a master diver who had salvaged wrecks off the coast of Connecticut. He later managed a grocery and marine supply store on the wharf across from Pequot Avenue (while his counterpart, Muriel McComber's father in *Ah, Wilderness!*, is the proprietor of a tug-boat supply store).

It was Maibelle's married sister, Arlene Fones, who encouraged Eugene to seek Maibelle's acquaintance. In the summer of 1912, a year after Maibelle's graduation from high school, Arlene and her husband, Byron — who worked for his father-in-law — were waiting

to move into a new house with their infant daughter, and briefly rented from James O'Neill the Pink House (occupied by the O'Neills until
1900).

Maibelle, who dropped in on her sister frequently, caught a
glimpse of Eugene now and then, as he did of her, for there was only
one house between the Pink House and the Monte Cristo cottage.
One Sunday toward summer's end, Eugene, on his bicycle, overtook
Arlene as she strolled along Pequot Avenue. He dismounted and
walked beside her, mumbling awkward pleasantries and then, sum-
moning his courage, "I don't know your sister well, but I'd like to."

Inviting Eugene to sit with her on her porch, Arlene gave him her
five-month-old daughter, Alma, to hold. Eighty-five years later,
Alma, still residing in New London, spoke of her mother's fond recollection of this trifling incident. "My mother was a very neighborly
woman who saw good in everyone and was always nice to Eugene,"
she said.

Arlene asked Eugene if he would be at the wedding of a mutual
friend, Bessie Young, planned for Tuesday evening at the Young
home on Pequot Avenue. Eugene said he would be there. "Well, then
you'll meet my sister," said Arlene.

Bessie had been Eugene's childhood friend. Her father, a deep-sea
diver, died in 1905 and her widowed mother accommodated boarders. The O'Neills took their meals there whenever Ella was without
domestic help. All the O'Neills had been invited to the wedding and,
although Ella declined, she insisted on loaning Bessie table napkins
for the reception, and gave her a wedding gift of two fine pieces of
cut glass.

"Mrs. O'Neill was very refined," Bessie recalled. "She always
wore a hat, even when she came up the block to have her meals at our
house. Often she'd skip a meal, and Mr. O'Neill would explain that
she was ill. I always felt there was something strange about her."
Bessie had no inkling the problem was morphine addiction.

As it happened, Eugene was assigned by the Telegraph to cover
the wedding. Concerned he would not be able to impress Maibelle
sufficiently in the role of reporter, even with the help of the small
mustache he had again cultivated, he got himself up in a black satin
cape and top hat borrowed from his father. He borrowed a bit of his
father's technique as well.

When he arrived at the Youngs, Eugene learned that Maibelle was
in an upstairs room, fluttering with the other attendants around the
bride. He stationed himself at the foot of the staircase and waited for

the bridesmaids to emerge. As he heard them take leave of the bride-to-be, he swept up the staircase, confronting Maibelle Scott on the landing. With a sweeping bow, he murmured, "At last, we meet," and fixed his piercing dark eyes on her startled gray-blue ones.

There was no time to pursue the effect, for Eugene was obliged to take notes for his story as well as make himself agreeable to the other guests, among them Mabel Ramage. After the ceremony, Eugene bundled up his cape and hat, mounted his bicycle and sped to the Telegraph where, inspired by thoughts of the delectable Maibelle, he wrote a story that appeared the next morning, September 25. While he was unable to work in Maibelle's name until the third paragraph, it led the list of attendants:

"A very pretty wedding took place last evening at 8 o'clock at the home of Mrs. Frances Young, 267 Pequot Avenue, when her daughter Bessie Eleanor Young was married to Percival Frazer Palmer of Noank . . . The bride wore a charming gown of crepe meteor [sic] over white satin trimmed with silk lace and carried a shower bouquet of Killarney roses . . .

"Miss Angenetta Appledom was the pianist and played both the Mendelssohn wedding march and the one from *Lohengrin*.

"The young ladies who served were: Miss Maibelle Scott, Miss Mildred Culver, Miss Jennie Strictland, Mrs. Byron Fones . . . "

Not trusting the effect of the cape to last until the next day, Eugene telephoned Maibelle at ten-thirty that night and asked if he could see her again. He need not have been anxious.

"I was terribly impressed with Eugene," Maibelle said some forty-five years later. "Aside from his being so handsome, he was vastly sophisticated — and, of course, I knew that he had been married and had a child."

Maibelle was bewildered when her parents expressed disapproval of Eugene. Only her sister, Arlene, who found Eugene unfailingly well-behaved, gave the match her blessing. Maibelle had assured her that Eugene was always sober and gentle. She also told Arlene she could not understand why his father thought it necessary to warn their father about him. James, suspecting the warmth of Eugene's feelings for Maibelle, doubtless feared another entanglement like the one with Kathleen.

When Maibelle learned that James had told her father she was too nice for Eugene, warning that he was unreliable and drank too much, she simply drew closer to him, wounded by the cruelty of the allegation. Surprisingly free of small-town prejudice, Maibelle had the self-confidence to trust her own judgment.

Even when James tried to enlist the help of her mother in breaking up the romance, cautioning Mrs. Scott that Eugene "fell for every pretty face he saw," Maibelle refused to believe anything bad of him. In rebuttal to those who attempted to tar his reputation, Eugene told her, "I am not responsible for filling any of the orphanages or cemeteries in New London." It never occurred to her to doubt him.

Maibelle realized there was nothing to be gained by flaunting her defiance and asked her sister's aid in concealing the relationship. Arlene, despite the fact that her husband also disapproved of Eugene, refused to join forces with her family.

Convinced it was nobody else's business and that her sister could be trusted, Arlene offered her home as a trysting place. Eugene, by prearrangement, would amble over from his house two doors away. Apart from these meetings, their dates consisted mostly of sedate walks on the outskirts of town.

They once risked going to the Lyceum Theatre to see *The Bohemian Girl*, so incensing the Scotts that Maibelle and Eugene foreswore further public appearances. There were only a few friends willing to chance censure by inviting them to their homes as a couple. Frederick Latimer and his wife were among those who had them to dinner on several occasions; and one time they spent a few hours together on a yacht belonging to a Pequot Avenue neighbor unconcerned about flouting the common disapproval.

Eugene, ever the romantic (not to say sentimentalist), had begun presenting Maibelle with love poems, some of which he considered too personal to submit to "Laconics." One of the first, "Rondeaux to Scotty," bewailed the sadness of his life until he met her, tritely citing her "hair in wanton disarray" and her "lips a chalice, love-filled to the brim." It ended, "(How could I help but weep for Yesterday/ Until you came?)" and was signed "E.G.O."

Despite the pressure to remain invisible as a couple, Maibelle and Eugene managed to see each other almost every day for more than a month. Often they met in the early afternoon in front of Mitchell's Woods, part of a large estate on Montauk Avenue, a thoroughfare parallel to Pequot, behind the O'Neill house.

They would walk toward Ocean Beach, a modest boardwalk and bathhouse establishment at the westerly tip of New London, about three miles from Monte Cristo Cottage. Or they might sit unobtrusively on the dock of the Pequot Casino, a private club at the mouth of the Thames, near the lighthouse.

Established in 1890 by socially prominent summer residents of the Pequot area, the club would not have dreamed of inviting an Irish touring actor like James O'Neill to join (and it is doubtful he would have applied for membership). The casino had two dining rooms, as well as a ballroom, a billiard room and tennis courts. At teatime Eugene and Maibelle could listen to "the sound of the waves and of distant dance music," as O'Neill described it in 1925 in the epilogue of his experimental play, *The Great God Brown*.

Since Eugene was required to report to the Telegraph by six o'clock, he and Maibelle separated before dusk. The relationship, as Maibelle depicted it, was conducted on a literary, as well as a romantic, plane; Eugene, as ever, could not help proselytizing and Maibelle was a dutiful pupil.

At nearly twenty-four, Eugene no longer spouted the radical jargon he attributed to Richard Miller in *Ah, Wilderness!* ("I'll celebrate the day the people bring out the guillotine again and I see Pierpont Morgan being driven by in a tumbrill!" and "Why shouldn't the workers of the world unite and rise? They have nothing to lose but their chains!") But he made it clear to Maibelle that he had not relinquished the basic radicalism he had first absorbed in Benjamin Tucker's book shop. He was still apt, for example, to sign his letters (only half in jest), "Yours for the revolution!"

Eugene instructed Maibelle in what to read, as he had Marion Welch seven years earlier. His first gift to her was *Thus Spake Zarathustra*, inscribed with a quotation from the text that he believed applied to the parental hostility toward their romance:

"Almost in the cradle we are given heavy words and values. 'Good' and 'Evil' such cradle-gift is called.

"And we — we carry faithfully what we are given, on hard shoulders over rough mountains! And when perspiring, we are told: 'Yea, life is hard to bear.'

"But man himself only is hard to bear! The reason is that he carrieth too many strange things on his shoulders.

"But he hath discovered himself, who saith: 'This is my good and evil.' Thereby he maketh mute the dwarf who saith: 'Good for all, evil for all.'"

Maibelle not only labored to understand *Zarathustra*, but tried to persuade her friends to read it — just one more incident that exacerbated her family's disapproval of Eugene.

The Adventure Years

Home from Honduras (and having found no gold), Eugene was adrift. With parental blessing he shipped out in 1910 as a passenger-apprentice on a bark, the Charles Racine. The voyage was to prove pivotal in shaping him as a writer.

Gustav Waage, the benevolent captain of the Charles Racine.

The tramp steamer, S.S. Ikala, on which Eugene worked his way home from Buenos Aires as an ordinary seaman. The ship was the setting in part for his early one-act sea plays. He later sailed as able-bodied seaman on two passenger liners.

The Abbey Players' 1911 New York visit was a revelation to O'Neill. Above is a scene from J. M. Synge's *Riders to the Sea*.

O'Neill wanted to be a "two-fisted Jack London 'he-man' sailor." He cherished his seaman's sweater and "mutual release" document.

EXORCISM

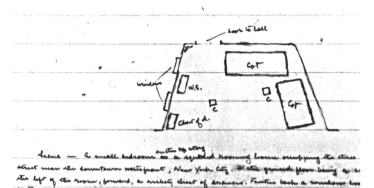

Scene — A small bedroom on the top story of a squalid rooming house occupying the stories street near the downtown waterfront, New York City. The ground floor being a ... the left of the room, forward, a rickety chest of drawers. Facing back a window ...

O'Neill's sketch for the set of *Exorcism*, the one-act play he based on his suicide attempt at Jimmy the Priest's, the flophouse where he lived after being at sea.

Jimmy the Priest's, at 252 Fulton Street near the Hudson River. It is one of three saloons O'Neill drew upon for the setting of *The Iceman Cometh*.

Pequot Avenue, looking toward the lighthouse, whose foghorn figures prominently in *Long Day's Journey Into Night*.

On the beach in New London (left to right): Arthur McGinley, unidentified man, Ed Keefe, O'Neill, unidentified man.

Frederick Latimer (top) was editor of the New London Telegraph, where O'Neill worked in 1912 — "the first one" who thought O'Neill "had something to say."

Dr. Joseph Ganey, who permitted Eugene free access to his library and often found him poring over Schopenhauer, Wilde or Zola at 3 in the morning.

Maibelle Scott was Eugene's passion in the summer of 1912 and was also a model for Muriel in *Ah, Wilderness!* Their romance flagged when Eugene was stricken with tuberculosis

Hart Cottage (top) at Gaylord Sanatarium, where O'Neill slept on an open porch while recovering from T.B. Catherine Mackay (above left) was a patient with whom O'Neill had a casual romance and who inspired the heroine of *The Straw*. O'Neill (middle, right) with two fellow patients. Dr. David R. Lyman (bottom) with two unidentified nurses and (on his right) Florence R. Burgess. Both Dr. Lyman (as Dr. Stanton) and Nurse Burgess (as Mrs. Turner) are characters in *The Straw*.

Taken - (cross my heart) - Jan. 1, 1914
New London, Conn.   Water - 39°

"The uniforms 'e wore
Was nothin' much before
An' rather less than 'arf o' that
be'ind."

Recovered from T.B., O'Neill began writing plays in
New London. Following Dr. Lyman's advice, he swam
in icy winter water (top left). He initiated a romance
with Beatrice Ashe (above) while awaiting his
father's consent to study playwriting at Harvard
under Professor George Pierce Baker (left).

Edward Crowninshield
Hammond, railroad
tycoon (left), and
Edward S. Harkness,
Standard Oil heir, two
of O'Neill's New
London nemeses,
whom he mocked in
his plays.

The biblical spectacle, *Joseph and His Brethren*, in which James doubled as Jacob and the 103-year-old Pharaoh; he is seated on throne (far right). As a favor to James, Jamie was given two minor roles in the production.

Brandon Tynan, a young actor in *Joseph and His Brethren*, with whom James strolled and attended church during the run. James infuriated both Jamie and Eugene by praising Tynan publicly as "my son."

Eugene kept pressing books on Maibelle, among them volumes of Schopenhauer and Wilde, and she obediently discussed them with him. They wrote each other several letters every day, even though they knew they were soon to meet. Most of the letters, far from centering on sentimental matters, dealt with Eugene's tutelage and his interpretation of philosophical passages he thought she might misunderstand.

Interspersed with his lectures, of course, were tender messages and a steady flow of poetry, not always his own. In one instance he sent her his "Sentiments as expressed by Arthur Symons":

> I wandered all these years among
> A world of women, seeking you.
> Ah, when our fingers met and clung,
> The pulses of our bodies knew
> Each other: our hearts leapt and sung
>
> . . . .
>
> Because God willed for us and planned
> One perfect love, excelling speech
> To tell, or thought to understand,
> He made our bodies each for each,
> Then put your hand into my hand.

Did she like it?, he asked in his letter. "Have you my Oscar Wilde with you? Just want to know, that's all." He then exhorted her to "Answer all questions this time like a good Big Girl." Maibelle was amused by the endearment, a response to her having chided him for patronizing her as his "good little girl."

He also gave her a handwritten transcription of Ernest Dowson's "Impenitentia Ultima," in this case without reference to its derivation. He had heard the poem recited time and again by Jamie, who felt a kinship with Dowson who, not incidentally, had drunk himself to death in 1900 at thirty-three. Eugene made no comment about the poem, other than to add a question mark enclosed in parentheses at its end, apparently to signal that his memory was not letter-perfect.

Eugene gave Maibelle a number of the original handwritten versions of the poetry that appeared in the Telegraph, as well as the original, penciled version of "Free." All the love poems he submitted to "Laconics" were written with Maibelle in mind. "Only You," which appeared on September 27, two days after he met her, illustrates his sentimental romanticism:

We walk down the crowded city street
    Thus, silently side by side
We loiter where mirth and misery meet
    In an ever refluent tide.

You thrill with the joy of the passing throng
    Or echo its weary sighs
You gaze at each face as it hurries along
    — But I only see your eyes —

I only see your eyes, my love,
    I only see your eyes
For happiness or misery
    Are only real when seen by me
Reflected in your eyes.

We walk down the crowded city street
    Lingeringly, side by side
You throb with the city's ceaseless beat
    While I in a dream abide.

For how can its harsh triumphant din
    Make me shudder or rejoice?
When the only sound in the dream I'm in
    Is the music of your voice.

The music of your voice, my love
    The music of your voice.
The world's vibrating symphony
    Seems vague and most unreal to me
I only hear your voice.

Maibelle and Eugene had an eager ally (in addition to Arlene) in Maibelle's best friend, Mildred Culver. Mildred shared Maibelle's opinion that Eugene was maligned by their elders and was convinced he had no ulterior intentions. "I think he loved her because he knew she loved his true self," Mildred reflected. "He wasn't used to her kind of girl; she was a complete surprise to him."

Mildred occasionally acted as go-between, delivering notes and helping to arrange secret meetings at her own house, often unoccupied because her mother was away teaching school. Mildred would leave Eugene and Maibelle alone in one of the rooms and keep a lookout for her mother, who held the same dim view of Eugene's reputation as Mrs. Scott. It was "Mid" Culver whom Eugene had in mind when he drew Mildred Miller in *Ah, Wilderness!* — the young woman who carried Muriel's notes to Richard.

According to Maibelle, she and Eugene were happy together and rarely quarreled. But on at least one occasion, he evidently misbehaved and felt constrained to apologize, which he did in the form of a sophomoric lampoon called "Love's Lament," published in the Telegraph on October 6:

> There ain't no nothing much no more,
>   And nothin' ain't no use to me;
> In vain I pace the lonely shore,
>   For I have seen the last of thee.
>
> I seen a ship upon the deep
>   And signaled this here fond lament:
> "I haven't did a thing but weep
>   Since thou hast went."
>
> Alas! fur I ain't one of they,
>   What hasn't got no faith in love.
> And them fond words of yesterday
>   They was spoke true, by heaven above!
>
> Is it all off twixt I and you?
>   Will you go and wed some other gent?
> The things I done, I'd fain undo,
>   Since thou hast went.
>
> O Love! I done what I have did,
>   Without no thought of no offense —
> Return, return, I sadly bid
>   Before my feelings get intense.
>
> I have gave up all wealth and show
>   I have gave up all thoughts of fame,
> But, oh! what joy 'twould be to know
>   That thou hadst came!

Although Eugene seldom showed Maibelle his brooding, somber side, he once recounted a softened version of his life at Jimmy the Priest's and his attempted suicide. He also told her that when the

appropriate time came, he would like to die by swimming out into
the moon's reflection past the point of no return.

He never alluded, however, to his painful relationship with his
parents and brother. When *Long Day's Journey Into Night* was published, Maibelle was aghast at its revelations.

"I have no recollection of Gene being disturbed about his family,"
Maibelle said. "He even took it calmly when James O'Neill warned
my parents against him."

Maibelle knew that Ella was ailing, but had no chance to observe
her at close quarters. She did know and like James, but could not
comprehend his attitude toward Eugene. She found Jamie intolerable. "He really was a drunk and a slob," she said. "And he had a
nasty way of looking at people."

Maibelle and Eugene began to talk of marriage after they had
been seeing each other for only a short time. While there seems no
reason to doubt her version of events, Eugene's motives are unfathomable.

He surely realized his father would oppose marriage to Maibelle
just as vehemently as to the hapless Kathleen. Eugene had barely
begun a new career and was not in a position (on his salary of twelve
dollars a week) to declare his total independence, either financially or
emotionally, from the "Old Man." Although he was about to turn
twenty-four, he appeared helplessly confused, oblivious to the burden he would be shouldering if he married Maibelle.

Despite her own naiveté, Maibelle, at eighteen, was the clearer-
headed of the two. If Eugene regarded his salary as sufficient on
which to marry, Maibelle thought otherwise, and suggested they
wait.

She understood that Eugene had faith in himself as a writer; he
often told her he would be a famous one, and she did not doubt him.
In fact, in an effort to be supportive, she enrolled in a shorthand
course at the local business college.

"I did it so that if Gene, after we were married, had a profound
thought in the middle of the night, I'd be able to leap out of bed, take
my pad and pencil, and record it for him."

If her intentions were laudable, her secretarial talents proved bor-
derline; on a test, she spelled asparagus, "asparroggross."

THIRTY-ONE

J AMES INSTALLED A HEATING SYSTEM IN MONTE CRISTO Cottage in the late summer of 1912, so that Eugene could continue at the Telegraph during the fall and winter. Despite this luxury, Eugene developed a bad cold and cough soon after his twenty-fourth birthday on October 16, and could not shake the symptoms.

He believed he had caught the cold riding his bicycle to work in a downpour and that a contributing factor might have been a severe chill that suddenly overcame him while swimming in the Sound in late September. Eventually he was bedridden with fever and night sweats.

Although too ill to report at the Telegraph, he continued to send poems to "Laconics." In one, "It's Great When You Get In," he described how it felt to plunge into the autumnal Sound:

> I felt like a frozen mummy
>   In an icy winding sheet.
> It took me over an hour
>   To calm my chattering teeth . . .
> So be warned by my example
>   And shun the flowing sea,
> When the chill winds of September
>   Blow sad and drearily . . .

On November 5, just before the presidential election, the Telegraph carried a lengthy tirade against political hypocrisy by "Eugene Gladstone O'Neill," entitled "The Long Tale." With apologies to Rudyard Kipling's "The Long Trail," the poem began:

There's a speech within the hall, echoes back from wall
    to wall
    Where the campaign banners swing;
And the voters sit so patient, listening to the tale
    so ancient,
    That the old spell binders sing.
You have heard the story of thieving Trusts
    And their lawless lust for gain;
You have heard that song — how long! how long?
    'Tis the same old tale again!
We have fallen for that same bull, dear lass,
    Many a season through,
Till we're getting fed up with the old tale, the cold tale,
    thrice-told tale,
Yes, we're just about sick of that Long Tale, the tale
    that is never new . . .

For more than two months Eugene had been living the closest thing to a normal life since his days at Betts Academy. He had a job he did not dislike, was appreciated for his poems in the Telegraph and had a loving girlfriend. But all at once this benign existence was threatened. While depressed about his illness, he did not at first suspect its severity nor, in fact, did anyone in his family.

It was not long before his mother, more than usually agitated, began making references to his "bad cold" — as does Mary Tyrone in *Long Day's Journey Into Night*; like Mary, she persuaded herself the symptoms would soon vanish.

In the play, the struggle that revolves around the younger son's illness takes place during a single, supercharged day in August; in actuality, the events of Eugene's illness and his mother's disintegration were played out gradually, not coming to a climax until the late fall.

O'Neill radically condensed time to create artistic truth, and in the play the "bad cold" seizes the younger son during a period when all four Tyrones are in residence at the cottage. In reality, Jamie O'Neill was absent, having checked himself into a sanatorium some days earlier to undergo one of his periodic cures for alcoholism. He was not — like his counterpart in the play — privy to the evolving seriousness of his younger brother's illness.

As for James O'Neill, although he had to visit New York every so often in search of a vehicle for the coming season, he could not help being aware of Eugene's intensifying symptoms. Ella, sliding once

again into a drugged daze — and with her habitual mistrust of doctors — was incapable of dealing with Eugene's illness. As always in
a crisis, it fell to James to take charge. Differing diametrically from the
play's James Tyrone, he arranged for Eugene to be seen by two reputable doctors: Daniel Sullivan, New London's leading surgeon, and
his assistant, Harold Heyer. While neither bore any resemblance to
the "quack" described in the play, Eugene had little faith in their competence.

Because Eugene ran a fever, Dr. Heyer at first diagnosed a recurrence of the Honduran malaria and prescribed quinine, which
Eugene said made him "feel mean." His condition was next thought
to be "muscular rheumatism" and finally, on November 15, his illness
was diagnosed as "pleurisy in the right back."

At that point Dr. Heyer ordered him to bed and called in a registered nurse (of whom there is no mention in *Long Day's Journey Into
Night*). Personally selected by Eugene, the nurse, Olive Evans (later
Maxon), was close to Eugene's age and had known him casually for
years. Her patience, understanding and humor lifted his spirits.

"Gene had a high fever and had to have cold bed baths to bring
his temperature down," Olive Evans recalled. "He was very shy and
modest, and I had to put him at ease when I bathed him by repeating
what I had often heard my nursing superintendent say to patients: 'I
think no more of washing a back than of washing that door.'"

Imprisoned by his illness, Eugene found his mind returning to
the freedom of the open sea, and it was at this point that he wrote
"The Call," in which he pined "once more to roam," poignantly
recalling his joy in lying "on the hatches/In the glowing tropic night/
When the sky is clear and the stars seem near/And the wake is a trail
of light . . . "

As Eugene's illness continued to worsen, Olive stayed by his side,
taking off only four hours a day. Fluid developed in his right lung
and his cough was unrelieved. Dr. Heyer, who visited daily, called in
Dr. Sullivan, who punctured Eugene's chest with a hollow needle to
draw fluid from his lung.

"It was terribly painful," Olive said, "but Gene was very brave;
there was hardly a grunt from him."

His despondency was reflected in his poetry for the Telegraph.
His thoughts flew back to the cynical carousing in New York with Ed
Keefe three years earlier, spurring him to write "The Haymarket,"
with its bitter references to "dull satiety," "breath of doom," "drunk-
en tears" and "choking sighs." The poem appeared on November 21,

with the even more desolate verse, "Noon"; it spoke of trees that "sway to and fro protestingly/Dancing as if to the weird melody/of anguished protest that the north wind screams," not to mention "The sere, dead leaves . . . Fleeing as if from nameless pestilence."

A few days later Eugene's pessimism culminated in his grimmest poem of all, "The Lay of the Singer's Fall." Reverting to thoughts of self-destruction, he described a gifted youth whose spirit was plagued by the devil of doubt; first his faith, then his heart, then his soul died. "When Truth and Love and God are dead/It is time, full time, to die!," says the Singer in the last stanza. The poem ends:

> And the Devil in triumph chuckled low,
>   "There is always suicide,
> It's the only logical thing I know."
>   — And the life of the singer died.

Once the liquid had been drained from his lungs on November 26, Eugene's fever subsided. But he was subject to occasional hemorrhages and, while allowed to leave his bed, it was only to sit in a chair in the sun. He occupied one of the two front bedrooms on the second floor, overlooking the Thames and the most cheerful in the house. In Jamie's absence, Olive slept in his room across the narrow hall.

Eugene sometimes showed Olive snatches of dialogue, sketches of characters and notations for settings of plays, including a description of a barge captain called Chris — an early version, as Olive later realized, of the father in *"Anna Christie."* He kept his notes in an old-fashioned bureau with divided drawers and informed Olive he had gone to sea with a vague hope of obtaining material for the writing he might want to do some day.

Olive, a less qualified judge than Frederick Latimer, nonetheless thought Eugene highly gifted: "A brilliant boy, but a little warped," as she put it. She did not hesitate to tell Eugene that in her opinion many of his ideas were "immoral."

"You are so naive," countered Eugene. "If I didn't want to be polite, I'd say stupid."

Having discovered Olive's weak spot, he attempted to shock her with stories of his love affairs. He told her about the half-starved waif with whom he shared a hovel in Buenos Aires, and described the derelicts with whom he lived at Jimmy the Priest's. Olive kept her composure.

"Later, other girls told me how he used to try to scandalize them," she said. "But he didn't only enjoy shocking women; he loved to shock men, too. A number of men I knew took a strong dislike to him — the man I later married was one of them."

Olive became an amused observer of Eugene's romance with Maibelle. Ella had learned of the notes passed between Maibelle and Eugene and asked Olive not to act as messenger. According to Olive, Ella's reason for discouraging the romance — unlike James's — was that Maibelle, as a small-town girl, was unsuitable; among other failings, she was not Catholic.

When Eugene began to feel stronger, Dr. Heyer permitted him to go outdoors for short periods. With Olive's collusion, Eugene persuaded his father to hire a carriage and driver, so that Olive could take him on ostensibly salutary outings.

After riding a few blocks, she left the carriage at his request, and Eugene headed for a prearranged meeting with Maibelle. After one such tryst Eugene came home enraged. Maibelle had refused to remove her veil to be kissed, he grumbled to Olive.

Expressing his genuine pain, Eugene sent Maibelle a poem, "To You":

> No more the throbbing pulses beating bliss;
>   The silences love made articulate
>   When clasped in close embrace impassionate
> Our lips became our souls in one long kiss.
>
> Have I not known enough of doubt and dearth
>   O God, great God, that Thou shoulds't sternly place
>   A wall between my lips and her fair face
> And make me taste of Hell while still on earth? . . .

Eugene told Olive that Maibelle was the only girl he ever loved. Soon after their tiff, he again met Maibelle with the same unsatisfactory result. This time he failed to come home long after dark. James telephoned an acquaintance at the Crocker House who volunteered to find Eugene. Two men finally brought him home — so drunk, according to Olive, that "he began smashing things."

"I don't think Gene cared at that point whether he lived or died," Olive said. "He was just desperate about Maibelle." The next morning Eugene, drawn and shaky, told Olive, "I yearn to see her all the time."

During her stay, Olive gradually became aware of Ella O'Neill's peculiar behavior. She remembered Ella staying mostly downstairs, sometimes playing the piano, but more often sitting, hands folded in her lap, on the veranda or in the parlor. (Doubtless for dramatic effect, O'Neill in *Long Day's Journey Into Night* depicted the mother's hands as too crippled by arthritis to make more than a feeble attempt to play the piano.)

In Olive's view, Ella did not seem overly anxious about Eugene's health. It is probable that what Olive mistook for emotional detachment was, in fact, Ella's determination to deny the seriousness of her son's condition, a state of mind conveyed (in this instance factually) by Mary Tyrone's behavior in *Long Day's Journey*.

Indeed, to Olive, Ella seemed more distressed about Jamie and his progress at the sanatorium. Once, hearing Ella sobbing quietly, Olive asked Eugene whether she should go to her.

"No, leave her alone," Eugene ordered.

Olive never saw Ella behave demonstratively toward her son, but she recognized affection in her voice when she spoke to him. "Not that there was much conversation between them," Olive observed. Once in a while Ella would offer Eugene an eggnog she had prepared and plead with him to sit in the sun. He would comply, but with irritation. On other occasions, Eugene would call downstairs — with tenderness — "Mama, will you please play something for me?"

While Olive discerned that the O'Neills were seldom overtly affectionate, neither did she witness behavior that remotely approached the hostility displayed in *Long Day's Journey Into Night*. Like others who had known the O'Neills, she was baffled when she read the play.

"I think Gene must have been out of his mind when he wrote that play," she said. What Olive, in her innocence, failed to understand, was that the O'Neills — skilled at concealment — would hardly have permitted themselves to confront each other before a stranger. And Olive had no inkling that Ella's frequent spells of vagueness were morphine-induced.

The O'Neills were keeping house in a sketchy fashion, employing only a cleaning woman. Eugene's meals were brought over in a basket by a young servant from the Young's house, as were Ella's. James ate out.

Olive was disturbed by Eugene's all-too-obvious antagonism toward his father. In truth, the intricacies of Eugene's constantly shifting emotions toward James defy rational interpretation.

"The Old Man and I got to be good friends and understood each other the winter before he died," Eugene wrote to Art McGinley in

1932, just after he had drawn an idealized James in *Ah, Wilderness!*
"But in the days [1912] you speak of, I was full of secret bitterness
about him — not stopping to consider all he took from me and kept
on smiling."

One reason for his resentment, Eugene told Olive, was that he
had been "dragged about" as a child during James's road tours. But,
in Olive's view, James appeared to be genuinely concerned about his
son.

"Of course, Mr. O'Neill was always a little theatrical," Olive said.
"When he arrived home for the weekend, he would step out of his
horse-drawn hack and come up the front steps with his arms flung
wide, expecting Mrs. O'Neill to rush into them in greeting, which she
did. Then he would go straight up to Gene's room."

"How are things going, son?" he would ask.

Eugene would mumble a curt reply and turn his back. He never
invited his father into his room and James would hesitate uneasily in
the doorway. With his own robust constitution, still apt to brag that
he had never been sick a day in his life, he must have felt cursed to
be burdened with an entire family of the weak or broken. He now
had on his hands not only a drug-addicted wife and an alcoholic
older son, but a younger son who (as he thought) was probably
dying.

It seemed that James's hope of setting Eugene on his feet was
again to be dashed — and this after only two months as a wage earn-
er on the brink of a respectable career. James agonized over the way
his son had wantonly brought his illness upon himself with reckless
living.

The friction between father and son was palpable. One Sunday
Olive heard Eugene ask his mother, "Has the Irish peasant gone to
Mass?" "Oh, Genie, please," Ella remonstrated.

James attended Mass every Sunday (unlike James Tyrone, who
puzzlingly is depicted as negligent about his religious observance).
Ella's relatives, in fact, were constantly after James to bring Ella along
to church. They had long since given up on Eugene.

At the end of November, Eugene's condition suddenly worsened
and it was then his doctors began testing for tuberculosis. Ella apparently was too dazed to fully comprehend their suspicions. James
understood all too well for he had grown up amidst the illness that
had long been the scourge of the impoverished Irish.

Consigning Eugene to Olive's care, Ella left him on Thanksgiving to join James, who had to be in New York on business. Eugene was accustomed to the family habit of ignoring holidays; James was usually on the road during Thanksgiving and Christmas, and holiday dinners more often than not were hasty meals between performances in drab restaurants near the theater. This lack of attention to the holidays had a lasting effect on Eugene, who grew up with scant sentiment for family celebrations of any kind.

With his father on tour nearly every winter, O'Neill once said, Christmas meant less than nothing. "As a boy," he elaborated, "I never disbelieved in Santa Claus. I had hardly heard there was one — not that I lacked my share of gifts, but that we never had much chance for a winter home and so Christmas was just a holiday without the usual associations."

Still, it is hard not to assume that his mother's desertion on this particular holiday, under the circumstances of his illness, did not wound him.

The retrospective bitterness O'Neill felt toward his mother is reflected in one surprisingly vicious note for *Long Day's Journey Into Night*: he described Mary Tyrone — when under the influence of morphine — as changing from "a vain happy, chattering girlishness" to "a hard cynical sneering bitterness with a bitter biting cruelty and with a coarse vulgarity in it — the last as if suddenly poisoned by an alien demon."

Abandoned by both parents on Thanksgiving, Eugene longed for Maibelle's company. She was unable to leave her own family celebration, however, and Eugene, overwhelmed by loneliness, asked Olive to call Mildred Culver. "I talked my mother into letting me go to visit Gene," Mildred recalled. "I made it a sob story — poor Gene, all alone and ill on Thanksgiving day." Early in the evening she wrapped herself in her brother-in-law's Navy boat cloak and walked through the softly falling snow to Eugene's house. She sat by his bed and talked to him about Maibelle.

A few days later, his illness was definitively diagnosed as a mild case of tuberculosis. Dr. Heyer advised a stay in a sanatorium, offering to assist James with the arrangements. Stunned by the bad news, Eugene met Maibelle that evening to tell her.

Tuberculosis in those days was regarded with dread, and those afflicted were held at arm's length. "But it didn't occur to me to be frightened of contagion," Maibelle later said, "and I kept on seeing him for a while, whenever he was well enough to get out of bed."

Early in December, Eugene received a further blow when Maibelle's parents, undoubtedly fearing contagion and more than ever opposed to the relationship, whisked her away for a vacation in Florida. "They were in the throes of breaking apart," Frederick Latimer recalled years later, adding that Eugene "was adrift in mind and spirit. And the mind was threatened. I was sorry for him."

While James did not cut corners on Eugene's medical costs and paid all of his son's personal expenses, both his generosity and his parsimony were episodic and often difficult to evaluate. His compulsion to turn off lights, for example, was a quirk on which O'Neill harped in *Long Day's Journey Into Night*, depicting James Tyrone's miserly concern for saving on electricity.

In fairness, it should be noted that this particular quirk was one James O'Neill shared with many householders in the early 1900's. In an era when a pound of ham cost 17 cents and a family of four could be well fed for under $60 a month, the charge of between $7 and $10 a month for the newly available electric light was out of all proportion. It cost fifteen times more to burn a light bulb in 1912 than in the late 1990's.

Theodore J. Liebler Jr., son of James's prosperous theater manager, was one who felt compelled to defend James's desire to save on electricity:

"In 1912, my family was worth about three quarters of a million dollars — and we always switched off lights," he said. "Like the O'Neills and most of their friends, we had started converting to electricity in the early 1900's, and we all tried to save on lights in those days. When electricity was first installed, the company figured that the users had to pay for the installation of dynamos and other equipment. They had to get some of their money back, so the original charges were high."

Far more difficult to comprehend is the instinctive tight-fistedness James exhibited once his son's tuberculosis was diagnosed — a point at which he seemed to panic.

James informed Eugene that he had decided to send him to the Fairfield County State Tuberculosis Sanatorium in Shelton, Connecticut, a few miles west of New Haven. The facility was run by a good friend of Dr. Sullivan, Dr. Edward J. Lynch. The sanatorium charged four dollars a week for those who could pay; those who could not were supported by the state. Mortified by this evidence of his father's stinginess, Eugene told no one, not even Olive, that his father was sending him to a state-operated facility.

Eugene's destination settled, James made a truly bizarre gesture. He called in New London's best tailor to outfit his son for what was essentially a pauper's institution. Unsurprised by his father's behavior, Eugene accepted this minor largess with a shrug, aware as he was of his father's contradictory nature.

Because Eugene was not sure of his strength, James asked Olive to stay in the living room during the fitting by the tailor, Charles Perkins. "Mr. O'Neill wanted me to be around all the time," Olive said. "He sat in a rocker while Mr. Perkins fitted Gene for a beautiful suit and overcoat, suggesting alterations and trying to be helpful, but Gene acted as though he didn't hear him; he was very critical about the fit, and would pinch in a place where a pin should go to mark an alteration. He just ignored his father."

On December 9, Eugene's signature appeared for the last time in the Telegraph, at the end of a poem, "To Winter." Evidently despair had given way to resignation, possibly even to the beginnings of hope, for the tone of this poem, in pointed contrast to his agonized outpourings of the month before, was whimsical:

> "Blow, blow, thou winter wind."
>   Away from here,
> And I shall greet thy passing breath
>   Without a tear.
>
> I do not love thy snow and sleet
>   Or icy floes;
> When I must jump or stamp to warm
>   My freezing toes.
>
> For why should I be happy or
>   E'en be merry,
> In weather only fitted for
>   Cook or Perry.
>
> My eyes are red, my lips are blue
>   My ears frost bitt'n;
> Thy numbing kiss doth e'en extend
>   Thro' my mitten.
>
> I am cold, no matter how I warm
>   Or clothe me;
> O Winter, greater bards have sung
>   I loathe thee!

For all the delight Eugene seems to have taken in his poetry, both public and private, he ultimately disparaged it. In 1929 he chided his early biographer, Barrett Clark, for "the seriousness with which you take it, the amount of space you give it," serving, as he said, "to create a wrong impression of my own opinion of it — now and in those days."

As O'Neill explained (making no reference to the handful of melancholy poems he wrote when he was bedridden), "I was trying to write popular humorous journalistic verse for a small-town paper, and the stuff should be judged — nearly all of it — by that intent." In 1931 he reluctantly permitted Clark and Ralph Sanborn to reprint some of the poetry for an O'Neill "Bibliography."

In a later disavowal, he declined permission to publish a volume of his collected poems. "It would be a shame to waste good type on such nonsense," he wrote to the would-be publisher. "They are merely very dull stuff indeed." Some years after that, he dismissed his poems as imitations of Kipling and others. "Dante Gabriel Rosetti," he said, "would have a chance for a pretty good lawsuit if he could get himself out of that grave and come back."

His serious poems, however, meant a great deal to him, as he declared in his mid-twenties. They were "not written without mental effort," he said; they represented, "better than prose could express, the soul of a mood." He continued to write poetry, most notably when he was in love, almost to the end of his life.

On the same day the Telegraph published "To Winter," the newspaper reported: "James O'Neill, the noted actor, will close his residence on Pequot Avenue today and will leave for New York, where he will begin rehearsing tomorrow for the wonderful scenic production, 'The Deliverer,' which will be played for the first time at the Century Theatre in about six weeks."

The play, subsequently retitled *Joseph and His Brethren*, was a lush biblical spectacle featuring fifty sheep, three camels, several donkeys and an elephant, in addition to ninety humans. Conceived by a popular writer named Louis N. Parker and mounted by George Tyler, the production pandered to the public enthusiasm for Eastern pageantry, inspired a bit earlier by Tyler's production of *Garden of Allah*.

Tyler had been reluctant to ask James to play the minor role of Jacob. "It was a queer feeling — and not altogether joyful either," Tyler said, explaining that he worshiped the ground James walked on. James insisted on doubling in the roles of Jacob and the 106-year-old Pharaoh because, he said, he would "be hanged" if he would wait in his dressing-room with nothing to do between the first and last acts, in which Jacob made his only appearances.

If Tyler had misgivings, James did not. He was looking forward to making a comeback on Broadway in his dual roles. He was gratified also that Tyler agreed to give Jamie the two minor roles of Naphtali, one of Joseph's brothers, and Ansu, Pharaoh's chief magician.

There was no mention of Eugene in the Telegraph story, but a brief separate item, headed "Goes to Shelton Today," announced he was "seriously ill with pleurisy" and was leaving New London "to take what is called the 'rest cure' for several weeks." The item failed to identify Shelton as the site of a state tuberculosis facility for the indigent.

James asked Olive to accompany him and Eugene as far as New Haven. Monte Cristo Cottage was closed for the season and Ella, according to Olive, arranged to stay for a few days with her New London relatives before joining James in New York. In *Long Day's Journey Into Night*, O'Neill implies that Mary Tyrone, in a drugged daze, cannot confront the fact that her son is to depart for a cure. In early notes for the play, however, her reaction was far more wrenching.

It is unclear why O'Neill deleted from the final version these angry lines, hurled by Mary at her husband: " . . . don't think you're going to send him away from me to a sanatorium, because you're not! I refuse to permit it, do you understand! You're up to your old jealous tricks but this time I'll never give in! . . . The same old trick of using any excuse to send my children away, when they need me above all!"

On the afternoon of December 9, Eugene, James and Olive boarded a train for New Haven, where James had ordered a car and driver to meet him and take him and his son the remaining few miles to Shelton.

Olive said good-by to Eugene at the station in New Haven. She had not been asked to accompany him on the last short leg of his journey; presumably neither father nor son would have wanted her to see Eugene's final destination. As Eugene stepped off the train in New Haven, a baggage truck with three coffins rolled across his path.

"My God," Olive remembered Eugene saying, "what a reception!"

Arriving by car in the gloom of late evening at the Fairfield County State Tuberculosis Sanatorium at Shelton, Eugene and his father were confronted with a primitive infirmary and a scattering of wooden shacks that housed patients, many terminally ill.

If James had misgivings about this crude and cheerless setting, once a farm, he was not deterred from consigning his son to Dr. Edward Lynch's care and taking his departure for New York. He was due there the next day for the first rehearsal of *Joseph and His Brethren*.

Dr. Lynch, who rose to superintendent and transformed the facility into a modern hospital rechristened Laurel Heights, never forgot his meeting with Eugene.

"He was tall and thin," Dr. Lynch recalled. "He was neatly dressed in a dark-gray, single-breasted suit."

Eugene was Fairfield's 547th patient and its most ephemeral. He stayed only two days. Although he had lived in worse hovels, he preferred not to die in one.

Dr. Lynch quickly assessed the depth of Eugene's misery and concluded his state of mind would not favor recovery. After ascertaining that Eugene, unlike the indigent patients, did have some choice in the matter, Dr. Lynch advised him to apply to Connecticut's Gaylord Farm Sanatorium, less than twenty miles north, in Wallingford.

"I told him he'd meet a better class of people at Gaylord," Dr. Lynch said, "and that, since Gaylord took only minimal cases, his chances for recovery there would be much better."

PART FIVE

REBIRTH

"If, as they say, it is sweet to visit the place one was born in, then it will be doubly sweet for me to visit the place I was reborn in — for my second birth was the only one which had my full approval."

— Letter from O'NEILL to the
doctor who cured him
of tuberculosis

THIRTY-TWO

IN THE OFT-TOLD VERSION OF HIS RECOVERY FROM tuberculosis, O'Neill spoke only of Gaylord Farm Sanatorium and never mentioned his fleeting, earlier stay at the state facility for the indigent at Shelton.

Even his relatives and close friends, including Maibelle and Olive, came to believe he had gone from his sick-bed in New London directly to Gaylord, the exemplary semiprivate institution where he actually underwent his cure. In later years, the brief item in the Telegraph giving his destination as Shelton had long been forgotten, and the shameful interlude would have remained hidden if not for O'Neill's own allusion to it in *Long Day's Journey Into Night*.

In the play he vented his long-suppressed fury, making much of James Tyrone's heartless intention of sending his son for treatment to an unnamed, state-run sanatorium for the indigent (which could only have been Shelton).

"Christ, you have to make allowances in this damned family or go nuts!" says Edmund Tyrone. Then, flying into a rage, he attacks his father in what is arguably the play's most savage speech: "It makes me want to puke! . . . to think when it's a question of your son having consumption, you can show yourself up before the whole town as such a stinking old tightwad! . . . Jesus, Papa, haven't you any pride or shame? And don't think I'll let you get away with it! I won't go to any damned state farm just to save you a few lousy dollars to buy more bum property with! You stinking old miser — !"

At the last moment James Tyrone is shamed into changing his mind, and agrees to send his son to a reputable, semiprivate sanatorium (also unnamed, but unquestionably Gaylord).

What is puzzling, not to say paradoxical, is that O'Neill the dramatist chose to contort the facts in his father's favor, since in real life James O'Neill did send Eugene first to Shelton and only later, under pressure, to Gaylord.

James O'Neill's motivation in first sending Eugene to Shelton may be explained, if not condoned, by his concern over his precarious financial status. Although his worth was somewhere between $100,000 and $200,000 in cash and real estate, he knew his income from the stage version of *Monte Cristo* was at an end. He was also distressed to learn that the Famous Players film version had to be shelved, due to the release of a three-reel *Monte Cristo* photoplay rushed into production by a rival company headed by William Fox.

"I remember how bitterly disappointed Mr. O'Neill was when it was decided the picture would not be released," Olive Evans recalled. Although James's version was shown the following year, it failed to earn the large royalties he had anticipated. But this did not deter him from subsequently appearing in minor roles in three more silent films: *God of Little Children* (released in 1917), *The Grain of Dust* (1918), and *The Courage of Marge O'Doone* (1920).

James complained to his barroom cronies that he felt like an old war horse put out to pasture, and he grew irritable even with Ella. At sixty-seven, his high-earning days were over and he saw the poorhouse again looming. Despite the unexpected offer to appear on Broadway at a salary of $400 a week, he had no guarantee the play would run, and his sons seemed ever more needful of his support.

He was convinced, moreover, as Edmund charges in *Long Day's Journey*, that tuberculosis was a fatal disease and that trying to cure it was a waste of money. His own father-in-law, after all, had been felled by what was then called "the consumption."

Writing from Shelton on December 11 to James O'Neill at the Lambs Club in New York, Dr. Lynch explained that Eugene planned to transfer to another sanatorium. He pointed out that while Eugene's condition was "emphatically in need of adequate treatment," his chances were "very good" for recovery.

It is not known by what means Eugene departed his dismal surroundings and managed to get to New York. Once there, he confronted his father and shamed him into arranging examinations by two specialists. The first, Dr. Livingston Ferrand, removed fluid from Eugene's chest and sent him on for further consultation to Dr. James

Alexander Miller, a pioneer in the treatment of T.B. and regarded as the country's leading chest surgeon.

On December 17, after examining Eugene, Dr. Miller wrote to the director of Gaylord, Dr. David R. Lyman. He described Eugene as being in "excellent general condition" and "a very favorable case," since he "has almost no cough or expectoration and no fever." He asked Dr. Lyman to let him know immediately if he could receive Eugene.

Dr. Lyman responded that a place would be available on December 24. Eugene, with his father's consent to pay the bills, promptly informed Dr. Lyman he would arrive at Gaylord on the afternoon of the date designated; that it happened to be Christmas Eve held little if any significance for him.

Although rehearsing for his January 11 opening of *Joseph and His Brethren*, James again accompanied Eugene, this time hiring a car for the eighty-mile trip to Gaylord. The car broke down in a blizzard, delaying their arrival until late evening. Eugene was cheered, however, at the sight of the sanatorium ablaze with Christmas lights and humming with good spirits.

According to one nurse, soon to become Eugene's friend, "Christmas was always celebrated in as big a way as was consistent with the patients' welfare — trees, decorations, small gifts, special entertainment, special menu and a relaxation of the rules — up to a point." Indifferent though he was to holidays, Eugene could not help but contrast the warmth of his reception at Gaylord with the dreariness of his arrival at Shelton.

His impressions of Gaylord have been accurately recorded in *The Straw*, written in 1918-19 and set mainly in what he called the "Hill Farm Tuberculosis Sanatorium."

The play's hero is a tubercular newspaper reporter named Stephen Murray who, though five years older than the ailing Eugene of 1913, is something of a self-portrait: " . . . a tall, slender, rather unusual-looking fellow with a pale face, sunken under high cheek bones, lined about the eyes and mouth, jaded and worn for one still so young." His intelligent eyes "have a tired, dispirited expression in repose, but can quicken instantly with a concealment mechanism of mocking, careless humor whenever his inner privacy is threatened."

In 1924, dedicating a volume of his plays to a nurse at Gaylord, O'Neill wrote: "I confess I believe there is a great deal of the 'me' of that period in 'Murray' — intentionally!" But according to the recollections of nurses, Murray seemed more a composite of Eugene and another patient who, like Eugene, had been a reporter on a Connecticut paper.

Gaylord Farm was small, nonprofit and to a degree experimental, in an era when T.B. was the leading cause of death in the United States and dreaded as the Great White Plague. James was not alone in believing it to be fatal; it was considered virtually incurable except in a high altitude such as the Swiss Alps or — in the United States — in the well-established sanatoriums at Saranac Lake in upper New York State and the mountains of Asheville in North Carolina.

The Wallingford sanatorium, situated amid 293 acres of rolling farmland and orchards — once the ancestral home of three generations of Doctors Gaylord — was still called a farm because its immense barnyard and dairy made it self-sustaining. The Blue Hill Mountains formed part of its smoky azure background, of which the most picturesque grouping was the Sleeping Giant, one flat hill representing the head, a broader one the paunch and a third, flatter and longer, the legs.

Established in 1904 with one doctor, one nurse and six patients, the sanatorium was financed largely by the region's rich businessmen who had established the Anti-Tuberculosis Society of New Haven. Aided as well by a modest annual state fund, it was dedicated to proving that tuberculosis could be arrested in any climate with plain good care and sufficient rest. Patients were charged seven dollars a week.

From the day of admission, Eugene felt reassured by the optimism and competence of the staff. Upon arrival he was put to bed and underwent a thorough examination. Confirming previous diagnoses that his case was a light one, the doctors recorded that his weight was 146, that he had recently lost five pounds and that his "top weight" had been 156; his "strength," though, was deemed "fairly good."

Also noted was that he caught cold easily, was subject to severe attacks of tonsillitis, was nervous and, though he could fall asleep easily, was in the habit of waking up six or seven times a night. The record stated further that he smoked, but had taken "very little" whiskey for the past eight months and "has always led a more or less *irregular* life."

Eugene's farfetched theory that "he may have gotten infected while visiting dives and tenement houses as reporter," was included in the record.

This was not among the varied reasons he gave to friends over the years in explaining the onslaught of the disease. Long after he had recovered, he told Art McGinley that he had probably "picked up" T.B. in the Argentine when he was a beachcomber; to the critic Kenneth Macgowan, with whom he later became associated in the production of his plays, he said he had contracted the disease at Jimmy the Priest's, where he had slept in a bed previously occupied by a man who had died of T.B.; to a theatrical press agent, Joe Heidt, he declared that the symptoms had been brought on by riding his bicycle in the rain in New London.

To the writer Benjamin De Casseres he offered a more elaborate explanation:

"I got such a dose of those germs — at least, this seems to me the reasonable dope — while living at Jimmy the Priest's with 'lungers' numerous among the lodgers of its airless rooms — cells, better — that later when I got run down after a long siege of booze, theatrical tour with its strain of free — not always — love and of pretending I was pretending to be an actor — the little bugs got me. And at that, thanks to a constitution from my father that I had done my damndest to wreck completely, I only contracted a very slight incipient case."

While he felt free to mythologize his own brief bout with T.B., it always irritated him when others attempted to glamorize the illness, sarcastically implying that it had somehow become the affliction of choice for writers. "Keats died of it," he told an interviewer, "and people like Stevenson had it, so if you want to do the right thing in a literary way, you get it." In a letter to his older son, he added Camille to his list, quipping, "*such* a *romantic* ailment for whores and writers."

While he could be jocularly dismissive in public about his own case of T.B., he actually worried for years over a possible recurrence. On one occasion, ten years after leaving Gaylord, he feared that the "little bugs" had returned to make an end of him. He was staying at the time with a friend, Eben Given, in Provincetown.

"Gene came down with tonsillitis," Given recalled. "He had a slight hemorrhage and he thought it was a recurrence of T.B.; he was convinced he was going to die. My father, who had some medical knowledge, examined him and was able to assure him that there was nothing wrong except a little burst blood vessel in his throat."

Acutely conscious of his health once he began writing, and always worried about the extent of the damage he might have done to himself in his derelict years, he hoarded physicians as an athlete collects trophies, exulting each time he bagged a new doctor.

Wherever he lived and worked, doctors became part of his family. They were his confidants and they listened patiently to his often exaggerated complaints of symptoms. When in his forties, he began to suffer from serious ailments, he depended on his doctors to keep him well enough to continue writing.

David Russell Lyman, the first of the many doctors O'Neill collected, was thirty-six, Buffalo-born and educated in Virginia. O'Neill called him Dr. Stanton in *The Straw*, describing him as "a handsome man . . . with a grave, care-lined studious face lightened by a kindly, humorous smile."

His gray eyes, wrote O'Neill, "saddened by the suffering they have witnessed, have the sympathetic quality of real understanding. The look they give is full of . . . the courage-renewing, human companionship of a hope which is shared."

The character based on Dr. Lyman might also have been partly influenced by a warmhearted and popular New London physician named J. G. Stanton.

"It was funny, *The Straw* opening in N.L. when there is so much autobiographical stuff in it connected with that town," O'Neill once told Ed Keefe. "When I wrote it three years ago [in 1919] of course I never dreamed of that coincidence — or I would never have lazily picked up actual names which, even if the stage folk were altogether different from the living, must have sounded rather mirthful. 'Doctor Gaynor' for Doc. Gayney [sic], for example — and 'Doctor Stanton'."

Once a T.B. patient himself, Dr. Lyman had joined the medical staff at Saranac and then, at only twenty-eight, had taken charge of Gaylord soon after it was founded. Assisted by a devoted registered nurse named Florence R. Burgess, a widow nine years his senior, he turned Gaylord into a model sanatorium where new methods were tested and proved. Mrs. Burgess became Mrs. Turner in *The Straw*: "a stout, motherly, capable-looking woman with gray hair."

In 1913, forty years before the advent of drugs able to cure most cases of T.B., Gaylord offered a regimen mainly based — in addition to rest — on fresh air and wholesome food, in a tranquil homelike environment. Its staff stressed the importance of self-care. Gaylord patients learned to consider themselves, upon discharge, as graduates of a benevolent alma mater. O'Neill himself, thoroughly indoctrinated, signed a letter to Dr. Lyman some years after leaving Gaylord: "Your alumnus, Eugene O'Neill." The patients regarded Dr.

Lyman, whom they affectionately called "Dr. David," as a heaven-sent savior. The mastery of each tortuous step toward recovery was rewarded by a privilege. Because his own case was slight, Eugene moved up the steps more rapidly than most patients.

During a couple of weeks of bed rest in the main building, Tuttle Infirmary — which accommodated thirty-one patients — he gained weight and strength and received permission to walk unescorted to the bathroom. His next earned privilege was an unassisted tub bath.

By the end of January, he was permitted to sit for an hour in a reclining chair and, soon after, with his weight up to 158 — a gain of twelve pounds — he was ready to move into Hart Cottage, one of several small dormitories. The gift of a New Haven businessman, Hart Cottage accommodated four patients. Because fresh air was deemed an essential part of treatment, Eugene slept on one of the cottage's two open porches, even in the bitterest cold.

By mid-February he was no longer plagued by a cough or fatigue and he had no pain, although he still had a slight "drawing" sensation at "the right base."

Gradually, he was allowed to leave bed for one meal, then two and finally three. Milk, of which an ample supply was produced on the farm, was a daily diet requirement and Eugene consumed large quantities. Next, he was invited to the main hall for social activities, such as card games and checkers. With a sense of true achievement, he reached the stage of regulated exercise: first, a daily walk of fifteen minutes, which was slowly increased to one hour in the morning and one hour in the afternoon.

To both staff and patients, Eugene was singled out as someone special because of his father's celebrity. Many of them had seen *The Count of Monte Cristo* at least once and, not long after Eugene's arrival, a nurse called his attention to an article in Vanity Fair about a rowdy champagne party and show produced by the Friars Club early in January at New York's Berkeley Theater.

The show, a mock-trial entitled "A Giggle," listed James in the cast as the defendant "charged with putting the bull in Bull Durham." Always the loyal clubman, James had long since learned how to put aside his domestic heartaches and carry on his public life. If he had managed to give a performance on the day his infant son, Edmund, died, he was not likely to allow Eugene's illness to deter him from taking part in a show called "A Giggle."

James did, however, make a point of visiting Eugene on his days off from *Joseph and His Brethren*, which, to his great joy, had become an instant hit and restored him to the limelight. He was never accompanied by Ella for, as he told Dr. Lyman, he feared that, weakened as she was by her addiction, she would have a low resistance to tuberculosis.

Toward the end of February, Eugene was making rapid progress toward recovery and was allowed a four-day visit to New London. The Telegraph reported his arrival, stating that he was "feeling fit as a fiddle," and adding that he was "receiving the congratulations of many friends on the successful outcome of his convalescence." On his return to Gaylord, Eugene began to form friendships; he was especially drawn to Mary A. Clark, the head nurse of the Infirmary whom, in *The Straw*, he portrayed as Miss Gilpin.

As self-consciously Irish as Eugene, Mary Clark shared his view of life as tragic but exhilarating; she could agree with him that the only true hero was one who struggled to triumph over his fate — even knowing the odds were against him. Thirty-three, tall, dark-haired, dark-eyed and strong-minded, she had come to the sanatorium as a patient in 1910 and stayed on to work after her recovery.

Along with a number of other nurses, Mary Clark became the recipient of the sort of light verse with which Eugene could not resist showering anyone of the opposite sex who seemed to take an interest in him. Although Dr. Lyman had sternly cautioned Eugene against any exertion, physical or mental, he evidently did not regard writing poetry as work.

In one of his poems, "Ballade of the Birthday of the Most Gracious of Ladyes," he called Mary Clark the "angel of old pneumothorax," and declared his devotion:

> Hope's Hebe to the fever-toss'd!
> (Some figure of speech, you'll agree)
> Kindest of bosses that e'er bossed!
> I'm almost glad to have T.B.
> Else I'd never have met you — see?
> And real true friendship's none so rife,
> With all my heart I shout to thee —
> Top of the morning and long life!

Writing to her ten years later, after she had published all four of the poem's stanzas in a hospital magazine at Eaglesville,

Pennsylvania, where she had become superintendent, O'Neill declared that although seeing the poem again had given him nostalgic pleasure he realized its literary merits were negligible. "But — whisper! — I think as a poet I'm a very good playwright."

Eugene stayed in touch with Mary Clark for many years, sending her several volumes of his published plays. In a collection containing *The Straw*, *The Emperor Jones* and a play called *Diff'rent*, he wrote: " . . . with affectionate remembrance of our friendship at Gaylord Farm and of her great and continued kindness to me while I was a patient there — the spirit of which kindness I have tried dimly to portray in 'The Straw' without, however, presuming to make any personal sketches out of the characters in that play."

The denial, of course, was automatic; he had by then fallen into the habit of insisting that no character in any play, however obvious the derivation, was based on an actual person. Aware that many of his plays contained recognizable characters, he believed this was the safest way to guard against recrimination.

There were two other nurses of whom Eugene grew fond, and who emerged as characters in the *The Straw*. One was Wilhelmina Stamberger, a tall, slender, blonde probationer (or nurse-in-training) of twenty-seven. She was, like Mary Clark, a former patient who had fought her way back to health. She and a second nurse, Katherine Murray, who had also been a patient, became the composite character, Miss Howard.

Wilhelmina Stamberger had the task of checking Eugene's weight every Saturday and spraying his throat with what she called "a vile concoction of Argyrol" to ward off tonsillitis. "I may have been the outward model for Miss Howard," she recalled, "but Katherine Murray was the one who used to have long chats with O'Neill. She had a wonderful gift of gab." Katherine was a native of New Haven, dark-haired with an oval face, and Irish Catholic to the core.

In fact, it was Katherine Murray who, hoping to bring him back to the Catholic doctrine, introduced Eugene to "The Hound of Heaven," by Francis Thompson, who wrote the poem in 1890, two years after almost dying of opium addiction in London and being rehabilitated by a compassionate clergyman.

Murray sent O'Neill a copy of the poem in New London, following his departure from the sanatorium. While it did not revive his lost faith, as Katherine Murray had hoped, the epic poem eventually became so familiar to O'Neill that he could recite all of its 183 lines. It had a profound influence on him for years to come, gradually taking precedence over the poetry of Baudelaire and Swinburne.

The further he withdrew, personally and artistically from his Catholic roots, the more keenly he felt the exhilarating terror of his flight, as exemplified by these lines of the poem:

> I fled Him, down the nights and down the days;
> I fled Him, down the arches of the years;
> I fled Him, down the labyrinthine ways
> Of my own mind . . .

Katherine Murray was among several nurses and patients who encouraged Eugene when he told them of his ambition to be a writer, thereby earning his undying gratitude. In acknowledgment of her friendship, he borrowed her surname for the hero of *The Straw*.

Ever more certain that writing was to be his life's work, he continued to make notes in his mind for future plays. Having suffered and searched and struggled, he was now convinced that writing was to be his justification for being born.

For seven years he had been in violent motion: hell-raising at Princeton, entangled in a foolish marriage, futilely prospecting in Honduras, disgracing himself on his father's vaudeville tour, seeking escape at sea, sinking to the depths in Buenos Aires and on New York's waterfront and, wherever he happened to be, whoring and drinking himself senseless. Now, no longer able to lash out physically, he was forced to internalize his rage, releasing it through writing and becoming a creator rather than a destroyer.

In 1921, shortly after *Beyond the Horizon* had brought him fame, O'Neill explained that before he fell ill he had had little sense of direction: "My ambition, if you call it that, was to keep moving — to do as many things as I could. I just drifted along till I was twenty-four and then I got a jolt and sat up and took notice. Retribution overtook me and I went down with T.B."

In the last interview he gave, in 1948, he was still eager to stress that if he had not been forced to look hard at himself in the sanatorium, he might never have become a playwright.

"There are times now when I feel sure I would have been, no matter what happened," he said, "but when I remember Buenos Aires, and the fellow down there who wanted me to be a bandit, I'm not so sure."

It was during his illness, he later elaborated, that his "mind got the chance to establish itself, to digest and valuate the impressions of many past years in which one experience had crowded on another with never a second's reflection." He began to mine his own psyche, searching for answers to his life's meaning, trying to face the sometimes painful truth about himself and the raw facts of his past. And this questing and confronting can be discerned in even the clumsiest of his literary beginnings.

"If a person is to get to the meaning of life," he reflected, "he must 'learn to like' the facts about himself — ugly as they may seem to his sentimental vanity — before he can lay hold on the truth behind the facts; and that truth is never ugly!"

He came to regard his recovery from tuberculosis and his simultaneous discovery that he wanted to be a playwright as his rebirth. He once described this period as "the time I should have been cast down by my fate — and wasn't." He felt, moreover, that the conquest of his illness had empowered him to challenge fate on other levels — and dare to believe he could win. After such a struggle, he said, "one's confidence in coming out on top in other battles ought to be increased ten-fold." The essential element in overcoming what appeared to be overwhelmingly negative odds, he believed, was something he came to think of and write about as "hopeless hope." This faith, first revealed to him at Gaylord, was "the greatest power in life and the only thing that defeats death."

Seven months after he had left the sanatorium he wrote to Dr. Lyman: "I am looking forward to some fine spring day when I shall be able to pay the Farm a visit . . . If, as they say, it is sweet to visit the place one was born in, then it will be doubly sweet for me to visit the place I was reborn in — for my second birth was the only one which had my full approval."

In a letter to Dr. Lyman six years later, he emphasized his deep gratitude for having been saved by Gaylord for his work. "My blessings on the Farm 'spring eternal,'" he wrote, "and the recollections of my stay there are, and always will be, among the most pleasant of my memories."

Only a Eugene O'Neill could have counted a bout with tuberculosis among his cherished moments. Certainly those moments, besides revealing his mission, were to influence his work for many years. He applied the knowledge of tuberculosis gained at Gaylord to several plays, beginning with *The Web*, which he wrote not long after leaving the sanatorium. The heroine is a victim of the disease, as is the hero of *Beyond the Horizon*, written in 1918, and, of course, the autobiographical protagonist of *Long Day's Journey Into Night*.

O'Neill's most distressingly tubercular heroine (and his most comprehensive depiction of the disease) appear in *The Straw*, which he wrote five years after he had left Gaylord.

Eileen Carmody was the name O'Neill chose for his heroine and she, too, had an actual counterpart at Gaylord. Her story, however, did not end as romantically as the fictitious Eileen's.

Eileen was modeled on Catherine Mackay, nicknamed Kitty, and, like Eileen, she belonged to a large Irish working-class family in the Connecticut town of Waterbury. A fellow patient once described her as "not really pretty, but a girl with depth."

In *The Straw* O'Neill wrote that Eileen possessed a "wavy mass of dark hair" surrounding an oval face that was "spoiled by a long, rather heavy, Irish jaw contrasting with the delicacy of her other features." He described her eyes as "large and blue, confident in their compelling candor and sweetness; her lips, full and red, half-open, over strong even teeth, droop at the corners into an expression of wistful sadness . . . her figure is slight and undeveloped."

When Eugene met Kitty in March of 1913, she was twenty-three, and seriously ill. She had been a patient at Gaylord a year earlier, but after a stay of only five months — and though she was still far from well — Dr. Lyman had reluctantly discharged her because, as the sanatorium report stated, she was "worrying greatly over home affairs."

Her mother was dead and nine young siblings at home clamored for her attention, a fact her father did not spare her on his visits. Kitty had an aunt and a grandmother in New Jersey and it was arranged for her to go there with the two youngest children. "Relatives can look after them and patient can sleep out and take cure there," Kitty's report read. "Patient worrying so, the above course seems best under the circumstances."

By the end of the year, however, Kitty's condition had deteriorated and she was readmitted to Gaylord. This time she was a charity case, since her father claimed he could no longer bear the expense. Her chances of arresting the disease were now considered only fair.

Kitty drew Eugene's attention almost at once and, as he invariably did with impressionable young women, he set about educating her. She responded with more fervor than Eugene had anticipated, creating a potential problem for the staff. Gaylord had a strict rule about emotional entanglements between patients: "Scatter your attention. Do not concentrate."

"The interference of the healthy heart with the cure of the sick lung is . . . a real problem to me," Dr. Lyman wrote with specific reference to Eugene and Kitty.

There were two infractions for which a patient could be asked to leave Gaylord: a love affair and drinking. Eugene, not surprisingly, was guilty of both. He pursued a romance with Kitty and occasionally sneaked into town after midnight for beer, returning at 4 A.M. Dr. Lyman later confided to Doc Ganey, whom he met in New London, that Eugene had been "a problem." That he did not send him away was probably due to the fact that Eugene was not there long enough for his misbehavior to be sufficiently documented.

For Kitty, the romance had serious consequences. Much sicker than Eugene, she knew that being dismissed from Gaylord would amount to a death warrant. But her infatuation made her reckless.

One of her roommates, Emma Halper, was aware of the extent of Kitty's involvement and was concerned. Emma considered herself responsible for the three patients with whom she shared a bungalow. She was the oldest and had had a long bout with tuberculosis. Years later, she expressed astonishment that the romance could have flourished as it did.

"Kitty was always in bed in our cottage at the proper time," Emma recalled, "and if she sneaked out later to meet Eugene, I certainly didn't know about it. They couldn't have had much time together during the day, either. One of the ways Gaylord had of enforcing the non-romance rule was the manner in which the patients' daily walks were scheduled; on one day the men would walk the Cheshire Road and the women would walk the Wallingford Road. Next day they'd switch. Patients of both sexes did congregate in the main hall at designated social hours, and that is where Eugene and Kitty met."

Emma first suspected Kitty's interest in Eugene when she came back from Mass one day, looking pensive. "Gene wasn't there," she said. Emma soon realized that Kitty was falling in love. It began with her borrowing books from Eugene; he had brought so many with him to Gaylord that the porter who cleaned his cottage used to mutter, "That man and his damned books."

As had recently been the case with Maibelle Scott, the relationship between Eugene and Kitty revolved around her being a dutiful student. But Eugene did not treat Kitty as gingerly as he had Maibelle. He mocked her Catholic faith and enjoyed shocking and confusing her. It was evident to the other patients that she cared far more for him than he for her.

As a matter of fact, Eugene still fancied himself in love with Maibelle. He wrote to her in Florida of his daily progress, sent her snapshots of himself and his nurses, and composed a tender love poem, "To Maibelle from a Recliner":

> Drowning I sit and watch the world glide by —
>> That working world which toils so far away —
>> My thoughts are listless as the clouds that stray
> Across the soft blue of the far off sky.
> The old despair seems scarcely worth a sigh
>> Remembering all the futile prayers men pray:
>> "Unborn Tomorrow and Dead Yesterday"
> And 'ere Tomorrow's birth perhaps we die!
>
> Yet life seems worth the living just to dream
>> Through the long hours in languid indolence,
>> To cease to wail with fretful impotence
> Against insensate Destiny; to seem
>> Thrilled as of old from eyes to finger tips
>> Your heart on mine, my lips upon your lips!

Eugene also wrote to Maibelle about his friendship with Kitty Mackay and received a cool response. Thrown off balance, he showed Kitty a picture of Maibelle and, in Emma Halper's presence, mockingly remarked, "She's through." He kept Olive Evans informed about his flirtations and sent her a poem he had written about Kitty, maintaining his reputation as a rake.

In addition to his love poetry and his paean to Mary Clark, Eugene also took the trouble to entertain his fellow-patients with a parody he called *Alice in Bacciland,* in which a character called the Cure Turtle invites the sanatorium's inmates to sample the curative brew of a Dr. Friedman: "'Lungers' let not your spirits droop/ But come take a shot of Friedman's soup."

By May 24, only five months after he had entered the sanatorium, his illness was deemed arrested and he was informed that he was free to leave Gaylord. He weighed 162, a gain of sixteen pounds since his admission, and was evaluated as being in "A-1 shape" with an excellent prognosis. His record noted: "Patient going home to take rest cure at his father's cottage at sea shore . . . Advised against strenuous exercise of all kinds for next year but can resume work in Fall."

Eugene wrote his father that he was ready to come home. In a letter to Dr. Lyman, James expressed his fear that Eugene's condition might still be contagious. Was it true, he asked, that no one, not even Eugene's "ailing mother," could become infected with tuberculosis by "living in the same house and eating at the same table" with Eugene? James went on to imply that, rather than jeopardize Ella's health, he would arrange to have Eugene go elsewhere for the summer.

If Dr. Lyman was surprised by this letter, he gave James only the slightest hint of it. He replied that in Eugene's case there was no danger of contagion, adding, "in his present condition he would not be a menace to anyone." Apparently James was shamed. He wrote to Eugene, asking him to return to New London. The total bill paid by James for his son's stay was $167.35.

Eugene left Gaylord on June 3, 1913, bursting with assurance about his future. Like his autobiographical hero in *The Straw*, Stephen Murray — who leaves knowing that Eileen is in love with him, but unable to reciprocate her love — Eugene regretfully said his farewells to Kitty. She was discharged six months later and returned to the tedium of her life in Waterbury and Eugene never saw her again.

O'Neill obviously felt that this was not a satisfactory ending for a play, and invented a somewhat mawkish one. In *The Straw*, Stephen returns four months after his discharge to find Eileen dying, and heroically determines to marry her, hoping to restore her will to live. To his astonishment he finds that he truly loves her, and convinces himself that her life can be saved.

"We'll win together. We can! We must!," says Stephen. "Happiness will cure! Love is stronger than — Oh, why did you give me a hopeless hope?" The implication, however, is that Eileen and Stephen will win through, clutching at "the straw" of the title.

But Kitty Mackay had no straw to grasp. Not quite a year and a half after having left Gaylord, she was dead.

CHAPTER
THIRTY-THREE

CHASTENED BY HIS ILLNESS, EUGENE RETURNED TO NEW
London with a renewed tolerance for his father and a deeper sense of
pity for his ailing mother.

During his summer break, before rejoining *Joseph and His Brethren*
for its tour in September, James evidently tried to regain Eugene's
affection by supporting his resolve to become a playwright. For once,
he put no pressure on his son to take a job, instead offering him the
leisure to write in New London after completing the three-month
convalescence ordered by Dr. Lyman.

Jamie, also in New London for the summer, continued in an alcoholic haze. He spent much of his time in the house, devoting himself
to his mother. When she was up to it, she accompanied him on short
motor trips. But Jamie sometimes felt put upon in his role as caretaker and grumbled to his cousin, Phil Sheridan, "I'm the goat for this
family — the nannygoat."

Jamie was beset by a further anxiety. He made no secret of his suffering from an unrequited love. Sheridan, McGinley and other barroom cronies, as well as Eugene, were aware that the object of his
worship was Pauline Frederick, starring as Zuleika in *Joseph and His
Brethren*. A beauty renowned for her cascade of glorious black hair,
she had been likened by more than one critic to Cleopatra.

She was unhappily married and Jamie had persuaded himself she
would marry *him* — if he agreed to give up drinking. He kept her
photograph in a silver frame on his bureau and grandiloquently sent
her roses throughout the summer.

There is no evidence, except for Jamie's own declaration to
friends, that Pauline ever considered marrying him, drunk or sober.
In any case, he could not manage to stay sober for more than a few
days at a time, and Pauline, also according to Jamie, continued to

refuse him.

During June, July and August, Eugene heeded Dr. Lyman's advice by swimming, walking and reading. He was seeing Maibelle again, but less often than before his illness.

"I had matured," Maibelle recalled, "and was less impressed with Gene's worldliness. Some of the glamour had worn off for me." Eugene did not importune Maibelle for he, too, was beginning to weary of the romance.

Although he had been warned not to focus on a writing routine until summer's end, Eugene could not resist jotting down notes for future work and wrote *A Wife for a Life*, inspired by his Honduran gold-mining adventure. The idea for the skit had actually come to him while touring with his father in vaudeville. Such skits were popular with well-known actors, who appeared in them on the vaudeville circuit between engagements in full-scale productions.

Eugene's skit hinged on contrived misunderstanding and ended with redeeming renunciation. The characters are two mining partners, young Jack and a nameless "Older Man," who suspects his much younger wife, Yvette — who has left him — had a lover. What he does not know is that Yvette's lover was Jack, nor does Jack realize that Yvette is the wife of the Older Man. Jack tells the Older Man about his love for "another man's wife":

" . . . he was a drunken brute who left her alone most of the time . . . I fell in love with her on the spot and the thought of how he treated her made my blood boil."

The Older Man, beginning to tumble to the truth, asks, "in stifled tones" (which Jack does not notice):

"What was the name of the mining town you mention? I've been in that country [Peru] myself — many years ago."

"San Sebastien," says Jack, naively. "Do you know it?"

The Older Man replies, "in a hoarse whisper," that he does.

Jack, still unaware that he is addressing Yvette's husband, tells him the rest of the story:

"I realized that the time had come and I told her that I loved her . . . Her lips trembled as she said: 'I know you love me and I — I love you; but you must go away and we must never see each other again. I am his wife and I must keep my pledge.'"

"You lie!" cries the Older Man, half-drawing his pistol.

"Why what do you mean? What is it?" asks Jack, still in the dark.

"Nerves I guess," says the Older Man. This satisfies Jack. After a few similar exchanges, the Older Man nobly sends Jack off to join

Yvette, who believes herself a widow. His curtain line is a paraphrase of the Bible: "Greater love hath no man than this that he giveth his wife for his friend."

In the typescript for *A Wife for a Life*, copyrighted on August 15, Eugene called it "A Play in One Act." He later amended this description, maintaining it "was not a play," but rather "a ten-minute vaudeville skit" that he had "dashed off in one night." In fact, he said, "my friends in vaudeville crudely insisted it was not a vaudeville skit, either." Nevertheless, he did bequeath it a special distinction by noting it was the first work he "wrote for the stage."

Despite his renouncement of the script as "the worst" thing he had ever done, he used an adaptation of the same biblical utterance twenty-eight years later in what he himself believed was "the best" thing he had ever done. In *Long Day's Journey Into Night* it is Jamie Tyrone who delivers the line, altered to: "Greater love hath no man than this that he saveth his brother from himself."

On completing *A Wife for a Life*, Eugene was confident it would find an audience, especially since James, in his eagerness to establish a rapport with his son, actually went so far as to offer to appear in it — if the backing could be found. But it is difficult to imagine that James, with the best will in the world, could have had much faith in its salability.

Eugene announced his achievement to his friends on the New London Telegraph, which obligingly published the following item: "Eugene O'Neill, son of James O'Neill the eminent actor, has written a vaudeville sketch . . . He expects to market it this fall. Mr. O'Neill has considerable literary talent, which was evidenced when he was a member of The Telegraph staff . . . This is his first venture into theater writing."

Some time later, Eugene admitted he had written it with an eye on the box office — his first and last such attempt, he said, perhaps forgetting that he did subsequently write one or two scripts he himself did not regard as purely esthetic efforts.

Having idled away the better part of the summer, Eugene was impatient to set to work. James had arranged for him to live and board with a neighboring family named Rippin when the Monte Cristo cottage was closed in September. While devoting himself to his new career, Eugene could continue to live a healthy outdoor life and breathe fresh sea air.

During his final few weeks at home, he devoted himself to writing two one-acters: *The Web*, which he later claimed as his "first play," and *Thirst* (originally entitled *Hunger*).

The literary one-act play had proliferated in Europe by the end of the 19th Century. It developed as a natural outgrowth of the long established short story form, popular with authors who wished to focus on the incisive expression of a single mood or idea. The form also lent itself to rapid completion and Eugene, untried as he was, thought it expedient to begin this way.

Continuing to write steadily after he moved in with the Rippin family, he completed four more one-acters, *Recklessness*, *Warnings*, *Fog* and *Children of the Sea* (later retitled *Bound East for Cardiff*), as well as the four-act *Bread and Butter*. Upon his return home after a seven-month stay at the Rippins', he wrote two additional short plays, *Abortion* and *The Movie Man*, and wound up his first full year as a playwright with the three-act *Servitude* — bringing his total output (not counting the vaudeville skit) to nine one-acters and two full-length plays.

"That's the year I thought I was God," he once told an interviewer, referring to the period between September 1913 and September 1914. "I'd finish one, and rush down to the post office to ship it off to Washington to be copyrighted before somebody stole it."

When Archibald MacLeish became Librarian of Congress years later, he told O'Neill he didn't "think there was much chance of anybody's wanting to steal them," and O'Neill ultimately agreed, stressing that of the lot, only *Bound East for Cardiff* was "worth remembering." He was right. From a literary viewpoint, all of the plays, except *Bound East for Cardiff*, groan with stilted dialogue and gratuitously violent plots.

It was as though, when he first began to write, he was suffering from a sort of multiple-personality disorder. With one part of his mind, he yearned to emulate the work of Ibsen and the other European innovators — to challenge, if not indeed negate, the traditions of his father's theater. "I suppose if one accepts the song and dance complete [sic] of the psychoanalyst," he once reflected, "it is perfectly natural that having been brought up around the old conventional theater, and having identified it with my father, I should rebel and go in a new direction."

With another part of his mind, however, he wanted to write plays that would be accepted for production — plays that therefore could not depart too radically from the conventional. And with yet another part he believed himself capable of tossing off trivia for vaudeville and the newly-opened field of photoplays — hack work that could earn him some money and buy him the time he knew he needed to develop into an uncompromising artist.

The dilemma was not an uncommon one in the life of a nascent artist. And regardless of his missteps, the plays of this period are worth inspecting as signposts to his mature achievement. They contain settings and characters significant for their authentic backgrounds, for their often audacious challenge of conventional values, and for their dogged probing of life's mysteries.

Eugene was already dealing not with mere individuals struggling against each other, but with their far more tragic battle against forces they could not control — the predestined workings of Fate. These frail beginner's efforts foreshadow the noble themes he was to pursue in ever greater depth and that were soon to awaken the trivial, contemporary theater from its self-satisfied torpor.

What is most immediately evident about these early plays is that, despite his professed sense of "rebirth," Eugene still had mayhem on his mind. In four of his first five plays — *The Web, Recklessness, Warnings* and *Fog* — various forms of betrayal are avenged or resolved by murder or suicide.

Three of them — *Thirst, Warnings* and *Fog* — deal with shipwrecks, perhaps unconscious symbolism for his own wrecked health. This choice of subject, however, was at least partly inspired by the sinking of the Titanic and by the graphic, protracted and widely reported hearings that began on April 19, 1912, the day after Titanic survivors arrived in New York.

Thirst is set aboard a steamer's life raft adrift in shark-infested waters, and *Warnings* is set partly aboard a foundering ocean liner, while *Fog* takes place on an oarless lifeboat drifting toward an iceberg. In these three plays, as well as *The Web*, he was hewing to his original intent of challenging the conventional commercial stage.

It is possible to discern Eugene's first shaky steps toward exposing social injustice and hypocrisy in *The Web* (originally entitled *The Cough*), even though he seems at times more intent on showing off his familiarity with New York's seamy street life than in revealing the social inequity that caused prostitution.

Written in a naturalistic style, the play was the first of Eugene's numerous attempts at dialect. An obstinate originality shines through in his emerging preoccupation with Man's futile struggle against his fate. The hope of a new life offered the tubercular prostitute, Rose, by

Tim, the sympathetic gangster, is doomed when Steve, the pimp, shoots him and frames Rose for the murder.

"She seems to be aware of something in the room which none of the others can see," Eugene wrote in his stage directions, " — perhaps the personification of the ironic life force that has crushed her."

The Web was not produced. "I love it, but I sure don't like it," O'Neill remarked thirty years later.

In his next effort, *Thirst*, Eugene engaged in his first flirtation with expressionism. Somewhat hysterical in tone, the play depicts three strangers — A Gentleman, A Dancer and A West Indian Mulatto Sailor — adrift on a life raft under a broiling sun that glares down upon them "like a great angry eye of God." The expository dialogue reveals that the Dancer was in the midst of entertaining the other passengers just as their ship foundered, that the Gentleman was in the audience, and that the captain guiltily shot himself as the ship went down.

The Dancer and the Gentleman, driven mad by thirst, suspect the silent Sailor of hoarding water. The Dancer offers herself to the Sailor, but he resists, denying he has water. The Dancer finally dies, and the Sailor takes out his knife, muttering, "We will live now . . . We shall eat. We shall drink."

The horrified Gentleman pushes the Dancer's body from the raft, the Sailor stabs the Gentleman and loses his own footing, and the two fall into the shark-infested water.

The play is notable as O'Neill's only brush, incipient as it was, with cannibalism — a subject entertained by the playwright who influenced him most, August Strindberg, in *The Father*, and for which, of course, both Aeschylus (in the myth of Atreus in *The Oresteia*) and Shakespeare (in *Titus Andronicus*) had set a literal precedent. Also shocking for its time was a stage direction calling for the Dancer, in her final frenzy of madness, to rip her bodice and expose her breasts, "withered and shrunken by starvation."

Answering a query from a reporter sixteen years after the play was produced in the summer of 1916 by the recently-formed Provincetown Players, O'Neill conceded there were those who doubtless "did think that one pretty frightful," adding he "would be the last to quarrel with their opinion."

Pleased that Eugene was already hard at work on his writing, James saw his son settled with the Rippins and left New London accompanied by Ella and Jamie to rejoin *Joseph and His Brethren*.

Eugene was no stranger to the Rippin household. His family had for several years, on and off, taken their meals there (as well as at the Youngs'). The Rippins' brown-shingle house at 416 Pequot Avenue was called the Packard. It had been built on an incline across the road from the O'Neills' home and was one of the few dwellings to spring up on the river side of the Avenue.

When a storm was brewing and the harbor crowded with schooners seeking shelter, boats tied up at the narrow Rippin dock to wait out the weather, their owners availing themselves of water from a capacious well at the side of the house. Below the back porch was the large dining room, where a select group of boarders were accommodated.

An unequivocal matriarchy, the Rippin family was dominated by Helen Maude, who towered both physically and psychologically over her slightly built, self-effacing husband, James. Helen Maude, the youngest of twenty children, had grown up forthright and resourceful in the English village of Whitney on-the-Wye.

Married in Rutland, England, she and James Rippin had arrived in New London one Guy Fawkes Day in the 1880's. Motherly, an excellent cook and a lively raconteur who had never lost her Cockney accent, Helen Maude had an endless supply of energy, humor and homely wisdom and was not easily awed by anyone — qualities she had passed on to her three attractive, unmarried daughters, Jessica, Emily and Grace (called Dolly), all in their twenties.

Jessica, who was still living in the Packard in the late 1950's, retained clear memories of the O'Neills. "James O'Neill wasn't the only celebrity who boarded here," she said. "People liked to come here. It was like a private home; my mother cooked, and my sisters and I helped serve. We didn't take in strangers."

The O'Neills, who did not care to sit in the communal dining room, were served in a private alcove facing the river. Awaiting their arrival, the Rippin sisters would observe James and Ella walking side by side with their sons following.

On reaching the house they would, in Jessica Rippin's phrase, "poke along, single-file, down the stairs to the dining room," the two sons always seating themselves between their parents. The Rippins referred to Jamie (then in his early thirties) and Eugene (in his twenties) as "the boys" — a somewhat disdainful recognition of their status as dependents. To all three Rippin sisters, the O'Neills appeared taciturn and moody, although never impolite. They struck Jessica initially as "a funny bunch."

The Rippins were among those few New Londoners aware that "there was something not quite right" about Ella, as Jessica put it. Emily, who served as chief waitress, recalled that, on several occasions, Ella seemed not to recognize her. "She looked pale and strange, and at first I thought she was sick. When she was like that, she'd push the plates away from her, not seeming to notice when food spilled from them onto the table or floor. Mr. O'Neill and the boys ignored her, and went on eating as though nothing were wrong."

Both Emily, the family beauty, and Jessica remembered their shock when Ella, after being served, once moved her arm in a wooden gesture, sweeping her plates and cutlery off the table. James, beyond making a brief apology, took no notice of the incident, nor did "the boys." Jessica and Emily began to suspect Ella drank. Their mother, assuring them Ella was "not that kind of woman," nonetheless had no satisfactory explanation for her behavior.

Sometimes, as had been the case when the O'Neills boarded at the Youngs', Ella did not turn up at all. "Mamma won't be down today," Eugene would say, "she doesn't feel well." A basket, often containing her favorite cornmeal muffins, would be prepared and Eugene or Jamie would carry it home.

Helen Maude was devoted to James O'Neill and he, despite his prejudice against the English, was willing to overlook her unfortunate origins — partly because she made exemplary corned beef and cabbage, as well as Irish stew. He treated her with utmost gallantry, often bowing before he addressed her and then assuming the stance of the old-style romantic actor, head thrown back, one shoulder held slightly higher than the other.

Once, greeting her as his Portia, he appeared in the kitchen after dinner and gave her lines to learn. The following evening he played a scene with her, to the delight of mother and daughters. He continued this amusement but, since James Rippin tended to sulk about it, the scenes were usually played behind his back.

Emily became as intimate a friend of Ella as any she cultivated in New London. Ella invited her on automobile rides, during which they would be driven several miles into the country. Though hardly loquacious, she once told Emily, without elaborating, that she had gone through two fortunes, and that was why her husband was careful about the money he allowed her. Another time she told her about Eugene's troubles with Kathleen Jenkins.

Now and then, escorted by Jamie, Ella dropped in on Helen

Maude in the evening. Jamie was always a welcome visitor at the Packard, even though the Rippins had been warned by a friend that he and his brother were "drunk and dissolute" and should be given a wide berth.

Jamie would keep them laughing. "We all loved him," Jessica recalled. "His only fault was liquor." The high-spirited Rippin women stood on little ceremony with Jamie and Eugene. Jamie, in fact, once took Emily for a walk and when they returned, Eugene teased, "What a drop from Pauline Frederick!"

When Eugene moved in with the Rippins in the fall of 1913 it was understood the accommodation was more in the nature of a personal favor to James O'Neill than a formal business arrangement.

"If Eugene comes to stay with us," Helen Maude cautioned James, "he'll have to live as simply as we do." James agreed to send the Rippins a weekly check of $13, of which $12 was to pay for his son's room and board and one dollar was to be his pocket money. Eugene found himself with no choice but to live a wholesome, sober life.

He was given a room that opened onto the back porch, which seemed suspended above the narrow beach. It commanded a view of the harbor and, across the river, the Groton shore with its sprinkling of stately homes. Eugene slept on the porch even on the coldest winter nights, simulating conditions at Gaylord's Hart Cottage. The Rippins hung rugs at one end of the porch to shelter him from the wind.

"After I left the San, I kept up the sleeping outdoors for over a year and kept pretty careful watch over myself," he later explained.

He fell asleep to the sound of breakers washing up on the beach below, and awakened to the shrill call of gulls. A black-and-white cat kept him company. "Friday used to climb to my porch on zero nights and crawl into the bed with me," he later reminisced, "leaving the rat he had killed thoughtfully on the floor for me to step on in case Nature called me to get up."

Shortly after he awoke every morning, Eugene set himself to work in his little room, writing with hectic intensity throughout his seven-month stay. "I write steadily four or five hours a day and feel able to keep it up forever," he reported to Dr. Lyman.

He evidently realized he was not likely to earn quick money from experimental one-acters such as *The Web* and *Thirst*. Succumbing to the impulse to support himself by writing photoplays, he spent several weeks grinding out the sort of silent-movie scenarios then gaining popularity. He sent them off to one producer after another, but even with his father's help could not sell them.

Embarrassed by his lack of success, he lied to Dr. Lyman in answering the pro forma questionnaire that reached him from Gaylord: To "What have you worked at the last year since May 1, 1913?" Eugene replied: "The Art of Playwriting — also prostitution of the same by Photo-play composition." In answer to "What have been your average weekly earnings when at work?" he put down "$30." Then he wrote a long-winded accompanying letter, in which he went to childish lengths to impress Dr. Lyman:

"Fearing that the answers on my question sheet may prove misleading in the case of one who is unjustly suspected of being a member of the more-or-less Idle Poor Class, I hasten to take advantage of your charitable offer to read the egotistic spasms of former patients.

"You must acknowledge that to ask a struggling young playwright with the Art for Art's sake credo how much he earns per week in terms of contaminating gold, is nothing short of brutal . . . while my adventures with High Art have been crowned with a sufficient amount of glory, I am bound to admit they have failed to be remunerative. Therefore, when I set down my earnings at thirty dollars a week, I am speaking in the main of the returns I have received from the 'Movies.'"

The Rippin sisters did not recall Eugene earning anything like $30 a week; it was their impression he made do with his paternal dollar-a-week allowance. As a matter of fact, Dolly paid for the postage when Eugene sent his manuscripts to producers and to the copyright office. He promised he would pay her back when he became famous. (He never did.)

None of the Rippin sisters believed there was a chance in the world Eugene actually would become famous. Jessica, for one, thought the plays he showed her were terrible. But she was impressed by his endurance. "He would work in his room, sometimes far into the night, banging away at his typewriter," she recalled.

Every so often he would ask one of the sisters to type a script from his handwritten draft. He had discovered he could not think creatively on a typewriter. Switching to a pencil, he found the words flowed. He once explained that the more concentrated and lost to himself his mind became, the smaller the handwriting. In his early one-act plays, he said, the handwriting was large by comparison with later work.

"The minute style grew on me. I did not wish it on myself, God knows, because it made it so hard to get my scripts typed — forced me to type a lot of them, which was a damned nuisance. I always hated typewriting and was very bad at it."

Eugene also soon realized he was wasting his time, not to say talent, trying to sell photoplays. For one thing, his recent discovery of Strindberg had renewed his desire to produce serious work.

"It was reading his plays when I first started to write, back in the winter of 1913-14," O'Neill said, in accepting the Nobel Prize in 1936, "that, above all else, first gave me the vision of what modern drama could be, and first inspired me with the urge to write for the theater myself. If there is anything of lasting worth in my work, it is due to that original impulse from him, which has continued as my inspiration down all the years since then — to the ambition I received then to follow in the footsteps of his genius as worthily as my talent might permit, and with the same integrity of purpose."

Eugene was under the spell not only of Strindberg's recently translated *The Dance of Death* but of Dostoevsky's *The Idiot*. To him both were tangible evidence that a writer could communicate "a powerful emotional ecstasy, approaching a kind of frenzy." These two works, he said, had "the feeling and sensation" he himself wanted to convey to an audience.

Strindberg was by far the stronger influence, for his philosophy of life and love was uncannily close to Eugene's own. In *The Dance of Death*, which struck an overwhelmingly responsive chord, Strindberg drew a portrait of a marital tug-of-war that evoked for Eugene the marriage of his parents. "It is called love-hatred, and it hails from the pit!" wrote Strindberg. Audiences had found the play's revelations repulsive, but Eugene recognized them as tragically true to life.

Though permeating the whole of O'Neill's body of work, Strindberg's sway is nowhere more visible than in *All God's Chillun Got Wings* (1923). Compare Jim's speech about his wife in that play — "I can't leave her. She can't leave me" — with Alice's speech about her husband in *The Dance of Death*: "We have been trying to part every single day but we are chained together and cannot break away." In reply to the family friend's comment, "Then he loves you," Alice says, "Probably. But that does not prevent him from hating me."

Even Strindberg's formula for suicide matched Eugene's. In *The Dance of Death*, Alice's daughter, Judith, suffering over the threat of separation from her young lover, speaks of killing themselves by swimming out into the sea until they drown. "There would be style in that," she says.

The Strindbergian theme is also apparent in Eugene's first full-length play, *Bread and Butter*, in which a thwarted husband declares, "We're two corpses chained together." It was Strindberg's *The Stronger* that inspired an early O'Neill one-acter called *Before Breakfast* — a two-character play in which the wife does all the talking and the bedeviled husband cuts his throat (as does the heroine of Miss Julie). And what could have resonated with Eugene more than this line from *The Father*, spoken by the Captain: "My mother did not want me to come into the world because my birth would give her pain."

Strindberg was more than a literary kindred spirit. His life, like Nietzsche's, became in some ways a pattern for O'Neill's own. The son of incompatible parents — his mother was a barmaid and his father believed he had married beneath him — Strindberg lived in constant torment; he was an iconoclast and a mystic, a bold theatrical innovator, often misunderstood and condemned. Like O'Neill, he was driven by furies, fated to disastrous relationships with his wives, mistresses and children. He died in May, 1912, the year O'Neill had attempted suicide.

The modern Swedish theater embraced O'Neill for what its practitioners recognized as a Scandinavian mentality. "We are accustomed to O'Neill's kind of drama," said Sven Barthel, the Stockholm critic who translated *Long Day's Journey Into Night* and other O'Neill plays into Swedish. O'Neill's plays, Barthel explained, evoked the storytelling of the ancient Scandinavian sagas. "In a sense," he added, "O'Neill is Strindberg. The two were wrestling with the same problem, which the Bible states as: 'For what shall it profit a man if he shall gain the whole world and lose his own soul?'"

Eugene's initial attempt to emulate Strindberg turned out to be more travesty than tragedy. Seemingly, he gave in to the insistent voice in his head spurring him to write something with a decent chance for production.

Recklessness, the first play he wrote at the Rippins, far from being innovative, was painfully close both in style and plot to the lurid melodramas of his father's theater. It was much the sort of play, in fact, Eugene himself had always despised.

The heroine, Mildred Baldwin, young, beautiful, voluptuous, is in love with the young, handsome, earnest chauffeur of her nasty, rich, middle-aged husband. "You have never loved me," says Mildred to her husband. "I have been just a plaything with which you amused yourself."

The husband discovers the liaison and sends the chauffeur off to die in a defective automobile, then thoughtfully arranges to have his body brought back to the house. On viewing her dead lover, Mildred shrieks and falls senseless to the floor. Soon after, she shoots herself.

"Mrs. Baldwin has just shot herself," announces the nasty, rich, middle-aged — and now triumphant — husband to a trembling housemaid. "You had better phone for the doctor, Mary." Curtain.

It is possible *Recklessness* was as much influenced by Boccaccio as by Strindberg. *The Decameron* was a volume that absorbed Eugene during his stay at the Rippins and he was surely familiar with Boccaccio's tale of a beautiful young noblewoman in love with a commoner, who kills herself when her lover is murdered by her father (rather than her husband).

Foolish as it is, *Recklessness*, completed in November, 1913 and apparently not copyrighted, embodies the biographical references present in most of O'Neill's plays: The marriage, of course, is unhappy. The setting in this case is the Catskills, where Eugene spent a childhood summer with his family in 1896; in the center of the room where the action takes place — as in *Long Day's Journey Into Night* — stands "a heavy oak table" on which rests "an electric reading lamp wired from the chandelier above"; Mildred, the star-crossed heroine, has the same reddish gold hair as Mary Tyrone in her youth.

Eugene had not yet learned how to blend his own vision with what was useful from his father's theater — at the same time sidestepping its hollowness and trickery. It was at the close of his career that he put the lesson he learned into simple words: "There are well-established rules for the theater as there are for painting and for music. The only ones who can successfully break the rules are the people who know them. A knowledge of rules is necessary, even if adhering to tradition is not."

Despite the profound influence Strindberg continued to exert on O'Neill's later work, his next play, *Warnings* (probably written in December), owes more of a debt to Conrad.

Marking Eugene's return to a more honest form of expression, it is a realistic play in two scenes about a middle-aged ship's wireless operator, James Knapp, who learns, between voyages, that he is losing his hearing. Terrified of forfeiting his job and his income and egged on by his wife, he conceals his handicap from the captain. On his next voyage his deafness leads to the ship's foundering. As passengers and crew are scrambling for the lifeboats, Knapp shoots himself.

The play seems to have been affected by Conrad's *The End of the Tether*, in which a sea captain stays in his job despite going blind. Having inadvertently caused his ship's sinking, he shoots himself.

Along with Conrad, there are also suggestions in O'Neill's work of London and Kipling. Because it is known that O'Neill was an avid reader of both authors, it is tempting to discern traces of London's *The Call of the Wild* and Kipling's *The Jungle Book* (first and second) in *The Hairy Ape* and *The Emperor Jones*. But it is impossible to know where the "influence" on an honest writer leaves off and where the inspired original work begins. O'Neill himself was rarely conscious of this process.

William Faulkner, commenting on the subject of literary influences, referred to the "matter of the writer reaching into the lumber room of his memory for whatever he needs to create the character or the situation, and the similarity is there, but not by deliberate intent." It came back, he said, "to the notion that there are so few plots to use that sooner or later any writer is going to use something that has been used." In the case of O'Neill, a marathon reader of classical and topical books since early childhood, the lumber room was packed.

Of more interest than the literary borrowings in the case of *Warnings* (as in most of O'Neill's plays) are its autobiographical elements: Knapp's marriage is not happy; his wife, Mary, complains — as does Mary Tyrone — of her difficult life as wife and mother; and she is suspicious, as is Mary Tyrone, of doctors who "make things worse than they really are." The ear specialist who has diagnosed her husband's deafness "is just tryin' to scare you so you'll keep comin' to see him," she says, echoing Mary Tyrone's complaint. James Knapp's fear of losing his income and persisting in a job for which he is no longer suited can be seen to reflect James Tyrone's fear of poverty and his persistence in milking the role of Edmond Dantes, for which he has grown too old.

Warnings (not produced in O'Neill's lifetime) is notable also as his first play to include children. He continued for a time to introduce children of various ages into his work, but it is clear from the perfunctory manner in which he tended to kill them off — the ruthlessly dispatched infant in *Desire Under the Elms* the most extreme example — that they were merely props to advance his plots. The children in his more mature works are no less wooden than the four in *Warnings*.

"I don't get them," says Stephen Murray, in *The Straw*, tersely mirroring O'Neill's own lifelong disenchantment. (In a 1914 letter he spoke of turning down a trip to the beach with friends: " . . . when I found out the children were to be taken along I backed out. A long trolley ride with a couple of playful brats is my idea of one of the tortures Dante forgot to mention in the *Inferno*.")

That January the critic, Clayton Hamilton, and his new bride stayed a weekend with the Rippins while seeking a summer house to rent. Hamilton, in his early thirties, was the drama critic of both The Bookman and Vogue, as well as a lecturer in playwriting at Columbia University. He had long been acquainted with James O'Neill both through his membership in The Players and his earlier visits to New London.

Instinctively hostile toward any friend of his father's, Eugene grumbled to Jessica that he found Hamilton patronizing. Jessica bristled, for she respected Hamilton above anyone she knew, and contrasted his cheerful outlook with Eugene's self-centered morbidity.

Hamilton's Rabelaisian sense of humor and gusto for life and art enraptured the Rippin sisters. Once described as a "snow-capped mountain of a man," Hamilton was prematurely white-haired, rotund and easygoing.

He referred to the Rippin sisters as "The Seventeen Daughters of the House of Rippin" and they called him "Mr. Ham" — except for Helen Maude, who called him "Mr. 'Am." Commenting on his magazine articles, she once said, "You write about such nice people. Eugene's are all so 'orrible."

Eugene at first struck Hamilton as withdrawn. "I looked the lad over. He had large and dreamy eyes, a slender, somewhat frail, and yet athletic body, a habit of silence, and an evident disease of shyness." Both Hamilton and his wife, Gladys, a slim, patrician woman, found Eugene less impressive to listen to than to look at. "I didn't pay any special attention when he came in," she recalled, "but suddenly I was aware of his two eyes and his silence sitting opposite me."

Eugene finally decided to give Hamilton the benefit of the doubt. Diffidently he asked Hamilton if, upon his return to New London for the summer, he would appraise his one-acters. Hamilton said he would, and advised Eugene in the meantime to concentrate on aspects of life he knew at first hand.

"Now it happened that the life that he knew best was the life at sea, because he had so lately been a sailor; and I made the obvious suggestion that this might be a fortunate fact," Hamilton later said.

"There had been several novelists of the sea and poets of the sea — Mr. Conrad and Mr. Kipling and Mr. Masefield, for example — but there never yet had been a dramatist of the sea. The average playwright knew nothing whatsoever of the sea; and any one who really knew the sea and who could learn to say something about it in dramatic form would find a new field open to him."

Eugene mulled over Hamilton's advice, but his next play, the one-acter *Fog*, while set on the sea, did not deal with the lives of sailors. Written at the Rippins' sometime in the winter of 1914, it was an experiment in symbolism and was both the most cryptic and psychologically revealing of his early plays.

In an oarless lifeboat, shivering with cold and barely able to see each other in an enshrouding fog, are seated A Poet, A Man of Business and A Polish Peasant Woman, who never utters a word, and who clutches to her breast A Dead Child. The play is the first literary indication of how haunted O'Neill was all his life by the ghost of his infant brother, Edmund.

Fog also foreshadowed the father-son antagonism O'Neill was to enlarge upon endlessly in future plays. And it introduced the brooding fog later to pervade *Long Day's Journey Into Night* and other plays.

The Businessman, a sketchy stand-in for the materialistic James O'Neill, assures the skeptical Poet that the fog will soon lift, leading to their rescue. "I've seen plenty like it at my country place on the Connecticut shore," he says, in a reference evoking New London.

The Poet, who looks like Eugene "with big dark eyes and a black mustache and black hair pushed back from his high forehead," confesses he has been contemplating suicide — a subject still much on Eugene's mind. Even more striking is the symbolism of the Woman and her Dead Child.

It is the Child's ghostly crying in his grieving mother's arms that alerts a passing ship to the drifting lifeboat. The Businessman is rescued, but the Poet remains in the lifeboat with the Dead Child and its mother, who has frozen to death. "I think I will stay with the dead," he says, gazing at their "still white faces with eyes full of a great longing."

From the the violent evidence of suicide and murder in these early one-acters it is clear that Eugene still seethed with inner rage. Far more noteworthy, however, is that he had found a way to channel his anger into the fumbling beginnings of art.

The writing he did between late summer of 1913 and winter of 1914, despite his wavering and confusion and lack of recognition, awakened his realization that — at least on paper — he could escape from a world whose hypocritical demands he was helpless to meet. Through writing he could create his own world, a world free of social restraints, set with his own idealistic standards. "My dream children," he called his plays.

"As long as you have a job on hand that absorbs all your mental energy you haven't much worry to spare over other things," he once lectured a young author, adding, "It serves as a suit of armor."

Writing gave him back the release he had found at sea, where he first experienced "the joy of belonging to a fulfillment beyond men's lousy, pitiful, greedy fears and hopes and dreams!" Without writing he had no life.

In 1924 he made a devastatingly revealing comment to Dr. Lyman, who had sent him a routine follow-up inquiry for Gaylord's records. In response to "How much [working] time have you lost from vacations?" O'Neill wrote: "Writing is my vacation from living — so I don't need vacations."

But there were backslidings — periods when writing alone was not enough to keep his demons at bay. Sometimes, like any writer, he would grow frustrated with a project not turning out as he wished. He would fall back on the familiar solace of alcohol, and it might be weeks, or even months, before he could stop.

Dr. Lyman had asked the wrong question. Eugene did lose working time — but not from vacations. He lost it from the destructive drinking binges he could not control.

CHAPTER
THIRTY-FOUR

EUGENE BELIEVED HE WAS NOW ENOUGH OF A COMMITTED writer to show his work to his father, hoping at last to receive a sign of approval. Accompanied by Art McGinley, he made a brief excursion in the winter of 1914 to visit his family in Hartford, where *Joseph and His Brethren* was on tour.

Entering the Hublein Hotel dining room before the evening performance, Eugene and McGinley found James and Jamie seated at opposite ends of the room. They were no longer on speaking terms, and Eugene and McGinley spent fifteen minutes with each of them.

Jamie sullenly observed that the camel in the first act was "the only regular guy in the company," even though the beast had not only trod on his foot during a recent performance but spat at him with what Jamie believed to be poisonous saliva.

"Look at him," James jeered, in his turn, "a thirty-five-thousand-dollar education and a thirty-five-dollar-a-week earning capacity."

At that, Jamie was doubtless overpaid. He had now taken to maliciously twisting his dialogue. In Chicago he delivered the line, "Let Reuben tell his own tale," as "Let Reuben smell his own tail." In another scene, seated at a table loaded with fruit, he chewed on grapes and aimed the pits at fellow actors.

His excuse for misbehavior was better than usual, or so he confided to McGinley. After yet another futile effort to give up drinking, he felt he had lost all hope of winning Pauline Frederick — if ever there had been anything to hope for. According to Brandon Tynan, who was playing the title role in *Joseph and His Brethren*, Jamie "stayed on the wagon for about two months. Then it got to be too much for him."

One night, Jamie's antics caused his father to break down on stage. Seated on Pharaoh's throne, James was about to deliver a lengthy speech — a trying time for him, now that his memory was not what it had been. In fact, recalled George Tyler, "the courtiers round Pharaoh's throne had to feed him his lines pretty steadily some nights."

As always, the supers were simulating rapt attention. Jamie, playing an old wise man dressed in a flowing white robe, was supposed to be equally absorbed. Drunker than usual, he swayed from side to side.

James's eye fell on his son and he faltered. Then he began silently to weep. The young actor, Leslie Austin, who had learned James's speech to be able to prompt him, was so overcome by James's anguish that he could barely utter the lines himself. It was after this episode that James ceased to speak to his older son. But he would not allow him to be dismissed from the company.

Longing for a sympathetic ear, James drew close to Brandon Tynan. Dublin-born and in his early thirties, Tynan endeared himself to James by his unaffected, boyish manner. He was among the promising actors who received James's fatherly affection, to the ill-concealed annoyance of both Jamie and Eugene — who dismissed Tynan as an "actor-yokel."

Tynan worshiped James for his dedication to his craft, the kindness with which he treated members of his company and for his dignified, yet affable, offstage deportment. He also shared James's devotion to Church and Ireland. During the run of *Joseph and His Brethren* the two fell into the habit of attending mass together every Sunday. They went on daily afternoon walks of several miles, James in his derby and dark chesterfield, Tynan in a snap-brim fedora and plaid sport coat. Although James was twice his age, Tynan had to step briskly to keep up.

As a favor, James asked Tynan to read the five scripts — *Thirst, The Web, Fog, Warnings* and *Recklessness* — that Eugene had left with him at the Hublein Hotel. James had read the plays himself but his son's choice of subject baffled him. "My God! where did you get such thoughts?" he expostulated.

Nevertheless, he made an effort to suppress his misgivings and augment his encouragement in the belief that Eugene was at least attempting to achieve independence. He even went so far as to show the scripts to George Tyler, who was politely dismissive.

In later years, trying to explain his father's attitude, Eugene O'Neill told an interviewer his father did believe in him "in a way," but did not see why he should write "the kind of plays" he wrote because there was "no market for them." His father, he said, "believed that I might someday amount to something — if I lived."

Tynan thought the scripts showed promise and sent them to Holbrook Blinn, a prominent actor, who was presenting experimental one-act plays at the Princess Theater, in a venture that heralded the little-theater movement in New York. Apart from vaudeville, Blinn's was the only significant venue that produced one-acters, encompassing "satire, light comedy, pure horror, 'punch,' froth and tragedy." Eugene was encouraged to believe that Blinn was interested in producing *The Web* and *Recklessness*; as it turned out, Blinn changed his mind. Years later, O'Neill could laugh about his disappointment.

" . . . I've just sold an extremely lousy one-act thriller (which Holbrook Blinn was was once going to do when he was running Grand Guignol at the Princess back in 1914)," O'Neill wrote to the Hollywood screenwriter, Robert Sisk. The play was *Recklessness*, and had been bought by a company called Educational Films. "Paid five thousand net. Which I thought was a good price for a forgotten dud of a one-act."

James also showed some of the scripts to his friend, the writer, Irvin S. Cobb. "I'm taking the liberty of asking you to read them and give me your opinion on their possibilities," he said to Cobb over cocktails at the Lambs. According to Cobb's later account, he (like Tynan) found them arresting. "I read them through — there were four scripts. And then, stirred to my very marrows by the brute strength here expressed, I reread them." Eugene's writing, he told James, had "raw, crude life in it — blood and muscle and guts," but he doubted any manager would produce the plays. James replied resignedly, "Exactly what I thought myself."

Eugene did receive encouragement of sorts from Richard C. Badger, the head of the Boston publishing company, Gorham Press, which had brought out work by such noted playwrights as Augustus Thomas and Rachel Crothers.

Badger agreed to publish Eugene's first five one-acters — with the stipulation he bear the printing cost; James, in a spurt of generosity, advanced the $450. On March 30, 1914, a contract was signed, guaranteeing Eugene twenty-five percent of the gross proceeds from the sale of the book, and Badger guaranteed to print a thousand copies in August.

When Eugene returned to the Rippins' from Hartford, he again immersed himself in work, outlining ideas for future plays and pursuing his literary education. "I read about everything I could lay hands on: the Greeks, the Elizabethans — practically all the classics — and of course all the moderns." Using a dictionary, he read Wedekind in the original German, since few of his plays had been translated.

His sporadic habit of note-keeping — to record the clamorous ideas inspired by his reading — now became compulsive. He also began to formulate his philosophy of tragedy, which he kept refining until it became the fundamental truth of his art. It was wrong, he insisted, to think of tragedy as unhappy. "A work of art is always happy," he said. "All else is unhappy."

Between sessions of concentrated writing and the hours he devoted to reading, Eugene swam, took long walks and wrote poetry. He also found time to flirt with all three Rippin sisters, calling Grace "Dolly of the luxuriant locks," describing her room as "the sanctum of charms," and referring to Emily as "Emily Belle."

"With his dollar a week he didn't have much to spend on girls or liquor," recalled Emily Rippin. "He'd often walk into town because he didn't have trolley fare. And quite often we would buy cigarettes for him because he couldn't afford them. As far as I know, he didn't drink; I certainly never saw him drunk during the seven months he stayed with us." (Evidently smoking was not regarded by Gaylord as deleterious for a recovering tubercular. According to Jessica Rippin, "Gene smoked a lot.")

Blending into his environment with ease, Eugene grew casual in his dress. He went about in old, dirty white ducks and his cherished American Line jersey, often going barefoot.

"He felt fancy dressing was for the capitalists; he had all those anarchist ideas," Jessica said. "He would write long, radical poems and read them to us. One of them was published in Emma Goldman's magazine [Mother Earth]."

Another poem appeared in a socialist newspaper, The Call, on May 17, 1914. Entitled "Fratricide," it denounced what he perceived as an unwarranted militaristic intrusion of American troops into Mexico on April 21. President Wilson, in retaliation for what he regarded as humiliating incidents by Mexico's revolutionary government — including the arrest of several American sailors and their commander in Tampico — ordered seven thousand American troops to occupy the Mexican port city of Vera Cruz.

"Fratricide" was an impassioned plea for pacifism and a defense of the labor movement led by the I.W.W., as well as an attack on profiteering and on his old enemy, Standard Oil.

The poem was naive, simplistic and long-winded but, unlike some of Eugene's earlier efforts, it did, at least, scan. Of its nineteen stanzas, these are typical:

Ho, ho, my friend, and think you so?
And have you not read history?
This much of war, at least, we know:
The jingoes are the first to flee.
The plutocrats who cause the woe
Are arrogant but cowardly . . .

The army of the poor must fight,
New taxes come to crush them down.
They feel the iron fist of Might
Press on their brows the thorny crown.
They see the oily smile of Right.
They don the sacrificial gown . . .

What cause could be more asinine
Than yours, ye slaves of bloody toil.
Is not your bravery sublime
Beneath a tropic sun to broil
And bleed and groan — for Guggenheim!
And give your lives for — Standard Oil . . .

Comrades, awaken to new birth!
New values on the tables write!
What is your vaunted courage worth
Unless you rise up in your might
And cry: "All workers on the earth
Are brothers and WE WILL NOT FIGHT!"

Fortunately for posterity, O'Neill came to understand that militancy was not his forte. After incorporating his ire into some of his earliest poems and plays, his political scorn gave way to a loftier concern for the human condition.

Eugene addressed most of his radical harangues to Jessica. Although he could, when he wished, summon charming manners, he seldom bothered to produce them for the Rippin sisters. "He slouched, shuffled and mumbled," Jessica remembered with distaste.

During much of the time Eugene boarded at the Packard, Jessica was working at a school in Philadelphia and came home only for weekends and holidays. Jessica, at twenty-five, tall and attractive, with brown hair and blue eyes, felt somewhat ambivalent about Eugene. She was apt to deprecate him with her cutting sense of humor for what she called his "parasitical" existence. At the same time, she was drawn to him, watching his "maneuvers," as she thought of them, with amusement.

"He was always trying to 'make' us," she said. His attempted seduction of Jessica began as an assault on her unenlightened mind; he gave her a copy of *The Decameron* and studied her expression as she read it. Jessica was embarrassed — and delighted. Eugene proceeded to regale her with salacious details of his encounters with accommodating women, which embarrassed her even more and delighted her not at all.

"He used to talk of those girls as 'pigs,'" Jessica said. One day he told her about his plan for "the perfect marriage." Jessica was shocked by his cynicism — precisely the reaction Eugene sought.

"My wife and I will live on a barge," he crowed. "I'll live at one end and she'll live at the other, and we'll never see each other except when the urge strikes us."

Although repelled by Eugene's ideas, Jessica took a perverse pleasure in his companionship. What made it even more enjoyable was that her father disliked him and disapproved of his presence. James Rippin, with three unmarried daughters, had not wanted Eugene as a boarder, but his wife laughed at his fears.

Even before Eugene began living at the Packard it was James Rippin's quaint habit, when the O'Neill "boys" paid a call in the evening, to station himself in the basement. When he thought the visit had lasted long enough, he would signal his daughters by banging on the furnace.

Jessica took care to give her father no cause for alarm, but, once in the early fall, she very nearly got into trouble. Eugene took her in his rowboat to a cove on the Groton side of the Thames, where they went blueberry picking. Eugene inadvertently sat down on a berry patch and, as they were about to row home, Jessica noticed, not without mirth, that his white ducks had been stained bright blue.

Fearful her father might think she had been dallying among the berries, she persuaded Eugene to sit in the water to try to soak off the evidence. But the ducks stayed blue. Jessica's heart was in her mouth when they arrived home. She distracted her father's cold eye from Eugene, permitting him to sidle into his room.

James Rippin's disapproval rankled Eugene. More than a decade later, he wrote to Jessica: "You astound me by what you say of your father's interest in articles about me! I had imagined I was forever in his bad graces. But perhaps he is looking for the resounding knocks, what?"

Eugene was not sufficiently intimidated to forswear sporadic attempts on Jessica's virtue. Jessica, however, claimed not to be interested in him romantically: "Who would want to kiss that cruel mouth?" she said.

Emily was slightly more receptive and judged Eugene less harshly. "He had a beautiful smile — when he smiled," she said. "But he could get a mean look on his face at times." It was Emily's job to help her mother with the running of the household and, because she was always at home, she was consistently exposed to Eugene's proselytizing. As in Jessica's case, the lessons began with *The Decameron*. "My father knew the book," Emily recalled, "and when he heard we were reading it he was furious; we had to hide it to finish it."

Not tall like her mother and sisters, Emily had hazel eyes, brown hair, a rosebud mouth and a seductively rounded figure. She was watched over with particular care by her father — though her mother was not concerned for her virtue.

Helen Maude felt she had done her maternal duty by warning Emily never to let a man kiss her until she was engaged. "I couldn't miss all those kisses," Emily protested, and her mother, smiling indulgently, responded that she was a bad girl. Helen Maude, perhaps foolishly, trusted Eugene.

"Gene was not a rapist," Emily declared. "You were safe with him as long as you wanted to be safe." After allowing Eugene to give her an experimental kiss, she concluded she wanted to be safe. Not that this put an end to her flirtation with him, which was regarded with suspicion not only by her father but her married brother, James Jr.

One day when Emily's parents went uptown, her brother, who had been visiting and was himself about to leave, changed his mind. "He was afraid to let me stay alone in the house with Gene," Emily said. "Later, when we walked uptown together, I told Gene why my brother had stayed home. From then on, he called my brother 'Mr. Platitude.'"

Eugene treated Emily — as he had Jessica — to dissertations on the women with whom he had romped. And he repeated his fantasy about married life aboard a barge, adding that when he grew tired of his wife he would leave her to drift and shift for herself. This image of a woman on a barge evidently stayed with him. Six years later he conjured it up as the setting for Anna Christie's love affair.

In his prattlings to Emily, Eugene seemed frozen in a pubescent sexuality. "He seemed very lustful," Emily said. "He'd go into details about the nights he'd spent with women, and how long he'd stayed with each of them."

The contrast between the Rippins' home and that of his own across the road doubtless threw him off balance. Helen Maude's good-natured, all-inclusive mothering was a revelation to him, and he could not have failed to compare her rational domesticity with his own mother's remoteness.

He did attempt to speak to Emily about his mother but managed no more than a halting effort. "My room was near Gene's, and he'd sometimes walk in and talk to me in the morning," she said. "I think he suspected I knew something was wrong with his mother." Once he told her that his mother had recently been in a sanatorium. "My mother was ill, but she's better now," he said.

Aware of the lack of warmth in Eugene's family, Helen Maude drew him into the bosom of her own. To express his fondness for her he often hovered nearby while she attended to domestic chores and listened to her homely advice, basking in her maternal strength.

Helen Maude was white-haired, hazel-eyed with a figure ample but not stout, and an erect carriage. Her most distinguishing feature was a smooth, unwrinkled complexion, unchanged until the day she died. Once, when Eugene had been complaining to Emily that most girls grew to look like their mothers, Emily said, "I guess I'll look like mine." Eugene regarded her with new interest. "That's all right," he replied.

Writing to Jessica some years later, he recalled how much the Rippins meant to him: "Your family gave me the most real touch of a home life I had had up to then — quite a happy, new experience for an actor's son! I've never forgotten to be grateful to all of you for it — above all your mother." Shortly before Helen Maude's death in 1941, he wrote Jessica that living in her home had helped him become the playwright he was.

That Christmas, Eugene experienced his first traditional family holiday. He sat by the side of Helen Maude while she sewed winter bathrobes as gifts for her daughters, and she was touched by his appreciation at receiving presents from all the Rippins on Christmas Day.

Later that evening he bought four boxes of candy for the Rippin women, confiding to Jessica it was the first time he had ever purchased a gift "for a girl." He had, however, presented Emily with a "Ballad to Emmy" three days before Christmas, which pleased and flattered her. In it he referred to her "form divine" and her "sparkling eyes."

"If he could get by on a poem," jibed the less susceptible Jessica, "that pleased him no end." Although Emily and Eugene continued their lighthearted flirtation, both were pursuing other romantic interests; Emily in fact was seeing the man she eventually married.

At this point, according to Emily, Maibelle Scott was Eugene's "strongest interest most of the time," but not his only one. "He always had a photograph of a girl in his room," Emily recalled, "but it was not always the same girl. And he'd moon about whichever was the current one, while playing some popular record like 'Song of Araby' or 'Tango' on the victrola."

On the coldest days of winter, Eugene tried to build up his health by taking dips from the Rippins' beach.

"At the risk of gaining a reputation for eccentricity before my literary fame warrants such an indulgence," he wrote to Dr. Lyman, "I have gone in swimming in this Long Island Sound at least once a week ever since I left Gaylord last June. I haven't missed a single week. The coldest the water has ever been when I took my plunge was thirty-three degrees. I haven't had a cold (hear me rap wood) nor has the Demon Tonsillitis, formerly a familiar spirit of mine, paid me a single visit. I thought this might interest you as a 'lunger's' experience."

He enclosed a snapshot taken by Emily that displayed a well-muscled, scowling young man dressed in a bathing suit, standing on a strip of beach with the water and the Groton shoreline visible behind him. On the photograph Eugene wrote, "Taken (cross my heart) — Jan. 1, 1914, New London, Conn. Water — 39°."

At his feet Eugene drew an arrow pointing to a patch of snow and beneath this he scribbled a quotation from Kipling: "The uniform 'e wore/Was nothin' much before/And rather less than 'arf o' that be'ind."

Emily remembered one cold day when her doctor was paying a house call. She was in bed with tonsillitis, and Eugene happened to walk past her door, wearing his bathing suit. "The doctor wanted to

know who that was and where he was going in that outfit," Emily
said. "I told him Gene was going swimming. The doctor went outside
and watched Gene run up and down the beach, which had clumps of
ice on it, and then plunge into the icy water. The doctor came back
and told me, 'That boy is crazy.'"

Although Eugene was supposed to have his meals with the family, Helen Maude thought he would be more comfortable eating
alone, and served him trays in his room. He ate ravenously with an
appetite well trained at Gaylord.

Helen Maude, like her daughters, noticed Eugene had a decided
tremor. "His coffee cup used to shake in his hands when he first came
to stay with us," Jessica recalled. "But after about four months the
trembling got better."

Eugene did not mention the tremor to Dr. Lyman, but did tell
him, "When I yawn or draw a deep breath unexpectedly, my pleura
utters a feeble, catching protest." He said he had no other symptoms.

Toward early spring, Eugene began to focus on what was to be his
first full-length play. He had been thinking about the characters and
plot for several months. It was to be the portrait of a young artist in
conflict with his family and his stuffy, small-town environment,
based on Eugene's own current struggles to become a playwright.

He decided to tell the story in a straightforward narrative style,
but instead of the conventional Broadway three-act form, he chose to
write it in four acts, foreshadowing his later experiments with double
and triple-length plays. It was his greatest challenge thus far and he
conscientiously scribbled notes for construction and dialogue for several weeks before writing a first draft, which he then painstakingly
continued to revise. He called the play *Bread and Butter*.

Despite its whiffs of Strindbergian rancor, it fell far short of his
ambition to write a Strindbergian play. It does contain many of the
autobiographical elements O'Neill explored throughout his career
and is, in fact, the earliest in a series of awkward precursors to *Long
Day's Journey Into Night*. It presents an idealistic and misunderstood
younger son, here called John Brown, who wants to be a painter, but
whose materialistic father denigrates his ambition and urges him
instead to become a lawyer.

John, who (like Eugene) went to Princeton, has black, "abnormal-
ly large dreamer's eyes" and "a finer, more sensitive" nature than the
rest of his family. His father, self-educated and self-made (like James

O'Neill), wears a symbolic "self-satisfied smile forever on his thin lips." There are scenes of sibling rivalry — the hero's two brothers representing different aspects of Jamie O'Neill's personality.

The play's first and fourth acts are set in two nearby houses in a coastal Connecticut town that could be New London. In both the Brown family's sitting room of Act I and in John's and his wife's home in Act IV, "an electric reading lamp wired from the chandelier above" rests on a table in the center of the room (as in *Long Day's Journey Into Night*).

The play's second and third acts are set in a painter's studio in New York, shared by several art students and an aspiring writer, that resembles the space Eugene shared with George Bellows, Ed Keefe and a series of other young men, including the illustrator, Ted Ireland. (In the play, a character named Ted is one of the studio's occupants.)

Too weak-minded to persevere in his study of art (he takes a job on the docks at one point to support himself), John eventually throws up his promising career as a painter (as Ed Keefe had been persuaded to do by his father) and allows his hometown sweetheart to persuade him to marry her and go to work for her father. Predictably, the marriage soon sours.

There are indications in the play that Eugene's affair with Kathleen Jenkins still weighed on his mind, and that he was trying to imagine what might have been the consequence of living with her as husband and wife. The wife in the play is called Maud, a name associated by Eugene (perhaps unconsciously) with that of Maude Williams — the woman who testified at his divorce trial as his partner in adultery.

The wife also sounds a bit like Mary Tyrone: as a character in *Bread and Butter* points out, Maud's "home life with [her] father was always so ideal." Following the play's most Strindbergian speech ("We're two corpses chained together," spoken by John Brown to his sister), Brown shoots himself.

Eugene received a copyright for the play on May 2, 1914, but continued to tinker with it. Oddly enough, it was during the same time he was writing the essentially hollow *Bread and Butter* that he outlined the genuinely tragic one-act play he eventually called *Bound East for Cardiff*, for which he received the copyright on May 14, only twelve days after *Bread and Butter*.

In *Bound East*, through the eyes of the dying sailor, Yank, Eugene first expressed his deep sympathy for the men with whom he had shipped to sea. Yank dwells on the hard life of a sailor and on his regret at never having settled down on a farm — "Just a small one, just enough to live on" — and he worries briefly that God might "hold it up against" him for having stabbed a man during a dock fight. He asks his shipmate, Driscoll, to buy a box of candy for a barmaid in Cardiff who has been good to him: "She tried to lend me half a crown when I was broke there last trip."

Though revisions were made in dialogue and stage directions, the play remained essentially the same as under the original title, *Children of the Sea*. The most significant changes included the deletion of a page in which Driscoll talks of having murdered a ship's officer, and revisions in Yank's final speech when he courageously confronts his own death:

"I was just thinkin' it ain't as bad as people think — dyin'," Yank says to Driscoll. " . . . I ain't had religion; but I know whatever it is what comes after it can't be no worser'n this." In the earlier version, Driscoll speaks the line, "Our Father who art in Heaven," but in the final script he makes the sign of the cross and only moves his lips "in some half-remembered prayer."

Eugene had hit upon the naturalistic-lyrical voice in which he believed he could "evolve original rhythms of beauty where beauty apparently isn't." Having already formed his conception of "the transfiguring nobility of tragedy . . . in seemingly the most ignoble, debased lives," he had at last achieved his ambition to "bring home to members of a modern audience their ennobling identity with the tragic figures on the stage."

As an insecure novice, however, he utterly failed to recognize how *Bound East for Cardiff* towered above his other early plays. It took a while before he saw *Bound East* as his first truly original work.

"Very important, this play!" he stressed to a critic in 1934. "In it can be seen — or felt — the germ of the spirit, life-attitude, etc. of all my significant future work . . . Remember in these U.S. in 1914 *Bound East for Cardiff* was a daring innovation both in form & content."

The "spirit" and "life-attitude" revealed by the play were innately tragic, the only aspect of life that O'Neill — even in his early maladroit efforts — was determined to express.

He believed tragedy had the meaning the Greeks gave it, "an urge toward life and ever more life"; to them, the spectacle of a performed tragedy released them from the petty greeds of everyday existence.

"When they saw a tragedy on the stage," he explained to an interviewer in 1922, "they felt their own hopeless hopes ennobled in art

... because any victory we *may* win, is never the one we dreamed of winning. The point is that life in itself is nothing. It is the *dream* that keeps us fighting, willing — living!"

A year earlier, in his "Credo" published in The New York Tribune, he expressed his contempt for those who failed to comprehend this doctrine:

" ... The people who succeed and do not push on to a greater failure are the spiritual middle classers. Their stopping at success is the proof of their compromising insignificance. How petty their dreams must have been! The man who pursues the mere attainable should be sentenced to get it — and keep it. Let him rest on his laurels and enthrone him in a Morris chair, in which laurels and hero may wither away together. Only through the unattainable does man achieve a hope worth living and dying for — and so attain himself. He with the spiritual guerdon of a hope in hopelessness is nearest to the stars and the rainbow's foot ... "

*B*ound East for Cardiff was the last play Eugene wrote at the Packard. Although he continued to take some of his meals there, he moved back into his own home soon after the play's completion. From then on, his relationship with the Rippins, though warm, was sporadic. Over a period of more than twenty years, he periodically sent them accounts of his professional and personal life.

When Dolly Rippin wrote to him after the opening of *Ah, Wilderness!* on Broadway to express concern that her mother was a character in the play, he hastened to deny it. Dolly was, of course, correct. O'Neill had given Essie Miller some of Helen Maude's maternal characteristics — as well as layering the Miller household with Rippin gaiety. But by then his standard disclaimer was in effect:

"Never believe reports ... about me or my work ... Always read the play or see it! The idea that your Mother is in *Ah, Wilderness!* is absurd — and, as you will see when you read the play, there is no 'rooming house' in it ... I make it a point never to put real people I have known into my plays. All my characters are my own fabrication ... Another thing: The time of *Ah, Wilderness!* is 1906, which was before I ever knew a Rippin!"

Chapter
THIRTY-FIVE

FOR A MAN OF SIXTY-NINE, JAMES O'NEILL HAD BEEN managing with surprising agility in his dual roles in *Joseph and His Brethren*, but he was beginning to feel the strain of his complex costume and makeup changes. At his entrance, he appeared in the loose robes of the 106-year-old Jacob, with makeup that emphasized pallor and wrinkles. In his second appearance, as Pharaoh, he was required to change into a tight-fitting costume and look swarthy. For the last act he had to change back to Jacob's flowing robes and wrinkles.

Once, just before the curtain rose, he entertained the backstage crew with a little jig and the stage manager noticed he was wearing street trousers beneath Jacob's robes. The stage manager scolded him for being slipshod and James apologized. Leslie Austin, waiting in the wings, was astonished at James's lack of temperament in accepting the reprimand.

"Most stars of Mr. O'Neill's stature would have exploded at such effrontery," Austen marveled. "But James O'Neill was a memorable exception. There was a man who breathed truth and sincerity."

One day, as the company was leaving Kansas City by train, Brandon Tynan handed Austin a telegram from his brother. "Mother died this morning," it read. "Don't leave the company."

"I sat in the coach, trying to make up my mind what to do," Austin recalled, "when Mrs. O'Neill, who had been told the news, slipped into the seat next to mine."

Although Ella's dependence on morphine had brought her to the verge of a breakdown at this time, she managed to pull herself together long enough to murmur some words of consolation.

"She was wearing something dark and her face was pale; she reminded me of my own mother. I don't remember what she said, but she sat with me for half an hour and then she kissed me on the cheek and left. I felt better, and must have told her I'd stay with the company, because Mr. O'Neill took her place next to me and told me I was doing the right thing in not leaving."

James told Austin that when, years earlier in San Francisco, he had received word of his own mother's death, he had continued playing "for the sake of the company and the theatre." (He did not mention he had also performed on the day of his infant son's death.)

Aware Ella's health was in jeopardy and that she could not go untreated, James at last resigned himself to giving up the remainder of the season and accompanied Ella to New York. An item in the New London Telegraph on March 26 stated that James "left *Joseph and His Brethren* at Indianapolis last week because of the illness of Mrs. O'Neill."

Holding little hope that yet another sanatorium was the solution, James suggested Ella turn for help to her devout Sheridan cousins.

According to Eugene's contemporary, Phil Sheridan, who was able to supply only sketchy details, Ella, evidently at the end of her rope, agreed. The Sheridans persuaded her to seek a cure through re-embracing her lost religious faith. One factor in her decision may have been that morphine was becoming more difficult to obtain. Concerned with the growing problem of addiction, Congress that year passed the Harrison Act, bringing the dispensing of all narcotics under strict Government supervision.

In *Long Day's Journey Into Night*, O'Neill foreshadowed this momentous event in his mother's life with a speech by Mary Tyrone. Some day, she declares, she will find her faith again, "— some day when the Blessed Virgin Mary forgives me and gives me back the faith in Her love and pity I used to have in my convent days, and I can pray to Her again — when She sees no one in the world can believe in me even for a moment any more, then She will believe in me, and with Her help it will be so easy. I will hear myself scream with agony, and at the same time I will laugh because I will be so sure of myself."

That "some day" had finally come. While waiting for the Sheridans to make arrangements for Ella, she and James stayed at the Prince George Hotel where, the year before, they had rented an eighth-floor suite consisting of a bedroom, parlor and bath. A comfortable apartment hotel on Twenty-eighth Street between Fifth and Madison Avenues, the Prince George was to serve as the O'Neills' New York residence until James's death.

Phil Sheridan recalled that Ella was put in touch with the

Carmelite nuns in Brooklyn, but could not remember further details. The only Carmelites in that borough in 1914 were a cloistered order housed in a block-square monastery surrounded by a high stone wall on St. John's Place in Crown Heights.

The nuns lived in minimal contact with the outside world but, according to Sister Constance Fitzgerald, historian of the Baltimore Carmelite Monastery, which spawned the Brooklyn branch in 1907, the Carmelites assigned two or three "Out-Sisters" to live in "out-quarters" on the monastery grounds. These nuns were in touch with the community and available to counsel parishioners.

It was entirely possible, said Sister Constance Fitzgerald, that the Out-Sisters could have responded to the request of a troubled woman such as Ella O'Neill, and arranged for her to be housed nearby, to pray with her and assist her on an ongoing basis to recover her spiritual equilibrium and help effect her cure.

At the beginning of May, apparently with Ella still struggling to regain her faith, James reestablished residence in the Monte Cristo Cottage and summoned Eugene home from the Rippins'.

"I had no idea I would have to leave 416 in such haste," Eugene explained in a letter to Jessica Rippin, who had taken a new job in Philadelphia as a dietician, "but Father was lonely, and had to solace himself with the comforting presence of his younger mistake." By then, however, James had left again to look after Ella in New York, and Eugene, alone and depressed, unburdened himself to Jessica (although making no reference to his mother's most recent bout of illness).

"The trees I can see from the window," he wrote, "remind me for some ridiculous reason of homely, skinny-legged girls in drenched bathing suits which cling to their unsightly members; the river is of a doleful grayness with wind spots here and there like patches of soot on a factory window-pane; Scott's dock looks exactly like the unsightly abortion which it is, and the tug boats putter around dejectedly; my row boat is slowly filling with water which I, with many a twinge in the back, will have to bail out tomorrow, God help me, poor wretch! . . . "

In sole possession of the cottage and too lazy to light the furnace, he was, he said, freezing to death, and would commit suicide if he "could find a tree strong enough to hang myself on." What appeared to be troubling him most was the momentary lack of a love object. His and Jessica's relationship had evidently deepened several weeks earlier, shortly before her departure for Philadelphia.

"Do you wonder I am sad?" he lamented. "I see lovers sporting all about . . . but, alas I am as sterile as Salmacis, as barren of delights as a frog is devoid of feathers . . . I seethe with longings; desire has me by the throat, and I — go for long rows or mow the lawn."

Not for the first time he tried, with Nietzschean arguments, to persuade Jessica to be his lover:

"Lord, hear my prayer! *I would sin!* What is sin? Tell me, sweet Jessica . . . Sin and its punishment, virtue and its reward; piffle upon piffle until everything in the world is turned upside down and all that is delightful is dubbed 'Bad' and all that is disagreeable and ugly 'Good.' The immortal Gods deliver me from Good and Evil!"

He declared that he longed "most ardently" for her return to New London in July, reminding her of their recent time together, characterizing it as "merely a provocation, a hint of wonders to come, of hours which we will both be able to treasure up and ponder over when we look back in after years and wish to justify our existence to ourselves."

Again, he stressed his "amorous loneliness" and his longing for "someone who will combine in the same proportion in which I have them spirit and body . . . who will be a joyous animal frank in her approval of her flesh and proud, not ashamed of it . . . who will practice not deadening restraint but exultant freedom."

"Teach me such a woman is possible," he pleaded. "Or don't you care to? . . . I would penetrate to the inner shrine and I hope that, as Lorenzo says in the *Merchant of Venice*: 'Fair Jessica shall be my torch bearer.'"

Neither his change of venue, his temporarily unfulfilled sexual longings, nor the crisis in his mother's health appeared to interrupt the creativity that had gripped Eugene since September, 1913.

Upon returning home, where he awaited the copyright for the recently completed *Children of the Sea*, he at once set to work — as he informed Jessica — "pruning the first act" of *Bread and Butter* (though he had received the copyright for it five days earlier). And to Dr. Lyman at Gaylord he wrote, with considerable hubris, "I am hard at work finishing a four-act play which, by God's grace, may see the footlights next season." But *Bread and Butter* was not produced and O'Neill ultimately disavowed it.

Eugene's next effort was *Abortion*, the one-act play about the former college baseball star, Jack Townsend, who has gotten a girl "into trouble." Evidently written at feverish speed, it is of interest partly because — even more than *Bread and Butter* — it reveals the powerfully lingering effects of his marriage to Kathleen Jenkins. That play, too, went unproduced.

While it rankled that none of his efforts had earned any money, he could take pride in having completed eight plays in eight months. Lasting literary value aside, this was no inconsiderable achievement for a man who had spent most of the preceding six years as a wastrel.

Eugene interrupted his busy work schedule toward the end of May. Both the New London Day and the Telegraph ran items on May 25 noting that James and his sons had left New London to visit Ella in Brooklyn where, the stories said, she was "ill." Three days later, the Telegraph announced that James and Eugene were back and that Ella was "greatly improved and will come here next week to spend the summer."

It is probable that all four O'Neills did indeed spend the remainder of the summer in New London. Ella resumed attending church regularly and — while it must have taken several months before her husband and sons could accept her transfiguration as permanent — it eventually became apparent to her family that, at fifty-seven, she had undergone a successful cure at last.

After his readjustment to family life, Eugene began a one-act farce he called *The Movie Man*, apparently pricked once again by the desire to write a play for money rather than for his own artistic satisfaction. He chose as his subject an episode from Francisco (Pancho) Villa's rebel uprising against the Mexican government. It was the great news event of the day and the most widely-read coverage was John Reed's for the Metropolitan Magazine.

When Eugene had visited his mother in New York in May, he doubtless looked up Louis Holladay, his early guide to Greenwich Village bohemia with whom he had stayed in close touch since his Princeton days. Holladay knew everyone worth knowing among the writers and artists through his sister, Polly. The cellar café in Washington Square that bore her name had become a bohemian crossroads, where she offered her patrons protective warmth. Theodore Dreiser was among the first to respond to Polly's welcoming personality and was soon trailed to the café by his friends.

Recently back from his assignment in Mexico, John Reed was another of Polly's coddled patrons. Although he and Eugene did not become close friends until nearly two years later, it is reasonable to assume they found themselves in each other's company at Polly's.

The flamboyant reporter loved to hold forth there about Pancho Villa's exploits, and it is more than likely that Reed's behind-the-scenes tales of the revolution partly inspired *The Movie Man*.

Eugene's fancy was seized by a particular episode that soon became widely circulated. In a deal bizarre even by Hollywood standards, the fierce and self-aggrandizing Villa, eager to see his exploits immortalized on film — for a price — had signed a contract on January 3, 1914, with Frank M. Thayer of the Mutual Film Corporation.

As described in an account of the early film industry, "It was agreed that Villa was to fight his battles as much by photographic daylight as possible." The rebel leader was to earn a percentage of the profits and received an advance of $25,000. At one point he staged a battle for the cameras on a hillside and, as shells exploded, dead and wounded flew into the air. The bodies, it was rumored, belonged to prisoners who had been planted as props on the hillside. Entitled *The Life of Villa*, the movie was completed in Los Angeles under the supervision of D. W. Griffith, but an ownership dispute arose and, so the account went, "the picture vanished."

The Movie Man is a one-act farce set in a suburb of northern Mexico; it describes the efforts of a couple of American entrepreneurs to persuade a Mexican general called Pancho Gomez to live up to the terms of a motion-picture contract, stipulating that Gomez fight his battles at the moviemakers' convenience.

The playlet mocks both the putative ideals of the Mexican Revolution and the brashness of American moviemakers, but in tone and plot it is every bit as slight as Eugene's early vaudeville skit. Despite his disclaimer in later years that he never again, after *A Wife For a Life*, wrote anything with an eye on the box office, *The Movie Man* reads as though he intended it for quick commercial success.

O'Neill later tried to explain, in a letter to the critic, George Jean Nathan, what it was that occasionally drove him, early in his career, to wander from his goal of writing plays "purely for their own sakes." Somewhat abashedly, he described this kind of lapse as a "form of recreation" falling between "the two serious extremes of art and money," and he characterized the works turned out during these lapses as "intermediate dramas" written "when one cannot remain inactive."

In any case, his hope of making money from *The Movie Man*, for which he received the copyright on July 1, soon evaporated. He was unable to market the play and, like all of his earlier efforts except

Children of the Sea / Bound East for Cardiff, he eventually disowned it. But he held on to the plot until 1916, when he rewrote it as a short story that was never published — the only short story other than "Tomorrow" and "S.O.S" that he is known to have completed. "S.O.S.," his final short story, which he adapted from his play, *Warnings,* was written in 1918 but not published in his lifetime.

"**M**y father doesn't think my plays are any good," Eugene told Clayton Hamilton in New London early that July. "He won't think of staking me." Reminding Hamilton of his promise to read his scripts, he gave him *The Web, Thirst, Recklessness, Warnings* and *Fog.* Hamilton assured Eugene they showed "appreciable promise."

The problem, Hamilton later recalled, was to get around the senior O'Neill: "Eugene did not want to be put to work; he wanted to write plays; and he did not relish the idea of another winter in New London." He asked Hamilton if he "could not get the old gentleman" to allow him to enroll in Professor George Pierce Baker's celebrated playwriting course at Harvard.

"Eugene allowed me to infer," Hamilton said, "with all due respect to Professor Baker, that his main idea was to get out of New London and that Harvard might be a good excuse; but his father was rather difficult to get around, because Mr. O'Neill had the ready argument that he had sent Eugene to college once before and that the boy had run away."

It was true that James did not have much confidence in his son's future as a playwright. Although he later came to regret and even vigorously deny his lack of faith, it was plainly his view at this time that his son was a parasitical dilettante. He did not intend to allow Eugene to become his permanent ward, as had Jamie. He began again prodding Eugene to take a job and every so often threatened to stop his allowance.

"If you want to write, why don't you write for a newspaper?" James asked, with what he deemed utter reasonableness. Eugene grumbled to his friends about his father's ultimatum. How could he be a playwright if he had to devote himself to a job?

Hamilton had a plan to persuade James. He suggested that Eugene apply to Baker directly, and if Baker was receptive, Hamilton would have the ammunition that might change James's mind.

George Pierce Baker had begun to teach English 47 at Harvard in 1905, at a moment when the American theater seemed to be shaking off its ingrained glibness and superficiality — albeit with painful slowness.

A very few insightful playwrights were attempting to say something of substance in dramatic form. In 1906, Langdon Mitchell's comedy, *The New York Idea*, was acclaimed for its original view of divorce and Percy MacKaye's *Jeanne d'Arc* reached for a poetic vision. In the same season the poet, William Vaughan Moody, presented *The Great Divide*, about a New England woman in conflict with the Westerner she marries. It was hailed for its subtlety and naturalness — qualities glaringly absent from most commercial productions. The Times critic, John Corbin, described it as the best American drama up to that time and Walter Prichard Eaton of the Sun called it the first drama "to find the American soul."

In Eugene's view, Moody had not gone far enough. "*The Great Divide* is a fine play for two acts and then it falls to pieces because it has to end happily," he later told an interviewer. "It was that way with practically all of them."

While two of the era's most popular playwrights, Clyde Fitch and Augustus Thomas, were still drawing audiences — the one with his facile and unrealistic comedies and the other with his luridly unrealistic melodramas — they both, in fact, were on their way out. Baker, somehow mystically attuned to the signs of an awakening, entreated his hopeful playwriting students:

"Write what you know to be true about your characters, and write nothing that you do not know to be true." He abjured them to "Get your material from what you see about you."

The course and its teacher became famous when one of Baker's early pupils, Edward Sheldon, wrote *Salvation Nell* while still in the class. He saw it produced on Broadway with great success in 1908, a year after he graduated magna cum laude.

Eugene had seen the play and found it better than *The Great Divide* (even though it, too, had a happy ending). In fact, he liked it enough to write about it to Sheldon some years later: "Your *Salvation Nell*, along with the Irish Players on their first trip over here, was what first opened my eyes to the existence of a real theater as opposed to the usual — and to me then, hateful — theater of my father, in whose atmosphere I had been brought up."

Often cited as a turning point, *Salvation Nell*, despite the essential triteness of its melodrama, was the closest thing to realistic native drama produced up until that time on the American commercial stage, and Sheldon was quick to credit Baker's role in its success.

During a walk through a Boston slum, Sheldon had chanced to observe a Salvation Army meeting and was beguiled by the young, attractive woman in uniform vivaciously preaching to a sorry-looking but attentive group on the street. Deciding he had found a fit subject for a play, he began to invent the details of a sordid past for the woman that would account for her presence on the street.

Obeying Baker's instructions to "write nothing that you do not know to be true," Sheldon haunted the slums of Boston, as well as of his native Chicago, observing at first hand other dedicated young Salvation Army women as they strove to save the souls of drunks and drifters.

The play was brought to the attention of Minnie Maddern Fiske, who had established a reputation for playing realistic drama — mainly Strindberg. She appeared in it first at the Providence Opera House and soon after on Broadway.

Most of the critics were awed. Vanity Fair, for example, declared *Salvation Nell*'s bare-knuckled realism was "from the heart of the times." Describing the heroine's situation — "She is good at heart . . . faithful in her relations with the Bowery brute with whom she lives in the unwedded state" — the critic asked, "Is her character and condition unfitted for the stage? We think not. Are the incidents seen in the barroom and in the areaways of the slums too gross for audiences? We think not.

"The intent is not to entertain us with the disagreeable or to make us acquainted with vice for our amusement. It is all incidental to the pity and sympathy which it should evoke . . . Here is a side of humanity . . . revealed to us and brought to the intelligent sympathy for the first time."

Not surprisingly, there was a strong dissenting minority determined to quell the new voices. It was led by William Winter of the New York Tribune, that sourest of critics, who had consistently disparaged the realism of Ibsen and Shaw. He seemed to regard *Salvation Nell* as a personal affront and dismissed it as "a piece of rubbish," warning potential audiences that they would find "their minds dragged through the gutter and drenched in the slime of the brothel."

The play's settings and dialogue did venture beyond what other American playwrights had attempted. Sheldon's daring departure from escapist Broadway fare was assuredly a leap forward. Nonetheless, the play's conventionally happy ending placed it in the category of melodrama, not tragedy — and Eugene strongly disagreed with the Vanity Fair critic who held it was "as true to life as is possible on the stage."

In Eugene's view, there was no reason why a modern play could not be every bit as "true to life" as a novel — as, indeed, were the plays of Ibsen, Strindberg and Shaw. Sheldon's play, much as Eugene saluted its innovative settings and dialogue, did not approach either the literary quality or the psychological honesty that he believed could be brought to the American stage — as he himself hoped ultimately to demonstrate.

While Eugene doubtless believed he would one day surpass Sheldon, he could not help but envy the ease of his early achievement. By 1913, the year before Eugene applied to Baker's course, and while he was just entering upon his own far more tortuous struggle to become a dramatist, Sheldon was already rich and famous, not to say something of a legend.

Within five years Sheldon had followed his *Salvation Nell* with six more plays, among them *The Nigger*, about a southerner who feels obliged to renounce his white fiancée, when he discovers he has Negro blood; and *The Boss*, which began as an exposé of a self-made man who has climbed his way — not always ethically — to the top as a newspaper owner — a play that disappointingly evolved into a romantic melodrama.

A cting on Clayton Hamilton's advice, Eugene wrote a letter to Professor Baker that was at once cocky and defensive:

"Let me explain my exact position . . . My university training consists of one year (Freshman) at Princeton University, Class of 1910 . . . All my life I have been closely connected with the dramatic profession. My father is James O'Neill, the actor, of whom you may perhaps have heard."

He went on to inform Baker that, while he had read "all the modern plays I could lay my hands on, and many books on the subject of the Drama," he realized such a system of study was inadequate. "With my present training I might hope to become a mediocre journeyman playwright," he declared "It is just because I do not wish to be one, because I want to be an artist or nothing, that I am writing to you." Eugene concluded by expressing the hope that Professor Baker would "look favorably upon this very earnest desire of mine to become your student."

Awaiting Baker's response, Eugene continued to make notes for new work and amused himself by pursuing the chimera of requited love. His romance with Maibelle Scott was drawing to an end and his attack on Jessica Rippin's virtue appeared doomed. Determined to miss no opportunity, however, he went so far as to slip a note addressed "To the Beautiful Unknown" under the door of a neighbor of Maibelle's sister, who was being visited by a young niece. Nor did Eugene cease to flirt casually with his former nurse, Olive Evans, or with Maibelle's friend, Mildred Culver. By then his eye had been caught by a spirited, dark-haired woman named Beatrice Frances Ashe, who was soon to become the sole focus of his ardor.

Many young women in that innocent era treasured autograph books, in which they invited friends to set down facetious or senti-mental remarks. Despite his status as a dramatist-in-the-making and his pose as a cynical man of the world, the nearly-twenty-six-year-old Eugene wrote in Mildred's book what might have seemed childish even in an eighteen-year-old: "I Hereby Confess that I love parsnips, that I once wrote a love letter to Lena Cavalleri [sic] in English, which I afterwards found out she cannot read, that I have read *Mademoiselle de Maupin* (sh!) and liked it, that I do not think State Street and Broadway have much in common, that politics are my idea of the acme of futility, that I voted for Eugene Debs because I dislike John D. Rockefeller's bald head."

He further declared that his "Idea of Utter Bliss" was "Being the tenor in a Broadway musical comedy and singing a kiss song — with appropriate pantomime"; that for him "The Acme of Discomfort" was "Trying to write a poem in this book with three people bending over my shoulder saying 'how clever'"; and that his conception of "The Supremely Ridiculous" was "Getting into a crowded car with the One Girl and her mother (?) and finding coin of the realm is in one's other suit — and Mother pays the fare."

Eugene seems to have been aware of his own arrested emotional development. In the mid-1930's, making notes for a play he never fin-ished, he described an apparently autobiographical character, Ernie Wade, as "a likeable boy who has never grown up as a complete per-sonality, a large part of him still held by adolescent romantic dreams."

By contrast with Eugene's somewhat juvenile contribution, Maibelle's entry in Mildred's book sounded almost urbane. She "con-fessed" to "having murdered my second husband just before marry-ing the first" and declared the custom of breakfast in bed to be the height of her ambition.

Late in the spring of 1914, Maibelle met a Coast Guard Academy cadet, Chester Arthur Beckley, at a dance in New London. Tall, hand-some and, according to his daughter's later account, the most sought-after cadet at the academy, he was snapped up by Maibelle from under the noses of her rivals.

She told Eugene she had fallen in love and was going to marry Beckley. They arranged to meet at Ocean Beach, so that he could return all her letters. She later burned them, together with all of his, saving only the poems he had sent her. She kept an inscribed copy of *Thirst* (which he later gave her) as well as an inscribed copy of *Thus Spake Zarathustra*. As Maibelle recalled, Eugene did not seem devas-tated by the parting.

Maibelle settled happily into the serene, conventional small-town life for which she had been conditioned. Her husband, after serving in World War I, resigned from the Coast Guard to become vice presi-dent of his father-in-law's marine salvage company in New London.

Never regretful of her choice, Maibelle lived to be ninety-five. She had two daughters, seven grandchildren, seven great-grandchildren and two great-great-grandchildren.

CHAPTER
THIRTY-SIX

Eugene's infatuation with Beatrice Ashe was like nothing he had experienced before. His sentimental romance with Maibelle Scott and his dalliances with the Rippin sisters, to say nothing of his short-lived affair with Kathleen Jenkins, however carnally motivated, paled beside the anguished intensity of his new love.

In Beatrice, not yet twenty, Eugene found what he had long been seeking: a woman who could love him with passion and was willing also to lavish on him the maternal understanding he craved. Unlike Kathleen and Maibelle, Beatrice inspired in him a worship that verged on the obsessional.

Beatrice was the only child of Peter Ashe, the superintendent of New London's trolley-car system. She lived with her father and mother, Mary Balfour Ashe, on West Street in the town proper. Though she moved in the same circles as Maibelle, Beatrice had a far more fanciful view of herself than did the more conventional young women of her class.

Beatrice had graduated from the Williams Memorial Institute in New London the year before and intended to enter Connecticut College in the fall of 1915. She had a pleasing, if untrained, soprano voice frequently heard in church, and was planning a career as a singer. "I used to drive my neighbors mad, practicing scales early in the morning," she once recalled.

Perhaps seeking to emphasize the contrast between the smooth whiteness of her skin and her shining dark hair, she affected a flamboyant style of dress. Jessica Rippin, for instance, recalled seeing her in a Scotch-plaid skirt and jaunty feathered cap. Maibelle remembered her in a skirt and blouse of bright purple, topped by a gold turban and big loop earrings. Her eyes, as Eugene remembered them, were "grey, green, flecked with golden lights."

According to Beatrice's account, Eugene asked a mutual friend to introduce them not long after his discharge from the sanatorium. During the late 1950's, she was guarded in interviews for this biography about the depth of her romantic commitment. She confided, however, that she had kept "sixty passionate" love letters and thirty poems that Eugene wrote to her between late July, 1914, and late July, 1916. She was planning, she said, to write her own book about her relationship with O'Neill.

She never did. Some time before her death in 1974, she sold the letters and poetry to the New York Public Library. They document, often with excruciatingly intimate detail, both the ardor and the frustrations of her liaison with Eugene.

Judging by the poetry he began writing to Beatrice in the summer of 1914, their mutual attraction must have been intensely physical. A close reading of all the surviving poetry and letters, however, suggests Beatrice, while feverishly demonstrative, set a barrier beyond which she would not yield, and that their passion was never technically consummated.

Some of their earliest fondling took place in a hammock on the grounds of Beatrice's house, a hammock Eugene described as "that confidant of all our joys and sorrows, our kisses and quarrels, that most hallowed of all spots . . . I love every inch of that dear old floating divan."

That summer they also trysted frequently on the secluded white sand beach that was part of the ninety-five-acre estate owned by the railroad tycoon, Edward Crowninshield Hammond. (The estate held the ice pond adjoining "Dirty" Dolan's pig farm — the pond that comically figures in both *Long Day's Journey Into Night* and *A Moon for the Misbegotten*.)

To get there, Eugene and Beatrice, who made no secret of their mutual enchantment, bicycled or sometimes rowed to Ocean Beach and were often seen by acquaintances as they waded through the shallow water of Alewife Cove to the Hammond beach. "How the few spectators used to stare when I carried you in my arms across the Cove!" Eugene later reminisced.

Alexander Campbell, a member of Doc Ganey's Second Story Club, recalled that he and his friends "were all jealous," when they observed the two walking down the beach. "She was a peach," he said.

Few others ventured onto the Hammond Beach for it was prominently posted with "No Trespassing" signs and was overlooked by

Walnut Grove Farm and its Victorian mansion that Hammond had
aptly christened "Ironsides." Beyond Ironsides, but not visible from
Hammond Beach, was Eolia, the Edward S. Harkness estate. For
Beatrice's amusement, Eugene would hurl epithets at both millionaires.

"There is a house on a distant hill, a cold, lonely/ugly millionaire's house," Eugene wrote petulantly in one stanza of an interminable prose-poem to Beatrice. "The world would say this is his
beach; he has a stamped/paper to prove it./We know better — and
we have our hearts to prove it./This is Our Beach!"

Eugene went on to extol their idyllic interludes in a torrent of
unrestrained lust that might have been expected to intimidate the vir-
ginal Beatrice; but she, although plainly lustful herself, was determined to preserve her technical virginity until married:

> Upon Our Beach we two lie, side by side — together!
> Before us the sea, sparkling, vibrant with motion,
> thrilling beneath the amorous sun's warm kisses . . .
> I turn to you, my Beloved. You are smiling at me. Your
> smile is tender and sweet. It sends a shiver of delight
> through me . . .
> We are in each other's arms. We are kissing each other.
> Lip to lip and limb to limb we lie.
> It is indiscreet. That dreary old fisherman might turn-
> around. But what do Love and Youth care for Mrs. Grundys
> and life-sick old fishermen?
> Your body clings to mine, — your beautiful body firm
> and supple as a tigress'. (There is sometimes a tigerish
> fierceness in you which I have noticed. I love you for it.)
> Our kisses redouble. They are fire. I see your face dimly
> through quivering half-closed lids. I murmur half-choked
> words or sobs of tenderness. The world is a great rose-col-
> ored flame of desire . . .
>
> There is a purple kiss upon your neck (necessitating
> much concealment). I am sorry; but it is your fault indeed.
> Why are you so sweet?
> Your limbs are beautiful, your breasts are beautiful —
> my lips yearn for them — your hips, your feet, your hands
> are all beautiful.
> I ache to possess you.
> Today, I love life . . .

In another shorter poem he described what appears to have been a night spent together indoors: " . . . Vague, white, upon a chair the clothes you wore — /And in the air your tangled hair's perfume/And in my arms the body I adore!"

This does sound as though the two were cohabiting; nonetheless, in his letters over the next months, Eugene often importuned Beatrice to surrender to him. Most of their quarrels, in fact, appear from Eugene's letters to have been triggered by his helpless hankering to consummate the relationship and her steadfast disinclination to comply — at least until they were married. Eugene usually assumed the blame for these quarrels.

"Whatever of our nights and days have been saddened or made imperfect it was always my swinishness to blame," he confessed at one point.

A few days later, after Beatrice evidently chided him for being lustful, he argued, "Of course I *want* you, too. What a poor gray shade I would be if I didn't! The touch of your soft skin, your kisses, your hair, all your loveliness has the power to send a shivering flame through my brain. My blood seethes and fumes, and at times I have forgotten — promises and all weary things, like the rabid immoralist that I am . . . I am proud of it! Soul without body is crippled as body without soul . . .

"Pardon this ethical philosophizing but you must understand the inherent innocence of my 'I want you's.' To mistake it for lust would be doing me an injustice. It is part of my love for you and is as strong and free from a sense of guilt as the love of my soul for yours . . . I want you with all my heart, I want you with all my body, I need you with all my soul!"

While still early in his siege of Beatrice, Eugene left her to take a week's cruise with friends on Long Island Sound. He kept her informed of his itinerary, reiterating his longing and love and declaring he would go on no more trips because he missed her "too horribly." He said he had dreamed of being married to her, deplored his lack of a "bank account" and, surprisingly, declared he was "bored with the sea."

Back in New London on July 29, Eugene complied with a request from Professor Baker, sending him two one-act plays from which he believed Baker would "be able to form a judgment" as to his "suitability" for admission to the course. The plays, evidently *Children of the Sea* and *Abortion*, convinced Baker of Eugene's suitability and he was notified he could enter English 47 in the fall. All that was needed now was James's willingness to pay the tuition.

When on August 17, *Thirst and Other One-Act Plays* was published, Eugene finally saw some tangible proof that his labors of the past year had not gone totally unrecognized. He proudly gave copies of the thin (168-page) gray-and-tan volume to friends and relatives. For sentiment's sake, he presented Maibelle with a copy, inscribed:

"To Scotty — In memory of all those sweet minutes and days and hours which have 'gone glimmering thro' the dream of things that were': 'Youth, take hand to the prayer of these!/Many there be by the dusty way,/Many that cry to the rocks and seas — /Give us, ah give us but Yesterday!'"

Indicating his strong conviction of future worth (which evidently outweighed any inclination to pen a more intimate signature), he signed himself formally "Eugene G. O'Neill." And four years later, in a dedication to his second wife, Agnes Boulton, he wrote:

"These First Five Stations of the Cross in my plod up Parnassus —
'I, also, have been afraid — —
but I know now that I had been gazing
at the sea too long, and listening to
the great silence.' . . . "

The euphoria of being a published author evaporated when, after a few months, Badger offered Eugene the unsold volumes (almost the entire edition) at thirty cents a copy.

"With the usual financial acumen of an author," O'Neill informed Mark Van Doren in 1944, "I scorned his offer as a waste of good money on my lousy drama!" He came to wish the *Thirst* plays had never been published, as he wrote to a would-be playwright seeking advice.

Eventually Badger found a buyer in Frances Steloff, who, in 1920, became the proprietor of a New York bibliophilic gold mine, the Gotham Book Mart. She bought Badger's stock for only $200.

She later admitted she never bothered to read the volume, but had heard of the promising young playwright whose work, by then, was being noticed. *Thirst* eventually became a collector's item, sold off by Steloff in the late 1950's at $150 a copy and netting her a profit of well over $100,000.

One person who received a complimentary copy of *Thirst* was Clayton Hamilton, who reviewed it in both the Bookman and the Nation.

"This writer's favorite mood is that of horror," he wrote in the Bookman in April, 1915. "He deals with grim and ghastly situations that would become intolerable if they were protracted beyond the limits of a single sudden act . . . He shows a keen sense of the reactions of characters under stress of violent emotion; and his dialogue is almost brutal in its power."

Unaware that the plays had been rejected by Holbrook Blinn, Hamilton added that "more than one of these plays should be available for such an institution as the Princess Theatre in New York."

O'Neill wrote to Hamilton in 1920, recalling how much the review had meant to him. "It held out a hope at a very hopeless time . . . It made me believe I was arriving with a bang; and at that period I very much needed someone whose authority I respected to admit I was getting somewhere."

In the same letter, O'Neill reminded Hamilton of an earlier favor:

"It was one day I met you down at the R.R. station in New London. I had just sent off the script of what was really my first long play."

The play was *Bread and Butter*, which he had sent to George Tyler. (In fact, as he later amended, he had sent Tyler two plays, not one.) He said he "innocently expected an immediate personal reading and a reply within a week — possibly an acceptance."

Hamilton, in Eugene's words, "slipped" him "the unvarnished truth and then sand papered it!" Hamilton told him: "When you send off a play remember there is not one chance in a thousand it will ever be read; not one chance in a million of its ever being accepted — (and if accepted it will probably never be produced); but if it is accepted and produced, say to yourself it's a miracle which can never happen again."

Eugene left the railroad station feeling "a bit sick." But the advice, as he later assured Hamilton, had been salutary. "I reflected that you knew whereof you spoke, that I was up against a hard game and might as well realize it and hew to the line without thought of commercial stage production. Your advice gradually bred in me a gloomy and soothing fatalism which kismeted many a rebuff and helped me to take my disappointments as all an inevitable part of the game."

O'Neill never could inure himself altogether to the artistic disappointments that variously beset him — what writer ever could? But

Hamilton's caution helped him to take philosophically the particularly humiliating rebuff from Tyler who, despite his professed loyalty to James, simply ignored the scripts from his son.

"Don't boast to me of the number of your rejection slips," O'Neill ruefully wrote years later to an aspiring novelist who had asked for his help. "Here's one rejection experience you will never tie: I sent my first two long plays to a famous Broadway producer. He was an old friend of my father's. That should have given me an 'in' one would think. Well, I waited and waited.

"Then I wrote letters. Never a reply. Then I wrote asking for my scripts back. Nothing happened. Finally a year and a half later, after a season in which he put on lousy plays and they all failed, he went into bankruptcy. Six months or so later I got my scripts back — from the Receiver. They were in the same wrapping in which I had sent them. It had never been opened!"

A few years after O'Neill got back his unread manuscripts, Tyler, once again in business, produced two O'Neill plays, *Chris Christofersen* and *The Straw*. It was then that Tyler confirmed what O'Neill already knew, that he had put the early scripts "away in a drawer and didn't even look at them."

Tyler told O'Neill that when he had received them, with the accompanying letter from James, he had said to himself, "Oh! So Jim O'Neill's son has been writing some plays. Well, they can't be any good, because plays by actors' sons are never good!"

In a later version of the story, Tyler evidently confused the two long plays Eugene sent him with some of the early one-acters James had asked him to read. In any case, he did remember accurately and with some embarrassment that he had failed to read anything at all written by Eugene.

"I didn't see any particular reason to suppose that Gene should be taken seriously," Tyler wrote. "I figured it was just run-of-mine paternal pride that made his father bring me those scripts of his. So I'd take them in and forget about them for a while — maybe read a little, but I wouldn't take oath I did that often, and I'm certain that I can't remember at all what they were like."

It was Tyler's recollection that he gave the scripts back to James "with the customary polite remarks about how Gene undoubtedly showed signs of talent, and deserved encouragement, but needed more development and had better wait a while."

James still had not consented, in mid-August, to pay for Eugene's tuition at Harvard, apparently having lost interest in his son's endeavor to become a playwright. It had perhaps slipped James's mind that nearly twenty years earlier, in an interview with the New York Mirror, he had emphatically stated that America needed a training school for persons who wished to learn the techniques of playwriting.

"Now and then," James had said, "a genius may write a play without any great degree of technical knowledge . . . The average writer for the stage, however, has to serve a dramatic apprenticeship of some sort before he is qualified to write a play of any practical value."

James seemed at this time to be more absorbed in investing in real estate and other commercial projects. He put some money into a device he believed would be "wonderful for the ladies" and for once he was right: it was the recently invented zipper.

Then, too, he was probably still unsure whether Ella's cure would be lasting. And he was once more caught up in his acting career. Toward the end of August, he went to New York to rehearse with Brandon Tynan, Pauline Frederick and Jamie, as well as some new cast members of *Joseph and His Brethren*, about to take to the road again.

The war in Europe, affecting international trade, was having a corollary effect on the health of the Broadway theater, and the new tour of *Joseph and His Brethren*, one of Liebler's big money-makers, was almost the firm's last hope of staying in business.

James's doubt about the wisdom of investing any further in his younger son's education was understandable. Finally, however, when Eugene's cousin, Lil Brennan, added her urging to Clayton Hamilton's, James gave in. But according to Hamilton, he still maintained "the boy would never amount to anything." On August 29, the New London Telegraph deemed it newsworthy to announce that Eugene had been admitted to Professor Baker's playwriting course.

Notwithstanding his obsessive pursuit of Beatrice, Eugene managed to embark on his second full-length play, *Servitude*, which proved to be as solemn as *The Movie Man* was jocose. It is perhaps the most schizophrenic of his early plays — influenced by Ibsen but compromised by a silly, happy ending.

Its attitude toward the materialism and rigid conventionality of upper-class society evokes *A Doll's House*, although the play's two female characters, Alice Roylston and Ethel Frazer, are based to some degree on Kathleen Jenkins and Beatrice Ashe. In one more instance of Eugene's continuing preoccupation with his guilt over Kathleen, it evolves that Alice was forced to marry because she was pregnant.

Her husband is David Roylston, who is yet another stand-in for Eugene, with an "ironical mouth . . . and keenly intelligent dark eyes." Despite his success as a "playwright and novelist" known for his idealism, he is in fact egotistical and treats his wife as a possession.

Ethel, endowed with some of Beatrice's characteristics (her beauty and her eagerness to absorb an artist's ideals), is married to George Frazer, a crass and wealthy Wall Street stockbroker, who professes to love her. But he, too, treats his wife as a possession and she has left him, turning to David (whom she knows only from his compassionate writings) for consolation and advice.

In a contrived denouement, Alice and Ethel meet and exchange personal histories, revealing Alice's fear that David would tire of her. George Frazer shows up and, after a failed attempt to shoot David, informs Ethel he has had a nervous breakdown and pleads with her to return to him. Both couples are reunited in a happy ending.

Eugene seemed as yet unable, despite his lofty goals, to rise above the stereotypical. His ideas were framed in a plot as forced as any on the commercial stage. *Servitude* was untrue to the life he knew, as was his earlier depiction of marital conflict in *Recklessness* (which had a silly, *un*happy ending). Its only aspect of note is Eugene's introduction of the thesis that "love means servitude," and that to serve a loved one is happiness — a theme to recur in later plays, most movingly exemplified by Nora Melody in *A Touch of the Poet*.

Blind to the shortcomings of *Servitude*, Eugene believed he had created a work both artistically honest and eminently producible. He copyrighted it on September 23, but it failed to find a producer. He later listed it as "destroyed."

For two more years he was fated to grope bravely but haplessly. He fashioned four additional one-acters and four full-length plays before he again found his voice with the three short sea plays that, together with *Bound East for Cardiff*, were ultimately packaged under the title *S.S Glencairn*.

A week before he was due to register at Harvard, Eugene went to New York to make one more attempt to enlist an agent or a manager. He checked into the Garden Hotel at Madison Square and Twenty-

Seventh Street, across the street from where Madison Square Garden was situated at the time. More rooming house than hotel, and possessing no elevator, it was a block and a half from the Prince George, where his parents lived.

The theater at that time was in one of its periodic states of flux, largely because of the advent of motion pictures. Broadway managers were looking for a new Clyde Fitch (who died in 1909), or a new William Vaughan Moody (who died a year later). They saw no possibility of making money with anything Eugene had to offer.

He turned to Beatrice for solace: " . . . if you could see the obstacles in the path of the prospective playwright as I have seen them today I'm afraid you'd feel like a soldier in the forlorn hope . . . Your love will be put to tests such as few loves are ever put to but *please, please* do stick for I have faith in the ultimate outcome, and without you — Oh, the thought is too unbearable! Your love is my whole life . . . where you are concerned, I am a deep well of tenderness bubbling over . . . How can I whisper, my lips against your heart, the love I feel, the passion of my longing for you?"

The rush of his passion for Beatrice had transformed the lofty truth-seeker into an abject fetishist. He referred piteously to the "faded stocking," the "dilapidated red bathing cap" and "your three pictures," that he carried with him — tokens that, in his loneliness, he cuddled, kissed and pressed to his heart.

PART SIX

THE EMERGING PLAYWRIGHT

"I want to be an artist or nothing."

— O'NEILL, applying for
admission to George Pierce Baker's playwriting course at Harvard

CHAPTER
THIRTY-SEVEN

BARELY WITHIN MINUTES OF ARRIVING IN BOSTON ON September 28, Eugene began bemoaning "the unkindness of the fate" that had separated him from his beloved "Bee." He wrote her that he felt like "giving the whole bloody business up" and rushing back to her "dear arms" and "sweet compassion."

Although planning to return to New London in four days for the weekend, he carried on as if their separation was to be of endless duration. There was a "great big emptiness inside," he wailed, and "there were tears" in his eyes.

Virtually all of his letters during the next nine months were dominated by despairing declarations of hunger for Beatrice's love and mothering and his obsessive yearning for the comfort of her breasts.

"I feel the impulse of the tired child who runs to his mother's arms and lays his head upon her breast, and sobs for no reason at all," he wrote to her. "Be my Mother!" Frequently addressing her as "Own Little Wife," he told her, over and over, sometimes writing twice in the same day, "I want you!" "I miss you!" "I need you!" "I love you!" "Please love me!" and "Please, Dear God, give me Bee!"

Beatrice seems not to have objected to the endearment of "Little Wife" — as long as it was understood this did not imply literal conjugal obligation.

If the feelings Eugene poured into his letters sometimes sounded almost unbalanced, he interspersed his outpourings with matter-of-fact accounts of his life in Cambridge, including reports of classroom discussions and comments about the plays he was writing.

He found room and board in a furnished apartment in a small house at 1105 Massachusetts Avenue not far from Harvard Square. The neighborhood was tranquil except for the "rumbling clamor" of the recently opened subway line coursing under the avenue, as

Eugene irritably noted in a poem written a few months after his arrival (entitled "Just a Little Love, a Little Kiss").

The apartment was occupied by a Mennonite family newly arrived from Hillsboro, Kansas. The address, one of several listed as offering rooms to students, had been posted on a bulletin board near the Harvard admitting office.

In need of a paying guest to share expenses, the family consisted of a married couple, Catherine and Bartel Ebel, and their two young sons; Catherine's brother, Daniel Hiebert; and Bartel's brother, August. Bartel was taking a postgraduate course in Greek at Harvard, his brother was studying art in Boston and Daniel was studying medicine at Boston University, while Catherine kept house for them all.

Uncomfortable with the family's religious devotion and unimpressed by Catherine's cooking — "so-so," as he wrote to Beatrice — he tolerated rather than liked them, with the exception of Daniel, who later became his doctor and close friend. "I eat with the family who all speak German and say grace before meals. S'nuff said!" Eugene reported to Beatrice.

August Ebel, who kept a diary, did not appear to feel slighted by O'Neill, nor did the rest of the family, for Eugene took the trouble to be mannerly. August did recall that Eugene rarely conversed at the dinner table and spent most of his time in his room. "His bed served him both by day and by night," noted August. During the day, August added, "he usually stretched out over it, a writing pad resting against his pulled-up knees, writing, writing, writing, or reading with the head of the bed pulled close to the large double window."

When Eugene paid an occasional visit to August and Daniel in the room they shared, he "assumed the air of one who has been around," August said. Disregarding his status as a guest in a religious home and not revealing he was the father of a four-year-old son, Eugene once remarked, "If I should ever have a son of my own I would see he be kept open-minded and not become hide-bound by any superstitious theological tenets, political palaver and so-called cultural imbecilities."

August evidently took this small outburst with humor rather than offense. In any case, Eugene seems to have made up for his lapse, at least in August's mind, by reciting poetry. He particularly remembered Eugene's rendition — "with depth of feeling" — of Swinburne's "The Garden of Persephone."

James had agreed to give Eugene, in addition to his tuition, ten dollars a week. With this "magnificent sum," as Carlotta O'Neill later characterized it, "he was to pay his board, his room, his streetcar fare, his laundry."

While Eugene often complained to Beatrice about not having enough spending money, he did receive a clothes allowance from his father that enabled him, in early October, to order a suit — "a fine one" — and "a wonderful pair of horsehide shoes."

Whatever James did for him, however, was never enough, and Eugene continued to carp about his pinched circumstances. It seems not to have occurred to him to supplement his income with a part-time job, apparently believing he had a divine entitlement to his father's support for however long it took to establish himself as a writer.

Eugene settled into his quarters, "a nice corner room on the ground floor with three big windows," as he wrote to Beatrice, and went off to attend his first class. He found Professor Baker to be "a fine man with a very fascinating personality."

The legendary George Pierce Baker, then forty-eight, was teaching two seminars, each limited to twelve students, one at Harvard and the other at Radcliffe, the affiliated women's college. Stage-struck since the age of six, when his parents gave him a toy theater during a year's illness at home in Providence, he grew up immersed in the history and lore of the theater from Shakespeare to Boucicault. A year after graduating from Harvard in 1887, he became an English instructor at Radcliffe, and shortly thereafter taught a course in the history of English drama at Harvard.

In 1903, believing that the sorry state of the contemporary American theater cried out for correction, he initiated a graduate course in playwriting at Radcliffe, hoping eventually to inspire a new school of naturalistic drama. Toward term's end, he invited his students to submit playscripts in lieu of term papers.

Two years later he introduced a similar course at Harvard, a course just barely tolerated by the university's entrenched English department, which held the elitist attitude that worthwhile theater had essentially ended with the Elizabethans. The modern American stage, Harvard's literary establishment believed, was beyond help and, in any case, Harvard was not a vocational school.

As O'Neill later noted, Baker had "no standing whatever with the English Department," whose faculty "thought playwriting stopped with Congreve and barely nodded to Baker when they passed him on the campus." When members of his class wanted to put on a play, O'Neill recalled, they "had to use the auditorium at Radcliffe."

Baker was once described by the theater critic, John Mason Brown, as "the least dogmatic of men." Brown, himself a former pupil, said Baker dared to teach the "unteachable subject" of playwriting with "no Golden Rules of Dramaturgy." "He did not pretend to be able to turn out playwrights in ten easy lessons," said Brown. "Indeed he did not claim to be able to turn them out at all. He was among the first to admit that dramatists are born, not made. But he did hope to be able to shorten the playwright's period of apprenticeship by granting him the same instruction in the essentials of his craft that the architect, the painter, the sculptor and the musician enjoyed in theirs."

Although Baker's students, according to Brown, sometimes found him "outwardly chilly," they generally responded to his "inner warmth." His blue-gray eyes, Brown added, "were always eager to light up with laughter behind his pince-nez, and when he was amused his somewhat portly body shook with merriment." Thomas Wolfe, another of Baker's students, immortalized him in *Of Time and the River*, calling him Professor James Graves Hatcher, "a man whose professional career had been made difficult by two circumstances: all the professors thought he looked like an actor and all the actors thought he looked like a professor."

Though not uncritical of the little vanities and crotchets of "Professor Hatcher," Wolfe found him imposing: "a well-set-up figure of a man . . . with an air of vital driving energy that was always filled with authority and a sense of sure purpose, and that never degenerated into the cheap exuberance of the professional hustler."

His pince-nez, Wolfe wrote, "dangled in a fashionable manner from a black silk cord; it was better than going to a show to see him put them on, his manner was so urbane, casual and distinguished when he did so."

When Eugene entered Baker's class in Massachusetts Hall, Baker was seated at the head of an oblong oak table, surrounded by his students, familiarly known as Baker's Dozen. Baker's methods, as Eugene soon discovered, were unorthodox, as he had no precedent at any other college.

He outlined the year's schedule: first his students were to select three short stories from any source and, with Baker's approval, settle on one to be dramatized as a one-act play. Next, they were to write an original one-act play and, toward the end of the term, a full-length play. They could also submit any other work for Baker's comment if they wished.

Eugene was pleased to find, as he wrote to Beatrice, that Baker wanted his students to begin "right away writing an adaptation of some short story." His mind, however, was as much on Beatrice as on Baker.

"I wish I could just give you a slight inkling of the aching vacuum your absence has left in my life," he wrote. "The world exists only in you."

After spending the weekend visiting with Beatrice in New London, he immediately wrote to her on his return to Cambridge, bewailing their separation. "I am thinking of last night and of all the wonder which is you, and my great desire moans from the depths of its abysmal aloneness; 'Give us, ah give us but yesterday!'"

He complained he could not sleep for thinking of her: " . . . And, oh, that time, that golden time-to-be, when dream and desire come true, when my glad mad heart shall beat against your own."

Two days later, returning from a swim in the YMCA "tank" (which he preferred to the more crowded University pool), he wrote to Beatrice that being enclosed in her love was "an immortality springing from the grave of my dead life." He seemed compelled to strip himself spiritually naked before her, seeking absolution as from a surrogate mother.

His compulsion to expiate grew more pronounced over the years, illustrated not only in his plays but in letters to the women he loved, to whom he endlessly apologized. The most telling example of his need to atone may be found in *A Moon for the Misbegotten*, in which he combined his own and his brother's cravings for absolution and transposed them to the character of Jamie Tyrone, who confesses his agonized guilt to the forgiving earth-mother, Josie Hogan.

"All of the sordid values the world has rubbed into me lose their cruel validity before your love," Eugene wrote to Beatrice. "When I look into your eyes I feel a sense of deep shame; I want to cry out and ask your forgiveness for being what I have been, to crave your indulgence for the grimy smears on my life, to pray your pity for the tattered wings of my spirit stained with the muck of the long road. I long for some clear well of the spirit wherein I could cleanse and purify my rag of life."

Although Eugene's painful preoccupation with past transgressions appeared, for the moment, to be taking precedence of all else, he did pause long enough to tell Beatrice of an interesting two-hour session with Baker.

"He sure is there with the acid wit . . . I look forward with *horror* to the time when he trains the batteries of his biting irony on the budding efforts of his class — particularly one member I know of. The slaughter will be frightful."

Eugene was hard at work on his first assignment. Baker had returned the short stories the students had submitted for adaptation, instructing them to write scenarios before beginning on the actual play.

"Have written about a thousand words of mine already," Eugene informed Beatrice, not mentioning it was a farce entitled *Dear Doctor*. "Baker has injected so many 'don'ts' into the work that it is fraught with difficulty to say the least."

Eugene's mind continued divided between his studies and his love. "My God, it's so hard to wait! . . . I want you! I want you! I want you!" he wrote, concluding, "'I am a prince of thwarted ecstasy/of unassuaged desire.'"

His romance with Beatrice was a tango of importunity on his side and of seductive retreat on hers. Her firm insistence on retaining her technical virginity apparently reduced Eugene to a state of panting adolescence. But his letters make clear he believed Beatrice would eventually surrender. "We have a future together, I am sure," he wrote, "that will more than compensate for the Present's sins of omission."

The following Saturday, returning from a Harvard football game — "a corker" — he informed Beatrice he had been concentrating on his scenario and had also begun work on an original one-act play. He was looking forward to his next visit to New London on the coming Friday, October 16, his twenty-sixth birthday.

"Had a great longing to pack my little bag and catch a rattler for New London today," he wrote, "but I reflected that my birthday would be more appropriate and I ain't rich enough to come both times . . . I had a wicked, wicked dream about you last night. It was very much — the afterwards."

On Sunday, he wrote to her again, begging her not to take down her hammock as she had threatened — "that confidant of all our joys and sorrows, our kisses and quarrels." "Spare it for the night of my birthday, at least. What if it be cold? We possess a sovereign remedy for all low temperatures — each other's arms — do we not? . . . Our Love is one of the open places, of the sand and sea, of clear fresh air."

Their reunion, whether in or out of the hammock, did little to refresh Eugene's outlook. A few days after he returned to Harvard he seemed to have lost all zest for life or creativity. He wrote to Beatrice that his work was "tiresome," his room "dismal," Cambridge "a bore," Boston "a frightful ennui of spirit" and Massachusetts "a dog's island."

Existence, he groaned, was "by-and-large insufferable and a blundering shame" — all because Beatrice was not with him. Having evidently promised her he would stay sober, he added that he had resisted the temptation to "seek a little oblivion" in drink: "Dear one, please, please, believe in the sincerity of my resolve to try and become worthy of you!"

By the following day he had come down with "La Grippe," to which he attributed his "terrific feeling of mental and physical depression." A week later, he told Beatrice he was still overcome with "Stygian gloom" and quoted Swinburne: "Say at night, 'Would God the day were here!' And say at dawn: 'Would God the day were dead!'"

His depression was preventing him from writing. "My brain is fallow and barren," he said. "I am not in harmony with myself. The ideas won't come . . . In fact this damn expedition of mine to Harvard's halls of learning is fast going to pieces on the rocks. I realize I have made a mistake — both from the standpoint of mental and physical well-being."

He counted the days until his next visit to New London for the Thanksgiving weekend. "I'll never be able to stick it as long as that —" he wrote Beatrice. He had been "filled full of gloom" reading Strindberg's *Married* — a collection of short stories that "especially harp on the fact of an insufficient income ruining so many lives by compelling them against the dictates of nature to waste their youth in waiting for each other."

The following day, he announced he had completed his one-act adaptation: "Thank God, for I took no pleasure in it at all. Stealing someone else's idea and fixing it up doesn't appeal to me when I have so many ideas of my own that I ought to be working."

A short while later, Eugene recovered his creative élan, and he joyfully reported to Beatrice: "Have been a positive glutton for work these past few days. (Oh, yes, I do get such industrious fits, strange as it may seem.) Have written my right hand into writer's cramp several times during the past week." He said he had "mapped out a tentative scenario" for a five-act play, which was "nothing if not grimly realistic and to the point."

The play was *The Second Engineer*, later retitled *The Personal Equation*. Heeding Baker's advice to write what he knew, Eugene drew upon his experience of the Liverpool dockworkers' and sailors' strike during his 1911 passage on the S.S. New York.

As he told an interviewer a few years later, "I don't think any real dramatic stuff is created, to use an excellent expression of Professor Baker, 'out of the top of your head.' That is, the roots of a drama have to be in life, however fine and delicate or symbolic or fanciful the development."

Except in *Bound East for Cardiff*, Eugene had not yet achieved that balance of realism, detachment and symbolism soon to emerge. In *The Second Engineer*, he set out to examine, not unsympathetically — but with the sort of doctrinaire rigidity that he himself later came to scorn — the forces that drove the early members of the militant labor movement.

The play was also inspired in part by an aspect of his father's character. James's thirty-year career in *The Count of Monte Cristo* must have been on Eugene's mind while he grappled with *The Second Engineer*. The title character is a man who weakly knuckles under to his superior officers and allows himself to be bullied by his son.

Even more significantly, perhaps, he is a man who has been content to dedicate himself for thirty years to his ship's engines, too timid to seek advancement in rank. This was Eugene's symbolic interpretation of James's inability to separate himself from the Count to seek greater stature as a Shakespearean actor.

Eugene must have felt dangerously daring in dealing sympathetically with the growing militancy of the labor movement.

"If [the play] is ever produced — and it never could be in this country — the authorities will cast me into the deepest dungeon of the jail and throw away the key," he wrote to Beatrice. "But one writes what one *must*, what one *feels*. All else is piffle. I will be [an] artist or nothing."

Convinced he was making genuine progress in that direction, he beseeched Beatrice to be his "goal," his "encouragement," his "ambition," his "end in life."

With renewed hope, Eugene decided to teach himself what he called "a reading knowledge" of both French and German, devoting an hour a day to each. "You see," he lectured Beatrice, "so many of the best plays by writers of the two countries — and they have the best writers — are never translated; Anglo-Saxon prudish hypocrisy being the principal reason."

He thought he would have no difficulty recovering his school French, but, while apprehensive about mastering German on his own, he was determined to try. With a flash of humorous insight, he asked, "Now what have you to say about the dauntless energy which has flamed up in me all at once — and, alas, if I know myself, is liable to flare out again just as suddenly!"

Trotting out the Emersonian argument against a foolish consistency, he made his case:

"However, what a tiresome person one would become to oneself if one were the same all the time! Positively not fit to live with! I have the faculty for assuming many roles and I always feel a certain curiosity as to what I shall do under given conditions. 'Know thyself!' What a mortal bore life would become if you did! It is the unexpected whims which change one's whole perspective, which make life fascinating — granting it ever could be so, what with its goodbyes and separations and other abominations."

In the same letter he made it clear he had by no means abandoned hope of bedding his beauteous Bee. "I've been thinking about 'Your Bet' regarding a certain Night-to-be. I hate to cast a skeptical slur upon your will power but I have a sneaking suspicion that the winning of said 'Bet' transcends the limits of human possibility."

By now, Eugene's classwork was beginning to win approval from Baker as well as his fellow-students. With obvious pride and pleasure, he informed Beatrice about his success with *Dear Doctor*: "My work comes on apace. Although Baker suggested a few minor changes in my one-act adaptation, which he read in class yesterday, his comments were very flattering." His classmates, Eugene said, "laughed their heads off."

Even his rivals, he said, acknowledged it was the best adaptation. Unfortunately, the short story itself seemed to have been stolen from a vaudeville sketch. "Two of my classmates declare they have seen a play built on almost the exact subject only not treated so well. Just my accursed luck, of course! Baker said: 'Well, if this has been done before it's a crime against Mr. O'Neill for I am certain this would be produced.'" Eugene discovered when he looked into the rights that his farce — whose plot has been long forgotten — had indeed been stolen from a vaudeville sketch. O'Neill later destroyed his manuscript.

As the time drew closer to his Thanksgiving vacation, Eugene hastened to assure Beatrice he was staying "strictly dry," and that his "most devilish libations" were chocolate milk shakes.

Evidently not wishing to burden Beatrice with the chore, he wrote to Dolly Rippin asking her to find him a rooming house for his six days in New London — one costing no more than ten dollars.

He made a point of letting her know that life in Cambridge was "not without its redeeming features," describing his activities on the production of a play written by a Radcliffe student of Baker's. "The sweet young things have their own theater, you know," he said.

Eugene's week in New London did not bring him any closer to winning the "'Bet' regarding a certain Night-to-be." They spent their first few days bickering about the status of their relationship: Beatrice was determined to remain a virgin until legally a wife — and Eugene could not support a wife.

In early December, back in Cambridge, he was remorseful over the bickering. "We'll not let our first Christmas days be anything like our first Thanksgiving ones were," he wrote to Beatrice. "We'll walk and be together all the time."

Again trying to subdue his romantic frustration, he tackled a different sort of writing project, while still developing *The Personal Equation*. He began to collaborate with Colin Ford, a classmate, on a long play aimed at Broadway, but uncompromisingly literary, making no concession to Broadway's glib dialogue and facile melodramatic tricks.

Ford was a well-to-do Yale graduate who had endeared himself to Eugene early in the term by mentioning he had read a review of *Thirst* and Eugene fell into the habit of dining with Ford and his wife.

"We have been head over ears writing out a structural synopsis of the plot, scenario of the acts, etc.," he wrote to Beatrice, "and are to start on the play itself immediately after Christmas vacation."

A precursor of such later O'Neill pageant-dramas as *Marco Millions* and *Lazarus Laughed*, the play, shortly to be given the title *Belshazzar*, was, he said, "founded on the fall of Babylon." Never a slouch when it came to research, however arcane, he (and Ford) were deep in reading about the customs and morals of the ancient city.

"I think I could find my way around if I were suddenly set down there before the temple of Bel or some other popular rendezvous in the year 650 B.C.," he said. "The play will be spectacular, have a distinctly Biblical atmosphere, and ought to hit the public square in the middle of their low brows." This last comment was obviously a reference to the low-brow *Joseph and His Brethren*. Eugene would show his father that pageantry in the right hands could be artistic theater.

Eugene claimed credit for "the plot and most of its ramifactions," but allowed that Ford had "all kinds of brains" and was strong in areas where Eugene was apt to be careless. "Vive Ford & O'Neill!" he crowed. "On to Broadway!"

On December 15, Eugene complained to Beatrice that the funds he expected from "the dear old Governor" for his trip to New London had not yet arrived, but he expected the money any day. He assured her he would be spending both Christmas Eve and Christmas Day with her.

"Where else would I spend it if I am to feel any of that 'peace on earth' emotion. Christmas without my Wife would be *Hamlet* without the melancholy Dane."

What truly elated him was Beatrice's announcement that she planned to go to New York with a friend the following winter to study and find a job. He told her they would live in Greenwich Village, where "we would be happy, very happy, working and living and loving — together." He assured her it was possible for them to marry "even under present straightened circumstances . . . if *we want to enough.*"

In a sudden burst of euphoria soon to evaporate, he informed her he would forswear his father's dole and become a dedicated wage-earner: "I'll work twenty-three hours out of twenty-four if it's necessary . . . Waiting for My Ship to arrive is fruitless . . . I hope for nothing next fall in the play line . . . This isn't gloom. It's common sense . . . It will take time! So let us cease to build on clouds and come down . . . to homes for human beings."

Chapter
THIRTY-EIGHT

During his christmas holiday in new london, Eugene must have reached some rapprochement with Beatrice that permitted him to rationalize their unconsummated relationship. They had visited their beach and held hands in the movies. Writing to her from Cambridge on January 6, 1915, he spoke of her "triumph" on the afternoon before he left New London:

"You have routed the Gene O'Neill of the Past. I am born again — your very own child . . . You have inspired my manhood with a great desire to be clean . . . Your clear girlhood or womanhood has put my unwholesome cynicism to shame."

He was now trying, he said, to "think only of Spring and Summer and our delightful future." His "one bright spot" was that Baker, the day before, had read his new one-act play to the class, probably the play he had mentioned to Beatrice in October. Called *The Sniper*, it was a realistic anti-war treatment of the kind of contemporary cause O'Neill was later to eschew.

Set on the outskirts of a Belgian village during the early days of World War I, it concerns an elderly peasant whose son has just been shot by the "Prussians." When the peasant learns that his wife, too, has been killed, he fires from his house on some Prussians and is himself shot down. The play ends when a priest, who has been praying for the peasant, looks down "with infinite compassion at the still bodies of father and son."

"Alas, the laws of men!" he says, as the curtain falls.

As Eugene reported to Beatrice, Baker "did not hesitate to say it was 'very good.'" He could now turn to his collaboration with Colin Ford on *Belshazzar*. He soon had a new concern, however. The long-running *Joseph and His Brethren* was about to close in St. Louis.

The news was broken to him by the young actor, Malcolm Morley, who had recently left the *Joseph* cast to enter Baker's class. "If this is true," Eugene wrote to Beatrice, "it will mean . . . that Father will be in an abominable humor and I may expect some severe judgments at his hands. Heigh-ho, t'was ever thus!"

He did not let the news dampen his ardent courting and he was soon again sending Beatrice poetry. In "Just a Little Love, a Little Kiss," he recalled a popular ballad of similar title that Beatrice often had sung to him:

" . . . Summer, indeed, is gone with all his rose"?/Ah, but the soul of Summer haunts me yet,/Conjured by this refrain, I can't forget, — /A song you sang at one soft twilight's close."

Within the next week, he dispatched six more poems, all more or less echoing the same theme, and ranging from the pseudo-lyrical to a besottedly idiotic paean to Beatrice's frostbitten nose.

Eugene had no trouble shifting gears from romantic fluff to serious literary effort. On January 11, he informed Beatrice he had completed the first draft of the scenario for the first three acts of *The Second Engineer*. But, he added, he was "in a quandary about how I shall end the daw-gun thing. I have one ending which delights my soul but — you know me . . . I do want to strive and give it a reasonably contented ending but my perverse mind doesn't seem to want to let me."

Eugene went on to tell Beatrice he had received a letter from his "unworthy Father," confirming that the tour of *Joseph and His Brethren* had indeed ended in St. Louis. His producers, Liebler and Company, had been losing $3,000 a day by the end of 1914 (and in early 1915 were forced to declare bankruptcy).

The theater generally was in financial doldrums, brought about partly by increasing competition from motion pictures and partly by economic uncertainty over the war in Europe — and James was in a state of near-panic. Roles for aging actors were few, but up until now he had depended on his loyal, longtime producers to come up, sooner or later, with work for him. Apparently of greatest concern to Eugene was the effect of his father's unemployment on his allowance. His parents were back in New York and he was just as happy not to be there to greet them. "I can guess the Pater's mood," he told Beatrice, "and he and I would get along like a cage full of wounded wild-cats."

Two days later Eugene was in a cheerier mood. He wrote to Beatrice that he was "all puffed out like a pouter-pigeon," after lunching in Boston with the family of a wealthy classmate from

California. Felton Elkins (called "Pinky" by his friends) had leased a Beacon Street town house complete with butler and chauffeur. Both Elkins's wife and her visiting mother, evidently having read *Thirst*, complimented Eugene on his work. When he returned home, he wrote Beatrice, he "did strut before the glass twirling my mustache with gusto and exclaiming with admiring satisfaction: 'Aha. Perhaps they were *not* kidding me. You may, with good luck, escape hanging yet.'"

Within a few days, however, he complained of awakening with "a beautiful sore throat and a delightful cold in the head." He was nonetheless hard at work on *Belshazzar*:

"I have succeeded in catching the mood in which the play should be written very well . . . I have also solved the difficulty of comic relief . . . I fear — and also hope — that the burden of writing most of the dialogue will fall on me. There doesn't seem to be much of the poetic fancy (creative) in Ford, and the lines in this play will have to be lifted out of every day conversation."

His cold turned into the tonsillitis he always dreaded and he was confined to the infirmary for three days. "Your letters," he wrote to Beatrice, "are the only gleams of sunlight in a world of abysmal darkness."

By the end of January — addressing her as "Beatrice O'Neill" — he felt well enough to solicit a fetish in the form of her "red flannel — (censored), or her nightie, or her pajamas . . . or something."

Explaining his lift of spirits, he described a recent private visit with Professor Baker:

"I went to his house at seven-thirty and he kept me there until half past ten, talking and smoking his gold-tipped cigarettes. He has a beautiful home on Brattle St. and the finest study I was ever in. We sat in front of the enormous open fire-place where a log fire was burning, and he made me open up and tell him the story of my life and adventures along the Ragged Edge. I did so with the plainest frankness and I saw that even he was forced to acknowledge that I have knocked about a bit. I did most of the talking and I held his interest all right for it is almost unprecedented for him to give up a whole evening to one student."

Baker analyzed Eugene's faults and virtues, calling his work "eminently worth while" [sic] and said he had the "stuff" in him and that "time and hard work would grind it out." Eugene said he had derived more value out of the visit "than of all the classes put together."

He failed to mention that Baker told him he did not think *Bound*

East for Cardiff (then still called *Children of the Sea*) "was a play at all," an opinion evidently accepted by Eugene with uncharacteristic meekness.

In addition to working with Ford on *Belshazzar*, he was still struggling with *The Second Engineer* in late March. He had reduced it from five to four acts, explaining to Beatrice that the play had undergone major changes and had "wandered into such unforeseen ramifications and complications, that it has me bewildered and a bit peeved."

In its final version, the play is set in the Headquarters of the International Workers Union in Hoboken, meant to stand for International Workers of the World. In Act I, plans are being hatched for a terrorist attack on the S.S. San Francisco, scheduled to depart shortly for England. The action continues in the home of the San Francisco's second engineer (Act II); in the "Fireman's fo-castle of the San Francisco, docked at Liverpool," (Act III, Scene I); in the engine room of the San Francisco, (Act III, Scene II); and in a hospital room in Liverpool (Act IV).

Unbeknownst to Thomas Perkins, the second engineer, his own son, Tom — a radicalized college dropout and sometime sailor with a background similar to Eugene's — has been selected to carry out the terrorist act of dynamiting the ship's engines.

At one point, Tom defensively tells his anarchist girlfriend, Olga Tarnoff, "I'm a college boy, if that one year I wasted in college makes me one." Presumably indulging in a bit of wish-fulfillment, Eugene depicts Olga as Tom's enthusiastic partner in bed, a liberated woman who sees no need for marriage. More than likely, Olga's attitude was inspired by Emma Goldman's zealous advocacy of free love.

The dynamiting fails and, in a melodramatic twist worthy of *The Count of Monte Cristo*, the young provocateur is accidentally shot by his father, trying to protect the San Francisco's engines. The play was a hash composed of one part pamphlet anarchism (courtesy of Benjamin Tucker and Goldman's Mother Earth); one part pseudo-Ibsen; and one part stale melodrama of the sort Eugene professed to despise.

He did not copyright the play and later dismissed it, along with the bulk of his other work for Baker, as "rotten," calling it "a rambling thing about a seamen's and firemen's strike."

George Pierce Baker appealed to Eugene as a person, but ultimately disappointed him as a teacher. Eugene was particularly offended when Augustus Thomas, regarded as the dean of American play-wrights, was invited by Baker to take over the class as guest lecturer for two three-hour sessions.

Thomas, who was fifty-eight, had been writing plays since four-teen. He had been an actor, newspaperman and advance agent for a mind reader; this last job had provided the background for his enor-mously popular *The Witching Hour*, produced in 1907. Eugene con-sidered Thomas the personification of all that was hackneyed on the Broadway stage.

Thomas, with a glibness that revolted Eugene, proceeded to define the method for writing a surefire Broadway success:

"Suggest the name of a star," he invited the class, it being an iron-bound convention of the Broadway stage of that era to write plays for the talents of specific actors. When a student suggested Margaret Anglin, Eugene scowled and hunched his shoulders in disgust — not because he recalled his backstage encounter with her as a child, but because he knew and despised her lurid acting style. Nonetheless, after several other names had been suggested, a vote was taken and Anglin won the lead.

"All right, we'll write a play for Anglin," said Thomas, and pro-ceeded to chart a scenario on the blackboard. "She's broad at hip, well-developed — so our story will have to fit a woman of that phys-ical type. She's no longer young or beautiful, so it must be a role for an older woman — a woman with deep emotions; we'll make her a mother — and since we have to have drama — a mother threatened with losing her child."

The students, with the exception of O'Neill, listened in awe and, catching fire from Thomas's swift outline of detail, offered refine-ments of their own. Within an hour Thomas had woven for them a full-length, standard melodrama:

"The mother lives in a puritan New England community. Her townspeople find out she's had a lover. They are shocked. They decide she's not a fit mother for the child. There's a great scene with Anglin, abandoned by all, defending her right to keep the child against all the world.

"If you write this up as a scenario," he told the class, "I will put in the dialogue, and guarantee a production."

Baker commented mildly that it sounded a little too commercial and Eugene, as he later recalled, "got up and left the room." Infuriated, he went straight to Boston to get drunk. He had not come to Harvard to study how to write carbon copies of the kind of palatable tripe then being consumed on Broadway.

Some years later, he summed up his feelings about that era, observing that a popular author was one who built up a thesis for three acts and then proceeded in the fourth act to knock over what he had constructed.

"The managers," he said, "felt they knew what the public would accept and the plays had to conform to their ideas. The very fact that I was brought up in the theater made me hate this artificiality and this slavish acceptance of these traditions."

Long before anyone else recognized that Augustus Thomas and other popular playwrights of the era were doomed, O'Neill saw through the hollowness of their facile posturing. He wanted the stage to come to grips with the big themes, the realities of life. Although failing to make much progress in that direction at Harvard, he loftily determined not only to write such plays but to compel the managers and public to accept them.

While his goals were sublime, Eugene's attitude at Harvard struck at least one classmate, Bruce Carpenter, as supercilious. Carpenter, who had begun acting professionally at fifteen, eventually settled down as an English professor at New York University.

"O'Neill fitted the old definition of a gentleman — 'A man who never offends, except intentionally,'" Carpenter said. "When I first met him I was impressed. I had seen his father play Monte Cristo and Marc Antony — the finest Marc Antony I have ever seen.

"I had come to Harvard from New York and had been on the stage and pretended to be older than I was and more educated. But I had nothing on O'Neill. He let us all know that he had shipped before the mast. He was very much the gentleman when he wanted to be, but he had an indifference almost bordering on contempt."

Very probably, Eugene simply took an impulsive dislike to Carpenter; and he rarely bothered to conceal such feelings. Carpenter interpreted his hostility as egotistical. "He seemed to feel the rest of us hadn't lived. I realize now there was something in his heart that he wouldn't let us see; I couldn't reconcile the O'Neill I knew at Harvard with the genius who later wrote such human plays."

According to Carpenter, Baker's method was to read a student's play aloud without revealing its author and often without identifying the characters by name or even by sex. Baker would then ask each student for comment. Carpenter said Eugene's would often be, "'Huh!'" and that nobody else would have dared be so abrupt.

Baker generally pretended to take no notice, viewing Eugene's

attitude with more understanding: "Because of his wider experience
of life, he seemed a good deal older than most of the men in the
course, although not really so in years. He seemed a little aloof,
though I never found him so personally. This, I think, came quite as
much from a certain awe of him in his fellow-students . . . as from any
holding apart by him."

Eugene, as Carpenter recalled, dressed more casually than most
of his classmates, who wore the Harvard costume of unpressed
Brooks Brothers suit, white shirt, tie, and a pummeled hat.

Eugene attended classes wearing corduroy trousers and flannel
shirt open at the throat. He saved the fine tailored suit lavished on
him by his father, mainly for evenings out. Carpenter recalled that
Eugene would slouch in his chair, often with a sneer on his face; he
could not remember ever seeing Eugene smile, or hearing him say a
pleasant word.

O'Neill came to believe Baker's course had been something of a
waste of time. He learned little from the actual class work itself, he
said. "Necessarily, most of what Baker had to teach the beginners
about the theater as a physical medium was old stuff to me." On a
much later occasion, he reiterated this opinion: "The course wasn't
much good to me, for they spent the whole first year on fundamen-
tals of the theater that I had learned in short pants."

O'Neill did acknowledge it was from Baker that he grasped the
essential technical procedure of writing a scenario before attempting
any actual dialogue — a rule he followed with only rare exceptions
throughout his career. In 1945, when illness forced him to cease writing, he took the trouble to answer at length an inquiry from an aspiring writer about his method of work.

In this remarkably candid letter he disclosed, among other salient
facts, that both *The Emperor Jones* and *The Hairy Ape* had been written
in ten days. In the case of the former, he said, "no scenario, just a few
notes in preparation." As for *The Hairy Ape*, it had been "dashed off
too, without much preparation." Both, he added, were "easy" plays:
"They just came to me."

After revealing that two other plays, *Desire Under the Elms* and *Ah
Wilderness!* had come to him in dreams — "I simply awakened with
these plays in mind" — he went on to explain his more usual method
of work:

"In my note book I write a line or so about anything that strikes
me as a basis for a future play — a character, or an incident, a memory, a story I hear or read, any fragment — Most of these never devel-

op (in the unconscious or wherever it is such germination happens) into ideas for plays. Some of them do."

In most cases, he explained, his original note for a play was apt to become "a lot of notes," which eventually germinated into a detailed scenario and "then waits." The scenario "finally becomes a first draft of a play which sometimes follows the notes, and sometimes does not." At that point he would have the first draft retyped "and again wait." After that, a second draft, "And so on until I feel I have put all I have to give into the play — and had cut all I felt was unnecessary, etc."

In an earlier and equally candid comment about the process of creativity, O'Neill conceded it was "undoubtedly true" that "an author is not always conscious of the deeper implications of his writings while he is actually at work on them, and perhaps never becomes fully aware of all he has revealed."

Apart from Baker's fundamental lesson on the importance of a scenario to the construction of a play, O'Neill was forever grateful for his teacher's encouragement at a time when he was in dire need of it.

"The most vital thing for us, as possible future artists and creators, to learn at the time (Good God! For anyone to learn anywhere at any time!) was to believe in our work and to keep on believing," O'Neill wrote after Baker's death. "He helped us to hope — and for that we owe him all the finest we have in memory of gratitude and friendship."

CHAPTER
THIRTY-NINE

THERE WAS A SIDE OF EUGENE'S LIFE AT CAMBRIDGE HE barely alluded to in his letters to Beatrice. While he teased her gently at times about the women he met at Radcliffe and through introductions by classmates, he never mentioned the bibulous evenings he spent on the town, since he had repeatedly promised her he would not drink.

One of his drinking companions was a classmate, William L. Laurence, who soon discovered he was not fitted for a career in the theater and ultimately became science editor of The New York Times (a role in which he gained international renown in 1945 after breaking the behind-the-scenes story of the atomic bomb). Laurence had read *Thus Spake Zarathustra* in the original German and, according to Carpenter, was the only member of Baker's class Eugene held in awe.

As an undergraduate, he had worked his way through Harvard, shoveling snow, tending furnaces, reading gas meters and tutoring students. A garrulous, proselytizing intellectual who possessed the sort of arcane literary knowledge Eugene could both admire and envy, Laurence had a background as filled with adventure and struggle as Eugene's.

A Latvian Jew, subject to an education quota in the port city of Libau where he grew up, Laurence had become his own teacher. He read German and English as well as Russian and, like Eugene, had devoured every book he could lay hands on. After discovering Nietzsche in the Libau library, he saved enough to buy a copy of *Zarathustra*, and (like Eugene) carried it with him wherever he went.

Stimulated by his reading, which included Ibsen, Dostoevsky and Gorky, Laurence became a precocious political activist, traveling about Russia trying to awaken the peasants to a sense of their social responsibility. The failure of the 1905 revolution put a stop to his activities and, not yet out of his teens, he was forced to flee. A copy of *Zarathustra* was his only luggage when he arrived in America.

Once there, Laurence turned his zeal from the Russian peasantry to his new compatriots. "I wanted to make people hate philistinism," he said. "I thought the state of literature and culture was generally poor in this country. Everything was so vulgarized. Even people who came here from Russia with taste and hopes became corroded. I wanted to instill the love of good literature in my friends."

Since Eugene was already a literary convert, Laurence went to work on his politics — not because they were conventional but because, so Laurence believed, they were confused.

"Intellectually," Laurence said, "Eugene was a philosophical anarchist; politically, a philosophical socialist. I tried to give him a sense of consciousness about the value of labor and the struggle between labor and capital. The play he wrote for the course [*The Second Engineer*] was a violent labor play. I thought it was the best one written. It had the same impact as [Gerhart] Hauptmann's *The Weavers*." Hauptmann had won the Nobel Prize two years earlier and his 1893 play, deeply admired by O'Neill, was the compassionate story of a revolt by German weavers against inhuman working conditions in their community.

Laurence remembered Eugene as "a strange, taciturn fellow" and thought he would make a good Mephistopheles for *Faust*.

"For some time, he didn't talk at all," Laurence said. "Then he began talking, and I found out he was the son of James O'Neill and that he had just had a volume of plays published." That clinched Laurence's interest in Eugene and he determined to make him a disciple — much as Eugene himself had done with various susceptible friends. According to Laurence, Eugene hungered to fill in the gaps in his education and often visited Laurence's room in Thayer Hall, overlooking Harvard Yard.

"We talked about Nietzsche, of course," Laurence recalled. "And I talked my head off about Ibsen's *Brand* and *Peer Gynt*. I told O'Neill they were expressions of the Nietzschean idea of the individualist." He also expounded on Gorky and it was at Laurence's suggestion that Eugene, early in November, decided to read *The Lower Depths*.

"Have been reading a play this afternoon which for pure unadulterated gloom just about bears off the palm," he wrote to Beatrice. "It is *The Lower Depths* by Maxim Gorki and, believe me, the depths are pretty low, to say the least."

When Eugene mentioned he had seen Nazimova in *Hedda Gabler*,

Laurence was able to provide firsthand information about her background: She had come to the United States as an exile the same year as Laurence, bringing her entire company, none of whom spoke English.

Renting the first floor of a three-story stable on East Third Street, they built a makeshift stage and installed benches. There they presented, in Russian, plays by Gorky, Ibsen, Chekhov and Dostoevsky. Sometimes during performances the stamping of hooves could be heard from upstairs. Admission was ten cents, but Laurence, when he could not pay, was allowed to attend anyway. He went every night.

He told Eugene about one backstage crisis, when the actors ran out of cigarettes, without which they refused to perform. Among them they could not produce the five-cent price of a pack of cigarettes. Laurence, momentarily flush, provided the nickel and they then gave an impassioned performance. Laurence told Eugene the actors were dedicated to great theater and not interested in making money. Eugene agreed with Laurence that was the kind of theater the country needed.

In common with Carpenter, Laurence claimed never to have seen Eugene smile. "He used to talk in monosyllables, saying a biting, cutting thing every once in a while."

The two men took long walks through Cambridge and Boston. Once, crossing the Charles River Bridge, Laurence told Eugene about a paper he had written for a course on rational and irrational fear. To prove his point, he tried to scare himself by walking to a cemetery at night, and before long he had found himself fleeing in terror. Eugene appeared greatly interested and Laurence later concluded that Eugene remembered the conversation when he conceived *The Emperor Jones*.

In the course of these nocturnal walks Eugene and Laurence sometimes got drunk. Compared with Eugene's earlier protracted binges, however, the Cambridge drinking episodes appear relatively mild — no more riotous, indeed, than the carousing of his fellow-students.

Eugene could not have accomplished the work he did, nor have given himself so intensely to his infatuation with Beatrice, had he not, during this time, been able to maintain long dry spells. This is not to say he forgot how to go on a bender.

"At times we were like a combination of Joyce's Bloom and Mulligan," Laurence said. "When we were drunk enough, we'd go to the Boston Common and stand under a huge elm and lecture passersby who, at that hour, usually consisted of sailors and their girls.

"We'd argue for universal sterilization, as the best solution for the human race. We maintained that the advantage of sterilization was freedom to fornicate to our hearts' content and put the abortionists out of business. We were loud, but our audiences seemed to be amused, and we somehow managed to escape arrest."

Eugene had the tact to stay away from his room in Cambridge during his weekend binges. Often he would not be seen by Hiebert or the Ebels from Friday to the following Monday. In their soberer moments, Eugene and Laurence, together with other classmates, would congregate at a Boston spaghetti diner to encourage each other's work and compare ideas.

Another classmate accompanying Eugene on the town was John V. A. Weaver, a Chicagoan, who sat beside him at the English 47 table. Baker predicted it would take Weaver eight years to get somewhere in the theatre and it was exactly eight years later that his first play, *Love 'Em and Leave 'Em* was produced. (It was forgotten in far fewer.)

Like Carpenter, Weaver at first found Eugene forbidding and unapproachable. As everyone else sat spellbound listening to Baker, Eugene "would writhe and squirm in his chair" and Weaver could hear him muttering "fearful imprecations and protests." To Weaver this was "delightful, fascinating anarchy."

Then one day, Professor Baker read aloud a particularly earnest and lugubrious student scenario. "Several of us gave timid suggestions," Weaver said. "It came O'Neill's turn. He waited some moments. Finally he said, without a smile, 'Cut it to twenty minutes, give it a couple of tunes and it's sure-fire burly-cue.'"

Weaver said the entire class "howled with laughter" and Baker smiled. "From that time until we all parted in June," said Weaver, "there was a new ease, a refreshing relaxation in the meetings."

In a version adjudged somewhat fanciful by other classmates, Weaver went on to describe a number of wild evenings spent by himself, Eugene and their wealthy classmate, Felton Elkins.

They "feasted amidst quiet elegance and flunkies," Weaver recalled. "Always, afterwards, we would go to some new show. Elkins would buy up a whole box, and once we were seated, tear up the rest of the tickets. He was a good scout. He knew what he wanted, and he could afford it. Why not?"

Describing another night when he, Eugene and Elkins drank ale in an Irish bar "until four in the morning," Weaver remarked, "It was just one of those nights. Ribald tales, anecdotes of experience, theorizing about the drama . . . We piled finally into a decrepit hack. We fell into O'Neill's room some time about five."

Weaver had with him a newly purchased copy of *Spoon River Anthology*, and at dawn, as he recalled, he was sitting on a trunk, Elkins was sprawled across the bed and Eugene was reading "poem after poem from that disturbing collection."

In his letters to Beatrice, Eugene Eugene, while avoiding descriptions of the pub-crawling evenings spent with Elkins and Weaver, did make passing references to dinners with Elkins and his wife in their Beacon Street town house and attendance at the theater with them.

While Eugene was happy to benefit from Elkins's largess at Harvard, he grumbled years later that his erstwhile friend spent his money only for show: "He was a tightwad except where his personal indulgence and vanity was concerned. He could cry poor on a waiter's tip with two grand in his wallet."

What impressed Weaver most about Eugene was the hypnotic effect he exerted on women — another aspect of his Harvard life he barely hinted at to Beatrice.

"Women were forever calling for Gene," wrote Weaver. "There was something apparently irresistible in his strange combination of cruelty (around the mouth), intelligence (in his eyes) and sympathy (in his voice) . . . One girl told me she could not get his face out of her thoughts. He was hard-boiled and whimsical. He was brutal and tender, so I was told. From shop girl to 'sassiety' queen, they all seemed to develop certain tendencies in his presence."

Though not averse to flirting, Eugene remained obsessively fixed on Beatrice. On February 5 he was still "anxiously awaiting the something" which had "been near to" Beatrice's skin. And on February 9 he asked pathetically "when do I get the something which has nestled close to your warm flesh? I tell you my lips are parched with thirst for it."

Eugene was now having second thoughts about working with Ford on *Belshazzar*. "The idea of collaboration is ridiculous but I have let myself in for it and there you are," he wrote to Beatrice. "I will write the whole play and Ford will get half the credit — if there ever is any. Of course he is much too fine a fellow and too good a friend of mine for me to ever let him have an inkling of this but, really, as far as the creative work goes, it will be all mine."

Abruptly shifting gears, he offered to send Beatrice (who still had not sent him the promised "something") semi-naked photographs of himself. The pictures had been taken by Daniel Hiebert for his brother-in-law, August Ebel, who needed them "for help in his studies of the nude."

"I run the risk of losing your love by this offer," Eugene quipped. "You may take one flash at me, unadorned — and say: 'So this is what they give green certificates [marriage licenses] with! Take it away!' Promise not to or I won't send them."

Beatrice, however, had other matters on her mind. She had apparently resumed a relationship with a former admirer who, unlike Eugene, had prospered, and was now pressing her to marry him. Evidently having abandoned her recent plan to go to New York the following winter, she informed Eugene that although she still loved him, she was finding it difficult to keep her suitor at bay. Eugene exploded.

"It is up to you to make a decision for once and for all time!!" he expostulated. " . . . If you love me, as you say, then *bury your dead*!! How often have I implored you to do that! You must! You must! I will have none of these specters of your past arising to mock my love and make me miserable!! I cannot and I will not bear it! I have work to do, work which must be done, and these phantoms come between me and my work, fill my heart with agony and my soul with misgivings, stifle inspiration and all creative joy. I will not bear it!

"My past is dead. There is not a single thread that binds me to it . . . I am yours free and unfettered! . . . My cosmos contains nothing, or rather no one, but you.

"I demand the same of you. I am worth, my love is worth, all of you or nothing at all! . . .

"You love me, you cry? Very well, then. Write to whatever-his-name-is and tell him in such a way that he cannot doubt, that he is out of your life forever. Be cruel! It will be the greatest kindness you can do him. It will be but simple justice to me who love you and am living and building for you . . . If you, confessing that you love me, were to marry him, you would be in my eyes such a mean and pitiful caricature of my ideal of you, that only hate and disgust would remain of my love!!"

With a mix of arrogance and trepidation, he enclosed one of the photographs of himself taken by Hiebert, challenging Beatrice to compare it with her suitor's and demanding pathetically "Which of us belongs to the future? . . . Which of us contains the most 'man?' . . . Look into our eyes! Who will be your lover and who your hus-

band down the long trail which leads from the green certificate? Who
has the most poetry, — and therefore, the greatest capacity for emotion in him? Then choose! For all time!"

Beatrice, at least for the moment, was cowed into choosing
Eugene. They spent a weekend together toward the end of February
and she allowed him to carry away her garter and some "tangled
hair" from her comb.

He began counting the days to spring, when, he vowed, he would
kiss her eyes, her hair, her lips, her ears, her nose, her neck, her breast
"and, in token of befitting humility, every small toe" on her "littlest
feet!"

More soberly, he reported that *The Sniper*, for which he received
the copyright on March 13, had earned "honorable mention" in the
one-act play competition. He did not win the award, he said, because
Baker — though he "thought it a stronger play than any of the others" — felt it would be injudicious for the Harvard Dramatic Club "to
put on a war play."

Baker instead chose a script — *Plots and Playwrights* — by a writer
long-since forgotten, named Edward Massey. A departure of sorts
from the traditional Broadway theater, and later produced by the
Washington Square Players off Broadway, it concerns a successful
playwright who confides to a young short-story writer that he is at a
loss for a plot. The short-story writer tries to demonstrate that material for drama exists in the apartments of a Greenwich Village rooming house; snatches of life are then acted out in each of three apartments, but with no attempt at a unifying plot.

The playwright points out that such a "play" would never be a
success on Broadway and, in a spoof of the Augustus Thomas school
of drama, proceeds to tie up the isolated scenes in a luridly melodramatic fashion. Massey's play represented the limits to which Baker
was prepared to encourage his students to revolt against conventional theater. For Eugene, still struggling to achieve his own revolution,
this was not nearly far enough.

Despite Baker's politically motivated rejection of *The Sniper*,
Eugene felt encouraged enough by its otherwise favorable reaction to
send it to his father in New York, asking him to try to interest a producer.

"Don't know whether he will accept the job as my agent or not
but I hope he does," he confided to Beatrice. "It's about time for
something to break my way in some manner or other."

But nothing did. Not only did Holbrook Blinn reject his work, the two other small, noncommercial theaters that had recently sprung up also turned down his scripts.

Disappointed but still gamely persevering, Eugene went on to tell Beatrice he had finished the first draft of *Belshazzar* — "complete in all its seven act glory!" — and that he and Ford were going to show it to Baker.

No script of the play survives; but in a draft of the short story, "Tomorrow," O'Neill made an odd, self-mocking reference to "a play in seven acts about the feast of Belshazzar & the Fall of Babylon." In the story, the narrator (representing O'Neill) says, "I never got past the first act but I remember it had lots of action. Eight Babalonian [sic] nobles fell on their swords in blank verse during this period. It was worse than an Artzibashef novel . . . "

Eugene was in "a frenzied state of mind" about what he was still calling his Engineer play: " . . . can't seem to fix in my mind what final form it will take," he said. "I know all the pangs of child-birth."

It is evident from a March 18 letter to Beatrice that she was again having serious doubts about her commitment, apparently even trying to squirm out of the relationship. Eugene's overwrought dependency was beginning to exasperate her and the high pitch of their passion seemed to be wearing thin. Then, too, Beatrice began to have misgivings about the wisdom of casting her lot with a penniless writer.

On the first day of spring Eugene, sounding anxious, reminded Beatrice she had sworn, the last time they were together, that she would never again doubt his love.

"You *knew* Our Love was all it should be! And now — why? why? why? . . . Can a few weeks of absence cause that difference? Then your love — your 'mother-love' even — is not worth the name, but is more correctly 'whim' . . . Perhaps you think the path ahead with me is too rough?"

He continued in a muddled frenzy to berate her: "There is only one love possible between us — all else is piffle and you know it. I don't want to be your father or uncle or brother. I want to be lover and husband — or nothing." Eugene concluded with a warning that if Beatrice could not with certainty assure him of her love, he would, as he put it, return to "the beast hunt of old times."

His letter drew the response he had hoped for. He received not only her assurance of true love, but was finally in possession of what he referred to as her "undervestie," which he took to bed with him at night, placing it on his pillow and dreaming "the old wonderful dreams over and over again." At last, he said, he was "in tune with the joy of Spring."

Eugene was also happy about good news from his father. *The Sniper*, he informed Beatrice, "has made a big hit with all the people he has had read it but they all say the vaudeville censors would not allow it unless I omitted all reference to Prussians, French, Belgians, etc."

Moreover, Holbrook Blinn (who had rejected his earlier plays) had assured him he would "seriously consider" the production of *The Sniper* if he sent it to him "after the war." (*The Sniper* was finally produced, not by Blinn, but by the Playwrights Theater, in 1917; O'Neill later listed it as destroyed.)

With the exception of *The Sniper*, Eugene's output at Harvard was unimpressive. In addition to *Dear Doctor*, *Belshazzar* and *The Personal Equation*, he also wrote a play called *The Knock on the Door*, subsequently destroyed. And yet, the plays he wrote in Baker's class were no worse than most of those turned out over the years in English 47 — at least according to Heywood Broun, the somewhat acerbic columnist and critic who had taken Baker's course.

"There is no denying the fact that a certain number of dramatists have come out of Harvard's English 47," wrote Broun. "But the course also has a splendid record of cures." He maintained facetiously that Professor Baker deserved the thanks of the community not only for Edward Sheldon and Eugene O'Neill but also for the number of "excellent young men who have gone straight from his classroom to Wall Street and the ministry and automobile accessories with all the nascent enthusiasm of a man just liberated from a great delusion.

"People who come to English 47 may talk about their plays as much as they choose but they must write them, too," he continued. "Often a cure follows within forty-eight hours after the completion of a play. Sometimes it is enough for the author to read a thing through for himself. But if that does not avail, there is an excellent chance for him. After his play has been read aloud by Professor Baker and criticized by the class, if a pupil still wishes to write plays, there is no question that he belongs in the business."

Describing the sort of plays written by Baker's students, Broun quipped that "Somebody has figured out that there are 2,983 more rapes in the average English 47 plays than in the usual non-collegiate specimen of commercial drama."

"We feel comparatively certain," he added, "that there is nothing in the personality of Professor Baker to account for this." Nowhere in the world, said Broun, was a woman quite so unsafe as in an English 47 play.

"When I was in English 47, I remember that all our plays dealt with Life. None of us thought much of it, at that. Few respected it and certainly no one was in favor of it . . . Some of the playwrights in English 47 said that Life was a terrific tragedy. In their plays the hero shot himself or the heroine or both, as the circumstances might warrant, in the last act.

"The opposing school held that life was a joke, a grim jest to be sure, cosmic rather than comic, but still mirthful. The plays by these authors ended with somebody ordering 'another small bottle of Pommerey' and laughing mockingly like a worldwise cynic. Bolshevism had not been invented at that time, but Capital was severely handled, just the same. All our villains were recruited from the upper classes.

"Yet capitalism had an easy time of it compared to marriage. I do not remember that a single play which I heard all year in 47, whether from Harvard or Radcliffe, had a single word of toleration, let alone praise, for marriage."

Professor Baker, explained Broun, was "wise enough to realize that it is impossible that he should furnish or even attempt to mold in any way the philosophy which his students bring into English 47 each year.

"He can't attempt to tell the fledgling playwright what things to say and of course he doesn't," Broun said. "When a man is done with Baker he has begun to grasp some of the things that he must not do in writing a play. With that much ground cleared, all he has to do is acquire a knowledge of life, to devise a plot and find a manager."

Baker by now had decided to introduce an advanced course in playwriting during the 1915-1916 academic year. Designated English 47, it was to consist of only four students — those who had taken Course 47 "with distinction."

Although he had found Eugene a difficult pupil at times, Baker chose him to be one of the four. And Eugene, despite his grumbling about Baker's leniency toward the commercial theater, was flattered to be selected. With no prospect of a New York production, he agreed to return to Harvard the following fall.

His immediate future apparently settled, he planned to spend a blissful summer in New London, combining his reunion with Beatrice with serious playwriting, and also trying again to earn some money writing movie scripts. Euphorically, he wrote to her of his high hopes:

"This summer of Ours . . . will be wonderful; must be! We are going to be very happy, You and I . . . How can we help being happy — even if we dare not the consummation? Our love is greater than mere desire, will prove itself so. You love and trust me? Content you! I will be worthy."

The summer turned out not to be as wonderful as Eugene had anticipated. To begin with, his father was finding it difficult to accept that his acting career — and his earning capacity — were coming close to an end. His outlook was not improved by the realization that his sons, despite all he had done to help them, still could not manage to live on their own.

James did not conceal his fretfulness at home, but kept up a brave front in public. Wishing to spare Ella the burden of housekeeping, he had once again arranged for his family to take their meals at the Packard, and the Rippins, who saw him almost daily, found him as gracious as ever.

James was cheered somewhat in midsummer when he was once again pressed to run for Mayor of New London. But he declined the offer and, in a ringing speech that finally squelched his nominators, declared: "Every politician seeking office aspires to the Presidency of the United States. If I were to enter politics, I should want to make that my goal and I can't be President because I was born in Ireland, God bless it!"

In addition to the pressure of his father's moodiness, Eugene had to contend with an unexpected lack of inspiration. The serious writing he had planned was not going well. The new foray into movie work was also a failure.

Worst of all, soon after he joined his family in the Monte Cristo Cottage, Beatrice fell ill with typhoid and was ordered by her doctor to recuperate quietly at home. Eugene sent her an eight-line poem, "Triolet of My Flower," referring to her as "rose of my heart." The poem was accompanied by three red roses.

Unable to escort her on the sort of ecstatic romps he had cherished the previous summer, Eugene was reduced to faithful visits and the writing of love poems dwelling on his longing: "Your body is warm and undulating/As the sand dunes./Eager with tremulous heat waves/Beneath my kisses/Your passions stretch upward/Their frantic, quivering hands."

Eugene somehow managed not to be cast down by despair. He eased his woes at various saloons in the company of old friends such as Art McGinley and Ed Keefe (and hoped Beatrice would not hear of his lapses).

Further consoling himself, he began a flirtation with a woman named Nina Jones, a student of Clayton Hamilton's spending the summer in the New London area. He had been put in touch with Nina by his Harvard classmate, "Pinky" Elkins. A letter he wrote Elkins in the early summer, thanking him for the introduction, included a somewhat guarded picture of how Eugene was passing the time. He liked Nina Jones very much, he said.

"On short acquaintance she seems to be all kinds of a regular person. It's a delightful treat to meet a girl whose bean is not simply a rendezvous for hair, and who is trying to do something worth while. Most of the God-bless-'ems in this locality have a large To Let sign painted on their more-or-less lofty brows."

Unlikely as it sounds, Eugene evidently toyed with the idea of collaborating with Nina on a play set in the reign of Louis XIII. Very likely the "collaboration" — which came to nothing — was a device to stay in Nina's company, without appearing disloyal to Beatrice. Nina, according to some of Eugene's New London cronies, fell in love with him.

Eugene also found amusement in attending the Yale-Harvard boat race. "I was lucky enough to have two Yale friends of mine as my guests over boat race," he wrote Elkins. Adding that he had "loafed so far," he said he intended "to dig in from now on."

He did work at his chosen craft during part of the summer, but was evidently unhappy with the results. He made notes for several plays and wrote a short piece entitled *Atrocity*, labeled a "pantomime," which he destroyed.

His efforts to sell movie scripts were faithfully documented — one might say over-documented — by the local newspapers. In August, the Day announced Eugene had been engaged as "a writer of scenarios" by the Eastern Film Company of Providence.

The company, reported the Day, had purchased a New Bedford whaling bark, to be anchored in the New London harbor and "used to stage a number of moving picture scenes" in which actors would "do all kinds of stirring deeds from the decks." The Day failed to follow up this report and it is not known how Eugene's venture into filmmaking ended. Not presumably in triumph.

Eugene continued to woo Beatrice as she convalesced, and she, of
course, continued to cling firmly to her chastity. "You grudging,
reluctant female!" he had scolded in one of his letters. And in a poem
entitled "Beyond the Great Divide," he once again rebuked her for
her prim inflexibility:

"We wait! — Love mocks us with sad scornful tears./We wait! —
the wine of life dries in the cup./We wait! — The feast grows cold, we
dare not sup./We wait! — a sickly conscience goads our fears . . . /We
wait! — While Life yawns wearily and sneers . . .

His enslavement was beginning to slacken, however. In addition
to his flirtation with the brainy Nina Jones (if indeed it was nothing
more than that), he could not, for example, resist making mock-love
to Emily Rippin whenever an occasion presented itself. When he was
introduced to her fiancé that summer, he murmured, "Emily, I wish
you'd let me be the father of your second child."

Nonetheless, he did celebrate Beatrice's charms on one occasion
in a very public way. "Speaking, to the Shade of Dante, of Beatrices,"
was published that July 5 in "The Conning Tower," a widely read column in the New York Tribune. The poem was much in the vein of his
earlier New London Telegraph contributions:

> "Lo, even I am Beatrice!"
>   That line keeps singing in my bean.
> I feel the same ecstatic bliss
>   As did the fluent Florentine
> Who heard the well-known hell-flame hiss.
>
> Dante, your damozel was tall
>   And lean and sad — I've seen her face
> On many a best-parlor wall—
>   I don't think she was such an ace.
> She doesn't class with mine at all.
>
> Her eyes were not so large or grey;
>   She had no such heart-teasing smile,
> Or hair so beautiful; and say,
>   I hate to state it, but her style
> Would never get her by today.
>
> I'm not denying that your queen
>   In your eyes may have been a bear.
> You couldn't pull the stuff I've seen
>   About her, if she wasn't there —

That soft poetic bull, I mean.

But just to call your rhythmic bluff
    I'll say, before I ring the bell
And kill this roundelay of fluff,
    Like Dante, I'd go plumtoel
For Beatrice — and that's enough!

The poem's publication caused a considerable stir in New London. Writing in The New Yorker, E. B. White once observed: "There are still plenty of writers alive today who will testify that the high point in their lives was not the first check in the mail from a publication but the first time at the top of the Tower looking down in the morning at the whole city of New York.

"Making the Tower was a dizzy experience. No money changed hands, and this made it unique . . . If you were skilled in French verse forms, you could even make love to your girl in full view of a carload of subway riders who held the right newspaper opened to the right page."

White's article was by way of an obituary for the Tower's originator, Franklin P. Adams, who signed himself "F.P.A." and who, according to White, "gave a young writer three precious gifts: discipline, a sense of gaiety, a brief moment in the sun."

Although Beatrice shared Eugene's moment in the sun, the celebrity was not enough to persuade her to succumb. She knew he had scant hope of having his plays produced in the foreseeable future and, since he refused to work at anything but his writing, there was no way he could support himself — let alone a wife.

Eugene, attributing (or professing to attribute) Beatrice's recalcitrance to the blandishments of her other admirers, wrote her the long-winded and whimsically entitled "Villanelle To His Ladye In Which Ye Poore Scribe Complaineth Sorely Because The Cursed Memory Of The Thousand Others Doth Poison His Dreams Of His Beatrice."

The poem read, in part: "I dream of all your lovers who have wooed/And gained your kiss, and won your subtle smile—/I am but one among a multitude."

Eugene had resigned himself to another nine months' apprenticeship at Harvard, but not to continued residence in Cambridge. He wrote to Daniel Hiebert on September 21, 1915, only a few days before the start of term, that he was coming back "to enter Professor Baker's second year course," but wanted "to locate in Boston this year," because Cambridge was "too darn dead." He asked Hiebert to find him a place to stay temporarily, informing him he would arrive on September 27, "about 2:15 P.M."

Eugene never did arrive.

What prevented his return to Harvard at the last moment is something of a mystery. On September 24, three days after he wrote to Hiebert, the New London Day reported that Eugene had accepted a job as the New York drama critic for a new Cincinnati weekly. Eugene himself later confirmed this in letters and interviews. But he never satisfactorily explained why he abruptly threw away the chance to continue working on his serious writing to take a job for which he surely had neither liking nor aptitude.

Most startling is that Eugene, evidently believing he had the means of spending the next nine months at Harvard, suddenly discovered he did not. Possibly James refused, at the last minute, to furnish an allowance (in addition to his tuition), telling him to find an after-class job to pay his living expenses.

In a letter to Baker four years later, Eugene "explained" why he had "failed to come back."

"I wanted to," he wrote. "It was none of my choice. I just didn't have the money, couldn't get it, and had to take a job as a New York dramatic critic on a new theatrical magazine. Oh, indeed, I wanted to come back!"

Baker was disappointed and later commented that while Eugene knew how to write well in the one-act form, he needed further study. "I was very eager that he should return for a second year of work in these longer forms, but did not know until later that, though equally eager, his means at the moment made this impossible."

When O'Neill later began to show his mettle, Baker not only became his ardent supporter but insisted that he always had been (entirely forgetting his disparagement of Bound East for Cardiff).

"He was a most delightful man to work with," Baker said on one occasion, of his often-sulky ex-pupil. "For he brought me maturity and wide experience. I asked him once whether his preference for grim and depressing subjects was not something of a pose. He replied in the negative, declaring that 'Life looked that way' to him following his experiences before the mast and all parts of the world. You watch him, for there's a great deal of poetry in his soul, although he's only just beginning to show you it's there."

Baker moved his English 47 workshop from Harvard in 1924, when Yale offered to build him the theater Harvard had denied him. With hindsight, O'Neill decided to dislike Harvard: when choosing, in 1942, where to deposit his manuscripts, he snubbed Harvard in favor of Princeton and Yale.

"Perhaps, as a just man, I should have asked Harvard if it wanted any," he wrote to his older son, Eugene Jr., then teaching at Yale "but I'm not a just man where Harvard is concerned (early Princeton influence, perhaps). I just don't like the damned place."

Preparing to depart New London at the end of September, Eugene asked Beatrice once again to elope with him, but she refused. Finally forced to acknowledge that his Bee was not the dauntless bohemian she played at being, he headed alone for New York's Greenwich Village.

Beatrice confided to Emily Rippin that her father was strongly opposed to the match. But in fact, she had already judged for herself that Eugene was a precarious marital prospect. She was not prepared to starve with him while he awaited recognition.

CHAPTER FORTY

"THE CONEY ISLAND OF THE SOUL," WAS HOW THE POET, Maxwell Bodenheim, described the Greenwich Village toward which O'Neill was heading in the fall of 1915.

The Village was a roller coaster of radical ideas, violent soul-searching and monumental egotism. From all over the country came eager young rebels, escaping the aridity of small towns, lured by the promise of freedom from judgmental elders and the rigid social pressures of the Victorian age.

Part slum, part boom town, part Paris Left Bank, the Village had remained a backwater while Manhattan continued to spring skyward and northward. Still fashionable were lower Fifth Avenue and the north side of Washington Square, presided over by Georgian mansions preening their elegant facades in the shadow of Stanford White's grand marble Arch.

On the south side of the Square were a row of low red-brick houses, less pretentious but comfortable, some of them divided into studio apartments. O. Henry had been among the first writers to reside there, although briefly.

In the early 1900's a black slum had taken root a few blocks south of the Square. Many of the old squat brownstones and brick buildings lining the area's erratic tangle of narrow intersecting streets were converted into rooming houses or cut up into small ramshackle flats whose low rents attracted Irish and Italian immigrants. It was not long before the cheap housing became a magnet for the adventurous.

Hungering for self-expression, many came to explore their newly discovered libidos and to pursue their various chimeras of love and art. Emancipated women lived alone or in freewheeling alliances, in sparsely furnished rooms where candles were the sole illumination and a batik mat the only decorative touch.

The new arrivals quickly found each other in musty saloons and cheap cellar restaurants, such as Polly Holladay's, or in the more continental cafés of the Brevoort and Lafayette Hotels, where they argued through the night about such burning issues as how to save humanity and reshape society.

One unchallenged conclusion was that "uptowners," representing middle-class mores and narrow tastes in literature, art and politics, were contemptible. Another universal point of agreement was that having fun was not sinful. If the Villagers, as they called themselves, sometimes sounded self-righteous, exhibitionistic or even slightly unbalanced, they were undeniably alive.

Some had money but few of them worried about it; that would have been bourgeois. Sex was a subject that assumed the nature of "a crusade," according to one Villager, Lawrence Langner, then a twenty-year-old patent expert who had arrived from London in 1910 (and who later became O'Neill's producer).

"When a young man and a young woman decided to live together without benefit of clergy," explained Langner, "it was then called 'free love,' and books and essays and plays were written about it. In fact free love soon became so respectable that no 'modern' young man would go out with a girl who was living with another man, with the result that these lovers were usually thrown on each other's company to such an extent that they became bored to distraction with one another and ultimately got married just in order to have a little more freedom."

Free love was often a topic at the newly celebrated salon in a brownstone at 23 Fifth Avenue, where Mabel Dodge, recently separated from a rich husband, collected the city's acclaimed and notorious.

They included writers, artists and activists: the self-styled "hobo poet," Harry Kemp, who had achieved notoriety in 1911 for attacking marriage as a form of "concubinage" when Upton Sinclair named him as correspondent in his divorce case; the rabble-rousing head of the I.W.W., William ("Big Bill") Haywood; the long-suffering anarchist, Emma Goldman; the iconoclastic novelists Theodore Dreiser and Sinclair Lewis; and the combative journalists, Lincoln Steffens and John Reed (soon to become Mabel's lover).

Mabel, originally from Buffalo, made no claim to beauty or wit but possessed a supreme self-confidence enabling her to infuse others with her enthusiasms — and she had the means to be generous to her friends.

"Her secret, I think," recalled Steffens, "was to start the talk going with a living theme" built around a controversial event currently in the news, which would be hotly debated.

She had gained public notice early in 1913 as an impassioned sponsor of the International Exhibition of Modern Art at the 69th Infantry Regiment Armory.

Including more than thirteen hundred Abstract works — from the Cubism of Braque and Picasso to the Fauvism of Matisse — the Armory Show, as it came to be known, drew outraged reviews from many established critics for its irreverent disregard for traditional rules of art. In fact, it managed to offend nearly everyone — with Duchamp's "Nude Descending a Staircase" provoking the greatest ire.

In her stark-white drawing room, furnished with French and Italian antiques, Mabel encouraged her guests to debate the new art, Freud, radical politics, women's' suffrage, Margaret Sanger's birth-control movement, muckraking journalism and how to keep America out of the war in Europe.

Disregarding the possible consequences to herself, Mabel permitted the I.W.W. agitator, Elizabeth Gurley Flynn, to make plans in her salon for a city-wide waiters' strike. It resulted in a rampage of restaurant and hotel window-smashing, finally subdued by the police.

On one memorable evening, she organized a peyote party by candle light, in a misconceived attempt to recreate an American Indian campfire cult ceremony, during which a number of her guests were stricken with violent hallucinations requiring emergency medical attention.

Among the most vocal Greenwich Villagers in 1914, the year before O'Neill's arrival, was a group of novelists, journalists and artists who had begun searching for ways to express avant-garde ideas in theatrical terms.

Undeterred by their amateurism, they dreamed of challenging the outmoded attitudes of the commercial stage with daring new concepts. It was their lofty ambition to transform the drama into an art form reflecting modern life as they thought it should be lived.

Soon to band together as the Washington Square Players, they weighed the possible means by which serious American writers could establish — away from profit-driven Broadway — a natural, cerebral, intimate theater currently the domain of European play-wrights.

They were aware that theirs was not the first such small-scale experimental stage in America. The "little theater movement," as it was then called, was already manifesting itself in such cities as Baltimore and Detroit and particularly Chicago, where an English director, Maurice Browne, was the guiding spirit of his aptly-named "Little Theater." Chicago was simultaneously giving birth to a liter-ary flowering, led by — among others — Vachel Lindsay, Sherwood Anderson and Carl Sandburg.

In New York, on March 11, 1912 (shortly after O'Neill had desert-ed his father's *Monte Cristo* tour and returned to the city), the pro-ducer, Winthrop Ames, opened his 299-seat Little Theater on Forty-Fourth Street west of Broadway, where he presented experimental full-length plays by both European and American writers that no commercial manager would have dreamed of mounting.

It was a year later — March 14, 1913 — that the actor, Holbrook Blinn, inaugurated his Princess Theater on West Thirty-Ninth Street. Blinn presented exclusively one-act plays, also deemed unfit for Broadway (but evidently regarded O'Neill's submissions as *too* dar-ing). The future Washington Square Players, like Blinn, seized on the one-act play as their medium, but were determined to go well beyond Blinn in choice of subject.

The event that catapulted the Washington Square Players into being can be traced to an evening in 1914 at the Liberal Club. With the motto, "A Meeting Place for Those Interested in New Ideas," the club, occupying the first floor of a Macdougal Street brownstone, had high ceilings and large open fireplaces and was a home away from home for the likes of Edna St. Vincent Millay and Upton Sinclair.

Among the charter members who prided themselves on their advanced beliefs was the passionately pro-labor journalist, Hutchins Hapgood, who later resigned when Emma Goldman was black-balled; the club, he felt, had failed the test of "liberality."

Members met to converse and, as often as not, to dance to the tunes of an ancient player piano — for their interest in New Ideas extended to the craze for such risqué ragtime steps as the Bunny Hug and the Grizzly Bear.

One day, returning to the Liberal Club after dining at the Brevoort, several members began to consider the possibility of rent-ing a theater, wondering where they might find an affordable down-town space. Albert Boni, who with his brother Charles had recently opened the Washington Square Book Shop next door to the Liberal Club, argued that a stage was not necessary for the presentation of plays.

The matter was resolved by Robert Edmond Jones, a club member with some recently acquired experience in the professional theatre. Jones (later to design some of O'Neill's major plays) had attended Harvard with Albert Boni and was just back from Germany, where he had studied stage design and witnessed the work of the master director, Max Reinhardt. Jones's presence alone — tall, red-haired and bearded — gave him an air of authority.

"Do you have to have a stage to put on a play, Bobby?" asked Boni.

"Of course not," answered Jones. "You can put on a play right here."

An adjoining wall of the Liberal Club had recently been broken through to allow members easier access to the book shop, which was becoming as much a social center as a commercial enterprise. Lawrence Langner and Edward Goodman, a free-lance journalist infatuated with the theater, suggested staging a production then and there.

Since the Boni brothers sold only books they deemed literary — D. H. Lawrence's *Sons and Lovers* was one of their best-sellers — they did not have hordes of customers, and nothing stood in the way of the impromptu performance.

The shop consisted of two large rooms, each thirty feet square, with ceilings fourteen feet high. They were divided by sliding mahogany doors, whose frames, Jones decreed, would serve as the proscenium. *The Glittering Gate*, by Lord Dunsany, an Irish writer known for his one-act parables, was selected as the vehicle because of its brevity and the presence of several copies of the play on the shop's shelves.

The only two roles — two dead Cockney burglars tying to enter Heaven — were quickly cast from among the group's members and Bobby Jones improvised a pair of columns with ten feet of wrapping paper to represent the Glittering Gate. Read by the actors from the text, the playlet was forthwith performed.

Jones may have proved his point, but the pleased participants still felt they needed a real theater, and they began to search in earnest. It was then they christened themselves the Washington Square Players and appointed Langner and Boni as business managers.

Goodman was designated the director because of his recent experience in writing, directing and producing experimental one-acters in partnership with another young Villager, Philip Moeller, for the Socialist Press Club.

Designated as leading lady was Ida Rauh, who, after receiving a law degree from New York University in 1905, had foregone a practice in favor of an acting career. An outspoken feminist, she kept her maiden name after her marriage in 1911 to the boyishly handsome Max Eastman. Like many of the radicals of that period, Eastman was a restless romantic, and Ida Rauh was but one in a series of wives and mistresses who floated through his life.

The son of two Congregational ministers from upstate New York, Eastman had taught philosophy at Columbia University before becoming the editor of the lusty antiestablishment magazine, The Masses. Theoretically run as a cooperative venture, the magazine published contributions from Carl Sandburg, Sherwood Anderson, Amy Lowell, Alice Duer Miller, Bertrand Russell, Maxim Gorky and Vachel Lindsay, none of whom were paid or expected to be.

"Nobody is trying to make money out of it," Eastman stated in a masthead credo. "A revolutionary and not a reform magazine; a magazine with a sense of humor and no respect for the respectable . . . a magazine directed against rigidity and dogma . . . printing what is too naked or true for a money-making press; a magazine whose final policy is to do as it pleases and conciliate nobody . . . "

The Washington Square Players were equally cocky about their aims. "We've got to assert the rights of the human soul," said Philip Moeller (later to direct several of O'Neill's major plays). "The American theatre has no place for the subtler nuances of drama. The whole system is wrong. The acting is mechanical, the production lifeless and the scenery . . . positively mid-Victorian. The trouble is that the whole system is commercial. The American theatre is aiming at nothing but the dollar."

In their manifesto, the Players declared preference would be given to American plays, but that they would also produce "the works of well-known European authors which have been ignored by the commercial managers."

On the day the group became a corporate body — although still lacking a theater — the writer, Hiram Kelly Moderwell, of Theater Magazine, interviewed several Players in the back room of the Washington Square Book Shop.

"The American theater, as it exists today, is all wrong," Edward Goodman told him. "There's just one thing to do — sweep the whole system away and begin all over. That's what we intend to do."

Langner, while not disputing Goodman, had more mundane things on his mind. "I wish I could find another subscriber," he said. "That would make six."

The Players devoted the next few months to soliciting subscriptions, in competition with the Neighborhood Playhouse, another little theater preparing to open on February 12 on the Lower East Side's Grand Street. Langner and his colleagues, having raised the money, but unable to find suitable space in Washington Square, settled for a small, reasonably priced theater uptown.

On February 19, 1915 (with O'Neill still at Harvard dreaming of future production), they presented their first bill to a sold-out audience at the Bandbox Theatre, on Fifty-seventh Street near Third Avenue.

It was a catholic mixture of one-act plays: *Interior*, in rhymed dialogue, by the Belgian poet, Maurice Maeterlinck; *Licensed*, by Langner (writing as Basil Lawrence, so as not to embarrass his associates in the legal world), dealing with an unmarried pregnant woman's plea for birth control; Edward Goodman's *Eugenically Speaking*, about a woman so intent on following Shaw's ideas about mating that she picks up a brawny streetcar conductor and invites him home. The final work was a satirical pantomime entitled *Another Interior*, in which the cast represented various foods entering a man's stomach.

The following morning the Tribune, the Herald and The Times glowed with praise. The Times was singularly prescient in predicting a successful future for the Washington Square Players which, only four years later, evolved into the Theater Guild, one of Broadway's most enduring and powerful producing companies for more than three decades.

Long before then, however, concern with success appeared to have shunted aside the Players' dedication to experiment — as Hiram Moderwell discovered on a return visit in 1917.

Finally gaining access to Goodman — now ensconced in a suite of offices on Forty-first Street — Moderwell was told that if he wished to learn about the Players' current activities he would have to see a Mr. Pennington about "the technical work," and a Mr. Lawson and Philip Moeller about "the scenery and production." All three, however, would be unavailable for some time because of their demanding schedules.

Goodman consented to make a brief statement about the company's "general aims and ideal" that illustrated how far it had departed from its original inspiration.

"We view with alarm the growing tendency of half-baked amateurs to usurp the field properly belonging to the trained professional," he said, evidently without a trace of irony. "They suppose that
what they call inspiration will take the place of years of practical
experience behind the footlights . . . I notice that there is still another
company starting up in Greenwich Village, where most of these
crackbrained schemes originate. Its directors complain that the
American theater is becoming commercial. Commercial! They forget
that every good theater is a commercial theater. There is just one test
of excellence in dramatic art — the box office!"

Langner, meeting Moderwell on his way out, confided he was
"trying to think of a scheme for keeping our subscription list to the
really nice people. It doesn't look right to have those Greenwich
Village nuts overrunning the place. It makes us look as though we
were just one of those amateur art theaters."

Among those who created the Washington Square Players and soon
to have an epiphanous effect on O'Neill's life, was George Cram
Cook. Forty-two years old, six feet tall and powerfully built, he had
enormous vitality and a contagious enthusiasm for history and the
arts. Originally from Davenport, Iowa, he was a Greek scholar and
writer; an admirer of Thoreau, he had been at various times a truck
farmer and a college English instructor.

After writing *The Chasm*, a novel propounding his socialistic philosophy, he was invited in 1912 by his friend Floyd Dell to be associate editor on the influential Friday Literary Supplement of the
Chicago Evening Post. Cook quickly became part of Chicago's explo-
sive avant-garde movement

He and Dell had met in 1907 when both were members of the
Davenport Monist Society, a group of "freethinkers" dedicated to
resisting the conventions and traditions of the era. Dell, in his twenties, was tall and slender with a broad forehead and pointed chin and
wore long sideburns. An avowed socialist since the age of fourteen,
he wanted to write novels and plays and it was not long before he left
Chicago for Greenwich Village.

By the spring of 1913, Cook himself lost interest in the Evening
Post and he, too, departed for the Village. But his main reason for
leaving was to rejoin the writer, Susan Glaspell, his lover of the past
five years. Having finally divorced his second wife, he married

Glaspell soon after his arrival in New York and they moved into a flat in Milligan Place.

Glaspell, in her late thirties, professed to be only thirty-one. She was a delicate, sad-eyed, witty woman who had been a reporter in Davenport, lived for a year in Paris and had published two novels and a collection of short stories. Along with Cook and Dell, she had been a member of the Davenport Monist Society.

Private and reclusive — Cook's diametric opposite in personality — Glaspell possessed a steely steadiness inherited from the pioneering women who had settled the Iowa prairies. Cook had quickly learned to lean on her quiet strength.

Cook, on the other hand, was flamboyant and volatile; as Glaspell once fondly described him, he had "a great shock of blue-white hair, pointing to a widow's peak above a clean line of very black eyebrows," and was "a passionate, gentle person" with "a big laugh." Susan worshipfully devoted herself in equal measure to him and to her writing; it was she who provided the backbone of their income.

Although not himself a writer of the first rank, Cook possessed a knack for sensing literary quality in others, and he knew how to stimulate their talent. Erudite and mystical, Cook, ubiquitously known as "Jig," regretted not having been born a Greek of the Fourth Century. He yearned for nothing less than to recreate the Athenian cradle of art and philosophy, and devoted his life to an ultimately futile effort to impose this fantasy on his surroundings.

Initially supporting the aims of the Washington Square Players, Cook continued to dream of a more idealistic theatre, existing solely for the expression of native American creativity, and inspiring the emergence of such talent: "a threshing floor," as he phrased it, "on which a young and growing culture could find its voice." Like O'Neill, he had been fired by the Irish Players during their 1909 tour of the United States.

He soon grew disillusioned with the Washington Square Players, maintaining that, despite the stated loftiness of their aims, they were not experimental enough. No small part of his disappointment stemmed from the Players' rejection of *Suppressed Desires*, whose authors happened to be himself and his wife.

The playlet satirized the craze among intellectuals for the emerging practice of psychoanalysis and poked fun at a married woman's obsession with her analyst's pedantic interpretations of Freudian theory.

The woman, Henrietta Brewster, insists that both her husband,

Stephen, and her younger sister, Mabel, visit the analyst. But when the analyst deduces that not only does Stephen unconsciously wish to leave his wife but that Mabel has a suppressed desire for Stephen, Henrietta's faith in psychoanalysis is shattered.

The Washington Square Players pronounced the play too much of a departure, asserting that Freud was as yet too little known — a stand disputed by Susan, who declared, "You could not go out to buy a bun without hearing of someone's complex." After staging the play for a one-night performance at the The Liberal Club on March 15, Jig, with Susan's concurrence, decided to break away from the Washington Square Players and attempt to establish a theater representative of his own quixotic view of what American drama should be. He imagined this theater as his "dream city."

"Why not write our own plays," he said, "and put them on ourselves, giving writer, actor, designer, a chance to work together, without the commercial thing imposed from without? A whole community working together, developing unsuspected talents. The city ought to furnish the kind of audience that will cause new plays to be written."

Cook had only the vaguest notion of how to summon his "dream city" into being. But before leaving New York that summer of 1915 for his vacation, he importuned all his friends to express their avant-garde ideas in the form of one-act plays that could be quickly completed.

Provincetown, where the Cooks had been vacationing since 1913, was a fishing settlement in Massachusetts, at the tip of Cape Cod. While its population had begun to fatten during the summer with writers and painters as well as tourists, it was relatively unspoiled.

The town prided itself on its whaling tradition and its place in American history as the first landfall of the Mayflower Pilgrims, who anchored in the harbor for five weeks during the winter of 1620 before sailing on to Plymouth. During four walking explorations in the mid-1800's, Henry David Thoreau savored Provincetown's natural beauty, later bringing it to the attention of the literary elite in his lectures and essays (and still later in his book, *Cape Cod*, posthumously published in 1865).

Among the Cape's devoted vacationers, beginning in the 1880's, were the touring stars of James O'Neill's generation. Lawrence Barrett and Joseph Jefferson built cottages there — the former in

Cohasset and the latter in Buzzard's Bay. They were visited by Edwin Booth and other actors, who later bought or rented properties in various communities up and down the Cape.

In the Provincetown that Eugene O'Neill was soon to call home, fishermen's houses, their wharves jutting into the bay, hugged the western edge of Commercial Street, the narrow thoroughfare that paralleled the harbor.

Further east were clustered a scattering of rooming houses, shops and unpretentious eateries, including Polly Holladay's, transposed for the summer from Washington Square to Commercial Street. The town's only other street, Bradford, was on the ocean side, but separated from the Atlantic by a mile and a half of towering dunes and scrub grass; Bradford and Commercial were connected by a maze of alleyways.

Provincetown's stable population was divided into three groups: descendants of the first Puritan arrivals; families of early Portuguese settlers; and "outsiders" — year-round residents like the doctor, shopkeepers and a sprinkling of artists and writers.

In 1899, the town had been claimed as an artists' colony by the painter, Charles Webster Hawthorne. Enchanted by the clear northern light, he established the Cape Cod School of Art, extolling the locale in advertisements as a "jumble of color in the intense sunlight, accentuated by the brilliant blue of the harbor."

After the painters came the writers. Among the first, in 1906, was Viola Roseboro, who liked to shock acquaintances by smoking in public. A novelist and chief literary editor of McClure's, she guided the careers of O. Henry and Willa Cather and was largely responsible for making McClure's a foremost literary magazine.

Known for the brilliant women editors and reporters on its staff, McClure's was also America's most influential muckraking publication, having aroused the country with Ida Tarbell's exposé of the Standard Oil monopoly and Lincoln Steffens's probes of big-city government corruption.

Two of Roseboro's writers at McClure's, Albert Vorse and his wife, Mary Heaton Vorse, arrived in Provincetown from New York with their children a year later, in search of a distant refuge. They bought an old whaling captain's house that they converted into a permanent residence and, having brought with them their freewheeling mores, they soon turned Provincetown into a Greenwich Village-by-the-sea.

Albert was a less successful writer than his wife, and it was she

A Charles Ellis painting depicts members of the Provincetown Players (from top left, clockwise): James Light, Christine Ell, "Jig" Cook, O'Neill, Charles Collins.

Emerging Playwright

Although O'Neill wrote steadily after he left Gaylord Sanatarium, he went unproduced until "discovered" in 1916 by George Cram ("Jig") Cook and his circle of enlightened artists.

John Reed, the journalist, urged O'Neill to join the new theater group in Provincetown, Massachusetts, where O'Neill won his first hearing with *Bound East for Cardiff*.

Emma Goldman, the anarchist admired by O'Neill, was part-model for the betrayed mother in *The Iceman Cometh*, set in 1912.

Terry Carlin was for some years O'Neill's mentor in nihilism and inspired the major character, Larry Slade, in *The Iceman Cometh*.

Clarence Darrow (right), who defended labor leader James B. McNamara in the Los Angeles murder case that figures in *The Iceman Cometh*.

Fisherman's shack in Provincetown that became the Wharf Theater, summer of 1915.

Contemporary Provincetown scene, painted by Bror Nordfeldt, a member of the Provincetown Players.

"Jig" Cook, godfather of the Provincetown Players, and his wife, the author Susan Glaspell, who wrote almost as many experimental plays for the group as O'Neill.

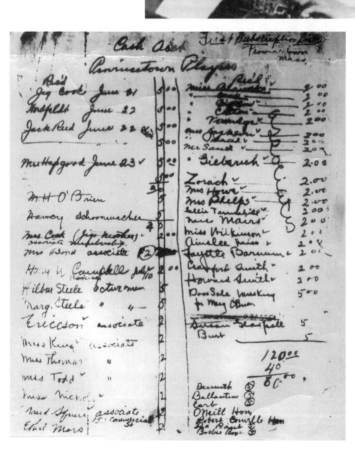

Provincetown Players' list of charter members. So broke he could not pay the minimum initiation fee, O'Neill (fourth from bottom) was given honorary status.

O'Neill in Provincetown, 1916. He fell in love with Louise Bryant, then living with John Reed (and soon to marry him). Their triangle was the talk of the village.

Provincetown, 1916. First row: Susan Glaspell, Beatrix Hapgood, Mary Vorse (owner of the fishing shack that became the Wharf Theater), Hippolyte Havel (model for Hugo Kalmar in *The Iceman Cometh*). Second row: Harry Weinberger (later O'Neill's lawyer), Hutchins Hapgood, the journalist and memoirist, and his older daughter, Miriam.

A gallery of persons who populated O'Neill's world during the years he was establishing himself as a playwright. Left, top to bottom: Mabel Dodge, Neith Boyce, William and Marguerite Zorach with baby and Harry Kemp.

Right, top to bottom: H. L. Mencken with George Jean Nathan, Max Eastman and his wife, Ida Rauh, Edward Goodman and Floyd Dell.

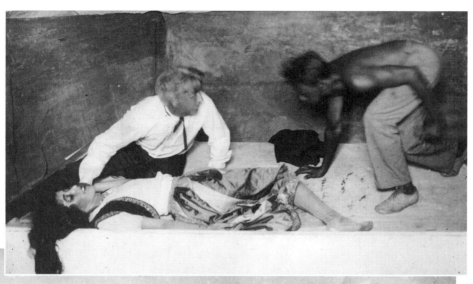

Above, a scene from *Thirst*, written in 1913 and produced in Provincetown in 1916 with Louise Bryant, "Jig" Cook and O'Neill (playing a "mulatto" sailor). Louise sent the nude photo of herself to Reed while he was away.

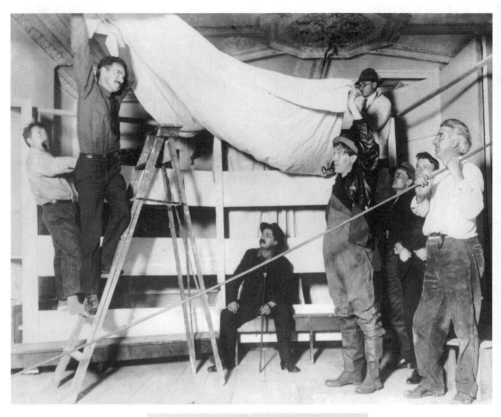

Preparing O'Neill's first New York production, *Bound East for Cardiff*, which opened November 3, 1916 at the Playwrights' Theater. O'Neill on ladder, Hippolyte Havel seated, "Jig" Cook at far right.

James O'Neill in *The Wanderer*, a biblical spectacle about the prodigal son, in which James, now seventy-one, played Jesse, the prodigal's father. It was his final role.

who provided the family's basic support. In 1908, Mary Vorse caught Albert among the dunes with the unmarried and predatory Viola Roseboro.

Mary Vorse left her husband — but not Provincetown — and retaliated by having an affair with the somewhat younger Wilbur Daniel Steele, a short-story writer from North Carolina whose career she was nurturing. The two remained friends after the affair ended in 1913, when Vorse married a reporter named Joe O'Brien and Steele married Margaret Thurston, a painter.

Among Vorse's recently arrived friends were the writer, Hutchins Hapgood, and his wife, Neith Boyce, a novelist. A self-styled "New Woman," Boyce continued to pursue her career after her marriage, retaining her maiden name. Like many — perhaps most — of her friends, she was married to a man who regarded fidelity as bourgeois and was flagrantly unfaithful.

Hapgood, in theory, was prepared to accord his wife the same freedom. But like the majority of his male contemporaries, he smugly relied on the greater psychological and practical difficulty for a married woman — especially one with children — to have affairs.

Balancing femininity, professional identity and attentive motherhood, Neith Boyce had little leeway for liaisons. Much as she, Mary Vorse, Susan Glaspell and their friends in the early 1900's vigorously denied the double-standard, it was not easily theorized away.

By the summer of 1915, Provincetown's ranks were swelled by American expatriates forced home from Europe at the outbreak of the war. From Boston they arrived by boat (the Dorothy Bradford, named for a Mayflower passenger who drowned in Provincetown Harbor soon after the ship anchored).

Whereas the trip from Boston took only three hours, the journey from New York was more roundabout, entailing overnight passage on a steamship that landed in Fall River, Massachusetts, where the traveler boarded a train to Middleboro, changing to another train for the snail-like final leg of the journey.

That summer, Jig Cook took a first step toward the realization of his "dream city." At ten o'clock on the night of July 15, he and Bobby Jones mounted *Suppressed Desires* on an improvised stage and with makeshift scenery in the home of the Hapgoods.

A curtain-raiser called *Constancy* was offered by Neith Boyce, who had begun writing plays the previous winter. She based it on the issue of fidelity that preoccupied her and her friends — in this instance the clamorous affair between Mabel Dodge and John Reed.

While Mabel herself was by no means an advocate of monogamy, she had reacted with violent jealousy to Reed's philandering during the past winter, providing Greenwich Village with some of its juiciest gossip.

In *Constancy*, the Mabel character, called Moira, has the last word. When the Reed character, Rex, returns to her after his most recent affair, confident of being again forgiven, she lets him know he has erred once too often. Informing him she no longer loves him, she calmly dismisses him.

Reed, who had spent part of the previous summer in Provincetown with Mabel, was now in Eastern Europe covering the war for both the Metropolitan magazine and the World, and Mabel had found a new lover, the painter, Maurice Sterne.

Jones sat the audience, made up of the Hapgoods' close friends, in the living room facing the wide seaside veranda. Neith, strikingly attractive with her auburn hair and green eyes, acted the role of Moira. Joe O'Brien, universally loved despite his chronic alcoholism, played Rex with some difficulty. (He fell ill during the summer and died that October.)

Behind the backs of the audience, Jones set the stage for *Suppressed Desires* and, when *Constancy* was over, the audience turned its chairs to face an alcoved room representing a studio in Washington Square, the setting for the Glaspell-Cook play, in which Susan and Jig played the wife and husband.

This casual double bill came to be revered as the birth of the Provincetown Players (the name they adopted formally the following year).

Stimulated by the success of their experiment, the Cooks, the Hapgoods and several other friends commandeered an old fish house at the end of a tumbledown, hundred-foot-long dock known as Lewis Wharf, purchased that July by Mary Vorse. Used occasionally as an artist's studio, the fish house was little more than a two-story shell perched on pilings. Jig and his friends set to work cleaning it up, dragging out the boats and nets and transforming it into a theater.

A five-dollar contribution by each of the thirty members provided for tools and equipment. Cook, who loved working with his hands, helped build the stage, with tin reflector-backed lanterns serving as footlights. At high tide the bay could be seen and heard and smelled through cracks in the ancient floor planking.

The miniature stage, only ten by twelve feet, was sectional and could be rolled several feet through the wide door that formed the theater's rear wall, providing an effect of distance. It was through this door, and another that faced west, that fishermen not too long since had hurled their catch of mackerel and cod.

When both doors were open, a realistic sea-backdrop was exposed that no producer could have bettered: the vast bay, dotted with blinking lights of passing vessels, and swept by the lighthouse beacon across the harbor.

Christened the Wharf Theater, Jig saw it, crude as it was, as the "shining object" on which artistic native drama could make its long-delayed arrival.

Publicly introducing their first season in late August, the troupe presented *Constancy* and *Suppressed Desires* and added two more short pieces: a satire by Cook called *Change Your Style*, which debated, with somewhat forced humor, the merits of Post-Impressionism as opposed to the scorned academic school of art.

Another character like Mabel Dodge, a rich eccentric named Myrtle Dart, made an appearance in the play ("in East Indian robe and turban") to buy and then return a Cubist painting by a character called Marmaduke Marvin, Jr. The real-life painters Charles Demuth and Bror Nordfeldt performed in this essentially trivial one-acter.

A parable called *Contemporaries*, by Wilbur Daniel Steele, rounded out the bill. Subtitled "An Episode of the Church Raids," it was inspired by the plight of the homeless men who sought refuge in New York's churches during a period of severe unemployment in the winter of 1914. It attempted to draw a parallel between the police intimidation of a radical labor leader who took up their cause, and the harassment of Jesus of Nazareth. The most serious-minded of the four playlets, it evidently impressed its audience despite a clumsiness of construction and dialogue.

There was not enough lumber on hand in Provincetown to build seats that first season, and patrons were obliged to carry their own chairs to and from the theater. They also had to carry umbrellas on opening night, against a heavy rainfall — which, at least, safeguarded them from fire, a constant threat.

During most performances, Mary Vorse recalled, "Four people stood in the wings with lamps in their hands to light the stage," and four more "stood beside the lamp bearers with shovels and sand in case of fire." Despite the primitive conditions, the opening bill received robust applause.

Returning to New York that fall, the triumphant Provincetowners thought longingly of their theater on the wharf and of the native drama they were trying to fan into existence. Inexperienced as they were as playwrights, actors and producers, they nonetheless made ambitious plans for the following summer's programs.

They were not to adhere to any precepts of the Broadway theater, which, Cook reaffirmed, existed solely as a money-making enterprise. They were to stumble and blunder and grope their way toward a native dramatic art. It was precisely their unfamiliarity with the conventional dramatic form that, in Cook's opinion, suited them to be pioneers on his threshing floor.

Entranced by the concept, Cook's friends warmed to the adventure ahead.

CHAPTER
FORTY-ONE

DURING THE NEXT TEN MONTHS IN NEW YORK, O'NEILL slowly sank into the kind of drunken dereliction that had defined the years before his "rebirth" in the tuberculosis sanatorium. For the second time in his life he was overwhelmed by the "great down-and-outness" he described in "Tomorrow."

O'Neill never explained what set him adrift again, any more than he fully explained why he failed to return to Harvard for a second year.

Between October 1915, and July 1916, he stopped writing plays — although he did write some poetry out of a habit that no amount of despair could ever break.

If he wrote letters to anyone during this interval they have not surfaced. In later correspondence (notably a long letter in the summer of 1916 to Beatrice Ashe) and in his recollections for later interviews, he touched glancingly upon aspects of those ten months. However, it is primarily through the memories of persons who encountered him in New York that this abject period can be reconstructed.

The abrupt way he suppressed the high-minded, fervid creator of the past three years suggests a defiant and childish fury: toward Beatrice, who did not love him enough to throw in her lot with him; toward the producers who would not take a chance on his work; and, most especially, toward his father, who had lost faith in him as a playwright.

That winter, in a possible rebuke to his drifting younger son, James espoused a romantic comedy called *Melody of Youth* by Brandon Tynan, to whom he openly referred as "my son." James volunteered to appear for a brief period in the twenty-line role of a blind Irish beggar without salary. In a letter made public by George Tyler, the play's co-producer, James wrote that he did not care how small the part was. "As one of the older generation of players," he stated, "I want to make a little offering to one of the most promising representatives of the younger generation."

As if this pronouncement was not wounding enough to Eugene, James characterized *Melody of Youth* as "my son's play" — a reference that likely reached Eugene's ears. It was hardly surprising, in view of his true son's disdain, that James should clutch at Tynan's proffered affection. Nor was it remarkable that the enmity between father and son accelerated.

O'Neill's deterioration was gradual. At first, he must have felt some sense of uplift amidst the cultural awakening in Greenwich Village, where the voice of the individual was encouraged — no matter how rebellious or outlandish.

Acquainted with the Village from earlier forays with Louis Holladay, he found a room on the second floor of a boardinghouse at 38 Washington Square West, the block adjoining Macdougal Street, where the Liberal Club was situated.

His rent was four dollars and fifty cents a week, "breakfast included," and his token salary from the magazine that had hired him as a dramatic critic presumably kept him in food and liquor for the next three months. Whether he was asked to write any trial reviews is not known; the magazine, as he later told Professor Baker, "never got beyond the promotion stage."

Undoubtedly aware of the theatrical ferment surrounding him, he felt shut out from it, having tried again and again to find a producer who would take a chance on his work. Not even the Washington Square Players, in their search for new scripts, would accept his plays. According to Edward Goodman, all the plays in the *Thirst* collection, as well as *Bound East for Cardiff*, were rejected.

Simmering over his failure to achieve production, he attempted to make a reputation as a poet. He submitted work that he described as "free verse" to Poetry magazine, The Little Review and the Masses, as well as to such lesser-known radical publications as Blast and The Flame. He later claimed to have done some writing for a new anarchist weekly, Revolt, helping to "get the paper out every week," until it was closed down after three months by Federal agents. "We all narrowly escaped getting a bit to do in the Federal pen," he recalled.

Although he shied away from those working in the experimental theater community, he did not lack for friends upon arriving in the Village. If his later report to Beatrice Ashe is to be credited, he was "a fixture there," who "knew everyone and was popular, if I do bouquet myself."

He found his friends, in his own words, "principally among Radicals of the Labor movement — I.W.W's and the Anarchist group. Also among the true native villagers — the Negro & Italian inhabitants of the quarter."

His closest friends were Louis Holladay and his sister, Polly, at whose cellar café beneath the Liberal Club he idled away much of his time, as well as in the café and bar Louis himself had recently opened in the cellar of 60 Washington Square South and dubbed the Sixty.

The cash for Holladay's venture was furnished by an alluring young woman named Louise Norton, as generous with her affections as with her money. Louis was in love with her but, as a free spirit, she would not commit herself, partly because she disapproved of his drinking.

At the Sixty, O'Neill, whose boardinghouse was nearby, was welcome to eat and drink on the cuff. Louis's cook was Christine Ell who, like Polly Holladay, was a prominent presence in the life of Village bohemia. An intimate of Polly, she too had run a small restaurant in Provincetown the previous summer, called The Oaks, on Bradford Street.

It was Christine who very probably suggested, at least in part, the character of the pure-hearted Josie Hogan, "so oversize she is almost a freak" but nonetheless "all woman," as O'Neill described her in *A Moon for the Misbegotten* some thirty years later. There are also elements of her personality and history in *"Anna Christie,"* and she was undoubtedly in O'Neill's mind when he drew the Mother Earth prostitute, Cybel, in *The Great God Brown.*

Although not Irish, Christine was, like Josie Hogan, a large woman — five feet nine inches tall, wide-hipped and big-breasted. Charles Demuth, Bror Nordfeldt and other artists painted her green-eyed, leonine face and thick, shining, untidy tawny hair. They tried to capture the quality of pain and love that lay under the surface of her bawdy smile. She was self-conscious of her bulk and made fun of herself. Also like Josie, she was convinced she was basically unattractive to men.

The illegitimate child of a Danish peasant woman and a Danish Army captain, she had been brought to America by her mother and stepfather and forced into domestic service and then into factory work. At fourteen she was seduced by her stepfather and, soon after, broke away from her family and began to have casual love affairs.

Christine believed herself an outcast until the day she chanced to hear Emma Goldman speak in Denver on society's responsibility for the abandonment of women of her class. Christine discovered that in espousing the concept of anarchy she could find the self-respect and dignity that had eluded her.

In New York, Christine married a carpenter named Lewis B. Ell to whom she was joylessly unfaithful. He alternated between moods of murderous jealousy and abject forgiveness. To Hutchins Hapgood, who first met Christine in Provincetown, she confided she was miserably unhappy. She hated herself for the way she treated Lewis, she said.

"Why is it that I must act as I do?" she asked Hapgood, weeping. "I long to have a perfect lover, one that satisfies me. Louis [sic] doesn't know how to express himself to me. If all goes well he is quiet, never says anything, and doesn't go out with me to the theaters or our parties. It is only when he is jealous that he can express himself, and I want him to be near me all the time and he cannot be. When I see how far away he is I cannot stand it. I try to console myself with other men, but Louis is always there in my thought, standing between me and them and making it impossible for me to realize the dream of my life, of an utter sympathy with some man. So I hurt him all the time, yet I know too that I help and stimulate him, that through me life is richer and more interesting to him."

The police closed down Louis Holladay's Sixty after only a few months because he had absentmindedly failed to obtain a liquor license. Christine then assisted Polly in her restaurant for a time and, later with her husband, she opened the first of her own small Village eating places. O'Neill followed her there, but he was in truth more interested in drinking than in eating.

It was Holladay who led O'Neill to a saloon that became one of the few places where he found himself completely at home. Formally known as "The Golden Swan," nicknamed the Hell Hole by its clientele, it became O'Neill's haunt for the next several years and was to form part of the composite setting for *The Iceman Cometh*. John Sloan and Charles Demuth were among the artists who painted its seedily picturesque interior.

Like any Irish saloon in any run-down neighborhood, the Hell Hole was filled with the smell of sour beer and the mingled cries of alcoholic woe and raucous laughter. Furnished with rude wooden tables and benches, its floor was covered with sawdust. The barroom — or "front room," in which women were not allowed — was entered from the corner of Sixth Avenue and Fourth Street. Above the doorway swung a wooden sign decorated with a tarnished, life-size gilt swan.

A few feet to the east was the "family entrance," a glass door that gave access to a small, dank, gaslit chamber known as the "back-room," whose tables clustered around a smoking potbellied stove. It was here that neighborhood wives and widows gathered to cry into their five-cent mugs of beer.

Between front and back rooms a stairway led to the gloomy region above, where the proprietor, an ex-prizefighter named Tom Wallace, lived and rented out rooms. Renamed Harry Hope in *The Iceman Cometh*, Wallace was large, lugubrious and clean-shaven. He was never seen to go outdoors, but every evening he emerged from his upstairs quarters to join his regular customers in the front room in shot after shot of five-cent whiskey.

For O'Neill, the Hell Hole must have stirred memories of Jimmy the Priest's, memories he perversely cherished. Here at the Hell Hole he could share the boozy pipe dreams of men every bit as dazed and deprived as the denizens of the old Fulton Street saloon where he had made his half-hearted attempt at suicide.

It was only in "the religious and Christlike security of the very bottom" that he could feel "free and himself," observed his friend, Elizabeth Sergeant, commenting on O'Neill's withdrawal into the Hell Hole's grim protectiveness. And what he found there was "tragedy, naked suffering reality [and] insight into the lives of the underdogs of the earth."

Saloon life was in O'Neill's blood, a heritage from his father and brother; the saloon was his home away from home — in New York, New London, Buenos Aires, Liverpool — wherever his wanderings took him. His attachment to the barroom is reflected in scenes from his plays, beginning with *The Long Voyage Home* and followed by *"Anna Christie," The Great God Brown* and *Ah,Wilderness!*; the barroom was central to his creativity until the end of his career and he set the action of two of his final plays — *A Touch of the Poet* and, of course, *The Iceman Cometh* — in saloons.

Of all the saloons he haunted with his Village friends, the Hell Hole lived longest in his mind. Mary Heaton Vorse once tried to explain its strange appeal for the young artists and writers like her-self who were to join O'Neill there soon after he became an habitué.

"Every night it happened that Wallace and his aged cronies fought and got tight together," she once wrote, recalling that their querulous roars could be clearly heard from the back room.

"Then, just before closing time they staggered off to bed, each man having been presented with a half pint of whiskey to sober up on the next day . . . Each man went to sleep with the knowledge that a pick-me-up was under his pillow. The gangsters, the truck drivers, the outsiders like ourselves were only an obligato to the Gargantuan drama of Wallace and his friends, their nightly wassailing and the clamor of their fights . . .

"The day of the Hell Hole got under full swing around 5 in the afternoon. Officially it closed at 2 in the morning, Wallace and his barkeeps cursing each other off to bed while Lefty Louis and John Bull tumbled the drunks out onto the pavement. If a few quiet people were finishing their beer in the back room they could stay."

Vorse sensed something menacing in the Hell Hole's atmosphere. "Something at once alive and deadly," as she put it long before O'Neill conceived of Hickey, the salesman of death in *The Iceman Cometh*.

"In spite of the Rabelaisian quality of Wallace and his companions the Hell Hole was sinister. It was as if the combined soul of New York flowed underground and this was one of its vents. Truly it was a hell hole and that was the fascination for Gene as well as the rest of us from a different world."

Members of a tough Irish street gang, the Hudson Dusters, were often found in the Hell Hole, as were anarchists (recently out of jail or on their way in), deposed politicians, gamblers, touts, pimps and "'hard' ladies of the oldest profession," as O'Neill once described them.

Order was maintained by Lefty Louie, who disliked women in saloons because, he insisted, they "brought trouble and police." He became Rocky Pioggi in *The Iceman Cometh*, while John Bull, his ham-fisted assistant, became Chuck Morello. Attached to the clouded barroom mirror was a portrait of Richard Croker, the Tammany Hall boss who had single-handedly controlled the politics of the city. Wallace, his longtime friend, embellished his portrait with crossed shillelaghs and a wreath of encircling shamrocks.

The mirror reflected shelves lined with plates of food; like most saloons of the era, the Hell Hole served free lunch to its drinking customers — and sometimes, inadvertently, to the neighborhood children who roller-skated through its swinging barroom doors, grabbing a fistful of food and skating out through the family entrance. Wallace would thrust his head out an upstairs window, shouting abuses.

Mounted on a wall alongside a grandfather clock in the back room was a glass case containing a bedraggled stuffed swan "floating" on gilded wooden lily pads. A dumbwaiter, shuttling supplies between the barroom and the upper region, served as a speaking tube for Lefty Louie below and Wallace above.

A large window was set into the Sixth Avenue side of the saloon, but such light as filtered through its dusty panes was dimmed by the massive structure of the elevated train tracks. The train's thunder periodically drowned out the barroom din.

With nothing much else on his mind, O'Neill learned the pattern of sounds made by the "El." He did not, perhaps, realize it at the time, but it was part of his education, his "life-experience," as it later pleased him to characterize the seemingly wasted months that preceded his true creative blossoming.

In his long one-act play, *Hughie*, written in 1942, he described the thoughts of the night clerk of a cheap West Side hotel in the Forties near the El. For the clerk (as well as for O'Neill) the El's predictable pattern of arrivals and departures became a mystical symbol of survival.

"The Clerk's mind remains in the street to greet the noise of a far off El train," O'Neill wrote. "Its approach is pleasantly like a memory of hope; then it roars and rocks and rattles past the nearby corner, and the noise pleasantly deafens; then it recedes and dies, and there is something melancholy about that. But there is hope. Only so many El trains pass in one night, and each one passing leaves one less to pass, so the night recedes too, until at last it must die and join all the other long nights in Nirvana, the Big Night of Nights. And that's life."

It was from the Hell Hole that O'Neill, twenty-four years later, drew most of the major characters who people Harry Hope's "Raines-Law hotel" in *The Iceman Cometh* — although the physical setting is a medley.

"The dump in the play is no one place but a combination of three in which I once hung out," he explained in a letter to a friend.

The places, although not specified, are readily identifiable: Jimmy the Priest's, still catering to the same sort of waterfront down-and-outers as during O'Neill's seafaring days and which he might have revisited in 1916; the Garden Hotel, where he sometimes slept and often drank; and, of course, the Hell Hole.

In point of fact, the three "dumps" had little in common other than as a source for the assorted drunks in *Iceman*. Jimmy the Priest's was the most degenerate, frequented almost exclusively by homeless sailors and half-dead, drunken derelicts; it was not a place that Mary Vorse and her friends would ever have patronized.

If hardly refined, the Hell Hole by comparison was several notches above in respectability. Its clientele included men who held jobs, in addition to the small circle of chronic alcoholics who slept most of the day and nightly joined Tom Wallace in drunken stupefaction.

Some of the work the men did was unsavory, even illegal, but they did earn a living of sorts, and went home to bed for at least part of the night. As for the Garden Hotel, its patrons were a mixture of the raffish and the respectable; when measured against the other two it was a veritable Hotel Astor.

*T*he Iceman Cometh is the third of the three tragedies that together with *Long Day's Journey Into Night* and *A Moon for the Misbegotten* form the powerful, culminating statement of O'Neill's creativity.

O'Neill set both *Iceman* and *Long Day's Journey* in 1912, proclaiming for posterity the significance of that year in his life. Indeed, the plays follow almost literally the chronology of O'Neill's youthful years, with *Iceman* (written first) set in "summer, 1912" and *Long Day's Journey* (which can be regarded as its sequel) set on "a day in August, 1912."

The two plays on the surface seem utterly disparate. Whereas *Long Day's Journey* studies an embattled, drug-and-alcohol-dependent family about to self-destruct, *Iceman* portrays a huddle of irredeemably drunken derelicts awaiting oblivion. They are, nonetheless, thematically similar — both fueled by O'Neill's preoccupation with illusion and destiny.

Moreover, *Iceman*'s mysticism is in many ways just as personally revealing, beneath its symbolism, as the candidly autobiographical *Long Day's Journey*.

References to O'Neill's suicide attempt in 1912 provide an example. In *Long Day's Journey*, Eugene (in the guise of Edmund Tyrone) realistically describes his effort to do away with himself at Jimmy the Priest's; in *Iceman*, he depicts the suicide in code, attributing the deed to the young turncoat anarchist, Don Parritt, who jumps from a fire escape (instead of trying to overdose on Veronal).

There is no doubt the two plays were linked in O'Neill's mind, for he noted the idea for each in his work diary on the same day, when he had all but given up hope for completing other work in progress.

"Read over notes on various ideas for single plays — decide do outlines of two [plays] that seem appeal most, and see — the Jimmy the P — H.H. — Garden idea — and N.L. family one," he wrote on May 6, 1939, when he was steeped in memories of his tragic youth.

So closely entwined were the two plays that he even transposed the essence of a deleted line from *The Iceman Cometh*. The line, Hickey's defiant "I am what life has made me, and anyone that doesn't like what I am can go to hell!" — turns up somewhat altered in *Long Day's Journey Into Night*, spoken by Mary Tyrone in defense of herself and her husband: "But I suppose life has made him like that, and he can't help it. None of us can help the things that life has done to us."

Although all of O'Neill's plays dwell in some degree on the past, he had, since the early 1930's, been completely submerged in it.

"I do not think that you can write anything of value or understanding about the present," he said, a few days before *The Iceman Cometh* opened on Broadway. "You can only write about life if it is far enough in the past. The present is too much mixed up with superficial values; you can't know which thing is important and which is not."

Clearly, O'Neill believed that in *Iceman* he had penetrated to the universal meaning he had been pursuing throughout his career.

" . . . there are moments in [*The Iceman Cometh*]," he wrote to his producer, Lawrence Langner, "that suddenly strip the secret soul of a man stark naked, not in cruelty or moral superiority, but with an understanding compassion that sees him as a victim of the ironies of life and of himself. Those moments are for me the depth of tragedy, with nothing more that can possibly be said."

Even though he had long since conquered his alcoholism by the time he set himself to write *Iceman*, he was still brooding about the chronic, debilitative drinking that had been his curse and nearly finished him off in his youth. Indeed, this preoccupation with alcohol continued to the end of his writing life. His two final full-length plays, *A Touch of the Poet* (begun in 1935 but not completed until 1942) and *A Moon for the Misbegotten* (completed in 1943), are as saturated with alcoholic guilt as *Iceman* and *Journey*.

Just as Harry Hope's is a composite of three saloons, the characters in *The Iceman Cometh* are a mixture of the people he met in those barrooms. In several instances, he embellished the characters with aspects of his own former self, as well as of Jamie, the ultimate barfly.

"All of the characters are drawn from life, more or less, although not one of them is an exact portrait of an actual person," he wrote to George Jean Nathan soon after completing the play, adding that the play was "written in exact lingo of place and 1912," as he remembered it, "with only the filth expletives omitted."

In the same letter, he hastened to assure Nathan, "The plot, if you can call it that, is my imaginative creation, of course." (Interestingly, O'Neill used similar words a year or so later to describe the plot of *A Moon for the Misbegotten* in his work diary. While he would base the play's "principal character" on his brother Jamie, the play was to be "otherwise entirely imaginary . . . ")

O'Neill gave conflicting accounts of how he created *The Iceman Cometh*'s most fantastically imagined character, the deluded Theodore Hickman, a hardware salesman known as Hickey. He told two friends from his Greenwich Village days that Hickey was suggested by a man known as "Happy," a collector for a laundry chain, who made regular Friday visits to the Hell Hole and, like Hickey, dispensed cheer and free drinks. Happy failed to appear one Friday, having absconded with the laundry funds, and was never heard from again.

Later, writing to George Jean Nathan, O'Neill confirmed that Hickey was in fact inspired, at least in part, by "a periodical drunk salesman, who was a damned amusing likeable guy." The salesman, he added, "did make that typical drummer crack about the iceman, and wept maudlinly over his wife's photograph and, in other moods, boozily harped on the slogan that honesty is the best policy."

Writing to Kenneth Macgowan ten months later, however, he unaccountably contradicted himself. "What you wonder about Hickey: No, I never knew him. He's the most imaginary character in the play."

A beguilingly plausible theory of Hickey's genesis, advanced by Brenda Murphy, professor of English at the University of Connecticut, is that he was based on Theodore Dreiser. O'Neill had recently met Dreiser at Polly Holladay's, where Dreiser enjoyed the company of such friends as Hutchins Hapgood and John Reed.

Seventeen years O'Neill's senior and long established as a novelist, Dreiser was a much gossiped about figure in the Village. At the time, he was embroiled in a censorship battle over his autobiographical novel, *The "Genius,"* in which the protagonist, Eugene Witla, describes his uncontrollable sexual urges and his guilt toward his cruelly misused wife. Like Hickey, Witla comes to hate his wife and wish her dead; and like Hickey's wife, Evelyn, Dreiser's wife, Sara, tolerated and forgave Dreiser time after time.

Adding credence to this theory, among other telling details, is O'Neill's physical description of Hickey, which closely matches Dreiser's. Then, too, there is Hickey's name — not only the first name, Theodore, but Hickman, a possible comment on Dreiser's rural Indiana background and bumpkin-like manners.

Since Dreiser, whose work O'Neill respected, was still alive when O'Neill finished writing *The Iceman Cometh*, it would have been natural for him to withhold the fact that he had borrowed aspects of the novelist's personality for the murderous salesman.

As for the rest of the inebriates who populate *The Iceman Cometh*, in O'Neill's depiction they are as much symbolic as real. In at least two instances, they have been embellished with traits evocative of O'Neill's own younger self and his relationship to his family. It is not difficult, for instance, to find emblematic traces of Jamie O'Neill as well as of Eugene in the guilt-ridden young anarchist, Donald Parritt, who is seeking to revenge himself on a neglectful mother — or in Willie Oban, the self-pitying Harvard-educated lawyer who prefers drunken indolence to the practice of law.

Both characters are composites, based partly on men who figured in sensational newspaper stories of the period — men whose histories happened to resonate with O'Neill's own circumstances.

Oban's background, as indicated by notes for *The Iceman Cometh*, closely parallels that of a son of the crooked securities dealer, Al Adams (and in fact Oban was initially given the name, Morris Adams). After serving time in Sing Sing, Al Adams, unchastened, went into yet another illegal business and finally committed suicide in 1906.

If not a physical match for Jamie, Oban surely sounds like him, expressing the same childish dependence on and resentment of his overwhelming father.

"Harvard was my father's idea," Oban drunkenly tells a fellow denizen of Harry Hope's saloon. "He was an ambitious man. Dictatorial, too. Always knowing what was best for me." Out of revenge, Oban declares, he made himself a brilliant student.

Then, explaining why he failed to live up to his promise (as had Jamie), Oban adds, "But I discovered the loophole of whiskey and escaped his jurisdiction." Despite his rebellion, Oban, like Jamie, still feels a powerful filial bond, as conveyed by his blurting, from the depths of an alcoholic dream, "Papa, papa!"

There are other similarities between Oban and Jamie. Oban's family periodically gives him "the rush to a cure." And Oban's derisive reference to his father as "the king of the bucket shops" (illegitimate establishments dealing in high-risk commodities) is suggestive of both Jamie's and Eugene's sarcastic references to James as "My father, the Count of Monte Cristo."

O'Neill's development of the suicidal eighteen-year-old Donald Parritt is infinitely more complex — so complex that O'Neill himself had difficulty in explaining it, although he made a stab at it in a letter to Nathan:

"The story of Parritt has a background of fact, too. The suicide really happened pretty much as shown in the play. But it was not the man the character of Parritt is derived from who bumped himself off that way. It was another person and for another reason."

The other person was, of course, James O'Neill's former press agent, James Byth, who killed himself by jumping from a fire escape at Jimmy the Priest's in 1913 and who also appears as Jimmy Anderson in "Tomorrow." (In the story, he jumps to his death at "Tommy the Priest's" in despair over his lost journalism career.)

More confusing still is that another character in *The Iceman Cometh* also is modeled on James Byth. This character, called James Cameron and nicknamed "Jimmy Tomorrow," does *not* jump to his death (as he does in the short story, "Tomorrow"), but merely sinks back into drunkenness at Harry Hope's, having, like Jimmy Anderson in "Tomorrow," failed to redeem his journalistic career.

Thus we have the real James Byth who jumped to his death at Jimmy the Priest's; the fictionalized Jimmy Anderson in "Tomorrow," who jumps at Tommy the Priest's; the similarly fictionalized James Cameron, who does *not* jump at Harry Hope's; and the young anarchist, Don Parritt, based on someone else altogether but who *does* jump at Harry Hope's.

Small wonder O'Neill would not take the trouble to explain all this to Nathan. (He also failed to mention that his own attempted suicide at Jimmy the Priest's in 1912 was a component of the Parritt episode.)

O'Neill made things easier for himself in a letter to Kenneth Macgowan a few months later. "Parritt is . . . almost entirely imaginary," he wrote. "His betrayal of the Movement derives from a real incident, but I never knew the guy, or anything about his mother, so

Parritt's personal history is my own fiction."

The "real incident" involved a twenty-four-year-old turncoat named Donald Vose, who was scathingly denounced by Emma Goldman in the December, 1915, and January, 1916, issues of Mother Earth, a few months after O'Neill arrived in the Village. A dedicated reader of the magazine, he surely read her account, not to mention the widespread newspaper coverage.

The story began some years earlier on the West Coast, the result of an ongoing enmity between the Structural Iron Workers Union of America and the employers' coalition known as the National Erectors' Association. The iron workers had been planting bombs on the West Coast in retaliation for the employers' anti-union tactics, such as fierce opposition to the closed shop and the dismissal of union sympathizers. The outcome was a bitter class struggle, with The Los Angeles Times relentlessly attacking the union in its editorials.

On October 1, 1910, at 1:07 A.M., a suitcase containing sixteen sticks of dynamite exploded in a narrow space, known as "Ink Alley," behind the Los Angeles Times building. The blast set a fire that trapped twenty-one machinists and other workers, who all died of suffocation.

When the Times was able to resume publication, it accused the Iron Workers union of setting the charge, and the city of Los Angeles hired the private detective, William J. Burns, to hunt down those responsible.

Among the chief suspects were two brothers, James B. and John J. McNamara, both ultimately arrested. The "McNamara Case," as it came to be known, was tried in 1911 and evidence was given that between 1909 and 1911 eighty-seven structures built by nonunion labor had been dynamited under orders from the McNamaras. The prosecution demanded the death penalty, which the brothers, keen to be martyrs, were eager to accept.

Lincoln Steffens had been sent to Los Angeles by a syndicate of leading eastern publications to probe the facts of "the story behind the story." A strong adherent of the labor movement and never a neutral observer, Steffens did not feel bound to maintain a journalistic distance.

Well acquainted with the defense lawyer, Clarence Darrow, who specialized in labor cases, Steffens approached him with an unorthodox, not to say presumptuous, plan. Steffens offered to organize a meeting of community and business leaders to find a compromise that would settle the case and calm the climate of vengeance and polarization gripping the city.

Under the compromise, agreed to by Darrow to spare the brothers from the gallows, James McNamara pleaded guilty. He accepted a life sentence in San Quentin, on condition his brother receive a lesser sentence. John McNamara was sentenced to fifteen years.

"It was my intention to injure the building and scare the owners," James stated in his plea. "I did not intend to take the life of anyone. I sincerely regret that these unfortunate men lost their lives. If the giving of my life would bring them back I would gladly give it."

The compromise was furiously disparaged by militant radicals, who believed the martyrdom of the McNamaras would have been a blessing for their cause. In their eyes, Darrow was forever discredited and Steffens derided for his interference.

Detective Burns was not content to let the case rest, convinced that two other men — Matthew A. Schmidt and David Caplan — were as culpable as the McNamaras. For three years, he hunted them from coast-to-coast, but they consistently eluded him.

Burns's surveillance targets included the Home Colony, an anarchist enclave near Tacoma, Washington, one of whose veterans, Gertie Vose, was an intimate friend of Emma Goldman. Burns, having marked Gertie's son, Donald Vose, as weak and disaffected, offered him $2,500 to turn spy. Donald accepted.

Burns suspected that Schmidt would sooner or later turn up at Mother Earth, Emma Goldman's headquarters in New York, and he devised a plan to capture him. He persuaded Donald to tell his mother he wanted to work for the movement in New York. Gertie Vose innocently wrote to Goldman asking her to take Donald in and look after him.

Goldman agreed and, when she returned to New York after her travels in September of 1914, she found Donald established, along with several other boarders, in the house on East 119th Street where Mother Earth was published.

Detective Burns and Goldman had long been sworn enemies. She had labeled him "a sneak" who "could not apprehend a flea." Burns, in turn, had denounced Goldman on numerous occasions, calling Mother Earth "the central power station" of the anarchist movement. He would have liked nothing better than to trap her.

"For the first time in eighteen years I saw the boy I had met as a child of six," Goldman later wrote. "My first impression of Donald Vose was not agreeable; perhaps because of his high pitched, thin voice and shifting eyes." In words echoing Goldman's, O'Neill in *The Iceman Cometh* describes Donald Parritt's personality as "unpleasant," due to "a shifting defiance and ingratiation in his light blue eyes and an irritating aggressiveness in his manner."

Goldman stifled her aversion, however, because Donald "was Gertie's son, out of work, wretchedly clad, unhealthy in appearance," and offered him continued shelter. He told her he was planning to return shortly to the West Coast, and that he was delaying his departure only until he could deliver a "message given to him by someone in Washington for M. A. Schmidt, the delivery of which was imperative." The message, of course, was a false one, dictated by Burns and designed to lead Schmidt into the trap.

Schmidt had been working in New York as a mechanic under an assumed name and did at last pay a visit to Goldman's house in late September to meet "a few friends." Among them were Lincoln Steffens, Hutchins Hapgood and Alexander Berkman (Goldman's former lover who had served fourteen years in prison for attempting to murder Henry Clay Frick in 1892). During the visit, Vose delivered the false message to Schmidt and then reported to Burns. However, presumably having collected part of his bribe, Vose did not leave New York as he had promised Goldman.

At the end of December, rumors reached Goldman that Vose was "spending a great deal of money on drink though he was not working." Her suspicions, however, were not yet fully aroused, for he continued to look shabby and "did not even have an overcoat." Some weeks later, he did leave for the West Coast and in mid-February of 1915 Schmidt was arrested. A few days later, Caplan, too, was apprehended.

"At once we realized that Donald Vose was the Judas Iscariot," wrote Goldman. "Soon positive proofs came from the Coast. It was Donald Vose who cold-bloodedly, deliberately betrayed the two men. It was the most terrible blow in my public life of twenty-five years. Terrible because of the mother of that cur; terrible because he had grown up in a radical atmosphere."

At the trial of Schmidt and Caplan, Donald Vose testified he had been in the employ of W. J. Burns, that he had been sent to New York to track down Schmidt and "was coached to pose as a radical."

"Donald Vose, you are a liar, traitor, spy," wrote Goldman. "You have lied away the liberty and life of our comrades. Yet not they but you will suffer the penalty." In her typically overwrought style, she added: "You will roam the earth accursed, shunned and hated; a burden unto yourself, with the shadow of M. A. Schmidt and David Caplan ever at your heels unto the last."

O'Neill, imaginatively carrying the Vose story beyond the actual facts, created in Donald Parritt a man who has betrayed his mother, Rosa (rather than her comrades), to "the Burns dicks" (as they are described in *The Iceman Cometh*).

Parritt turns up at Harry Hope's, apparently seeking understanding and sympathy from his mother's former lover, Larry Slade. Concealing his guilty secret, he professes to be deeply concerned over his mother's arrest, claiming it was by the merest good luck he was not himself arrested with her and her companions.

O'Neill (who never met Gertie Vose) envisioned the betrayed Rosa Parritt partly in terms of Emma Goldman. The offstage Rosa is described by her son as an aggressively free woman who, like Goldman, has no qualms about taking one lover after another, but whose dedication to the movement supercedes all personal commitment.

Parritt gives himself away with almost every word and gesture. It is soon evident to Larry Slade that Parritt's motive was not the money. It was his long-suppressed hatred of his mother — not unlike the submerged hostility O'Neill felt toward his own mother, and which he was minutely analyzing in *Long Day's Journey Into Night* during the same period he was writing *The Iceman Cometh*. There is a clearly discernible parallel between Parritt's betrayal (to the law) of his mother's radical activity, and O'Neill's betrayal (to the public) of his mother's secret drug addiction.

"She used to spoil me and make a pet of me," Parritt whines in the play. "Once in a great while, I mean. When she remembered me. As if she wanted to make up for something. As if she felt guilty . . . " In the end, it is Parritt's newly acknowledged truth that he hated his mother and his remorse over his treachery that impels him to commit suicide.

It was the disillusioned anarchist, Terry Carlin, who doubtless filled in O'Neill on any details of Donald Vose's betrayal not gleamed by him from Goldman's account. O'Neill had met Carlin at the Hell Hole during the Schmidt-Caplan trial and he became the model for Larry Slade in *The Iceman Cometh*.

Carlin was an old friend of both Emma Goldman and Gertie Vose and had spent time with Donald Vose after his arrival in New York; in fact, he had been in Goldman's house, according to her account, when Vose delivered his false message to Schmidt. Whether Carlin harbored any suspicion at that time of Vose's duplicity is not known.

Carlin, as Larry Slade — the "one-time Syndicalist-Anarchist" — became in O'Neill's depiction a pivotal figure, second in importance only to Hickey. He is the character in *Iceman* whom O'Neill portrayed closest to life; for it was Carlin, of all the people O'Neill knew during this period, who made the most searing impression on him. Indeed, Carlin was to dominate O'Neill's thinking for years to come.

CHAPTER
FORTY-TWO

O'NEILL COULD NOT HAVE WRITTEN *THE ICEMAN COMETH* without having been a friend of Terry Carlin any more than he could have written *Long Day's Journey Into Night* without having been the son of James O'Neill.

In *The Iceman Cometh* he depicts Larry Slade as a man of sixty — "tall, raw-boned, with coarse straight white hair, worn long and raggedly cut." The description, as confirmed by his contemporaries, fitted Carlin in virtually every detail:

"He has a gaunt Irish face with a big nose, high cheekbones, a lantern jaw with a week's stubble of beard, a mystic's meditative pale-blue eyes with a gleam of sharp sardonic humor in them . . . His clothes are dirty and much slept in. His gray flannel shirt, open at the neck, has the appearance of having never been washed. From the way he methodically scratches himself with his long-fingered, hairy hands, he is lousy and reconciled to being so . . . his face [has] the quality of a pitying but weary old priest's."

Hutchins Hapgood, who knew Carlin as well as anyone, described him as "a complete bum, so complete that it was magnificent." When O'Neill first met him in the Hell Hole, Carlin was in his fifties, his hair not yet turned white. He had long yellow teeth and the irises of his eyes were flecked from a gunpowder explosion.

Unkempt and unclean by choice, Carlin had not worked for years but, relying entirely on his Irish charm and eloquence, he always found someone to keep him in liquor. Even such practiced storytellers as Jack London and Theodore Dreiser were enraptured by the mythic quality of his yarns.

On his first visit to the Hell Hole, Carlin ordered one whiskey after another. Finally the bartender suggested payment. When Carlin, according to Hapgood, "blandly and sweetly" said he had no money, "the bartender, captivated, like so many others before and since, by the beautiful ragged bum, said, 'Have another.' Believe it or not, this was not so uncommon in the old days of the New York saloon; but of course Terry was a remarkable person and a fascinating person; his talk was an asset to any saloon." Carlin not only was treated to as much drink as he wanted, but was also offered a room upstairs, rent-free.

Like Benjamin Tucker, O'Neill's earlier mentor, Carlin was a philosophical anarchist to whom both socialism and communism were anathema. It was Nietzsche he worshiped, wrapping himself in the image of his spiritual and intellectual superman. By his own standards, Carlin was a compassionate man, but to those who could not follow the mystical turn of his mind he appeared cold-blooded, even inhuman, particularly in his stony refusal to judge or offer guidance.

He had been present, for example, at Mabel Dodge's peyote party. The only guest who had used drugs and had a precise knowledge of their danger, he made no attempt to warn the others they were courting severe impairment. Hapgood at one point began to worry about the effect peyote might have on him, and beseeched Carlin: "Terry, I am afraid of this thing. What do you advise me to do?"

Carlin regarded Hapgood "with abysmal disapproval."

"Hutch," he said, "you surely know that I have too much respect for you to give you any advice. The worst crime . . . is to interfere with another personality. Such things are sacred."

Hapgood persisted. "Shall I stay here or go away?" Carlin did not answer, but Hapgood interpreted his silence as an indication he should leave, and triumphantly declared, "You've answered my question, Terry!"

Carlin was furious. "That's a lie!" he shot back.

"He continued to protest," wrote Hapgood, "for, in his state of mind, I had accused him of the greatest transgression possible."

In another instance involving Carlin's credo of noninterference, one witnessed by O'Neill, he passively stood by while a friend killed himself with an overdose of heroin. It was this episode that O'Neill drew on in *The Iceman Cometh*, when Larry Slade silently condones Donald Parritt's suicide.

Born Terence O'Carolan, he shortened his last name for reasons of his own. Like James O'Neill, he sprang from Irish peasant stock and his family, too, migrated to America when he was a boy. The

O'Carolans, including mother, father and their seven children, settled in New York in the 1860's and tried to subsist on the father's salary of eight dollars a week.

Also like James, Carlin went to work at an early age. While he could be as winning and outgoing as James, he was far more sensitive to the social injustice he saw in and around the sweatshop that employed him. It was not long before he embraced anarchy as a creed.

Carlin worked for ten years, until he was twenty, as a journeyman tanner and currier, and soon excelled at his trade, but his heart was not in it. He spent his spare time with books, giving himself a remarkable, if one-sided, education.

Like the O'Neills, the O'Carolans were an emotionally interdependent family. "We clung desperately to one another long after the necessity was past," Carlin once informed Hutchins Hapgood, who described him at length in his book, *An Anarchist Woman* — the story of Marie, a young woman adrift, whom Carlin saved from a career of prostitution and molded into a passionate philosophical anarchist. (Whatever details of Carlin's life, loves and philosophy were not imparted by him directly to O'Neill, were to be found in Hapgood's book, which had been published in 1909.)

Carlin, like O'Neill, had a dearly loved brother named Jim, whom he once described as "my other ego." It was an experience involving Jim that decided Carlin in his early thirties to become a social exile. Jim, who had a good job with a Pittsburgh tannery and owned stock worth the substantial sum (for that day) of $25,000, asked Carlin, an expert in the leather-tanning field, to come to Pittsburgh.

Jim's firm was losing thousands of dollars a week because of a flaw in the manufacturing process, and Jim thought his brother could find and correct it. Carlin had been happily living in a Chicago slum, working only occasionally to provide the bare necessities for himself and Marie.

"It was with the utmost repugnance that I quit my happy slum life," Carlin wrote to Hapgood, "but I loved Jim, and it was the call of the ancient clan in my blood. When I arrived in Pittsburgh, without a trunk, and with other marks of the proletarian on me, Mr. Kirkman, the millionaire tanner, showered me with every luxury — every luxury except that of thought and true emotion. Never before did I realize so intensely my indifference to what money can buy. My private office in the shop was stocked with wines and imported cigarettes; but I was not so well off as in my happy slum."

Carlin finally found the source of the trouble in an obscure process. "I had put no price on my services," he said. "For Jim's sake, I had worked like a Trojan, physically and mentally, for a month. With unlimited money at my disposal, I had drawn only twenty dollars altogether, and this I sent to Marie, to keep the wolf away."

Kirkman had been saved a fortune and he offered Carlin the job of running the shop at a large salary and the chance to buy $2,000 worth of stock. Carlin refused, explaining he would do nothing to exploit the workers and would permit no one to be discharged for incompetency. He had never met a man he could not teach, he said.

Carlin departed with nothing but his railroad fare to Chicago, though Jim assured him that Kirkman would send him between $500 and $1,000 for his services. Within a few days, Jim found that Kirkman had no intention of sending Carlin a cent; Kirkman was angry at the spurned offer, and used the excuse that no written or verbal contract had been made for Carlin's services. In spite of having a wife and children to support Jim retired from the firm in protest.

Crushed by the disaster he had brought upon Jim, Carlin marveled at the lopsidedness of a world in which love of money could play such a vindictive role.

"Mr. Kirkman thought all the world of Jim and could not run the shop without him," Carlin wrote to Hapgood. "Nor could he recover from the blow, for he loved my brother, as everybody did. Mr. Kirkman died a few weeks afterward, and after a year or two the firm went into the hands of a receiver. All this happened because of a few paltry dollars, which I did not ask for, for which I did not care a damn — and this is business! I heartily rejoice, if not in Mr. Kirkman's death, at least in the dispersion of his family and their being forced into our ranks, where there is some hope for them."

Carlin could never shake off the torment of his brother's tragedy. "Jim was one of the maimed ones in my family," he said, pointing out that years earlier "defective machinery and a surgeon's malpractice made one arm useless. The Pittsburgh affair broke up his beautiful home."

Although Jim O'Carolan and Jamie O'Neill had been maimed by life in different ways, the resemblance between the two was startling and provided yet another bond between Carlin and O'Neill. In his last years, Jim O'Carolan withdrew from life, as O'Neill believed Jamie was doing.

"I have . . . a desire to be considered a dead one," Carlin's brother wrote, "and am doing all but the one thing that will make my wish a reality. I am long tired of the game . . . The chase for dollars I am performing here is very disgusting to me . . . It is a hell of a life and I wish it were done."

Jim O'Carolan had been dead many years when Carlin and O'Neill met, but Carlin still held poignant memories of him. "He died of that great loneliness of soul which made of his wasted body a battered barricade against the stupidity which finally engulfed him," Carlin said. Some years later, O'Neill voiced very similar sentiments when his own brother died.

Their lost faith also bound O'Neill and Carlin. "Though we were Catholics on the surface," Carlin once said, describing his family during their early years in America, "we were pagans at bottom." Carlin liked to repeat his brother's deathbed comment, when it was proposed that a priest be sent for: "I hire no spiritual nurse."

"There must be some meaning," Carlin said, "for all this ancient agony. Oh, that I might expand my written words into an Epic of the Slums, into an *Iliad* of the Proletaire! If an oyster can turn its pain into a pearl, then, verily, when we have suffered enough, something must arise out of our torture — else the world has no meaning . . . It cannot be that I came up out of the depths for nothing.

"If I could pierce my heart and write red lines, I might perhaps tell the truth. But only a High Silence meets me, and I do not understand . . . I feel like a diver who has nigh strangled himself to bring up a handful of seaweed, and so feels he must go down again — and again — until he attains somewhere the holy meaning of Life."

Carlin left it to O'Neill to pierce his heart and write red lines. In a way clearly discernible in his plays, O'Neill became Carlin's literary voice. In May of 1944, after playing back a recording he made of a brief speech written for Terry's alter ego, Larry Slade, O'Neill confided to his producer, Lawrence Langner, that he vividly recognized himself in Slade's lines. No longer able to use a pencil, he had been experimenting with a dictating machine sent to him by Langner.

"When I played the record back," he wrote to Langner, "and listened to the voice that was my voice and yet not my voice saying: 'I'm afraid to live, am I? — and even more afraid to die! So I sit here, my pride drowned on the bottom of a bottle, keeping drunk so I won't see myself shaking in my britches with fright, or hear myself whining and praying, "O Blessed Christ, let me live a little longer *at any price!* If it's only for a few days more, or a few hours even, let me still clutch greedily to my yellow heart this sweet treasure, this jewel beyond price, the dirty, stinking bit of flesh which is my beautiful little life!'" — well, it sure did something to me. It wasn't Larry, it was my ghost talking to me, or I to my ghost."

Incessantly expounding upon Eastern philosophy, Carlin presented O'Neill with *Light on the Path*, a slender volume published by the Theosophical Society in London in 1884. The book, a dissertation on ancient Eastern mysticism, crystallized for O'Neill his own mystical inclinations.

The wisdom in the treatise — according to its introduction by a mysterious "M.C." — supposedly had originated some centuries earlier with a sage influenced by "a dynasty of Perfect Men" (who claimed to have ruled the continent of Atlantis before it was lost beneath the sea). The author was subsequently identified as Mabel Collins, who was thirty-three when she transcribed this wisdom, which had been revealed to her in a manner she did not deem necessary to explain.

Light on the Path was crammed with Hindu, Buddhist and Taoist advice on how to find the "right path" to life. It exhorted the reader to seek this path "by plunging into the mysterious and glorious depths of your own inmost being."

The philosophy of one of O'Neill's early mentors, Strindberg, seemed at some points to echo the teaching of *Light on the Path*. Strindberg indeed had learned both Chinese and Japanese and had become a scholar of Oriental wisdom, sometimes referring to himself in his letters as "Buddha."

O'Neill's inborn affinity for the occult had already manifested itself in his one-act play, *Fog*, and was to inform much of his future work. In 1925, he described himself as "a most confirmed mystic," explaining that he was "always, always trying to interpret Life in terms of lives, never just lives in terms of character." He was, he said, "always acutely conscious of the Force behind — (Fate, God, our biological past creating our present, whatever one calls it — Mystery, certainly)."

The mysticism of the East was but one of the interests Carlin shared with O'Neill during long nights spent in the Hell Hole. Other subjects that occupied them were the plight of the underdog and a mutual concern for prostitutes, whose hopeless struggle O'Neill had recently depicted in *The Web*.

"The kind of prostitution you contemplate is no worse than the kind often called marriage," Carlin once told a friend of Marie's who was considering a career in the streets:

"Selling your body for a lifetime is perhaps worse than selling it
for an hour or for a day. Perhaps you will be better off so than in
domestic drudgery. It is a choice of evils, but if you are very brave
and courageous you may perhaps get along without either. But if
forced to one or the other, I recommend prostitution. It may be worse
for you but, as a protest, it is better for society, in the long run."

Marie herself became a primary inspiration for Anna Christie.
Marie (as O'Neill portrayed Anna), had tried being a "nurse girl"
before taking to the streets. After being rescued by Carlin, Marie
eventually abandoned him and went off to a mountain retreat. The
sense of being washed clean, of being reborn, that Anna found at sea
on her father's barge, was doubtless based on Marie's description of
the peace she found in the hills of California.

"I am intoxicated by all this beauty and love the very air and
earth," Marie wrote to Carlin. " . . . I feel newborn and free . . . At
night I sleep as I have never slept — a deep dreamless slumber. I
awake to a cold plunge in the stream. Oh, it just suits me! Everything
in the past is dead . . . I have become happy, healthy, and free."

Echoes of Marie's sentiments can be found in the speech O'Neill
wrote for Anna:

" . . . It's like I'd come home after a long visit away some place
. . . why d'you s'pose I feel so — so — like I'd found something I'd
missed and been looking for . . . And I seem to have forgot — everything that's happened — like it didn't matter no more. And I feel
clean, somehow — like you feel yust after you've took a bath. And I
feel happy for once — yes, honest! — happier than I ever been anywhere before!"

Marie also could have been pointing the way for a Nina Leeds
and the asides of *Strange Interlude* when she wrote of a friend to
Hapgood:

"I am fascinated by Rose . . . I always like to be near her when
there is no one else around. She reveals herself to me then; in fact
quite throws off the mask which all women wear. In order to encourage her to do this, I apparently throw down my own mask. Oh, how
I gloat over her then, when she shows me a side of her life and
betrays secret thoughts and feelings to me half unconsciously!
Sometimes I succeed in having her do this when there is a third person present, and the look of hatred which passes across her face when
she perceives she has made a mistake, is a most interesting thing to
see."

Marie's concept of "the mask" was rooted in Carlin's philosophy. "Words only conceal thought," he was apt to say, "and do not express it" — a comment that O'Neill repeated to countless friends as his own.

By the time he met O'Neill, Carlin had retired from life, like Larry Slade in *The Iceman Cometh*, and he made no pretense whatever at being civilized. "I am very 'crummy,' badly flea bitten, overrun with bed bugs," he confided to Hapgood, "but, redemption of it all, I am free and always drunk."

He was also, on occasion, drugged. "I had to seek surcease in my old remedy of hashish and chloroform, which was a change from suffering to stupidity," he said. He stayed drunk, or drugged, content to sleep where he could, eat what little he could beg — and talk to anyone who would listen.

Battling his own despair, O'Neill allowed himself to be influenced by what was most destructive and dangerous in Carlin's nihilistic doctrine. As always when he felt misunderstood and unappreciated, O'Neill withdrew ever more deeply into drink. Like Cornelius Melody, the haughty, embittered, self-pitying and self-deluded hero of *A Touch of the Poet*, he took refuge in quoting from Byron's *Childe Harold*:

> I have not loved the World, nor the World me;
> I have not flattered its rank breath, nor bowed
> To its idolatries a patient knee,
> Nor coined my cheeks to smiles, — nor cried aloud
> In worship of an echo: in the crowd
> They could not deem me one of such — I stood
> Among them, but not of them . . .

Several people who encountered O'Neill during the winter of 1916 were convinced he was willfully drinking himself to death.

Although his employment as a drama critic with its token salary had evaporated early in 1916, O'Neill put up a brave front, as always, for Dr. Lyman, when Gaylord's periodic questionnaire found him in New York. Describing the boardinghouse at 38 Washington Square West as a "hotel," he maintained he was being paid twenty-five dollars a week as a "dramatic critic" and said he spent "six or seven" hours a day writing.

There is no evidence of any writing he did at the Washington Square address except for a short poem he preserved, called "The Stars" and inspired by the war in Europe:

> Stars shoot
> Over the blinding blaze of shrapnel
> Over the torn fields
> And the torn bodies;
> Like sedate, amusing fireworks
> Set off for the laughter
> And the wonder of children.
> Stars shoot. —
> The harmless and kindly stars.
>
> I think the jaded gods,
> Bored by the stench and the slaughter,
> Are holding carnival
> And throwing confetti.

Soon after returning the questionnaire to Dr. Lyman, O'Neill was dispossessed from his boardinghouse because his rent was forty-six dollars in arrears. His landlady, Adele Marchesini, insisted that he leave behind his trunk with the bulk of his possessions, permitting him to take only his manuscripts and an armful of books.

In 1924, thanking a friend who had sent him an inscribed copy of a book, O'Neill wrote, "I owned it once before when it was first published by the Bonis — but a hard-hearted landlady on the Square requisitioned it, along with my trunk and extra clothes and other books for a matter of neglected rent. Although I've been prosperous since I've never quite had the nerve to go back and reclaim my possessions, if still there." Some months after recalling the episode, however, he did screw up the courage to go back. He paid his bill and ransomed the trunk.

With scant means of support, O'Neill had to depend on Carlin, whose career as a parasite had taught him innovative survival techniques. They often stayed up most of the night getting drunk and did not go to bed at all, merely catnapping with their heads on a back-room table at the Hell Hole, like the characters in *The Iceman Cometh*. Tom Wallace, if in a generous mood, might allow them to flop on a bed upstairs without sheets or pillows, using their coats as blankets.

When they felt the need for more comfortable shelter, they resorted to a stratagem Carlin had found reliable. They dispatched a presentable-looking friend to inquire of one or another Village real-estate agent about available rooms.

After casually inspecting the premises, the friend would surreptitiously press a lump of clay against the door latch upon leaving, to prevent it from locking. Then he would tell Carlin the address, and Carlin and O'Neill would move into the empty flat with a couple of old mattresses and with orange crates to hold their books and whiskey bottles.

If they could not find mattresses, they slept on newspapers or burlap sacks. The arrangement was a bare notch above the improvised housing of O'Neill's days "on the beach" in Buenos Aires. He and Carlin sustained themselves on handouts from friends, the Hell Hole's free soup, and oysters bought cheaply by the sack at the Fulton fish market.

In the spring of 1916 O'Neill and Carlin were joined by a temporarily affluent, if alcoholic, newspaper reporter, Jack Druilard, who was able to pay a month's rent on a spacious unfurnished basement flat on Fourth Street between Washington Square and Sixth Avenue, a few doors from the Hell Hole.

Because the three occupants tossed their refuse into a corner and let it accumulate, the premises came to be known as the "Garbage Flat." Writing to a friend many years later, O'Neill said he remembered the flat "fondly and vividly."

"I ought to," he added. "I christened it . . . it continued to be unfurnished except for piles of sacking as beds, newspapers as bed linen, and packing boxes for chairs and tables. Also, it remained unswept. Toward the end of our tenancy, there was a nice even carpet of cigarette butts, reminding one of the snow scene in an old melodrama. And — well, in short, the name I gave it was by no means in any way a libel."

By this time O'Neill, like Carlin, was in an advanced state of alcoholism. He had reached the point where he could not survive without a shot of whiskey on awakening in the morning. There is no apter description of his inebriated state of mind than in some of the narrator's lines he deleted from "Tomorrow," written only a few months later:

"I gave myself up to this fit of suicidal melancholia. I wandered in that grey country of alcohol in which all worldly hopes are as naught and the great longing one for annihilation. Ah, to fall asleep and never wake again to cower before the fetish of life."

Robert Carlton Brown, a contributing editor to The Masses since

1912, and a well-paid fiction writer for popular magazines, often drank with O'Neill at the Hell Hole.

"I liked him because of his Irish temperament, his wanting to drink and his love for travel," Brown recalled. They sometimes talked literature and poetry, and O'Neill once showed Brown a poem entitled "Ashes of Orchids," written, he said, in Buenos Aires. Brown was appalled by O'Neill's physical condition.

That March, Brown and two colleagues led an insurrection against the Masses editor, Max Eastman, demanding his title be abolished and decisions be made by a consensus of all twenty-one contributing editors. Eastman's only apparent loyalist, clinging to his own title, was his associate editor, Floyd Dell (not long since the editor of Chicago's Friday Literary Supplement).

Eastman refused to give in and Brown, together with several other editors, resigned. Eastman, aware of Brown's heavy drinking, was less than devastated. "He had contributed nothing for six months and was due for removal in any case," Eastman said.

With no more editorial responsibilities, Brown could devote his attention to O'Neill. "Often, he had no place to sleep," Brown said, "and sometimes, after a night of drinking at the Hell Hole, I'd take him with me to the apartment of a friend in Washington Square who was out of town.

"I'd buy a pint of whiskey before we went to sleep somewhere around dawn, fill an eight-ounce tumbler and put it near Gene's bed. He looked so weak I thought he was going to die. Sometime during the next afternoon I'd be awakened by a low, feeble call. He'd want me to help him lift the glass to his lips."

Brown was convinced it was Carlin — for once eschewing his philosophy of nonintervention — who saved O'Neill's life by forcing him to take food. Carlin would amble over to the Hell Hole with an empty tin container to bring back soup for O'Neill in one or another of the flats they shared. Yet Carlin, typically, did nothing to discourage O'Neill from wallowing in his drunken state.

One day, according to Brown, Carlin returned with soup and whiskey to a recently appropriated flat on Third Street, furnished with the unexpected luxury of a big brass bed. O'Neill was lying on the bed, awake and trembling, but with determination in his eyes. He told Carlin he had made up his mind to go on the wagon.

Carlin, who knew as much about alcoholism as any physician, warned him against quitting cold, aware that sudden withdrawal could bring on delirium tremens. Carlin suggested tapering off and then sticking to a regimen of moderate drinking. O'Neill insisted he had to quit completely and at once. Shaking his head pityingly, Carlin drank up the whiskey he had brought and departed, leaving O'Neill twitching on the bed.

Carlin rounded up ten of the most unsavory characters he could find, including an aged whore, a trembling drug addict and an assortment of street thugs. He sent each, in turn, to stare in silence at O'Neill, who was finally so unnerved by this staged preview of the D.T.'s that he abandoned his plan to quit cold and pleaded for a drink — which Carlin cheerfully supplied.

FORTY-THREE

BACK TO HIS WANDERING IN THAT "GREY COUNTRY OF alcohol," O'Neill landed with Carlin in an abandoned loft on Fulton Street, not far from Jimmy the Priest's. The new space was conveniently close to the wholesale fish market with its supply of cheap oysters, but distressingly distant from the one source of whiskey where his credit was always good — the barroom of the Garden Hotel.

When he could not come by free liquor at the Hell Hole at Fourth Street, he was obliged to travel even further uptown, to the Garden on Twenty-seventh Street. He navigated by subway, as indicated in the two-stanza "Lament of a Subwayite." The second stanza drolly expressed his resignation:

> Great words of fury sputter in my brain
>> And I am tempted to cry out in heat
> "A seat! A seat! My kingdom for a seat!
>> Why should I bend and break beneath the strain?"
> Methinks I hear the song the harsh wheels sang:
>> "They also pay who only stand and hang"

Arriving at the Garden, trembling from liquor deprivation and the exertion of his trip, O'Neill would prop himself against the bar. The bartender, who knew him well, would place a shot glass in front of him, toss a towel across the bar, as though absentmindedly forgetting it, and glide away.

Hanging the towel around his neck, O'Neill would grasp both the glass of whiskey and one end of the towel in his right hand, while he clutched the other end of the towel with his left. Using the towel as a pulley, he would laboriously hoist the glass to his lips, his hands shaking violently. He was barely able to pour the whiskey down his throat, and sometimes he spilled it. Small wonder that O'Neill admired bartenders as "the most sympathetic people in the world."

James O'Neill, joined occasionally by Jamie, had stayed at the Garden on and off since 1911 and Eugene had at times slept there at his father's expense. Louis Bergen, one of four bartenders at the hotel, recalled a past period when James and both sons lived in rooms on the first floor — evidently during one of Ella's sanatorium cures.

"Every morning James O'Neill and the boys would come into the bar, and Mr. O'Neill would go through a routine of giving each boy his daily allowance," Bergen said.

"Usually, there'd be an argument. The old man would tell the boys they'd never amount to anything. The boys drank the bar rye — ten cents a shot, from a bottle I kept on ice; it was the worst thing you could drink. I knew it would kill Jamie eventually. The old man liked Old-Fashioneds; he'd usually wait until I wasn't busy, so I could take time to fix one the way he liked it. I'd crush the orange in it for him."

When Bergen realized Jamie and Eugene were out of funds, he would ask, "How are you fixed?" If they shook their heads ruefully, he would place a bottle before them and busy himself at the other end of the bar.

"The old man was very generous to me," Bergen added. "He offered to set me up in a café once. He also wanted me, at one time, to take care of some property he owned in New Jersey. I turned down his offers, because I liked it at the Garden. It was a good bar; good food and no phony liquor."

Regulars of the barroom knew Bergen as a repository of James O'Neill lore. "One day," according to a favorite story, "the old man knocked off early from rehearsals and came into the bar, where everyone was placing bets on the day's big race — the annual Brooklyn handicap. Some of Mr. O'Neill's friends coaxed him to place a bet, but he didn't like to gamble on horses. Finally, though, he asked what horses were running, and when he heard that one of the entries was Irish Lad, he decided to place a ten-dollar bet on him.

"The odds on Irish Lad were forty to one, and everyone laughed at Mr. O'Neill. He asked who was riding Irish Lad, and when he was told it was a jockey called Frankie O'Neill, he bet another ten dollars. Someone called out that his colors were green and white, and Mr. O'Neill put down another ten dollars. By this time everyone in the bar was laughing like crazy.

"Irish Lad won, and then nobody laughed except Mr. O'Neill."

When Jamie had the cash, he would place racetrack bets for

Bergen as well as for himself. As for Eugene, Bergen recalled, his interest in horse racing had given way to a passion for six-day bicycle racing at Madison Square Garden across the street from the hotel.

Although James, no longer touring, now lived with Ella at the nearby Prince George, he continued to frequent the Garden Hotel for drinks and for a meal in the back-room restaurant now and then.

According to an Irish porter at the Prince George named Dan Foley, the O'Neills followed a routine that seldom varied: Every morning at about 8:30 or 9, James breakfasted in the public dining room. He then joined his cronies at The Players or the Lambs, serene in the knowledge that Ella (entirely recovered from her morphine habit) could be trusted to remain contentedly on her own.

Soon after James left the Prince George, Jamie arrived from the Garden Hotel, where he now lived at his father's expense, to visit his mother — a daily duty he rarely shirked. He sometimes brought her freshly baked rolls for her morning coffee.

"He'd give his mother a couple of kisses and stay with her for two or three hours," Foley recalled. "He helped himself to his father's whiskey. I'd see him leave, all smiles." After Jamie's visit, Ella, as ever fashion-conscious, sometimes shopped. Lord and Taylor, where (according to O'Neill's later description) she knew "everyone," was among the stores she favored.

James returned to the hotel at about four in the afternoon, to resume the ritual of what had at last become a calm and congenial married life. At six, he escorted Ella to the dining room and, following dinner, they often attended the theater. On some evenings, Ella might return alone to their suite while James joined friends in the Prince George Tap Room, where women were not allowed. Or, if James felt reasonably sure he would not encounter Jamie or Eugene, he might stroll the short distance to the Garden Hotel.

"I used to go over to the Garden Hotel bar on my way home after work," Foley recalled. "Jamie was usually there drinking, and sometimes his brother was with him. One night I remember seeing Gene and Jamie on the sidewalk outside the hotel, with their arms around each other. They were talking and kissing each other, both as high as kites."

Finding it ever more painful to watch the thirty-seven-year-old Jamie disintegrating and the twenty-seven-year-old Eugene still drifting, James continued to ease his conscience by keeping them on the dole. As often as not, he would leave them their daily dollar at the cashier's cage of the Prince George Hotel. After all these many years,

Jamie and Eugene still sullenly clung to their father. And he, as ever, was incapable of abandoning them.

The barroom of the Garden Hotel was a gathering point for those who worked at Madison Square Garden. "The circus men who stayed there I knew very well," O'Neill once said. "Not only the circus men, but the poultry men, the horse breeders and all others who displayed their wares at the old Madison Square Garden. Used to meet them all in the bar."

He neglected to mention the fight promoters, six-day bicycle racers, racketeers, sportswriters and show-business people who basked in its lively atmosphere. Among the clientele was the policeman who in 1906 had arrested Harry Thaw for shooting Stanford White in the rooftop cabaret of Madison Square Garden. Another regular was a man nicknamed "the Colonel," who had married the elderly proprietress of his boardinghouse when he could no longer afford to pay his rent. There was a doctor who had been barred from practice for public drunkenness, and a young department store publicity man named Frank, married to a vacuous blonde beauty. "What do you talk to her about?" O'Neill once asked Frank, to the amusement of bartender Bergen.

"Gene spoke so seldom," recalled Bergen, "that a lot of people thought he was a dummy. But when he did say something, it had meaning." Bergen knew O'Neill wanted to be a playwright and used to watch him scribbling in the "Bartender's Guide," a notebook that listed recipes for mixed drinks along with dates of current sporting events. Several blank pages at the end provided space for notations.

One Garden patron, later described by O'Neill as an "old chum," was a circus man named Bill Clarke, who performed as "Volo the Volitant." As a bicycle stunt rider, he propelled himself down a steep incline and turned a loop in the air.

An observant Catholic, Clarke, known by his friends as "Clarkie," always said a Hail Mary before launching his daredevil feat. Despite his prayers, he fell and broke his back. By the time O'Neill met him, he had become a megaphone man touting tickets on Times Square for a Manhattan sightseeing bus service.

Compared with O'Neill in the winter of 1916, Clarke was affluent, and he often paid for his chum's drinks. Like O'Neill, he was willing to drink anything when out of funds, and he sometimes sampled wood alcohol flavored with Worcestershire sauce. Down on his luck in later years, Clarke was one of several former drinking companions whom O'Neill, after achieving success, helped support.

A second circus man befriended by O'Neill at the Garden, Jack Croak, once worked in the ticket wagon of the Willard Shows and had in fact been a sparring partner of Jess Willard, the champion heavyweight boxer (a title lost to Jack Dempsey in 1919). Croak had also traveled with a tent show called Sells Circus through the West Indies, and it was his experiences on that tour that gave O'Neill the idea for *The Emperor Jones.*

"He told me a story current in Haiti concerning the late President Sam," O'Neill recalled. "This was to the effect that Sam had said they'd never get him with a lead bullet; that he would get himself first with a silver one. My friend, by the way, gave me a coin with Sam's features on it, and I still keep it as a pocket piece. This notion about the silver bullet struck me, and I made a note of the story." In *The Iceman Cometh,* Croak (possibly with some of Clarkie's characteristics added) became Ed Mosher, "one-time circus man."

At the Garden Hotel, O'Neill also met a chambermaid who liked to engage him in conversation, especially about her love affair with Rudy, a waiter, who had died. During his final creative years, O'Neill planned to base a character on her in a projected series of forty-minute sketches, under the collective title, *By Way of Obit.* All were to concern people O'Neill had known, and all featured one character speaking to an indifferent listener about a dead person.

O'Neill conceived the series as "quiet tragedies of New York," but the only play he completed was *Hughie,* about the Broadway gambler down on his luck. It was his idea to depict the chambermaid intercepting a guest departing his room for the bar, and haranguing him about her dead Rudy.

Also at the Garden Hotel, O'Neill met a man who remained a friend for many years, a brawny, big-featured Scotsman named William Stuart. Known to everyone as "Scotty," he had fought in the Boer War (like Piet Wetjoen and Cecil Lewis in *The Iceman Cometh*). Once apprenticed to a wood carver who worked on ships, Scotty earned his living by teaching a wood-carving class at a settlement house in Greenwich Village.

Scotty, who later performed in several of O'Neill's one-act sea plays was, in O'Neill's words, "a bit of a rough-neck," who had "seen the 'hard' side of the world." He knew "ships and the men on them by heart."

Tough as he might be, Scotty was no match for the Hudson

Dusters. Two of the gang members, believing Scotty had defrauded them in a furniture deal, confronted him in the Hell Hole one day. According to Maxwell Bodenheim, drinking there at the time, O'Neill's intervention saved Scotty from bodily harm.

O'Neill, said Bodenheim, "managed to smother their rage and induced them to forego their intended vengeance."

"He did this," continued Bodenheim, "with a curious mixture of restrained profanity, mild contempt, and blunt camaraderie, which showed that he shared the spirit of these roughnecks and yet failed to share it. His spirit was made up of almost equal parts of deeply artic-ulate proletarian and surface poet, with both blended to an undistin-guishable whole."

Organized in the late 1890's, when other vicious gangs like the Gophers, the Five Pointers, the Marginals and the Pearl Buttons ter-rorized Manhattan, the Dusters commandeered an old building on Hudson Street as their clubhouse. To the helpless fury of their law-abiding neighbors, they entertained waterfront prostitutes at all-night parties, with refreshments supplied free of charge by neighbor-hood merchants.

No one dared complain, for the Dusters were easily offended. One local saloon keeper, who refused to donate six kegs of beer for a party, was subsequently robbed of his entire stock and his establish-ment wrecked.

The Dusters bore names like Kid Yorke, Circular Jack, Goo Goo Knox, Rubber Shaw, Honey Stewart and Ding Dong. Many were cocaine addicts and their drug-inspired courage was a menace to the police.

One of their daring feats of revenge was perpetrated shortly before O'Neill came to the Village, and was still well-remembered. A policeman named Dennis Sullivan, assigned to the Charles Street Station, declared his intention of singlehandedly smashing the Hudson Dusters. He arrested ten of them and the gang set out to teach Sullivan a lesson.

On a night when he was about to arrest another Duster in Greenwich Street, four of them assaulted him. They grabbed his coat, nightstick, shield and revolver, and beat him unconscious with black-jacks and stones. They rolled him on his back and ground their heels in his face for punctuation.

Sullivan was hospitalized for weeks, and the triumph of the Dusters was joyously celebrated not only locally but by gangdom at large. A member of the Gophers, One Lung Curran, the acknowledged poet laureate of the West Side gangs, was so impressed by the Dusters' feat that he was moved to congratulate them in verse:

> Says Dinny, "Here's me only chance
> To gain meself a name;
> I'll clean up the Hudson Dusters,
> And reach the hall of fame."
> He lost his stick and cannon,
> And his shield they took away,
> It was then that he remembered
> Every dog has got his day.

One Lung wrote half a dozen additional stanzas describing the attack in detail, and the Dusters had the ditty printed and distributed among Village saloons and barbershops. The legends about One Lung Curran and Ding Dong made a permanent impression on O'Neill. Their names were on a list of more than eighty he jotted down among his early notes as possible designations for characters in *The Iceman Cometh*.

Accompanied by Scotty Stuart or Robert Brown or Terry Carlin, O'Neill wove between the Garden Hotel barroom and the Hell Hole but, when the proprietors would not extend their hospitality beyond the designated closing hour, he was likely to move on to Polly Holladay's or Romany Marie's.

Polly's and Marie's were among the dimly lit Village caves that served food and coffee throughout much of the night. The two women knew their customers by their first names and were willing to stake those who could not pay.

Polly Holladay was living with a man whom O'Neill had first met at Benjamin Tucker's bookstore. He was Hippolyte Havel, a former lover of Emma Goldman and a familiar Village figure, once likened to a ragged chrysanthemum.

Born in Bohemia, then a part of Austria, of a gypsy mother, Hippolyte had worked with Karl Marx on an anarchist publication in Germany. On the run from the law, he was picked up and placed in the mental ward of a German prison. The psychiatrist Krafft-Ebing pronounced him sane — an opinion not unequivocally shared by Hippolyte's Village friends.

Released from the mental ward, he remained in prison, from

which he escaped and made his way to London. It was there he met
Emma Goldman, who helped him reach Chicago, where he joined
her radical circle and edited the anarchist newspaper,
Arbeiterzeitung.

O'Neill had portrayed Hippolyte in *The Personal Equation*, as the
minor figure, Hartmann (a member of the "International Workers
Union"). In that early play, he is depicted as "an undersized man"
whose "head is massive, too large for his body, with long black hair
brushed straight back from his broad forehead. His large dark eyes
peer near-sightedly from behind a pair of thick-rimmed spectacles."

A frequenter of the Hell Hole, Hippolyte Havel evolved in *Iceman*
as Hugo Kalmar ("one-time editor of Anarchist periodicals" whose
surname is a conjunction derived from Karl Marx). O'Neill's description of him mirrors his earlier portrait of Hartmann: "a small man"
who "has a head much too big for his body, a high forehead . . . black
eyes which peer near-sightedly from behind thick-lensed spectacles."
Both Hartmann and Kalmar wear mustaches, as did Hippolyte
(although neither wears the goatee that was his real-life trademark).

That winter, Hippolyte was doing double duty as Polly's lover
and cook, and he was the center of attention at the restaurant. His
temper tantrums often erupted into drunken and profane denuncia-
tions — delivered in his middle-European accent — of those he
labeled "bourgeois pigs!" He was fond of spouting the final lines of
the forty-line poem, "Revolution," by the 19th century German poet,
Ferdinand Freiligrath: "The day grows hot, O Babylon! 'Tis cool
beneath the willow trees!"

The poem, with its biblical and Marxist allusions, had first been
published in America in March 1910, in Emma Goldman's Mother
Earth, which Hippolyte helped edit.

Whether O'Neill remembered the final lines from reading them,
or from hearing Hippolyte recite them over and over, they stuck in
his mind. He gave them first to the rebellious Richard Miller in *Ah,
Wilderness!* and, seven years later, to Hugo Kalmar in *Iceman*. In each
case, he slightly misquoted the lines: "The days grow hot, O Babylon!
'Tis cool beneath thy willow trees!"

Polly and Hippolyte did not live peacefully, for Polly had a rov-
ing eye and, though Hippolyte was theoretically committed to sexual freedom, he tended to lose his perspective where Polly was concerned. Polly's grievance against Hippolyte was of a different sort.

One night, after Hippolyte had made an especially noisy scene at
the restaurant, she complained to Hutchins Hapgood that her lover

was not acting in good faith because he had not committed suicide. "He promised me over and over again," she said, "but he just won't keep his word."

When Hippolyte once denounced Polly in Hapgood's presence for being unfaithful, the embarrassed Hapgood queried Polly's brother, Louis, about their accelerating battles. "Why shouldn't they if they like it?" said Louis. "And they seem to. They're always at it."

Christine and Lewis Ell sometimes joined them in a four-sided battle. According to Hapgood, the four were often "huddled together in the restaurant" and "this communism developed its usual difficulties: jealousies, nerves, drunkenness as a relief and physical enormities" (which Hapgood did not specify). He went on to quote Christine as saying, "The trouble was that we were all so close together that we felt each other's vibrations."

O'Neill was drawn to Polly's partly because he enjoyed listening to Hippolyte, partly because he was apt to find Louis there. However, he found it more peaceful at Romany Marie's, in Washington Place, where no liquor was served but where he could bask in the proprietor's maternal aura. A buxom, flamboyant woman of thirty with a heavily accented, throaty voice, Marie came from a family of conservative Romanians. She pretended to be a gypsy, bedecking herself in jewelry and gaudy colors. Her husband, Damon Marchand, a translator for immigrants at Ellis Island, assisted her in the restaurant.

"There was never a question of anyone having enough to eat," Marie once said, "as long as there was food on my stove." In lieu of liquor, Marie served her strong brew of Turkish coffee.

One day, six Hudson Dusters paid a visit to the restaurant.

"It was early in the evening and our place was packed," recalled Marie, "but when they came in, the customers quietly began to melt away."

Marie watched helplessly as her restaurant emptied, and regretted O'Neill's absence. She knew he had somehow managed to establish a rapport with the gang.

"Give us the strongest drink you have in the house," one of the Dusters demanded.

"The strongest drink is Turkish coffee," Marie said nervously.

"Serve it," ordered the tough.

Marie served three rounds of coffee, her husband watching apprehensively from the kitchen. Then Marie, knowing she could call on O'Neill for protection, looked the leader straight in the eye and told him, "You've had enough coffee." She presented her bill, which came to $4.50, certain the thugs would consider it exorbitant. To her astonishment, the leader reached into his pocket and brought out the cash, pushed back his chair and swaggered out, followed by his men. They made straight for the Hell Hole, where they encountered O'Neill.

"That Romany Marie is some dame," the leader told him. "She put us out of her place, and made us pay for our coffee. Her husband was scared, but she wasn't." O'Neill, upset, asked the Dusters to stay out of Marie's. His request was obeyed.

The Dusters valued O'Neill's friendship. They knew he was the son of "Monte Cristo" and were in awe of his education. They also knew he had knocked about and could talk their language, and that, like them, he carried his Irish heritage like a banner. The Dusters referred to him as "the Kid," or their "old pal, Gene." When a fight broke out in the Hell Hole, one of them was always sure to shout, "Look out for the Kid!"

Early that winter, one of the Dusters — doubtless Ding Dong, reputed to be a talented thief — noticed that O'Neill was going about in a jacket lined with newspapers to keep out the cold. He urged O'Neill to take a walk up Sixth Avenue, select a coat in any store and let him know his choice; the coat would be delivered to him the following day.

O'Neill was touched, but declined the offer.

Later that winter, O'Neill resumed his acquaintance with John Reed, who had become the enfant terrible of American journalism, as well known for his political activism as for his impassioned reporting. He had recently returned from covering the war in Europe and was happy to rejoin his friends at the Hell Hole.

At twenty-eight, Reed was only a year older than O'Neill. Six feet tall, curly-haired, green-eyed, with a generous mouth and pugnacious chin, he could look by turns the raffish adventurer and the melancholy poet. A flamboyant, uninhibited, often witty conversationalist, he had a candid opinion about everything. His friends found his throbbing enthusiasm for his pet subjects irresistible.

Previously Reed and O'Neill had known each other only slightly, and they were surprised to discover how much they had in common. Reed, his early imagination fired like O'Neill's by London and Conrad, had felt the lure of the sea and, like O'Neill, had dreamed of becoming a "he-man" writer. He marveled at O'Neill's youthful daring in having shipped out and at his adventures in Honduras, Buenos Aires and Liverpool.

Always interested in the stage as a means of dramatizing injustices toward the working man, Reed was absorbed by O'Neill's vast knowledge of the theater. O'Neill, in turn, admired Reed as the quintessentially daring foreign correspondent, and was absorbed by his tales of his feats in Mexico and his more recent adventures on both the western and eastern European battlefronts.

While Reed was as gregarious and exuberant as O'Neill was moody and introverted, both were inveterate romantics and idealists. Both wrote poetry and shared similar views about Life and Art — including a mutual distrust of capitalists and self-appointed authority figures. Like O'Neill, Reed had explored the Haymarket and the Tenderloin and had often lingered on Manhattan's downtown waterfront.

Drawn to the city's underbelly, O'Neill and Reed were immersed in sympathy for the downtrodden, especially prostitutes, and could listen with endless fascination to their tales of woe.

Both, in fact, had written about prostitutes in 1913, their works in each case greeted with a lack of enthusiasm; just as O'Neill's one-acter, *The Web*, could not find a producer, Reed's short story, "Where the Heart Is" — about a Haymarket dime-a-dance girl — was rejected by every mainstream magazine until finally accepted by The Masses (for no pay). That same year The Masses also published Reed's one-act play, *Moondown*, about working girls forced to sleep with their bosses.

Reed and O'Neill also had in common a background of poor health and both had become excellent swimmers in compensation for their inability to excel at other sports. In addition, they had led lonely childhoods and felt special and set apart. But while O'Neill tended to retreat into the seedy world of derelicts and embrace it as his own, Reed — with his more conventional middle-class background and his optimistic view of life — had learned how to live in two worlds.

Both men also shared an affinity for the murky ambiance of the barroom, although Reed, unlike O'Neill, drank socially rather than compulsively. Of course, they held this affinity for the tavern in common with many of their literary mentors — particularly Jack London, whose classic description of the saloon's seductive ambiance was surely familiar to both Reed and O'Neill:

"Here life was always very live, and sometimes even lurid, when blows were struck, and blood was shed, and big policemen came shouldering in . . . In the saloons, even the sots, stupefied, sprawling across the tables or in the sawdust, were objects of mystery and wonder." London, who began drinking at seven, wrote those words in his widely read *John Barleycorn*, a partly autobiographical tract against liquor published in 1913, as well as serialized in the Saturday Evening Post.

Just as the singing of chanteys was the bond that united sailors aboard a ship, so was the croaking of sentimental songs the glue that held together the barroom inebriates in maudlin camaraderie. O'Neill could sing them all, as he could the songs of the sea.

The writer, Malcolm Cowley, recalled hearing O'Neill, during drinks in a Greenwich Village saloon, huskily render a verse of "Whiskey Johnny": "Whiskey is the life of man,/(Whiskey—Johnny),/Oh, I drink whiskey when I/ca—a—an/(Whiskey for my Johnny)."

In *The Iceman Cometh*, which, of all O'Neill's plays, dwells most explicitly and relentlessly on the alcoholic mystique of the barroom, he subtly displays his expertise. Just before the final curtain, when the barroom drunks have regained the hopeless hope Hickey has tried to deny them, they all begin to sing, catching fire from Harry Hope, who "starts the chorus of 'She's the Sunshine of Paradise Alley.'"

In his stage directions, O'Neill writes: " . . . instantly they all burst into song. But not the same song. Each starts the chorus of his or her choice . . . " O'Neill then lists the titles of the twelve different songs that twelve of the barroom habitués howl, including such popular ballads as "Waiting at the Church" and "You Great Big Beautiful Doll," as well as Hugo Kalmar's choice of the French Revolutionary "Carmagnole."

"A weird cacophony results from this mixture and they stop singing to roar with laughter . . . " writes O'Neill. He has made his point.

Reed had arrived in Greenwich Village from his native Portland, Oregon, in the spring of 1911, at the same time that O'Neill, recently back from Buenos Aires, moved into Jimmy the Priest's. Reed had begun his career at twenty-four, as contributor to the American magazine, a job arranged by Lincoln Steffens, who lived in Reed's apartment building at 43 Washington Square South — a place, Steffens once said, "where youth lived and reds gathered."

Reed's embrace of the radical movement and his emergence as an activist-journalist was not sparked until the spring of 1913, when he covered the strike of 25,000 silk-mill workers in Paterson, New Jersey.

Organized by Big Bill Haywood's I.W.W., the strike was going badly. One evening at Haywood's Greenwich Village apartment, Reed heard him expound on the pitiable working conditions and low pay prevalent in the mills. The newspapers, Haywood charged, had blatantly ignored the strikers' side of the story, and Reed went to Paterson to see for himself.

As soon as Reed arrived, a detective ordered him off the street. Reed argued he was breaking no law, but was nonetheless arrested. He spent four days in jail before a friend bailed him out. He then joined the strikers long enough to confirm the callousness of the mill owners and the brutal tactics of the police. Haywood, he now believed, had rightly accused the press of unfair reporting.

Returning to New York, Reed wrote a vehement eyewitness account that appeared in The Masses in June 1913, under the heading "War in Paterson." Finding it impossible to stand by any longer as a neutral observer, he made up his mind to abandon what he decried as "the hypocrisy" of objectivity. The story, which brought him considerable notoriety, set his style of passionate participatory journalism from then on.

Mabel Dodge, who had been at Haywood's apartment when he expounded on the origins of the strike, suggested a pageant to raise money for the strikers. Reed volunteered to write a script depicting — in action and song — the brutality of the mill owners and the police.

When it was decided to rent Madison Square Garden for the event, Reed persuaded Robert Edmond Jones, a former Harvard classmate, to design a gigantic set representing a silk mill, on a stage to hold a thousand strikers with their wives and children. Spectacular and moving as it was, the pageant did not draw sufficient contributions and the strike was lost.

Having worked closely together on the pageant, Reed and Mabel inevitably became lovers. The affair, entered upon with headlong passion, soon turned rocky, and it was not long before Reed leaped at the chance to escape Mabel's possessiveness. He accepted an assignment from the Metropolitan to cover the great news event of the day, Pancho Villa's revolution in Mexico (the inspiration a year later for O'Neill's one-act comedy, The Movie Man).

Reed on horseback, wearing a sombrero, galloped into battle with the formidable Villa. Enthusiastically submitting himself to a life of daily hazard, he was shot at and pursued by enemy forces and nearly perished from thirst in the desert, all the while churning controversy with his graphic partisan accounts of the rebel cause.

In one dispatch, he wrote of a meal taken with Villa's soldiers on the march: "At noon we roped a steer, and cut his throat. And because there was no time to build a fire, we ripped the meat from the carcass and ate it raw."

The Metropolitan advertised Reed's stories as "word pictures of war by an American Kipling," and also compared him to Stephen Crane and Richard Harding Davis. They did not exaggerate, for Reed's gift of imagery and dramatic detail truly gripped his readers. Not surprisingly, the Metropolitan openly acknowledged Reed as its pet.

Until 1912, when the magazine was bought by the multimillionaire, Harry Payne Whitney, it devoted itself to the fiction of such as Conrad, Kipling and Booth Tarkington. Whitney brought in H. J. Wigham, the British Fabian Socialist, to transform the magazine into a voice of provocative social commentary, and Wigham in turn invited contributions from an eclectic group that included George Bernard Shaw, Walter Lippmann, Havelock Ellis and Lincoln Steffens — as well as Theodore Roosevelt, who violently opposed socialism.

A story in circulation held that when Reed and Roosevelt chanced to meet in the offices of the Metropolitan the air crackled with animosity.

"Villa is a murderer and a rapist," Roosevelt snapped at Reed.

"Well, I believe in rape," retorted Reed.

Roosevelt extended his hand. "I am glad, John Reed," he said, "to find that you believe in something. It is very necessary for a young man to believe in something."

With his popularity soaring after his success in Mexico, Reed did not lack for other choice assignments. When the war broke out in Europe, he instantly headed for the battlefront, first covering the French and German sides and later the eastern European front. In the late fall of 1915, he returned to New York to begin preparing a book based on his articles. It was not long after that he encountered O'Neill and warmly befriended him.

When he learned of O'Neill's failed efforts to get his plays produced, Reed encouraged him to keep on writing. The one thing that concerned him was O'Neill's ruthless drinking. Believing that even a small measure of recognition might lighten his friend's melancholy,

Reed tried to intercede for him at the Metropolitan. Sonya Levien
Hovey, wife of the Metropolitan's managing editor, Carl Hovey, and
herself on the staff of the magazine, recalled that Reed introduced
Eugene to her husband as a potential contributor.

Although grateful for Reed's support, O'Neill was not yet ready
to arise from his drunken depths. The few extant O'Neill poems from
that period, most written while drinking in the Hell Hole, are bleak
and cynical. "Good Night" is representative:

> Put out the light!
> Let us sleep!
> Pull down the shade
> Let us hide
> From the meaning wink
> Of the worldly stars
> From the smirk
> Of the sated moon
> Peering
> There
> Through the window pane
> Dirty with tears
> Of old rains.
>
> Patter, patter, patter,
> Go the little feet
> Of the little people —
> Bound whither?
>
> Chatter, chatter, chatter
> Runs the little talk
> Of the little people
> As they lie to each other.
>
> Put out the light
> Let us sleep!

O'Neill also composed a brief verse, "Revolution," initially entitled "Tiger." The poem, however, had nothing to do with the social
revolutions of either Freiligrath or William Blake. While somewhat
cryptic, it appears to refer to the artistic revolution O'Neill envisioned
for the American theater; it can be read as a sardonic attack on the
experimental groups that were vastly pleased with their own daring
but — to O'Neill's mind — had made only the most tepid departures:

Tiger, tiger!
How beautiful you look!
How strong you seem!
How somnolent you are!

Have you tested the bars of your cage,
Have you found them too strong,
Is that why you doze?

See the crowds watching you
With their timid, curious eyes!

Tiger, tiger!
You are proud of your stripes
But are you a tiger
Or merely an overgrown
Alley cat?

Although unrelated to Blake's "The Tyger," the poem is an early indication of O'Neill's admiration for the poet's work, which he doubtless knew from the collection edited by Edwin J. Ellis and William Butler Yeats, a literary idol.

O'Neill declared himself honored when Yeats, in 1932, asked him to join the newly organized Irish Academy, explaining that while other literary academies held little meaning for him, "Anything with Yeats, Shaw, A. E. [Houseman], O'Casey, Flaherty, Robinson in it is good enough for me."

For Christmas, 1927, O'Neill gave Carlotta Monterey, soon to be his wife, Geoffrey Keynes's 1925, three-volume edition of *The Writings of William Blake.*

Referring in his inscription to the traditional assumption that Blake's grandfather was an Irish O'Neill (or O'Neil), he wrote: "As a patriotic Irish clan egotist I want to give you all the O'Neill you can endure without fetching a shriek — so what gift more to the point than the immortal beauty (reproduced) of the grandest of all O'Neills, past, present & to come?"

Although O'Neill's discontent in the winter of 1916 was due largely to his failure to receive professional recognition, it is fair to conjecture that his unhappiness was compounded by his separation from Beatrice, as the final stanzas of another poem scribbled in the Hell Hole attest:

Dirty
Bricks
Of buildings!
Sallow
Window shades!
Even the cats
Yowl
For freedom
From their backyards.

Underdrawers
On the lines
Between
Firescapes [sic]
Loose their
Evanescent
Charm

Ah, Love
Indecent,
Beautiful,
How I miss you!

O'Neill's affair with Beatrice appears to have frozen into a state of irresolution, although he professed to still be in love with her. She evidently made at least one trip to New York while he was living in Greenwich Village; O'Neill, as he later wrote to remind her, had asked a mutual friend to bring her downtown to meet him for dinner at Christine's restaurant, but somehow the plan miscarried.

" . . . I wanted oh, so much to see you," he protested. "I didn't dare go to you myself for I thought you must hate me . . . If you had come down it would have saved me many nights and days of hell when I longed for you so hopelessly. I would have cried in your arms and you would have forgiven me, Dear Old Big Heart."

Despite his longing, however, he did not scruple to take advantage of more accessible prospects. He had, in fact, returned, as he had once threatened Beatrice he would, to "the beast hunt of old times." As usual, he did not have to hunt far; in spite of his ragged condition, both emotional and physical, he found that women continued to gravitate to him.

For a while, he amused himself with Beckie Edelson, a former lover of Big Bill Haywood. A committed labor organizer who had recently undergone a hunger strike in jail, she was also a sensual and appealing woman who found time to flit from man to man.

O'Neill was at last beginning to realize it was hopeless to expect Beatrice ever to fling away her provincial attitudes and adopt the freedom of the women who surrounded him in the Village. He envied John Reed, who had recently found a new love, and was living with her in Washington Square.

Having rested from his European assignment and nursed the bruises from his on-again-off-again affair with Mabel Dodge, Reed had gone in November to visit his mother in Portland, where he met Louise Bryant. She was as free from conventional restraints as Beatrice Ashe was fettered by them. With scant if any misgivings, Bryant left her husband, a Portland dentist named Paul Trullinger, to join Reed early in January.

Lyrically in love, Reed wrote to a friend, "I think I've found Her at last. She's wild, brave, and straight — and graceful and lovely to look at." He brought her to his ramshackle apartment at 43 Washington Square, not far from the boardinghouse O'Neill had recently been obliged to leave.

Their domestic arrangements, like those of most of their friends, were casual in the extreme. Neither was concerned with material comfort — although Reed by now was earning an adequate living. He proudly displayed Louise to all his friends, including O'Neill.

Louise was undeniably wild — and brave, too, in the sense of being recklessly eager to squander herself. And she was undeniably lovely, with chestnut hair heightened by a blonde sheen, eyes that could deepen from gray to violet, a slender figure, and a provocative, gamine quality that enabled her to look far younger than her age. She had attempted journalism in Portland with some success and was determined to make something of herself as a writer.

Mabel Dodge, on hearing of Reed's new love, decided he was simply taking jealous revenge. "He had to stiffen inside himself and feel coldly toward me so as not to mind too much," wrote Mabel, with characteristic egoism. Mabel could not resist inventing a flimsy excuse to size up her replacement.

"One late afternoon I knocked at [Reed's] door," she wrote. "It was opened by a very pretty, tall, young woman . . . who held a lighted candle in her hand.

"'Is Jack Reed here?' I asked.

"He appeared suddenly behind her with rumpled hair and hurt eyes . . .

"'This is Louise Bryant,' he told me gravely.

"'How do you do?' I asked, but she didn't tell me. 'Reed, I came to ask you for your old typewriter, if you're not using it.'

"'Louise is using it,' he said.

"'Oh, all right. I only thought . . .'"

Hurrying on after this pathetic revelation, Mabel recovered her equilibrium sufficiently to record her acid summary of Louise's character:

"The girl was clever with a certain Irish quickness and very eager to get on. I think Reed was a stepping stone, and through him she met a lot of people she never would have known otherwise. It had not seemed to me that she cared very much for him."

Indeed, Reed introduced Louise to his editors and her writing career began to advance. But although ambitious, she seemed even more eager for romance and adventure than for fame. She was also very much subject to her emotions; while devoted to Reed, she found it difficult to resist anyone who seemed to need her.

Like many Village couples, she and Reed had a tacit agreement that love must be free, and Reed made no bones about his own frequent — if mostly inconsequential — dalliances.

Louise was less forthright. She yearned to be all things to all men, but she seemed to want each of her lovers to believe he was the only one.

A facile fabricator, Louise had a tendency to mythologize herself. O'Neill began to fantasize a love affair with Louise, even while he still yearned for his impregnable Beatrice — although he felt guilty about desiring the woman who belonged to his good friend.

In mid-May, he learned that Reed and Louise were planning to spend the summer in Provincetown; Reed told O'Neill about the experimental theater on Mary Vorse's wharf. Although he had not been in Provincetown the previous summer, Reed had had long talks with Jig Cook during the winter and had, in fact, become his ardent disciple.

He was caught up in Cook's dream of creating an American theater that would be the equivalent of the Dionysian dance. Having seen native drama in Mexico, Reed agreed that such theater could be created out of group spirit and free expression on an experimental stage. He urged O'Neill to come along and participate.

O'Neill's long mood of despair was drawing to an end. Perhaps he had needed the plunge into the depths once again to make him aware of the possibilities of life. Miraculously, he had survived the damage he had inflicted on himself. When Terry Carlin agreed to accompany him, O'Neill decided to take Reed up on his suggestion.

"It was the late John Reed who first brought me to Provincetown," O'Neill acknowledged seven years later in an interview with a Boston newspaper. He did not say precisely what motivated him to go. It might have been the hope of finally finding a platform for his work, or the fantasy that Louise would fall in love with him — or, perhaps, a desire to be once again near the sea.

Summering in New London did not seem to be an option. Regarding himself as a failure, he was unwilling to face his parents or, for that matter, the boyhood friends who would expect him to have made his mark by now.

Whatever it was that propelled him to Provincetown, it was a step that probably saved his life. It most certainly proved crucial to his emergence at last as an acknowledged playwright.

PART SEVEN
RECOGNITION

"What I am after is to get an audience to leave the theatre with an exultant feeling from seeing somebody on the stage facing life, fighting against the eternal odds, not conquering, but perhaps inevitably being conquered. The individual life is made significant just by the struggle . . . "

— O'NEILL, in an interview four years after his first Broadway production, *Beyond the Horizon*, in 1920

Chapter
FORTY-FOUR

WHEN JIG COOK AND SUSAN GLASPELL HASTENED BACK to Provincetown in the spring of 1916 to revive their theater on the wharf, they had no inkling of the epic moment awaiting them. Cook announced a season of four bills of one-act plays to begin in mid-July and managed to enlist a subscription audience of eighty-seven, each paying $2.50 for a pair of tickets to each program. Flush for the moment, the Provincetown Players, as they had decided to call themselves, installed suitable lighting and purchased lumber for permanent benches.

Reed and Bryant rented a large white clapboard house at 592 Commercial Street. Reed's painful recurrence of a chronic kidney ailment did not inhibit him from filling the house with guests. He had hired Hippolyte Havel to be his cook for the summer, paying him, according to Bryant, "something like $80 dollars a month." Few of Reed's friends could have indulged in such an extravagance, but Reed, as "one of the most popular writers in America" — in Bryant's words — was also among the highest paid.

"He made at that time about twenty-five thousand dollars a year," she said. "We used to spend it as he made it." In taking on Hippolyte, Reed perhaps was responding to a comment once made by Theodore Dreiser, that Hippolyte was "one of those men who ought to be supported by the community, he is a valuable person for life, but can't take care of himself."

Hippolyte's menus were inventive and his after-dinner conversation provocative. Once, after Reed had expounded on some radical cause, Hippolyte furiously accused him of being "a parlor socialist," to which Reed retorted, "And you're a kitchen anarchist!" Reed's house resounded to the quarrels and reconciliations of Hippolyte and his fickle love, Polly Holladay, who had joined him in Provincetown.

Although Reed reveled in the company of his friends, at times he found that the bustle of his household exacerbated the fatigue caused by his illness. Thus, during June, he welcomed the magazine assignments that afforded him periodic escapes — even though they meant parting from Louise.

When he was on assignment — covering presidential conventions, for example — Reed exchanged ardent love letters with Louise. In one letter, she enclosed a nude photograph of herself lying against the dunes, inscribing it: "This is to remind you of 'The Dunes' and Please, Honey, take good care of yourself out there." Reed replied he was "thinking about the dunes all the time." A week later he wrote, " . . . O how I wish I was in my sweetheart's arms in bed together!"

Reed was apt to issue casual invitations to friends encountered during his travels, and Louise found herself called upon to entertain people who presented themselves as houseguests, and whom she had never met. That summer she was hostess to the painters, Marsden Hartley and Charles Demuth (who had portrayed Marmaduke Marvin Jr. in Wilbur Daniel Steele's *Change Your Style* the summer before).

O'Neill later drew on the personalities (and combined names) of the two painters for the character of Charles Marsden in *Strange Interlude*. The imaginary Marsden, congenitally ill at ease with women, is depicted as possessing "an indefinable feminine quality." Although he is a writer rather than a painter, he is, like both Hartley and Demuth, a committed and somewhat beleaguered bachelor.

Max Eastman, who lived across the street with his wife, Ida Rauh, and their young son, described the comings and goings at the Reed house as "a spectacle." He thought Louise an indifferent housekeeper and called their summer home "barnlike," but conceded that a "large assortment of interesting males was provided with abundant nutrition . . . and beds to sleep on."

Eastman's somewhat sour view of the Provincetown group might have sprung from his own personal malaise that summer. He was planning to leave Ida, one of the group's committed members.

Hutchins Hapgood, on the other hand, relished every aspect of his relationship with them. "The original Provincetown group," he wrote, "were workers; they lived pleasantly together, made love, had occasional bouts with Bacchus, and did what more conventional people would call unseemly things, but they had a rather steadfast general purpose in life, a quiet persistency in trying to express themselves more truthfully in writing or painting than is fashionable, and they cared really little for the big successes, measured by money, of the world."

Among the Provincetowners that summer was E. J. ("Teddy") Ballantine, an actor who had come from England with Mrs. Pat Campbell's production of *Pygmalion*, and who threw himself eagerly into all activities. He was married to Emma Goldman's niece, Stella, a would-be actor herself, who had invited her aunt to visit them and their baby for a month.

Goldman was grateful for the respite from the emotional problems that regularly beset her. In Provincetown with her family, she wrote, "I would rest and perhaps find peace, peace." (Duty to the Cause called poor Emma away well before her month was up.)

The Balantines also invited Stella's brother, Saxe Commins, a medical student at the University of Pennsylvania, who later switched to dentistry. Commins was soon to forge a lifelong bond with O'Neill — first as his dentist and later as his editor.

Commins's kinship with Goldman provided him entree to the writers, artists and political radicals of Greenwich Village. "It was through Jack Reed and Louise Bryant that I first met Eugene O'Neill," Commins noted in a memoir introducing his extensive correspondence with O'Neill.

The Ballantines apparently were not aware that they, along with their expected houseguests, were targets of a lurking cultural bias typical of many of the era's most enlightened thinkers and writers.

Writing to Reed in mid-June, for example, Louise told him, "Hip and I . . . called on Stella and got reports of the Jewish invasion soon to take place in Provincetown . . . " A day or two later, Stella visited Louise "with more reports of the Jewish invasion." Derisively, Louise added, "It's going to be a sort of New Jerusalem at that end of town."

It is clear that at least some of Provincetown's dedicated liberals and humanitarians shared in the embedded atavistic bigotry. Even Hippolyte, once Goldman's lover, manifested this reflexive bias. Informing Reed that their landlord was coming to make a requested repair, Louise wrote, "He is a little fresh Jew and Hippolyte almost dies when he is around. He says he forgets about the Brotherhood when fresh Jews appear."

Louise was unabashed at expressing these sentiments, for she believed that Reed (though with more reserve) shared them. At Harvard, Reed, considered something of a misfit and snubbed by classmates during his freshman year, was finally befriended by a Jewish youth.

"We were always together, we two outsiders," he later recalled. "I became irritated and morbid about it — it seemed I would never be part of the rich splendor of college life with him around — so I drew away from him . . . It hurt him very much, and it taught me better. Since then he has forgiven it, and done wonderful things for me, and we are friends."

While individual Jews apparently were acceptable as friends — especially if they served a useful purpose — somehow, in groups, they were seen as a threat. In any event, Reed did not find it necessary to chide Louise for her attitude.

When Reed returned to Provincetown on June 21, he was surprised to learn that O'Neill had yet to arrive. Reed had invited him to to stay at his house and encouraged him to join the Players.

O'Neill had in fact reached the Cape with Carlin in mid-June, but chose not to go directly to Provincetown, pausing instead in the adjoining village of Truro. O'Neill was in no hurry. For one thing, he dreaded groups of any kind. An even stronger deterrent was his long history of professional rebuff. To approach Cook's theater, he needed to collect his courage.

Then, too, O'Neill was back on a meager allowance from his father. Although living was cheap in Provincetown, it was even cheaper in the hull of the wreck on the Truro beach where he and Carlin established squatters' rights.

Carlin read and O'Neill swam, gradually working off the effects of his derelict winter. He did not quit drinking, but did attempt to moderate his intake — all the while keeping a watchful eye on the theatrical cauldron a few miles down-Cape. He, of course, had no more intimation than Cook that the Provincetown summer of 1916 would come to symbolize the turning point of the American stage, or that his was to be the voice responsible.

Toward the end of June, with funds exhausted, Carlin persuaded O'Neill to accompany him to Provincetown, where he planned to ask Hutchins Hapgood to "lend" him ten dollars. Hapgood produced the cash.

As Louise Bryant remembered it, O'Neill and Carlin presented themselves at the Reed house early one morning, before anyone but Hippolyte was awake. Professing great distress, Hippolyte reported to Louise that O'Neill was drunk. "Don't have anything to do with those two bums. You'll be sorry if you do," he warned her. But Louise ordered him to serve O'Neill and Carlin breakfast.

After helping O'Neill drink some coffee from a cup he could bare-ly hold in his shaking hands, she asked him what he planned to do. He told her he "wanted to get a place where he could live simply," and she suggested the empty fisherman's shack diagonally across Commercial Street.

O'Neill and Carlin moved in and, according to Louise, "Gene set-tled down to try to get off drink. I helped him do that. It was quite a task."

Hapgood, in a letter to Mabel Dodge on July 1 inviting her to visit, wrote: "There is a bunch here now in addition to the usual Provincetonians ... Jack's house is full of guests." He added that Carlin and O'Neill had taken a "studio" and that the "play fever is on."

O'Neill and Carlin slept in hammocks. Louise maintained that O'Neill — if not Carlin — took most of his meals at the Reed house, but others present that summer recalled that both O'Neill and Carlin often ate from cans, tossing them out their back door. They occasion-ally cooked the fresh catch offered by the Portuguese fishermen.

A long poem entitled "Silence," dated "7/9/16," is an indication of O'Neill's muddled state of mind as he tried to taper off alcohol. Intermingling metaphorical whores with metaphorical nuns in its eleven stanzas (and alternately invoking Death and Love), he began:

> The earth,
> Stripped bare of sound,
> Lies at the feet of Silence,
> Like a nude whore,
> Gross, sentimental, sweaty,
> Dreaming of love.

And in a later stanza:

> Silence,
> Pale, ivory-skinned,
> A naked nun
> With a rosary of great black pearls
> Hanging between her breasts, — Silence
> With cool lips kisses me,
> And gives me her rosary
> Of dead centuries
> To play with.

Two days before the Players were to present their first bill, some costumes hanging near a stove caught fire. The flames, before they could be subdued, blackened two walls of the theater and destroyed the curtain. Ever the resourceful entrepreneur, Cook had the uncharred walls stained black to match the burned ones, hung them with old fishing nets for added atmosphere and replaced the curtain.

On July 15, the Provincetown Players bravely rang up the curtain with three one-act plays. Heading the bill was *Freedom*, a satire by Reed that had been turned down by the Washington Square Players, about the divergent ideas of four men who are not free. The second play was *Winter's Night* by Neith Boyce, about two brothers in love with the same woman. The bill ended with *Suppressed Desires*, the previous summer's success. All seats were filled, but there is no record of O'Neill having been in the audience.

Though thirteen dollars had been the largest outlay for any of the productions, the treasury was depleted. To supplement subscriptions, single admissions at a dollar each were solicited for the next three bills. Provincetown's growing summer colony was only too eager to embrace its new entertainment and the money flowed in.

The Players, however, were experiencing difficulty coming up with a second bill. Wilbur Steele had completed a one-acter, *Not Smart*, about the hypocrisy of Provincetown's sexual mores, and several others in the group, including Louise Bryant, submitted scripts. However, there was no agreement on three plays strong enough to carry the next program, already announced for the end of July. The Players were in near-panic.

Enter O'Neill.

It is no surprise that accounts of what happened next differ dramatically. Understandably, many of those involved — gauging the dimensions of the legend with hindsight — were eager to claim a share in the discovery of O'Neill as a playwright.

The most widely accepted version is Susan Glaspell's, recounted in a memoir published eleven years after the event and following her husband's death: Happening to encounter Carlin as he strolled about Provincetown, greeting friends, she asked him forlornly, "Haven't you a play to read to us?"

"No," answered Carlin, "I don't write, I just think, and sometimes talk." He said his friend, Gene O'Neill, "has got a whole trunk full of plays." This part of the story is patently apocryphal, for O'Neill's trunk was still impounded at 48 Washington Square West and, in any case, his entire output consisted of the *Thirst* volume and a few typed manuscripts.

According to Glaspell, it was arranged for O'Neill to be at the Cook's house during the final vote to determine which three one-acters would compose the Players' second bill. The gathering included Harry Kemp, the "hobo" poet, and his wife, Mary Pyne. Reed and Louise were of course present and — in Glaspell's version — *Bound East for Cardiff* was read aloud by Frederic Burt, a professional actor, while O'Neill sat alone in the dining room, afraid to listen.

Harry Kemp told a rather different story in an article published three years after Glaspell's version (and in which he made no reference to her account). Kemp, an alcoholic, was under numerous misapprehensions:

He described Carlin as being "close upon seventy," when in fact he was in his fifties; he placed O'Neill and Carlin in quarters they would not actually occupy until the following summer; and he confused Eugene's history with Jamie's, stating the rift between Eugene and his father "came because the son refused to be an actor."

Kemp's account nevertheless contains kernels of fact not commonly acknowledged. It might very well be true, for instance, as he maintained, that O'Neill initially proffered the group "a book of one-act plays for perusal, for the printing of which he admitted he had somehow paid." While Kemp did not mention the book's title it could only have been *Thirst and Other One-Act Plays*. The group did, in fact produce *Thirst* later that summer.

Of particular note is Kemp's account of a reading by O'Neill himself, at Reed's house, of a play whose title he does not give, but which must have been *The Movie Man*, the farce about a filmmaker's staged battle scene during the Mexican Revolution. The play had not been published, but Kemp was able to sum up the plot convincingly from memory, observing it was "frightfully bad, trite and full of the most preposterous hokum."

Kemp went on to describe a subsequent meeting, at which it was O'Neill himself (not Frederic Burt) who "delivered in his low, deep, slightly monotonous but compelling voice the lines of a one-act play" that was obviously *Bound East for Cardiff*. "This time," wrote Kemp, "no one doubted that here was a genuine playwright."

There was scarcely anyone in that supremely egoistical group who did *not* write a memoir of that period, and Hutchins Hapgood, in his autobiography, gave yet another version, published nine years after Kemp's. He claimed it was his wife, Neith Boyce, not Susan

Glaspell, who "discovered" *Bound East for Cardiff*:

"Gene came to a meeting of the little group at one of the houses and sat on the floor, perfectly silent, listening intently — a striking figure, his young face gaunt and taut-mouthed, his eyes burning. After that meeting, he gave us the manuscript of *Bound East for Cardiff* to read. Neith took it to Jig and said, 'We have got to do this play.' Jig read it and agreed."

Perhaps O'Neill himself should be allowed the final word: "*Bound East for Cardiff* was the first play I read to the Provincetown Group," he wrote many years later to a member of the Associated Press who was preparing a biographical work.

Whatever the details, there is no doubt the group's response to the play's vitality and originality was instantaneous and wholehearted. Reed congratulated him and Louise regarded O'Neill with new interest. As for Cook, he was stunned. He realized at once that he had found the dramatist who could express his idea of native theater. Susan Glaspell said, in a line quoted time and again, "we knew what we were for." The voting was a mere formality and *Bound East for Cardiff* was put into rehearsal under O'Neill's own supervision, scheduled to open less than two weeks later, on July 28.

O'Neill was dazzled to find himself at long last among kindred spirits who recognized his worth. The validation of his talent renewed his faith in himself, a stronger tonic than any amount of drink (although he still needed that crutch) and it had come just in time. Whether he could have survived another winter of hopelessness is questionable.

"Have been busy directing rehearsals of my play *Bound East for Cardiff*," O'Neill crowed on July 25, three days before the opening. He was responding to a letter from Beatrice Ashe that had found its way to Provincetown, in which she appealed for advice on what to do with her young life. His reply rang with the lofty tone of preachment he had often employed when writing to her from Harvard:

"I can sympathize with all my heart with your indecision. It is hard to go and just as hard to stay . . . One way or the other, choose you must . . . My advice is always the same . . . there is no happiness outside of self-development. One's duty to oneself must forever stand first of all duties."

And then, typically, he dissolved into the childish whimpering that had also marked his Harvard correspondence:

"Bee! Bee! You mustn't stay! . . . Can you see yourself, wild, wayward bird-soul that you are, caged in a home, propagating with a husband-man? Or clutching your virginity to the miserable, stagnant end?"

Addressing her as "My Own," and referring to her in the body of this long letter as "Glorious One" and "Own Sweetheart," he seemed, even yet, to be trying to talk her into bed. He assured her he was still her "lover who is willing to put his life in your dear hands and live and love it out with His Lady in such manner and under any conditions which are pleasing to her."

Asking if she would consider traveling to Provincetown, he said she would be welcome to stay in John Reed's house, leading her to believe she would be chaperoned by Louise, whom he described as Reed's "wife" (certain she would refuse if she knew that Reed and Louise were unmarried). O'Neill ended with his relentless and all-too-familiar refrain: "I love you, I want you, I need you so!"

Despite his entreaties, there is a sense in the letter that his passion no longer burned at white heat. Indeed, had Beatrice accepted his invitation, he would probably have panicked, for at that very time he was yearning for Louise, and had nearly convinced himself she was ready to reciprocate.

Beatrice did not accept O'Neill's invitation, and it was soon apparent the romance had come to an end. Whether she ever regretted her decision is a matter for speculation. She returned to college, but while still a student, and doubtless still a virgin, dropped out to be married. Like Maibelle Scott, she married a serviceman — in her case a U.S. Naval Academy cadet, James Edward Maher.

Also like Maibelle, who concluded she had matured beyond O'Neill, Beatrice ultimately felt oppressed both by O'Neill's neediness and his apparent inability to stay sober. She told Emily Rippin that Maher, in contrast to O'Neill, did not demand to be mothered. What Maher wanted was a companionable wife and a family. And yet, unlike Maibelle, Beatrice saved and treasured O'Neill's love letters and poetry throughout the years of her marriage.

Settling into the life that clearly suited her, Beatrice raised two sons, had seven grandchildren and three great-grandchildren. She was a church soloist for twenty-five years, voted Republican, was a member of the Navy Wives, the Garden Club, the Lucretia Shaw Chapter of the Daughters of the American Revolution, the New London Historical Society and the Congregation Pequot Chapel.

When she died at eighty in 1974 she was buried in Arlington National Cemetery beside her husband, who had achieved the rank of Vice Admiral. Despite her solid affiliations, the New London Day in its obituary chose to acclaim her as "a former girlfriend of the famous playwright, Eugene O'Neill."

O'Neill reflected his residual frustration and bitterness about Beatrice in *Strange Interlude*, written twelve years after the end of the affair. Nina Leeds, the play's Everywoman, is a fantasy distillation of the significant women in his life.

The Beatrice-like aspect of her character surfaces in Nina's sanctimonious refusal to consummate her love for her soldier-lover before he goes off to war to be killed. She then spends the rest of her life punishing herself for it.

There are aspects of Beatrice as well in *Ah, Wilderness!*, written sixteen years after the end of the affair. She, along with Marion Welch and Maibelle Scott, must have been lurking in O'Neill's unconscious during the final days of August 31, 1932, for he awoke on the morning of September 1 with the plot and characters of his nostalgic New London love story "fully formed and ready to write."

His romantic dalliances with the three young New London women had taken place, of course, in three different years — none of them, as it happens, in 1906, the year of the play's action: the Welch flirtation in the summer and fall of 1905; the Scott romance in the fall of 1912; and his courtship of Ashe from summer 1914 to summer 1916.

O'Neill, however, was skilled at compressing, refracting and transcending the events of his life. By this time he was accustomed, as are all creative writers, to playing God: rearranging life as it suited him, killing off those he disliked, besting those who threatened him, recomposing lovers, parents, friends — and most of all himself — to conform to his fantasies.

It is not surprising, therefore, that in *Ah, Wilderness!* he reconfigured his blighted romance with Beatrice, making particular reference to her demand for temperance to win her. In the play's bittersweet comic twist, he created an unrequited romance between the middle-aged bachelor, Sid Davis, and the spinster aunt, Lily Miller (who shares a first name with O'Neill's spinster cousin, Lil Brennan).

Lily will not marry Sid unless he keeps his promise to stay sober, and Sid is incapable of doing so. (O'Neill had yet another real-life model on whom to draw: Jamie's inability, according to his own account, to stay sober so that Pauline Frederick would agree to marry him.) It appears that O'Neill in his imagination was condemning Beatrice to clutch her virginity "to the miserable, stagnant end."

In spite of the Players' eagerness to befriend him in Provincetown, O'Neill kept somewhat aloof. At one point, while he was writing, he went so far as to nail a sign reading "Go to Hell" to the front door of his shack.

For companionship he preferred the fishermen and the men of the Coast Guard station who stood lonely watch over the town's treacherous waters. The firshermen were from the Azores, "people of pride and character," as Mary Vorse described them, "a mixture of Sudanese Negro, who were a proud and superior warrior race, and of Arab and Portuguese." Like the sailors O'Neill once lived among, he found these men to have no affectations.

In his view, the self-styled intellectuals of the summer colony flaunted their pretensions. He was not comfortable mingling with them and competing with their small talk. No one, not even the few he respected and who put him at ease, ever found him chatty.

Only when a subject arose that held profound importance for him, did he condescend to talk — and then it was sometimes all but impossible to interrupt him; he could in these rare moments carry on a monologue in a low, halting voice until he had presented every facet of his argument.

His social unease was one reason he continued to drink, although in Provincetown his binges were less destructive than in New York. He seemed able to sober up from time to time, according to many of the Provincetowners, especially when he set himself to write. Although he had come to understand that he was indeed an alcoholic, always balanced on the edge of a chasm, he was still a long way from dealing squarely with the problem.

The O'Neill-Carlin shack had a long ramp running almost to the water's edge. Kyra Markham, an actress in her early twenties who lived next door, retained for many years an image of O'Neill about to plunge into the bay.

"Day after day," she recalled, "he would stand leaning against the wide door frame, gazing out to sea, literally for hours and hours. When at last he had drunk his fill of gazing, or the sun, or whatever held him so immobile, he moved swiftly, but not running, into the water and began to swim. He swam straight out without swerving to right or left. Sometimes his head became a tiny dot in the distance and sometimes he went so far that I could not see him at all and would worry about him."

Markham was recovering that summer from an unhappy love-affair with the lustful Theodore Dreiser, whom she had met in Chicago when she was twenty. At the time, she was acting at Maurice Browne's Little Theater and having an affair with Floyd Dell.

Dreiser, nearly twice her age, was smitten with both her beauty and her sharp mind. He took her away from Dell and soon after brought her to Greenwich Village. But he was as faithless to Markham as he was to all his other women and she finally left him. She was attracted to O'Neill, but realized he had eyes only for Bryant.

As for Bryant, she was as much a spellbound observer of O'Neill's marathon swims as was Markham. Although Reed was an excellent swimmer, she acknowledged O'Neill's superior prowess. She watched him from her window and, when he returned, joined him on the beach.

With Reed now back in Provincetown, Louise fretted about his ill health and was restless when he shut himself away to write his magazine articles. "Jack came and went," Louise noted, "and did his writing in another little cottage nearby. He always had a separate workroom, he didn't like writing in the same house he lived in."

It soon became plain to their friends that Louise was in search of distraction, and no one was surprised when she gravitated toward O'Neill.

Her far from subtle signals were difficult to overlook. Because of his loyalty to Reed, O'Neill hesitated to respond and for a time even took pains to conceal his ardor. It was not easy, however, for Louise behaved and dressed seductively.

Her appearance left a marked impression on at least one observer. William Carlos Williams, who was making a reputation as a poet (while earning his living as a physician), described Louise's allure in "a heavy, very heavy, white silk skirt so woven that it hung over the curve of her buttocks like the strands of a glistening waterfall." He added, "There could have been nothing under it, for it followed the very crease between the buttocks in its fall."

Nevertheless, Louise was obliged to resort to a direct approach. Using Terry Carlin as emissary, she sent O'Neill a note: "I must see you alone. I have to explain something, for my sake and Jack's. You have to understand."

Characteristically combining truth and romantic invention, Louise told O'Neill that Reed was soon likely to have a kidney operation and that his condition prevented him from having sexual relations. They had been living together as brother and sister, she said.

Despite Reed's apparent good spirits and enthusiasm for his

work, Louise confided, he was, in fact, preparing himself for death and she was helping him face this grim prospect. Although their liaison now was sexless, she loved Reed and would never leave him.

It was true Reed's doctor had advised him to enter a hospital for tests and a probable operation in the near future. But in view of his recent passionate letters to Louise while away on assignment ("O how I wish I was in my sweetheart's arms in bed together!") — not to mention the nude photo she sent him anticipating "all the nice months" following his return — it is unlikely they were living the ascetic life Louise described.

Not even the hesitant O'Neill could mistake Louise's communication for anything but an invitation, particularly when she further assured him that Reed would understand her need for consolation and would not blame either of them.

Reed was, in truth, bracing himself for his probable operation in the fall. Though he seldom allowed his illness to depress him, he did at times dwell on his own death, turning to verse as a way of coming to grips with the prospect, as in the first stanza of his poem,"Fog":

"Death comes like this, I know/Snow-soft and gently cold;/Impalpable battalions of thin mist,/Light-quenching and sound-smothering and slow."

O'Neill, in his naiveté, apparently accepted Louise's account. Why she felt it necessary to resort to such a subterfuge is puzzling. Reed had always made it clear that however much he was in love with a woman, he never wanted to own or be owned by her, and Louise professed to feel the same way. Perhaps she understood that O'Neill, unlike most of his unfettered contemporaries, preferred to concentrate on one woman at a time, and would be more inclined to capitulate if she persuaded him Reed was, at least temporarily, impotent. When it came to getting what she wanted, she invented a scenario to suit the occasion.

O'Neill and Louise became lovers. Some years later, in confessing the details of the affair to his second wife, Agnes Boulton, he said he pitied as well as admired Louise, and that she became for him "a great woman, something out of the old Irish legends, betrayed by life" — exactly what Louise wished to convey.

During a forlorn and unstable childhood, Louise had learned to escape into make-believe, forming a lifelong habit of substituting romantic invention for drab facts. Few of her friends knew the truth about her early life.

To some she confided that her grandfather had been the younger son of an Irish lord, to others that she was related to Oscar Wilde, and to others still that her father had been an Irish officer in the British army. In one instance she referred to him as a "general." Always vague about details, she rarely mentioned her mother or spoke about the life she had lived before arriving in Portland in 1909.

She was born Anna Louise Mohan in San Francisco, on December 5, probably in 1885. She began lying about her age in her early twenties and continued to drop years as she grew older — always successfully, because her looks remained youthful.

Her father, Hugh J. Mohan, born in the Pennsylvania coal town of Minersville on March 9, 1848, worked in the mines as a youth. He later became a reporter for various newspapers, including three in San Francisco — the Chronicle, the Mail and the Daily Globe.

Not long after Louise's birth, the family moved to Reno, Nevada, where Mohan, a heavy drinker, abandoned them when Louise was three. Her mother, Anna Louisa Mohan, obtained a divorce, a trauma Louise could never bring herself to confront.

Instead, she maintained from early childhood that her father had died when she was "two or three," leaving her mother grief-stricken and herself an inconsolably lonely child. In 1892, Anna Louisa Mohan married Sheridan Bryant, a railroad conductor, whose name Louise adopted.

Although she was an indifferent student in high school, Louise entered the University of Nevada in 1904 and after her sophomore year transferred to the University of Oregon, where she joined a sorority and led an otherwise conventional life. It was not until she left college that she began to develop a social conscience. According to friends she later made in Portland, she worked for six months in a Seattle canning factory, as a sort of sociological experiment.

This brief exposure to the grim working conditions and pitifully low wages that prevailed in factories at the time turned her into a determined social rebel. On her return to Portland, she began to feel that a middle-class existence was more a fringe existence than a real life. Not that it was easy to shake off the bonds of conformity.

For a time she was obliged to make her living as a society reporter for a local weekly tabloid. Her escape from dreary gentility was to rent a houseboat on the Wilamette River, where Reed, as a boy, had learned to swim. There she met Paul Trullinger, a member of the lively houseboat colony. It did not take her long to captivate the handsome young dentist and they were married on December 16, 1909 by an Episcopal minister, although she had been christened a Catholic.

Both Paul and Louise held a liberal view of marriage, presaging the life Louise was soon to adopt in Greenwich Village. She kept her maiden name and rented a studio where she painted and wrote, and where Paul never intruded.

The two often appeared together at artists' gathering places in downtown Portland, attended concerts and art exhibits and occasionally the theater and, while the couple's unconventional style of life earned the disapproval of some of their acquaintances, the arrangement seemed to work for a time.

After five years, the marriage began to sour. Then John Reed visited his mother in Portland, fell in love with Louise and persuaded her to come east with him.

CHAPTER
FORTY-FIVE

THE LOVE AFFAIR BETWEEN O'NEILL AND BRYANT BECAME the gossip of the moment in the tightly knit Provincetown community.

What Reed's position was, no one could quite understand. Some believed he was ignorant of the affair, while others thought it conformed to his view of an open relationship. He continued to be loving toward Louise and proud of her; nor did he waver in his affection and admiration for O'Neill, and the three continued their amicable participation in the theater on the wharf.

Mabel Dodge, arriving on the scene in midsummer, was apprised of the situation and, meeting Reed on the street, let him know she stood ready to console him. Candid as always, she recalled, "I thought Reed would be glad to see me if things were like that between him and Louise — but he wasn't."

Despite O'Neill's preoccupation with Louise he found his way back to concentrated writing and began work on a one-act play, *Before Breakfast*. Like all the one-acters he wrote during the next two years, *Before Breakfast* was composed in the comfortable assurance he would have an experimental stage on which to produce it.

The play is a monologue delivered by a shrewish wife, embittered by her forced marriage to an unsuccessful writer. Her incessant nagging leads to her husband's offstage suicide.

O'Neill himself obviously was the model for the suicidal husband, Alfred, of whom nothing is seen by the audience except his hand, when it reaches from the wings for a bowl of shaving water. At the end, his voice is heard in a death gurgle, as he slashes his throat with a razor. Even O'Neill's brief stage note about the hand is autobiographical: "It is a sensitive hand with slender fingers. It trembles . . ."

O'Neill wished to test the staying power of an audience subjected to a one-character diatribe — an attempt that paved the way for the expository monologues he subsequently wrote into his long plays. Evidently he and the Players did not consider *Before Breakfast* quite ready for production that summer. It was not staged until the following December in New York.

Having recovered his stride, O'Neill next wrote "Tomorrow," his short story about the alcoholic Jimmy Byth. It is clear from this story that he was becoming increasingly concerned about his own struggle with alcohol. (He borrowed the title — consciously or subliminally — from a short story written by Conrad in 1903 and adapted by the novelist two years later as the one-act play, *One Day More*.)

Without pause, O'Neill then began work on a three-act play including a prologue and epilogue called *Now I Ask You*. In late July, he noted that he was "half through the first act." His object in writing the play is obscure. He characterized it as a comedy, but it is difficult to find a witty line in the labored dialogue.

With a nod or two to Nietzsche, Ibsen and Shaw, the play purports to satirize the concept of free love. It echoes the O'Neill-Bryant-Reed triangle, but treats the fictional situation far more casually than the actual one. As he confided to Terry Carlin, "When Louise touches me with her fingernail, it's like a prairie fire."

In the play, Lucy (who can be seen as a caricature of Louise) has married Tom (a stereotyped conventional businessman) with the understanding they are not bound to fidelity. However, the moment that Gabriel (a brooding, egotistical poet and something of an O'Neill self-parody) makes love to Lucy, Tom begins to sulk. And when Tom in turn pretends to make love to Gabriel's wife, Leonora, Lucy falls into a jealous fury.

The play, an odd departure from O'Neill's earlier, didactically expressed determination to bring literary substance to the American theater, is more of a piece with the commercially intended *The Movie Man*. Possibly O'Neill was not entirely sober while writing it and, even more possibly, he permitted Louise to influence its composition. The two frequently discussed each other's projects and O'Neill took time to encourage Louise with her writing, which was generally more ambitious than inspired.

Louise, for her part, dedicated herself to promoting O'Neill's work, along with her attempts to curb his drinking. She herself did not drink, very likely because of her father's alcoholism; in fact, in her letters to Reed, she frequently made disparaging comments about the drinking of others, including Hippolyte Havel. All her friends were aware she was trying to keep O'Neill sober, and was, to a degree, succeeding.

That summer, both wrote poetry they tried to sell. Having spent hours in silent contemplation of the sea's edge and its creatures, O'Neill appears to have been imbued with the predatory aspects of nature.

In "Moonlight," he addresses a beach spider: Are you pale/With the weariness of watching/Love,/The eater and the Eaten/ Loathsome Spider? And in "Tides," originally entitled "Flotsam," he contrasts the "dancing grasses" and "the calm of the land" with "stinking seaweed," "dead fish" and crabs sidling by, "Searching for carrion."

Other O'Neill poems probably were inspired by his love for Louise. At least one, "On the Dunes" (among Louise's papers when she died) was a revised version of an untitled poem he had written in New London the summer before, when he was still wooing Beatrice.

No doubt he felt that the "Beloved" addressed in the original version could just as aptly be applied to Louise, and that his description of a beloved young woman's body would serve just as well for a Louise reclining against the dunes of Provincetown as for a Beatrice lolling on the warm sands of New London. Both versions contain the same passionate stanza (with only slight variations):

> Your body is warm and undulating
> As the sand dunes
> Eager with tremulous heat waves.
> Beneath the kisses of my desire
> Your passions reach upward
> Their quivering fingers.
>
> I shall come to you
> In the delirium of noon . . .

Louise, perhaps in response, wrote "Six Poems" (subtitled with the Roman numerals I to VI, each consisting of five short lines) that might have applied either to O'Neill or to Reed. Since the poems were intended for publication, she was obliged to be oblique. They contained such phrases as, "He is more beautiful to me," and "So does your soul kindle mine." The only verse with a title, Number IV, is dedicated "To a Swimmer," and does seem to suggest O'Neill:

Ah me!/When sun and wind/And the water . . . caress you/How can I who am flesh, withhold/My love?

Number V, however, is more suggestive of the periodically absent Reed:

Empty/And silent as/Midnight . . . are the grey hours/When I cannot touch you or hear/Your voice.

The eager audience at the Wharf Theater was enraptured by *Bound East for Cardiff* when it led the second bill on July 28. "I may see it through memories too emotional, but it seems to me I have never sat before a more moving production," wrote Susan Glaspell a decade later.

On the tiny stage arranged to represent the forecastle of the S.S. Glencairn, Jig Cook played the dying sailor, Yank. Teddy Ballantine, who had helped O'Neill with the staging, portrayed a crew member, as did Reed, Harry Kemp, Wilbur Daniel Steele and Frederic Burt.

O'Neill himself, undaunted by his acting disaster in the vaudeville version of *The Count of Monte Cristo*, spoke one line as the Second Mate: "Isn't this your watch on deck, Driscoll?" He doubled as prompter, breathing so nervously behind a partition that he distracted the other performers.

The scenic effects were largely supplied by nature. "It's rather a curious coincidence that my first production should have been on a wharf in a sea town," O'Neill drily recalled. Fortunately, others who witnessed the performance described their own vivid impressions — none with more sense of occasion than Susan Glaspell:

"The sea has been good to Eugene O'Neill. It was there for his opening. There was a fog, just as the script demanded, fog bell in the harbor. The tide was in, and it washed under us and around, spraying through the holes in the floor, giving us the rhythm and the flavor of the sea while the big dying sailor talked to his friend Drisc of the life he had always wanted deep in the land, where you'd never see a ship or smell the sea.

"It is not merely figurative language to say the old wharf shook with applause."

Bound East for Cardiff so overwhelmed the audience that the two other plays on the bill faded into the background. One was Wilbur Steele's light domestic comedy *Not Smart*, the other a stilted parable by Louise Bryant called *The Game*, in which Reed jauntily portrayed "Death"; other characters were "Life," "Youth" and "The Girl." *The*

Game did come to be regarded as a minor tour de force, mainly due to its stylized acting and a striking abstract set designed by the sculptor, William Zorach, and his wife, the artist Marguerite Zorach.

In the audience was Adele Nathan, the director of a "little theater" in Baltimore called the Vagabonds. Nathan, who happened to be vacationing in Provincetown, had been searching for one-act plays by Americans to put on at her own theater and was impressed. She sought out Jig Cook, telling him she would pay for plays the Vagabonds could use, and he invited her to his house.

"Next afternoon practically the entire group from the Wharf was there to meet me," Nathan recalled. "Each had at least one manuscript clutched in a hot little hand." O'Neill's name was the only one she knew because, as she recalled, *Thirst and Other One-Act Plays* had "been read eagerly and rejected unanimously" by the Vagabonds.

She told O'Neill she had found *Bound East for Cardiff* gripping and offered him fifteen dollars for the right to produce it. But O'Neill had no copy of the play. Rehearsals, she was informed, had been conducted from a single working script, now in sad condition. O'Neill offered to make a clean copy and deliver it before she left Provincetown at the end of the week.

"He was not a good typist," she observed. "He made innumerable corrections in ink. The stage directions and offstage noises he had added almost illegibly in blue and red pencil." But he took good care to sign his name clearly to the script. It was the first money he ever earned for a playscript.

In early August, the Players presented their third bill, notable for a one-acter by Susan Glaspell called *Trifles* (which Saxe Commins obligingly typed). The play was based on a story Glaspell had written as a reporter about a woman in Des Moines convicted of murdering her husband.

In the play, the wives of the men investigating the case find a series of apparently trifling domestic clues — overlooked by the less attuned men — that establish the motive for the murder. With its clever feminist sensibility, *Trifles*, like *Suppressed Desires*, went on to a life as a stock-company staple.

Also on the bill was a revival of *Constancy*, Neith Boyce's satire of the Reed-Dodge love affair. Most titillating to those Provincetowners in the know, however, was Reed's one-acter, *The Eternal Quadrangle*, which, like O'Neill's *Now I Ask You*, satirized marriage and free love and seemed to be sending his friends and colleagues a pointed message: that he was aware of Louise's involvement with O'Neill and could handle it. In fact, both Louise and Reed performed in the play with evident sangfroid.

Although Louise tended to dissemble about her love affair with O'Neill, she did allude to it many years later in a letter, describing a farcical incident that occurred one night during the summer of 1916. It involved a somewhat unstable young man Reed had occasionally employed, named Fred Boyd.

"Boyd," explained Louise, "is in the last analysis a little conceited Cockney who Jack picked up abroad to use as secretary because Jack said he was a perfect machine." When Boyd arrived in America, however, he began drinking too much and Reed constantly had to bail him out of scrapes.

When the war broke out in 1914, Boyd, from Provincetown, attempted to cable the Kaiser, the Czar, the President of France, and the Emperor, demanding they call off the war. Later, he ran about town brandishing a revolver. Ultimately, he was arrested for preaching sabotage. He returned to Provincetown in the summer of 1916, but Reed had no work for him.

"He was usually drunk," Louise said. "Jack rented a room for him in the town and he ate at our house. One morning he arrived about four. Staggered into our bedroom and asked Jack for $40. Jack asked him what he wanted it for. He said that he had to kill Eugene O'Neill because I was untrue to Jack and Gene was the culprit."

Presumably Boyd wanted the money to buy a gun. Reed's response was to kiss Louise and tell Boyd to go home to bed. Later that day, according to Louise's account, Reed informed O'Neill: "Boyd was drunk last night and shooting off his face around town. If you hear any stories don't pay any attention to them. And I wish you and Terry Carlin would take all your meals with us for a while."

For their fourth bill on September 1, the Players chose to revive the previous summer's *Contemporaries* and *Change Your Style* (in which Stella Ballantine appeared as the Mabel Dodge character). In a gesture part loyal and part quixotic, they also decided to stage O'Neill's *Thirst*.

Louise portrayed the thirst-crazed Dancer and O'Neill, so deeply tanned he needed no makeup, played the taciturn "West Indian Mulatto Sailor," who entertained the notion of dining on her. Jig Cook played the role of the Gentleman who shared the raft with them.

The production gave O'Neill and Bryant a chance to play (with deadly earnestness) a scene of attempted seduction, one remarkable for its clumsy dialogue and preposterous action. After considerable discussion, it was decided not to follow literally O'Neill's stage direction that the dancer expose her breasts, although Louise indicated she might be willing to do so. Even with this omission, it is a wonder, given O'Neill's avowal that Louise's fingernail touch could ignite a prairie fire, that his scenes with her did not incinerate him on the spot:

> DANCER: (*putting her hand on [the sailor's] shoulder she bends forward with her golden hair almost in his lap and smiles up into his face*): I like you, Sailor. You are big and strong. We are going to be great friends, are we not? (*The Negro is hardly looking at her. He is watching the sharks.*) Surely you will not refuse me a little sip of your water.
>
> SAILOR: I have no water.
>
> DANCER: Oh, why will you keep up this subterfuge? Am I not offering you price enough? (*Putting her arm around his neck and half whispering in his ear.*) Do you not understand? I will love you, Sailor! Noblemen and millionaires . . . have loved me, have fought for me. I have never loved any of them as I will love you. Look in my eyes, Sailor, look in my eyes! (*Compelled in spite of himself by something in her voice, the Negro gazes deep into her eyes. For a second his nostrils dilate — he draws in his breath with a hissing sound — his body grows tense and it seems as if he is about to sweep her into his arms. Then his expression grows apathetic again. He turns to the sharks.*)
>
> DANCER: Oh, will you never understand? Are you so stupid that you do not know what I mean? . . . I have promised to love you — a Negro sailor — if you will give me one small drink of water. Is that not humiliation enough that you must keep me waiting so? . . . Will you give me that water?
>
> SAILOR: (*without even turning to look at her*): I have no water.
>
> DANCER (*shaking with fury*): Great God, have I abased myself for this? Have I humbled myself before this black animal only to be spurned like a wench of the streets? It is too much! You lie, you dirty slave! You have water. You have stolen my share of the water. (*In a frenzy she clutches the sailor about the throat with both hands.*) Give it to me! Give it to me!
>
> SAILOR: (*takes her hands from his neck and pushes her roughly away. She falls face downward in the middle of the raft.*) Let me alone! I have no water.

William Zorach recalled that the setting included a sea cloth with someone wriggling around underneath it to represent the ocean. O'Neill insisted on it, but this throwback to the scene in which Monte Cristo escapes from the Chateau d'If into the sea did little to enhance the production. Though there is no record of a mass exodus, the play was not a success and was not produced again in O'Neill's lifetime.

Determined to end their season with éclat — and to raise a few more dollars — the Players presented a "Review Bill": *Bound East for Cardiff*, the unchallenged hit of the summer, along with *Suppressed Desires*, by now a staple, and *The Game*.

On September 10, the Boston Sunday Post took note of the season on the wharf. Under the headline, "Many Literary Lights Among Provincetown Players," the article described them as the "Last Word in Modernity," and marveled that "The Provincetown Players are so modern that they not only write about modern things but satirize them." The author of the article was sufficiently prescient to single out O'Neill for special notice (although misspelling his name):

"It begins to look as if the American drama may be the richer for the fun and the work of the Provincetown Players this summer. They have put on two plays by Eugene O'Neil, a young dramatist whose work was heretofore unproduced and who, they are confident, is going to be heard from in places less remote than Provincetown."

Having turned down assignments to return to Mexico and Europe, Reed had been spending more time in Provincetown, partly because his illness was slowing him down and partly because he was reluctant to leave Louise. Consequently, he devoted much of his energy to the Players in August and September and, as the summer drew to a close, joined Jig Cook in proposing they take their theater with them to New York that winter.

Glaspell expressed concern over their plan. Mostly she was anxious for her husband.

"I was afraid people would laugh at him, starting a theatre in New York — new playwrights, amateur acting, somewhere in an old house or a stable . . . I said I did not think we were ready to go to New York; I feared we couldn't make it go. 'Jack Reed thinks we can make it go,' Cook said. Those two were the first to believe — adventurers both, men of faith."

O'Neill later described Cook as "the dominating and inspiring genius of the Players." He was the next in the series of older men to notably influence O'Neill's life. Just as James took under his wing young actors like Tynan and called them "son," so Eugene attached himself to older men like Carlin — and now Cook — who, unlike his father, gave him the encouragement and support to be himself.

O'Neill's senior by fifteen years, Cook was the same height as Eugene but heftier, with broad shoulders. Idealist that he was, he could be pontifical, vain and over-sensitive, and could be hurt by any slight of his well-meant guidance.

Despite these failings, there is no doubt O'Neill owed him a great deal. He was the first person who was willing to devote his full time, talent and energy to making sure O'Neill had the hearing he deserved.

O'Neill once observed that Cook was "impatient with everything that smacked of falsity or compromise." He represented "the spirit of revolt against the old worn-out traditions, the commercial theater, the tawdry artificialities of the stage."

Cook was equally laudatory of O'Neill. "You don't know Gene yet," Cook told his friend, Edna Kenton, a writer he had first met when she was part of the flowering Chicago literary circle. Kenton had arrived in Provincetown in early September, became a founding member of the Players and, later that year, a member of the group's executive committee. "You don't know his plays," Cook said. "But you will. All the world will know Gene's plays . . .

"Some day this little theatre will be famous; some day the little theatre in New York will be famous — this fall the Provincetown Players go into New York with *Cardiff* on their first bill. We've got our group of playwrights and they've got to have their stage. Gene's plays aren't the plays of Broadway; he's got to have the sort of stage we're going to found in New York."

Although he looked to Cook for practical support, O'Neill was more comfortable in Glaspell's company. Tireless reader that he was, he knew some of the short stories she had been publishing in magazines since 1903, and doubtless had read her recently published third novel, *Fidelity*; he respected the views she expressed through her protagonists — perceptive women trying to free themselves from the societal conventions imposed on them by the men in their lives, unable to fathom their restlessness.

O'Neill regarded Glaspell as a woman of experience and achievement and did not hesitate to seek her counsel. He was drawn to her lively mind and warmth of spirit and they became good friends, discussing each other's plays, exchanging ideas on technique. Though her recent attempt at playwriting was more Cook's idea than her own, she went at it seriously.

She undoubtedly described to O'Neill her knowledge of German expressionism gained during her year abroad in 1908; she was to experiment with aspects of the form, particularly in her use of lighting and sound effects, even before O'Neill employed his own "expressionistic" stage effects in *The Emperor Jones* and *The Hairy Ape*.

Glaspell and O'Neill soon came to be regarded by critics of the day as the twinned experimental backbone of the Players. Glaspell provided eleven plays — only three less than O'Neill — before the group disbanded in 1923, by which time O'Neill had surpassed her.

On the night of September 5, the Players gathered at Reed's house to draw up their manifesto. Earlier in the day, Reed and Cook had met on the stage of the Wharf Theater to draft some basic "resolutions," which they now presented. Among such a group of individualists, however, agreement on a credo was not easily achieved and the debate at times grew stormy.

"Organization is death!" cried Hutchins Hapgood with rebellious fervor.

The manifesto, finally worded so broadly as to render it almost inoperable, resolved, among other specifications:

"That it is the primary object of the Provincetown Players to encourage the writing of American plays of real artistic, literary and dramatic — as opposed to Broadway — merit.

"That such plays be considered without reference to their commercial value, since this theatre is not to be run for pecuniary profit . . . "

It was also resolved that "the President shall cooperate with the author in producing the play under the author's direction. The resources of the theatre . . . shall be placed at the disposal of the author . . . *The author shall produce the play without hindrance, according to his own ideas.*"

No playwright could have asked for anything more utopian. O'Neill's only suggestion, one he felt needed to underline the author's unchallenged primacy, was that the name, "The Playwrights' Theater," be added to the already-approved "The Provincetown Players." The amended name was unanimously adopted.

Never falsely modest, O'Neill was aware that he stood on the brink of recognition as an original voice in the shaping of a modern American theater. What he had in mind was the kind of experimental "Intimate Theatre" born in Stockholm in 1907 to present "Chamber Plays" — new works, primarily by Strindberg. Supremely confident of his own potential, O'Neill very likely envisioned the Playwrights' Theatre as America's Intimate Theatre and himself as the future Strindberg.

Only two officers, the president and the secretary, were to be paid. Jig Cook, subsequently voted in as president, received $15 a week, as did the secretary-treasurer, Margaret Nordfeldt, a homeopathic doctor married to the painter, Bror Nordfeldt.

Cook was entrusted to find a theatre that would fit The Players' pitifully slim working budget of $320, composed of the $80 left after the summer's productions and eight contributions of $30 each, made by the better-heeled members. O'Neill, penniless, was pronounced an honorary member.

Enjoining everyone to "write another play," Cook departed for New York to find a suitable — and affordable — space.

O'Neill, Reed and Louise remained in Provincetown to enjoy the post-season serenity, putting off their departure for New York to October 1; O'Neill gave his forwarding address to publishers to whom he submitted work as Jack Reed's apartment at 43 Washington Square South.

Reed was still uncertain about when he would have his operation and increasingly concerned about how he would support himself and Louise while confined to a hospital. He asked the advice of a writer friend, David Carb, who had played the role of The Captain in *Bound East for Cardiff*. Carb had recently entered Johns Hopkins Hospital in Baltimore for a similar procedure and he chided Reed for his reluctance to have the operation.

"We will make rendezvous at the undertaker's or the cemetery if you don't get some sense knocked into you," Carb wrote. "I'm quite as broke as you — broker — you can sell your stuff. And it's worth going into debt for . . . I'm pawning all I ever hope to make to see it through. Think it over, Jack — you can raise the money easily — about $10 a day it costs — and when you are well, plug like hell to pay up . . . it's quite easy to work here. Bring your typewriter and get well . . . . Won't you do it? It's mere common sense — you aren't well. You can't work much — actually your earning capacity is lessened — If it's the money part that deters you — it's really economy."

Carb's advice made sense to Reed. Taking advantage of the quiet that had descended on Provincetown with the withdrawal of its summer visitors, he wrote a couple of potboilers for Collier's and the Metropolitan.

O'Neill busied himself polishing *Before Breakfast* and making notes for future projects. As for Louise, she worked on her poetry and continued to divide her time between O'Neill and Reed, pleased to be regarded as essential to each but unwilling to commit herself unequivocally to either.

CHAPTER
FORTY-SIX

O'NEILL, REED AND BRYANT RETURNED TO GREENWICH Village bound together in their strange tangle of friendship, desire and deceit. It had been scarcely four months since O'Neill had pulled himself out of his despondency and now, back in the city where he had so often approached shipwreck, he was reveling in a new love and anticipating his long-overdue New York debut.

The Players had unanimously agreed that O'Neill was to be the cornerstone of their season. With Louise's encouragement, he struggled to stay relatively sober and, to Jig Cook's delight, he was brimming with ideas.

Cook felt sure that if O'Neill could resist slipping back into his barroom habits, he would soon write a worthy sequel to *Bound East for Cardiff*. Cook was himself a hearty drinker, but he knew well the difference between his own bibulous conviviality and O'Neill's incapacitating drunkenness.

As for Reed, apparently unconcerned about sharing Louise, and still anxious about his impending operation, he was now preoccupied with the war, having no faith in Wilson's ability to keep America out of it. Heading ever more precipitously into radical activism and spurning all pretense of journalistic detachment, he devoted himself to writing anti-war articles and addressing pacifist rallies.

Louise, occupied with poetry and other writing, unlike either of her lovers, was as yet unsure of the direction she wished her career to take. Reed encouraged her to pursue journalism and continued to introduce her to magazine editors, urging her to send them articles. Determined to hold onto Reed and worried about his health, she nonetheless contrived to maintain her grip on O'Neill.

That O'Neill eventually came to understand this duplicity is apparent from still another aspect of Nina Leeds, the heroine who represents Everywoman in *Strange Interlude*. While he endowed the young Nina with Beatrice Ashe's unassailable virginity, so did he bestow on the mature Nina the sexual freedom pursued by Louise Bryant.

He describes Nina's "gloating" pleasure in her dominance over both her lover and her husband. Nina is married to a man who cannot have children — symbolic of the putatively impotent Reed; Nina secretly takes her husband's best friend as lover — ostensibly to become pregnant but actually, in O'Neill's symbolism, to be sexually fulfilled.

Reed invited O'Neill to stay in one of the warren of rooms he and Louise rented in the brownstone on Washington Square and, although O'Neill appreciated Reed's generosity, he did not, like Reed, share Louise willingly.

Louise later destroyed her letters from O'Neill but, in light of the epistolary evidence of his jealous demands on Beatrice and other women with whom he became romantically involved, it is safe to assume that he chafed and sulked about not having Louise to himself, and pressed her to choose between him and Reed.

That choice was one Louise did not want to confront. She evidently was convinced she could placate both lovers, even if the effort, at times, taxed her ingenuity.

For the moment, she could put off O'Neill with the excuse of awaiting Reed's kidney operation, knowing it would be churlish of O'Neill not to agree. In all probability, she did not tell O'Neill — at least for a time — that her divorce from Trullinger had been granted in July, and that she and Reed were planning to marry.

Certain of her hold on O'Neill even at a distance, Louise agreed with Reed they should spend less time amid the distractions of the city. They decided to buy a country house where they could do some serious writing, and settled on Croton-on-Hudson, in Westchester County.

Their house had once been rented by Mabel Dodge, who had led the way to Croton for artists and writers in search of a retreat within commuting distance of New York. Reed and Louise planned to move to Croton after Reed's operation, meanwhile holding onto their Greenwich Village lodgings.

Doubtless it required all the guile Louise could summon to break the news of her anticipated move, and O'Neill's thralldom must have been severely tested. She appears, however, to have propitiated him by renewing her efforts to help sell his work. He, in turn, remained hopeful of winning her at last.

In spite of the confused relationships, O'Neill was perfectly willing to accept not only Louise's but Reed's continued efforts on his behalf. Reed tried to interest Carl Hovey in publishing "Tomorrow" in the Metropolitan.

Hovey acknowledged O'Neill could write, informing Reed, "This thing is genuine and makes a real man live before you." Nonetheless, he turned it down because, he said, "With all its fine sincerity and effectiveness, there is a kind of over-emphasis and sense of repetition which makes the story drag."

Reed did manage to place an O'Neill poem with Max Eastman in The Masses. Entitled "Submarine," it was undoubtedly linked to the national concern over German U-boats.

The torpedoing of the Lusitania, in May of 1915, was still fresh in the public mind. On October 7, a few days after O'Neill's return to New York, Americans were outraged to learn that the captain of a German U-53, arrogantly availing himself of neutrality regulations, was permitted to berth briefly in Newport, Rhode Island, even though he had been attacking Allied shipping in the Atlantic and intended to continue doing so as soon as he left his safe harbor.

O'Neill's "Submarine," however, was metaphorical and can be read, like his earlier "Revolution," as yet another onslaught on the complacent American theater by an advancing Redeemer (himself):

> My soul is a submarine.
> My aspirations are torpedoes.
> I will hide unseen
> Beneath the surface of life
> Watching for ships,
> Dull, heavy-laden merchant ships,
> Rust-eaten, grimy galleons of commerce
> Wallowing with obese assurance,
> Too sluggish to fear or wonder,
> Mocked by the laughter of waves
> And the spit of disdainful spray.
>
> I will destroy them
> Because the sea is beautiful.
>
> That is why I lurk
> Menacingly
> In green depths.

Despite all the complications of their personal lives, O'Neill, Reed and Bryant were closely following the progress of the Playwrights' Theater. The space Jig Cook had found was in familiar territory, at 139 Macdougal Street, near the southwest corner of Washington Square and close by the Liberal Club, Polly Holladay's restaurant and the Washington Square Book Shop.

An ancient brownstone, it was owned, as were Numbers 133 (a stable), 135 and 137, by Jenny Belardi and her sister, Mary. A handsome, amiable woman in her forties, Jenny had longed for an acting career but, to please her mother, went into business, successfully managing a men's clothing store and saving enough to buy the Macdougal Street brownstones in 1904.

When Cook pronounced the three-and-a half rooms of the parlor floor of Number 139 suitable for conversion into auditorium, stage and dressing room, Jenny Belardi, still stagestruck and comfortable in the company of the artists and bohemians who were her Liberal Club and book shop tenants, was pleased to rent the space for fifty dollars a month.

"Mrs. Belardi was an Italian who appreciated our 'teatro' more than one American landlord in ten thousand would have done," recalled Edna Kenton. She was pleased to add her name to the Provincetown Players' list of subscribing members and often waited patiently when the rent was late.

On October 7, the Players met at John Reed's apartment to vote for the three short plays to begin their season: *Bound East for Cardiff*, *The Game* and a comedy called *King Arthur's Socks*, by Floyd Dell (Max Eastman's associate editor on The Masses). Scheduled to open November 3 and to run for five nights, the three plays were immediately put into rehearsal.

As in Provincetown, Louise supervised *The Game*, in which Reed, despite his ill health and impending operation, insisted on repeating his role as the jaunty personification of "Death." Teddy Ballantine took over the direction of *King Arthur's Socks* from its panicky author. O'Neill, as earlier, supervised the staging of his own play. Jig Cook was once again cast as the dying sailor, Yank, and for the important role of Driscoll, O'Neill cast his friend, Scotty Stuart.

Though Stuart was an amateur, O'Neill later said that he was the only performer "who ever really looked and acted like a 'salt' instead of an actor in war paint." (While Stuart appears to have managed well enough in the mostly nonprofessional *Bound East*, ultimately he did not live up to O'Neill's expectations. Three years later, at

O'Neill's urging, he was cast in *Chris*, the failed precursor of *"Anna Christie,"* and was soon fired. "He hasn't the instinct for the stage," O'Neill regretfully concluded. "They've given him every chance to pick up, but he just simply can't make it.")

O'Neill also cast a new friend, Frank Shay, as one of the sailors. Unlike Stuart, Shay was not interested in a stage career. He had recently bought the Washington Square Book Shop from the Boni brothers, and was planning to publish the texts of the Provincetown Players' one-acters in a pamphlet series.

As fiercely proud of his heritage as O'Neill, Shay enjoyed nothing better than a verbal joust over which of them was descended from the more illustrious Celtic line. The two were a striking physical contrast — Shay, with his blazing blue eyes, shock of tawny hair and sandy mustache, and O'Neill, dark-eyed, dark-haired, dark-mustached and glowering — as they traded extravagant proofs that each was descended from the purest, the strongest, the most ancient of clans.

By the end of October, the renovation of the parlor floor at 139 Macdougal Street was completed. The Players now had an auditorium forty-four feet long by fifteen feet wide, and a barely adequate stage that measured fourteen by ten-and-a-half feet. Tiered benches, precariously supported on stilts, could seat one hundred and forty. They had low wooden backs that added élan but little comfort.

The walls of the auditorium were painted a soft, dark gray, while the proscenium arch had been hand-decorated in vermilion, gold, violet and blue by William Zorach, Charles Demuth and Bror Nordfeldt among others.

The curtain, as Edna Kenton described it, "was a poor affair at first, common bag canvas, transparent and disillusioning," but they could afford nothing better; and they installed a bare minimum of lighting.

The theater was obliged to operate as a private club, with tickets sold by subscription only, to sidestep various city building ordinances. And so, with Jig Cook laboring over the reconstruction, other company members mailed copies of a circular announcing their aims to a select list of a thousand New Yorkers, offering an "Associate Membership" and a season subscription for a fee of four dollars.

Among those chosen to receive the circular were four theater critics described by Edna Kenton as "friends" of the Players (but whose names she did not supply). They were invited to become subscribing members, not reviewers. The circular stressed the Players' declared intention of experimenting for the sake of their own artistic growth, and invited the sympathetic support of patrons who would not measure them by Broadway standards.

The circular did not say so, but the Players were guided by Cook's impassioned battle cry: "We promise to let this theater die rather than let it become another voice of mediocrity." To the company's gleeful surprise, three hundred subscriptions came in almost immediately and another two hundred — the maximum they could accommodate — within the next two months.

Seeking no publicity, the Players nevertheless were treated to a small story in The Times on October 27. Based on the circular, the article announced the company would present "ten new plays, under the personal direction of the authors, a new bill to be staged each two weeks."

The productions would be "simple in stage settings, and, except for two salaried officers who will devote their entire time to the work, the members will receive no financial return, either for their plays or services." Some twenty members of the group were listed, O'Neill among them.

The Players nervously opened their doors to their subscription audience on Friday, November 3. The theater was unheated, the single dressing room was no bigger than a closet, the scenery was ragged and the makeshift costumes were sewn by Jig Cook's mother. The under-rehearsed actors were barely competent by professional standards.

None of these details concerned O'Neill. What did matter was that with *Bound East for Cardiff* heading the bill, he had at last achieved his first New York hearing as a bona fide playwright.

Moreover, according to his own account, his father was in the audience and liked the play. It is more than probable that James was accompanied by Ella, with whom he continued to enjoy a calm and companionable old age, his main regret that his acting days were in abeyance.

Bound East for Cardiff was clearly the hit of the opening bill. There can be little doubt that James permitted himself a prickle of pride, or that Ella was pleased that Eugene was finally receiving recognition. How she and James reacted to their son's bohemian milieu is a matter for conjecture, but it is more than probable that Eugene introduced his parents to Jig Cook and others of the group, including Louise.

Only one of the subscribing critics who attended the first bill ignored the injunction against reviews; on November 13, the Evening

Sun ran an unsigned and somewhat smart-alecky article citing the background of the Provincetown Players, and summed up their initial presentation:

"The first piece of their first bill on November 3, *The Game*, a morality play by Louise Bryant, was so amateurish that the less said about it the better. The Zorachs' decoration was fair.

"The second piece, Eugene O'Neill's *Bound East for Cardiff*, was delightful. The setting, a wall of bunks in the ship's fo'c's'le, fitted the little stage perfectly."

After praising the cast as "capital sailors," the writer declared, "The play was real, subtly tense and avoided a dozen pitfalls that might have made it 'the regular thing.'" (He appeared to have found *King Arthur's Socks* amusing, although his comments were a bit garbled.) Apart from this minor notice, the first bill produced scarcely a murmur from the theater at large.

The Players settled into a harum-scarum existence of writing, rehearsing, set-building and acting. Everything except the writing was accomplished on a scrupulously amateur scale. Practically any young visitors to the Village could affiliate themselves with a production if they showed the proper enthusiasm for the troupe's artistic aims — and if they lacked professional training. Any would-be actors who demonstrated during auditions that they knew too many of the facile Broadway poses, were rejected.

While lacking professional standards and discipline, the Players were determined to enjoy themselves. They shrugged off the last-minute scrambles about misplaced costumes, half-painted sets and defecting cast members. And in spite of all their fumbling and stumbling, the subscription audiences spread the news that here was a group worth watching.

Traditional Broadway was oblivious of the fuse that had been ignited in Greenwich Village. Uptown, apart from the première of George Bernard Shaw's *Getting Married*, the critics encountered little challenging fare: *Old Lady 31*, by Rachel Crothers; *Good Gracious, Annabelle*, by Clare Kummer; a revival of *Ben-Hur*; and *The Century Girl*, a play with music by Victor Herbert and Irving Berlin.

It is likely that Jamie took the trouble to travel downtown to see what his brother had wrought — although probably not on the same evening as his father. Jamie's reputation as a drunk had finally put an end to his own stage career at thirty-eight.

Now living entirely on the paternal dole, Jamie spent much of his time lounging on the sidewalk in front of the Film Café on Seventh

Avenue at 49th Street, an all-night saloon where bit players, gamblers and assorted Broadway know-alls gathered.

Sometimes joined by Art McGinley, in New York seeking a better newspaper job, Jamie would exchange gossip with friends and ogle women passersby. According to McGinley, it would infuriate Jamie when an employed actor he knew strolled by without greeting him. "And to think, I once got him a job with the Old Man's company," he would sneer to McGinley.

McGinley failed to find a newspaper job, and Jamie introduced him to his Garden Hotel circus acquaintances, who engaged him to do publicity work.

He and Jamie roomed together for a time in one of the cheap hotels lining the side streets of the West Forties, the sort of hotel O'Neill later depicted in his one-act play, *Hughie*, whose protagonist, Erie Smith, was, as O'Neill once explained, "a type of Broadway sport I and my brother used to know by the dozen in far-off days."

Although Erie is a down-on-his-luck gambler with delusions of grandeur, he is unmistakably modeled on Jamie, the failed actor, who has frittered away his essence to become little more than facade. But it was a facade to which he clung.

McGinley remembered that Jamie "always looked like a Dapper Dan, even if he had only one suit; his shoes were always shined." He also recalled that Jamie once uncharacteristically permitted himself to be baited into a fistfight with an equally drunk John Barrymore in front of the Lambs Club. "Jamie sported a shiner for a few days," McGinley said.

Predictably, there were times when Jamie's drinking brought him to the brink of delirium tremens. Shuddering, he would comment, "The Brooklyn Boys are after me." The phrase, explained McGinley, referred to a parade of little men in derbies who passed in lockstep through walls and bolted doors.

James and Ella had long since realized Jamie could not live with them without constant friction, but thought Eugene, entering a productive life, might again fit under their wing. They had tried to persuade him, when he first returned to New York from Provincetown, to move into the Prince George with them.

They realized he would need James's continuing financial support until, and if, he managed to earn a living as a playwright. Eugene himself had made a gesture of reconciliation, though he was still smoldering over James's public espousal of Brandon Tynan as his "son." But he declined to live with his parents, at least for the time, preferring to bunk with Reed and Louise.

As earlier, O'Neill stretched his pittance by allowing Polly Holladay to treat him to meals. And he could eat cheaply at the Samovar, a club established early during the Players' first season out of a "desperate need" — as Edna Kenton put it — for a place where members could meet and talk. One flight above a junk shop, the Samovar was adjacent to the Hell Hole on Fourth Street, a block from the Playwrights' Theater. It was operated by a trained nurse named Nani Bailey, who, in need of a rest, had vacationed in Provincetown the summer before.

Nani was so swept up in the activity on the wharf that she became a member of the Players, postponing her return to nursing to open the Samovar, which quickly prospered.

John Reed's entry into Johns Hopkins was scheduled for November 12. On the 9th — the day the Provincetown Players ended their initial five-day run — he and Louise were secretly married in Peekskill, not far from their new country house.

As Louise recalled in her memoir, Reed said, "Well, honey, I think we'll have to get married, because I might die, and there seems a very good chance that I will, and I want you to have everything I've got."

Louise saw Reed off at the station. They had agreed she should not incur the expense of a hotel room in Baltimore until it was known if and when he would have his operation. She herself was not feeling well and had seen a doctor who tentatively diagnosed an intestinal infection.

She wrote to Reed a few hours after he left: "Oh, I hope you are feeling cheerful. I had a lump in my throat as big as the Woolworth Tower when I left the Station and it still comes back any moment."

O'Neill, living in Reed's apartment, found himself in the uncomfortable position of having to console Louise for Reed's illness, while wanting nothing more than to make love to her. Marguerite and Bill Zorach, who lived next door to the Reeds' apartment, and in whom Louise sometimes confided, were among a number of friends aware of O'Neill's and Louise's dilemma.

Louise told Marguerite of her faith in O'Neill's writing and said that O'Neill's need of her was the justification for her relationship with him. And yet, she said, Reed needed her, too. "You have no idea what it's like living with Jack," she said. "His war images come back to him — he goes through hell."

The triangle continued to beguile the Villagers, who could not fathom which man Louise truly loved. In her letters to Reed she went to as much pains to mislead him about her feelings for O'Neill, as she did to misguide O'Neill about her intentions toward Reed.

In one letter, written just hours after Reed's departure, she casually mentioned that O'Neill and Nani Bailey had invited her to dinner. "I'll weep in the middle of it if they aren't careful," she said, and added, "Oh, honey-heart — everyone's been pouring out love over you all day long and it's nice to have the little secret about us when they do."

Reed, responding the next day, ignored the mention of her dinner companions and anxiously asked her to write at once about how her "insides" were faring. "I'm really worried about them," he said. "You must spare no expense and pains to get that fixed up — *at once.*"

O'Neill's euphoria at having Louise more or less to himself was cut short by her lingering illness. The setback gave him a reason to resume his uncontrolled drinking — although, as with most alcoholics, any excuse, or none at all, would have served. Despite Louise's efforts, he could no more stay sober for her than he could for Beatrice.

Jig Cook's fears had materialized. Having given up any pretense of writing, O'Neill had no new work for the second bill on November 17.

On the bill were *Suppressed Desires* (finally, to the Cooks' satisfaction, being presented in New York); *Enemies,* a dialogue between a husband and wife, by Hutchins Hapgood and Neith Boyce, which satirized their own unhappy open marriage; and Reed's *Freedom,* previously produced in Provincetown and staged in his absence by Bror Nordfeldt.

Compounding O'Neill's misery and providing fresh justification for his backsliding, Louise left New York before the end of the bill's five-day run to be with Reed for his operation on November 22. She stayed until assured by his doctor that he was out of danger. Immediately after her return to New York on November 26, she wrote, "Oh Darling, the hospital was so white and cold and efficient I hated to leave you there."

At her apartment, she found O'Neill in a sorrier state than when she left. Although her own health had taken a turn for the worse, she summoned the strength to begin packing up hers and Reed's belongings for shipment to Croton, while O'Neill reluctantly moved his own scanty possessions into his parents' apartment at the Prince George.

It was "pretty dismal," she wrote to Reed, to camp out in the apartment with only "a chair and a cot." But she decided to remain in town, on learning that O'Neill's monologue, *Before Breakfast*, written in Provincetown, was scheduled to lead the third bill on December 1. At Cook's urging, she agreed to serve as prompter, hoping her presence would keep O'Neill sober through the production.

From all accounts, Louise was successful. O'Neill cast Mary Pyne as the shrewish wife, whose hideous nonstop nagging leads to her husband's suicide.

Knowing his father had time on his hands and encouraged by his positive reaction to *Bound East for Cardiff*, O'Neill invited him to look in on a rehearsal of *Before Breakfast*, even though he realized his father inevitably would find the subject matter distasteful.

Indeed, James is reported to have asked, "My son, why don't you write more pleasant plays?" Nonetheless, James gallantly tried to be helpful.

Members of the company, some cherishing childhood memories of *Monte Cristo* touring their hometowns, recalled James's grandiose presence when he came to inspect *Before Breakfast*. Hutchins Hapgood described him as "a striking figure with fur-collared coat, gold-headed cane and a diamond ring on his finger."

Like others, Hapgood observed a certain amount of friction between father and son. "He did not approve the diction or 'business' of the actress; he began to show her how acting was done, how points were made, with the voice and gesture of Monte Cristo," said Hapgood.

As James was leaving, some of the Players "spoke to him about Gene's gifts and promise" and, as Hapgood noted, he agreed with them "benignly," saying, "Yes, yes, I think the boy has something in him."

According to a contemporary history of the Provincetown Players, "O'Neill Senior tried to instill in Mary Pyne some of the histrionic technique of an era which the Players had no wish to revive, while O'Neill Junior stalked up and down muttering his displeasure." Though willing to acknowledge his father's contribution, O'Neill bridled at stories that James had been called in to *direct* the play. His recorded reaction to such accounts was, "Nuts!"

"There was no question of him directing," said O'Neill. "I got him down to make suggestions on the acting. He made some I didn't agree with, but some I thought were fine and which the actors were glad to follow."

In speaking of "the actors," O'Neill presumably meant himself, as well as Mary Pyne, since he portrayed the play's only other character — the offstage Alfred. Pyne, who tied back her lustrous red hair and concealed her alabaster complexion with the makeup of a pinched virago, had the sense to do everything James told her to do, grandiloquent gestures, melodramatic inflections and all. James, gratified, told her: "You are a most intelligent young actress. I don't need to give you any further instruction." (Presumably she toned down the performance after James's departure.)

The program, which included Neith Boyce's *The Two Sons* and *Lima Beans*, a verse play by Alfred Kreymborg, received no reviews. The audience no doubt was stumped by *Lima Beans*, subtitled "A Conventional Scherzo," so advanced that not even the Players understood it. (Its cast of characters included "the Curtain" and in his stage directions Kreymborg loftily wrote: "If there must be a prelude of music, let it be nothing more consequential than one of the innocuous parlor rondos of Carl Maria von Weber.)

Kreymborg was the editor of Others, a magazine dedicated to the radical movement in poetry. It was printed at cost by a Russian anarchist who lived in the Bronx and called himself Mr. Liberty. O'Neill showed Kreymborg some of his own poems, but Kreymborg rejected them as "rather sketchy."

Before Breakfast is noteworthy as O'Neill's final appearance as an actor. He acknowledged that he cast himself because he wanted to measure from the stage audience reaction to the lengthy monologue.

"How much are they going to stand of this sort of thing before they begin to break," O'Neill mused. According to Edna Kenton, his experiment with *Before Breakfast* enabled him to write *The Emperor Jones*, much of it a monologue. "The matter of monologue had been settled — an audience could be made to take it and like it," Kenton said.

Whatever satisfaction O'Neill might have derived from the presentation of *Before Breakfast*, it was soon overshadowed by depression over Louise's departure for Croton, and her continued ill health. If she was as forthcoming about her illness to O'Neill as she was to Reed, they both had grounds for concern. In Croton, she suddenly felt so ill that she hurried back to New York to see her doctor.

She wrote to Reed: "You remember I told you that I began to feel my insides again, well, I got really ill out in the country and Dr. Lorber examined me and ordered me to bed under special care or in a hospital . . . here I was with a high temperature and the Dr. threatening a serious operation."

Harry Lorber was a forty-year-old, Polish-born physician, who had fought his way up from a Lower East Side, impoverished childhood, to a Park Avenue practice.

Always interested in the arts and sympathetic to its young practitioners, he was a favorite of the Greenwich Villagers, who knew him fondly as "Dr. Harry." It was he who had been summoned during Mabel Dodge's peyote party three years earlier, to treat some of the overdosed guests. Described by Dodge and Hapgood as "discreet," he doubled as psychologist to any Villager in need of a confidant.

Louise's friend, Beckie Edelson (who had once dallied with O'Neill), came to the rescue. "I'm to stay in bed at her house under Dr. Lorber's care," Louise wrote to Reed, assuring him that Beckie's was as good as a hospital because — though she required special care — "the *principal* thing" was "quiet and rest."

"It's the only way I can keep from having an operation," Louise said. And then, in an uncharacteristic and somewhat incoherent burst of nastiness, she told Reed, "They think maybe that I got it from your condition."

Reed responded with alarm. If she was concealing anything about the seriousness of her illness, he would leave "on a stretcher if necessary and get carried to New York" to be with her. But he was not so distraught that he allowed her accusation to go unchallenged.

"I didn't mind what you said about my infecting you — if it were true — but I had been awfully careful to find out about that . . . " And then, fully aware of what he was implying, and not without a certain malice of his own, he asked, "Are you *sure* . . . that it isn't a tubercular infection?"

A number of Louise's friends believed her illness was the result of a botched abortion. Had that been the case, she would — in that era before antibiotics — very likely have died. It is more probable she had an ovarian abscess that, given her sexual activity, as well as both Reed's and O'Neill's, might have been caused by a venereal disease (in those days not uncommon).

As it was, she was fortunate to recover as rapidly and fully as she did. Nor did she require an operation, and by mid-December she was convalescent. Reed, by then, had been discharged from Johns Hopkins and the two went to Croton to rest.

Whatever promises Louise might have made to O'Neill about a future together, it must have been quite clear to him that she had no plans to include him in her life during the coming months. She intended, once she and Reed had both regained their strength, to accompany him to China on assignment for the Metropolitan.

She and Reed underlined their new purpose in life by sending Jig Cook their resignations from the Provincetown Players. Although both frequently took the train to New York, they essentially severed themselves from their old crowd.

Too distraught over Louise to resume his writing, O'Neill was living a hand-to-mouth existence. Although he had reluctantly accepted his parents' shelter at the Prince George, he sometimes slept at the Garden Hotel, and often spent his nights in the Hell Hole. He had hit an overwhelming roadblock.

O'Neill had hoped by now to see some of his other early one-acters mounted at the Playwrights' Theater — *The Web*, for example, or perhaps *Warnings, Recklessness* or *Abortion*. But Cook did not think those plays worthy of O'Neill; he wanted plays of the caliber of *Bound East for Cardiff*. Despite O'Neill's own later dismissal of the plays, he was angered by Cook's rejection.

The Players' fourth bill, on December 15, had no play by Eugene O'Neill.

CHAPTER
FORTY-SEVEN

Two DAYS BEFORE CHRISTMAS 1916, JIG COOK TOOK worried note of O'Neill's worsening condition. Writing to Susan Glaspell, who was visiting relatives in Iowa, he told her that O'Neill, because he was not seeing Louise, was "nearing the snapping point of suspense" and that his "nervous tension is a thing that I feel instantly when I see him."

Mary Vorse was another observer of O'Neill's misery and ferocious drinking. "There was no such darkness as Gene's after a hangover," she wrote. "He would sit silent and suffering and in darkness. You could have taken the air he breathed and carved a statue of despair of it."

Nearly as debilitating as O'Neill's alcoholism, and of course related to it, was his all-but-incapacitating inability to mature emotionally. (Did he drink because he could not mature, or was he unable to mature because he drank?) At twenty-eight, he was still dependent on his father, and embroiled for the second time in two years in a needy and frustrating love affair. Once again, he was unable to pull himself together to concentrate on his writing.

Because O'Neill had written no new play since *Before Breakfast*, the Players, for their fifth bill on January 5, resignedly mounted *Fog* from the *Thirst* volume. O'Neill cast his New London boyhood friend, Hutch Collins, in the play, despite their estrangement of the year before.

O'Neill resented Collins's rude and callous attempt to insinuate himself into Greenwich Village life. Collins, he grumbled, "went at Bohemia as if he thought it was a place where you sponged without gratitude and made no pretense of return"; he "acted like a surly, silent bore," said O'Neill, "and so anathema is his name."

Somehow, Collins had redeemed himself by early 1917. No longer anathema, he played the Business Man, whose ideology clashes with that of the Poet, as they drift, together with the Peasant Woman and her Dead Child, in a lifeboat through the fog banks of Newfoundland.

At the time *Fog* was going into rehearsals, James O'Neill, at seventy-one, had impulsively accepted an offer to come out of retirement. He was about to begin rehearsals of his own in a new play called *The Wanderer*. He took the time, however, to look in once more at the Playwrights' Theater and offer fatherly advice.

James was familiar with *Fog*, having paid for its publication three years earlier (and been as baffled by it as he was by the other *Thirst* plays). Having weathered the suicide scene of *Before Breakfast*, he was gamely prepared to deal with *Fog*'s grim symbolical ending.

Although there was nothing he could do about it, James was distressed that Eugene refused to regard the theater as a medium for inspiration and uplift. William Carlos Williams, who had recently played a role in Kreymborg's *Lima Beans*, recalled that during a rehearsal, "the father would often interrupt the course of the play and when he did the son would be closely attentive."

The two plays that accompanied *Fog, A Long Time Ago* by Floyd Dell and *Bored* by John Mosher, were not much better. Jig Cook, seemingly unable to impose the discipline necessary for sustained artistic results, sorely felt the loss of John Reed's flair for organization.

The Players showed signs of faltering.

"We have hardly any good interesting plays and if we don't get them, we're going to peter out," Cook wrote to his wife.

O'Neill, drunk or sober, was too self-absorbed to concern himself with the Players' problems, except as they directly affected him. He attended some meetings to vote on play selection and policy, but did not participate in the productions of fellow writers. Even when it came to his own plays, his supervision was evidently somewhat hit-or-miss.

"O'Neill could make anybody work for him," Harry Kemp once said. "It was a joke to see him cast the plays. He'd go out and walk up and down the street in front of the theater, and if he saw somebody he wanted, he got him. Artists, ironworkers, wealthy idlers, penniless strikers . . . that Irishman could kid them into anything."

It had become obvious not only to O'Neill but to most of the other writers that personal supervision of their own plays, not to mention participation in other productions, left little time for creativity.

By now, the selection of plays for each bill, rather than being the democratic process of twice-weekly group readings and discussion originally intended, had been ceded by mutual consent to Edna Kenton and Susan Glaspell. They found it to be an onerous task.

"Periodically," wrote Edna Kenton, "we would glance at each other across some dinner table, realizing that one of the many nights was upon us when the scores of pounds of manuscripts must be read," when the time had come to "thin the trash from the possible, the possible from the 'perhaps,' through to the 'really goods' and the few 'musts.'"

Foreign plays were sent back unread and certain works were instantly seen as unmountable on the Players' cramped stage — such as the five-act Civil War epic with a cast of forty submitted in all innocence by an aspiring (and never again heard from) playwright from Montana.

The theater's good reputation was beginning to spread. In November 1916, Frank Shay brought out the first of his pamphlet series, The Provincetown Plays, including *Bound East for Cardiff*. The second contained no play by O'Neill, but the third in December included *Before Breakfast*. All three pamphlets were reviewed in January in the Evening Globe (New York), which called the plays "almost uniformly interesting, at least to read."

The writers represented, wrote the Globe's critic, N. P. Dawson, "are sometimes gleeful and sometimes severe, but generally unerringly sure."

He praised Susan Glaspell and Jig Cook together as "clever burlesquers," and called Glaspell (writing solo) "the sober realist"; Floyd Dell was "the pale amorist," John Reed "the satirist," Louise Bryant "the moralist." Neith Boyce and Hutchins Hapgood were characterized by Dawson as "the sex-problemers," and he hailed O'Neill as "the thriller." The plays, he concluded, provided "first-class and really refreshing literary entertainment."

Heywood Broun, who had switched in 1915 from sportswriter to drama critic of The Tribune, was less laudatory. While faintly praising both Glaspell and O'Neill, he declared there was "only a little gold dust" to be found among the published plays. O'Neill, he conceded, had struck a rich "Kipling vein" in *Bound East for Cardiff*, which he described as owing "more to the creation of mood and atmosphere than to any fundamentally interesting idea or sudden twist of plot."

Frank Shay had printed 1,200 copies of this first paperback edition, priced at fifty cents. Most were distributed free to writers, actors and others interested in the Provincetown group, and the pamphlet brought O'Neill no more income than had *Thirst*.

The fortuitous arrival in early January 1917 of Nina Moise, who had staged some plays with small stock companies in California and Massachusetts, raised the faltering spirits of the Players. Moise wanted to act and was planning to audition for the Players, until a friend told her the company had all the actors it needed; what was urgently wanted was a director with professional experience.

With Jig Cook's approval, Moise was assigned to direct one of the plays already in rehearsal for the sixth bill, *The Dollar* by David Pinski, the prolific Yiddish playwright. Set to open on January 26 but behind schedule, the bill included Neith Boyce's *Winter's Night* (reconstituted from Provincetown) and a trifle — also directed by Moise — called *Pan* by Kenneth MacNichol.

"I'd never seen anything like it," Moise later said. "The actors didn't know enough not to bump into each other."

As Edna Kenton recalled, "Under Nina Moise's skilled touch, *The Dollar*, none too much in itself, became an expertly played, smooth-running comedy. For the first time on that experimental stage, a trained director had been in full charge of one play, and the result spoke for itself, not only in that play but in the rest of the bill. The other players had picked up hints and had acted on them."

Moise was asked by the all-but-defeated amateurs to stay on. She accepted and moved into a three-dollar-a-week garret on Washington Square. "I wasn't paid anything, and I rarely went north of Fourteenth Street again," she later recalled.

Not only did she become the Players' resident director but her effectiveness prompted the Players to swallow their pride and, as Kenton put it, "to call in outside aid when we needed it."

As O'Neill's career faltered, his father's unexpectedly revived. *The Wanderer* opened on February 1 at the Manhattan Opera House to warm reviews. Adapted by Maurice V. Samuels from a German play produced by Max Reinhardt in Berlin, it was yet another biblical spectacle, set in Jerusalem — this time dealing with the legend of the prodigal son.

The sort of play that James found uplifting, it was produced by Morris Gest and William Elliott with the assistance of none other than David Belasco, the onetime irrepressible stage manager of *The Passion*, who well remembered the 1879 riot in San Francisco incited by James's portrayal of Jesus.

Belasco, now a power on Broadway, anticipated no such disturbances over James's role as the prodigal's father, Jesse. Indeed, James drew high praise for the "patriarchal grandeur" of his performance.

The play was likened to *Ben-Hur* by the Evening World's critic, who hastened to describe the "Oriental orgy in which girls threw themselves down and hung their heads over the edge of the stage." There were a dozen curtain calls on opening night — "Calls for the author, bravos for the actors and cheers for the scenery."

Predictably, Eugene thought the play a waste of his father's ability, while James stubbornly held to his belief that the "modern" theater was thoroughly wrongheaded. As with *Virginius* and *The Passion*, he was convinced *The Wanderer* was "classic drama."

In what might be construed as an oblique disparagement of his son's efforts, James declared in an interview: "I would not have returned to the stage in any other kind of play, because when one has acted on the legitimate for fifty years as I have, with such great actors as Edwin Booth and Edwin Forrest, it is impossible to be resigned to the commonplaces of the modern style of play."

The Wanderer, he continued, "has the old heart quality in it, the appeal that the public cannot resist." He compared it to plays like *The Count of Monte Cristo*, "eternally human" plays dealing in "love, heroism, filial devotion, ideals and passion that go to make up our lives to-day as they did 3,000 years ago in Jerusalem."

What James mildly characterized as "the modern style of play" had been vilified a few months earlier by David Belasco. The new experimental theaters, he fumed, not only were "devoted to false ideals," but had never before "been so vicious, vulgar and degrading."

He went on to attack their work as "the wail of the incompetent and the degenerate." They were, he raged, "the haven of those who lack experience and knowledge of the drama," and he declared he must "take this stand more firmly than ever and endeavor to protect our drama, the stage and the legitimate theater of America from those who would make a freak of it."

On February 16, the Playwrights' Theater presented its seventh bill — again behind schedule — calling it the "War Bill." O'Neill offered *The Sniper*, the anti-war play that had earned "honorable mention" in George Pierce Baker's class, but had been turned down for political reasons by both the Harvard Dramatic Club and Holbrook Blinn (who said he would consider it after the war).

In the Players' view, the time had come for *The Sniper*. It was directed by Nina Moise, with Cook and Ida Rauh in the cast. Moise, said Edna Kenton, was just what the Players needed: "a tyrant, velvet-gloved if possible, but always with the iron hand." O'Neill watched appreciatively as Moise took control of his play, the first of four O'Neill one-acters she was to direct.

She and O'Neill became confidential friends. Although Nina lent nothing discernible of her personality to his 1928 play, *Strange Interlude*, the first part of the drama is set in the period when he knew her, and her name evidently sprang to his mind when he was creating Nina Leeds.

"I didn't like Gene when I first met him during the production of *The Sniper*," Moise recalled. "He was morose, sullen, uncommunicative." It was not long, however, before she fell under the spell of his "moody, tormented eyes" and felt the power of the man, "terribly potent, terribly lonely." He told her of his love for Louise: "She's the only woman I love or ever will love." Nina was moved, even though she thought he was exaggerating.

Nina was wary of O'Neill's hard-drinking friends and rarely joined them at the Hell Hole. She did join O'Neill one night at a party, timorously watching the guests drink, herself holding an untouched glass of punch — a blend of wine and gin. When O'Neill taunted her about her abstinence, she impulsively drained her glass.

"You're a god-damned fool," said O'Neill, with a mocking grin. "I wouldn't drink that trash." He took a deep draught from a bottle he carried with him.

On another occasion he sat with Nina in her room until five in the morning, talking about his past. "You know, Nina, somewhere in the world I have a son."

Nina, predictably, gasped.

"Don't be so god-damned sentimental," said O'Neill. "I've never seen him."

With habitual dramatic flair, he murmured, "Nina, I make the poet's plea in *Candida*."

Nina was caught off guard and stammered an inadequate answer. She had forgotten that the poet's name was Eugene. Later, rereading the Shaw comedy, she found that the poet, like O'Neill, wore a "haunted, tormented expression" and was shy and awkward.

In the last-act scene to which O'Neill had referred, Candida is confronted by the husband who needs her and the poet who worships her, and asks each what inducement he has to offer for her love.

The poet's plea is: "My weakness. My desolation. My heart's need." Nina was distressed to think that if only she had remembered Candida's answer ("That's a good bid, Eugene") it would have had the virtue of being both graceful and noncommittal; for Candida, of course, rejects the poet.

Nina was soon to learn that although O'Neill was interested in hearing how his plays were received, he rarely witnessed an opening performance of his work. After one first night, she asked, "Gene, how did you like it?"

"I didn't see it," he replied. "The theatre on opening night is no place for a nervous man. When I finish writing a play, I'm through with it."

He added that "a play may be damn well acted from an acting standpoint, and still be far from the creator's intention." Some of his plays had featured excellent acting, he explained, but never had there been a production he recognized as being "deeply" his play. "That's why I never see them," he said. "A play is written about living and is seen on the stage as acting."

He nearly always attended rehearsals, however, making additions or deletions of dialogue, and sometimes suggesting changes in stage business. "Gene was concerned with plays, not theatre," Moise observed. "His plays were foolproof and almost director-proof."

O'Neill also tried to make his plays actor-proof, specifying every nuance of each role. His stage directions sometimes are impossible to take literally, demanding a character turn pale, or sweat, or — in one instance — chew gum "like a sacred cow forgetting time with an eternal end."

Actually, they are important road signs for the intelligent performer, and many of O'Neill's actors expressed gratitude for them. His actors were also aware he had the experienced craftsman's knowledge of the number of words a performer can handle comfortably on each intake of breath.

"I was practically brought up in the theater . . . and I know all the technique of acting," he once said. "I know everything that everyone is doing from the electrician to the stagehands. So I see the machinery going round all the time unless the play is wonderfully acted and produced . . . in my own plays, all the time I watch them, I am acting all the parts and living them so intensely that by the time the performance is over I am exhausted — as if I had gone through a clothes wringer."

Two weeks before *The Sniper* opened on February 3, 1917,

President Wilson severed relations with Germany, and America found itself in the throes of war fever. That same week, Carl Hovey informed Reed that, in view of the changed world situation, the Metropolitan could not justifiably invest in his assignment to China.

Hovey asked Reed if he could propose a more relevant assignment, but both knew that because of Reed's outspokenly bitter opposition to America's entry into the war, his services were no longer acceptable.

Reed had lost not only a lucrative assignment, but the pleasure and romance promised by a trip to the Far East with Louise. All mainstream magazines were now closed to him, as he refused to adopt their conformist view of the war.

He made up his mind he would write nothing that did not express his hatred of capitalism and that did not encourage social revolution. He participated in pacifist demonstrations and continued to express his views in The Masses, which welcomed (but did not pay for) them.

"I know what war means," he wrote in the Masses on April, 1916. "I have been with the armies of all the belligerents except one . . . War means an ugly mob-madness, crucifying the truth-tellers, choking the artists, side-tracking reforms, revolutions and the working of social forces . . . Whose war is this? Not mine."

The cancelling of the China trip was equally a blow to Louise. She had dreamed that, once in China, she could file free-lance articles that would lead to employment by a mainstream publication.

Continuing to hope for magazine assignments and fearing that she, like Reed, would be boycotted, Louise was not ready to espouse Reed's views publicly, even though she agreed with them in principle — as, indeed, did O'Neill and the rest of the Village's artistic community. They were united in their conviction that the banking interests and munitions makers were creating the propaganda pushing America into the war.

With Reed engaged in anti-war activity, Louise was once again under-occupied — and perhaps regretful that she had cut herself off from the Players and O'Neill. She might not have been aware that O'Neill himself had by now virtually severed himself from the Players.

With ever fewer worthwhile one-acters being submitted, the Players were tentatively considering long plays for their next season. O'Neill offered them *The Personal Equation* (like *The Sniper* written in Baker's class). According to the company's sketchy minutes, O'Neill read two acts of the play on February 21, and outlined the other two before a selection committee. O'Neill's mood did not improve when the Players turned it down.

On a visit to New York from Croton, Louise learned from Jamie O'Neill that Eugene, still nominally living with his parents at the Prince George, had gone missing. His mother was worried about him, Jamie said, and thought Louise might be able to coax him home.

"So I went to the Hell Hole," recalled Louise. "Gene was there, I don't know how long he had been there. He hadn't washed or shaved for days, but I managed to get him to go with me.

"We went outside and tried to find a taxicab, but none came along, so we got into a Fifth Avenue bus. When we got to Twenty-eighth Street I wanted Gene to get off with me. He was in an ugly mood and said he wouldn't get out . . . But I finally got him out and to his hotel and to bed. I was to take the subway to the Forty-second Street station, and just as I was going down into the tube Gene came running after me and stood at the top of the stairs, shouting. But I had got into a train, and off I went."

It might have been soon after this incident that a remorseful, if not quite sober, O'Neill, sat down in the Garden Hotel to scribble a poem called "Eyes":

> I gazed in the mirror
> And smiled at myself —
> But my eyes could not smile.
> They were dead souls,
> Imprisoned.
> How could they smile?
>
> Yet I must meet her —
> And so I shaved,
> Shuddering
> At the horror
> In the mirror.
>
> And a little later
> I met her at the train,
> And kissed her,
> And smiled —
> But my eyes could not smile.
>
> I longed to close them.

Why could they not smile?

And her eyes,
Eager with the desire of love,
Stared accusingly;
Then filled with tears
When they saw
The dead.

According to Louise, O'Neill telephoned her "a few days" after the episode on the bus, "very sober, and apologized, and said he would like to see me. So I came into town again and we had a serious talk. He decided he'd go to Provincetown and go to work. He'd be all alone down there and could settle down."

There was no play by O'Neill on the eighth bill. He had, by mid-March, fled the Village for the insularity of Provincetown. He had come to realize, as had Louise and Reed, that it was impossible to write amid the distractions of the city, that he needed more than a locked door to protect him. It was difficult to say no to a friend seeking a drinking companion or a good argument. He needed complete seclusion, a wide, physical barrier between himself and his friends.

"Although I have spent a good deal of time here and ought to be used to the city," he said some years later, "I have never written a line in New York. It's too jarring, too hectic."

He was, however, perfectly aware that the principal inhibiting factor was alcohol, and he later admitted as much. His uncontrolled drinking during more than twenty years appears to have matched if not exceeded that of almost any other contemporary alcoholic American author (several, like him, Nobel Laureates).

Many years after giving up alcohol, he ruefully confessed: "After I'd had a quart and a half of bourbon, I could walk straight and talk rationally, but my brain was nuts. If anybody suggested that I climb up the Woolworth Building, I'd be tickled to death to do it."

As it happened, O'Neill was the only one among his literary alcoholic contemporaries who, at forty, managed to stop drinking and go on to produce his greatest work.

Jack London was a suicide at forty; Hart Crane (who became a friend of O'Neill) was a suicide at thirty-three; and Scott Fitzgerald had drunk himself to death by forty-four. The best work of both

Ernest Hemingway and William Faulkner was behind them by their forties, although, like O'Neill, both survived into their sixties. Alcohol killed Faulkner at sixty-six, and Hemingway shot himself at sixty-two.

Most if not all of these writers began drinking early, like O'Neill, and alcohol at times appears to have stimulated their imaginations. Unlike O'Neill, however, the others made their marks in their twenties. In O'Neill's case, the early onset of alcoholism seems to have delayed his literary blossoming, as he did not hit his stride until nearly thirty.

O'Neill understood he was dependent on alcohol, and even conceded that it did, in some ways, release his imagination, but stoutly maintained he could not and did not write plays while under its influence — and there is no reason to doubt him.

Early in his career, O'Neill insisted that a writer needed all his "critical and creative faculties" when working. "I never try to write a line when I'm not strictly on the wagon," he said. "I don't think anything worth reading was ever written by anyone who was drunk or even half-drunk when he wrote it. This is not morality, it's plain physiology. Dope I know nothing about, but I suspect that even De Quincey was boasting what a devil he was!"

He was vehement in his assertion that "altogether too much damn nonsense has been written since the beginning of time about the dissipation of artists. Why, there are fifty times more real drunkards among the Bohemians who only play at art, and probably more than that among the people who never think about art at all. The artist drinks, when he drinks at all, for relaxation, forgetfulness, excitement, for any purpose except his art."

Toward the end of his career, having long since quit drinking, he was still defending himself against the "absurd" legend that he had written plays when drunk. It was when he was *not* writing, he said, that he drank. "I'd drink for a month and then go out and snap out of it by myself. It was during these periods that I wrote."

He was not entirely correct, however, in his assumption about the drinking habits of other writers. Faulkner, for one — a fourth-generation alcoholic who began drinking as an adolescent — claimed he could not write *without* the stimulation of drink.

Fitzgerald, on the other hand, apparently concurred with O'Neill. He regretted having drunk heavily while writing *Tender Is the Night*, later explaining that "a short story can be written on a bottle, but for a novel you need the mental speed that enables you to keep the whole pattern in your head."

O'Neill attributed his own drinking to a need to combat his "highly introspective, intensely nervous and self-conscious" nature. "I drank to overcome my shyness," he once said. But the reasons went deeper.

A comment by one of his favorite poets, the dissolute Baudelaire, with regard to Poe's drinking, might aptly be applied to O'Neill. Poe, said Baudelaire, drank "barbarously, with a speed and dispatch" that suggested "a homicidal function, as if he had to kill something inside himself, a worm that would not die."

There is a mass of anecdotal data indicating that alcoholism is an illness of epidemic proportions among contemporary American writers. O'Neill, being *Irish*-American, was doubly damned, for drink has always been seen as the Irish curse. Andrew M. Greeley, the writer and priest — perhaps over-eager to make his point — has written that "The Irish are twenty-five times more likely than the typical American to suffer from alcoholism."

At the end of March, with O'Neill in Provincetown, the Players presented their concluding production — a "Review Bill" of four plays which, in O'Neill's absence, omitted *Bound East for Cardiff*. The Players had initially promised a season of ten bills, but they had "run out of plays and strength" and were "literally spent in body and spirit," as Kenton recalled.

With the audience packed along the narrow planks "like herring," according to Kenton, the "Review Bill" was a huge success. At last, all the critics came down to the theater and "wrote us up glowingly though they paid, every man of them, for the privilege of doing it."

Burns Mantle, in the Evening Mail, wrote that he counted it a "civic duty" to report that the Players' achievement "is as sound as it is modest," adding, "We never thought anything could live a year in New York without a press agent."

Writing in Vogue, Clayton Hamilton congratulated the Provincetowners for making "no attempt to compete against the established theater of commerce," seeking "no reward for their endeavors either in money or in reputation."

He pointed out, however, that their staging was "for the most part unworthy of serious consideration" and that their acting was "amateurish and uncertain." He concluded that "the plays produced by the Provincetown Players are strangely interesting and strikingly impressive."

After reelecting Jig Cook as president, the Players scattered, committed to return in early fall.

"Even knowing we did it, I am disposed to say what we did that first year couldn't be done," Susan Glaspell wrote. "I can see Jig, say, an afternoon of dress rehearsal, coat off, sleeves up, perspiring as any other laborer perspires, lifting, pounding, working to help finish a set; wrestling with a stage-manager who says a certain thing can't be done, checking up on props — himself going over to Sixth Avenue for some of them — yes, sweeping the theater, if the woman who should have done it failed to come . . . he works through till performance time — works as if it were death which waits if the thing is not done."

It was, in fact, a *birth* at which Cook and the other Players had presided. Despite the brash failures and sometimes dubious triumphs, those five months of the first season, from early November 1916 to late March 1917, eventually were to be emblazoned in the annals of theater history as the birth pangs of the modern American drama.

Actually, O'Neill's only significant offering that first season, as he himself came to realize, had been *Bound East for Cardiff*. His four plays — though more than anyone else's contribution — did not measure up in quality to Jig Cook's high expectations.

In the end, O'Neill himself preferred to forget *Fog* and *The Sniper*, and decided to preserve *Before Breakfast* only as an interesting experiment. It was not until the following season that he was to begin earning his rightful place as the cornerstone of the Playwrights' Theater.

Chapter
FORTY-EIGHT

Rather than being "all alone" in Provincetown, as he had intimated to Louise, O'Neill was accompanied by a friend from Greenwich Village. Harold DePolo, a spewer of short stories for pulp magazines, was mockingly described by O'Neill as "story-a-minute DePolo." Hard-drinking and self-indulgent, he left his wife and children at home to join O'Neill for what he thought would be a brief lark.

O'Neill and DePolo first moved into the Atlantic House, an unpretentious hotel that boasted a sign, "GUESTS HEATED." The proprietor, also the chef, amused himself by shouting a customer's order to the kitchen, then hurrying to his stove to cook it.

Far removed from New York, O'Neill found he was able to resume his writing in spite of sporadic breaks for drinking with DePolo, who divided his own time between writing and playing poker. Possibly Louise had bestowed a temporary serenity by offering some hope for a future together. In any case, O'Neill was sufficiently motivated to complete three one-act plays in rapid succession before the end of March, and a fourth by the end of April. All were good enough to be produced and one of the four, *The Moon of the Caribbees*, was a small poetic gem.

O'Neill luxuriated in Provincetown's early-spring isolation. He felt spiritually at one with the windswept dunes, the roiling ocean and the pulsing tides of the bay with its canopy of circling sea gulls.

Taking long, invigorating walks across the dunes, he had his first taste of how it might be to live there year-round. A picture of spring-time Provincetown in the days before it became a populous resort has been drawn by Mary Heaton Vorse:

" . . . there is a bloom of wild fruit, which spreads like a bridal veil, of shad and juicy pear and wild cherries and beach plum, growing in great quantities where the dunes and the wood meet . . . All through the season there are blueberries and huckleberries . . . The back country is so wild that it abounds with little creatures. Many of them, like the rabbits and puff adders and toads, have turned dune-color. Foxes slide through the underbrush . . . There is seldom a time when there are no gulls soaring and sweeping over the Bay. Some of the gulls come from as far as Plymouth for the rich pickings from the Provincetown boats."

O'Neill wrote in his room and occasionally, believing the cold sea air was good for his lungs, wrapped himself in a blanket and wrote on the beach. Before long, however, he was in trouble.

That spring, Provincetown, even more than the rest of the country, was swept up in furor over the war. America's entry now appeared inevitable. Threats of German U-boat action were a daily topic of conversation on the exposed Cape and safety precautions along the coast were tightened.

O'Neill was not popular among the patriotic villagers; known as an intimate friend of "the radical John Reed," he was believed to share Reed's pacifist views. A natural object of suspicion, he was mistrusted by the local constabulary the way Smitty was suspected by his shipmates of being a German spy in *In the Zone* — which O'Neill was to write within a few weeks.

On March 28, five days before President Wilson asked Congress for a declaration of war against Germany, O'Neill and DePolo returned from a walk across the dunes and sat down to a meal in a rival hotel grandly named the New Central. A local constable, Reuben O. Kelley, informed them they were under arrest.

The charge, he said, was vagrancy, but it soon evolved that the arrest had been made at the instigation of the chief of the United States radio station in North Truro, who had somehow arrived at the notion that O'Neill and DePolo were German spies.

Constable Kelley, it seemed, had trailed O'Neill across the dunes, hiding while he watched him take out "an instrument that flashed in the sun"; he leaped to the conclusion that O'Neill was using a "wireless gadget" to signal an enemy ship. The "gadget" turned out to be a typewriter.

As the Provincetown Advocate reported the next day, the arrest was made "for the purpose of ascertaining if O'Neill and DePolo were the men" who had been seen "prowling about the radio grounds during the past ten days." A Secret Service agent arrived that evening from Boston to question the suspects.

According to the Advocate, the incident resulted in a memorable stir: "All manner of rumors were rife Wednesday afternoon and evening regarding incidents of the arrest . . . Statements to the effect that the arrested men drew revolvers upon the arresting officer, that the pair were found armed, that plans of the radio station and grounds and Provincetown Harbor were found in the possession of the pair were all wholly false statements."

As the article summed up, O'Neill and DePolo "were fully able to explain the reason for their presence" and to describe their movements "in manner satisfactory to their inquisitors." O'Neill preserved the story in a scrapbook and enjoyed embellishing the episode.

"I was the victim of war hysteria," he said in one account. "We were having dinner in a hotel in town one evening when some Secret Service men pounced on us at the point of a revolver and carried us to the lockup in the basement of the Town Hall." He added that they were held incommunicado for twenty-four hours. "They wouldn't even let us see a lawyer."

On April 2, Wilson, addressing a joint session of Congress, asked for a declaration of war. On the same day, Reed addressed a pacifist rally in Washington attended by thousands, at which he reiterated, "This is not my war and I will not support it."

In Provincetown, Constable Kelley, aware of O'Neill's connection with Reed, remained unconvinced of his innocence. He appointed himself O'Neill's shadow, and took to steaming open his mail. If he happened to see O'Neill before his mail had been officially delivered, Kelley would present a brief résumé of what he could expect: "Well, you got a letter from your mother, Gene, but your girl's forgot you today."

His girl, in fact, had achieved some success on his behalf. After Carl Hovey rejected his short story, "Tomorrow," Louise recommended it to Waldo Frank, an editor of The Seven Arts, a literary magazine, and Frank told Louise he would consider it. Frank's co-editors were James Oppenheim, Louis Untermeyer and Van Wyck Brooks, and among the magazine's contributors were Robert Frost, Amy Lowell, Theodore Dreiser and Sherwood Anderson; The Seven Arts had recently featured an essay by Reed called "This Unpopular War."

On March 26, O'Neill sent Frank his "working copy" of "Tomorrow," saying he hoped it would "prove to be something in the line" of what he was looking for, and explaining that he would send "the plays Louise mentioned" as soon as he had them typed.

"Our magazine was very serious, almost religious," Waldo Frank said. "We considered ourselves the organ of cultural nationalism. We were disciples of Walt Whitman and were creating the voice Whitman wanted.

"Louise was just around; she was a 'flaming youth' girl, an Irish beauty, thin, with pale skin, very romantic. She was intellectually alive and responsive, although not profound. She told me about O'Neill, and said he had written a story we might want. We laid our main stress on stories, although we used poetry and nonfiction articles, too."

Frank accepted "Tomorrow" conditionally, suggesting some changes. O'Neill, recovered from the trauma of his arrest two days earlier, devoted an afternoon and evening to revising and cutting the manuscript and, either unwilling or unable to retype it, returned it with his handwritten corrections. Conceding that Frank's editorial suggestions were valid, he said he had shortened the story by "about a thousand words" and hoped he had thereby "sharpened" it.

Among his numerous deletions was a six-paragraph postscript that did not come to light until the original manuscript was made available to scholars many years after O'Neill's death.

The deleted postscript is noteworthy mainly for its revelation of the liberal-minded O'Neill's callous aping of the social and literary bigotry of his day. Mindlessly, he permitted himself to refer to the manager of a theatrical booking office as "a fat little Jew."

He made no mention of that particular phrase in his letter to Frank, merely conceding, "The postscript goes overboard. You are quite right about it." When he wrote the story, he explained, he had "planned it as the first of a series of Tommy the Priest's yarns in which the story-teller was to hog most of the limelight — a sort of Conrad's Marlow — and once I had that idea I couldn't let go, and it rode me into the anti-climax."

A few days later, Frank agreed to publish the revised story and O'Neill sent him, at his request, a neatly typed page of biographical data for the magazine's "Notes on Names" department. Frank paid O'Neill fifty dollars for the story, the first respectable sum he had earned from his writing, and it was published in the June issue.

O'Neill, at the time, regarded the story as "pretty devastating stuff," but jested about its publication some twenty-five years later, saying he doubted whether his editors "were as overwhelmed by its hideous beauty as I was."

On April 30, O'Neill sent Frank the three one-acters he had

recently completed: *The Long Voyage Home* (originally entitled *Homeward Bound* and set in the London waterfront saloon where Olson, the hapless drunken sailor from the crew of the Glencairn, is shanghaied); *The Moon of the Caribbees* (his mood piece about the same crew, anchored off an island in the West Indies, originally entitled *The Moon at Trinidad*); and *In the Zone* (also about the Glencairn's crew, whose members mistakenly believe their shipmate, Smitty, is a spy).

O'Neill described them as "units in a series I have been writing intended to depict different phases of modern merchant-sailor life on board ship and in sailor-town ashore." He did not include *Bound East for Cardiff* because Frank Shay had published it after its New York production.

"The fact that I use several of the same characters in each play may be misleading," he wrote to Waldo Frank, explaining they were not intended to "form a connected story," but, rather, were each "complete in itself."

He said he had used "members of the same crew on the one ship throughout only because, judging from my own experience as a sailor, I thought I had, in the majority of these characters, picked out the typical mixed crew of the average British tramp steamer."

Frank accepted only *In the Zone*, praising "its real color." He paid O'Neill another fifty dollars for it, but The Seven Arts shut down before the play could be published.

By mid-May, Harold DePolo had gone home and O'Neill moved into an apartment of four small rooms above a general store on Commercial Street, near the Wharf Theater. Harry Kemp, who lived with Mary Pyne across the hall, described the flat as "sketchily furnished," with "two beds, a Morris chair, several kitchen chairs, a kitchen table, a small sitting-room table, a three-burner oil stove." O'Neill's back windows, Kemp recalled, "gave on a magnificent view of bay and harbor."

The proprietor of the store and apartments was John A. Francis, the most generous and accommodating of landlords. Of Irish and Portuguese descent, Francis was a native of Provincetown and probably its most beloved resident. In the evenings, ignoring a sign that read "Please loaf in the back room," the sea captains and fishermen congregated around his front-room cracker barrel, smoking, chewing tobacco and basking in his geniality.

A rotund, baby-faced man whose kindly eyes peered over steel-rimmed glasses, Francis was so tenderhearted that people often wondered how he eked out a living. He never collected rent on his apartments — known by all as "Francis's Flats" — from anyone who seemed hard up. He extended unlimited credit and frequently accepted paintings from artists in lieu of payment.

Francis loved O'Neill, as he loved all strays, and subsidized him for nearly a year. O'Neill returned his affection and, when a friend sent him Francis's obituary in 1937, O'Neill expressed his genuine sorrow: "He was a fine person — and a unique character. I am glad the article speaks of him as my friend. He was all of that, and I know he knew my gratitude, for I often expressed it."

Unfazed by Waldo Frank's rejection of *The Long Voyage Home* and *The Moon of the Caribbees*, O'Neill sent them to The Smart Set toward the end of May. Smugly styling itself "a magazine of cleverness," it was edited by George Jean Nathan and H. L. Mencken, both possessed of an absolute faith in their ability to recognize cleverness when they saw it. Happily for O'Neill, they saw it in his plays.

The Smart Set tended to provoke debate in intellectual circles because Nathan and Mencken, though often brilliant, were sometimes vulgar and always irreverent. One leaflet issued from the magazine's offices announced, "A woman Secretary is in attendance at all interviews between the Editors, or either of them, and lady authors. Hence, it will be unnecessary for such visitors to provide themselves with either duennas or police whistles."

While The Smart Set was decidedly iconoclastic, O'Neill wondered if it was nonconformist enough to publish his two submissions. In his letter to Mencken, he elaborated on what he had told Waldo Frank about the plays ("merchant-sailor life on a tramp steamer as it really is — its sordidness inexplicably touched with romance by the glamor of far horizons"). He added that he had "never seen anything of this kind in The Smart Set," and had "small hope of it being the type of material you desire."

Knowing that virtually every contemporary writer of fiction regarded an appearance in The Smart Set as a literary triumph, O'Neill could barely believe it when Mencken replied that he liked the plays.

Soon after, O'Neill received a letter from Nathan, who served as the magazine's drama critic, accepting both one-acters for publication and paying him $75 for each. O'Neill was stunned by his triumph. In 1922, after having won two Pulitzer Prizes, he said that acceptance as a playwright by The Smart Set was "the first recognition of any kind that I received."

Nathan's letter of acceptance marked the beginning of a long friendship. Six years O'Neill's senior, Nathan had been a drama critic since 1908, first for the New York Herald and later as a contributor to Harper's Weekly, among other publications. He had been co-editor of The Smart Set since 1914.

Having studied in Germany, Nathan was an advocate of the European drama, endearing himself to O'Neill by praising the plays of Strindberg and Ibsen, and ridiculing, often with wild abandon, the plays of such sacrosanct Americans as Augustus Thomas and Eugene Walter. Nathan throve on controversy and loved stepping on toes. He was a gallant fighter in any intellectual cause he believed in and, from the beginning, he believed in O'Neill.

"In O'Neill [the American] theater has found its first really important dramatist," Nathan wrote in an introduction to the volume entitled *The Moon of the Caribbees and Six Other Plays of the Sea*.

"To it he has brought a sense of splendid color, a sense of vital drama and a sense of throbbing English that no native playwright before him was able to bring . . .

"O'Neill came into the American theater at a propitious moment . . . Just as this drama seemed about to be laid low by unremitting stereotyped dullness and preposterous affectation, he jumped upon the scene with a bundle of life and fancy under his arm, hurled it onto the stage, and there let it break open with its hundred smashing hues to confound the drab and desolate boards. Instantly — or so it seemed — the stage began to breathe again . . .

"The essential difference between O'Neill and the majority of his contemporaries in the field of American drama lies in the circumstance that where the latter think of life (where they think of it at all) in terms of drama, O'Neill thinks of drama in terms of life."

The Smart Set published *The Long Voyage Home* in October 1917 and *The Moon of the Caribbees* in August 1918. The latter was by far O'Neill's favorite of his one-act plays. It was, as he later said, his "first real break with theatrical traditions." It was also the first of his plays that belonged thematically with his later work.

"Once I had taken this initial step," he said, "the other plays followed logically."

The break with tradition, he maintained, lay in the play's disregard for plot or action, and its concentration on pure, poetic mood. Dreamy and fragile, it probes the sensibilities of a group of lonely seamen afloat under a West Indian moon, and examines their varied responses to a group of native women who board the Glencairn offering liquor and sex.

With *The Moon of the Caribbees*, O'Neill achieved the goal he had all along sought: to reveal the souls of his characters by depicting them in their natural environment, and not (like the despised Augustus Thomas) by wedging them into artificial situations and then melodramatically extricating them.

People whose lives were "bright and easy," O'Neill said, were continuously dramatized. "Why not give the public a chance to see how the other fellow lives? Give it an insight into the under dog's existence, a momentary glimpse of his burdens, his sufferings, his handicaps?"

There were, to be sure, stumbles and setbacks to come, and many a bout of protracted drinking. But never again did O'Neill succumb to such a despairing and extended period of aridity as he had endured the previous winter. From the spring of 1917 in Provincetown, he wrote steadily and with increasing authority.

In the midst of negotiating the sale of the Glencairn plays, O'Neill wrote *Ile*, based on Provincetown lore as relayed by Mary Vorse. During one particularly arduous voyage to the Arctic region in 1903, a ruthless whaling captain named John Cook drove his men to the point of mutiny. The crew confronted him over his insistence on staying at sea for two years to harvest his quota of whale oil (or "'ile," in the local dialect).

His wife, Viola, accompanied him on the brig he had named for her and, according to Vorse, she went mad — partly from the unbearable loneliness and monotony, partly from witnessing her husband's psychological and physical harshness to his men. Captain Cook continued to sail after whale until 1916, but his wife never again accompanied him. She spent the rest of her deranged life ashore in Provincetown.

During full moons, she could be heard wailing hymns. She took pains to keep all her kitchen knives sharp and had a habit of greeting her husband, when he returned from a voyage, with "There's blood on the deck, John Cook! What do you know about that, John Cook?" It was rumored that Cook barricaded his door when he retired for the night.

When he was away, his wife would be heard talking to herself in her yard. While brushing out his shore clothes, which included a derby hat, she would chant: "Never better a pair of legs went into any pants than Johnny Cook's legs" and "Never a better head went in any hat than Johnny Cook's head." When she hung up his drawers, she would say, "Takes a big rear to fill these drawers!"

O'Neill advised Mary Vorse to write the story, but when she said she knew the Cook family too well to write about them, he told her he would like to use the material for a play.

Assigning Cook the name of his father's old New London acquaintance, Captain Keeney, O'Neill set the play aboard the whaling ship Atlantic Queen, in 1895, in the becalmed icy Arctic Sea. The opening scene quickly foretells the plot:

"Two years we all signed up for are done this day," growls the ship's steward to Ben, the shivering cabin boy. "Blessed Christ! Two years o' this dog's life, and no luck in the fishin', and the hands half starved with the food runnin' low, rotten as it is; and not a sign of him turnin' back for home! . . . What is it he thinks he's goin' to do? Keep us all up here after our time is worked out till the last man of us is starved to death or frozen? We've grub enough hardly to last out the voyage back if we started now. What are the men goin' to do 'bout it? Did ye hear any talk in the fo'c's'tle?"

Ben whispers that the men are planning to mutiny if the captain does not "put back south for home to-day," and the steward expresses his doubt this will happen.

"All he thinks on is gittin the 'ile — 's if it was our fault he ain't had good luck with the whales. I think the man's mighty nigh losin' his senses." The crew does attempt to mutiny, but Captain Keeney swiftly subdues them, mainly by force of his adamant personality.

His wife, Annie, already half-mad from the confinement of two years at sea — despite Keeney having installed a small organ for her to play — pleads with him to head for home at once. But his determined pride will not permit him to give up until he has harvested his quota of oil.

Consciously or not, O'Neill could not help imposing on the story elements of the troubled marriage of his parents, eerily foreshadowing Long Day's Journey Into Night.

When Annie complains she cannot bear "this prison cell of a room," she could be Mary Tyrone (and Ella O'Neill) bewailing the second-rate hotel rooms of James's tours. Annie further laments that she had wanted to be by her husband's side in "the vigorous life of it all," hoping to see him as "the hero" he was made out to be in "Homeport." This has the ring of Mary Tyrone's articulated disappointment at the difficult life of a matinee idol's wife.

Similarly, when Captain Keeney protests he had warned Annie of the hardships, her words of forgiveness echo Mary Tyrone's condescending phrases: "Oh, I know it isn't your fault, David. You see, I didn't believe you. I guess I was dreaming about the old Vikings in the story books and I thought you were one of them."

When Annie finds that her husband is deaf to her pleas to return home, she snaps. Unwilling to acknowledge her madness (read drug addiction), Keeney orders the crew onward in pursuit of whales. In the end Annie is found playing a hymn "wildly and discordantly" on her organ — evoking the drugged Mary Tyrone at her piano in the final act of *Long Day's Journey Into Night*.

It was not until after *Ile* had been produced that O'Neill encountered Mrs. Cook near her home in Provincetown. One night, as he was walking along a snowy street, he noticed her some ten paces ahead. Suddenly a black cat crossed her path. She gave it a kick that sent it sailing onto the steps of a barber shop several yards away, and called out in a clear voice, "No goddamn black cat is going to cross my bow!"

Louise Bryant came to Provincetown in mid-May to see O'Neill and found him "sitting in his room quite alone and working."

He was "thunderstruck" to see her, she declared in her unpublished memoir. "I took a room in a house nearby and stayed a week, till I got a telegram from Jack saying, 'The fruit trees are in bloom.'" Louise did not immediately act on Reed's subtle plea that she return to Croton.

O'Neill had been worrying about being drafted. As he told Louise, Art McGinley and others, he had no intention of going into the Army. Although he had claimed exemption on the grounds he was "an arrested tubercular case," he was uncertain the excuse would be honored. He wrote nervously to Dr. Lyman, asking if he would need a certificate from him.

"I am not trying to dodge service," he said, not with total candor, "but from what I hear, conditions in the camps and at the front are the very worst possible for one susceptible to T.B . . . . I want to serve my country but it seems silly to commit suicide for it." He told Dr. Lyman he had tried to enlist in the Navy, but had been rejected "for minor defects" which, he understood, would "not count in the draft." But his offer of voluntary Naval service seems somewhat suspect, in view of his implacable anti-war sentiments.

Soon after Louise's arrival in Provincetown, O'Neill decided he had better take up a position of watchful waiting in New London, where he was listed by his draft board as eligible to serve in the Army, along with 2,579 other New London men between the ages of twenty-one and thirty-one.

Louise agreed to accompany him on her way back to Croton. Assuring the Cooks and Terry Carlin and other friends, who had by now arrived for the summer, that he would return as soon as he had straightened out his draft status, he headed with Louise for the Monte Cristo Cottage, as yet unoccupied, pending the return of his parents. *The Wanderer*, which had extended its run into June, was to suspend performances for the summer before beginning a road tour on September 20.

"Gene brought Louise Bryant to have dinner at our house," Jessica Rippin recalled many years later. "It was obvious that he thought she was pretty terrific." Emily added that O'Neill made no secret of being in love with Louise. After dinner he asked Jessica and Emily what they thought of her. The sisters were noncommittal, but later agreed privately that she was "sloppy."

When Bryant returned to Croton, she found that Reed, anticipating her arrival, "had gone out at dawn to pick wood violets and put them all over the house." Her pleasant surprise at this loving gesture was quickly rent by Reed's confession of a recent casual affair. Incomprehensible as it may seem in view of her own behavior, Bryant flew into a blind fury. Refusing to understand or forgive, she decided she must go abroad at once as a war correspondent.

Reed meekly acquiesced. He arranged for her accreditation to the Bell Syndicate, provided her with letters to friends in Europe and paid for her passage. O'Neill was devastated when he received word of Louise's precipitate departure.

An indication of Bryant's distraught state may be gleaned from her dealings with the Passport Office. Her passport photograph shows her as hollow-cheeked, with dark rings under her eyes, mouth agape, wearing a wrinkled, open-neck shirt. When her passport was issued on June 1, 1917, a State Department official clipped the following note to her application:

"I suppose I will have to issue a passport to this wild woman. She is full of socialistic and ultra-modern ideas, which accounts for her wild hair and open mouth. She is the wife of John Reed, a well-known correspondent." (She gave her age as twenty-seven, although she was approaching her thirty-second birthday.)

On June 9, shortly before boarding the Espagne for her crossing to France in the submarine-infested waters of the Atlantic, Louise hastily scribbled a note to Reed:

"Please believe me, Jack — I'm going to try like the devil to pull myself together over there and come back able to act like a reasonable human being. I know I'm probably all wrong about everything. I know the only reason I act so crazy is because it hurts so much, that I get quite insane, that's all . . . I love you so much. It's a terrible thing to love as much as I do."

Whether her uppermost emotion was jealousy over Reed's affair, bewilderment at her own violent reaction, or frustration over a shattered fantasy of life with both Reed and O'Neill, it is probably safe to assume she had not anticipated that the triangle could turn into a quadrangle. One thing was clear from her letters, however: even in her incoherence she was intensely attached to Reed and frightened at the thought of losing him.

Reed responded two days later — even though he knew Bryant would not receive his letter until she reached France: "In lots of ways we are very different, and we must try to realize that, while loving each other. But of course on this last awful business, you were humanly right and I was wrong. I have always loved you, my darling, ever since I first met you — and I guess I always will . . . I know that the one thing I cannot bear any more is consciously to hurt you, honey."

CHAPTER
FORTY-NINE

$\mathbf{O}$'NEILL HAD REGISTERED FOR THE DRAFT IN NEW LONDON on June 5, 1917 and, like a prisoner at the dock, tremulously awaited his fate. The word from Dr. Lyman had not been reassuring; he wrote that only the examining Army surgeon could decide whether to exempt a former tubercular patient from service.

To ease his anxiety, O'Neill kept up the prodigious reading that was almost as intoxicating an escape from life as writing and drinking. At times, he caroused with his old Second Story Club cronies, most often with Art McGinley, who had also returned to New London to register. As the only one among them unwilling to go to war, O'Neill was uneasy in their company. Even Doc Ganey had volunteered to serve as an Army physician, despite being over the draft age.

The New London Day reported the absence of any anti-draft sentiment, describing the spirit of the registrants as "very pleasing" to the Mayor.

"It was only what was to be expected," said a city spokesman. "The people of New London are patriotic and realize that this is a duty and a privilege. It is only in the great centers, such as New York, with its great foreign population that any resistance will be made. New England is all right; it is God's country."

To O'Neill's probable dismay, his old mentor, Frederick P. Latimer — now writing exclusively for the Day — published an impassioned and lengthy editorial championing the draft.

"The nation will be better, and in the end happier, for its part in righteous conflict," declared Latimer. "We had been thinking and living too much for ourselves, too little for the common good . . . If the Germans had sinned in an over-worship of the state, we had sinned by losing a right and adequate regard for the state . . . The offering of our sacrifice is not for war, but for peace . . . for the annihilation of injustice and lawlessness worse than war, more unendurable than death."

O'Neill's parents, returning to New London in mid-June, were ready to celebrate their son's recent literary triumph. But they found him anxious about his draft status and miserable over Louise's departure.

His anti-war sentiments, which he did not bother concealing at home, were predictably unacceptable to his chauvinistic father. It was not long before the partially submerged father-son friction exploded once again.

Wallowing in a state of put-upon adolescence, Eugene baited James mercilessly. He expounded his anarchist-pacifist jargon, which echoed his earlier tirades against his father's religious faith and the creaky *Count of Monte Cristo*.

Some of his outrage had already been vented in a poem of fifteen stanzas that he had given to Louise before her departure for France. In the poem he railed at the injustice of society (and, by implication, at his father's conformist views). Sounding as though written when he was less than sober, it was entitled "The Louse," and is typified by these verses:

> I am the Louse of Society,
> The Idler,
> I toil not
> Neither do I spin
> And yet I live and grow fat
> Upon the blood of fools —
> (Of workers).

> Have I no social conscience?
> Do I think I am right?
> Right?
> Wrong?
> Oh self-styled Anarchists! . . .

> Do you curse the injustice of it
> You who sweat through hours of slavery
> That I may sneer down at you
> From my height of indifferent ease?
> Do you demand what I have
> For your miserable children?

Do you hate me?

———————-

Then come!
Crush me for the louse I am!
Take what I have stolen from you!
You are a hundred and I am one.
You are strong and heavy-muscled.
I am weak and soft with fat.
The victory will be yours
So easily!

———————-

Cowards!
Reply to my challenge! . . .

———————-

Do you believe in God?
Do you hope to get even with me
When you soar from the Pauper's Field
Into the Great Perhaps?

———————-

God is a judge.
And who should know the justice of judges
Better than you?
God is the king of heaven.
Since when have you found mercy in kings?
God is a father.
Remember the beatings you received from
    your own! . . .

O'Neill received his deferment from military service, but continued to brood and drink. His depression reached its depth in mid-August, when he received word from Louise, who had returned from France. She was leaving at once for Russia with Reed, also exempted from military service (because of his kidney condition).

Reed was to report on the looming revolution for The Masses and The Call, among the few publications willing to run his dispatches. (Because neither could afford to pay his passage, the money was raised by friends.)

Bryant, who had forgiven Reed his misstep, was exhilarated by her recent venture as a foreign correspondent. She had proved her worth to the Bell Syndicate, whose editors now condescended to assign her to cover the revolution from "the woman's point of view." Continuing to hold out a vague promise of one day returning to O'Neill, Bryant sailed with Reed from New York on August 17.

O'Neill, all too aware that he had been unable to offer her any comparable opportunity, went on a serious binge.

Art McGinley, cheerfully awaiting his summons from the draft board, tried to console him. It was McGinley's recollection that Jamie was not in New London that summer and that Eugene had taken over his brother's abusive role toward their father — with a vengeance. Both James and Ella, McGinley said, seemed greatly distressed by Eugene's behavior.

"Gene came home in his cups one night," McGinley said, "and told his father it had just dawned on him that he was the worst actor in America." He quickly amended his statement: a maladroit actor named Corse Payton was the worst. "You are the second worst," he exclaimed.

James had had enough. He summoned McGinley and urged him to take Eugene back to Provincetown, offering to pay their way.

"Gene needs a change," James grumbled. "I think it would be a good thing for both of us if there were at least a temporary separation."

McGinley regarded the incident as something of a joke: "We left New London by popular request. There was no shedding of tears in the public square when Gene and I departed."

O'Neill noted without humor the period of his final stay in the only permanent home he had ever known. In a spare entry in the cyclical chart he made of his life some thirty years later, he set down, for the year 1916-1917: "last of N.L. home."

The two exiles, far from sober when they boarded the Provincetown boat in Boston, shared their bottle with members of the crew, until the captain, getting wind of their activities, threatened to put them in irons. When they arrived in Provincetown, Terry Carlin and Jig Cook were waiting to greet them.

O'Neill and McGinley moved into the same four-room apartment O'Neill had occupied earlier in the season; Terry Carlin had been living there rent-free since O'Neill's departure, and stayed on for the rest of the summer at James's expense.

It was that summer O'Neill painted on the rafters of one of the rooms (with slight variations and the addition of exclamation marks) the opening incantation from *Light on the Path*, the tome of Eastern mysticism Carlin had given him: "Before the eyes can see, they must be incapable of tears! Before the ear can hear, it must have lost its sensitiveness! Before the voice can speak, it must have lost the power to wound! Before the soul can fly, its wings must be washed in the blood of the heart!"

Jig Cook and Susan Glaspell began laying plans for the production in New York of the new plays O'Neill had written in Provincetown during the early spring.

"As it fell out," Edna Kenton observed, "there was no summer season that year at Provincetown. But do not think the little empty theater was not used, as the crystal globe is used to focus the outer eye and evoke vision for the inner. There was a summer season there — a summer season of writing — far more important just then for the experimental stage shut away behind locked doors in Macdougal Street until October."

In Louise Bryant's absence, Jig tried to coddle his cherished playwright, encouraging him to eat when he seemed inclined to neglect himself and imploring him not to squander his money on liquor.

O'Neill focused on his writing during the rest of the summer, but was dissatisfied with his output: a one-act comedy entitled *The G.A.N.*; a "novelette — sea theme," called *S.O.S.* and a short story, "The Hairy Ape," containing "the germ idea" of his later play of the same title. He destroyed all three efforts.

"Gene would spend a few weeks swimming, boating, fishing," according to McGinley. His swimming had grown even bolder than the year before; he would swim miles to reach the fishing boats, and often boarded them to the astonishment of the crews; more than once the fishermen warned him that he would surely drown.

"Then he would decide to go to work," McGinley said, "and all else would be off his slate. I have seen him work from sun-up all through the long day and into the small hours of the next morning. He would shut himself up and pound away at the typewriter hours on end. He would write something, not like it, and then rewrite it until he was satisfied with the result. He had a tenacity that was amazing."

After a sustained work period, there would come several days of drinking, when he was joined by McGinley and Carlin.

"I was definitely the unlettered member of the aggregation," recalled McGinley. "The conversation was often so far above my level, it might have been in another tongue. The whole colony was preaching internationalism — one world, one flag and so on.

"They used to call me 'McGinley the Patriot' because I admired Wilson and supported the country's stand in the war." (A few months later he was drafted into the Army and served in France, along with three of his seven brothers.)

Bewildered one day by a conversation about psychoanalysis, McGinley told O'Neill he did not know what some of the Provincetowners were talking about.

"Don't pay any attention," O'Neill said. "A lot of them are pretenders."

McGinley was flattered (although it came to nothing) when Cook, trying to line up a cast for the fall production of *The Long Voyage Home*, suggested McGinley as "a natural for the part of the drunken Russian sailor."

O'Neill's cash from his magazine sales had just about run out. His father had arranged for him and McGinley to eat at a hotel, but the paid-for meals were mostly liquid. The eight-dollar weekly allowance sent by James also went mainly for liquor. The two lived primarily on oatmeal, prepared in their apartment in a battered double-boiler.

"We cooked oatmeal the first night we were there and six weeks later we were still eating oatmeal," McGinley said. One day, finding the beach littered with squid, they tried to cook them. They quickly went back to oatmeal.

Many years later, writing to his older son, who had recently met McGinley, O'Neill reminisced about the warmth of their friendship — and about one episode in particular during the summer of 1917:

"He and I got in some of the craziest stunts together. Sometimes it was his alcoholic inspiration and sometimes mine, but it was always nuts. Did he tell you of the time at Francis' flats in Provincetown when he was visiting Terry Carlin and me, and we sent him to town to buy some hootch (his money), and on his return he got to the top of the last flight of stairs where we were eagerly awaiting. He had a quart under each arm and a straw hat on. To our horror, he wavered and plunged back down the stairs, through the window at the foot of the stairs taking it with him, and wound up on the roof of Francis' store. He pulled himself together, still sound in wind and limb, still with a quart under each arm and his straw hat on, and marched up the stairs to us. It was a deeply moving moment and Terry and I were profoundly touched. As Terry remarked with feeling: 'Well, thank Christ, the whiskey didn't break its neck!'"

Leaving some personal possessions in the safekeeping of his accommodating landlord, O'Neill returned with the rest of the Players to New York that fall. He brought with him his melancholy over

Louise's desertion, seemingly determined to proclaim his martyrdom to all his friends. But lovelorn though he was, his second season as a produced playwright proved much more satisfactory than his first.

O'Neill and Cook agreed that *In the Zone* was not experimental enough for the Playwrights' Theatre. Evidently forgiving the Washington Square Players for their earlier rejection of his work, O'Neill gave the play to them. On October 31, it opened at their uptown Comedy Theater in a bill featuring three other one-acters. Because the Washington Square Players had become successful enough to pay their playwrights, O'Neill began earning royalties (small as they were) for the first time.

The critics, albeit mostly second-stringers who received no bylines, attended the first night, for the Comedy, unlike the Playwrights' Theater, offered complimentary tickets to reviewers. They singled out *In the Zone* for high praise.

The Times devoted three quarters of its review to the O'Neill play, describing it as "heartfelt" and "tense with excitement," a play "of a very high order, both as a thriller and as a document in human character and emotion."

The Evening World declared that the producers "fired their best shot" with *In the Zone.* The Herald applauded it as well and The Globe's Louis Sherwin wrote, "I don't know where this young man got his knowledge of the speech of seafaring men, but this is the second play he has written about them with remarkable power and penetration." A dissenting voice, the Sun, took O'Neill to task for being repetitious — a charge he was to hear often during his career.

The reviews were generally so laudatory and the audiences so enthusiastic that O'Neill suspected *In the Zone* was, after all, not a very good play. He found further support for this view when, soon after the opening, he received an offer to send it on a vaudeville tour.

Any other neophyte playwright (or for that matter any established one) would have jumped at such a chance to extend the life of a play. O'Neill, however, initially rejected the offer, made by the recently formed but already flourishing booking partnership of Albert Lewis, a nineteen-year-old actor, and Max Gordon, an advance publicity man recently out of high school, later to become a prominent Broadway producer.

Lewis and Gordon presented only one-act plays for vaudeville, and usually had about fifteen shows on the Keith or Orpheum circuits running simultaneously. Lewis, who picked the plays Gordon subsequently booked, had earlier rejected *Bound East for Cardiff* as "too highbrow for vaudeville." He was convinced, however, that *In the Zone* would be a hit.

After spending several days trying to track down O'Neill, he was put in touch by Edward Goodman, still at the helm of the Washington Square Players. Lewis made his offer but, he said, O'Neill "thought the vaudeville proposition was degrading."

Unwilling to take no for an answer, Lewis persuaded Martin Beck, then in charge of the Orpheum Circuit, to see *In the Zone*. Beck told Lewis that if he could stage the play as well as the Washington Square Players, he would guarantee a twenty-five to forty-week booking.

"This was a terrific proposition," Lewis said, "and O'Neill finally decided that he just couldn't turn it down; he really needed the money."

O'Neill received a $200 advance and $70 a week in royalties, but had to split fifty-fifty with the Washington Square Players. Lewis staged the play with Horace Brahan, a well-known actor, in the leading role of Smitty. Early in 1918, he and Gordon sent it to Proctor's Theatre in Newark, then to the Palace in Chicago, where it immediately began drawing large audiences. It toured for thirty-four weeks and could have run longer, as O'Neill later pointed out, had it not been terminated by the flu epidemic and the armistice.

Although grateful for the money, O'Neill later repudiated *In the Zone* as "the least significant" of all the plays he preserved, calling it "a conventional construction of the theater as it is." He went on to disparage it as "too facile . . . too full of clever theatrical tricks." To O'Neill, its long run proved "conclusively . . . there must be 'something rotten in Denmark.'"

The play, he insisted, "in no way represents the true me or what I desire to express. It is a situation drama lacking in all spiritual import — there is no big feeling for life inspiring it. Given the plot and a moderate ability to characterize, any industrious playwright could have reeled it off."

To emphasize his point, he contrasted *In the Zone* with *The Moon of the Caribbees*, which, he said, was "an attempt to achieve a higher plain of bigger, finer values." O'Neill explained that the latter worked "with truth," whereas the former substituted "theatrical sentimentalism." He illustrated the point with the character of Smitty, who appears in both plays:

"Smitty in the stuffy, grease-paint atmosphere of *In the Zone* is magnified into a hero who attracts our sentimental sympathy. In

The Moon, posed against the background of that beauty . . . his sil-houetted gestures of self-pity are reduced to their proper insignifi-cance . . . "

On November 2, two days after *In the Zone* opened at the Comedy Theater uptown, *The Long Voyage Home* led the first bill of the second season at the Playwrights' Theater downtown. Nina Moise directed and Jig Cook, Hutch Collins and Ida Rauh were in the cast. The bill included a thin comedy by Susan Glaspell about an emancipated woman, called *Close the Book*, and a murky "dramatic poem" by James Oppenheim called *Night*.

The Long Voyage Home, unlike *In the Zone*, received scant notice in the press, mainly because the critics were reluctant to buy their own tickets. Then, too, the production was something of an anticlimax, after the play's appearance in the The Smart Set's October issue.

The opening was celebratory nonetheless, for the Playwrights' Theatre had been refurbished. For one thing, the seats had been given higher backs; but having also been narrowed, they were only frac-tionally more comfortable. The backstage accommodations had been greatly enhanced and the actors and technicians were less constrict-ed than during their first season.

The floor above the parlor had been acquired for use as cloak-room, lounging room, business office, dressing rooms and scenery storage. Moreover, in early December, Christine Ell was invited by the Players to install a small restaurant in the space; it took the place of the Samovar, which had closed when Nani Bailey enlisted as a war nurse in France (where she later died).

"In the afternoons," recalled Kenton, "Christine would bring in pots of tea, several packages of biscuits, salty and sweet, a jar of jam or a wedge of cheese, and then sit down again to the peeling of pota-toes or the stringing of beans for dinner while she talked with us on aesthetics or free will vs. determinism or the latest upset in our always creaky machinery of 'organization.'"

Christine was more than a good cook and conversationalist. She was a gifted mimic and often provided the chief amusement at par-ties with an imitation of Mary Vorse growing drunk in her ladylike way at the Hell Hole, or of Ida Rauh, who was mockingly called the "Duse of Macdougal Street," practicing grimaces before a mirror, or of Theodore Dreiser's unrestrained cursing.

But the pathos of Christine's personality was always close to the surface. To O'Neill, acutely aware of her inner agony, she personified what he once called "a female Christ." She possessed a strangely vir-

ginal quality and concealed a delicacy of spirit in her hulking body —
paradoxical traits later reproduced by O'Neill in the character of Josie
Hogan in *A Moon for the Misbegotten*.

Toward year's end, two members of the Players' staff were finally
put on salary. One was Nina Moise, rewarded with the new title of
general coach, and the other was Lewis Ell, the property-man-cum-
carpenter. Ell also designed an occasional set, walked on in minor
roles, and immortalized himself to the Players as the author of a sign
backstage: "Cloze the door was you born in a stabel."

The Players also acquired several new unpaid members who
were to become stalwarts. Among them was James Light, a slender,
handsome intellectual, on a scholarship at Columbia University. He
had studied at Pittsburgh's Carnegie Tech, where he majored in architecture and painting.

One day he looked critically at his drawings, concluded he would
never be as good as the two painters he most admired, Michelangelo
and El Greco, and abandoned painting forthwith. He transferred to
Ohio State University to study English literature and philosophy
before coming to New York.

Seeking a place to live in Greenwich Village that October, Light
ran into Charles Ellis, another former Ohio State student, in New
York to study painting at the Art Students League. They decided to
share a large room above the theatre at 139 Macdougal Street. While
unpacking, Light heard sounds of hammering below and went to
investigate.

"There were four people there — Jig Cook, Hutch Collins, O'Neill
and Lewis Ell," Light said, recalling his introduction to the
Provincetown Players. "Ell was doing the hammering. He was working on the benches in the auditorium. The other three were on the
floor, a half-bottle of whiskey near them, shooting craps. They asked
me to join them, and since I had a few dollars in my pocket, I did.
O'Neill's hands were very big and the others watched him suspiciously when he picked up the dice."

The game over, Light and O'Neill fell into conversation. O'Neill
mentioned swimming, Light's sport at Ohio State, and a bond was
quickly established. Light, whose father had been a carpenter and
builder, then ventured to criticize the construction of the benches. He
pointed out that the job could be more efficiently handled with a rip-
saw. Jig Cook promptly turned over the project to him.

"I started sawing immediately," Light said. He was also pressed into service as an actor. Susan Glaspell's *Close the Book* had not been completely cast, and one day when Light happened to pass by with an armload of books, looking professorial, an actor suggested him for the role of Peyton Root, an English instructor.

Light acquitted himself so well as both carpenter and actor that he became permanently attached to the Players. He attended lecture courses at Columbia, but abandoned his plan for a degree.

By this time, Light's roommate, Charles Ellis, also had been pressed into service, first, like Light, working on the physical side of productions and, somewhat later, as an actor. That same year, Cook discovered another gifted amateur — Edna St. Vincent Millay. Recently out of Vassar and already preceded by a reputation as a poet, she asked Cook for a role and was engaged for Floyd Dell's play, *The Angel Intrudes*, on the Players' third bill.

Millay, who was living in the Village with her sisters, Norma and Kathleen, told them about her new job, but did not suggest they join her. It was Charles Ellis who finally drew Norma into the group, where she became one of its leading actresses.

"Charlie started taking out Vincent [as Edna Millay was known] and ended up living with me," Norma Millay recalled with satisfaction, adding casually, "We were married in 1921 — my mother thought it was high time."

The Wanderer began its tour at Philadelphia's Metropolitan Opera House on September 20 and, on October 11, James O'Neill celebrated his fiftieth anniversary as an actor. He could look back with a mixture of wonder and melancholy at the day when, as a rough-edged youth of twenty-two, oblivious of his brogue, he had been plucked from a Cleveland poolroom to walk on stage in Dion Boucicault's *The Colleen Bawn*.

The Wanderer was to be his last play. After a half century in the theater, he had read his final press notices. Nevertheless, he was still uttering the sort of public pronouncements about the stage that made his son shudder — comments that to Eugene seemed like oblique slaps at his own efforts.

"There is but one kind of acting for me — that of the classic drama," declared James to a reporter for the Philadelphia Record, lumping *The Wanderer* with the plays of Shakespeare.

James did manage to leave his tour long enough to attend a performance of *The Long Voyage Home,* and told his son he liked it. He was trying hard to enjoy Eugene's good fortune, if still baffled by his choices of subject.

When *The Wanderer* tour reached Boston, James, accompanied by Ella, stayed in a quiet family hotel run by a Miss Fritz, who whimsically called her establishment the Fritz-Carlton. Both James and Ella struck up an acquaintance with an eighteen-year-old student named Harry Crowley, who worked as a desk clerk and hoped to go on the stage. Crowley remembered James as remarkably spry for a man of seventy-one. He would occasionally cross the hotel lobby to Crowley's desk in a lively hornpipe.

Ella always walked a little behind her husband. At sixty, she dressed in dark colors and was gray-haired but, according to Crowley, her posture was erect. He recalled her open delight when she saw the October issue of The Smart Set featuring Eugene's play. (Later, she showed the magazine to a young relative. "Isn't this wonderful?" she said. "Eugene has made seventy-five dollars!")

O'Neill himself was basking in his newfound literary and pecuniary success, and was not displeased to learn he was being talked about outside Greenwich Village. His first significant personal publicity came on November 4, 1917, in the Sunday drama section of The New York Times, two days after the première of *The Long Voyage Home.* "Who Is Eugene O'Neill?" asked the headline.

The four-hundred word answer reported that he was the son of James O'Neill, knew the sailors in his plays because he had been one of them and had not lost touch "with those of his friends who reckoned the time of day not by the hands of a clock but by bells."

The article ran in a space surrounded by ads for current Broadway productions: *Tiger Rose,* by William Mack, at the Lyceum, and *Polly With a Past,* by Guy Bolton and George Middleton, at the Belasco; Morris Gest's production of *Chu Chin Chow*; and the Charles Dillingham and Florenz Ziegfeld Jr. production of *Miss 1917.* There was also a racy ad for the new Theda Bara movie, *Cleopatra,* at the Lyric: "What Anthony paid for Cleo's clothes/Only the Great Sahara knows./In Thedapatra she wears a rose!"

The Provincetown Players' second bill opened on November 30 and included *Ile,* also directed by Moise, with Hutch Collins playing Captain Keeney. James Light made his debut in a play by Rita Wellman (who had caused a minor flurry the year before with her anti-war *Barbarians*). Also on the bill were two plays by Maxwell Bodenheim.

None, not even *Ile*, was a notable success. Nevertheless, according to Edna Kenton, O'Neill's increasing fame swelled the theater's subscription audience "to such an extent that for the rest of the season we played seven nights regularly."

Although *The Moon of the Caribbees* was ready, O'Neill and Cook hesitated to produce it on their shallow stage. Apart from its large cast of two dozen men and women, the play needed an illusion of distance to create the effect of a tropical island surrounded by sky and sea; they decided to postpone production until the following season, when the Players hoped to move into a new theater with a deeper stage.

With his reputation building and his financial status improved, O'Neill, by the end of 1917, was for the first time about to earn enough to live on. (In 1919 he was at last able to tell Dr. Lyman truthfully that he had been supporting himself by his writing. In response to the Gaylord Farm questionnaire that year, he said that during 1917 and 1918 he had earned an average of $40 a week from playwriting.)

O'Neill celebrated his success with his friends in the Hell Hole, where he still, on occasion, felt compelled to compose a stanza or two of verse, reading like symptoms of a monstrous hangover. One surviving poem, "'Tis of Thee," compared the city's buildings to "Frozen gray phalluses" and pleaded he be allowed to "sing my masochistic song."

Now and then O'Neill drifted four blocks north of the Hell Hole to a tavern at Eighth Street and Sixth Avenue, called Columbia Gardens, where Jig Cook and Susan Glaspell had first made their plans to produce plays in Provincetown. Less sinister in its atmosphere than the Hell Hole, it was run by a red-faced Irishman, Luke O'Connor, who wore stiff high collars that squeezed his neck and who possessed an old-country temperament that never failed to charm O'Neill.

O'Connor's greatest pride was that the poet, John Masefield, had once worked for him as a bar boy. Masefield remained loyal after he achieved fame and from time to time sent a copy of his latest book to O'Connor, who kept the volumes behind the bar and needed no urging to display them to his customers.

He was further respected for his generosity in cashing personal checks. The writer, Holger Cahill, for whom O'Connor once cashed a fifty-dollar check, told him: "Gee, Luke, that was nice of you. Don't you ever get any rubber checks?" O'Connor vanished for a moment behind the bar, reappearing with a stack of checks a foot high, all of which had bounced.

The saloon, decorated with cut-glass mirrors and tall Chinese vases, was across the street from night court. Like the Hell Hole, it was rarely referred to by its formal name, but simply as O'Connor's — or, jocularly, The Working Girls' Home, a name bestowed by Mary Heaton Vorse after observing a trio of prostitutes push through the saloon's swinging doors one day.

To O'Connor's, on occasion, came Jamie O'Neill, seeking his brother. He was torn between a wish to disparage and a grudging sense of pride in Eugene's achievement.

"See my brother's play last night?" he once asked Romany Marie. "Isn't he great?"

"Why aren't you?" retorted Marie.

"Someday I'm going to be," answered Jamie, with heavy irony.

At thirty-nine, his face had become flabby from alcohol, his eyes puffed and glazed. But he still kept up a mechanical pretense of being a Broadway playboy and behaved as though slumming when he looked in on his brother at O'Connor's, the Hell Hole, Romany Marie's, or Polly Holladay's.

So futile was Jamie's present, so dismal his future, he was forced to take refuge in his sorry past. Holger Cahill described Jamie coming into the Hell Hole "looking down his long nose." Jamie's attitude was so patronizing, according to Cahill, that a bouncer once asked Eugene why he stood for it, and offered to punch Jamie for him.

One time, Cahill and Jamie were engaged in a discussion at O'Connor's about comedy and tragedy in literature and Jamie said, "People think my life is a comedy, but it's a goddam tragedy."

"Gene and his brother were both soaked in self-pity," observed Cahill. "Jamie was jealous of Gene; he once told me Gene was overrated."

The new psychic rivalry between brothers who for so long had been so close reached its apogee that year. Both knew Jamie's life was spent and Eugene's was about to skyrocket.

If this knowledge made Jamie sullen, it made Eugene gentle. He treated Jamie with tenderness and affection. But the worshipful kid brother had long since vanished, and in his place was the determined artist set on his chosen path.

IN THE SPRING OF 1918, O'NEILL CONCLUDED HE HAD taken the short play form about as far as it could go. "To be candid, I am rather fed up with the one-act play at present and am starting a new long one," he wrote to Edward Goodman, who had inquired whether there was "another *In the Zone*" available for production by the Washington Square Players.

Expanding on his reasons a decade later, he cautioned a would-be playwright who had sent him some short plays not to "waste any more time" on one-acters. "There's a time to write them — and a time to stop writing them because you've reached the stage where your need of expression is bigger than one act — *must* be bigger!"

The "new long" play that had begun to brew in O'Neill's mind the previous summer was *Beyond the Horizon*. He was not quite ready, however, to abandon altogether the one-act form. Allowing time for his full-length play to ferment, he outlined a long one-acter called *The Rope*. Like *Ile*, it evoked the sort of raw, uncompromising character conflict that became a hallmark of his future work.

The Rope derived loosely from the parable of the prodigal son — oddly the same source for *The Wanderer* (and for that matter Conrad's *Tomorrow*). O'Neill, who always attended his father's performances, surely had been to see *The Wanderer* at least once since its opening in February, 1917. Even while deploring its grandiloquence, he must have been struck by the original story's application to his father and himself.

He was the returned prodigal who (in his father's view) had "wasted his substance in riotous living." Although Eugene had not, like the New Testament's prodigal (nor like his counterpart in *The Wanderer*) confessed that he had sinned, he believed his father had tentatively acknowledged his regeneration.

Eugene doubtless wanted to be re-embraced by his father. But at the same time, yielding to his artistic vision, he could not resist twisting the parable. He realized his father would condemn *The Rope* as irreverent mockery. Even worse, Eugene knew his father would view it as a thinly veiled defiance of his own values — which of course it was. Instead of being inspirational, as *The Wanderer* aspired to be, *The Rope* was harshly ironic and bitter.

Set in a barn "on top of a high headland of the seacoast," evidently suggested by a Truro farm, *The Rope* was a significant step in O'Neill's artistic development — a bridge to the deeply tragic plays to come. In particular, it embodied the germ of plot and character for the major three-act play, *Desire Under the Elms*, completed five years later.

One of the characters in *The Rope*, Abraham Bentley, is a grotesque earlier version of the tough old farmer, Ephraim Cabot, in *Desire*. Bentley is a "tall, lean, stoop-shouldered old man of sixty-five . . . His face is gaunt . . . His eyes peer weakly from beneath bushy black brows . . . " Though ten years older, the more fully-developed Cabot is also "tall and gaunt . . . but stoop-shouldered from toil . . . His eyes are small . . . and extremely near-sighted . . . "

Like Jesse in *The Wanderer*, Bentley in *The Rope* literally regards himself as the father of a prodigal and quotes the New Testament word for word:

"Bring forth the best robe and put it on him; and put a ring on his hand, and shoes on his feet: And bring hither the fatted calf, and kill it; and let us eat, and be merry: For this my son was dead, and is alive again; he was lost and is found."

In *The Wanderer*, on the other hand, the lines are paraphrased, perhaps in the author's misguided belief he could improve on them. "A coat for my son — the best my chest contains!" exclaims Jesse. "He has gone out and traveled stonier roads — and yet returned to us! Spread a great feast where all are welcome . . . He who was lost, is found! He who was dead is mighty now among the living!"

Bentley, like the self-righteous Cabot of *Desire*, is held responsible by one of his children — in this case his daughter, Annie — for having driven his first wife to her death with overwork, and then married a flamboyant younger woman.

Annie's half-brother, Luke, has run away from the farm as an adolescent, having stolen some of his father's money, and returns after five years of adventuring, hoping to claim the rest of his father's hoard.

Here the intricacies of family relationships and plot differ from *Desire Under the Elms*, but the similarity of theme is still evident. Both plays, of course, were rooted in O'Neill's own submerged feelings toward his father and mother.

The rope of the title refers to a noose that Bentley has rigged up to a rafter in the barn; he has indicated, with demented cheerfulness, that it awaits his son Luke's return.

When Luke, a ruffian almost as unpleasant as his father, shows up, his father indicates the rope and suggests he hang himself. Luke sneers and superstitiously avoids touching it. He then plots with Annie's husband to steal the rest of Bentley's money, convinced it is hidden somewhere on the farm.

The ironic twist comes when Bentley's granddaughter, a slightly imbecilic child of ten, enters the barn alone, climbs on a chair, and grabs at the suspended noose, planning to use it as a swing. At her touch, the rope separates from the beam, and a bag of twenty-dollar gold pieces drops to the floor. Bentley's little joke turns out even better than he had planned. The child, an infant spendthrift, sends each coin in turn spinning over the edge of a cliff, into the ocean. The curtain comes down as she flings handfuls of gold into the sea, gleefully calling out, "Skip! Skip!"

The child's name is Mary, frequently O'Neill's symbolic designation for his ailing and often helplessly childlike mother. There are also little girls named Mary in *Beyond the Horizon* and *The Straw*, both written the same year as *The Rope*.

The Marys in *The Rope* and *Beyond* are sickly, either in mind or body. The Mary in *Beyond* actually goes to the extreme of dying, and the Mary in *The Straw* — to stretch the symbolism a bit further — is the sister of a tubercular on the point of death. None of the Marys, incidentally, is a recognizable human child. The Mary in *Beyond* is just one of a series of children in O'Neill's plays killed off by one device or another.

While the demented Abraham Bentley was by no means literally based on James, Eugene did give Bentley a somewhat reminiscent obsession with money and a possessiveness about land. And he gave the son, Luke, his own smoldering anger at being unable to win his father's wholehearted approval.

Perhaps O'Neill even fantasized his actor-father performing in the role of Bentley. Appearing in a play by Eugene would have betokened James's genuine acceptance of his prodigal son turned successful playwright. James had, after all, once offered to act in his son's early vaudeville skit, *A Wife For a Life*; and, long after his father's death, O'Neill continued in his imagination to cast him in his plays, most notably as Cornelius Melody in *A Touch of the Poet*.

"What that [play] needs," O'Neill told George Jean Nathan, "is an actor like Maurice Barrymore or James O'Neill, my old man. One of those big-chested, chiseled-mug, romantic old boys who could walk onto a stage with all the aplomb and regal splendor with which they walked into the old Hoffman House bar, drunk or sober." It was "tough" trying to find such an actor, he said. "Most actors in these times lack an air."

Even if James might have considered playing a role like Cornelius Melody, he would certainly not have agreed to appear onstage as the unsavory Abraham Bentley, or in any play that mocked a biblical parable. Had not the stubbornly old-fashioned actor recently declared there was "but one kind of acting" for him — "that of the classic drama" — or that it was "impossible to be resigned to the commonplaces of the modern style of play"?

Eugene was just as stubbornly convinced that *his* was the enlightened new American theater, and he could never have written the kind of play his father would have championed. Thus, the subterranean antagonism, professional and familial, flowed on.

It was the duality — the tension between the poetic ideal and the lure of materialism — that dictated the theme of *Beyond the Horizon*.

O'Neill described the play, which was to take shape over the next two years, as "a simon pure uncompromising American tragedy." Here he expressed for the first time on a large scale his deepening philosophy of the need to cling to any shred of hope — even a "hopeless hope" — for the sake of survival.

With various embellishments, the story has been told by a number of O'Neill's friends that the play's title was suggested by a conversation he had in Provincetown with a retarded boy named Howard Slade.

"One day Howard was sitting on a railroad wharf at the town pier," according to O'Neill's friend, Eben Given. "Gene was there waiting for a boat to come in with its catch. 'What's out there, Gene?' asked Howard.

"'Where?'

"'Oh, way out there.'

"'The horizon.'

"'And what's beyond the horizon?'"

Although the story may be true, the O'Neill scholar, Travis Bogard, has pointed out that any reader during the first quarter of the twentieth century would have recognized "in the title's imagery what might be called the 'Horizon Syndrome,' an affliction that manifested itself in countless inspirational poems, stories and short plays" to express "a somewhat vaguely defined freedom of spirit."

Beyond the Horizon, like much of O'Neill's work, was written on several levels, all so well blended by the undefinable catalyst of his genius that even he was probably unaware where they merged.

He drew elements for the play's physical setting from his immediate surroundings. The farm on which it is set was one he had seen tucked away in the hills of Truro, beyond Pilgrim Heights. Great poplars lined the approach to the farmhouse and the roar of the sea could be heard in the near-distance. A byway across the dunes, called the Atkins-Mayo Road, lent its name to the two families around whom the play revolves.

O'Neill's thwarted romance with Louise Bryant and his uneasy friendship with John Reed inspired some aspects of the plot. The play evolves in one respect as a triangle: the two Mayo brothers are in love with the same girl, Ruth Atkins.

O'Neill wrote himself into the part of Robert Mayo, the younger brother, described as having "a touch of the poet." Robert makes a tragic mistake when he declares his love for Ruth and commits himself to staying with her on the farm, instead of following the sea as he had planned. By winning, he ironically loses. In some ways the story is yet another fantasized projection of what O'Neill felt would have happened had he stayed trapped in a marriage to a woman of middle-class mores like Kathleen Jenkins.

As for the hardier older brother, Andrew, there is something of John Reed's lust for adventure and daring in the character; having lost Ruth, he takes Robert's place as a sailor.

It was pure art, however, that enabled O'Neill to alter the unresolved personal situation among himself, Reed and Louise into one in which the poet wins the girl and loses his soul, while the adventurer grows materialistic in the face of a poetic experience he cannot appreciate. Moreover, O'Neill's retrospective fury at Louise for forsaking him is reflected in a scene in which Ruth confesses to Robert that she really loves Andrew, not him. "You — you slut!" Robert fumes.

On another level, the sibling rivalry between Andrew and Robert reflects O'Neill's relationship with Jamie. He added the ingredient of father-son antagonism, infusing the Mayo family with some of the passions and conflicts governing his own family. James O'Neill's disappointment that Jamie had not followed him successfully in the theater, is echoed by the farmer Mayo's adamant unforgiveness of Andrew when he abandons the farm. The father's first name, significantly, is James.

One influence that might have been unconscious (and was never mentioned by O'Neill) was T. C. Murray's *Birthright*, which had greatly moved him when he saw it produced by the Abbey Players in 1911. It depicted a hardened Irish farmer and his two sons. While the younger, Shane, shares his father's devotion to the farm, it is the elder son, Hugh, a dreamer, who is destined to inherit it. Shane ships out to find a new life in America.

On still another level, O'Neill drew on his experiences as a sailor and as a tubercular, fusing literal fact with artistic symbolism. Robert Mayo dies of tuberculosis — initially insisting, as does Mary Tyrone in *Long Day's Journey Into Night*, that the malady is just a cold. And both Ruth and Robert resignedly acknowledge, as does Mary in *Long Day's Journey*, that no one can help what life has done to them.

If James Mayo is a New England version of James O'Neill and if Andrew Mayo is part Reed, part Jamie and part symbol, Robert is, aside from O'Neill himself, also part Olson (the model for the Swedish seaman in *The Long Voyage Home* who has run away from the farm and longs to return).

This last example of how inspiration struck was conceded by O'Neill. "At exactly the right moment," when he was "floundering about in the maze of the novel-play," O'Neill said, the real-life Olson turned up in his memory.

"I thought, 'What if he had stayed on the farm, with his instincts? What would have happened?' But I realized at once he never would have stayed, not even if he had saddled himself with the wife and kids. It amused him to pretend he craved the farm. He was too harmonious a creation of the God of Things as They are. As well expect a sea gull to remain in a barnyard — for ethical reasons.

"And from that point I started to think of a more intellectual, civilized type — a weaker type from the standpoint of the above-mentioned God — a man who would have [Olson's] inborn craving for the sea's unrest, only in him it would be conscious, too conscious, intellectually diluted into a vague, intangible, romantic wanderlust. His powers of resistance, both moral and physical, would also probably be correspondingly watered. He would throw away his instinctive dream and accept the thralldom of the farm for, why for almost any nice little poetical craving — the romance of sex, say.

"And so Robert Mayo was born, and developed from that beginning, and Ruth and the others, and finally the complete play."

A few months later, he further elaborated on the play's genesis, stressing that he had "never written anything which did not come directly or indirectly from some event or impression" of his own.

"But these things," he said, "often develop very differently from what you expect. For example, I intended at first in *Beyond the Horizon* to portray in a series of disconnected scenes the life of a dreamer who pursues his vision over the world, apparently without success or a completed deed in his life.

"At the same time, it was my intention to show at last a real accretion from his wandering and dreaming, a thing intangible but real and precious beyond compare, which he had successfully made his own. But the technical difficulty of the task proved enormous and I was led to a grimmer thing: the tragedy of the man who looks over the horizon, who longs with his whole soul to depart on the quest, but whom destiny confines to a place and a task that are not his."

Also present in the play is a sampling of the knowledge O'Neill absorbed from his continuous and often arcane reading. Along with the influence of *Light on the Path* (whose "wisdom" he had painted on the rafters of his Provincetown flat), he had been greatly impressed by his vast reading about the Orient, and his yearning to see it is attributed to Robert Mayo in these lines:

"Supposing I was to tell you that it's just Beauty that's calling me, the beauty of the far off and unknown, the mystery and spell of the East which lures me in the books I've read, the need of the freedom of great wide spaces, the joy of wandering on and on — in quest of the secret which is hidden over there beyond the horizon."

Whatever combination of environment and intuition sparked *Beyond the Horizon*, it marked the first realization of O'Neill's long-held dream of writing tragedy on a grand scale.

Tragedy was "the core" of O'Neill's work, as the eminent critic, Joseph Wood Krutch, pointed out some years after O'Neill's death — "Tragedy in the sense of that word that never really changes." No other American writer for the stage, argued Krutch, "has so constantly produced plays which so closely approximate the Aristotelian ideal."

O'Neill, however, needed no one to speak for him about tragedy.

As early as 1913, at the tuberculosis sanatorium, he had formulated his own view of tragedy's tonic effect. Ten years later, he made one of innumerable attempts to explain his devotion to the dramatic form from which he rarely deviated after conceiving *Beyond the Horizon*:

"I have an innate feeling of exultance about tragedy. The tragedy of Man is perhaps the only significant thing about him . . . What I am after is to get an audience to leave the theatre with an exultant feeling from seeing somebody on the stage facing life, fighting against the eternal odds, not conquering, but perhaps inevitably being conquered. The individual life is made significant just by the struggle . . .

"The struggle of man to dominate life, to assert and insist that life has no meaning outside himself where he comes in conflict with life, which he does at every turn; and his attempt to adapt life to his own needs, in which he doesn't succeed, is what I mean when I say that Man is the hero. If one out of ten thousand can grasp what the author means, if that one can formulate within himself his identity with the person in the play, and at the same time get the emotional thrill of being that person in the play, then the theater will get back to the fundamental meaning of the drama, which contains something of the religious spirit which the Greek theatre had. And something of the exultance which is completely lacking in modern life."

Although O'Neill referred to *Beyond the Horizon* somewhat casually as a "novel-play," the description was meaningful. The play did have the largeness of theme, the psychological depth of character and the literary aspirations of a novel.

Moreover, like his works to come, it was boldly self-revelatory — a long-acknowledged tradition of the great novelist but rarely if ever displayed by an American dramatist. Indeed, there had been times before he wrote *Beyond the Horizon* when O'Neill had actually contemplated being a novelist — and, in fact, his published plays soon were to sell like novels. But the stage was what he knew. Success as a novelist, in any case, would not have enabled O'Neill, with his unresolved Oedipal striving, to triumph over his father and his father's theater.

In its time, *Beyond the Horizon* was perceived as a play of such tragic sweep and grandeur that it dwarfed the efforts of American playwrights who had come before.

The play found an adventurous producer, John D. Williams, willing to take a chance on it for Broadway in early 1920 — albeit as a series of special matinees. Critics at once recognized it as the first authentic American tragedy (although it was ultimately dated by its somewhat stilted language and self-conscious technique). Alexander Woollcott of The Times led the chorus of praise, calling it "an absorbing, significant, and memorable tragedy, so full of meat that it makes most of the remaining fare seem like the merest of meringue."

O'Neill's emergence underlined the timidity of "innovations" by William Vaughan Moody and Edward Sheldon, who had attempted to elevate standards but succumbed to the stony dictum of the business-driven Broadway managers demanding happy endings. Moody and Sheldon believed with the managers that there would *be* no audiences if presented with fare that probed for truth beneath life's surface. Unlike O'Neill, Moody and Sheldon dared not send audiences home troubled by the need to think.

What was required to break this mold was O'Neill's blend of vision, self-assurance, persistence and daring, not to mention his innate gift of storytelling. To find the way, he had spent four years writing twenty plays — with only two, *Bound East for Cardiff* and *The Moon of the Caribbees*, surviving as theater milestones.

By the time O'Neill, at the age of twenty-nine, was pondering *Beyond the Horizon*, he had already accumulated virtually all the material he would ever need to transfigure the American theater. With the experiences of family conflict and betrayal embedded in his soul and mind, he became his own endlessly fascinating tragic hero.

Seeking to illuminate the present, he dwelled on the past — his own partly real and partly mythologized past. He knew better than anyone that the stuff of his own life contained all the elements of compelling drama:

The obsession to own land as a hedge against poverty — an Irish characteristic exemplified by his father; his parents' embittered, yet ardent marriage; the infusion of theater into his blood during his first seven years; his unending struggle against his Catholic heritage; the shock of discovering he was an unwanted child — a substitute for his dead infant brother — and his conviction that he was responsible for his mother's morphine addiction; the Irish chauvinism transmitted to him by his father; the duality of his father's nature — gifted artist and frightened materialist — from which he sought to interpret the battle between man's poetic striving and the compulsive greed he predicted would destroy America's soul.

Then there was the hero-worship of and gradual disillusionment over his cynical older brother; his precocious radicalism; his early lust for adventure at sea and in foreign lands; his lifelong compassion for the downtrodden; the dreadful malaise that compelled him to soak himself in alcohol; his conflicted relations with women; his consuming passion for books that imbued him with the political, mystical and historical theories he was to weave into his work; and most of all, his unshakable conviction that he was an artist who would give birth to a new American theater.

In the eternal haunting by his family, in the life he had already lived before thirty, he was fully possessed of the tragic plots and themes and leading characters that were to infuse both the least and the greatest of his work.

Now he had only to bleed and weep endless tears for the sake of his artist's dream. No one expressed his creative struggle as tellingly as the equally haunted Tennessee Williams: "O'Neill gave birth to the American theater and died for it."

ACKNOWLEDGMENTS

I n addition to the hundreds of individuals and scores of libraries, organizations and publications that helped us prepare our earlier biography, numerous auxiliary sources contributed to our expanded — and we hope vastly enriched — new volume. We despair of being able to convey to them all the thanks they deserve, but we will try.

We can never sufficiently applaud Travis Bogard for the support he gave us over the years. Travis, who died in 1997, was the most knowledgable and devoted of O'Neill scholars, always happy to hear our theories and give us his own; we have greatly missed these exchanges. Equally, we can never repay the assistance of Brooks Atkinson, former drama critic of The New York Times, who guided us in countless ways, and who in 1956 first suggested that we undertake a seminal biography of O'Neill.

It was Brooks who urged O'Neill's reclusive widow, Carlotta Monterey, to meet with us. We thank her for allowing us to interview her over a period of years, in the late 1950's and early 60's, and for sharing with us her memories of her life with O'Neill. She not only permitted us to record her at length, but presented us with a number of signed photographs and books, as well as important documents such as O'Neill's autopsy report. We thank also O'Neill's first wife, Kathleen Pitt-Smith, who agreed to give us her then still-painful recollections of her brief marriage. And, of course, we were grateful to be able to draw upon *Part of a Long Story*, the memoir by O'Neill's second wife, Agnes Boulton, as well as her letters from O'Neill on deposit at Harvard.

We are especially grateful to the uniquely qualified friends who took the time and trouble to read this volume in manuscript form and give us their thoughtful editorial suggestions: Jackson Bryer, Linda Healey, Michiko Kakutani, Robert Marx, Frank Rich and Patricia Willis.

Ms. Willis, curator of the Beinecke Rare Book & Manuscript Library, Yale University, was enormously helpful in tracking down the most minute details in the library's O'Neill collection. Additionally, the library's former curator, Dr. Donald C. Gallup, who assisted with our original biography, continued to aid us in our new research. Among others of Ms. Willis's staff at the Beinecke, Miriam Spectre was especially helpful in getting archival material into our hands expeditiously, as was Adam J. Marchand. Also at Yale, for their great help with our earlier book, we thank James T. Babb and Steve Kezerian.

Robert Marx, until recently executive director of the New York Public Library for the Performing Arts, not only read our manuscript but went out of his way in helping to resolve many of our research problems. His colleague, Robert N. Taylor,

curator of the Billy Rose Theater Collection, was also extremely obliging, as was
Jeremy McGraw, photo librarian. For their help at the Public Library with our earli-
er book, we thank George Freedley and George Myers. At the library's Berg
Collection, we are grateful for the ample assistance of Rodney Phillips, its curator,
and his assistant, Stephen Crook. And, for his earlier help at the Berg, we thank John
Gordan.

We deeply appreciate the new research painstakingly gathered in Ireland over a
period of many months by Brian O'Neill, a retired Kilkenny farmer and self-taught
historian, who tracked down myriad family birth records and other vital documents,
including church listings and land deeds.

Our very special gratitude, also, to Patrick Ryan, a Kilkenny-born O'Neill scholar, now a reporter in Dublin; he probed records in numerous institutions and recruited an army of native researchers, who helped him pursue innumerable clues that
yielded hitherto unknown facts about the O'Neill family. Mary Mallett and Jeanne
Mallett, descendants of James O'Neill, were also of great assistance in tracing the
family's roots.

We are indebted to Gustav Adolph Waage, of Stavanger, Norway, grandson of
Captain Gustav Waage, who carried O'Neill to Buenos Aires on the Charles Racine.
He graciously gave us information from the ship's log and other valuable data, as
well as photographs of his grandfather and the ship.

Steven Kennedy Murphy, a director and devoted O'Neill scholar, was of enor-
mous help in unearthing new material for us at Harvard's Houghton and Widener
Libraries and at Yale's Beinecke Library, as well as in New London and
Provincetown.

Our special thanks to Howard Fishman — a theater scholar by day and a jazz
musician by night — who spent many days tracking down letters and photographs
at the Beinecke Library, as well as at the New York Public Library and the Fales
Collection at New York University; we are grateful to him also for combing our manuscript for accuracy.

We could not have presented our new picture of O'Neill's New London without
the ongoing assistance of Sally Pavetti and Lois McDonald, curators of the city's
Monte Cristo Cottage, who doggedly searched old city records and photo files; they
never turned down a request from us, no matter how arcane it might have seemed
at the time.

In New London, too, we were greatly helped by Morgan McGinley, editor of the
editorial page of the New London Day, and his assistant, Greg Stone. Robert Nye,
City Clerk in Waterford, Conn., was of much assistance, as was, earlier, Elizabeth T.
Roath. Also, for his earlier assistance at the New London Public Library, we thank
Frank Edgerton. For help with our early research in New London, too, we are grate-
ful to the Lawrence Memorial Hospital; also the New London County Historical
Society; St. Joseph's Church and St. Mary's Cemetery; Harkness Memorial State Park

(Connecticut State Park and Forest Commission, Waterford).

Of invaluable and ongoing aid has been Diane Schinnerer, past president of Tao House (O'Neill's former residence in Danville, Cal.) and the director of the Tao House Library. Among various research tasks, she provided us with a complete file of the known O'Neill letters (more than 3,000 collected by Travis Bogard and Jackson Bryer, but only a limited number used in their *Selected Letters*). Like Ms. Pavetti and Ms. McDonald, she has performed these daunting labors out of devotion to O'Neill. At Tao House, we also thank James Kantor.

Frederick C. Wilkins, editor of the Eugene O'Neill Review at Suffolk University, has been most helpful to us over many years, as have his former assistants, Bernadette Smyth and Ingrid Bandle Strange. At Connecticut College, New London, we are indebted to Brian Rogers for his great help with this book; and for our earlier research at Connecticut College, we thank Hazel Johnson.

At the University of Texas, where much of our own O'Neill collection is housed, we thank Thomas Staley, Don Carleton, Kathy Henderson and Cliff Farrington. And at the Museum of the City of New York, we thank Robert Macdonald and Marty Jacobs; we acknowledge also the earlier help at the Museum of May Davenport Seymour.

We proffer our special thanks to a number of individuals who provided us with valuable information or guidance:

Dr. Harley J. Hammerman, the preeminent O'Neill collector, who graciously gave us copies of significant documents and photographs.

Samuel (Biff) Liff, senior vice-president of the William Morris Agency, who has been an avid supporter of our new work from its beginning.

Adele Heller, who before her death in 1997, kept the Provincetown Players' reputation alive in its Massachusetts birthplace.

Among the Irish institutions and researchers recruited by our Kilkenny sleuth, Patrick Ryan, we are much obliged to his mother, Mary Ryan, who transcribed Kilkenny documents dating from the mid-1800's; also, to the following in Dublin: Brian Donnelly, National Archives; National Library; Land Valuation Office; Irish Met Service, Glasnevin; Iarnrod Eireann, Heuston Station; Canadian Embassy; British Embassy; Dr. Patricia Lysaght, Irish Folklore Dept. University College; Dr. Anthony Clare, director St. Patrick's Psychiatric Hospital.

Additionally, in Ireland: J. S. Beach, Shane's Castle, County Antrim; Public Library, Kilkenny City; John Kirwan, Kilkenny Archeological Society; Captain O. P. Foley, Harbor Master, New Ross, County Wexford; Jim Rees, County Wicklow. And beyond Ireland: New Ross Historical Society, Nova Scotia; Edward Laxton, Oxford, England; J. Gordon Reid, Merseyside Maritime Museum, Liverpool; Guild Hall Library, London Corporation; Lloyds of London; Canadian National Archives.

We will always be indebted, as well, to the numerous researchers throughout the United States who, beginning in the mid-1950's, helped us unearth facets of the

O'Neill family's early history. Chief among them were Robert Siegel, in Cleveland, and Oscar Godbout, on the West Coast.

Other major sources of material to which we are much indebted are: Princeton University Library and Alexander P. Clark and Alexander D. Wainwright; Dartmouth College and Bella C. Landauer, Donald D. McCuaig, Marcus A. McCorison and Professor Kenneth Robinson; Harvard University's Widener and Houghton Libraries and William Van Lennep; St. Mary's College and Marion McCandless and S. Robert Johnson; Cornell University and Julie Hayden (Mrs. George Jean Nathan); University of Oregon and Horace W. Robinson; Fordham University and Burt Solomon; University of Washington Library and Jessica Potter; University of Pennsylvania and Neda M. Westlake. At Notre Dame University's Hesburgh Memorial Library, we are grateful to Peter Lysy and Dr. Wendy Clauson Schlereth; and for earlier help, we thank James E. Armstrong. At Coumbia University's Rare Book and Manuscript Library we thank Jean Ashton; also at Columbia, we thank Kenneth A. Lohf. At the Newbury Library, we thank Amy Nyholm; at the Boston Public Library, Richard C. Hensley and Marjorie Bouquet; at the Library of Congress we are grateful for the help given us by Jan Lauridsen, Jeanne Smith, Alice Birney, Gail Kennon and Mary Gray; and, for their earlier help, Richard S. McCartney and David C. Mearns; we were assisted also by Actors Equity and Alfred Harding; the South Street Seaport Museum and Peter Neill and Charles L. Sachs; the Statue of Liberty-Ellis Island Foundation and Stephen A. Briganti; and the now-defunct O'Malley's Book Shop.

Also, the American Merchant Marine Institute and Frank Braynard; the Church of St. Ann (N.Y.) and the Rev. John P. Healey; the Euthanasia Society of America and Dr. Robert L. Dickinson and Mrs. Robertson Jones; the General Service Administration; National Archives (Washington, D.C.) and F. R. Holdcamper; the Marine Society of the Port of New York; the Mystic Seaport Museum and Malcolm D. McGregor; the National Institute of Arts and Letters; the George M. Cohan Music Publishing Co; the Office of the Chief Medical Examiner (N.Y.); Bellevue Hospital; Norwich State Hospital (Conn.); Laurel Heights Sanatorium (Conn.) and Dr. Kirby S. Howlett Jr. and Dr. Edward J. Lynch.

Also, The Players and Pat Carroll; the Episcopal Actors' Guild and Mrs. Helen Morrison; the Seaman's Institute, Sailors Snug Harbor, and Arthur Cochrane and Frederick S. McMurray; Stamford Historical Society and M. E. Plumb; United States Lines and Richard Harris; Mount St. Vincent-on-Hudson and the Sisters of Charity; the College of Mount St. Vincent, with particular thanks to Mother Mary Fuller and Sister Marie Jeanette; De La Salle Institute; Veterans Administration Hospitals in the Bronx, Manhattan and Bath (N.Y.); Probate Court, Salem, Mass; and special thanks to the Gaylord Farm Sanatorium and Howard Crockett, Reba Maisonville and director Sterling B. Brinkley.

Among the reference libraries and morgues of newspapers and magazines that provided information, first and foremost was The New York Times, where we received the tireless and invaluable research assistance of Linda Amster and Jeffrey Roth, as well as Dirk Johnson and his wife, Margaret Shannon, who tracked down documents and newspaper clippings in Chicago archives.

Other newspaper archives we consulted were the New York Herald Tribune; the New York Journal-American; the New London Day, the Oakland (Cal.) Tribune, the Boston Globe, the Providence (R.I.) Journal and Evening Bulletin, the Lynne (Mass.) Item, the Oregon Journal, the Oregonian, the Salem (Mass.) Evening News, the Seattle Post-Intelligencer, the Seattle Times, Time magazine and Variety.

We also are grateful to the following persons for their extraordinary support (many of them acknowledged in the text of both this and our earlier book — and most of them long since gone): S. N. Behrman, Dr. Philip Weissman, Clara Rotter, Leonard Harris, John Mason Brown, Kenneth Macgowan, Frances Steloff, Irving Hoffman, Robert Downing, Russel Crouse, Saxe and Dorothy Commins, Agna Enters, Arthur McGinley, David and Esther Habin, Ben and Ann Pinchot, Elliot Norton, Lawrence Langner, James Joseph Martin, Charles O'Brien Kennedy.

We thank, as well, the following persons and their organizations: Christopher Cahill, editor-in-chief, The Recorder, Journal of the American-Irish Historical Society; Christopher Gray, Office for Metropolitan History; Glenn C. Peck, Allison Gallery (N.Y.); Eric Widing, Christie's; Frank De Rosa, spokesman for the Brooklyn Catholic Diocese; Mary George, Firestone Library, Princeton University; Prof. Brenda Murphy, University of Connecticut; Bonnie Levinson, New York Public Library; Heidi Shepard, Connecticut College; Beverly C. Muldoon, City & Town Clerk, Norwich, Conn.; Michael Kelly, Fales Collection, New York University; Richard Cathal Fossett, Public Record Office, Kew, Richmond, Surrey; Debbie Lee, Williams School, New London; Elaine Mirone Ehrhardt, Cincinnati genealogist; Eleanor Tritchler, Buffalo genealogist; Joseph Silinonte, genealogist; Brother Luke Salm, New York District archives, Manhattan College; Paul Kutta, National Railway Historical Society.; Carol A. Dickson, Smithsonian Institution; Rev. T. Gerard Connolly, Fordham University archives; Brother Carl Malacalza, De La Salle archives; Rev. Msgr. Donald Sakano, Holy Innocents Church.

We ask the reader to bear with us while we list (at what may seem interminable length) those others, some living and some departed, who helped in one way or another with our new, as well as our earlier, research:

Shirlee and Robert Lantz, Dorothy Des Granges, Alma Wiess, Marc Bruno, Peter Macgowan, Alma Fones Eshenfelder, Dorothy Des Granges, David Burnham, Thomas Burke, John Catanzariti, Richard Shepard, Nick Tsacrios, Winfield Aronberg, Barbara Burton, Dr. and Mrs. Louis Bisch, E. J. Ballantine, Claire Bird, Mrs. Fred Boyden, Louis Bergen, Alfred B. C. Batson, Mrs. Chester A. Beckley, Agnes Casey, Professor Bruce Carpenter, Bennett Cerf, Bio De Casseres, Jasper Deeter, Eddie Dowling, Dorothy Day, Eben Given, Phyllis Duganne Given, Charles Ellis, Norma

Millay Ellis, Waldo Frank, Arlene Fones, Dr. Shirley C. Fiske, Lillian Gish, Mrs. Samuel S. Greene, Mrs. Pete Gross, Dr. and Mrs. Joseph Ganey, Mrs. Clayton Hamilton, John Hewitt, Joe Heidt, Ralph Horton, Mrs. Smith Ely Jelliffe, Edna Kenton; Alexander King, Joseph Wood Krutch, Louis Kalonyme, Manuel Komroff, Ed Keefe, James and Patty Light, Ruth Lander, Armina Marshall Langner, William L. Laurence, Romany Marie, Mrs. W. E. Maxon, Dr. Frederic B. Mayo.

Also: Jo Mielziner, George Middleton, Beatrice Ashe Maher, Phillip Moeller, Ward Morehouse, Frank and Elsie Meyer, Joseph A. McCarthy, Elizabeth Murray, Mrs. Matt Moran. Nina Moise, Mr. and Mrs. Dudley Nichols, George Jean Nathan, Patricia Neal, Sean O'Casey, Dr. Robert Lee Patterson, Florence Reed, Arthur Leonard Ross, Jessica Rippin, Robert Rockmore, Selena Royle Renavent, Paula Strasberg, Mrs. Earl C. Stevens, Lee Simonson, Wilhemina Stamberger, Bessie Sheridan, Mr. and Mrs. Phil Sheridan, Claire Sherman, Mrs. E. Chappell Sheffield, Mai-mai Sze, Pauline Turkel, Brandon Tynan, Allen and Sarah Ullman, Alice Woods Ullman, Carl Van Vechten, Fania Marinoff, Mary Heaton Vorse, Mrs. Jacob N. Wolodarsky, Charles Webster, Richard Weeks, Francis (Jeff) Wylie, Norman Winston, Mary Welch, Stark Young, William and Marguerite Zorach, Elizabeth Shepley Sergeant, Ilka Chase, Mrs. Barrett H. Clark, Mrs. Sherwood Anderson.

Also: Jacob Ben-Ami, Walter Abel, Mr. and Mrs. Egmont Arens, Leslie Austin, Margaret Anglin, Dr. Frank L. Babbott, Frank D. Brewer, Charlotte E. Betts, Mary Bicknell, Pincus Berner, Robert C. Brown, Bessie Breuer, Albert Boni, Lillian Brennan, Jeanie Begg, Jennie Belardi, Mark Barron, Charles Burns, Samuel H. Bradish, Frederick Brisson, Mark Crane, Dan D. Coyle, Joseph Corky, Holger Cahill, George Canessa, Mrs. Frances Cadenas, Edith Corwin, Ed Kook, Dr. Saul Colin, Melville Cane, Mrs. Albert B. Carey, Carmen Capalbo, Stanley Chase, Harry T. Crowley, Louis Calta, Frank Conroy, Alexander Campbell, Bosley Crowther, Padraic Colum, Aileen Cramer, Cheryl Crawford, Edward Choate, Arthur Cantor, Gloria Cantor, F. V. Chappell, Alexander H. Cohen, Jack Cunningham, Bernard Clark, Joe Cronin, Warren Carberg, Arthur Daley, Harrison Dowd, Jack Dempsey, Olin Downes, Zelda Dorfman, Thomas F. Dorsey Jr., Barbara Dubivsky, Lawrence E. Davies, Ruth Dutro, John D. Davies, Milton I. D. Einstein, Manny Eisler, Leon Edel, Max Eastman, Donald Friede.

Also: Daniel Foley, Mrs. Hall Furber, Lynn Fontanne, John Fenton, Bijou Fernandez, Robert Flanagan, Emily Rippin Griswold, Howard Mortimer Green, Paul Green, Max Gordon, Ruth Gilbert, Dr. Karl Ragner Gierow, Edward Goodman, Brother Angelus Gabriel, Mrs. Joseph Girdansky, Carol Grace. Howard Mortimer Green, Jess Gordon, David Golding, Margalo Gilmore, Marjorie Griesser, G. E. Birard, Dr. Gordon Hislop, A. Arthur Hall, Sam Hick, Mrs. Walter Huston, Sol Hurok, Sonia Levien Hovey, James Hammond, Helen Hayes, Theresa Helburn, Dag Hammerskjold, John Houseman, Mabel Hess, Inez Hogan, Riga Hastings, John Cecil Holm, Granville Hicks, Ann Harding, Robert Hassett, Margaret Heyer, Arthur

Hughes, Blanche Hayes, Sara Heller; Grace Hackmeir; Dr. Daniel Hiebert, Harry Hyams, Don Hartman, Dr. Andrew Harsanyi, Edward Hubler, Catharine Huntington, Louis Isaacs, Dr. Oswald Jones, Bill Johnson, Denis Johnston, Don Janson, Sybil V. Jacobson, Dr. Robert Klein, Alfred Kreymborg, Leon Kramer, Sadie Koenig, Margaret Kaplan, Gilbert Kahn, Theodore Liebler Jr.

Also: Bonnie Lefave; Mrs. William T. L'Engle, Claire Luce, Alfred Lunt, Frank Leslie, Dr. Sidney Lenke, Scott Lindsley, Louise Larabee, T. H. Latimer, J. Anthony Lewis, Gloria Vanderbilt, Edward Lazare, David Lawrence, Kyra Markham, Nickolas Muray, Mary Morris, Mrs. Julian Moran, Aline MacMahon, W. Somerset Maugham, Thomas Mitchell, Robert Manning, Marcella Markham, Philip McBride, Mrs. Harold J. McGee, Gilbert Miller, James Meighan, Walter Murphy, Mrs. Richard J. Madden, Dr. Merrill Moore, Warren Munsell. Mabel Ramage Mix, Bert McCord, Alan D. Mickle, Richard Maney, Sal J. Miraliotta, Edward R. Morrow, Albert C. Nathanson, Dr. and Mrs. John Norris, Daniel O'Neill, Arnold Newman. Dr. W. Richard Ohler, Clifford Odets, Hal Olver, Henry O'Neill, Dr. B. N. Pennell, Albert J. Perry, Augustus Perry, Joseph Plunkett, Karl Pretshold, Mrs. Percy Palmer, Seymour Peck, Brother Basil Peters, David F. Perkins, Coddington Pendleton, Judge S. V. Prince, Prof. Norman Pearson, Arthur Pell, Dorothy Peterson, Sidney Philips, Stavros Peterson, Frank Payne, Susan Pinchot, C. N. Pollock, Stephen Philbin, James Francis Quigley, José Quintero, George Reynolds, Sawyer Robinson, George Ronkin.

Also: George Ross, William Brennan Rogers, Jason Robards, Jane Rubin, Jay Russell, A. M. Rosenthal, Lennox Robinson, Harold D. Smith, James Shay, Mrs. Eunice Saner, Paul Shyre, Mrs. Henry Bill Selden, Dr. Thomas B. Stoltz, Robert Sisk, Arnault G. Schellenberg, Mrs. John Sloan, Louis Sobol, James Shute, Arthur Shields, Bernard Simon, Oliver M. Sayler, Dr. Daniel Sullivan, Wilbur Daniel Steele, John Snow; Mrs. George E. Shay, Dr. Kenneth J. Tillotson, John Tucker, Edna Tyler, Clara A. Weiss, Arthur G. Walters, Phyllis Cerf Wagner, Richard Witkin, Thornton Wilder, Richard Watts Jr., Mary Williams, Edmund Wilson, Dr. Sophus Keith Winther, Robert Weller, Ted Williams, Mr. and Mrs. Laurence A. White, Stephen Weissman, Stephen Watts, William Weart, Arthur W. Wisner, Peggy Wood, Sam Zolotow.

Our special thanks to the following persons who helped us research or obtain photographs: Jeffrey Roth, Thomas Burke, Warrie Price, Ken Cobb, Morgan McGinley. Brian G. Andersson, Glenn C. Peck, Eric Widing, Andrew Schoelkoph, Richard T. York, Meredith Ward, Elizabeth Barnett, Brian Rogers, Noni Korf Vidal, Sheila Tremper, Annette Marotta, Frank Goodman, Roberta Clouet, Eugene C. Cushman, Lester H. Heller, Allen Reuben, Kathy Flynn.

And, finally, we salute Louis Silverstein, former assistant managing editor of The New York Times and preeminent innovator of newspaper design, who volunteered to help lay out the illustrations for our book.

SELECTED BIBLIOGRAPHY

In addition to the sources listed below, other books, newspaper and magazine articles are cited in the End Notes.

ALEXANDER, DORIS (I) *The Tempering of Eugene O'Neill*, Harcourt Brace & World, New York 1962.

ALEXANDER, DORIS (II) *O'Neill's Creative Struggle*, Pennsylvania State University Press, University Park, Pa. 1992.

ASBURY, HERBERT *Gangs of New York*, Alfred A. Knopf, New York 1928.

ATKINSON, BROOKS *Broadway*, Macmillan, New York 1970.

BARLOW, JUDITH E. *Final Acts*, University of Georgia Press, Athens 1985.

BARNES, ERIC WOLLENCOTT *The Man Who Lived Twice*, Charles Scribner & Sons, New York 1956.

BARRETT, ANDREA *Ship Fever*, W. W. Norton, New York/London 1996.

BASSO, HAMILTON "The Tragic Sense," The New Yorker, February 28 (I); March 6 (II); March 13 (III) 1948.

BOGARD, TRAVIS (I) and JACKSON R. BRYER editors, *Selected Letters of Eugene O'Neill*, Yale University Press, New Haven and London 1988.

BOGARD, TRAVIS (II) editor, *Eugene O'Neill Complete Plays* (3 Volumes: 1913–1920; 1920–1931; 1932–1943). The Library of America, New York 1988.

BOGARD, TRAVIS (III) editor, *The Unknown O'Neill*, Yale University Press, New Haven 1988.

BOGARD, TRAVIS (IV) *Contour in Time: The Plays of Eugene O'Neill*, Oxford University Press, New York 1972.

BOULTON, AGNES *Part of a Long Story*, Doubleday, Garden City 1958.

BOWEN, CROSWELL (with SHANE O'NEILL) *The Curse of the Misbegotten*, McGraw-Hill, New York/Toronto/London 1959, and "The Black Irishman," PM, November 3, 1946.

BRUSTEIN, ROBERT *The Theater in Revolt*, Atlantic-Little Brown, Boston 1964.

BRYANT, LOUISE "Christmas in Petrograd," unpublished memoir (circa 1936), Granville Hicks collection, Syracuse University Library, Department of Special Collections.

BRYER, JACKSON editor, "The Theater We Worked For," The Letters of Eugene O'Neill & Kenneth Macgowan, Yale University Press, New Haven 1982.

CARGILL, OSCAR, N. BRYLLION FAGIN, WILLIAM J. FISHER editors, *O'Neill and His Plays*, New York University Press, New York 1961.

CLARK, BARRETT H. *Eugene O'Neill, the Man and His Plays*, Robert McBride, New York 1929; revised Dover Publications, New York 1947.

COLLINS, MABEL (writing as "M. C.") *Light on the Path*, Theosophical Publishing Co., New York 1897.

COMMINS, DOROTHY editor, "Love and Admiration and Respect," the O'Neill-Commins Correspondence, Duke University Press, Durham 1986.

CRICHTON, KYLE *Total Recoil*, Doubleday, Garden City 1960, and "Mr. O'Neill and the Iceman," Collier's, October 26, 1946.

DARDIS, TOM *The Thirsty Muse*, Ticknor & Fields, New York 1989.

DELL, FLOYD *Homecoming*, Kennikat Press, Port Washington, New York/London 1961.

DEUTSCH, HELEN and STELLA HANAU *The Provincetown: A Story of the Theater*, Farrar & Rinehart 1931.

EASTMAN, MAX *Enjoyment of Living*, Harper & Bros., New York 1948.

EASTMAN, MAX *Love and Revolution*, Random House, New York 1964

EGAN, LEONA RUST *Provincetown As a Stage*, Parnassus Imprints, Orleans, Mass. 1944.

ENGEL, EDWIN *The Haunted Heroes of Eugene O'Neill*, Harvard University Press, Cambridge, Mass. 1953.

ESTRIN, MARK W. editor, *Conversations with Eugene O'Neill*, University Press of Mississippi, Jackson & London 1990.

FALK, DORIS *Eugene O'Neill and the Tragic Tension*, Rutgers University Press, New Brunswick, N.J. 1958.

FLOYD, VIRGINIA (I) *Eugene O'Neill at Work*, annotated & edited, Frederick Ungar Publishing New York 1981.

FLOYD, VIRGINIA (II) *Eugene O'Neill, A World View*, Frederick Ungar Publishing, New York 1979

GALLUP, DONALD (I) editor, *Eugene O'Neill Poems*, 1912–1944, Ticknor & Fields, New Haven/New York 1980.

GALLUP, DONALD (II) editor, "Eugene O'Neill Work Diary 1924–1943," Yale University Library, New Haven 1981.

GALLUP, DONALD (III) *What Mad Pursuits!*, Beinecke Rare Book & Manuscript Library, Yale University, New Haven 1998.

GARDNER, VIRGINIA *"Friend and Lover," The Life of Louise Bryant*, Horizon Press, New York 1982.

GELB, ARTHUR and BARBARA *O'Neill*, Harper & Bros., New York 1962; revised Harper & Row, New York 1973.

GELB, BARBARA *So Short a Time*, W. W. Norton, New York 1973.

GERBER, DAVID A. *The Making of an American Pluralism*, University of Illinois Press, Urbana/Chicago 1989.

GLASPELL, SUSAN *The Road to the Temple*, Frederick A. Stokes, New York/Toronto 1927.

GOLDMAN, EMMA *Living My Life*, Garden City Publishing, New York 1931.

GOODWIN, DONALD W., M.D. *Alcohol and the Writer*, Penguin Books, New York 1990.

HAMILTON, CLAYTON *Conversations on Contemporary Drama*, Macmillan, New York 1925.

HAMILTON, G.V., M.D. *A Research in Marriage*, Albert & Charles Boni, New York 1929.

HAPGOOD, HUTCHINS (I) *A Victorian in the Modern World*, Harcourt, Brace, New York 1937.

HAPGOOD, HUTCHINS (II) *An Anarchist Woman*, Duffield, New York 1909.

HARRINGTON, JOHN P. *The Irish Play on the New York Stage, 1874–1996*, University Press of Kentucky 1997.

HELLER, ADELE & LOIS RUDNICK editors, *The Cultural Moment*, Rutgers

University Press, New Brunswick, N.J. 1991.

HICKS, GRANVILLE *John Reed*, Macmillan, New York 1936.

KENTON, EDNA Unpublished mss. Fales Library, New York University, and revised unpublished ms. Gelb collection. Also, *The Provincetown Players and The Playwrights' Theater 1915–1922*, edited by Travis Bogard & Jackson Bryer, published in The Eugene O'Neill Review, Vol. 21, Nos. 1 & 2, 1997.

KINNE, WISNER PAYNE *George Pierce Baker and the American Theater*, Harvard University Press, Cambridge 1954.

KREYMBORG, ALFRED *Troubador*, Boni & Liveright, New York 1925.

KRUTCH, JOSEPH WOOD *The American Stage Since 1918*, George Baraziller, New York 1957.

KRUTCH, JOSEPH WOOD Introduction, *Nine Plays by Eugene O'Neill*, Modern Library, New York 1954.

LANGNER, LAWRENCE *The Magic Curtain*, E. P. Dutton, New York 1951.

LASCH, CHRISTOPHER *The New Radicalism in America 1889–1963*, Knopf, New York 1965.

LOCKRIDGE, RICHARD *Darling of Misfortune Edwin Booth: 1833–1893*, Century, New York/London 1932.

LUHAN, MABEL DODGE *Movers and Shakers*, Harcourt, Brace, New York 1936.

MADDUX, PERCY *City on the Wilamette*, Metropolitan Press, Portland, Ore. 1952.

MADISON, CHARLES A. *Critics and Crusaders*, Henry Holt, New York 1947.

McCANDLESS, MARION Family Portraits, Saint Mary's College, Notre Dame, Ind. 1952

MOODY, RICHARD *Edwin Forrest, First Star of the American Stage*, Knopf, New York 1960.

MORGAN, CHARLES H. *Painter of America*, Reynal, New York 1965.

NATHAN, GEORGE JEAN (I) *"As Ever, Gene," The Letters of Eugene O'Neill to George Jean Nathan*, edited by Nancy L. Roberts & Arthur W. Roberts, Fairleigh Dickinson University Press, London/Toronto 1987.

NATHAN, GEORGE JEAN (II) *The Intimate Notebooks of George Jean Nathan*, Alfred A. Knopf, New York 1932.

NIETZSCHE, FRIEDRICH *The Philosophy of Nietzsche*, Modern Library, New York 1954.

O'FAOLAIN, SEAN *The Great O'Neill*, Mercier Press, Cork/Dublin 1986.

O'NEILL, EUGENE *Inscriptions: Eugene O'Neill to Carlotta Monterey O'Neill*, edited by Donald Gallup, Yale University Library, New Haven, 500 copies privately printed 1960.

O'NEILL, EUGENE *"Children of the Sea" and Three other Unpublished Plays*, edited by Jennifer McCabe Atkinson, NCR, Washington, D.C. 1972.

O'NEILL, PATRICK *History of the San Francisco Theater, Vol. XX: James O'Neill*, San Francisco Writers' Program of the WPA in Northern California, 1942.

QUINN, ARTHUR HOBSON *A History of the American Drama from the Civil War to the Present Day*, Harper & Brothers, New York/London 1927.

RANALD, MARGARET LOFTUS *The Eugene O'Neill Companion*, Greenwood Press, Westport, Conn./London 1984.

REED, JOHN *Insurgent Mexico*, D. Appleton, New York 1914.

ROBINSON, PHYLLIS C. *The Life of Willa Cather*, Holt, Rinehart & Winston,

New York 1983.

RUGGLES, ELEANOR *Prince of Players*, W. W. Norton, New York 1953.

SANBORN, RALPH & CLARK, BARRETT H. *O'Neill Bibliography*, Random House, New York 1931.

SERGEANT, ELIZABETH SHEPLEY   *Fire Under the Andes*, Alfred A. Knopf, London, New York 1927.

SHAUGHNESSY, EDWARD L. *Down the Nights and Down the Days*, University of Notre Dame Press, Notre Dame, Ind. 1996.

SHEAFFER, LOUIS *O'Neill Son and Playwright*, Little, Brown, Boston/Toronto 1968.

SKINNER, RICHARD DANA *A Poet's Quest*, Russell & Russell Inc., New York 1964.

STEFFENS, LINCOLN   *The Autobiography of Lincoln Steffens*, Harcourt,Brace, New York 1931.

STIRNER, MAX *The Ego and His Own*, Libertarian Book Club, 1963.

TIMBERLAKE, CRAIG *The Bishop of Broadway*, Library Publishers, New York 1954.

TYLER, GEORGE C. & J. C. FURNESS   *Whatever Goes Up*, Bobbs-Merrill, Indianapolis 1934.

VORSE, MARY HEATON *Time and the Town*, Rutgers University Press, New Brunswick, N.J. 1991.

WEISSMAN, PHILLIP, M.D. *Creativity in the Theater*, Basic Books 1965.

WINTER, WILLIAM *The Life of David Belasco*, Moffat, Yard, New York 1913.

WOODHAM-SMITH, CECIL *The Great Hunger*, Penguin Books, New York 1991.

Key to Abbreviations in End Notes

Authors of books and articles cited in End Notes by last names are fully credited
with their works in Selected Bibliography.

A/BG	Arthur and Barbara Gelb
ABO	Agnes Boulton O'Neill
AHQ	Arthur Hobson Quinn
AMcG	Arthur McGinley
AW	Alice Woods
(bibliog)	Selected Bibliography
BA	Brooks Atkinson
Berg	Berg Collection, New York Public Library
Beinecke	Beinecke Rare Book and Manuscript Library, Collection of American Literature, Yale University
BC	Bennett Cerf
CMO	Carlotta Monterey O'Neill
EK	Edward Keefe
ER	Emily Rippin
ESS	Elizabeth Shepley Sergeant
Fales	Fales Library, New York University
GCC	George Cram Cook
GCT	George C. Tyler
GJN	George Jean Nathan
HH	Hutchins Hapgood
Houghton	Houghton Library, Harvard University
JG	Dr. Joseph Ganey
JJM	James Joseph (Slim) Martin
JL	James Light
JWK	Joseph Wood Krutch
JMcC	Joseph McCarthy
JR	Jessica Rippin
KJP	Kathleen Jenkins Pitt-Smith
KM	Kenneth Macgowan
LB	Louise Bryant
LDJIN	*Long Day's Journey Into Night*

Locke	Robinson Locke Scrapbooks, Theater Collection, New York Public Library
LL	Lawrence Langner
LS	Louis Sheaffer
MHV	Mary Heaton Vorse
MSB	Maibelle Scott Beckley
MW	Marion Welch
MZ	Marguerite Zorach
NB	Neith Boyce
NYT	The New York Times
OEM	Olive Evans Maxon
O'N	Eugene O'Neill
O'N Jr.	Eugene O'Neill Jr.
PP	Provincetown Players
PS	Philip Sheridan
RC	Russel Crouse
SC	Saxe Commins
SG	Susan Glaspell
SL	Selected Letters of Eugene O'Neill, Yale University Press 1988
TC	Terry Carlin
WSP	Washington Square Players
WDS	Wilbur Daniel Steele
WZ	William Zorach

END NOTES

CHAPTER ONE

NERVES AND MUSCLES. "Necropsy #16,697," Boston, 11/28/53, 9 A.M. — "16 hours after post mortem." Copy given A/BG by CMO. **(p. 3)**

EMOTIONAL STRESS. Ibid. **(p. 4)**

BE FINISHED." To AHQ 4/30/41. *Selected Letters of Eugene O'Neill*, edited by Travis Bogard & Jackson R. Bryer, Yale University Press: New Haven & London, 1988. Bogard and Bryer state their choices were culled from more than three thousand surviving letters: "What is most remarkable about the bulk of O'Neill's correspondence is that a man forced by his genius to seek undisturbed solitude should reach forth so continually to maintain contacts with the exterior world . . . By the letters, O'Neill managed to live in the outer world without entering it deeply, and by their means, he generally kept the outer and inner planes of his being in balance . . . " (Copies of a number of included letters were supplied by A/BG.) **(p. 4)**

CAN'T ESCAPE!" CMO diaries, Beinecke. **(p. 5)**

THE HOPE." NY Tribune 1/13/21. **(p. 5)**

AND GOD." JWK introduction, *Nine Plays by Eugene O'Neill*, Random House, NY 1954. **(p. 5)**

A REVELATION." "Making Plays with a Tragic End: an Intimate Interview with Eugene O'Neill, Who Tells Why He Does It," Malcolm Mollen, Philadelphia Public Ledger 1/22/22. **(p. 6)**

ANIMAL CRACKERS, 1930; burlesque of stage asides in *Strange Interlude*. **(p. 6)**

MICKEY MOUSE). 1934 Broadway musical, *Anything Goes*. **(p. 6)**

IDIOTIC REVIEWS." To Warren Munsell 2/18/34, *SL*. **(p. 6)**

MODERN THEATER," Ibid. **(p. 7)**

MYSTERIOUS SORROW." NYT Magazine, S. J. Woolf 10/4/31 & 9/15/46. **(p. 7)**

JUST PEOPLE." To Malcolm Mollan, probably early Dec. 1921. *SL*. O'N was responding to questions for an article in Philadelphia Public Ledger 1/22/22. **(p. 7)**

SIX-FOOT FRAME. His precise height, according to various medical records, was six feet and a quarter inch. **(p. 7)**

CREATIVE STRUGGLE. Lengthy interview, tape-recorded by A/BG at NYT 10/2/56, for NYT's Sunday Drama Section 11/4/56, under Seymour Peck's byline. A/BG were present at the interview, together with BA (whose colleague Arthur Gelb was at the time); tape of the interview with a 20-page, single-spaced transcript, are in A/BG collection. Much of the material pertaining to O'N's struggle in writing *LDJIN* was later expanded upon by CMO and tape-recorded by A/BG. She often repeated the same stories as though having memorized them, with slight variations. For the quotations in this text A/BG have used what they regard as the clearest version. **(p. 8)**

AND HIMSELF." A/BG interviews with CMO. **(p. 8)**

LOVE WITH DEATH," *LDJIN*, Edmund, Act IV. **(p. 9)**

MINE OWN." James O'N, conversant as he was with Shakespeare, felt free to bowdlerize a line from *As You Like It*, in which Touchstone characterizes Audrey, the unkempt country wench he plans to marry, as "A poor virgin, sir, an ill-favour'd thing, sir, but mine own . . . " **(p. 9)**

OUTSIDE THEM." To KM 4/8/21, Bryer (bibliog). **(p. 10)**

A DAY'S JOURNEY Notebook entries 6/25/39, Beinecke. **(p. 10)**

LONG DAY'S JOURNEY: O'Neill Work Diary 6/26/39 (bibliog). **(p. 10)**

ABLE TO FORGET." To GJN 6/15/40, *SL*. **(p. 10)**

MOTHER AND SONS Undated notes for "N[ew] L[ondon] play," Beinecke. **(p. 10)**

DAY'S INSURRECTION. Scenario, June, '39. Beinecke. **(p. 10)**

I BELIEVE." O'Neill Work Diary (bibliog). **(p. 11)**

IN ACT IV. O'Neill Work Diary 4/1/41 (bibliog). **(p. 11)**

THAT'S FINISHED." A/BG interviews with CMO. **(p. 11)**

HAUNTED TYRONES." Dedication to *LDJIN*. **(p. 11)**

SWEEP AND POWER, To GJN 2/8/40; and to O'N Jr. 4/28/41, *SL*. **(p. 11)**

YOU READ IT." 1/30/41. *"As Ever, Gene," The Letters of Eugene O'Neill to George Jean Nathan*, London and Toronto: Associated University Presses, 1987. **(p. 11)**

RECORD ANYWHERE." Ibid. **(p. 11)**

AFTER HIS DEATH To Random House, 11/29/45, *SL*; and A/BG interviews with BC and SC. **(p. 11)**

WORK OF ART. Seven years earlier O'N had to defend himself against what were recognized by friends and relatives as autobiographical elements in *Ah, Wilderness!* **(p. 11)**

THE SHIMMY." 5/13/44, *SL*. **(p. 11)**

SEMI–INVALID. "Necropsy #16,697" (see earlier ref). **(p. 11)**

MOON SUCCESSFUL." "Tennessee Williams: 'I Keep Writing. Somehow I Am Pleased,'" NYT, Michiko Kakutani 8/13/81. **(p. 12)**

AMERICAN THEATER. Directed by José Quintero, starring Colleen Dewhurst and Jason Robards, the production was the dramatic hit of the '74 season. **(p. 12)**

MORE THAN EVER!" *Inscriptions: Eugene O'Neill to Carlotta Monterey O'Neill*, New Haven, Privately Printed, 1960. The volume contains love letters, poetry and play inscriptions preserved in the Beinecke Library. Copy given to A/BG with handwritten inscription from CMO. **(p. 13)**

OF HIS ESTATE. O'N's Last Will and Testament, signed in Boston 5/28/51; and a document naming CMO as sole trustee of O'N's literary properties "published and unpublished," signed 3/3/52; copies given to A/BG by CMO. **(p. 13)**

WRITTEN TO HER. Letter from CMO to BA, from Hotel Shelton, Boston 5/22/54. A/BG collection. **(p. 14)**

PLEASES ME A LOT." O'Neill Work Diary 9/4/41 (bibliog). **(p. 14)**

AS A PLAY." To BC 6/13/51, *SL*. **(p. 14)**

FIVE–ACT VERSION. O'N's work notes for *LDJIN*, Floyd I (bibliog). **(p. 14)**

"NEST EGG." A/BG interviews with CMO. (Had she obeyed her husband's instructions, CMO, the same age as O'N, could not have released the play until she was 90.) **(p. 14)**

GALLUP SAID. O'N Newsletter, Summer-Fall 1985. **(p. 15)**

GULLIBLE PERSON.)" CMO diaries, Beinecke. **(p. 15)**

UNCOMPROMISING." BC to CMO, 7/6/54 Butler Library, Columbia U. **(p. 16)**

AM O'NEILL" A/BG interview with BC's widow, Phyllis Wagner; CMO also said this more than once to A/BG during interviews. **(p. 16)**

SHE WROTE. CMO diaries, Beinecke. **(p. 16)**

SO TO SPEAK!" CMO to BA from Ritz-Carlton Hotel, Boston, 8/6/54. A/BG collection. **(p. 16)**

FELT FOR HIM!" A/BG collection. **(p. 17)**

ITS HISTORY. As of March 1997, it had sold 1,111,300 copies in the English version alone. CMO chose Yale U. Press because of her ties to Yale, whose Beinecke Library housed the O'Neill collection. For some reason, the Press elected to print the word, "Into," in the play's title, as "into," though O'N, in all ms. versions of the play and in letters, spelled the word with an upper-case "I" — with but one apparently absentminded exception — and the title in that form was picked up almost universally. "While there are memos and notes from the manuscript editor about styling, there is nothing in [the file] about the capitalization of 'into' in the title," writes Charles Grench, Editor in Chief, in a letter to B/AG, 9/11/97. He quotes Donald Gallup, former curator of the O'N collection: "O'Neill regularly capitalized prepositions in all his titles" — a fact confirmed by at least two of those titles, *Desire Under the Elms* and *Days Without End.* **(p. 17)**

REASON WHY.") Essay by Tom Olsson, Floyd II (bibliog). **(p. 17)**

REACHING NEW YORK. NY Herald Tribune, This Week Mag. 1/29/56. **(p. 17)**

LIKE YOU," SHE SAID. *If You Don't Dance, They Beat You*, José Quintero, Little, Brown, Boston-Toronto, 1974; also, A/BG interviews with Quintero. **(p. 19)**

TANGIBLE TO ME." "Saving O'Neill and Himself," NYT, Mel Gussow 8/26/98. **(p. 19)**

CELEBRATION." Quintero memorial pamphlet, "Lines in the Palm of God's Hand," South Coast Press 1999. **(p. 20)**

CONDITIONS!" Quintero collection, U. of Houston. **(p. 20)**

HAD JUST LIVED. Witnessed by A/BG. **(p. 21)**

CLASSIC TRADITION." NYT 11/8/56. **(p. 21)**

INTO NIGHT. NYT 11/18/56. **(p. 21)**

PULITZER PRIZE. Wolcott Gibbs of The New Yorker failed to deliver a timely review, leaving after the second act; he later confided to A/BG that it had "cut too close." He went back, and his review — when he turned it in a week late (Nov. 24) — was considerably short of a rave; it was, in fact, rather muddled. Although he found the play "impressive," he wrote: "In the face of a formidable body of opinion to the contrary, I seriously question whether *Long Day's Journey Into Night* will survive as a major contribution to the drama of our time, but it is a courageous one, and I hope its writing gave its author peace." **(p. 21)**

TEARS AND BLOOD," Dedication *LDJIN.* **(p. 22)**

CHAPTER TWO

ONE YEAR OLDER. Quinlan's age has been calculated from his death certificate 5/25/1874 when he was 41. There is a discrepancy in the record regarding Bridget's age: on Mary Ellen's birth certificate Bridget gave her age as 25, making her one year older than her husband; when she died in New London 7/28/1887, her age on her death certificate was given as 60, making her six years older than her husband; but on her New London tombstone her birth date is 1829, making her four years older. **(p. 24)**

"FANCY GOODS."   References to Quinlan's business, Cleveland City Directory (Cleveland Public Library). **(p. 24)**

HER CLASSROOM.   *The Broad Highway*: A History of the Ursuline Nuns in the Diocese of Cleveland, 1850-1950, Sister Michael Francis Hearon, Cleveland, 1951; *The Order of Saint Ursula*, Mother M. Justin McKiernan, O.S.U., Ursuline Provincialate, New Rochelle, NY, 1945; and "Ella O'Neill and the Imprint of Faith," Edward L. Shaughnessey, O'N Review, Vol.16,#2, 1992. **(p. 24)**

AND TOBACCO.   Business was under Quinlan and Spirnaugle. (Spirnaugle had been a bartender). Cleveland City Directory, 1870-1871. **(p. 25)**

ON THE STAGE.   A/BG interviews with CMO and members of Brennan and Sheridan families, including William Rogers Brennan, Claire Brennan Sherman, Bessie Sheridan, Irene Moran and PS. **(p. 26)**

IN CONTEMPT."   Notebook June 1939, Beinecke. **(p. 26)**

IRISH WOMAN."   Beinecke. **(p. 26)**

BOARDING SCHOOL.   A/BG interviews with CMO and Brennan and Sheridan families. **(p. 26)**

SOUTH BEND, INDIANA.   Quinlan's name appears on his daughter's matriculation entry 9/11/1872. Research about St. Mary's for A/BG by Marion McCandless, Alumnae Secretary, St. Mary's College (former Academy), and by James E. Armstrong, Secretary of Alumni Association, U. of Notre Dame. Also from *Family Portraits* by McCandless, Notre Dame 1952. **(p. 26)**

MATINEE IDOL.   A/BG interviews with CMO about O'N's family history, as confided to her over the years. Also A/BG interviews with Brennan and Sheridan families. **(p. 26)**

BECOME NOTRE DAME.   Research by McCandless, Armstrong, etc. (see earlier ref). **(p. 27)**

EXPLICIT WILL.   Quinlan's Will 11/5/1872, Cleveland Probate Court. **(p. 27)**

BEFORE THEN."   Ibid. **(p. 27)**

DIGNIFIED DESIGNATION.   McCandless research (see earier ref). **(p. 27)**

BECOME A NUN.   A/BG interviews with Dr. Louis C. Bisch, psychiatrist friend of O'N, and psychiatrist Philip Weissman. Also Dr. Weissman's essay, "O'Neill's Conscious and Unconscious Autobiographical Dramas," in *Creativity in the Theater*, Dell Publishing, NY 1965. (While it may be of no significance, it should probably be noted that Mary was also the name of O'N's paternal grandmother.) **(p. 28)**

PIANO TECHNIQUE.   Data from McCandless aunt, Loretta Ritchie, classmate of Ella O'Neill. **(p. 28)**

YEARS LATER.   Mother Elizabeth's name before becoming a nun was Harriet Redman Lilly. McCandless research (see earlier ref). **(p. 28)**

ACADEMIC RULES.   McCandless. **(p. 29)**

QUINLAN'S ESTATE.   Probate Court records, Cleveland. **(p. 29)**

HALF IN LOVE.   A/BG interviews with Bessie Sheridan, Irene Moran and PS. **(p. 30)**

CHAPTER THREE

WORE ON STAGE.   Except when other sources are cited, data on James O'N is from extensive A/BG interviews with contemporary actors (mainly Charles Webster, John Hewitt, Bijou Fernandez, Brandon Tynan); with relatives (Phil and Bessie Sheridan, Irene Moran); family friends (Arthur McGinley, Edward Keefe, James Rippin family, Mrs. Clayton Hamilton) and James O'N's scrapbooks at Beinecke and Robinson Locke scrapbooks, NY Public Library. (Locke was editor and publisher of the Toledo Blade.) Also Elizabeth Robins letters and diaries, Fales. **(p. 32)**

WAS A CARESS. San Francisco Chronicle 8/3/1879 and various newspaper articles in scrapbooks at Beinecke and NY Public Library. **(p. 33)**

O'NEILL ONCE SAID. *Total Recoil* (bibliog). **(p. 33)**

INTO SHAKESPEARE." Basso, Part III (bibliog). **(p. 33)**

OF AN ORGAN." Theater Magazine, "James O'Neill — The Actor and The Man," Ada Patterson, April 1908. **(p. 33)**

THE BALCONY." A/BG interview with Perkins. **(p. 34)**

IN MY LIFE." Theater Magazine, April 1908 (see previous ref). **(p. 34)**

JIMMY KISSED HER." Unsourced, undated clipping, James O'N's scrapbook, Beinecke. **(p. 34)**

SPRING OF 1851. NY State Buffalo Census 1855 of "the Inhabitants in the Eighth Ward," 6/25/1855; on that date the O'N family had been living there four years. **(p. 34)**

MALEVOLENT FAIRIES; "Pesonal Reminiscences" by James O'Neill, Theater Magazine, Dec. 1917: " . . . while I was still a lad in skirties my parents emigrated to America and settled in Buffalo." **(p. 35)**

DEATH IN 1920. Ibid. **(p. 35)**

YEAR, HOWEVER." To Lawrence Estavan 1/15/40, *SL*. Estavan was preparing a monograph published as "Volume XX, James O'Neill, History of the San Francisco Theater." Compiled by the Workers of the Writers' Projects Admistration in Northern California, 1942. O'N did not document the source of his information, but it might have been his father's headstone — which, in turn, might have been inscribed with an erroneous date; the month and day, Oct. 14, were correct. **(p. 35)**

NEW LONDON. Connecticut Bureau of Vital Statistics, which gives the precise date of James O'N's death — 8/10/20 at "74 years, 9 months, 27 days" — states he was born 10/14/1845. (Ella did not know his mother's maiden name but gave his father's first name as Edward.) Ella, perhaps, did not personally supervise the inscription on her husband's headstone, and was unaware that a mistake had been made by the stonecutter (a not uncommon occurrence), for the date engraved for James's birth was 1846, rather than 1845. That just such an error was made seems possible from O'N's correspondence about the grave markers in the O'N family plot.

"I've always had an aversion to visiting graves," O'N wrote to his lawyer, Harry Weinberger 9/27/37, *SL*. "I don't know what sort of stones are over my Father, Mother and Brother," he added, suggesting Weinberger send someone to New London to "locate plot and note down all details of what kind of stones over whom, condition of plot, etc." Weinberger reported back about the five members of the family who were buried in St. Mary's cemetery and enclosed a design by a local firm for a proposed monument. O'N specified the wording: "James O'Neill, actor, Born 1846 Died 1920." Letter to Harry Weinberger 3/8/38, *SL*. **(p. 35)**

ABOUT THE PAST." To Lawrence Estavan 1/15/40, *SL*. **(p. 35)**

LONG DAYS JOURNEY. O'Neill Work Diary 1/5/40 (bibliog); O'N read the outline completed June 1939, and wanted "to do this soon . . . " **(p. 35)**

HE HAD SIX.   To Lawrence Estavan 1/15/40, *SL.* **(p. 36)**

OF HIS TIME.   "Personal Reminiscences," Theatre Magazine, Dec. 1917 (see earlier ref). An even earlier article in the NY Clipper 9/29/1900 also referred — in almost the same words — to James's birthplace: "His childhood was passed in the shadow of the grey cathedral, its historic roundtower, and among its monastic ruins. He played in the mossy moat of Strongbow's ancient castle . . . " **(p. 36)**

NORE RIVER.   Tinneranny is twelve miles from Thomastown, sometimes wrongly cited by scholars as James O'N birthplace. **(p. 36)**

AOIFE, IN 1171.   Kilkenny City Public Library. Some scholars believe the castle referred to by James (and situated in Kilkenny City) was the reconstructed 12th-century landmark, Kilkenny Castle, originally built by William the Earl Marshall. But this castle was never known as Strongbow's Castle, having been built after his death; and since it was eighteen miles north of James's home, the shadow it cast on his birthplace could only have been figurative. **(p. 36)**

THAT PERIOD.   Documentation for the life and times of the O'N family in Kilkenny, and their early years in the U.S. is somewhat incomplete and sometimes contradictory. Apart from James himself and what can be gleaned from *Long Day's Journey Into Night*, there are four principal sources of information:

The first consists of handwritten records of births in Tinneranny, in the district of Rosbercon, originally bound in a volume called "Baptismal Book of the Parish of Rosbercon." They were later transferred to a loose-leaf journal and are the property of the Rosbercon Parish Catholic Church, South-East County Kilkenny. They have been closely examined and chronicled by Brian O'Neill, who upon retiring as a Tinneranny farmer traced the O'N geneology. These ecclesiastical records have also been transferred to the computerized database of the Kilkenny Archaeological Society's headquarters at Rothe House in the City of Kilkenny. A copy on microfilm is on file at the Kilkenny City Public Library Administration Building.

The locale is confirmed in a legal pension document filed in 1865 in Washington, D.C., on behalf of James's mother, Mary, who signed it with an "X." Perhaps because she spoke Gaelic and could not write English, she supplied the data for the document orally (in broken English) and the locale was recorded as "Ross Barracon." National Archives, Washington, D.C. Joint Affidavit, Army Pension — Mother's Case, 9/27/1867. According to Mary's interment record at St. Joseph's Irish Cemetery in Cincinnati, she was 68 when she died in 1878, which agrees with her baptismal birth record in Tinneranny, 5/10/1810.

The second source consists of anecdotal and historical research by Brian O'Neill and other Kilkenny natives, who consulted newspaper files, shipping and court records and other local documents. A principal researcher was Patrick Ryan, a Kilkenny-born free-lance journalist.

The third source is an unpublished manuscript by a great-nephew of James O'N, Manley William Mallett, based on anecdotal information derived from two of James's sisters and a nephew. The manuscript, "My Eighty-four Ancestral Families," was written for his children in 1979 and largely based on information obtained in 1937 from Mallett's uncle, Frank A. Kunckel. Kunckel derived his facts from his mother, Stasia Kunckel, and an aunt, Josephine Sears, both sisters of James O'N. (Stasia was Mallett's grandmother and Josephine his great aunt.)

The O'Neills, whose oldest child was eighteen in 1851 when they left Ireland, according to the manuscript, could not have been married any later than 1833. Mallett maintains that the father was born Edmund (not Edmond) and cites the fact that one of his daughters, Adelia, named her first son Edmund after her father (and a daughter, Mary, after her mother). But his name is given as Edward (by Ella O'Neill) on James O'Neill's death certificate. A copy of Mallett's type-script, in the possession of Jeanne M. Mallett, a niece of Manley, was given to A/BG. (An earlier, handwritten document, entitled "The O'Neills," was written for his children by Mallett in 1974, of which the 1979 typescript is an expanded version.)

The fourth source is the NY census for Buffalo in 1855, four years after Edmond O'Neill's family arrived there from Ireland. Additional material about Edmond and his family is given in his death records, filed with the Chief Secretary's Office in Dublin, which lists him as Edmond Neile of the townland of Tinneranny.

Since all these sources contradict each other at some points, their factual value is noted and weighed either in the text or an endnote. **(p. 36)**

THEIR CIRCUMSTANCES. *Irish Families — Their Names, Arms and Origins*, Edward MacLysaght, Hodges Figgis & Co, Dublin 1957. **(p. 37)**

YEARS HIS JUNIOR According to Mary's interment record, St. Joseph's Cemetery, Cincinnati, 8/16/1878, she was 68 when she died, indicating she must have been born in 1810, making her twenty years younger than her husband. However, other records indicate she was seventeen years younger: the Buffalo census of 1855 lists her age as 48 and her husband's age as 65; a pension application in 1864 lists her age as 57. **(p. 37)**

RICHARD TOTTENHAM. Primary Land Valuation, Rosbercon, Sept. 1850. **(p. 37)**

OTHER FARMERS. A/BG interviews with Brian O'Neill (see earlier ref). **(p. 37)**

IS CURSED!" Ibid. **(p. 38)**

WORK HOUSE." *The Story of Kilkenny*, Robert Wyse Jackson, Mercier Press Dublin, 1974. **(p. 39)**

NOT YET SIX. Allowances must be made for misapprehensions and errors in spelling and dates (on the part of recorders in Ireland and census takers in Buffalo) and for memory lapses (on the part of Manley Mallett's family and probably of Mallett himself). While all three principal sources of information about the O'Neill family agree that five girls were born to Edmond and Mary in Ireland, they disagree on at least three of the girls' names and on several of their birth-dates. All three sources, moreover, note the births of three boys — but they are not in each case the same three boys.

According to the Tinneranny birth records, Mary, the eldest O'Neill child, was born in 1832, but the 1855 Buffalo census lists her birthdate as 1833. She herself gave contradictory ages on various documents (and Mallett gives her birthdate as 1842 — patently an error).

Also according to the Tinneranny records, Mary was followed in 1834 by a boy named James; since neither Mallett nor the 1855 Buffalo census makes any mention of a boy born on that date, it may be assumed that he died in infancy — and that the same name was bestowed on a boy who came later. Next in age was a boy christened Richard after his maternal grandfather. Mallett does not supply his date of birth, and he is mysteriously absent from the Tinneranny records; according to the Kilkenny Archeological Society, which does not have him in its geneological data base, it is possible he was born elswhere in the region. But, according to the Buffalo census, he was born in 1836. Richard was followed by Josephine (Mallett's great aunt), whose birthdate he gives as "1837/38"; in the 1955 Buffalo census she is listed as Johana, born in 1839; and she appears in the Tinneranny birth records as "Oney" (possibly a pet name), with a birth date of 1837 — probably the correct one.

Anna was next, born, according to Mallett, in 1838 — a date confirmed by the Buffalo census (which gives her name as Anne); there is no Anna listed in the

Tinneranny birth records; as with Richard, she, too might have been born outside of Kilkenny. The fourth girl born was Adelia (or Delia), also called Bridget — the name under which she is listed both in the Buffalo census, which agrees with Mallett's birthdate of 1843, and the Tinneranny records, which gives her birth date as 1841.

There are three different birth dates given for Edward (or Edmond), the next child: the Tinneranny records cite the year as 1843, Mallett thinks he was born either in 1840 or 1841, and the Buffalo census places his birth in 1845 (which is known to be incorrect). The second son to be given the name James — who was to become Eugene's father — is listed in the Tinneranny records with his correct birthdate, 10/14/1845; (the dates given by Mallett and the Buffalo census are wrong). Stasia, the last child born in Ireland to Edward and Mary, is listed in the Tinneranny records (her name given as Anastatia) as having been born in 1848, although according to both Mallett and the Buffalo census she was born in 1849. **(p. 39)**

MOTHER COUNTRY.   Buffalo Historical Society and Public Library. **(p. 39)**

"GREAT INDIA."   Manley Mallett (see earlier ref). **(p. 39)**

FOUR DAYS LATER).   According to Ledger, Harbour Master's Office, New Ross, and Lloyd's List, Guild Hall, London, the India sailed Apr. 5 for Quebec (docking first for one day in Waterford) with "emigrants." The ship's home port was listed as Liverpool; the owners were William Graves & Son of New Ross and the ship's commander was John Willis. According to the Merseyside Maritime Museum, Liverpool, the India was built in 1847 and registered at New Ross, 8/3/1850. According to the National Archives in Dublin, the India's displacement was 726 tons, making it one of the largest ships operating in the area at that time. **(p. 40)**

THEIR SERVICES."   Many facts about Kilkenny in the 1850's herein cited were drawn from two biweekly newspapers, the Kilkenny Journal and the Kilkenny Moderator, microfilm files, Kilkenny City Library. **(p. 40)**

THEM ASHORE.   *The Great Hunger, Ireland 1845-1849*, Cecil Woodham-Smith, Penguin Books 1991; and *Ship Fever*, Andrea Barrett, W. W. Norton, NY/London 1996. **(p. 40)**

IN NEW YORK.   *An Emigrant's Narrative: Or A Voice From The Steerage*, William Smith, New-York: Published By The Author, 1850. The only known copy is at Harvard College Library. **(p. 40)**

SUPPOSED TO.   Ledger, Harbour Master's Office, New Ross, and National Archives, Dublin. **(p. 40)**

ON MAY 11,   Lloyd's List, Guildhall Library, London. **(p. 40)**

ARRIVING IN BUFFALO.   Malcolm Mallett states that the O'Neill family "apparently" made "the rest of the trip . . . from Quebec City or Montreal to Buffalo, New York by land." **(p. 40)**

AND EIGHTH WARDS.   *The Making of an American Pluralism, Buffalo, New York, 1825-60*, David A. Gerber, U. of Illinois Press, Urbana and Chicago 1989. **(p. 40)**

WITH THEIR CHILDREN.   NY State Census for Buffalo, 1855 (research by genealogist Ellie Adler Tritchler). **(p. 41)**

OWN DWELLING.   *Second Looks, a Pictorial History of Buffalo and Erie County*, Scott Eberle and Joseph A. Grande, Donning Company, Norfolk, Va. 1987. **(p. 41)**

CHILDREN TO NINE.   Buffalo census (see earlier ref). She was christened Margaret. **(p. 41)**

DRINK AND VIOLENCE.   *The Making of an American Pluralism* (see earlier ref). **(p. 41)**

TWIN SISTER.   Manley Mallett says: "The death of his son, Dick, probably caused him . . . to think of a last look at his home land." Brian O'Neill suggests that Edward was visited by the Banshee of the O'Neills, sometimes seen as well as heard — a spirit whose appearance foretold a person's death and was regarded as a summons to return home to die. **(p. 41)**

FOR THE FAMILY. According to National Archives, Washington, D.C., Mother's Army Pension, 9/27/1865: Mary O'Neill states her son, Edward "contributed to his mother's support for at least six years dating from about the year 1858." **(p. 42)**

FURNITURE FACTORY Ibid. **(p. 42)**

FOLLOWING YEAR. Edmond's death certificate, the coroner's report and other records pertaining to the case are in the Chief Secretary's Office Registered Papers, National Archives, Dublin. He was listed (once again minus the "O'") as Edmond Neile . **(p. 43)**

JUNE 7, 1862." National Archives, Washington, D.C., Affidavit for Army Pension — Mother's Case, 9/27/1865 (see earlier ref). According to Mallett, family descendants in the United States — ignorant of the inquest — believed Edward died of strychnine, mistaken by his niece for baking soda. **(p. 43)**

GILBERT V. HAMILTON. The document was among papers O'N left behind in the Bermuda home he had shared with his second wife, Agnes Boulton. The papers were either overlooked by the emissary O'N sent to retrieve them during divorce proceedings, or deliberately withheld by Agnes. The document was loaned to Louis Sheaffer, an O'Neill biographer, by Agnes's daughter, Oona O'Neill Chaplin, after Agnes's death in 1968. In a letter from Sheaffer to Oona 9/27/84, he states he has sold the document to a private collector [Dr. Harley J. Hammerman of St. Louis, who provided a copy to A/BG]. **(p. 43)**

SENTENCE OF DEATH. "Shanty Life Along the Sea Wall," Irish Times, Edward Patton June-July 1995. **(p. 43)**

FOOD TO EAT." O'N wrote Lawrence Estavan 1/15/40 (see earlier ref): "My father's parents were extremely poor, from his story. When he was only ten years old he had to start working in a machine shop for fifty cents a week." **(p. 44)**

FIND THIS FUNNY.) "James O'Neill — the Actor and the Man," Theater Magazine, April 1908. **(p. 44)**

KILKENNY'S BOAST." "Personal Reminiscences," Theater Magazine, Dec. 1917. The "college" was actually a Protestant grammar school in Kilkenny City called St. John's College; it later became Kilkenny's County Hall and Arts Promotion Office. **(p. 44)**

FLESHLY PLEASURES. According to Mallett, Josephine "apparently was well-established in the Cincinnati area before her father died and no doubt was instrumental in moving the family from Buffalo." According to the 1860 Census, at least three members of the O'Neill clan were living in Cincinnati: Stasia, now eleven, was listed as living with a married sister, Anne (sometimes Ann, or Anna) Jones (wife of James Jones, a file-maker) and next door to another married sister, Mary (wife of Patrick, a machinist). **(p. 45)**

UNDER HER WING. "My Eighty-four Ancestral Families" (see earlier ref). The name of her last husband was William A. Sears. She lived in Ohio during the last twenty-two years of her life and despite her religious conversion was buried in Toledo's Catholic Cemetery of Calvary, at the insistence of her sister, Anastasia. The date of her age and death are confirmed by an obituary in the Toledo Blade 12/20/33. **(p. 45)**

GALLERY GOD." Theater Magazine, Dec. 1917 (see earlier ref). **(p. 45)**

NOW SIXTEEN. According to Mallett, "If James O'Neill's story of living in Norfolk with a sister is true, only Josephine could have met the description . . . " **(p. 45)**

JULY 18, 1865.   Army Pension Records, National Archives (see earlier ref). **(p. 45)**

EIGHT DOLLARS.   Army Pension Records, National Archives (see earlier ref); affidavit by Captain William Worth, 9/27/1866. O'N had been told about Edward's career by his father. "I remember him saying one brother served in the Civil War — an Ohio regiment I suppose — was wounded, never fully recovered and died right after the war." Letter to Lawrence Estavan 1/15/40 (see earlier ref). **(p. 45)**

I SHOULD DO."   Theater Magazine, April 1908. **(p. 46)**

CHERISHING IT . . . "   Theater Magazine, Dec. 1917. **(p. 46)**

WITHOUT INTEREST."   To A. M. Palmer 5/17/1887, Harvard Theater Collection, Pusey Library. **(p. 46)**

TO REMAIN."   Ibid. **(p. 46)**

WITH HIS MOTHER.   Although James claimed to have made his stage debut in 1867, he had listed his occupation as "actor" a year earlier in the Cincinnati City Directory of 1866, giving his address as 238 East Pearl Street, the same as listed for his mother. His next appearance in the City Directory was 1869, when he and his mother resided at 100 Kilgour Street. **(p. 46)**

FOR THE SCENE.   Theater Magazine Dec. 1917. **(p. 46)**

WITHIN TWO YEARS.   Kilkenny Journal 3/19/1862. **(p. 46)**

GRANDLY SUMMED UP.   *Dion Boucicault* by Richard Fawkes, Quartet Books, London 1979. **(p. 47)**

THE DUMAS NOVEL.   *The Career of Dion Boucicault* by Townsend Walsh, Benjamin Blom, NY 1915. **(p. 47)**

FOOL OF MYSELF."   Unsourced newspaper clipping dated 2/1/04, NY Public Library. In a version James gave in 1911 (evidently wishing to bury his embarrassing breach of theatrical etiquette), he modified this account, claiming the role did require him to speak one line: "My lady, why not take me?" Cincinnati Times Star 10/19/11. And in a still later version he recalled the line as: "Miss Chute, take me." Cleveland Leader 2/22/14. **(p. 47)**

LATER RECALLED.   To A. M. Palmer 5/17/1887 (see earlier ref). **(p. 49)**

THAT BROGUE."   Theater Magazine, Apr. 1908 (see earlier ref). **(p. 49)**

OFFENDING DIALECT.   Ibid. **(p. 49)**

THE FULL EIGHT.   Theater Magazine, Dec. 1917. **(p. 50)**

OLD COMEDIES."   Ibid. **(p. 50)**

I COULD FIND."   Ibid. **(p. 50)**

FOR THE GALLERY.   Cleveland Public Library. **(p. 50)**

BE ABLE TO."   Chicago Chronicle 2/28/1894, "Actors Off The Stage," Eve Brodlique. **(p. 51)**

CHAPTER FOUR

PERSONAL CHARM."   A/BG interviews with Brandon Tynan and Charles Webster. Tynan appeared with James in 1913 in *Joseph and His Brethren*, Webster in the 1912 *Count of Monte Cristo*. **(p. 52)**

MEN IN VICE."   *Prince of Players* by Eleanor Ruggles, W. W. Norton, NY 1953. **(p. 53)**

GAVE UP DRINKING.   Ibid; and "The Romance of Mary Devlin Booth," Anne M.

Fauntleroy, Ladies Home Journal, Sept. 1904. **(p. 53)**

HEREIN MENTIONED."   James O'N scrapbook, Beinecke. While the letter is signed by J. A. Butler of 1128 Michigan Ave., the article is undated & unsourced. Booth and James O'Neill appeared together in *Macbeth* early March 1873. **(p. 54)**

EXQUISITELY COMBINED."   Theater Arts, "Greatest of Juliets," Albert E. Johnson, Aug. 1957. **(p. 54)**

BACKSTAGE JEALOUSIES.   Ibid. **(p. 54)**

BACK TO LIFE."   "How Miss Neilson Raised the Dead" by James O'Neill. Unsourced, undated. Locke. **(p. 55)**

ADMIRABLE TASTE."   Chicago Tribune 4/8/1873, 4/9/1873. **(p. 55)**

DID NOT DO."   To A. M. Palmer, 5/17/1887 (see earlier ref). **(p. 55)**

INTO HIS ARMS."   A/BG interview with Brandon Tynan, who said this was a widely circulated anecdote among actors. Neilson's comment about James as the best Romeo is also cited in Chicago Chronicle 2/21/1887 & Chicago Tribune "Theater Notes" 11/2/02. **(p. 55)**

AN EGOTIST."   James O'N scrapbooks, Beinecke, unsourced article 1873. In letter to the editor of the Chicago Tribune (undated but probably the same year) a John McLandburgh echoed these sentiments, cautioning that James could achieve greatness only by "hard, unceasing, cheerful toil." **(p. 55)**

"WORK, WORK, WORK!"   Chicago Times Herald 2/21/1897. **(p. 56)**

IN THE COUNTRY."   7/27/1873. **(p. 56)**

NEW YORK THEATER.   It was leased by a series of managers who presented the sort of trashy Gallic melodramas Booth despised. **(p. 56)**

HAD A MARRIAGE.   His wife died at 31, 11/13/1881 — Booth's 48th birthday — and Booth, though seemingly always stoical in the face of disaster, eventually turned morbid, as illustrated by a letter he wrote in 1885, eight years before his death. It was meant as a condolence to his friend, the critic William Winter, who had just lost his son; in it Booth recalled the loss of his first wife, Mary Devlin:

" . . . I thank God for her early death, — which spared her the sufferings she would have endured, in the misfortunes that so frequently have befallen me.

"I cannot grieve at death. It seems to be the greatest boon the Almighty has granted us. Consequently, I cannot appreciate the grief of those who mourn the loss of loved ones, particularly if they go early from the hell of misery to which we have been doomed.

"Why do not you look at this miserable little life, with all its ups and downs, as I do? At the very worst, 'tis but a scratch, a temporary ill, to be soon cured by that dear old doctor, Death . . . " *Prince of Players* (see earlier ref). **(p. 56)**

MET IN LIFE."   A/BG interview with Brandon Tynan; as told to him by James O'N. **(p. 56)**

BOOTH BOIL."   NY Dramatic Mirror 6/24/1899. **(p. 56)**

MY CAREER."   Chicago Tribune 3/7/1874 described a performance in which James alternated with Booth in *Othello*. **(p. 57)**

HUNDRED WOUNDED.   *Astor Place Riot* by Richard Moody, Indiana U. Press, Bloomington 1958. **(p. 57)**

PLAY IAGO."   Boston Transcript 1/12/1900. **(p. 57)**

LAST REHEARSAL."   Ibid. **(p. 58)**

NOT NEED IT."   Ibid. **(p. 59)**

OF HIS ADVICE."   Ibid. **(p. 59)**

THE SCENE."   Chicago Tribune 3/7/1874. **(p. 60)**

KINDLY TO ME." Chicago Chronicle "Actors Off The Stage," Eve Brodlique 2/28/1894. **(p. 60)**

OF THE WORLD." Divorce petition by "Nettie O'Neill," Superior Court Chicago 9/7/1877. **(p. 60)**

WERE TYPICAL. To A. M. Palmer 5/17/1887 (see earlier ref). **(p. 61)**

INSTANTLY KILLED. Various Chicago newspapers including the Tribune 6/29/1876. **(p. 62)**

CHAPTER FIVE

STELLAR EMINENCE." NY Public Library Theater Collection clipping file, undated. **(p. 65)**

PAMPERED DAUGHTERS. A/BG inteviews with CMO about O'N family history. **(p. 67)**

POTENTIAL HAZARDS. Ibid; also A/BG interviews with Brennan and Sheridan families. **(p. 67)**

DAUGHTER'S TROUSSEAU; Cleveland Probate Court disbursement records of Thomas Quinlan estate; reports were by Bridget's brother-in-law John Brennan, administrator, and by Bridget from 1876 to 1884, when Bridget rendered final accounting. **(p. 67)**

CATHOLIC WEDDINGS. "St. Ann's On East Twelfth Street New York City 1852-1952" by Henry J. Brown, published by St. Ann's 1952. The old St. Ann's, further downtown on no-longer-fashionable Eighth Street, became a variety house. **(p. 67)**

IN CLEVELAND. His store was at 465 Detroit Ave, Cleveland City Directory. **(p. 68)**

A YEAR LATER. James purchased her grave site at St. Joseph's Cemetery, Cincinnati: Interment Record 8/16/1878. **(p. 68)**

ONCE COMPLAINED. Manley Mallett (see earlier ref). **(p. 68)**

THE EVENT." 6/30/1877. **(p. 68)**

STRINDBERG'S MUMMY. A/BG interviews with SC. **(p. 71)**

SEA-MOTHER'S SON. O'Neill Work Diary 3/8/27 (bibliog). **(p. 72)**

MOTHER DEATH." Ibid. Entries 10/6/28 – 7/23/31. **(p. 72)**

THE MOUNTAINS, San Francisco Evening Post 6/30/1877. **(p. 73)**

IN GENERAL" To AHQ 6/13/22, SL. **(p. 73)**

DRESSER DRAWERS. Research by Marian McCandless (see earlier ref). **(p. 74)**

O'NEILL'S TALENT. Ritchie's niece, Marion McCandless (see earlier ref) wrote to A/BG 4/28/58: "George Jean Nathan's mother, Ella Nirdlinger ex-75 of Fort Wayne, Indiana, was also a member of this class of 1875 here. She did not remain to graduate, however." **(p. 74)**

SUITABLE ALIMONY. NYT 9/8/1877. Also records of Circuit Court Chicago. **(p. 75)**

FIRST TO LAST." Ibid. **(p. 75)**

CHOKED VOICE. Chicago Tribune 9/8/1877. **(p. 76)**

HE QUIPPED. Chicago Tribune 9/9/1877. **(p. 76)**

THE PRESENT." Chicago Tribune 9/16/1877. **(p. 76)**

HIS PATERNITY. Ibid. **(p. 76)**

A HUSBAND." Ibid. **(p. 76)**

SEAMAN'S CHILD).   Alexander I (bibliog). **(p. 77)**

HONORABLE WAY."   Chicago Tribune 9/16/1877. **(p. 77)**

OR IN FACT."   Ibid. **(p. 77)**

LAWRENCE BARRETT.   The tradition of never missing a performance was carried to its extreme by Barrett himself; a few years later, ill with pneumonia, he honored a commitment to perform with Edwin Booth. During the third act, he whispered to Booth that he could not continue and the curtain was rung down. He died two days later. *Darling of Misfortune* by Richard Lockridge, The Century Co., NY 1932. **(p. 77)**

IN CHICAGO.   Chicago Inter-Ocean 10/24/1877. Also records of Circuit Court Chicago. **(p. 77)**

FURTHER ARGUMENT.   Ibid. **(p. 78)**

FOR HER SUPPORT.   Ibid. **(p. 78)**

WAS DISMISSED.   Chicago Circuit Court record (#25927-1263), 12/6/1877. **(p. 78)**

WOMAN, HONEY?   Chicago News, Amy Leslie, 7/10/09. **(p. 78)**

CHAPTER SIX

YEARS EARLIER.   Unsourced clipping, NY Public Library Theater Collection. **(p. 79)**

HIS ARRIVAL.   The Argonaut 3/2/1878. **(p. 79)**

HIS INVESTMENTS.   To A. M. Palmer 5/17/1887 (see earlier ref). **(p. 80)**

FELLOW BACK . . . "   From GCT to O'N 12/13/20. **(p. 80)**

RUIN HIM."   To Lawrence Estavan 1/15/40, SL. **(p. 80)**

"WILD WEST" SHOW.   *Fifty Years in Theatrical Management 1859-1909* by M. B. Leavitt, Broadway Publishing Co., NY 1912. **(p. 80)**

YIELDING DIVIDENDS.   Letter from O'N to Milton Salsbury (Nate Salsbury's son) 5/17/1922, SL. **(p. 80)**

LONG AGO!"   To O'N Jr. 1932 (probably Jan. 8), SL. **(p. 81)**

HIS ASSISTANCE."   San Francisco Chronicle 8/3/1879. **(p. 81)**

SEPTEMBER 10, 1878.   O'N to Lawrence Estavan 1/15/40, SL. **(p. 81)**

NINA VARIAN.   Argonaut 4/27/1879. **(p. 82)**

DAVID BELASCO.   Timberlake (bibliog); also "Six Decades of Belasco Stage Magic," Montrose J. Moses, Theater Guild Magazine, Nov. 1929. **(p. 82)**

OPERA HOUSE.   Background of James in *The Passion* from "History of the San Francisco Theater," Vol. XX, James O'Neill; also Winter (bibliog); and Boston Sunday Journal 9/16/1900. **(p. 82)**

A MONASTERY.   "History of the San Francisco Theater," Vol. XX; and Winter (bibliog). **(p. 83)**

WOULD KILL ME."   Dramatic Mirror 10/27/1880. **(p. 84)**

JEWISH–OWNED ESTABLISHMENTS.   "History of the San Francisco Theater," Vol. XX; and William Winter (bibliog). **(p. 84)**

TO PROSECUTION.   Theater Magazine, April 1908. **(p. 84)**

DEGRADE RELIGION."   Timberlake (bibliog). **(p. 84)**

THEIR NOSES."   San Francisco Newsletter 4/19/1879. **(p. 85)**

DOLLARS EACH. "History of the San Francisco Theater" Vol. XX; and Winter (bibliog). (p. 85)

LATER REMARKED. Letter to A. M. Palmer 5/17/1887. (p. 85)

THE CHARACTER." Timberlake (bibliog). (p. 85)

PART IN IT." *Between Actor and Critic*, Selected Letters of Edwin Booth and William Winter, Princeton U. Press, NJ 1971. (p. 86)

WITHDRAWING THE PLAY, *Annals of the New York Stage*, George C. D. Odell, Vol XI, 1879-1882, Columbia U. Press NY, 1939. (p. 86)

AS AN ACTOR." Theater Magazine, Dec. 1917. Salmi Morse drowned in the Hudson River some years later, an apparent suicide. (p. 86)

JAMES'S REPERTOIRE, *Annals of the New York Stage* (see earlier ref). (p. 86)

WELL–RECEIVED. Adapted from a French melodrama by Adolphe D'Ennery and Eugene Cormon, the story concerns a soldier imprisoned on trumped-up murder charges, whose daughter, when she grows up, proves his innocence. (p. 86)

BOOTH'S THEATER. Robins diaries and letters, Fales. (p. 86)

TO WATCH THEM." 7/10/1882, Fales. (p. 87)

ESTABLISHED REPUTATION." Fales. (p. 87)

FOOTHOLD THERE." 11/29/1881, Fales. (p. 87)

HIS KINDNESS." 3/23/1882, Fales. (p. 88)

HER DIARY. 7/10/1882, Fales. (p. 88)

BAD TOBACCO." Diary 10/28/1882, Fales. (p. 89)

TOGETHER & TALK . . . " Diary 7/15/1882, Fales. (p. 90)

AN AMERICAN KING. In letter to A. M. Palmer 5/17/1887 James forgetfully called the play *The American King* and attributed its authorship to one "Con. Murphy." (p. 90)

OF THE YEAR. Dazey wrote his only successful play, *In Old Kentucky*, some years later. (p. 90)

THE CHANCE." To her father, C. E. Robins 11/9/1882, Fales. (p. 91)

AND JUST MAN." Ibid. (p. 91)

JAMES O'NEILL INSTEAD. Details of Thorne's illness and death, NYT obit 2/11/1883. (p. 91)

THAN HIS AGE.) Letter to her grandmother 6/18/1882, Fales. (p. 91)

PASSION OR MAGNETISM." 1/12/1883. (p. 92)

SOMEWHAT MAGNETIC." 1/12/1883. (p. 92)

THE PLAY." Theater Magazine, April 1908. (p. 93)

MONTE CRISTO. Robins diary 3/7/1883, Fales. (p. 93)

ASTUTE DEALS. Pittsburgh Gazette 2/13/10. (p. 94)

FORTY–NINTH STREET. Register of births, NYC Dept. of Records and Information Services Municipal Archives. James, about to turn 38, gave his age as thirty-four; Ella, 26, gave hers as 23. O'N inexplicably gave his brother's birthplace as St. Louis when writing to Lawrence Estavan 1/15/40, *SL*. This error has been perpetuated by a number of O'N scholars. (p. 94)

HIS FATHER. Some of James's friends, unaware of Edmund's middle name, assumed he had been named for Edmond Dantes. (p. 94)

3 WKS OLD." Letter to her grandmother 10/9/1883, Fales. (p. 94)

SOME TIME. San Francisco News Letter 6/28/1884. (p. 95)

CHAPTER SEVEN

JOHN BRENNAN. After John's death Elizabeth continued in New London until her death at 79; NL City Hall records 12/29/1890. **(p. 96)**

LONDON DAY. A/BG interviews with Morgan McGinley, editorial page editor of the Day and grandson of John McGinley. **(p. 97)**

SECTION OF TOWN. Research by Sally Pavetti and Lois MacDonald, curators of restored Monte Cristo Cottage. **(p. 97)**

AND A BARN. Deed to property 8/16/1884 was in Ella's name; seller was Gurdon A. Lester, a grocer. City Hall Transfer of Property Records, Volume #74. **(p. 98)**

DWELLING ON PEQUOT. Thomas Dorsey, local broker who had extensive real estate dealings with James, told A/BG it was built 1705. **(p. 98)**

FOLLOWING SUMMER: A/BG interview with Thomas Dorsey. **(p. 98)**

FOR MARCH 1, Denver Times 3/2/1885. **(p. 99)**

NEW YORK ALONE. Rocky Mountain News 3/5/1885. **(p. 100)**

EDMUND DIED. Death certificate NY City Dept. of Records Municipal Archives states Edmund was attended from 2/27/1885 to 3/3/85 by Dr. J. E. Stillwell, 150 E. 21st St. Cause of death was "Measles; Laryngitis." Dr. Stillwell stated last time he "saw him alive" was March 3. **(p. 100)**

HARD ONE. Denver Republican 3/5/1885. **(p. 100)**

VILLAINOUS A LIGHT. Act IV draft, Beinecke. **(p. 100)**

VIA DOPE." Notes, Beinecke. **(p. 101)**

ME LEAVE HIM!" Handwritten early draft of *LDJ* Act III, Beinecke. **(p. 101)**

SO HORRIBLE — : Act V handwritten scenario, Beinecke. **(p. 101)**

AS A GIRL. O'N's self-analytical document (see earlier ref). **(p. 102)**

SOUTH BEND, INDIANA, *School Days at Notre Dame* Vol. IV, Charles Warren Stoddard, 1936 U. of Notre Dame Archives; also E O'N Review, Vol. 15 #2 & Vol. 16 #2, articles by Edward L. Shaughnessy. **(p. 102)**

DECEMBER 7, 1885. Day Book, Hesburgh Memorial Library Archives, U. of Notre Dame. **(p. 102)**

COMPLETE MODERNIZATION. NL Day 4/16/10; "'News of New London 25 Years Ago,' (4/16/1885)." Architects were Gove & Strickland. **(p. 102)**

THE THAMES. A/BG interviews with PS and Alma Weiss, who sometimes led tours of Pequot area. The Pequot House was destroyed by fire 1908. **(p. 103)**

THEIR CARRIAGES. Notes about Pequot Avenue in early 1900's by Frances E. Hubbard, July 1969, Beinecke. **(p. 103)**

MONTGOMERY, ALABAMA: Fales. **(p. 103)**

TO COLUMBUS. Probably Columbus, Ga. **(p. 103)**

BETTER ADVANTAGE." Undated letter from Grace Raven to ER, Fales. **(p. 103)**

JUNE 9. NL Day 5/31/1887. James rented house to Chicago Judge Egbert Jameson. **(p. 104)**

THREE YEARS. Death Certificate 5/12/58, Office of City Clerk New London. **(p. 104)**

RELATIVES. A/BG interviews with Brennan family. Bridget's will left Ella and her brother William several parcels of land in Cleveland; NL Probate Court 7/11/1887. **(p. 104)**

BECOME A NUN). Letter from O'N to Sister Mary Leo 2/6/25, *SL*. Raven began her stage career as "Nita Sin" but her real name was Grace Middleton. **(p. 104)**

HAVE EVER MET." 11/14/1886, Fales. **(p. 104)**

SAD AND ILL."   8/24/1887, Fales. **(p. 104)**

DISTRICT SCHOOLHOUSE.   Property was bought from Michael and Susan Moriarity, City Hall Deed Records, Volumes #72 and #78. Research by Pavetti and McDonald (see earlier ref). Also NL Day, 3/15/1887. The 1840 date was estimated by Edgar de N. Mayhew, an expert on American furniture and interiors. **(p. 105)**

REMODEL IT,   NL Day 3/15/1887. **(p. 105)**

SEPTEMBER 5, 1887.   NL Day 8/27/1887. **(p. 105)**

TRIP ABROAD."   Fales. **(p. 105)**

BETTER ABILITIES."   San Francisco News Letter 12/31/1887. **(p. 105)**

AFFECTION FOR."   A rare reference to Ella's brother, William Quinlan; none of the family's descendants interviewed by A/BG were aware Ella had a brother. **(p. 106)**

CHAPTER EIGHT

A DAUGHTER!"   A/BG interview with Claire Brennan Sherman. **(p. 111)**

THREE BOYS."   Boulton (bibliog). **(p. 111)**

OATS AND HAY.   NYT 5/19/1890. **(p. 112)**

MME. MODJESKA.   NYT 2/28/1888. **(p. 113)**

MASSACHUSETTS.   Dramatic Mirror 10/27/1888. **(p. 113)**

TOO MUCH PAIN"   "Gen[eral] notes" for what he was then calling "*N.L. play*" — "*A Long Day's Journey,*" Beinecke. **(p. 113)**

BE PROUD OF."   Line reads: "It is too bad Edmund could not have lived and we might have had one son we could be proud of." Scenario, Act IV, Beinecke. **(p. 114)**

PLACE," SHE SAYS.   Actual lines read: "I loved you so much because you were you and you were Eugene, too . . . I wanted you to take his place." Typescript, Act 3, Beinecke. **(p. 114)**

BREAST–FED HIM.   As an infant O'N must have imbibed a certain amount of morphine-laced medication with his mother's milk, but whether this had any lasting effect is a matter of medical conjecture; there is no evidence that the obsessively self-analytical O'N himself ever considered this a significant possibility. **(p. 115)**

GOOD LOOKING . . ."   " Letter dated "Sunday." Beinecke. **(p. 115)**

EASE HER PAINS.   A/BG interviews with CMO, to whom O'N gave repeated accounts of his birth. **(p. 116)**

AFFAIR IN 1926.   12/10/26, SL. **(p. 116)**

I POSSESS."   Letter to Lawrence Estavan 1/15/40, *SL*. **(p. 117)**

OUT TO ME."   NY World, Flora Merrill 7/19/25. **(p. 117)**

LOOK AROUND.   A/BG interview with JL. **(p. 117)**

WAS BORN.   PM, John S. Wilson 9/3/46. **(p. 117)**

FROM THE CITY.   AP, Mark Barron 10/13/46. (A 33-story office building was erected on the site in 1972, nineteen years after O'N's death.) **(p. 117)**

BECOME BROADWAY."   NYT Magazine, S. J. Woolf 9/15/46. **(p. 117)**

WAS LATE."   To Charles O'Brien Kennedy 12/6/48, *SL*. Kennedy directed O'N's *Diff'rent.* **(p. 117)**

RED–HANDED O'NEILLS."   Letter to AHQ 4/3/25, *SL.* **(p. 118)**

IRELAND AS EUGENE.   When Owen Roe's forces arrived in Kilkenny in 1642, Papal Nuncio John Baptist Rinuccini referred to Owen Roe O'Neill as "Eugenius O'Nellus." (In Greek "Eugene" means "well-born.") **(p. 118)**

NIALL'S HAIR.   *A Treasury of Irish Folklore* by Padraic Colum, Crown Publishers, NY 1954; and A/BG correspondence with Colum. It was with Owen Roe's forces the O'Neill clan arrived in Kilkenny in 1642 to prepare for battle with English parliamentarians. *A Dictionary of Irish Biography* by Henry Boylan, Gill and Macmillan Ltd., Dublin 1988. **(p. 118)**

HAVE OVERLOOKED."   PM, Croswell Bowen 11/3/46. **(p. 118)**

GAVE IT UP.   Boston Globe, Charles A. Merrill 7/8/23. **(p. 118)**

GAELIC CHIEFTAINS.   Mercer Press, Cork & Dublin 1942. **(p. 119)**

PLAY ABOUT HIM."   7/28/43, *SL.* **(p. 119)**

FAITH HAS LAPSED.   A/BG interviews with numerous American-Irish who claim they fit the description "Black Irishman." **(p. 119)**

"ACTOR'S CHURCH."   Holy Innocence Church was built 1870. Its baptismal register, Entry 137, lists the patrons (godparents) as John O'Neil and Annie Connor. **(p. 119)**

BEAUTIFUL BABY."   Quoted in NY Tribune 5/26/18. **(p. 120)**

"FIRST PUBLICITY."   After his death CMO gave clipping to Museum of the City of NY with note dated 4/18/54: "It was his first publicity." (There had, in fact, been several earlier newspaper mentions of his birth.) **(p. 120)**

PROFICIENCY IN STUDY."   Scholastic Magazine, Notre Dame U. Archives 5/7/1887. **(p. 120)**

SCHOOL MAGAZINE.   "To Rev. President Walsh," Hesburgh Memorial Library, Notre Dame U. 12/20/1890. **(p. 120)**

BASEBALL TEAM.   Ibid. **(p. 121)**

JAMES DECLARED,   Tyler (bibliog). **(p. 121)**

SERIOUS THAN COLIC.   Ibid. **(p. 121)**

JOURNEY INTO NIGHT.   A/BG interview with Claire Brennan Sherman. Story confirmed by CMO, who heard it many times from O'N. **(p. 122)**

"YOU MIGHT," HE SAID.   New Republic 4/7/58. **(p. 123)**

DRESSING ROOMS."   NY Daily News, Fred Pasley 1/25/32. **(p. 123)**

MARVELOUS THING."   A/BG interview with JJM, O'N barroom crony during Provincetown Players days. **(p. 123)**

WITH A RESPITE.   NY Public Library Theater Collection. **(p. 123)**

OF THE INDIAN.   Typewritten notes by ESS 8/3/46, Beinecke. O'N in his self-analytical document wrote he was two years old when he had typhoid fever but ESS notes say he was three. **(p. 124)**

AMERICAN HISTORY.   PM, Croswell Bowen 11/3/46. **(p. 124)**

INDIANS AND BLONDES."   Ibid **(p. 124)**

SOON AFTER "WEANING."   Some scholars have read the word "weaning" as "meaning." A printed transcription of the original chart created for an exhibition at Yale U., 1988, (labeled "Diagram Showing Family") renders the word as "weaning." A/BG have examined the original document at Beinecke and believe the word is "weaning." **(p. 125)**

THEM TO AMERICA.   A/BG interview with ESS and LS Collection, Conn. College. Additional information in letter from Gertrude Mahoney Shea to BA 2/29/56.

Ms. Shea wrote that Sandy recently was employed as nurse to her father, Cornelius A. Mahoney, who lived in the Barrett House until his death in 1888. Ms. Shea's mother knew Ella O'Neill and "agreed to let her have the nurse Sarah Sandy for the infant Eugene O'Neill." Sandy "was devoted to my mother and for the next 30 years used to visit her occasionally." **(p. 125)**

OF THOSE PLACES . . ."   To Shane O'Neill, late Sept. 1928, *SL*. **(p. 126)**

PARK IN MEMPHIS.   NY Daily News, Fred Pasley 1/24/32. **(p. 126)**

OF HIS MOUTH.   Beinecke. **(p. 126)**

UNBELONGING AS EUGENE.   A/BG interview with ESS. **(p. 126)**

MOMENT'S NOTICE.   Letter from Gertrude Shea to BA 2/29/56 (see earlier ref). **(p. 127)**

VIRTUOUS OR VILE."   NY Times Magazine, S. J. Woolf 10/4/31. **(p. 128)**

CIRCLING SEA GULLS.   When presenting picture to the Beinecke, O'N wrote on its back: "1893 or '94, probably — not addicted to drama then . . . " **(p. 128)**

INCLUDING MEASLES   Gaylord Farm Sanatorium medical records, 1913. **(p. 128)**

OFTEN PALE.   Ibid **(p. 128)**

EXASPERATE ME."   Letter to CMO 1/23/27, *SL*. **(p. 128)**

CHAPTER NINE

EXCITED CHATTER.   Details of James Jr.'s discovery of mother's drug addiction recounted to A/BG by CMO. **(p. 129)**

ELLA'S AFFLICTION.   Ibid. **(p. 129)**

AFTERNOON OFF.   Locke. **(p. 130)**

FRIEND, JAMES O'NEILL."   Notre Dame U. Archives. **(p. 131)**

THAT JANUARY.   Ibid. **(p. 131)**

OF HIS INTENT."   *Macbeth*, Act I, Scene VII, line 25: "I have no spur/To prick the sides of my intent, but only/Vaulting ambition, which o'erleaps itself/And falls on th' other —" **(p. 131)**

TIMES FOR COAL).   The train, however, departed almost every hour; the NY-D.C. corridor was even then one of the busiest in the country. *Travelers Official Guide of the Railways Steam and Navigation Lines in the United States and Canada* June, 1893 edition. And the Museum of the City of NY. **(p. 132)**

AT GEORGETOWN."   Notre Dame U. Archives. **(p. 132)**

JAMES HENRY O'NEILL.   Research by Jon Reynolds, Georgetown U. archivist, from Rector's Entrance Registry 1850–1900; he registered from 134 Pequot Avenue, NL Conn. and gave his winter address as Barrett House. **(p. 132)**

"POCKET MONEY."   Ibid. **(p. 132)**

CLASSICS 50.   Georgetown U. Archives: ledger labeled "Marks" 1888–1908. **(p. 133)**

"TRIP TO ATLANTA."   Ibid. **(p. 133)**

ATTACHMENT IN LIFE."   Letter from Gertrude Shea to BA 2/29/56 (see earlier ref). **(p. 134)**

BE SENT AWAY.   A/BG interviews with CMO and ESS. **(p. 134)**

NEW SEASON.   Letter from O'N to Lawrence Estavan 1/15/40, *SL*. **(p. 134)**

DRILY REPLIED.   Anecdote circulated in NL and related to A/BG by AMcG, EK and

JG (local friends of O'N). **(p. 135)**

AS DISASTROUS." Sergeant (bibliog). O'N, often displeased with articles about him, was impressed by ESS's sensitive grasp of the early influences on his character. Soon after meeting her, he confided the history of his mother's morphine addiction, bestowed on very few intimates. In A/BG interview with ESS, she said she was revealing this confidence only in view of the posthumous publication of *LDJIN*. **(p. 135)**

ANYONE ELSE!" Boulton (bibliog). **(p. 136)**

JAMES H. O'NEILL. St. John's catalogue, Fordham U. Archives, Duane Library. **(p. 136)**

DEBATER. Ibid. **(p. 136)**

THE ESTATE FONTHILL. "The Man and his Castle," the Fonthill Dial, College of Mount St. Vincent, Fall 1951 Vol. XXXV No.1. **(p. 137)**

HEART–MELTING SMILE. Research conducted for A/BG by Mother Mary Fuller and Sister Marie Jeanette, College of Mt. St. Vincent, 1957. **(p. 137)**

JOSEPHINE BRENNAN. A/BG interviews with PS and Claire Brennan Sherman. **(p. 137)**

SPEAK TO JOSEPHINE. Ibid. **(p. 137)**

HER NINETIES. Congratulating her on her 91st birthday O'N wrote to her daughter, Agnes Brennan: "I always remember with deep gratitude how kind she used to be to me when I was a boy and how I used to look forward to her visits at Pequot Avenue." 4/14/31, *SL*. **(p. 137)**

MCCARTHY IN 1930.) 9/2/30, *SL*. **(p. 139)**

OVER AGAIN!" Letter from CMO to Donald Gallup 7/24/54, *What Mad Pursuits* by Gallup, Beinecke Rare Book & Manuscript Library, Yale U., 1998. **(p. 139)**

DUELING SCENES. A/BG interview with Philbin. **(p. 140)**

REDEMPTION TAKES PLACE." O'N explaining *The Iceman Cometh* to cast during rehearsal late Sept. 1946: quoted in Bowen (bibliog). **(p. 140)**

FROM THEMSELVES." John Loving in *Days Without End*. **(p. 141)**

WOODEN BRIDGES. An artificial lake, Lake Marian, was in fact built on St. Mary's campus in 1907; in 1953 a statue (Our Lady of Fatima) was erected there. McCandless research (see earlier ref). **(p. 141)**

AND KIPLING." Sergeant (bibliog). In *A Touch of the Poet* (written 1935-1942), Cornelius Melody, modeled partly on James O'N, quotes "Childe Harold" at length. **(p. 142)**

CHAPTER TEN

JAMES O'NEILL." Chicago Circuit Court archives. **(p. 143)**

RESOLVED IN 1900. Ibid. **(p. 144)**

MANUFACTURER'S AGENT.) Chicago Directory, 1906. Alfred Hamilton O'N made one further appearance in the O'N's lives. In June, 1922, not quite two years after James's death, a Chicago lawyer wrote Eugene demanding to know why Alfred, as the "son of James O'Neill, Sr. by his first wife" was not listed in papers filed in the Surrogate Court of NL as an heir to James O'N's property. Evidently receiving no answer, the lawyer wrote again August 23 saying "your half brother, Mr. A. H. O'Neill is anxious to hear from you to know when you are going to notify all the heirs of your father's estate of the disposition to be made of the real estate which he owned, or the proceeds thereof." No record exists in the Court indicating Alfred obtained any share of the estate. **(p. 144)**

CRIME WAS DISCOVERED. A/BG interviews with AMcG, EK and PS. **(p. 144)**

FORDHAM MONTHLY.) Duane Library, Fordham U. Research by Father T. Gerard Connolly. **(p. 144)**

DEGENERATE PALATES." Fordham Monthly, Dec. 1898, signed "Thiman Ina Hurry" a mocking pseudonym used by Jamie as disclosed in the Monthly's issue of Feb. 1899. Duane Library, Fordham U. **(p. 145)**

JAMES H. O'NEILL. Ibid. **(p. 145)**

TEAM MEMBER. A/BG interviews with AMcG and PS (story told them by Jamie). **(p. 145)**

RECORD STATED. Fordham U. records. **(p. 146)**

LAW SCHOOL. Ibid. **(p. 146)**

MOUNT ST. VINCENT, Boy students were kept only until twelve. **(p. 146)**

MAY 24, 1899. Sister Marie Jeanette research (see earlier ref). **(p. 147)**

FELLOW?" SHE ASKED. A/BG visit, 1957. **(p. 147)**

HALF MILLION. Lower East Side Tenement Museum. **(p. 147)**

LUMBER COMPANY. A/BG interviews with AMcG. **(p. 147)**

A GREAT JOKE!" To Shane O'N, late September 1928, SL. **(p. 148)**

DUMAS NOVEL. A/BG interview with David Perkins, actor in *The Musketeers*. **(p. 148)**

HORSE–PLAY." Dramatic Mirror 5/23/1891. **(p. 148)**

WAYS OF GENIUS. A/BG interview with BA. **(p. 150)**

FOR THE THEATER." Boston Sunday Globe, Charles A. Merrill 7/8/23. **(p. 150)**

NOW AND THEN." AP Newsfeatures "Dramatist is Home to Stay," Mark Barron 10/13/46. **(p. 150)**

OF THE ERA. Information about Liebler and Tyler supplied by Liebler's son, Theodore Liebler Jr; also Tyler (bibliog). **(p. 150)**

INTO EXISTENCE. Ibid. **(p. 151)**

WITHOUT FINANCIAL RISK. Ibid. **(p. 151)**

SEVERE COLD. Locke. **(p. 151)**

HE EXPLAINED. Chicago Chronicle 2/28/1897. **(p. 152)**

SIX MONTHS EARLIER. NY Dramatic Mirror 6/24/1899. **(p. 153)**

OF THEIR BIRTH." Ibid. **(p. 154)**

FOR ANY PRODUCTION." Tyler (bibliog). **(p. 154)**

JUST GIVEN HIM." Several newspapers described the railway as coal-burning and large enough for Eugene and a companion to sit in and drive about on track laid out on the grounds of his house — obviously an exaggeration concocted by a press agent. **(p. 154)**

MRS. O'NEILL'S MEMORY." Letter from Theodore Liebler Jr. to A/BG, 4/13/57; and follow-up interviews with Liebler. **(p. 155)**

CHAPTER ELEVEN

(AT 134 PEQUOT AVENUE). A/BG interview with Thomas Dorsey. **(p. 159)**

MONTE CRISTO COTTAGE. The misconception was discovered when a new search of

Jamie's and Eugene's still-surviving school records revealed that they gave their home address in 1894 as Number 134 Pequot Avenue (the address of the Pink House). That the O'N's were living at that address was then confirmed by a search of the NL City Directory by curators of Monte Cristo Cottage. The Directory listed James O'N as residing at that address during various years from 1887 until 1900. **(p. 159)**

PEQUOT AVENUE.   Monte Cristo Cottage archives. **(p. 159)**

LEAN–TO KITCHEN.   Ibid. **(p. 160)**

FOURTH BEDROOM.   Ibid. **(p. 161)**

FATHER'S PIANO.   Ibid. **(p. 161)**

"IT IS IN HER."   In the note (2/22/40) under the heading, "Weather Progression," O'N tracks the fog's increasing density through the action of the play. **(p. 161)**

MONTE CRISTO COTTAGE.   Boston Sunday Journal 9/2/1900. **(p. 161)**

THREE TOGETHER.   Only two prints (in slightly different poses) survive. Beinecke and Locke. **(p. 162)**

HER FRIENDS.   Beinecke. **(p. 162)**

HAVE ONLY ONE."   O'N to Katherine M. Black, a San Francisco friend of James and Ella, 6/21/31. In a second letter 7/14/31, O'N mentions that his father's trunk, "in which he kept all his photos was lost (or stolen!) a year or so before his death." LS collection, Conn. College. **(p. 162)**

DAY'S STANDARDS).   A/BG interview with David A. Perkins. **(p. 163)**

SIXTH AVENUE.   "M/M James O'Neill" are listed at this address (with five other residents) in the 1901 edition of Phillip's Elite Directory, NY Historical Society Library. The address is also listed as the O'N residence in De La Salle record book for 1900. The building no longer exists. **(p. 163)**

RUINED THE SCENE.   Boston Herald 5/16/09. **(p. 163)**

BROTHER BACKSTAGE.   A/BG interview with Theodore Liebler Jr. **(p. 163)**

CENTRAL PARK.   *The Christian Brothers in the United States, 1848-1948* by Brother Angelus Gabriel, McMullen, 1948. (The Christian Brothers eventually sold the site to the Barbizon Plaza Hotel.) **(p. 164)**

PROFESSIONAL PARENTS,   De La Salle archives and Mahattan College archives; and *The Christian Brothers in the United States* (see earlier ref). **(p. 164)**

NEARLY FIFTEEN.   A/BG interviews with CMO. **(p. 165)**

CONSISTENTLY RESISTED.   De La Salle archives, Individual Student Averages 1901-1902. **(p. 166)**

MERRY BIRDS."   Program, "An Evening with the Senior Students of De La Salle Institute, Institute Hall, Thursday Evening, March 21, 1901." **(p. 166)**

SO PROMPTLY.   O'N to Katherine M. Black 6/21/31, LS collection, Conn. College. **(p. 167)**

COFF MEDICINE."   Fall 1901, *SL*. **(p. 167)**

EXTREMELY WELL TOO."   Unsourced newspaper clipping, Locke. **(p. 167)**

WAS THE STAGE."   Unsourced newspaper clipping 11/9/01, NY Public Library Theater Collection. **(p. 168)**

SIR HENRY."   NY Herald 10/30/01. **(p. 168)**

TO THE FAITH."   NY Daily News, Fred Pasley 1/25/32. **(p. 168)**

MACHINE SHOP.   A/BG interview with ESS. **(p. 169)**

CHAPTER TWELVE

OF REDEMPTION."   Sergeant (bibliog). **(p. 170)**

AND RESEARCH."   Stamford Historical Society. Many details about the academy and its headmaster, William Betts, were provided by his daughter, Charlotte E. Betts, in interviews with A/BG. **(p. 170)**

WELL–SYSTEMATIZED NOTEBOOKS."   Stamford Historical Society (see earler ref). **(p. 170)**

FIVE HUNDRED DOLLARS.   Ibid; and A/BG interview with Arthur G. Walter, Betts instructor. **(p. 171)**

TOP COLLEGE."   A/BG interview with O'N schoolmate Howard Mortimer Green. **(p. 171)**

FELLOW STUDENTS."   To O'N Jr. 7/9/44 SL. **(p. 171)**

FIT TO IMPOSE.   A/BG interview with Walter (see earlier ref). **(p. 172)**

HEADMASTER'S BED.   O'N confessed this prank in a letter to William Betts 6/7/23, Charlotte E. Betts Collection. **(p. 172)**

WAS FLATTERED.   A/BG interview with Howard Mortimer Green (see earlier ref). **(p. 172)**

FOOTBALL TEAM.)   Letter from O'N to MW 10/10/05, SL. **(p. 173)**

IN 1905.   Ibid. **(p. 173)**

FRIED BROWN.   A/BG interview with Howard Mortimer Green. **(p. 173)**

IN HIS LIFE.   Dr. Patterson was O'N's orthopedist at Doctors Hospital in early 1948 and was interviewed after O'N's death by A/BG. **(p. 174)**

ITS BETRAYALS."   Sergeant (bibliog); and A/BG interview with ESS. **(p. 174)**

CHURCH ALONE.   A/BG interviews with CMO, ESS, AMcG, EK and PS, to all of whom O'N told this story. **(p. 174)**

ANY KIND.   Edward L. Shaughnessy, O'N scholar who made a study of O'N's "Catholic Sensibility," states that "a crucifix or a holy picture on the wall . . . was ubiquitous in the pious Catholic household of the period . . . One can only suppose that the Tyrones held it to be in dubious taste to flaunt their faith by such open displays of piety. *Down the Nights and Down the Days*, U. of Notre Dame Press, Notre Dame, Indiana 1996. **(p. 175)**

WITHOUT END.")   To many of O'N's non-Catholic admirers the sentiments did not ring true. In particular, they questioned the dogmatically Catholic pronouncement of the last act, when the hero declares: "At last I see! I have always loved! O Lord of Love, forgive Thy poor blind fool! . . . Thou art the Way — the Truth — the Resurrection and the Life, and he that believeth in Thy Love, his love shall never die!" The play's disparagers proved justified. Although *Days Without End* suggested O'N had re-embraced his faith, it was soon evident he had been unable to do so. Shortly after the play's failed production O'N slipped back into apostasy. **(p. 175)**

WORK" AT BETTS.   To "Professor" 9/17/04, SL. **(p. 175)**

THE MASSES."   "Bringing an Old Play Up to Date," unsourced probably March, 1904. Locke. **(p. 176)**

STATION PLATFORMS.   A/BG interview with Fernandez. **(p. 176)**

BACK WAS TURNED.   A/BG interview with Meighan. **(p. 176)**

YOUNG ACTOR!"   Unsourced clipping 8/17/02. Locke. **(p. 177)**

CRITICS' RIDICULE.   A/BG interview with John Hewitt, a company member. **(p. 178)**

FUMED OFFSTAGE.   Ibid. **(p. 178)**
SUCH EFFRONTERY.   Ibid. **(p. 178)**
YOU FEELING, LADDIE?"   Ibid. **(p. 178)**

CHAPTER THIRTEEN

TOO CLOSE."   Basso, Part III (bibliog). **(p. 181)**

MY FRANKENSTEIN!"   Jamie (or O'N) clearly made the common error of confusing Frankenstein, the doctor, with the monster he created. Several scholarly treatises have argued this might not have been an error, maintaining Jamie *knew* Frankenstein was not the monster, and that O'N was suggesting a confused Jamie really meant to say his younger brother had created *him*, rather than the other way around. This seems farfetched in view of the line, "I made you!" that precedes "You're my Frankenstein!" **(p. 181)**

INSIDE YOU!"   Crossed out in typescript (Act IV), Beinecke. **(p. 181)**

THE INDIVIDUAL."   Letter to O'N Jr. 1/27/37. This letter, discovered by Judith E. Barlow at the Beinecke, is cited in her book, *Final Acts*, U. of Georgia Press, Athens, 1985. **(p. 182)**

EASY FOR HIM."   PM, Croswell Bowen 11/3/46. **(p. 182)**

ETERNAL SLAVE."   7/24/05, *SL.* **(p. 184)**

PACE THAT KILLS!'"   8/5/05, *SL.* **(p. 184)**

THE RACETRACK.   Research by Library of Congress. **(p. 184)**

THE 'PONIES.'"   Letter probably late August, *SL.* **(p. 185)**

EN PENSÉE."   Ibid. **(p. 185)**

UNCOLLECTED DEBT.   A/BG interview with EK, to whom O'N told history of farm. **(p. 185)**

TO MARION.   Early Sept, 1905, *SL.* **(p. 185)**

YOURSELF KILLED.'"   Crichton (bibliog). **(p. 185)**

VERGIL, TRIG, ETC."   Letter to MW 9/29/05, Beinecke. **(p. 185)**

TO FIND OUT."   Letter 11/11/06, *SL.* **(p. 186)**

DEGRADED TASTES.)"   12/12/06, *SL.* **(p. 186)**

GIRL FRIENDS."   Crichton (bibliog). **(p. 186)**

ANNA LAUGHLIN.   A/BG interview with Howard Mortimer Green (see earlier ref) and A. Arthur Halle, another O'N schoolmate. **(p. 186)**

ABOUT ACTING?"   NY Journal American 8/26/46. **(p. 186)**

WISE GUY."   Life, Tom Prideaux 10/14/46. **(p. 186)**

FOLLOWING SEASON.   James O'N to Slevin 6/17/06, published NYT, 7/8/06. James had signed a contract 10/15/05, paying Slevin $1,000 and agreeing to additional royalties of 3 to 10 percent of the gross receipts, NY Telegraph 4/9/07. **(p. 187)**

THE PEOPLE."   Ibid. **(p. 188)**

ONES DEPARTED."   Several scholars maintain that James's claim of having sat on the porch of his "old home" was an invention, citing as evidence that Kilkenny area houses of the era did not have porches. But according to the House Valuation of Tinneranny, circa 1850, the O'N house did have a porch. **(p. 188)**

IN THE WORLD.'   James produced Slevin's play during the 1906–07 season but it apparently did not fare well. According to the NY Telegraph 4/9/07, James toured it throughout the West "and made a favorable impression in the principal part"; but Slevin accused him of not paying the promised royalties and brought suit against him in early April 1907, demanding payment of "between $1,500 and $2,000." **(p. 188)**

NOWHERE AT ALL!'   "Chats about James O'Neill," unsourced clipping 7/25/06. Locke. **(p. 188)**

CALL THAT WORK?'   A/BG interview with AMcG. **(p. 188)**

SAME PERIOD.   Ibid. **(p. 189)**

WORDS COME OUT!'   Crichton (bibliog). **(p. 189)**

ON THE STAGE.'   Basso Part III (bibliog). **(p. 189)**

CHAPTER FOURTEEN

WICKED OPPORTUNITY.'   Archives Museum of the City of NY. **(p. 190)**

MONTH OF SEPT.'   1/3/33, Commins (bibliog). **(p. 190)**

EXACT OPPOSITE.'   To "Mr. Maxwell" 5/8/45, SL. **(p. 190)**

HAD NO YOUTH.'   PM, Croswell Bowen 11/3/46. **(p. 190)**

WISHING OUT LOUD.'   Basso, Part II (bibliog). **(p. 190)**

OF PEOPLE.'   1/3/33 Commins (bibliog). **(p. 191)**

SPENT YOUTH —"   To O'N Jr. 1/14/33, SL. **(p. 191)**

STRONGEST INFLUENCE.'   To Moeller 8/19/33, SL. **(p. 191)**

KHAYYAM, ETC).'   Letter to O'N Jr. 5/13/33, SL. **(p. 191)**

CHANDELIER ABOVE.'   In *The First Man* (1921), also set in "Bridgetown," O'N again described "a great rug" that "covers most of the hardwood floor." (This being an upper middle-class home, there are no wires dangling from a chandelier.) **(p. 192)**

"GETTING OLD.'   Beinecke. **(p. 194)**

MAN I ENVY.'   A/BG interview with AMcG. **(p. 195)**

HIS METHODS.   A/BG interview with PS. **(p. 195)**

OF WEAKFISH.   BA, NYT 10/8/33; and in a letter to SC 1/[12]/33, O'N wrote: "How I remember the dinners in New London! I feel I've caught them." Commins (bibliog). **(p. 196)**

HIS CHARACTER.'   Letter to Lawrence Estavan 1/15/40, SL. **(p. 196)**

ONCE USED TO.'   Letter to AMcG 12/15/33; copy given to A/BG. **(p. 196)**

OF NOSTALGIA.   A/BG interview with Russel Crouse, then press agent for *Ah, Wilderness!* **(p. 197)**

FOR BIGAMY.   BA, NYT 10/8/33. **(p. 197)**

DEEP STUFF!'   A/BG interview with EK. **(p. 197)**

"HILARIOUSLY TOGETHER.'   Letter to SG 1/29/19. **(p. 197)**

I BELIEVE";   Clark (bibliog). **(p. 198)**

CÉSAR FRANCK;   Basso Part III (bibliog). **(p. 198)**

RAG TIME TUNE.   NL Telegraph 9/17/12. Also Sanborn & Clark (bibliog). **(p. 198)**

CALMS OF CAPRICORN.   East Bay Books, Berkeley, Cal. 1993. **(p. 198)**

OR SCHOPENHAUER.   A/BG interview with JG. **(p. 199)**

THE SEAMSTRESSES.''   A/BG interview with Ada Rovetti White's son, George C. White, founder of Eugene O'Neill Center, Waterford, Conn. **(p. 199)**

IN THE GROUP.   A/BG interviews with EK, AMcG and Alexander Campbell. **(p. 200)**

JAMIE OR EUGENE.   A/BG interview with AMcG. **(p. 200)**

BOYHOOD DAYS.''   Letter to BA 8/16/31, *SL.* **(p. 201)**

FULLY RECOVERED!''   Ibid. **(p. 201)**

BARE KNUCKLES.   A/BG interviews with EK and AMcG. **(p. 202)**

A MONTH.   1912 City Directory. **(p. 203)**

ESTATE INVESTMENTS.   NL Land Records Vol. 115 10/25/09, City Clerk's Office; also NL and Waterford Land Records 1890–1909. **(p. 203)**

AND WATCHMEN.   In 1952 it became a state park. **(p. 203)**

BY DOLAN.   Robert M. Nye, Town Clerk and Municipal Historian, Waterford. **(p. 203)**

MIND FOR YEARS.   O'N began thinking of Harkness, Hammond and Dolan — and doubtless the Montauk Inn — in the early 1930's when he began his 11-play cycle about the rise and fall of an Irish-American family. In *A Touch of the Poet*, the only cycle play he completed, he gave his rich Yankee villain yet another variant of the two names: "Harford" (rather than "Harder" or "Harker"). Drawing on his memory of Dolan, as well as his own father, O'N created Cornelius Melody, a proud, ambitious but defeated man, who ultimately reveals himself as the son of a shebeen keeper whose family in Ireland shared a hovel with pigs.

The incident in *A Touch of the Poet*, wherein an Irish crony of Melody kicks Harford's lawyer off his property, presages the scene in *A Moon for the Misbegotten* in which Phil Hogan expedites the departure of Harder from his farm. And Melody's tavern, though situated near Boston in the year 1828, resembles in atmosphere and clientele the Montauk Inn of the early 1900's. Moreover, Melody's daughter, Sara, is an earlier, if slightly more refined, version of Phil Hogan's daughter, Josie, in *A Moon for the Misbegotten.* **(p. 204)**

ONCE REMARKED —   Journal American, Louis Sobol 11/13/46. **(p. 204)**

CHAPTER FIFTEEN

PECULIARLY ITS OWN.''   Letter 5/7/45, *SL.* **(p. 205)**

NEVER SO INSULTED!''   A/BG interview, Lillian Brennan. **(p. 207)**

FORTY–FIVE POUNDS.''   A/BG interview with Sheridan sisters. **(p. 207)**

FOR ITS INHABITANTS.   Floyd I (bibliog). **(p. 208)**

"MAIN TENANT."   "Untold Tales of Eugene O'Neill," Theater Arts, Gladys Hamilton, Aug. 1956. **(p. 208)**

CONSIDERED ACCEPTABLE.''   A/BG interview with Edith Chappell Sheffield. **(p. 209)**

I'VE LOST INTEREST.''   A/BG interview with JG. **(p. 209)**

TEN YEARS.''   Undated clipping, given to A/BG by AMcG. **(p. 210)**

TURNING A HAIR.   A/BG interviews with AMcG and EK. **(p. 211)**

RELATIVELY CALM.   Notes about Pequot Avenue in early 1900's by Frances E. Hubbard, July 1969, Beinecke. **(p. 211)**

EDMOND DANTES,   Sword was acquired by Monte Cristo Cottage archives. **(p. 212)**

HOTEL'S OFFICES.   A/BG interview with Campbell. **(p. 212)**

HER ANATOMY.   A/BG interviews with AMcG, EK, Campbell. **(p. 213)**

WANT A DRINK?'"   Crichton (bibliog). **(p. 213)**

CHAPTER SIXTEEN

AMOUNT OF WORK."   Letter to George Pierce Baker 7/29/14, *SL*. **(p. 214)**

"ONLY REAL FRIEND."   A/BG interviews with CMO. **(p. 215)**

"POISONOUS TONGUE.")   Letter to ABO 1/23/20, *SL*. **(p. 215)**

FREELY ABANDON THEM."   Madison (bibliog). **(p. 216)**

BELONG TO THEMSELVES."   Ibid. **(p. 216)**

BUT NEVER MARRIED.   Ibid. **(p. 216)**

SUCH A STROKE."   Ibid. **(p. 216)**

THE UNITED STATES."   NY Herald 4/12/08. **(p. 217)**

ETHICS EVER WRITTEN."   Ibid. **(p. 217)**

SAME YEAR.   Publisher was W. Scott, National Union Catalog, Book #542. **(p. 217)**

COLLEGE CURRICULUM.   Boston Sunday Post, Olin Downes 8/29/20. **(p. 217)**

HER WAR CRY."   Madison (bibliog). **(p. 218)**

INTELLECTUAL CHANNELS."   NY Herald 4/12/08. **(p. 218)**

A TOY GUN.   Goldman (bibliog). **(p. 218)**

HER MEMOIRS.   Letter from O'N to Anarchist Aid Society 2/8/28, LS Collection, Conn. College. **(p. 219)**

TO LIVE IT!"   1/29/27, *SL*. **(p. 219)**

OUT OF IT.'")   Bowen (bibliog). **(p. 219)**

NO LONGER CONCEDE."   To critic and poet-essayist, Benjamin de Casseres 6/22/27, *SL*. **(p. 220)**

TO MEMORY.   Among O'N's papers at Yale are nine sheets of paper covered in his minute handwriting of laboriously copied quotations from Nietzsche. **(p. 220)**

PHYSICAL COLLAPSE.   While both suffered from deteriorating diseases, O'N's ailment was a degenerative nervous disorder, whereas Nietzsche died insane, ravaged by syphilis. **(p. 220)**

CHAPTER SEVENTEEN

OVER–CUTTING."   Letter to Baker 7/29/14, *SL*. **(p. 221)**

INSIDE OF HIM?"   Boston Sunday Post, Olin Downes 8/29/20. **(p. 221)**

IRON COT.   University Hall was later rebuilt as Holder Hall. **(p. 222)**

THE WEEKEND. "Episodes of Eugene O'Neill's Undergraduate Days at Princeton," Princeton U. Library Chronicle Spring, 1968. Also A/BG interview with Weeks. **(p. 222)**

HAVE MANY." A/BG interview with Horton. **(p. 223)**

CHARACTERISTIC. A/BG interview with Weeks. **(p. 224)**

IN SENTENCES." Sergeant (bibliog). **(p. 224)**

HEED HIM." A/BG interview with Weeks. **(p. 224)**

FROM SLEEPING." To GJN 12/7/31, Nathan (bibliog). **(p. 224)**

FOUR BEERS. A/BG interviews with Horton and Weeks. **(p. 225)**

HER SLIGHTINGLY. He referred to the Widow in "Ballard of Old Girls" published NL Telegraph 8/28/12/; it was a parody of François Villon's "Where Are the Snows of Yesteryear?" Reprinted in Gallup (bibliog). **(p. 225)**

LOBSTER SALAD. A/BG interview with Horton. **(p. 226)**

PLAY HE ATTENDED. Letter to Hans Olav, 5/13/38, SL. Play opened at Princess Theater 11/13/06 and after 40 performances went on tour; it reopened at the Bijou 3/11/07 for 32 performances, then again went on tour. **(p. 226)**

CONVENTIONAL ACTING. *Stanislavsky on the Art of the Stage*, by David Magarshack, Hill & Wang, NY 1961. **(p. 226)**

TO IBSEN." Boston Sunday Post, Olin Downes 8/29/20. **(p. 226)**

YEARS FROM NOW." Letter to Hans Olav 5/13/38, SL. **(p. 226)**

SECOND SEMESTER. Files of V. Lansing Collins, then Secretary of Princeton U. and formerly the instructor who passed O'N in French. **(p. 227)**

FRESHMAN YEAR. A/BG interviews with Horton and Weeks, who described the celebration to O'N after he had left campus. Incident also described in Nassau Herald, "Class History" [1910] by Leslie Roy Kendrick. **(p. 227)**

SOMETHING DREADFUL." Letter to BAM 11/7/14, SL. **(p. 227)**

WHERE HE LIVED." Nathan (bibliog). **(p. 228)**

OF VODKA." Basso Part I (bibliog). **(p. 228)**

RESPECT FOR." Crichton (bibliog). **(p. 228)**

TOLERATE THAT." A/BG interview with Weeks. **(p. 228)**

MAY 8. Secretary of Princeton U. files. **(p. 229)**

SCHOLASTIC STANDING." Ibid. Also John D. Davies, former editor, Princeton Alumni Weekly; and A/BG interview with Weeks (who in his later published account with Hastings remembered — incorrectly — that the incident occurred later in the semester). **(p. 229)**

THAT YEAR." 6/7/23, Charlotte E. Betts collection. **(p. 230)**

HELL RAISING." NY Times Magazine, S. J. Woolf 10//4/31. **(p. 230)**

A NEUROSIS!" "To O'N Jr 6/1/42, SL. **(p. 230)**

CHAPTER EIGHTEEN

AND RELATIVES. NY Herald Tribune, "Eugene O'Neill at Close Range in Maine," David Karsner 8/8/26. **(p. 233)**

BECOME A PARENT. Sergeant (bibliog). **(p. 234)**

("JIMMY TOMORROW"). "Tomorrow" appeared in The Seven Arts 6/2/17. **(p. 234)**

PURE INVENTION.   Edinburgh U. records indicate he never matriculated; Reuters has no record of his employment. **(p. 234)**

CHURCH TOWN, ILLOGAN,   Birth Certificate General Register Office, Southport, England. **(p. 234)**

PRESS AGENT.   Dramatic Mirror 8/10/1895. **(p. 235)**

APRIL 30, 1904.   Byth's obituary in Billboard states he "was responsible for the Boer War Spectacle at the St. Louis Exposition." **(p. 235)**

BEN VILJOEN.   *The Boer War* by Edgar Holt, Putnam & Co. Ltd., London. **(p. 235)**

CRUCIAL BATTLE;   Although Piet Wetjoen's name combines both "DeWet" and "Viljoen," his character is based solely on DeWet. **(p. 235)**

REGIMENTAL FUNDS.   In the play Lewis's personality and background are modeled on yet another Boer War soldier, Major Adams, a drinking crony at Jimmy-the-Priest's. **(p. 235)**

MONTE CRISTO."   NY Herald 9/17/07. **(p. 235)**

ONE CRITIC,   NY Telegraph 9/17/07. **(p. 235)**

WILL EVER KNOW."   NY Sun 9/17/07. Despite his gallant curtain speech, James's faith in his immortality was unjustified. Less than a dozen years after his death, audiences had not only forgotten he had ever played anything but *Monte Cristo*, they had all but forgotten him as anyone other than the father of Eugene O'Neill. **(p. 236)**

LONG AGO PLAY."   NY Telegraph 9/17/07. **(p. 236)**

THEIR PROGRESS.   A/BG interview with Sadie Koenig. **(p. 236)**

DISAPPOINTED HER.   Ibid. **(p. 236)**

HOURS READING.   "I never took it seriously," he later admitted to Arthur Hobson Quinn 6/13/22, *SL.* **(p. 236)**

ENGLISH LANGUAGE."   Chicago Record 2/5/08, Locke. **(p. 237)**

GOOD SUPPORT."   O. L. Hall, Chicago Journal 2/7/08, Locke. **(p. 237)**

GOOD PROMISE."   NY Herald 9/17/07. **(p. 237)**

FINAL CURTAIN."   Chicago Record Herald 1/9/08. **(p. 241)**

CHAPTER NINETEEN

FOR JAMIE.   The play was by actor-manager, Wilson Barrett. **(p. 242)**

OF SARDINES.   *This Fabulous Century* Vol. I 1900-1910, by the Editors of Time-Life Books. **(p. 242)**

NARROW COTS.   Morgan (bibliog); and A/BG interviews with EK. **(p. 243)**

— AND LIES!   NL Telegraph, "Laconics" 11/21/12; also Gallup (bibliog). **(p. 245)**

HE ANSWERED.   PM, John S. Wilson 9/3/46. **(p. 246)**

O'NEILL'S REACTION.   A/BG interviews with Norman Winston. **(p. 246)**

MORE FUN."   Life, Tom Prideaux 10/14/46. **(p. 247)**

CHORUS GIRLS."   Basso, Part I (bibliog). **(p. 247)**

TAKE HIS PLACE.   A/BG interview with Charles Grant, the roomer whom O'Neill replaced. **(p. 248)**

YEARS LATER.   American Magazine, Mary B. Mullett, Nov. 1922. **(p. 248)**

LACK OF DIRECTION.   Morgan (bibliog). Also A/BG interview with EK. **(p. 248)**

THIRTY YEARS LATER.   Letter to Shane O'N 1/18/40 *SL*. **(p. 249)**

"DECADENCE MANOR."   Morgan (bibliog). **(p. 249)**

FIRE TO DRY.   A/BG interviews with EK. **(p. 249)**

FROZE TO DEATH."   To Shane O'N 1/18/40, *SL*. **(p. 249)**

(TED) IRELAND.   Morgan (bibliog); and A/BG interviews with EK. **(p. 250)**

CHAPTER TWENTY

DISREPUTABLE, REFUSED.   A/BG interviews with EK. **(p. 251)**

LIFE HUMDRUM.   Most of the information about Kathleen Jenkins is from A/BG interviews during the late 1950's and early 1960's (when she was Kathleen Pitt-Smith), and supplemented by what CMO recalled of O'N's confidences to her. **(p. 251)**

BEEN THERE SINCE."   Letter to CMO 10/23/26, *SL*. **(p. 252)**

ST. LOUIS.   St. Louis Star 6/21/09. **(p. 253)**

ALL HER LIFE.   A/BG interview with KJP. **(p. 254)**

HURTING HER.   A/BG interviews with CMO. **(p. 254)**

THE HOLDING.   A/BG interview with Mrs. Earl C. Stevens and research by Horace W. Robinson, former professor of speech and drama, U. of Oregon. **(p. 255)**

"THEATRICAL" INFLUENCES.   Ibid. **(p. 255)**

THE RELATIONSHIP.   A/BG interviews with CMO and KJP. **(p. 255)**

TIME BEING.   A/BG interviews with KJP. **(p. 255)**

GILPIN OFFICIATED.   Division of Vital Statistics & Administration, NJ State Dept. of Health. **(p. 255)**

AS ZION, NEW JERSEY,   Ibid. **(p. 256)**

ACTUAL ADDRESS.   Ibid. **(p. 256)**

FOR ALL THREE.   In Boulton (bibliog) O'N's second wife gives a different version of the romance and marriage, but it contains factual errors that make it difficult to credit — such as placing Kathleen's absent father on the scene and citing Jersey City, rather than Hoboken, as the place where Eugene and Kathleen were married. More notably, Boulton gives no hint that the marriage was forced by Kathleen's pregnancy. **(p. 256)**

CHAPTER TWENTY-ONE

HAD ANTICIPATED.   Letters to his parents are at Harvard U. Library. **(p. 257)**

SON EUGENE."   11/9/09, *SL*. **(p. 258)**

LEMON LEAVES"   Christmas Day 1909, *SL*. **(p. 260)**

A LIZARD."   NY Daily News, Fred Pasley 1/25/32. **(p. 260)**

I AND YOU.   Beinecke. The poem was acquired from the Seven Gables Bookshop, which had bought it in 1963 from O'N's second wife, ABO. **(p. 261)**

SPANISH HONDURAS."   NY World, Charles P. Sweeney 11/9/24. **(p. 261)**

CHATTERING TEETH.   A/BG interview with Stevens's widow. **(p. 262)**

YEARS LATER.   Basso Part I (bibliog). **(p. 262)**

CALL IT QUITS.   A/BG interview with Stevens's widow. **(p. 262)**

NO GOLD."   Letter to AHQ 6/13/22, *SL.* **(p. 262)**

PLAY A PART."   Letter to Stevens 10/22/22, *SL.* **(p. 262)**

GREATLY APPRECIATIVE."   Sunday Oregonian 11/29/36. (Neuberger evidently was unaware O'Neill had long since dropped his middle name.) **(p. 263)**

HAVE AROUND!"   Copy of letter 12/5/36 given to A/BG by Stevens's second wife (and widow). **(p. 263)**

QUIXOTIC ADVENTURE.   A/BG interview with Stevens's widow. **(p. 263)**

PREVIOUS NOVEMBER.   St. Louis Star 3/15/10. **(p. 263)**

THE MARRIAGE.   NY World 5/7/10. **(p. 264)**

HIS SITUATION.   A/BG interview with Konig. **(p. 264)**

WORK FOR YEARS."   St. Louis Star 3/15/10. **(p. 265)**

"ROSE–PETAL HANDS."   St. Louis Star Chronicle 9/8/08. **(p. 266)**

MAINSTAY."   Source of clipping undecipherable. Locke. **(p. 266)**

VIOLA ALLEN.   12/9/20, *SL.* **(p. 266)**

HIS FRIENDS."   NY Daily News, Fred Pasley 1/25/32. **(p. 266)**

EMPTY SEATS."   A/BG interview with Liebler Jr. **(p. 267)**

SAILING SHIPS."   Letter to AHQ 6/13/22, *SL.* **(p. 267)**

WE WERE OFF."   Boston Sunday Post, Olin Downes 8/29/20. **(p. 267)**

STAVANGER, NORWAY.   A/BG interview with Gustav Adolf Waage, grandson of Captain Gustav Waage. Like his grandfather, Gustav, and father, Severin, Gustav Adolf had been a sea captain for the same company, Sigval Bergensen Line of Stavanger, Norway. **(p. 267)**

BLACK CAP.   Ibid. **(p. 268)**

SHIP'S WORK.   Ibid. **(p. 268)**

LATER RECALLED.   Clark (bibliog). **(p. 268)**

TAKE CARE OF . . ."   A/BG interview with Gustav Adolf Waage (see earlier ref). And LS Collection, Conn. College. **(p. 269)**

FIND JOBS.   A/BG interview with Gustav Adolf Waage. **(p. 269)**

CHAPTER TWENTY–TWO

OF DISASTER.   A/BG interview with Frank Meyer, friend of O'N Jr. **(p. 271)**

OF THE WORLD.   A/BG interview with Louis Kalonyme, friend of O'N (who also called himself Louis Kantor). **(p. 272)**

IN OUR HAIR.   Pleiades Club Yearbook, NY, April, 1912 (editon limited to 500 copies). O'N's first published work. **(p. 274)**

FOR SPEED.   The ship was 200 feet long with a 38–1/2-foot beam and a gross weight of a little over 1,600 tons. A/BG interview with Gustav Adolf Waage. **(p. 274)**

WITH THE MEN.   A/BG interview with Manuel Komroff, later one of O'N's editors, with whom he discussed his life at sea. **(p. 275)**

APPEALED TO ME."   American Magazine, Mary B. Mullett Nov. 1922. **(p. 275)**

SOCIAL HYPOCRISY."   Theater Magazine, Carol Bird June, 1924. **(p. 275)**

HIS SUITCASE.   LS Collection, Conn. College. **(p. 276)**

WITH THE CREW.   A/BG interview with Gustav Adolf Waage. **(p. 276)**

THE SAME TIME.   A/BG interviews with former seaman JJM, with whom O'N shared many details of his life at sea. **(p. 276)**

CAUGHT HIM."   Letter to Nichols 4/27/40, SL. **(p. 276)**

LIFE ITSELF!"   O'N paraphrased these lines from *LDJIN* in an interview five years after completing the play (but ten years before it was published). "He still speaks of the nights when he used to lie on the bowsprit as of a deep religious experience," wrote Tom Prideaux (Life, 10/14/46), quoting O'N: "As I watched the spray beating against the ship and looked back at the big moonlit sails, I felt synchronized with the rhythm of life." **(p. 277)**

"PRAYER BOOK."   Report to A/BG by NY Seaman's Institute (6/5/57). **(p. 277)**

GOOD SAILOR."   Ibid. **(p. 278)**

SMALL ORGAN.   A/BG interview with Gustav Adolf Waage. **(p. 278)**

BECOMES ELECTRA).   According to "WPA History Project," Library of Congress, many of the most beautiful of these melodies originated in the South, as did the words. "Negro seamen from the Southern states were great for chanteys. They had fine voices and liked to sing; they were good sailors, too." **(p. 278)**

OF THE SEA."   Boston Sunday Post, Olin Downes 8/29/20. **(p. 278)**

RIGHT HAND.   The Reporter, Malcolm Cowley 9/5/57. **(p. 279)**

LOUDEST FOGHORN.   A/BG interviews with JJM. **(p. 279)**

POOP DECK.   Ibid. **(p. 279)**

SHIP ITSELF."   American Magazine, Mary B. Mullett Nov. 1922. **(p. 280)**

SPRANG OPEN.   A/BG interviews with JJM. **(p. 280)**

BOOKS INCORRECT?"   Letter to Pace 11/7/34, SL. **(p. 281)**

CLIPPER SHIPS."   NY Herald Tribune, Marguerite Young 9/3/46. **(p. 281)**

TRANSFORMING EXPERIENCE.   Letter [probably April, 1917] to Waldo Frank, editor of The Seven Arts, who had asked O'N for a biographical note, and letter to AHQ 6/13/22, both in SL. He also told Barrett Clark the voyage had lasted sixty-five days. Olin Downes, perhaps inadvertently misquoting O'N in Boston Sunday Post 8/29/20, said the period at sea was sixty-*nine* days. The Charles Racine, according to Gustav Adolf Waage, "came to a sad end." Sold to another company not long after Eugene's voyage, she hit rocks near Mozambique, drifted and eventually came to shore, never to sail again. **(p. 281)**

CHAPTER TWENTY-THREE

SUSTAINED PATTERN."   Letter to CMO 11/27/26, SL. **(p. 282)**

EXPERIENCED AT SEA   Ibid. **(p. 282)**

DOCKS IN FACT."   Clark (bibliog) & NY Herald Tribune 8/8/26. **(p. 282)**

CONGENIAL BAR.   A/BG interviews with Frederick Hettman. **(p. 282)**

A DRAFTSMAN.   Letter to Waldo Frank, April 1917, *SL*. **(p. 283)**

ROOMING HOUSE.   A/BG interviews with Hettman. **(p. 283)**

OF QUITTING.   Letter to Waldo Frank, April 1917, *SL*. **(p. 283)**

ENTERTAINMENT."   NY Times, Louis Kalonyme 2/21/24. **(p. 283)**

SOBER PIANIST."   NY World, 1/6/29. **(p. 283)**

WORLD WAR I."   A/BG interview with Rockmore, who said conversation took place aboard a chartered boat in 1926. **(p. 284)**

TIME PLEASANTLY."   NY Times, Louis Kalonyme 12/21/24. **(p. 284)**

DORIAN GRAY."   Ibid. **(p. 284)**

YARDARM," HE SAID.   NY Daily News, Fred Pasley 11/24/32. **(p. 285)**

AND RETURN."   Letter to Waldo Frank, April 1917, *SL*. **(p. 285)**

AFRICA, AND RETURN."   Clark (bibliog). **(p. 285)**

THE COUNTRY.   "Eugene O'Neill Able-Seaman," by Louis Kantor (Louis Kalonyme), Provincetown Playhouse program 11/23/24. And NY Times Magazine, S. J. Woolf 9/15/46. **(p. 285)**

OF THE SHIP.   NY Tribune, Philip Mindil 2/22/20. **(p. 286)**

COMPLETE DESTITUTION."   Clark (bibliog). **(p. 286)**

DIED THERE."   Basso Part III (bibliog). **(p. 287)**

AS A BED."   A/BG interview with Sherwood. **(p. 287)**

HALF–STARVED WAIF.   A/BG interview with Olive Evans Maxon, who nursed O'N when he was ill in NL in 1912. **(p. 287)**

SHIP'S GALLEY.   A/BG interview with Robert Carlton Brown, short-story writer to whom O'N gave these details. **(p. 287)**

THE WORLD.   The I.W.W. was organized by 43 labor unions in Chicago in 1905 to unite unskilled and skilled workers. **(p. 287)**

HORRIBLE ENOUGH).   A/BG interviews with Frederick Hettman and JJM. **(p. 287)**

I SAW IT."   NY Times, Karl Schriftgeisser 10/6/46. **(p. 287)**

CRITICIZED."   "When I First Met Eugene O'Neill," Bulletin of the American Women's Club, March 1927. **(p. 288)**

ON THE SEA."   Boston Sunday Post, Olin Downes 8/29/20. **(p. 288)**

SAW AND HEARD.   A/BG interview with Olive Evans Maxon. **(p. 288)**

OR DESTROYED),   The definitive 3-volume collection, *Complete Plays*, lists fifty plays. It includes the unfinished, highly tentative draft of a manuscript entitled *More Stately Mansions*, which in the opinion of A/BG should not have been included in this otherwise authoritative collection. A/BG count of fifty plays includes the one-acter, *Exorcism*, produced in 1920 by the Provincetown Players; no copies of the manuscript have surfaced. **(p. 288)**

INTEGRAL PART.   The number and variety of these settings illustrate O'N's sustained preoccupation with the subject:

A steamer's life raft, adrift in a tropic sea (*Thirst*, 1913).

A section of boat deck of the S.S. Empress (*Warnings*, 1914).

The life boat of a passenger steamer adrift off the Grand Banks of Newfoundland (*Fog*, 1914).

The forecastle of the S.S. Glencairn, on the North Atlantic (*Bound East for Cardiff*, 1914).

Fireman's forecastle of the San Francisco, docked at Liverpool (*The Personal*

Equation, 1915).

A section of the main deck of the Glencairn, at anchor off an island in the West Indies (*The Moon of the Caribbees*, 1916).

The seaman's forecastle on the Glencairn, somewhere in the submarine zone (*In the Zone*, 1916).

The captain's cabin on board the steam whaling ship Atlantic Queen in the Arctic Ocean (*Ile*, 1916).

The main deck of Columbus's flagship, on a calm sea off the West Indies (*The Fountain*, 1920).

The barge Simeon Winthrop at anchor in the harbor of Provincetown and at dock in Boston (*"Anna Christie,"* 1920). The barge also appears in an earlier version of the play (*Chris Christophersen*, 1919).

The fireman's forecastle, a section of the promenade deck, and the stokehold of an ocean liner on the Atlantic (*The Hairy Ape*, 1921).

The poop deck of the royal junk of the Princess Kukachin, at anchor in the harbor of Hormiz, Persia (*Marco Millions*, 1923–24).

The afterdeck of a cabin cruiser anchored in the Hudson River (*Strange Interlude*, 1926–1927).

The stern of a clipper ship moored at a wharf in Boston (*Mourning Becomes Electra*, 1929–1931).

Seven additional plays deal with sailors or the influence of the sea (although containing no scenes set aboard ship): *The Long Voyage Home*, *Where the Cross is Made* (later expanded into the full-length play, *Gold*), *The Rope*, *Diff'rent*, and *Beyond the Horizon* (all written between 1916 and 1920); and, of course, *Long Day's Journey Into Night*. **(p. 288)**

CHAPTER TWENTY–FOUR

LIKE HELL."   NY Daily News, Fred Pasley 1/24/32. **(p. 289)**

THAT BECKONED.   Research report to A/BG by NY Seaman's Institute. **(p. 289)**

OF ORDERS."   American Magazine, Mary B. Mullett, Nov. 1922. **(p. 290)**

AND MARMALADE."   Crichton (bibliog). **(p. 290)**

YET TO MEET.   Letter to Waldo Frank 4/30/17, copy given to A/BG by Frank. **(p. 290)**

TRIP DOWN."   Article by O'N, NY Times 4/11/20. **(p. 291)**

COCONUTS.   NY Daily News, Fred Pasley 1/24/32. **(p. 291)**

TO THE SEA.   Published in NL Telegraph 11/19/12. **(p. 291)**

A BIG THING."   Letter to Barrett Clark 5/8/19, SL. **(p. 292)**

JUST CRAZY."   Clark (bibliog). **(p. 292)**

TEN–FOOT POLE."   Crichton (bibliog). **(p. 292)**

HOTEL LUCERNE.   A/BG interviews with Theodore Liebler Jr, who said that James O'N's producer, George Tyler — at James's behest — maintained contact, however tenuous, with Eugene, even when Eugene was out of touch with his family; it was through the Liebler and Company office (via Tyler), for example, that Eugene's dollar-a-day allowance often was paid. **(p. 292)**

THE DRUMMER.   The Toledo Blade, for example, noted that while Watts was not "a great role," Jamie played it "admirably," adding, "The last time he was here he was in company with his distinguished father," and "his present part suits him much better" than his previous roles in *The Count of Monte Cristo* and *Abbé Bonaparte*, 11/15/10. **(p. 292)**

UNLOADING PRODUCE. Tax map and photos, Ellis Island & Castle Garden Research Inc. by Brian G. Andersson, Dept. of City Planning. **(p. 293)**

MONTH'S RENT. NY World, Charles P. Sweeney 11/9/24, & A/BG interviews with Kalonyme. **(p. 293)**

UPSTAIRS ROOMS. The law was introduced in NY State Legislature by Sen. John Raines to molify prohibitionists. **(p. 293)**

TOLD KALONYME. NY Herald Tribune 11/16/24. **(p. 293)**

FOR SIXTY. 1910 Federal Census. At least one writer has reported that no women were to be found there, but according to the census, Rose Swartz lived there with her husband, A. A. Swartz, a "show business performer" — obviously at the end of their rope — and their five young children, one of them an 11-year-old girl, Lillian. **(p. 293)**

DO WITH THIS.) South Street Seaport Museum. **(p. 293)**

GROG SHOP." Description of setting for an early autobiographical one-act play, *Exorcism*. **(p. 293)**

IN ALL MEN." PM, Croswell Bowen 11/3/46. **(p. 294)**

KATHLEEN JENKINS. A/BG interviews with Louis Kalonyme. **(p. 294)**

JAMES J. CONDON. Trow's and R. L. Polk & Co.'s New York City Directories, 1905–1919. **(p. 294)**

IN COMPARISON." NY World, Charles P. Sweeney 11/9/24. **(p. 294)**

102ND STREET. 1910 Federal Census. **(p. 294)**

ROBBED THEM. A/BG interviews with JJM and JL, O'N friend during Provincetown Players days in Greenwich Village. **(p. 295)**

FIRE ESCAPES. A/BG interviews with JJM. **(p. 295)**

HE RECALLED. American Magazine, Mary B.Mullett, Nov. 1922. **(p. 295)**

THAT YEAR. 1920 World Almanac. **(p. 296)**

CHAPTER TWENTY–FIVE

TO $27.50). Shipping Articles, National Archives, Washington, D.C. **(p. 297)**

TWENTY KNOTS, *Great Passenger Ships of the World*, Vol I, 1858-1912, by Arnold Kludas. Additional research (in late 1950's) relating to a seaman's life aboard the S.S.New York and S.S.Philadephia in 1911 conducted by Frank O. Braynard, director of the Bureau of Information of the American Marine Institute; Frederick S. McMurray of Sailors Snug Harbor; Richard Harris of the United States Lines; New York Seaman's Institute; and A/BG interview with Arthur Cochrane, who sailed numerous times on both the New York and the Philadelphia. **(p. 297)**

STROLLING THE DECK. A/BG interviews with JJM. **(p. 297)**

ANY ROMANCE." Boston Sunday Post, Olin Downes 8/29/20. **(p. 297)**

GOOD–SIZED TOWN." Mary B. Mullett, American Magazine, Nov. 1922 (see earlier refs). **(p. 298)**

ENGLISHMAN HE WAS. The Shipping Articles Roberts signed before departing NY included stipulations against flogging and other forms of corporal punishment by the master and his officers. National Archives, Washington, D.C.; and A/BG interview with Arthur Cochrane. **(p. 298)**

TRANSATLANTIC LINERS.") 1/6/27, SL. **(p. 299)**

OF REPAIRS. Letter from O'N to Ralph E. Whitney 3/11/41, SL, and A/BG interview with James Francis Quigley, a seaman who befriended O'N in Liverpool. **(p. 299)**

THE QUAYS. NYT 6/30/11. **(p. 299)**

WENT UNMET. NYT 7/4/11. **(p. 299)**

LOCK THEM OUT. NYT 8/12/11–8/15/11. **(p. 299)**

LEFT THEIR JOBS. NYT 8/16/11, 8/17/11. **(p. 300)**

THIRTY–SEVEN YEARS. Starbuck Perry oral history interview by William Wood at Sailors Snug Harbor, Staten Island: The WPA Life Histories Collection, Library of Congress. Starbuck, then 85, lived to 90. Aspects of Starbuck's life confirmed in A/BG interviews with John Francis Quigley. **(p. 300)**

OUT TO SEA." The WPA Life Histories Collection, Library of Congress. **(p. 301)**

BLACK EYES. A/BG inteview with Quigley. **(p. 303)**

THE OTHER. American Magazine, Mary B. Mullett Nov. 1922. **(p. 303)**

WAS DRISCOLL." Ibid. **(p. 303)**

THAT I DID." To Ralph E. Whitney 3/11/41, SL. **(p. 303)**

TOUGH CUSTOMER." American Magazine, Mary B. Mullett, Nov. 1922. **(p. 303)**

UNITED STATES. Register of Deaths at Sea, J. Driscoll, Public Record Office, Kew, Richmond, Surrey, England; and General Register Office of Shipping and Seamen, Cardiff, Wales. **(p. 304)**

HIS MATES." NYT, Louis Kalonyme Dec. 1924. **(p. 304)**

ASHORE VERY LONG." WPA Life Histories Collection, Library of Congress. **(p. 305)**

MID–AUGUST, American Magazine, Mary B. Mullett, Nov. 1922. The ship's repair might have been delayed, as was the case with other passenger ships, by the strike, which did not subside until the end of August. **(p. 305)**

TO NEW YORK. Dept. of Commerce & Labor, Bureau of Navigation Shipping Service, Washington, D.C. **(p. 305)**

AUGUST 19. Shipping articles, SS Philadelphia, lists E. G. O'Neil [sic], "AB," as one of two crewmen transferred from the SS New York on 8/19/11. His wages "per month" were $27.50. **(p. 305)**

CAME TO $14.84. Mutual Release document, Dept. of Commerce and Labor, Bureau of Navigation Shipping Service, Washington, D.C. **(p. 306)**

LOVED IT ALL." NL Telegraph, 11/22/12. **(p. 307)**

STRAYED, OR STOLEN." Letter to Whitley, 3/11/41 (see earlier ref). **(p. 308)**

OFF THE HOOK. Sandy Hook, near NY harbor. **(p. 308)**

UNDER ME." Letter to CMO, 11/27/26, SL. **(p. 308)**

ON THE FLOOR. CMO was confusing O'Neill's "flat . . . where he slept on the floor" with Jimmy the Priest's waterfront saloon-cum-rooming house; the "flat" was of a later period, and was in Greenwhich Village. **(p. 308)**

VERY EXCITING.'" A/BG interview with CMO. **(p. 308)**

DRISCOLL'S APPEARANCE." NYT, Louis Kalonyme 12/21/24. **(p. 309)**

BROUGHT ON BOARD." Register of Deaths at Sea, Public Record Office, Surrey, England; and Certified Extract from a Return of Death, General Register Office of

Shipping and Seamen, Cardiff, Wales. He was listed as J. Driscoll, 37, "leading fireman"; the exact place of death was given as "Lat. 47° 25'N. Long. 28° 49'W. **(p. 309)**

WHO KNEW HIM.   Letter to Ralph E. Whitney 3/11/41, *SL*. **(p. 309)**

THE HAIRY APE."   NYT, Louis Kalonyme 12/21/24. **(p. 309)**

COMPANY OFFICE).   A/BG interviews with Theodore Liebler Jr. **(p. 310)**

YOU A LESSON!"   Act II, Beinecke. **(p. 310)**

CHAPTER TWENTY-SIX

CARRIED ON."   NY Daily News, Fred Pasley 1/24/32. **(p. 311)**

OLD SWEDE."   Clark (bibliog). **(p. 311)**

THE PRIEST'S."   NY World, Charles P. Sweeney 11/9/24. **(p. 311)**

REMEMBERED HIM: A/BG interviews with JJM, JL and Louis Kalonyme. **(p. 311)**

WORK HE KNEW."   NYT, Louis Kalonyme 12/21/24. **(p. 312)**

HIS BARGE."   Ibid. **(p. 312)**

FELL OVER."   Ibid. In the second interview, O'N said Chris was found frozen "in a great cake of ice." Charles P. Sweeney, NY World, 11/9/24. Twenty-four years later, in the last interview he ever gave, O'N again recounted Chris's sad story: " . . . On Christmas morning he was found in the river, frozen to death. He must have fallen in." Basso Part II (bibliog). **(p. 312)**

WORK OF ART.   Oddly enough, on 10/22/17 — five years after the real-life Chris, according to O'N, was found frozen in the river, and two years before he wrote *Chris Christophersen* — the New York Marine Police found a man's body floating near the Statue of Liberty. The man was identified in a small New York paper, the Norwegian News, as "Christian Christophersen," a not uncommon Scandinavian name. This incident occurred on a warm October night, not on a frigid Christmas Eve, as described by O'N. If he saw this item — which is unlikely — it could have jogged his memory about his own Chris; but in that case, he would doubtless have mentioned the coincidence in his detailed interviews. (Some students of O'N's life and work maintain that the 1917 Chris was the "real" Chris, and claim, for no explicable reason, that O'N was "lying" about when and how Chris died.) **(p. 312)**

DISORDERLY CONDUCT."   Tyler (bibliog). **(p. 313)**

AT THEMSELVES."   A/BG interview with O'Casey. **(p. 313)**

TREACHEROUS SEA.   "Like the Old Woman in *Riders to the Sea* I feel I've won to that spent calm where neither joy nor sorrow over anything exist," O'N later wrote to ABO 2/16[?]/20, *SL*. **(p. 314)**

OTHER COMPANY."   Boston Sunday Globe, Charles A. Merrill 7/8/23. **(p. 314)**

TOURED AMERICA."   Ibid. **(p. 314)**

THE BABY."   A/BG interviews with KJP. **(p. 314)**

CHURCH STREET),   Details of the divorce proceedings, Westchester County Archives — Supreme Court, White Plains, NY File #1673 (1912), County Clerk's office. **(p. 315)**

FORTY–SEVENTH STREET.   Ibid. **(p. 315)**

THE MORNING."   Ibid. (p. 316)

DIVORCE PAPERS.   Ibid. (p. 000)

SIXTH AVENUE.   A/BG interviews with Norman Winston and Russel Crouse. (p. 316)

NIGHT'S PLAY.   This was the same Canfield who subsequently opened the gaming house in Saratoga, where Eugene had gambled as a teeneager (and described in a letter to his then girlfriend, Marion Welch). (p. 316)

UNDERWORLD CRIMES.   A/BG interview with Russel Crouse. (p. 316)

SILENT PARTNER.   Beansy was shot on July 15, 1912. (p. 316)

LEFTY LOUIE.   "The Great Waterways Convention, A Study in Prophecy (With apologies to *Hiawatha*)", NL Telegraph, 8/26/12. (p. 316)

NEW ORLEANS."   A/BG interview with Norman Winston. Mary Heaton Vorse confirmed this story. (p. 317)

BECOMING DESPERATE."   To Joseph McCarthy 2/18/31, *SL*. (p. 317)

PLACE TO GO."   Life, Tom Prideaux 10/14/46. (p. 318)

IN VAUDEVILLE."   NY Tribune, Philip Mindil 2/22/20. (p. 318)

ABOUT A YEAR."   2/18/31, *SL*. (p. 319)

CHAPTER TWENTY-SEVEN

TO RETURN."   Letter to Joseph McCarthy 2/18/31, *SL* and A/BG interview with Norman Winston. (p. 320)

BONANZA.   Life, Tom Prideaux 10/14/46. (p. 320)

WAS EXPERIENCE."   Crichton (bibliog). In his letter to Joseph McCarthy 2/18/31 O'N wrote, "I braced him for the fare north, but he could not see it." (p. 320)

ROLE OF NORTIER.   Much of the information about the vaudeville tour is from A/BG interviews with Webster. (p. 320)

ORPHEUM CIRCUIT."   Letter to Joseph McCarthy 2/18/31, *SL*. (p. 321)

OF OUR STAGE."   Cincinnati Commercial, 10/16/11. (p. 321)

TIME OF LIFE."   Cincinnati Times Star Inquirer, 10/19/11. (p. 321)

YEARS FROM NOW."   A/BG interview with actor Brandon Tynan. Interestingly, this jibe of Jamie's is echoed in the opening scene of *"Anna Christie,"* when the young but dissolute Anna confronts her father's aging dissolute mistress, Marthy. "I got your number the minute you stepped in the door," sneers Marthy. And Anna replies: "Well, I got yours, too, without no trouble. You're me forty years from now . . . " (p. 321)

YOUR PLAY, SIR."   O'N told this story to a number of friends; the actor, E. J. Ballantine, recounted it in the NY Herald Tribune, 1/6/29. (p. 322)

PATERNAL PRIDE.   A/BG interview with Webster. (p. 322)

STOPPED TALKING."   Crichton (bibliog). (p. 322)

PUNK ACTOR."   NYT Magazine, Richard L. Neuberger 11/22/36. (p. 322)

HAD TERMINATED."   Letter to Joseph McCarthy 2/18/31, *SL*. (p. 322)

MEMORY OF IT."   Letter to director Charles O'Brien Kennedy, 10/29/38. Copy given to A/BG by Kennedy. (p. 323)

PLAYING HAMLET."   Letter to Lawrence Estavan 1/15/40, *SL*. (p. 323)

WHITE RATS!"   To Donald Pace 5/7/34, *SL*. **(p. 323)**

OF ACROBATS.   NYT Magazine, S. J. Woolf 9/15/46. **(p. 323)**

DRUNKEN FROLIC.   Letter to Joseph McCarthy 2/18/31, *SL*. **(p. 324)**

THE AUDIENCE.   A/BG interview with O'N friend, Eben Given. **(p. 324)**

"AH WILDERNESS!"   A/BG interviews with AMcG (as told to him by O'N). In the rowdy barroom scene of *Ah, Wilderness!* the bartender threatens to "call Sullivan from the corner" and have the prostitute, Belle, "run in for street-walking!" **(p. 324)**

A SPEECH.   A/BG interview with Eddie Dowling, director of 1946 première of *The Iceman Cometh*. **(p. 324)**

TOLD A FRIEND.   A/BG interview with Charles O'Brien Kennedy. **(p. 325)**

EUGENE'S CONQUEST.   O'N embellished this episode when he told it to friends, including Russel Crouse, Dudley Nichols and Norman Winston. **(p. 325)**

TO MORPHINE.   A/BG interview with Webster. **(p. 326)**

DRUNKEN MISBEHAVIOR.   Sheaffer (bibliog). **(p. 327)**

DURING THE MEAL.   Anecdote confirmed by A/BG interview with Charles O'Brien Kennedy, to whom O'N told it. **(p. 327)**

TOO DRUNK."   A/BG interviews with AMcG. **(p. 327)**

MY CHILDREN!'"   Letter to Robert Sisk 4/24/42, Beinecke. **(p. 328)**

OPERA HOUSE.   NY Tribune 5/28/12; Boston Post 6/11/12. **(p. 328)**

CHAPTER TWENTY–EIGHT

BRAIN–DROWNING DRUNK"   The phrase, often used by O'N, appears in letter to Harold de Polo postmarked 5/9/28, *SL*. **(p. 329)**

THEIR ROPE.   A/BG interviews with JJM, JL, Louis Kalonyme. **(p. 329)**

IN HIS ROOM.   A/BG interview with Dr. Robert Lee Patterson, who attended O'N in his 50's. **(p. 329)**

THE PRIEST'S   The third form of Jimmy the Priest's in O'N's writings: in "Tomorrow," it is "Tommy the Priest's" and in *"Anna Christie"* it is "Johnny-the-Priest's." **(p. 330)**

PEACEFULLY TO SLEEP."   Nathan II (bibliog). **(p. 330)**

LENGTHY MONOLOGUE.   Boulton (bibliog). **(p. 330)**

OR DESTROYED.   ABO kept many letters from O'N, later selling them to Harvard U. Under her divorce agreement she was restrained from quoting from O'N's letters; she did not publish her memoir until after O'N's death, but CMO was alive and might have brought an action. ABO appears to have got around the restraint by attributing O'N's words in her memoir not to his letters but to her putatively retentive memory. **(p. 330)**

A STROKE.   The Library of Congress was unable to find a copyright or script for "Exorcism." **(p. 332)**

MIDDLE OF MARCH . . ."   (Italics are A/BG's). Beinecke. Also Floyd I (bibliog). **(p. 332)**

CALLED NORDSTROM.   Deutsch & Hanau (bibliog). **(p. 332)**

SWALLOWS POISON . . ."   NYT 4/4/20. **(p. 333)**

A FUTURE.   The theory has been advanced by some O'N scholars that his suicide attempt took place in January, 1912 (just prior to joining the *Monte Cristo* tour), rather than in late March (after his shameful retreat from the tour) and that it was an immediate response to the trumped-up adultery on 12/29/11, required to obtain his divorce from KJP. But nothing supports the January date except the shaky memory of actor Jasper Deeter, who played Ned Malloy in *Exorcism* and who, according to Sheaffer (bibliog), was somehow able to dredge up a "memory" of the play, and thought he recalled that the protagonist's suicidal despair in *Exorcism* was the result of a sordid divorce proceeding. Deeter was exhaustively interviewed by A/BG in 1957 and 1958 (thirty-eight years after the play's production) and at the time he said he remembered hardly anything about the plot of *Exorcism*; certainly he recalled nothing about Malloy's suicide attempt being the result of sleeping with a prostitute to establish grounds for adultery. And surely such a striking plot component would not have escaped the notice of three theater critics, none of whom made mention of it. Indeed, the theory would seem to be incontrovertibly contradicted by the biographical details of *Exorcism*. According to Woollcott's summary of the plot, Ned Malloy realizes that "the devils have gone out of him," that he is "a new person, the life ahead is life in a new world . . . " This "new world" was obviously the NL summer Eugene looked forward to as a reporter, and not his earlier enforced stint in a job he despised — acting with the *Monte Cristo* vaudeville tour. It seems unlikely that O'N, as someone newly chastened and enlightened following a suicide attempt, would engage in the spectacularly self-destructive behavior he displayed during the tour with his father. The bad behavior is dismissed by LS with the peculiar claim that O'N simply lied to everyone about his drunken carousing during the tour and that he was, in fact, sober and on good terms with his father throughout.   **(p. 333)**

DEATH WISH."   A/BG interview with Dr. Bisch. **(p. 333)**

COMPLETED PLAYS.   *More Stately Mansions* is not included in this count because O'N left it as an unfinished, rough draft, which he believed he had destroyed. The "lost" manuscript turned up after his death and was "completed" by others. **(p. 334)**

FOLKS MAD."   To R. W. Cottingham 5/12/44, *SL*. **(p. 334)**

CALLING "TOMORROW").   O'Neill Work Diary (bibliog). Entry dated 6/7/39: "(— get fine title, *The Iceman Cometh* instead of tentative *Tomorrow* one I had)." **(p. 334)**

ROAD TO—MORROW."   O'N in several instances hyphenated the word in the text, as well as in letters, but the title was not hyphenated in the published version. **(p. 334)**

TOMORROW HAD COME."   In NY World interview with Charles P. Sweeney 11/9/24 O'N said the real Jimmy "was going to get himself together and get back to work. Well, he did get a job and got fired. Then he realized that this tomorrow never would come. He solved everything by jumping to his death from the bedroom at Jimmy's." **(p. 335)**

OR 7, 1913.   James Byth's death certificate #8100 gives date of death as June 6, while NYT 6/8/13 gives it as June 7. According to the Actors' Fund, which paid his funeral expenses, Byth was buried in Evergreen Cemetery in Brooklyn on June 10. **(p. 335)**

BADLY SHAKEN.   A/BG interview with Emily Rippin, to whom Ella told this story. **(p. 337)**

OF MANHATTAN."   Westchester County Archives, Supreme Court, White Plains, File #1673 (1912), County Clerk's office. **(p. 337)**

OF THE CHILD.   Ibid. **(p. 337)**

ME THE LEAST."   A/BG interviews with CMO. **(p. 37)**

CAMERA SOON."   NY Herald 7/9/12. (p. 337)

LEGITIMATE STAGE."   Letter to Lawrence Estavan 1/15/40, *SL.* (p. 338)

ART McGINLEY).   A/BG interviews with AMcG and EK. (p. 338)

CHAPTER TWENTY-NINE

GARDEN VARIETY."   Boston Sunday Post, Olin Downes 8/29/20. (p. 339)

ALREADY ADEQUATE.   A/BG interview with Latimer's son, T. H. Latimer. (p. 339)

A LIVING."   Boston Sunday Globe, Charles A. Merrill 7/8/23. (p. 339)

THE TELEGRAPH.   Some years later he became sports editor of the Hartford Times. (p. 340)

HIMSELF IN PRINT."   Letter to A/BG from T. H. Latimer 3/21/60. (p. 340)

HIS SALARY."   AMcG told A/BG this was a widely circulated story among reporters on both the Telegraph and the Day. (p. 340)

MY FATHER."   Letter from O'N to his lawyer, Harry Weinberger 9/28/42, *SL.* (p. 340)

HOSPITAL YESTERDAY."   A/BG interview with AMcG. (p. 341)

COULD SAY IT."   Clark (bibliog). (p. 341)

'ALL WET.'"   Ibid. Latimer had by then sold his interest in the Telegraph. (p. 341)

SUMMED UP.   Ibid. (p. 342)

HIS INCOME   Payroll records NL Day 1912. (p. 342)

'YES, SIR.'"   Philadelphia Public Ledger 1/22/22. (p. 342)

HE HAD TO."   Ibid. (p. 343)

SMALL TOWN."   Undated clipping, Hartford Times, "O'Neill Started Writing as New London Reporter," by A. B. McGinley, given to A/BG by AMcG. (p. 343)

BUM REPORTER,"   A/BG interviews with Russel Crouse and BA. (p. 343)

LOW ORDER."   Journal of the Outdoor Life, June 1923, Vol. XX. (p. 343)

THE DAY   A/BG interviews with AMcG. (p. 343)

OF GENIUS."   Providence [R.I.] Journal 12/6/31. (p. 343)

THROUGH HERE.   This was the same Dorsey from whom James O'N bought real estate and who figures as an offstage character (called McGuire) in *LDJIN.* (p. 344)

THE SPECTATORS."   8/18/12; although the story was unsigned, AMcG said O'N wrote it. (p. 344)

TAFT NEVER DOES.   NL Telegraph 9/2/12. Also Gallup (bibliog). (p. 344)

IN THE BARS."   "For the Waterways Convention's In The Morning." (With apologies to Rudyard K's "Danny Deever"). NL Telegraph. Also Gallup (bibliog). (Gallup gives the dates as "sometime before the Waterways Convention in New London, 3–4 Sept, 1912). (p. 345)

OUR PORRIDGE.   NL Telegraph 8/26/12. Also Gallup (bibliog). (p. 346)

SUNDAY NIGHT.")   NL Telegraph 9/23/12. Also Gallup (bibliog). (p. 346)

SHUT-EYE CANDIDATE."   NL Telegraph 10/3/12. (p. 348)

WAS UNTRUE.   A/BG interview with AMcG. (p. 348)

NEVER MAKE IT."   Ibid. (p. 348)

SCOTT'S SUPREMACY.   A/BG interviews with EK and AMcG. (p. 349)

TO YOU BOYS."   Ibid. (p. 349)

NO MONEY HERE."   A/BG interviews with AMcG. (p. 351)

INDEPENDENCE.   A/BG interviews with Peterson and Ramage. (p. 351)

CHAPTER THIRTY

IN ANOTHER.   A/BG interview with MSB's daughter, Dorothy Des Granges. (p. 353)

ADVENTURE–LACED PAST.   Information about MSB's romance with O'N from A/BG interviews with her and her friends and family; also with AMcG, EK and JG. At time of interviews she was Maibelle Scott Beckley. (p. 353)

EARLY AGE!"   A/BG interviews with Lillian Gish. (p. 353)

DISSOLUTE WAYS.   A/BG interviews with MSB. (p. 354)

I'D LIKE TO."   A/BG interviews with Arlene Scott Fones. (p. 355)

EUGENE," SHE SAID.   A/BG interview with Alma Scott Fones Eshenfelder, Arlene's daughter. (p. 355)

ADDICTION.   A/BG interview with Bessie Young. (p. 355)

THE WEDDING.   A/BG interviews with MSB. (p. 355)

GRAY–BLUE ONES.   Ibid. (p. 356)

HAD A CHILD."   It is noteworthy that in setting *LDJIN* during summer 1912 O'N — while including many pertinent facts of his family's and his own past — omitted reference to his marriage and his son. As Freudians who have studied the play are quick to point out, however, Kathleen Jenkins is symbolically present as Cathleen, the house maid, the only non-family member. Also worth noting is the offstage cranky cook named Bridget, who might be a symbolic stand-in for the deceased Bridget Quinlan, Ella O'N's mother. (p. 356)

ABOUT HIM.   A/BG interviews with MSB and Arlene Fones. (p. 356)

"E.G.O."   MSB's private collection, copy given to A/BG. (p. 357)

TENNIS COURTS.   A/BG interview with Alma Wies, widow of Dr. Carl Wies, prominent member of the club. Years later, after a fire had partly demolished the casino, Mrs. Wies bought and remodeled it as a private dwelling for herself. (p. 358)

BIG GIRL."   MSB's private collection, copy given to A/BG. (p. 359)

LETTER–PERFECT.   He had in fact mis-transcribed numerous words and phrases — writing, for example, " . . . *Yet* before the sand *in the glass* is run and the silver *cord* is broken . . . " instead of Dowson's " . . . before the sand is run and the silver thread is broken . . . " And, from another stanza: " . . . *And when the terrible torrents* fall and my *soul is* carried under . . . " instead of Dowson's " . . . Before the ruining waters fall and my life be carried under . . . " (p. 359)

YOUR VOICE.   Also published in Gallup (bibliog). (p. 360)

SURPRISE TO HIM."   A/BG interview with Mildred Culver Greene. (p. 360)

THOU HADST CAME!   Also in Gallup (bibliog). (p. 361)

CHAPTER THIRTY-ONE

DREARILY . . ."   NL Telegraph 9/28/12. Also Gallup (bibliog). **(p. 363)**

NEVER NEW . . .   Also Gallup (bibliog). **(p. 364)**

BROTHER'S ILLNESS.   A/BG interview with PS, who accompanied Jamie to sanatorium and kept in touch during his stay. **(p. 364)**

COMPETENCE.   A/BG interviews with OEM, O'N's nurse. **(p. 365)**

"FEEL MEAN."   Notes of interview 8/3/46 with ESS, Beinecke. **(p. 365)**

RHEUMATISM"   Ibid. **(p. 365)**

RIGHT BACK."   Gaylord records. **(p. 365)**

WASHING THAT DOOR!"   A/BG interviews with OEM. **(p. 365)**

TRAIL OF LIGHT . . ."   NY Telegraph 11/19/12. (Additional stanzas of "The Call" given in Ch. 23.) **(p. 365)**

HIS LUNG.   According to Gaylord records, "1,000 cc. fluid was drawn from chest." **(p. 365)**

"CHOKING SIGHS."   Text of sonnet given Ch. 19. **(p. 365)**

PESTILENCE."   Both poems Gallup (bibliog). **(p. 366)**

SINGER DIED.   NL Telegraph 11/27/12. Also Gallup (bibliog). **(p. 366)**

ON EARTH? . . .   4th and 5th of six stanzas. MSB's private collection. **(p. 367)**

ON SMILING."   12/10/32, SL. **(p. 369)**

ON EUGENE.   A/BG interviews with PS. **(p. 369)**

USUAL ASSOCIATIONS."   Journal of the Outdoor Life, June, 1923. **(p. 370)**

ALIEN DEMON."   Barely decipherable handwritten scenario notes for The Long Day's Journey (sic), Act IV, June 1939, Beinecke. **(p. 370)**

ABOUT MAIBELLE.   A/BG interview with Mildred Culver Greene. **(p. 370)**

SORRY FOR HIM."   Clark (bibliog). **(p. 371)**

LATE 1990'S.   Edison Electric Institute, Washington, D.C. **(p. 371)**

WERE HIGH."   A/BG interview with Liebler. **(p. 371)**

CONTRADICTORY NATURE.   Letter to Lawrence Estavan 1/15/40, SL. **(p. 372)**

LOATHE THEE!   Also Gallup (bibliog). **(p. 372)**

THAT INTENT."   Clark (bibliog). **(p. 373)**

AN O'NEILL "BIBLIOGRAPHY."   Sanborn and Clark (bibliog). After O'N's death various verses were included in a number of scholarly publications, most notably Gallup (bibliog). **(p. 373)**

STUFF INDEED."   Letter to Francesco Bianco 2/3/36. Copy given to A/BG by Frances Steloff, rare book dealer. **(p. 373)**

COME BACK."   Crichton (bibliog). **(p. 373)**

OF A MOOD."   Letter to BAM 11/12/14, SL. **(p. 373)**

ONLY APPEARANCES.   Tyler (bibliog). **(p. 374)**

ABOVE ALL!"   Handwritten notes for Act III, crossed out. Beinecke. **(p. 374)**

SINGLE-BREASTED SUIT."   A/BG interviews with Dr. Lynch. **(p. 375)**

CHAPTER THIRTY-TWO

REAL ESTATE,   A/BG interview with Theodore Liebler Jr. **(p. 380)**

O'DOONE (1920).   Internet Movie Database. **(p. 380)**

FOR RECOVERY.   Laurel Heights Sanatorium records; also letter to A/BG 9/3/57 from Dr. Kirby S. Howlett Jr., who succeeded Dr. Edward Lynch when he retired 1954. "It should be pointed out," Dr. Howlett wrote, "that diagnoses and evaluations at that time [1913] were made on the basis of history and physical examination, because it was before the days when the chest X-ray was considered a sine qua non to complete pulmonary diagnosis." **(p. 380)**

NO FEVER."   Gaylord records. **(p. 381)**

DATE DESIGNATED;   letter to Dr. Lyman 12/20/12, *SL*. **(p. 381)**

TO A POINT."   A/BG interviews with Wilhelmina Stamberger, retired nurse, then in her 70's. **(p. 381)**

INTENTIONALLY!"   Dedication to Mary A. Clark, Gaylord nurse. **(p. 381)**

CONNECTICUT PAPER.   A/BG interviews with Wilhelmina Stamberger. **(p. 382)**

IRREGULAR LIFE.   Gaylord records. **(p. 382)**

A BEACHCOMBER;   A/BG interviews with AMcG. **(p. 383)**

DIED OF T.B.;   A/BG interviews with KM. **(p. 383)**

IN NEW LONDON.   A/BG interviews with Joseph Heidt. **(p. 383)**

INCIPIENT CASE."   8/11/27. Copy of letter given to authors by de Casseres's wife, Bio. **(p. 383)**

YOU GET IT."   Crichton (bibliog). **(p. 383)**

AND WRITERS."   To O'N Jr. 7/14/40, *SL*. **(p. 383)**

HIS THROAT."   A/BG interview with Eben Given. **(p. 383)**

J. G. STANTON.   Unpublished memoir, Frances E. Hubbard, July 1969. Beinecke. **(p. 384)**

'DOCTOR STANTON."   Letter headed "Monday" with no month or year; envelope postmarked 11/23/21, *SL*. **(p. 384)**

AND PROVED.   A/BG interview with Wilhelmina Stamberger and Emma Halper Wolodarsky (former patient). **(p. 384)**

EUGENE O'NEILL."   Gaylord records. **(p. 384)**

RIGHT BASE."   Ibid. **(p. 385)**

BERKELEY THEATER.   Vanity Fair 1/11/13. **(p. 385)**

BULL DURHAM."   A/BG interview with Wilhelmina Stamberger. **(p. 385)**

TUBERCULOSIS.   Gaylord Farm records. **(p. 386)**

CONVALESCENCE."   2/21/13. **(p. 386)**

AGAINST HIM.   A/BG interview with Arthur W. Wisner, friend of Mary Clark, whose brother, Bernard Clark, gave him her letters shortly after her death in 1957. **(p. 386)**

LONG LIFE!   Second stanza of four-stanza poem, dated 5/24/13, Gallup (bibliog). **(p. 386)**

PLAYWRIGHT."   8/5/23, *SL*. **(p. 387)**

GIFT OF GAB."   A/BG interview with Stamberger. **(p. 387)**

YEARS TO COME,   Letter to Mary A. Clark 8/5/23, *SL*. **(p. 387)**

WITH T.B."   NY Tribune, Philip Mindil 2/22/20. **(p. 388)**

NOT SO SURE."   Basso III (bibliog). **(p. 388)**
REFLECTION."   Journal of the Outdoor Life June 1923. **(p. 389)**
NEVER UGLY!"   American Magazine, Mary B. Mullett, Nov. 1922. **(p. 389)**
AND WASN'T."   Letter to Dr. Lyman, [Summer 1914] *SL*. **(p. 389)**
TEN–FOLD.   Journal of the Outdoor Life June 1923. **(p. 389)**
DEFEATS DEATH."   NY Tribune, Philip Mindil 2/22/20. **(p. 389)**
FULL APPROVAL."   [Summer 1914] *SL*. **(p. 389)**
MY MEMORIES."   Gaylord records. **(p. 389)**
WITH DEPTH."   A/BG interview with Emma Wolodarsky. **(p. 390)**
HOME AFFAIRS."   Gaylord records. **(p. 390)**
ONLY FAIR.   Ibid. **(p. 390)**
AND KITTY.   A/BG interview with Emma Wolodarsky. **(p. 391)**
AT 4 A.M.   A/BG interviews with JG and Dr. Frederick B. Mayo, O'N's doctor in later years in whom he confided. **(p. 391)**
AS IT DID.   A/BG interview with Emma Wolodarsky. **(p. 391)**
DAMNED BOOKS."   Ibid. **(p. 391)**
YOUR LIPS!   Private collection of MSB. **(p. 392)**
ABOUT KITTY,   A/BG interview with OEM. **(p. 392)**
FRIEDMAN'S SOUP."   Beinecke. **(p. 392)**
WORK IN FALL."   Gaylord records. **(p. 392)**
FOR THE SUMMER.   Ibid. **(p. 393)**
WAS $167.35.   Ibid. **(p. 393)**
SAW HER AGAIN.   A/BG interview with Emma Wolodarsky. **(p. 393)**
SHE WAS DEAD.   Kitty Mackay died 5/17/15. Gaylord Farm records. **(p. 393)**

CHAPTER THIRTY–THREE

NANNYGOAT."   A/BG interviews with PS. **(p. 394)**
HIS BUREAU   Boulton (bibliog). **(p. 394)**
THE SUMMER.   A/BG interviews with PS. **(p. 394)**
TO REFUSE HIM.   A/BG interviews with PS and AMcG. **(p. 394)**
VAUDEVILLE.   Clark (bibliog). **(p. 395)**
ONE NIGHT."   O'N's handwritten note on another early play, *The Web*, donated to Princeton U. 1944. **(p. 396)**
SKIT, EITHER."   Nassau Sovereign (Princeton), Dec 1946. **(p. 396)**
FOR THE STAGE."   Notation in O'N collection, Princeton U. **(p. 396)**
HAD EVER DONE,   Clark (bibliog). **(p. 396)**
HAD EVER DONE.   O'N to Sean O'Casey, 8/5/43, *SL*. **(p. 396)**
COULD BE FOUND.   A/BG interviews with JR. **(p. 396)**
THEATER WRITING."   8/20/13. **(p. 396)**
ATTEMPT, HE SAID,   Clark (bibliog). **(p. 396)**
ESTHETIC EFFORTS.   O'N to GJN 6/20/20, *SL*. **(p. 396)**

"FIRST PLAY,"   O'N to Mark Van Doren 5/12/44, *SL. The Web* was copyrighted 10/17/13, Library of Congress. **(p. 397)**

HUNGER).   Beinecke. **(p. 397)**

FULL–LENGTH PLAYS.   In 1937 O'Neill made a "List of all plays ever written by me, including those I later destroyed," in which he noted "where and when they were written." For 1913 he lists *The Web* and *Thirst*, written "Our house — New London, Conn"; for 1914 he lists *Abortion*, also written "Our House"; he lists *The Movie Man* as written 1916 in Provincetown — obviously a mistake, since the copyright on file at the Library of Congress is 6/1/14. He lists the remaining plays (*Recklessness*, *Warnings*, *Fog*, *Bound East for Cardiff* and *Bread and Butter*) as written in 1914 at "Rippins', New London." In a second document, written in 1946 and headed "Cycles" — charting his life from the year of his birth in segments of seven years — he sometimes contradicts (either absentmindedly or deliberately) his own earlier documentation in "List of all plays . . . " Both documents at Beinecke. **(p. 397)**

STEAL THEM,"   Crichton (bibliog). *Thirst, The Web, Warnings, Fog* and *Recklessness* were published 1914. **(p. 397)**

"WORTH REMEMBERING."   O'N to AHQ 6/13/22, *SL.* **(p. 397)**

NEW DIRECTION."   NY World, Flora Merrill, 7/19/25. **(p. 397)**

YEARS LATER.   O/N to Mark Van Doren, 5/12/44, *SL.* At Van Doren's request O'N donated the original manuscript to a World War II Bond Drive; it was later presented to Princeton U. **(p. 399)**

THEIR OPINION."   To R. W. Cottingham 5/12/44, *SL.* A "revised" manuscript of *Thirst* is dated Fall, 1913. **(p. 399)**

STRANGERS."   A/BG interviews with JR. **(p. 400)**

EXPLAINED.   Journal of the Outdoor Life, June 1923. **(p. 402)**

TO GET UP."   Letter from O'N to Jessica and Dolly Rippin 8/18/25, copy given to A/BG by Rippins. **(p. 402)**

DR. LYMAN.   Letter dated Summer 1914, describing his work habits currently and during previous year. **(p. 402)**

THE 'MOVIES.'"   Summer, 1914, *SL.* **(p. 403)**

WORDS FLOWED.   Basso III (bibliog). **(p. 403)**

BAD AT IT."   "Eleven Manuscripts of Eugene O'Neill by Marguerite Loud McAneny." Princeton U. **(p. 404)**

OF PURPOSE."   O'N began his speech by acknowledging his debt to "that greatest genius of all modern dramatists, your August Strindberg." **(p. 404)**

AN AUDIENCE.   A/BG interview with Manuel Komroff. **(p. 404)**

OWN SOUL?'"   This Week Magazine, "O'Neill's Last Premiere" by Harry Heintzen, Stockholm 1/29/56. **(p. 405)**

TRADITION IS NOT."   NYT Magazine, S. J. Woolf 9/15/46. **(p. 406)**

HAS BEEN USED."   "A Plank in Faulkner's 'Lumber Room,'" by Donald P. Duclos, Northeast Modern Language Association Convention, Boston 4/3/87. Reprinted in E O'N Newsletter, Summer-Fall, 1987. **(p. 407)**

THE INFERNO.")   To BAM 11/1/14, *SL.* **(p. 408)**

SO 'ORRIBLE."   Theater Arts, "Untold Tales of Eugene O'Neill," Gladys Hamilton Aug. l956. **(p. 408)**

SHYNESS."   Vogue, "Seen on the Stage," Clayton Hamilton 4/1/20. **(p. 408)**

OPPOSITE ME."   A/BG interview with Mrs. Clayton Hamilton. **(p. 408)**

OPEN TO HIM."   Hamilton (bibliog). **(p. 409)**

WINTER OF 1914,   The copyright records for *Thirst, Recklessnes, Warnings* and *Fog* have been either misplaced or lost; a search by the Library of Congress failed to turn them up. **(p. 409)**

EARLY PLAYS.   *Fog* was presented at the Playwrights' Theater, Jan. 5, 1917. **(p. 409)**

CALLED HIS PLAYS.   Letter to BAM, 2/18(?)/15, *SL*. **(p. 410)**

OF ARMOR."   Letter to Patrick O'Neill 9/18/40, *SL*. **(p. 410)**

CHAPTER THIRTY-FOUR

EARNING CAPACITY."   A/BG interview with AMcG. **(p. 411)**

OWN TAIL."   A/BG interview with Brandon Tynan. **(p. 411)**

SOME NIGHTS."   Tyler (bibliog). **(p. 412)**

LINES HIMSELF.   A/BG interview with Austin. **(p. 412)**

"ACTOR–YOKEL."   Letter from O'N to GCT 12/9/20, *SL*. **(p. 412)**

KEEP UP.   A/BG interview with Tynan. O'N softened his view after Tynan sent him a photograph in 1948 of himself and James posing during one of their walks. "I knew and loved your wonderful Dad — as did everyone who knew him," wrote Tynan on the back of the photograph." Museum of the City of New York. In a letter 12/6/48, *SL*, O'N asked Charles O'Brien Kennedy to thank Tynan for the photo. Tynan also gave a copy of the photo to A/BG. **(p. 412)**

EXPOSTULATED.   Basso I (bibliog). **(p. 412)**

IF I LIVED."   NY Daily News, Fred Pasley 1/27/32. **(p. 413)**

HOLBROOK BLINN,   A/BG interview with Tynan. **(p. 413)**

AND TRAGEDY."   Theater Magazine, "A Theater of Thrills" June 1913. **(p. 413)**

RECKLESSNESS;   letter from O'N to Dr. Lyman, Summer 1914, *SL*; and NL Telegraph 8/20/14. **(p. 413)**

A ONE–ACT."   7/4/32, *SL*. **(p. 413)**

THOUGHT MYSELF."   NY Herald Tribune 3/19/33. **(p. 413)**

THE MODERNS."   Clark (bibliog). **(p. 414)**

UNHAPPY."   Philadelphia Public Ledger Sunday Magazine, "Making Plays With a Tragic End," Malcolm Mollan 1/22/22. **(p. 414)**

"EMILY BELLE."   Letter to Jessica Rippin 5/7/14, *SL*. **(p. 414)**

BAREFOOT.   1914 questionnaire, Gaylord records. **(p. 414)**

[MOTHER EARTH]."   Research by Winifred L. Frazer turned up no poem signed by O'N in any issue of Mother Earth. She did find an "unsigned contribution in the issue of May 1911," which she points out has striking similarities to O'N's poetry of 1912. The poem, ("With apologies to the literary executors of O. Khayyam"), is entitled "The American Sovereign" and attacks one of O'N's favorite subjects, the robbing by capitalism of the Working Class. *E.G and E.G.O. Emma Goldman and "The Iceman Cometh,"* the University Presses of Florida, Gainesville, 1974. **(p. 414)**

KNOCKS, WHAT?"   To "Dear Dolly & Jessica & Rippins in General:" 8/18/26. Copy of letter given to A/BG by JR. **(p. 417)**

BAD GIRL.   A/BG interview with ER. **(p. 417)**

YOUR MOTHER."   2/4/19, *SL*. **(p. 418)**

PLAYWRIGHT HE WAS. A/BG interviews with JR. **(p. 418)**

'LUNGER'S' EXPERIENCE." Summer 1914, *SL*. **(p. 419)**

OTHER SYMPTOMS. 1914 questionnaire, Gaylord records. **(p. 420)**

HALF–REMEMBERED PRAYER." Penciled script, Museum of City of NY. **(p. 422)**

APPARENTLY ISN'T." O'N to AHQ 4/3/25, *SL*. **(p. 422)**

FORM & CONTENT." Letter to Richard Dana Skinner, who was writing a critical study of O'N's plays [July ?], 1934, *SL*. **(p. 422)**

WILLING — LIVING!" American Magazine, Mary B. Mullett, Nov. 1922. **(p. 423)**

RAINBOW'S FOOT . . . " NY Tribune 1/13/21. **(p. 423)**

KNEW A RIPPIN!" O'N to Grace (Dolly) Rippin 10/16/33, *SL*. **(p. 423)**

CHAPTER THIRTY–FIVE

RELIGIOUS FAITH. A/BG interviews with PS. **(p. 425)**

CROWN HEIGHTS. Brooklyn Catholic diocese records. **(p. 426)**

EFFECT HER CURE. A/BG interview with Sister Constance Fitzgerald, who explained that the Brooklyn Carmelite monastery was one of the most rigid of the 65 in the country in its interpretation of cloistered Carmelite life, and it continued to grow more isolated with time. In May 1997, the five remaining sisters who maintained the monastery burned their records, vacated the premises and found shelter in other convents. **(p. 426)**

YOUNGER MISTAKE." 5/7/14, *SL*. **(p. 426)**

FOR PHILADELPHIA. Ibid. **(p. 426)**

TORCH BEARER.'" Ibid. **(p. 427)**

NEXT SEASON." Summer 1914, *SL*. **(p. 427)**

CURE AT LAST. A/BG interviews with CMO. **(p. 428)**

THE MOVIE MAN, See footnote Ch. 33 re: where and when written. **(p. 428)**

AS POSSIBLE." *A Million and One Nights — A History of the Motion Picture Through 1925*, Terry Ramsaye, Simon & Schuster NY, 1926. **(p. 429)**

PICTURE VANISHED." Ibid. **(p. 429)**

BOX OFFICE, Clark (bibliog). **(p. 429)**

REMAIN INACTIVE." 6/20/20, *SL*. **(p. 429)**

DISOWNED IT. *The Movie Man* was published, to O'N's anger and disgust, from the typescript on file at the Library of Congress, in an unauthorized volume entitled *The Lost Plays of Eugene O'Neill*, NY, New Fathoms Press, 1950. The volume also included *The Sniper, Abortion*, and *A Wife for a Life*, all of which he had wanted to forget, and for which he had failed to renew the copyright. All O'N's plays for which scripts were extant — including those he disavowed or listed as "destroyed" — are published (with notes on the texts) in Bogard II (bibliog). **(p. 430)**

HIS LIFETIME. Bogard III (bibliog). **(p. 430)**

STAKING ME." A/BG interview with Mrs. Clayton Hamilton. **(p. 430)**

"APPRECIABLE PROMISE." The Bookman, April 1915. **(p. 430)**

HAD RUN AWAY." Hamilton (bibliog). **(p. 430)**

TO A JOB?   A/BG interviews with AMcG, EK and Rippins. **(p. 430)**

AMERICAN SOUL."   Atkinson (bibliog). **(p. 431)**

ALL OF THEM."   Crichton (bibliog). **(p. 431)**

ABOUT YOU."   Speech by Sidney Howard 2/23/35 at National Theater Conference in New Haven, Kinne (bIbliog). **(p. 431)**

BROUGHT UP."   2/21/25, SL. **(p. 431)**

AND DRIFTERS.   Barnes (bibliog). **(p. 432)**

ON BROADWAY.   Sheldon biographer Eric Wollencott Barnes maintains it was Sheldon's agent, Alice Kauser, who brought the play to Mrs. Fiske, whereas Baker biographer Wisner Payne Kinne claims it was Baker. **(p. 432)**

THE BROTHEL."   Barnes (bibliog). **(p. 432)**

ON THE STAGE."   *Theatre, U.S.A.*, Barnard Hewitt, McGraw-Hill NY, Toronto, London 1959. **(p. 433)**

ROMANTIC MELODRAMA.   After two flops, Sheldon wrote a fourth successful melodrama, *The High Road*, about a woman with a disreputable past who achieves the pinnacle of respectability as the wife of a presidential candidate. Finally, he wrote another huge hit, *Romance*, loosely based on the career of the Italian opera singer, Lina Cavalieri (whose name he thinly disguised as Cavallini) and which marked the peak of his success. Barnes (bibliog). **(p. 433)**

YOUR STUDENT."   7/16/14, SL. **(p. 433)**

LENA CAVALLERI.   The singer, who spelled her name Lina Cavalieri. **(p. 434)**

ROMANTIC DREAMS."   Notes for what O'N was then calling *Bessie Bowen*. Beinecke. **(p. 434)**

HER AMBITION.   Entries shown to A/BG by Mildred Culver. **(p. 434)**

HER RIVALS.   A/BG interview with Dorothy Des Granges (MSB's daughter). **(p. 435)**

GREAT–GREAT–GRANDCHILDREN.   Ibid. **(p. 435)**

CHAPTER THIRTY–SIX

NOT YET TWENTY,   BAM was born Norwich, Conn. 12/2/1894. State Bureau of Vital Statistics. **(p. 436)**

YEAR BEFORE   Williams Memorial Institute, class of 1913 official transcript. **(p. 436)**

RECALLED BEATRICE.   A/BG interview with BAM. **(p. 436)**

LOOP EARRINGS.   A/BG interviews with Rippins and MSB. **(p. 436)**

GOLDEN LIGHTS."   "Upon Our Beach," Summer 1914 (before Sept. 22), Gallup (bibliog). **(p. 436)**

SANATORIUM.   A/BG interview with BAM. **(p. 437)**

FLOATING DIVAN."   O'N to BAM 10/11/14, SL. **(p. 437)**

LATER REMINISCED.   O'N to BAM 11/1/14, SL. **(p. 437)**

PEACH," HE SAID.   A/BG interview with Campbell. **(p. 437)**

"IRONSIDES."   In 1996 Hammond and thirteen relatives were exhumed from the Cedar Grove Cemetery and reburied on the site of the Hammond estate, which by then had become home to the Eugene O'Neill Theater Center. "I think the fact that the man who threw [O'Neill] off that beach will now be spending eternity on his ground would have amused him," said George C. White, Center founder. NYT, 10/7/96. **(p. 438)**

OUR BEACH!"   "Upon Our Beach," Gallup (bibliog). **(p. 438)**

I ADORE!"   "Full Many A Cup Of This Forbidden Wine," probably written summer 1914, Gallup (bibliog). **(p. 439)**

ONE POINT.   To BAM, 11/1/14, *SL*. **(p. 439)**

ALL MY SOUL!"   To BAM 11/7/14, *SL*. **(p. 439)**

WITH THE SEA."   To BAM dated 7/22/14, 7/24/14, 7/26/14, Berg. **(p. 439)**

TO THE COURSE.   To Baker 7/29/14, *SL*. **(p. 439)**

GREAT SILENCE. . . ."   Dedication dated 12/28/18, Houghton Library, Harvard U. **(p. 440)**

LOUSY DRAMA!"   Letter, 4/27/44, Princeton U. **(p. 440)**

SEEKING ADVICE.   To a "Mr. Maxwell" 5/8/45, *SL*. **(p. 440)**

OVER $100,000.   A/BG interview with Steloff. **(p. 440)**

THE NATION.   In letter to Felton Elkins June(?) 1915, O'N mentions the two reviews, as well as one in the Baltimore Sun, *SL*. **(p. 441)**

GETTING SOMEWHERE."   4/6/20, *SL*. **(p. 441)**

NOT ONE.)   Letter to Hamilton 4/5/35, Berg. **(p. 441)**

HAPPEN AGAIN."   Letter to Hamilton 4/6/20, *SL*. In his later letter to Hamilton (4/5/35, Berg), O'N recalled the advice with a slight difference: "Always remember when you send in a script that there is about one chance in a hundred it will ever be read, one chance in a thousand that, if read, it will ever be accepted, one chance in fifty thousand that, if accepted, it will ever be produced, and, if produced, one chance in a million that it will succeed." **(p. 441)**

OF THE GAME."   4/6/20, *SL*. **(p. 441)**

BEEN OPENED!   To Patrick O'Neill (no relation) 7/11/40, Dartmouth. These facts are described in almost identical language in a later letter to another aspiring writer, Mr. Maxwell, 5/8/45, *SL*. **(p. 442)**

NEVER GOOD!"   American Magazine, Mary B. Mullett, Nov. 1922. **(p. 442)**

WAIT A WHILE."   Tyler (bibliog). **(p. 442)**

TO ANYTHING."   A/BG interviews with Mrs. Clayton Hamilton. **(p. 443)**

"DESTROYED."   It was included without his permission in *Lost Plays of Eugene O'Neill*. **(p. 444)**

TO HIS HEART.   To BAM 9/21/14, *SL*. **(p. 445)**

CHAPTER THIRTY-SEVEN

IN HIS EYES.   9/28/14, Berg. **(p. 448)**

MY MOTHER!"   2/5/15, Berg. **(p. 448)**

LITTLE KISS").   1/9/15 Gallup (bibliog). **(p. 450)**

FOR THEM ALL.   A/BG interviews with Daniel Hiebert, later to practice medicine in Provincetown, Mass., where he renewed his friendship with O'N. **(p. 450)**

TO BEATRICE.   9/30/14, *SL*. **(p. 450)**

HORSEHIDE SHOES."   O'N to BAM 10/7/14, *SL*. **(p. 451)**

FASCINATING PERSONALITY."   9/30/14, *SL*. **(p. 451)**

RADCLIFFE."   Crichton (bibliog). **(p. 452)**

WITH MERRIMENT."   Kinne (bibliog). **(p. 452)**

IF THEY WISHED.   A/BG interviews with classmates Bruce Carpenter and William L. Laurence. **(p. 453)**

SHORT STORY."   9/30/14, *SL*. **(p. 453)**

ONLY IN YOU."   Ibid. **(p. 453)**

AGAINST YOUR OWN."   10/6/14, *SL*. **(p. 453)**

MY DEAD LIFE."   10/9/14, *SL*. **(p. 453)**

RAG OF LIFE."   10/8/14, *SL*. **(p. 453)**

WILL BE FRIGHTFUL."   10/7/14, *SL*. **(p. 454)**

UNASSUAGED DESIRE.'"   10/9/14, *SL*. **(p. 454)**

OF OMISSION."   Ibid. **(p. 454)**

THE AFTERWARDS."   10/10/14, *SL*. **(p. 454)**

FRESH AIR."   10/11/14, *SL*. **(p. 454)**

WORTHY OF YOU!"   10/21/14, Berg. **(p. 455)**

DEPRESSION."   To BAM 10/22/14, Berg. **(p. 455)**

WELL–BEING."   10/29/14, Berg. **(p. 455)**

EACH OTHER."   11/1/14, *SL*. **(p. 455)**

BE WORKING."   11/2/14, *SL*. **(p. 455)**

TO THE POINT."   11/7/14, *SL*. **(p. 456)**

DEVELOPMENT."   Boston Sunday Post, Olin Downes 8/29/20. **(p. 456)**

"END IN LIFE."   11/7/14, *SL*. **(p. 456)**

HUMAN POSSIBILITY."   11/8/14, *SL*. **(p. 457)**

BE PRODUCED.'"   ll/12/14, *SL*. **(p. 457)**

VAUDEVILLE SKETCH.   Clark (bibliog). **(p. 457)**

MILK SHAKES.   11/16/14, Berg. **(p. 458)**

YOU KNOW," HE SAID.   11/18/14, *SL*. **(p. 458)**

ALL THE TIME."   12/10/14, *SL*. **(p. 458)**

LOW BROWS."   12/12/14, *SL*. **(p. 458)**

TO BROADWAY!"   Ibid. **(p. 459)**

HUMAN BEINGS."   12/15/14, Berg. **(p. 459)**

CHAPTER THIRTY-EIGHT

CYNICISM TO SHAME."   *SL*. **(p. 460)**

DELIGHTFUL FUTURE."   1/7/15, *SL*. **(p. 460)**

BELSHAZZAR.   Ibid. **(p. 460)**

EVER THUS!"   1/8/15, *SL*. **(p. 461)**

SUNG TO HIM: Song by Adrian Ross and Low Silesu written 1912. **(p. 461)**

TWILIGHT'S CLOSE.   Gallup (bibliog). **(p. 461)**

FROSTBITTEN NOSE.   The poems, written between Jan. 10–15 were: "Just Me N' You," "Ballade Of The Two Of Us," "Impression," "Rondeau, To Her Nose," "A Dream of Last Week," and "Lament for Beatrice." Gallup (bibliog). **(p. 461)**

ST. LOUIS.   1/11/15, *SL.* **(p. 461)**

WILD–CATS."   Ibid. **(p. 461)**

HANGING YET."   1/13/15, *SL.* **(p. 462)**

CONVERSATION."   1/17/15, *SL.* **(p. 462)**

ABYSMAL DARKNESS."   1/21/15, Berg. **(p. 462)**

PUT TOGETHER."   To BAM 1/31/15, *SL.* **(p. 462)**

PLAY AT ALL,"   Clark (bibliog). **(p. 463)**

A BIT PEEVED."   3/28/15, *SL.* **(p. 463)**

FIREMEN'S STRIKE."   Clark (bibliog). A copy of the script was found among O'N's papers at Yale after his death and subsequently published in Bogard II (bibliog). **(p. 463)**

A PRODUCTION."   Details of Thomas's lecture related to A/BG by Bruce Carpenter. **(p. 464)**

LEFT THE ROOM."   Clark (bibliog). **(p. 464)**

TO GET DRUNK.   A/BG interview with Bruce Carpenter. **(p. 464)**

THESE TRADITIONS."   NYT Magazine, S. J. Woolf 10/4/31. **(p. 465)**

HUMAN PLAYS."   A/BG interview with Carpenter. **(p. 465)**

APART BY HIM."   Letter from Baker to Barrett H. Clark, Jan. 1926, Clark (bibliog). **(p. 466)**

STUFF TO ME."   Clark (bibliog). **(p. 466)**

SHORT PANTS."   Crichton (bibliog). **(p. 466)**

UNNECESSARY, ETC."   Letter to Mr. Maxwell 5/8/51, *SL.* **(p. 467)**

HAS REVEALED."   Letter from O'N to Richard Dana Skinner, *Eugene O'Neill, A Poet's Quest*, Russell & Russell NY 1964. **(p. 467)**

AND FRIENDSHIP."   "Professor G. P. Baker," by Eugene O'Neill, NY Times 1/13/35. **(p. 467)**

CHAPTER THIRTY–NINE

MY FRIENDS."   All Laurence's quotes are from A/BG interviews. **(p. 469)**

SAY THE LEAST."   11/2/14, *SL.* **(p. 469)**

THE MEETINGS."   NY World, "I Knew Him When," John V. A. Weaver 2/21/26. **(p. 471)**

WHY NOT?"   Ibid. **(p. 471)**

HIS WALLET."   O'N to Robert Edmond Jones 7/2/44, *SL.* **(p. 472)**

HIS PRESENCE."   NY World, John V. A. Weaver 2/21/26. **(p. 472)**

BE ALL MINE."   In the 1937 list O'Neill made of "all plays ever written by me . . . " he noted: "(*Belshazzar* written in ostensible collaboration with Colin Ford but I did most of it)." **(p. 472)**

WON'T SEND THEM."   2/14/15, *SL.* **(p. 473)**

FOR ALL TIME!"   2/18[?]/15, *SL.* **(p. 473)**

FROM HER COMB.   Letter to BAM 3/1/15, *SL.* **(p. 474)**

A WAR PLAY."   3/2/15, *SL.* **(p. 474)**

MANNER OR OTHER."   3/12/15, *SL*. **(p. 474)**

ARTZIBASHEF NOVEL . . ."   O'N subsequently deleted this passage. Bogard III (bibliog).
(p. 475)

CHILD–BIRTH."   To BAM 3/12/15, *SL*. **(p. 475)**

OF OLD TIMES."   3/21/15, *SL*. **(p. 475)**

"AFTER THE WAR."   3/28/15, *SL*. **(p. 476)**

AS DESTROYED.)   It was unearthed years later in the copyright office and included in
The Lost Plays of Eugene O'Neill. **(p. 476)**

SUBSEQUENTLY DESTROYED.   Beinecke. **(p. 476)**

FIND A MANAGER."   Vanity Fair, "Nipping the Budding Playwright in the Bud,"
Heywood Broun, Oct. 1919. **(p. 477)**

"WITH DISTINCTION."   Kinne (bibliog). **(p. 477)**

BE WORTHY."   5/12/15, *SL*. **(p. 478)**

GOD BLESS IT!"   NL Day 8/28/15. **(p. 478)**

RED ROSES.   Typescript of poem at Berg; also Gallup (bibliog). A penciled note in
BAM'S handwriting at bottom of poem reads: "When I had typhoid 3 red roses
came." (Note probably written at time she sold O'N's letters and poetry.) **(p. 478)**

QUIVERING HANDS."   Written in NL, Summer 1915. Gallup (bibliog). **(p. 479)**

LOFTY BROWS."   Probably June 1915, *SL*. **(p. 479)**

LOUIS XIII.   NL Day 7/16/15. **(p. 479)**

FROM NOW ON."   Probably June 1915, *SL*. **(p. 479)**

HE DESTROYED.   Clark (bibliog). **(p. 479)**

THE DECKS."   NL Day 8/11/15. **(p. 479)**

HIS LETTERS.   1/11/15, *SL*. **(p. 480)**

AND SNEERS . . .   Probably 1915, Gallup (bibliog). **(p. 480)**

SECOND CHILD."   A/BG interview with ER. **(p. 480)**

THAT'S ENOUGH!   Gallup (bibliog). An earlier version of poem, given to Beatrice, is at
Berg. **(p. 481)**

IN THE SUN.   New Yorker 3/7/31. **(p. 481)**

"TOO DARN DEAD."   *SL*. **(p. 482)**

TO COME BACK!"   6/8/19 *SL*. **(p. 482)**

IMPOSSIBLE."   Clark (bibliog). **(p. 482)**

IT'S THERE."   Speech at NY Town Hall to League for Political Education, NY Times
3/7/26. **(p. 482)**

DAMNED PLACE."   6/1/42, *SL*. **(p. 483)**

SHE REFUSED.   A/BG interviews with AMcG and ER. **(p. 483)**

CHAPTER FORTY

GREENWICH VILLAGE   NYT, Meyer Berger 2/10/54. **(p. 484)**

MORE FREEDOM."   Langner (bibliog). **(p. 485)**

HOTLY DEBATED.   Steffens (bibliog). **(p. 486)**

MEDICAL ATTENTION.   Hapgood (bibliog); Eastman (bibliog); Dodge (bibliog). **(p. 486)**

"LIBERALITY."   Hapgood (bibliog). **(p. 487)**

PRESENTATION OF PLAYS.   Information about Liberal Club and the start of Washington Square Players has been pieced together principally from A/BG interviews with Albert Boni, Lawrence Langner, Ida Rauh (via her friend, Alice Woods), Max Eastman, Edward Goodman, Philip Moeller, Robert Edmond Jones, Mary Heaton Vorse, William & Marguerite Zorach and Jennie Belardi, as well as letters, articles and books. **(p. 488)**

THE DOLLAR."   Theater Magazine, "Two Interviews" Nov. 1917. **(p. 489)**

MAKE SIX."   Ibid. **(p. 490)**

ART THEATERS."   Ibid. **(p. 491)**

BIG LAUGH."   Glaspell (bibliog). **(p. 492)**

ONE'S COMPLEX."   Ibid. The play was in fact produced by the WSP in 1917 when Freud had become better known (and after its production in 1916 by the PP in NY). **(p. 493)**

BE WRITTEN."   Glaspell (bibliog). **(p. 493)**

ALLEYWAYS.   Description of Provincetown and its inhabitants in 1915 is from letters and A/BG interviews with among others: MHV, WDS, AW, WZ, MZ, E. J. Ballantine, Charles Ellis, Kyra Markham. Also books by: Egan, Vorse, Hapgood, Deutsch & Hanau, Luhan, Heller & Rudnick, Glaspell (all bibliog). **(p. 494)**

THE HARBOR."   Egan (bibliog). **(p. 494)**

LITERARY MAGAZINE.   Robinson (bibliog). **(p. 494)**

HAPGOODS.   Letter from HH to his father Charles Hapgood 7/7/15 and letter from NB to Charles Hapgood 7/17/15, both at Beinecke. **(p. 495)**

INTO A THEATER.   Vorse (bibliog). **(p. 496)**

THE HARBOR.   A/BG interviews with MHV, WDS, WZ, MZ. **(p. 497)**

CASE OF FIRE."   Vorse (bibliog). **(p. 497)**

CHAPTER FORTY-ONE

"MY SON."   The Lamb Script Vol. XXIV May/June 1954. **(p. 499)**

YOUNGER GENERATION."   NY Sun 2/13/16. **(p. 500)**

EUGENE'S EARS.   A/BG interview with Tynan. **(p. 500)**

"BREAKFAST INCLUDED,"   Crichton (bibliog); also Brooklyn Eagle, Robert R. Haslett 12/19/26. **(p. 500)**

PROMOTION STAGE."   6/8/19, SL. **(p. 500)**

HE RECALLED.   Letter to BAM 7/25/16, SL. **(p. 500)**

BOUQUET MYSELF."   7/25/16, SL. **(p. 501)**

THE QUARTER."   O'N's penciled corrections on proof of Barrett Clark's book (bibliog). **(p. 501)**

HIS DRINKING.   A/BG interviews with Carl Van Vechten; also handwritten undated letter from Van Vechten to Edna Kenton: "Snappy Stories has snapped up a filthy bit I did about Louise N. (who by the way is having her latest affair with Louis Holliday [sic] who is starting a new one of 'those restaurants' at 60 W.Sq.S.)." Rare Book and Manuscript Library, Columbia U. **(p. 501)**

BRADFORD STREET.   Rust (bibliog). **(p. 501)**

UNFAITHFUL.   Ell sometimes spelled his name "Louis." **(p. 502)**

INTERESTING TO HIM."   Hapgood (bibliog). **(p. 502)**

MUGS OF BEER.   A/BG interviews with MHV and JL. Also NY World, Mary Heaton Vorse 5/4/30. **(p. 503)**

OF THE EARTH."   Sergeant (bibliog). **(p. 503)**

THEIR FIGHTS . . .   NY World, Mary Heaton Vorse 5/4/30. **(p. 504)**

LEFTY LOUIS   This was not the Lefty Louis who helped ambush the gangster, Herman "Beansy" Rosenthal in 1912 and whose name figures in O'N's 1912 poem, "The Waterways Convention, a Study in Prophecy." **(p. 504)**

DIFFERENT WORLD."   NY World, Mary Heaton Vorse 5/4/30. **(p. 504)**

DESCRIBED THEM.   Letter to ABO [12/2?/19], SL. **(p. 504)**

AND POLICE."   NY World, Mary Heaton Vorse 5/4/30. **(p. 504)**

TO A FRIEND.   To KM 12/15/40, Bryer (bibliog); and to GJN he wrote, " . . . the scene, Harry Hope's dump, is a composite of three places." 2/5/40, SL. **(p. 505)**

WHICH IS NOT."   NYT, "The Iceman Cometh," Karl Schriftgeisser 10/6/46. **(p. 507)**

POSSIBLY BE SAID."   8/11/40, SL. **(p. 507)**

OF COURSE."   2/8/40, SL. And to KM he wrote, "The characters all derive from actual people I have known — more or less closely or remotely — but none of them is an exact portrait of anyone. The main plot is, of course, imaginary. 12/15/40, Bryer (bibliog). **(p. 508)**

ENTIRELY IMAGINARY . . . ")   O'Neill Work Diary 10/28/41 (bibliog). **(p. 508)**

HEARD FROM AGAIN.   A/BG interviews with JJM and JL. **(p. 508)**

BEST POLICY."   2/8/40, SL. **(p. 508)**

IN THE PLAY."   12/30/40, Bryer (bibliog). **(p. 508)**

BUMPKIN–LIKE MANNERS.   Paper by Professor Brenda Murphy, U. of Conn. **(p. 509)**

MORRIS ADAMS).   Beinecke. **(p. 509)**

COMMODITIES)   According to Dictionary of Word and Phrase Origins Vol. II, Harper & Row, NY 1967: "Bucket shops were once very active institutions, operating on the fringes of respectability and offering stocks, bonds and commodities in small lots to speculators. Their business was actually a form of gambling — more direct and far less scrupulous than regular dealings of the stock market." **(p. 510)**

ANOTHER REASON."   2/8/40, SL. **(p. 510)**

MY OWN FICTION."   12/30/40, Bryer (bibliog). **(p. 511)**

NEWSPAPER COVERAGE.   Goldman also describes the incident in her autobiography, Living My Life, which O'N had in his library. According to Winifred Frazer, writing in E O'N Newsletter (Winter 1884) she detected the book's title among others on a library shelf in a photograph of the interior of a house lived in by O'N in the early 1930's. Other facts about the case are from Steffens (bibliog) and accounts in NYT and NY Sun between 1911–1915. **(p. 511)**

APPREHEND A FLEA."   Mother Earth, April 1915. **(p. 512)**

CHAPTER FORTY-TWO

IT WAS MAGNIFICENT."   Hapgood I (bibliog). **(p. 516)**

RENT–FREE.   Ibid. **(p. 517)**

TRANSGRESSION POSSIBLE."   Ibid. **(p. 517)**

OF HEROIN.   On 1/22/18 Louis Holladay induced TC to give him the heroin. **(p. 517)**

ANARCHIST WOMAN   All quotes by TC and his companion, Marie (the "anarchist woman" of the title), are from Hapgood II (bibliog). **(p. 518)**

MY GHOST."   5/13/44, *SL.* **(p. 521)**

THIRTY–THREE   According to Beinecke, Collins was born 1851 and died 1927. **(p. 521)**

LETTERS AS "BUDDHA."   *Alchemy and the Orient in Strinderg's Dream Play* by Leta Jane Lewis, as noted in *Eugene O'Neill and Oriental Thought, A Divided Vision,* by James A. Robinson, Southern Illinois U. Press, Carbondale & Edwardsville 1982. **(p. 521)**

MYSTERY, CERTAINLY)."   Letter to AHQ 4/3/25, *SL.* **(p. 521)**

AND FREE."   Hapgood II (bibliog). **(p. 522)**

NOT OF THEM . . .   Numerous friends interviewed by A/BG attested to O'N's tendency to quote Byron. **(p. 523)**

DAY WRITING.   Gaylord questionnaire 1916. **(p. 523)**

THROWING CONFETTI.   Dated 1915 with typed address "38 Washington Square/ NYC," Gallup (bibliog). **(p. 524)**

ARMFUL OF BOOKS.   In A/BG original biography (1962) this episode was erroneously described as taking place in fall, 1917. **(p. 524)**

STILL THERE."   To Benjamin de Casseres 3/21/24. Copy given to authors by Mrs. de Casseres. **(p. 524)**

RANSOMED THE TRUNK.   Brooklyn Eagle," Robert R. Haslett 12/19/26. **(p. 524)**

A LIBEL."   To J. J. Douthit 11/30/43, *SL.* **(p. 525)**

FETISH OF LIFE."   Ms of "Tommorrow," Princeton U. Library; in Bogard III (bibliog). **(p. 525)**

EASTMAN SAID.   Eastman I (bibliog). **(p. 526)**

THEY SHARED.   A/BG interview with Brown. **(p. 526)**

DELIRIUM TREMENS,   Among O'Neill's papers at Beineke is an article vividly describing delirium tremens, "Alcohol and the Nervous System" by Sir James Purvis-Stewart, senior physician to Westminster Hospital, London, published in the British Medical Journal, The Practitioner, Oct. 1924. In a datebook called "Scribbling Diary for 1925" (also at Beineke) O'N noted 1/22/25 he had read the article and found it "very interesting and applicable to me . . . " **(p. 526)**

CHEERFULLY SUPPLIED.   A/BG interview with Robert Carlton Brown. **(p. 527)**

CHAPTER FORTY-THREE

JIMMY THE PRIEST'S.   A/BG interview with Robert Carlton Brown. (James Condon finally closed his place shortly after a police investigation into the deaths of five patrons from wood alcohol poisoning. NY Tribune 12/29/19. **(p. 528)**

AND HANG"   Written "probably in NY, 1915." Gallup (bibliog). **(p. 528)**

IN THE WORLD."   A/BG interview with Louis Bergen, bartender at Garden Hotel. **(p. 529)**

MORNING COFFEE.   A/BG interviews with Foley. **(p. 530)**

SHE FAVORED.   Letter from O'N to ABO 12/1[?]/19, *SL*. **(p. 530)**

PRINCE GEORGE HOTEL.   A/BG interviews with Foley. **(p. 530)**

ALL IN THE BAR."   "A Eugene O'Neill Miscellany," NY Sun, 1/12/28. **(p. 531)**

NOTATIONS.   A/BG interviews with Bergen; and NY Sun, "A Eugene O'Neill Miscellany" 1/12/28. **(p. 531)**

IN THE AIR.   NY Sun, "A Eugene O'Neill Miscellany" 1/12/28. **(p. 531)**

BUS SERVICE.   A/BG interviews with Louis Bergen. **(p. 531)**

WORCESTERSHIRE SAUCE.   Ibid. **(p. 531)**

HELPED SUPPORT.   Letter from O'N to Harry Weinberger 11/27/34, *SL*. **(p. 532)**

THE STORY."   NY Sun, "A Eugene O'Neill Miscellany" 1/12/28; also NY World, "Back to the Source of Plays," Charles P. Sweeney 11/9/24. **(p. 532)**

DEAD RUDY.   Notes of interview with O'N by ESS 8/3/46, Beinecke. **(p. 532)**

GREENWICH VILLAGE.   A/BG interview with Holger Cahill, writer and Stuart's friend **(p. 532)**.

BY HEART."   Letter to GCT 8/6/19, *SL*. **(p. 532)**

UNDISTINGUISHABLE WHOLE."   New Yorker, "Roughneck and Romancer," Maxwell Bodenheim 2/6/26. **(p. 533)**

THE POLICE.   Asbury (bibliog). **(p. 533)**

BARBERSHOPS.   Ibid. **(p. 534)**

ICEMAN COMETH.   Handwritten notes, Beinecke. **(p. 534)**

ARBEITERZEITUNG.   Goldman (bibliog) & Hapgood I (bibliog); also A/BG interviews with members of PP. **(p. 535)**

WILLOW TREES!"   Background of poem is described in Modern Drama, "'Revolution' in *The Iceman Cometh*," Winifred L. Frazer, March 1979. **(p. 535)**

KEEP HIS WORD."   Hapgood I (bibliog). **(p. 536)**

ALWAYS AT IT."   Ibid. **(p. 536)**

VIBRATIONS."   Ibid. **(p. 536)**

ON MY STOVE."   A/BG interview with Marie Marchand. **(p. 536)**

WAS OBEYED.   Ibid. **(p. 537)**

PAL, GENE."   Letter to ABO [12/2?/19], *SL*. **(p. 537)**

DECLINED THE OFFER.   A/BG interviews with JJM and JL. **(p. 537)**

FOR NO PAY).   Eastman I (bibliog). **(p. 538)**

EVENING POST.   John Barleycorn, the personification of malt liquor, was popularized by Robert Burns in *Tam O'Shanter*: "Inspiring bold John Barleycorn/What dangers thou canst make us scorn!" **(p. 539)**

MY JOHNNY)."   The Reporter 9/5/57. **(p. 539)**

REDS GATHERED."   Steffens (bibliog). **(p. 539)**

ATE IT RAW."   Reed (bibliog). **(p. 541)**

IN SOMETHING."   Story was told to A/BG in 1958 by Sonya Levien Hovey, widow of the Metropolitan's editor, Carl Hovey. In March 1916 she had described the incident in the Metropolitan Bulletin, the magazine's house organ, in which she quoted Roosevelt as saying, "Villa is a murderer and a bigamist," and Reed as retorting that he believed in "bigamy." In that more prudish era, she explained, she feared offending both Roosevelt and her readers had she used "rape." **(p. 541)**

POTENTIAL CONTRIBUTOR.   In her 1958 interview with A/BG, Sonya Hovey (by then a Hollywood screenwriter) obviously confused some of the details involving O'N's introduction to her husband. She said Reed had described O'N to her husband as "a talented young man who had to get away and had nowhere to go" and suggested that he accompany him to Mexico. Her husband, she said, gave O'N $300 to cover expenses for any articles he might submit. She recalled having received several short pieces from O'N, but could not remember their substance or precisely when they were submitted. Obviously they were not from Mexico, since O'N never went there. **(p. 542)**

LET US SLEEP!   One of four poems dated "Hell Hole — 1916"; since O'N was in Provincetown between June and Oct. 1916, the four poems could have been written either between Jan. and June, or between Oct. and Dec. of that year. Donald Gallup in a letter to A/BG (12/10/98) notes he is unable to pinpoint the dates of these poems. **(p. 542)**

ALLEY CAT?   Dated "Hell Hole, 1916." Gallup (bibliog). **(p. 543)**

BUTLER YEATS,   *The Works of William Blake: Poetic, Symbolical, and Critical*, Edited by William Butler Yeats and Edwin John Ellis, 3 vols., London, Bernard Quaritch, 1893. **(p. 543)**

ENOUGH FOR ME."   Letter to O'N Jr. 11/11/32, *SL*. According to a letter from Lennox Robinson to A/BG (7/19/57), "Some years ago, when an appeal was made to Members of the Academy for a small, annual subscription to pay postage and other office expenses, Mr. O'Neill sent us a small m.o. on his bankers which was cashed annually until his death." **(p. 543)**

TO COME?"   *Inscriptions: Eugene O'Neill to Carlotta Monterey O'Neill*, Yale U. Library, New Haven, 1960 (edited by Donald Gallup and 500 copies privately printed). O'N evidently accepted Yeats's claim that Blake was descended from the O'N clan. "A certain John O'Neil," explained Yeats, "got into debt and difficulties, these latter apparently political to some extent; and escaped both by marrying a woman named Ellen Blake, who kept a shebeen at Rathmines, Dublin, and taking her name." According to Yeats, this John O'Neill (now John Blake) had a son James "by a previous wife or mistress," who also adopted the name Blake and it was James who eventually fathered William Blake. But Yeats's information rests on hearsay from a family member and has never been substantiated. *The Collected Works of W. B. Yeats Vol. VI*, prefaces and introductions, edited by William H. O'Donnell, MacMillan NY 1989. **(p. 543)**

I MISS YOU!   Untitled, dated "Hell Hole — 1916." Gallup (bibliog). **(p. 544)**

BIG HEART."   7/25/16, *SL*. **(p. 544)**

MAN TO MAN.   A/BG interview with Robert Carlton Brown. **(p. 545)**

IN JANUARY.   Granville Hicks Collection, Syracuse U. Library. **(p. 545)**

TO LOOK AT."   To Sally Robinson 12/18/15, John Reed collection, Houghton Library, Harvard U. **(p. 545)**

CHARACTERISTIC EGOISM.   Luhan (bibliog). **(p. 545)**

MUCH FOR HIM."   Ibid. **(p. 546)**

A BOSTON NEWSPAPER.   Boston Globe, Charles A. Merrill 7/8/23. In E O'N Newsletter article, "Turned Down in Provincetown: O'Neill's Debut Re-examined," Spring 1988, Gary Jay Williams attempts to discredit O'N's perfectly straightforward assertion that it was Reed who brought him to Provincetown. Williams states: "Contradicting the Gelbs' story [in their 1962 biography] that 'in later years' O'Neill 'acknowledged' that Jack Reed brought him to Provincetown, is a holograph note that O'Neill made in the margin of Barrett Clark's manuscript used in preparation of the 1947 edition of the Clark biography; the page is reproduced there (following p. 22), and in it O'Neill says he knew none of the group until he came to Provincetown."

Clark's text reads, in part: " . . . O'Neill spent the winter of 1915–16 in Greenwich Village, New York, where he found congenial companions chiefly among the group that were to found the Provincetown Players next year: George Cram Cook, Susan Glaspell, Frank Shay, Frederick Burt, Mary Heaton Vorse, Willbur Daniel Steele, Hary Kemp, "Teddy" Ballantine, Neith Boyce and Hutchins Hapgood."

O'N's marginal note reads, "No, Never met any of these until I went to Provincetown." Why Williams leaped to the unwarranted conclusion that Reed was one of this group, even though Clark did not list him, is baffling.   (p. 546)

CHAPTER FORTY–FOUR

DOLLARS A MONTH." Bryant (bibliog); unpublished, undated memoir written not long before her death in 1936. (p. 551)

HE MADE IT." Ibid. (p. 551)

OF HIMSELF." Hapgood I (bibliog). (p. 551)

OUT THERE." Undated, Houghton. (p. 552)

ALL THE TIME." Telegram from Reed to LB 6/10/16, Houghton. (p. 552)

BED TOGETHER!" 6/18/16 Houghton. (p. 552)

SUMMER BEFORE). Bryant (bibliog). (p. 552)

TO SLEEP ON." Eastman I (bibliog). (p. 552)

THE WORLD." Hapgood I (bibliog). (p. 553)

ACTIVITIES. A/BG interview with Ballantine. (p. 553)

PEACE, PEACE." Goldman (bibliog). (p. 553)

CORRESPONDENCE WITH O'NEILL. Commins (bibliog); in the posthumously published memoir SC dated his first meeting with O'N as 1914, which as his wife noted was obviously wrong. (p. 553)

END OF TOWN." Both letters dated 6/12/16, Houghton. (p. 553)

FRESH JEWS APPEAR." 6/9/16, Houghton. (p. 553)

ARE FRIENDS." "Almost Thirty," by John Reed, The New Republic, 3/15/36 and 3/29/36. The "Jewish boy" was very likely Walter Lippman, who was at Harvard with Reed and later became a friend. (p. 554)

JUNE 21, Telegram to LB 6/20/16, Houghton. (p. 554)

SQUATTERS' RIGHTS. A/BG interviews with Kyra Markham, actress, and Bessie Breuer, writer. (p. 554)

THE CASH. Hapgood I (bibliog). (p. 554)

QUITE A TASK." Bryant (bibliog). (p. 555)

FEVER IS ON." Luhan (bibliog). (p. 555)

PORTUGUESE FISHERMEN. A/BG interviews with Kyra Markham, Mary Ellen Boyden (daughter of Mary Heaton Vorse) and others. (p. 555)

AFRAID TO LISTEN. Glaspell (bibliog). (p. 557)

BE AN ACTOR." Theater Magazine, "Out of Provincetown: A Memoir of Eugene

O'Neill," Harry Kemp April, 1930. **(p. 557)**

PREPOSTEROUS HOKUM." If, as seems likely, O'Neill did give a reading of *The Movie Man* in the summer of 1916, it may explain his confusion about when he wrote it. According to his own listing, he did, in fact, write a short story made from the play that summer, which he destroyed. **(p. 557)**

GENUINE PLAYWRIGHT." Theater Magazine, Harry Kemp, April 1930. **(p. 557)**

AND AGREED." Hapgood I (bibliog). **(p. 558)**

BIOGRAPHICAL WORK. Letter to R. W. Cottingham 5/12/44, *SL*. **(p. 558)**

WE WERE FOR." Glaspell (bibliog). **(p. 558)**

ALL DUTIES." 7/25/16, *SL*. **(p. 558)**

NEED YOU SO!" Ibid. **(p. 559)**

A FAMILY. A/BG interviews with ER. **(p. 559)**

PEQUOT CHAPEL. Conn. College Alumnae Survey 2/2/67. **(p. 559)**

EUGENE O'NEILL." 1/21/74, 1/22/74. **(p. 560)**

READY TO WRITE." O'Neill Work Diary (bibliog). **(p. 560)**

HIS SHACK. A/BG interview with Kyra Markham. **(p. 561)**

AND PORTUGUESE." Vorse (bibliog). **(p. 561)**

WORRY ABOUT HIM." Letter to A/BG from Markham 5/9/57. **(p. 561)**

HE LIVED IN." Bryant (bibliog). **(p. 562)**

IN ITS FALL." *The Autobiography of William Carlos Williams*, New Directions, NY 1951. Williams evidently met Louise when he took a role at PP in Alfred Kreymborg's *Lima Beans*, Dec. 1916. **(p. 562)**

TO UNDERSTAND." Boulton (bibliog). **(p. 562)**

SISTER, SHE SAID. Ibid. **(p. 562)**

LEAVE HIM. Reed, LB and O'N confided in a number of friends that summer and the following winter in NY. Among those interviewed by A/BG about the triangle were WZ and MZ (who lived for a time next door to the Reeds in NY), MHV, Kyra Markham, E. J. Ballantine, EK and AMcG. Some details also in Boulton (bibliog). **(p. 563)**

AND SLOW." According to Hicks (bibliog) the poem was accepted by Scribner's Oct. 1916 but not published until Aug. 1919. **(p. 563)**

BETRAYED BY LIFE" Boulton (bibliog). **(p. 563)**

BRITISH ARMY. B. Gelb (bibliog). Interviews with: Katherine Caldwell and her mother, Sara Bard Field, a companion-in-arms in the Portland suffrage movement; Dean Collins, friend of Paul Trullinger; and the second Mrs. Trullinger. **(p. 564)**

A "GENERAL." Bryant (bibliog). **(p. 564)**

PROBABLY IN 1885. Her birthdate is difficult to pinpoint. San Francisco birth records before 1906 were destroyed during the earthquake. Office of Records, Washoe County, Reno, Nev., lists her birthdate as 1885. Registrar's offices of the U. of Oregon, which she attended, lists her birthdate as 1887. Her first marriage certificate, 12/16/09 in the Multnomah County Clerk's Office, Oregon, lists her age as "over 18" and the age and date on her second marriage certificate, 11/9/16, Peekskill, NY, lists her birthdate as 1890. **(p. 564)**

DAILY GLOBE. S.F. Chronicle records and California Historical Society. Mohan is last listed in the SF city directory in 1886. **(p. 564)**

LOUISE WAS THREE. Reno District Court. **(p. 564)**

LONELY CHILD. Bryant (bibliog). **(p. 564)**

LOUISE ADOPTED. Office of County Recorder, Washoe County, Reno. **(p. 564)**

UNIVERSITY OF OREGON   Registrar Office records at both Universities. **(p. 564)**

A REAL LIFE.   B. Gelb (bibliog). Interviews with Katherine Caldwell and her mother, Sara Bard Field. **(p. 564)**

DECEMBER 16, 1909   Multnomah County Clerk's Office. **(p. 565)**

EAST WITH HIM.   It may be of interest to note that in Bryant (bibliog) she did not mention, in describing her romance with JR, that she was married. **(p. 565)**

CHAPTER FORTY–FIVE

BUT HE WASN'T."   Luhan (bibliog). **(p. 566)**

FIRST ACT."   Letter to BAM 7/25/16, SL. **(p. 567)**

PRAIRIE FIRE."   A/BG interviews with AMcG, who said he was told this by TC. **(p. 567)**

JEALOUS FURY.   In his "List of all plays ever written by me . . . "(noted earlier) O'N said it was written In "Fisherman's Shack, Provincetown," in 1916, after *Before Breakfast*; he did not copyright it until 5/23/17. Not produced or published in his lifetime, it first appeared in *"Children of the Sea"* edited by Jennifer McCabe Atkinson, NCR, Washington, D.C. 1972, and is included in Bogard II (bibliog). **(p. 567)**

SPIDER?   Gallup (bibliog). **(p. 568)**

FOR CARRION."   Reed collection, Houghton. **(p. 568)**

DELIRIUM OF NOON . . .   Original untitled poem ends, "I am only a seagull/Dolefully squawking/When it would sing." Gallup (bibliog). In the version kept by LB these lines have been dropped. "On the Dunes" is in Reed collection, Houghton. **(p. 568)**

WITHHOLD/MY LOVE?   The Masses, Oct. 1916. **(p. 569)**

HEAR/YOUR VOICE.   Ibid. **(p. 569)**

DECADE LATER.   Glaspell (bibliog). **(p. 569)**

OTHER PERFORMERS.   A/BG interview with WDS. **(p. 569)**

DRILY RECALLED.   American Magazine, Mary B. Mullett, Nov. 1922. **(p. 569)**

WITH APPLAUSE."   Glaspell (bibliog). **(p. 569)**

A PLAYSCRIPT.   Letter, Adele Nathan to NYT Magazine 10/6/46. **(p. 570)**

OBLIGINGLY TYPED).   Commins (bibliog). **(p. 570)**

A REVOLVER.   Hapgood I (bibliog). **(p. 571)**

FOR A WHILE."   Letter from LB to Corliss Lamont 11/4/35, Houghton. Lamont was in touch with Granville Hicks, Reed's biographer, who refused to communicate with LB; she was attempting to counter what she feared was Boyd's misinformation about Reed and herself. **(p. 571)**

THE PRODUCTION.   A/BG interview with WZ and MZ. **(p. 573)**

THAN PROVINCETOWN."   9/10/16. **(p. 573)**

MEN OF FAITH."   Glaspell (bibliog). **(p. 573)**

OF THE STAGE."   Clark (bibliog). **(p. 574)**

IN NEW YORK."   Introductory essay by EK to *Greek Coins*, George Cram Cook, George H. Doran Co., NY 1925. **(p. 574)**

REBELLIOUS FERVOR.   Kenton (bibliog). **(p. 575)**

UNANIMOUSLY ADOPTED.   Ibid. **(p. 575)**

AFFORDABLE — SPACE.   Ibid. **(p. 576)**

WASHINGTON SQUARE SOUTH.   "On the Dunes," as well as "Tides," both given to LB, contained handwritten notes at bottom: "Until Oct. 1st (Provincetown, Mass.). After that (c/o Jack Reed 43 Washington Sq. So., New York City)." Reed collection, Houghton. **(p. 576)**

REALLY ECONOMY."   Houghton. **(p. 576)**

CHAPTER FORTY–SIX

GRANTED IN JULY,   Multnomah County Clerk's office; divorce was granted 7/7/16. **(p. 579)**

STORY DRAG."   Letter to Reed from Hovey 10/11/16, Houghton. **(p. 580)**

IN GREEN DEPTHS.   The Masses, Feb. 1917. In a letter to Ralph Sanborn, an early O'N bibliographer, O'N said he was delighted the poem was unsigned because it showed "what lousy verse a man can write when he is determined to be a poet." 10/3/30, Dartmouth Library. **(p. 580)**

DOLLARS A MONTH.   Kenton (bibliog). **(p. 581)**

RENT WAS LATE.   Ibid. **(p. 581)**

INTO REHEARSAL.   Ibid. **(p. 581)**

WAR PAINT."   Letter from O'N to GCT 9/25/19, *SL*. **(p. 581)**

CAN'T MAKE IT.")   Letter to ABO 2/16?/20, *SL*. **(p. 582)**

VOICE OF MEDIOCRITY."   GCC as quoted in Glaspell (bibliog). **(p. 583)**

NEXT TWO MONTHS.   Kenton (bibliog). **(p. 583)**

LIKED THE PLAY.   "*Bound East for Cardiff* and *The Long Voyage Home* were among plays he saw at the Provincetown that he liked." Letter from O'N to Lawrence Estavan 1/15/40. *SL*. **(p. 583)**

BIT GARBLED.)   The Sun critic was Stephen Rathbun, who probably wrote the review. **(p. 584)**

SNEER TO McGINLEY.   A/BG interviews with AMcG. **(p. 585)**

FAR–OFF DAYS."   Letter from O'N to GJN 6/19/42, *SL*. **(p. 585)**

BOLTED DOORS.   A/BG interviews with AMcG. **(p. 585)**

GEORGE WITH THEM.   Ibid. **(p. 585)**

REED AND LOUISE.   Ibid. **(p. 586)**

EVERYTHING I'VE GOT."   Bryant (bibliog). **(p. 586)**

BACK ANY MOMENT."   Letter headed "Sunday afternoon at 5." Houghton. **(p. 586)**

THROUGH HELL."   A/BG interviews with WZ & MZ. **(p. 586)**

AT ONCE."   11/13/17 Houghton. **(p. 587)**

LEAVE YOU THERE."   LB to Reed 11/26/16, Houghton. **(p. 587)**

AND A COT."   12/2/16, Houghton. **(p. 588)**

SERVE AS PROMPTER   Undated letter, LB to Reed, Houghton. **(p. 588)**

PLEASANT PLAYS?"   A/BG interviews with EK & JL. Other members of PP quoted slightly different versions of this remark. **(p. 588)**

SOMETHING IN HIM."   Hapgood I (bibliog). **(p. 588)**

HIS DISPLEASURE."   Deutsch & Hanau (bibliog). **(p. 588)**

"NUTS!"   O'N to Lawrence Estavan 1/15/40, *SL.* **(p. 588)**

GLAD TO FOLLOW."   Ibid. **(p. 588)**

FURTHER INSTRUCTION."   A/BG interviews with EK and JL. **(p. 589)**

"RATHER SKETCHY."   A/BG interview with Kreymborg. **(p. 589)**

LENGTHY MONOLOGUE.   Kenton (bibliog). **(p. 589)**

KENTON SAID.   Ibid. **(p. 589)**

SERIOUS OPERATION."   12/6/16, Houghton. **(p. 590)**

YOUR CONDITION."   Ibid. **(p. 590)**

INFECTION?"   Undated letter, Houghton. **(p. 590)**

CONVALESCENT.   LB's symptoms and treatment were reviewed at A/BG's request by a prominent gynecologist, Dr. Beth Lieberman, NY University Hospital. **(p. 590)**

HELL HOLE.   A/BG interviews with AMcG; and Bryant (bibliog). **(p. 591)**

CHAPTER FORTY-SEVEN

I SEE HIM."   12/23/16 Berg. **(p. 592)**

DESPAIR OF IT."   Vorse (bibliog). **(p. 592)**

IS HIS NAME."   O'N to BAM 7/25/16, *SL.* **(p. 592)**

CLOSELY ATTENTIVE."   LS collection, Conn. College. **(p. 593)**

TO HIS WIFE.   12/11/16 Berg. **(p. 593)**

INTO ANYTHING."   NY Herald Tribune 3/17/29. **(p. 593)**

FROM MONTANA.   Kenton (bibliog). **(p. 594)**

LITERARY ENTERTAINMENT."   1/20/17. **(p. 594)**

TWIST OF PLOT."   1/30/17. **(p. 594)**

EACH OTHER."   A/BG interview with Moise. **(p. 595)**

LATER RECALLED.   Ibid. **(p. 595)**

HIS PERFORMANCE.   Evening World, Charles Darnton 1/2/17. **(p. 596)**

OF THE STAGE."   Ibid. **(p. 596)**

THE SCENERY."   NY Mail, Burns Mantle 2/2/17. **(p. 596)**

IN JERUSALEM."   NY Sun 4/1/17. **(p. 586)**

FREAK OF IT."   NY Herald 1/7/17. **(p. 596)**

IN THE CAST.   Bill included *Ivan's Homecoming* by Michael Gold and *Barbarians* by Rita Wellman, also directed by Moise. **(p. 597)**

CARRIED WITH HIM.   A/BG interview with Moise. **(p. 597)**

REJECTS THE POET.   Ibid. **(p. 598)**

THROUGH WITH IT."   Ibid. **(p. 598)**

AN ETERNAL END."   O'N's stage directions, *The Great God Brown.* **(p. 598)**

CLOTHES WRINGER."   NY Herald Tribune 11/16/24. **(p. 598)**

SELECTION COMMITTEE.   A/BG interviews with Pauline Turkel, an administrator of the Provincetown Players; and Deutsch & Hanau (bibliog). **(p. 600)**

OFF I WENT."   Bryant (bibliog). **(p. 600)**

THE DEAD.   Garden Hotel 1917. Gallup (bibliog). **(p. 601)**

SETTLE DOWN."   Bryant (bibliog). **(p. 601)**

EIGHTH BILL.   For this bill, which ran from Mar. 9–14 and included *The Prodigal Son* by Harry Kemp, *Cocaine* by Pendleton King and *The People* by SG, the Players called in the professional actors, Frederic Burt and Margaret Wycherly, to direct two plays, and turned the third over to Nina Moise. "For the first time in our history," wrote Edna Kenton (bibliog), "we brazenly emblazoned the names of three directors, all of them 'professionals,' on our program." **(p. 601)**

TOO HECTIC."   NY World, Flora Merrill 7/19/25. **(p. 601)**

LAUREATES).   *The Thirsty Muse: Alcohol and the American Writer*, Tom Dardis, Ticknor & Fields, NY 1989. **(p. 601)**

TO DO IT."   Life, Tom Prideaux 10/14/46. **(p. 601)**

EXCEPT HIS ART."   Clark (bibliog). **(p. 602)**

THAT I WROTE."   PM, Croswell Bowen 11/3/46. **(p. 602)**

IN YOUR HEAD."   *Alcohol and the Writer*, Donald W. Goodwin M.D., Penguin Books, NY 1990. **(p. 603)**

HE ONCE SAID.   PM, Croswell Bowen, 11/3/46. **(p. 603)**

WOULD NOT DIE."   *Alcohol and the Writer*, Donald W. Goodwin M.D., Penguin Books, NY 1990. **(p. 603)**

AMERICAN WRITERS.   Ibid. **(p. 603)**

FROM ALCOHOLISM."   *Why Can't They Be Like Us?*, Andrew Greeley, Dutton, NY 1971. **(p. 603)**

PRESS AGENT."   4/4/17. **(p. 603)**

IS NOT DONE."   Glaspell (bibliog). **(p. 604)**

CHAPTER FORTY–EIGHT

STORY–A–MINUTE DEPOLO."   A/BG interviews with AMcG. **(p. 605)**

COOK IT.   A/BG interviews with MHV. **(p. 605)**

PROVINCETOWN BOATS."   Vorse (bibliog). **(p. 606)**

GERMAN SPIES.   Provincetown Advocate 3/29/17. **(p. 606)**

A TYPEWRITER.   Ibid; and later account, unsourced article in NY Public Library archives, "Provincetown Before the War, And a Bohemian Gene O'Neill," probably summer 1940. **(p. 606)**

THE SUSPECTS.   Provincetown Advocate 3/29/17. **(p. 606)**

IN A SCRAPBOOK   Beinecke. **(p. 607)**

SEE A LAWYER."   Boston Sunday Globe, Charles A. Merrill 7/8/32. **(p. 607)**

YOU TODAY."   Vorse (bibliog). **(p. 607)**

HAD THEM TYPED.   O'N to Frank, 3/26/17. Copy given to A/BG by Frank. **(p. 607)**

ARTICLES, TOO."   A/BG interview with Waldo Frank. **(p. 608)**

SOME CHANGES.   Letter from Frank to O'N 3/30/17, Beinecke. **(p. 608)**

"SHARPENED" IT.   O'N to Frank 3/31/17, *SL*. **(p. 608)**

LITTLE JEW."   The original ms with deletions at Princeton U. Library; also published in Bogard III (bibliog). **(p. 608)**

ANTI–CLIMAX."   3/31/17 *SL*. **(p. 608)**

REVISED STORY   Letter from Frank to O'N 4/17/17; copy given by Frank to A/BG. **(p. 608)**

DEPARTMENT.   O'N to Frank, April 1917, *SL*. **(p. 608)**

AS I WAS."   To Mark Van Doren 5/12/44, *SL*. **(p. 608)**

IS A SPY).   All three penciled scripts in Museum of City of New York archives. **(p. 609)**

SAILOR–TOWN ASHORE."   Letter from O'N to Frank 4/30/17; copy given by Frank to A/BG. **(p. 609)**

TRAMP STEAMER."   Ibid. **(p. 609)**

REAL COLOR."   Letter from Frank to O'N 5/17/17, Beinecke. **(p. 609)**

BAY AND HARBOR."   Theater Magazine, April 1930. **(p. 609)**

NEARLY A YEAR.   A/BG interview with Eben Given, artist and Provincetown friend of O'N. **(p. 610)**

EXPRESSED IT."   To GJN 8/30/37, Nathan I (bibliog). **(p. 610)**

END OF MAY.   O'N to Mencken 5/26/17, *SL*. **(p. 610)**

YOU DESIRE."   Ibid. **(p. 610)**

I RECEIVED."   American Magazine, Mary B. Mullett Nov. 1922. In this article, O'N mistakenly says his *first* submissions to The Smart Set consisted of "three 'fo'c'sle' plays." According to his 1917 correspondence, he in fact submitted three plays to Seven Arts and only *two* plays to The Smart Set — although he later submitted a third play, *Ile*, to The Smart Set. **(p. 611)**

TERMS OF LIFE."   *The Moon of The Caribbees and Six Other Plays of the Sea*, Modern Library, NY 1923. **(p. 611)**

THEATRICAL TRADITIONS."   Brentano's Book Chat, "Eugene O'Neill: Writer of Synthetic Drama," Malcolm Cowley, July/August 1926. **(p. 611)**

FOLLOWED LOGICALLY.   NY World, Flora Merrill 7/19/25. **(p. 611)**

HIS HANDICAPS?"   Theater Magazine, Carol Bird, June 1924. **(p. 612)**

WROTE ILE,   "List of all Plays . . . " (noted earlier); *Ile* was published in The Smart Set, May 1918. **(p. 612)**

IN PROVINCETOWN.   A documentary film, "Hunting the Sperm Whale," recording Cook's final voyage on the brig Viola, 1916, is at Pilgrim Monument Museum, Provincetown. **(p. 612)**

THESE DRAWERS!"   Vorse (bibliog); and A/BG interviews with MHV. **(p. 613)**

CROSS MY BOW!"   A/BG interviews with MHV and Eben Given. **(p. 614)**

IN BLOOM."   Actual words of telegram Reed sent (May 18): "Peach tree blooming and wrens have take[n] their house." 5/18/17, Houghton. **(p. 614)**

IN THE DRAFT."   Undated letter, probably June 1917, *SL*. **(p. 614)**

THIRTY–ONE.   NL Day 6/5/17. **(p. 615)**

"SLOPPY."   A/BG interview with JR and ER. **(p. 615)**

OVER THE HOUSE."   Bryant (bibliog). **(p. 615)**

PRECIPITATE DEPARTURE.   A/BG interviews with AMcG, JR and ER. **(p. 615)**

CORRESPONDENT."   State Department records, Washington, D.C. **(p. 615)**

MUCH AS I DO."   Houghton. **(p. 616)**

HURT YOU, HONEY."   6/11/17 Houghton. **(p. 616)**

CHAPTER FORTY-NINE

FROM SERVICE. 6/29/17, Gaylord records. **(p. 617)**

GOD'S COUNTRY." 6/5/17. **(p. 617)**

THAN DEATH." 6/5/17. Editorial unsigned but according to NL Day historian Gregory N. Stone it was written by Latimer. **(p. 618)**

MONTE CRISTO. A/BG interviews with AMcG. **(p. 618)**

YOUR OWN! . . . Handwritten on four sheets of paper and never published, poem (originally entitled "Flotsam") is at Houghton. **(p. 619)**

SERIOUS BINGE. A/BG interviews with AMcG. **(p. 620)**

OF N.L. HOME." Events in O'N's life arranged in 7-year cycles beginning with birth and ending 1946 when *The Iceman Cometh* marked final Broadway production of his lifetime. Beinecke. **(p. 620)**

GREET THEM. A/BG interviews with AMcG. **(p. 620)**

HAD GIVEN HIM: O'N to Silvio Bedini, son of his caretaker on his Ridgefield, Conn., estate. (O'N mistakenly identified the volume as *The Illumined Way*, a sequel to *Light on the Path*.) SL. **(p. 620)**

THE HEART!" The two final lines in the original text read: "Before the voice can speak in the presence of the Masters it must have lost the power to wound. Before the soul can stand in the presence of the Masters its feet must be washed in the blood of the heart." **(p. 620)**

UNTIL OCTOBER." Kenton (bibliog). **(p. 621)**

SAME TITLE. O'N to Richard Dana Skinner [July?], 1934, SL. **(p. 621)**

SEVEN BROTHERS.) A/BG interview with Morgan McGinley, editorial page editor of NL Day and AMcG's nephew. **(p. 621)**

BREAK ITS NECK!'" 4/28/44, SL. **(p. 622)**

WAS DEGRADING." A/BG interview with Lewis. **(p. 624)**

THE ARMISTICE. O'N to Barrett Clark 5/8/19, SL. While O'N does not give the exact dates of the vaudeville tour, it evidently ran January–November 1918 (Armistice Day was 11/11/18). **(p. 624)**

IN DENMARK.'" Ibid. **(p. 624)**

FINER VALUES." Ibid. **(p. 624)**

PROPER INSIGNIFICANCE. Ibid. Despite O'N's disparagement of *In the Zone*, it turned out to be — in conjunction with *Bound East for Cardiff*, *The Long Voyage Home*, and *The Moon of the Caribbees* — a minor classic of the stage. Under the title *S.S. Glencairn* these four one-acters are revived regularly throughout the world. **(p. ?)**

FEMALE CHRIST." A/BG interviews with MHV. **(p. 625)**

THE DICE." A/BG interviews with JL. **(p. 626)**

HIGH TIME." A/BG interviews with Ellis and Millay. **(p. 627)**

HE LIKED IT. O'N to Lawrence Estavan 1/15/40, SL. **(p. 628)**

HORNPIPE. A/BG interviews with Crowley. **(p. 628)**

DOLLARS!'") A/BG interview with Claire Brennan Sherman. **(p. 628)**

MASOCHISTIC SONG." Dated "Hell Hole 1917," Gallup (bibliog). **(p. 629)**

HAD BOUNCED. A/BG interview with Cahill. **(p. 630)**

DOORS ONE DAY. A/BG interviews with MHV. **(p. 630)**

CHAPTER FIFTY

SQUARE PLAYERS.   6/28/18, *SL.* **(p. 631)**

BIGGER!"   O'N to Leo B. Pride 11/12/29. A/BG private collection. **(p. 631)**

THE HORIZON.   O'N to Richard Dana Skinner [July?] 1934, *SL.* **(p. 631)**

THE ROPE   "List of all plays . . . " (as noted earlier). **(p. 631)**

AMERICAN TRAGEDY."   O'N to R. W. Cottingham 5/12/44, *SL.* **(p. 634)**

THE HORIZON?'"   A/BG interview with Given. Story confirmed in Clark (bibliog): "Harry Kemp told me [Clark] that once a feeble-minded boy of six formed a deep affection for O'Neill and O'Neill took pains to be kind . . . One day the two were . . . looking out over the Atlantic. The boy wondered what was beyond Europe? 'The horizon,' answered O'Neill. 'But what,' persisted the lad, 'is beyond the horizon?'" **(p. 635)**

COMPLETE PLAY."   Article by O'N, NYT 4/11/20. **(p. 637)**

ARE NOT HIS."   Boston Sunday Post, Olin Downes 8/19/20. **(p. 637)**

ARISTOTELIAN IDEAL."   NYT Magazine "Why the O'Neill Star is Rising," 3/19/61. **(p. 637)**

MODERN LIFE."   NY Tribune, "Young Boswell Interviews Eugene O'Neill," 5/24/23. **(p. 638)**

SPECIAL MATINEES.   Williams was an early member of George Pierce Baker's Harvard playwriting course. **(p. 639)**

OF MERINGUE."   2/3/20. **(p. 639)**

DIED FOR IT."   A/BG interview with Williams, 1956. **(p. 640)**

CHRONOLOGICAL TABLE OF O'NEILL'S COMPLETED PLAYS

Year Completed	Title	Year Completed	Title
1913	*A Wife for a Life*	1920	*Gold*
	The Web		*"Anna Christie"*
	Thirst		*The Emperor Jones*
1914	*Recklessness*		*Diff'rent*
	Warnings	1921	*The First Man*
	Bread and Butter		*The Hairy Ape*
	Servitude	1922	*The Fountain*
	Fog	1923	*Welded*
	Bound East for Cardiff		*All God's Chillun Got Wings*
	Abortion	1924	*Desire Under the Elms*
	The Movie Man	1925	*Marco Millions*
1915	*The Sniper*		*The Great God Brown*
	The Personal Equation	1927	*Lazarus Laughed*
1916	*Before Breakfast*		*Strange Interlude*
	Now I Ask You	1929	*Dynamo*
1917	*Ile*	1931	*Mourning Becomes Electra*
	The Long Voyage Home	1932	*Ah, Wilderness!*
	The Moon of the Caribbees	1933	*Days Without End*
	In the Zone	1939	*The Iceman Cometh*
1918	*The Rope*	1941	*Long Day's Journey Into Night*
	Beyond the Horizon	1942	*A Touch of the Poet*
	The Dreamy Kid		*Hughie*
	Where the Cross Is Made	1943	*A Moon for the Misbegotten*
1919	*The Straw*		
	Chris Christophersen		
	Shell Shock		
	Exorcism (unpublished)		

CHRONOLOGICAL TABLE OF DATE & PLACE OF FIRST PRODUCTION DURING O'NEILL'S LIFETIME (IN NEW YORK UNLESS OTHERWISE NOTED)

Thirst	Sept. 1, 1916, Wharf Theater, Provincetown, Mass
Fog	Jan. 5, 1917, Playwrights' Theater
Bound East for Cardiff	Nov. 3, 1916, Playwrights' Theater (i)
The Sniper	Feb. 16, 1917, Playwrights' Theater
Before Breakfast	Dec. 1, 1916, Playwrights' Theater
Ile	Nov. 30, 1917, Playwrights' Theater
The Long Voyage Home	Nov. 2, 1917, Playwrights' Theater

The Moon of the Caribbees	Dec. 20, 1918, Playwrights' Theater
In the Zone	Oct. 31, 1917, Comedy Theater
The Rope	Apr. 26, 1918, Playwrights' Theater
Beyond the Horizon	Feb. 3, 1920, Morosco Theater
The Dreamy Kid	Oct. 31, 1919, Playwrights' Theater
Where the Cross Is Made	Nov. 22, 1918, Playwrights' Theater
The Straw	Nov. 10, 1921, Greenwich Village Theater
Chris Christophersen	March 8, 1920, Apollo Theater, Atlantic City (ii)
Exorcism (unpublished)	March 26, 1920, Playwrights' Theater (iii)
Gold	June 1, 1921, Frazee Theater
"Anna Christie"	Nov. 2, 1921, Vanderbilt Theater
The Emperor Jones	Nov. 1, 1920, Playwrights' Theater
Diff'rent	Dec. 27, 1920 Playwrights' Theater
The First Man	March 4, 1922, Neighborhood Playhouse
The Hairy Ape	March 9, 1922, Provincetown Playhouse
The Fountain	Dec. 10, 1925, Greenwich Village Theater
Welded	March 17, 1924, Provincetown Playhouse
All God's Chillun Got Wings	May 15, 1924, Provincetown Playhouse
Desire Under the Elms	Nov. 11, 1924, Greenwich Village Theater
Marco Millions	Jan. 9, 1928, Guild Theater
The Great God Brown	Jan. 23, 1926, Greenwich Village Theater
Lazarus Laughed	Apr. 9, 1928, Pasadena Community Playhouse, Pasadena, Cal. (iv)
Strange Interlude	Jan. 30, 1928, John Golden Theater
Dynamo	Feb. 11, 1929, Martin Beck Theater
Mourning Becomes Electra	Oct. 26, 1931, Guild Theater
Ah, Wilderness!	Oct. 2, 1933, Guild Theater
Days Without End	Jan. 8, 1934, Henry Miller Theater
The Iceman Cometh	Oct. 9, 1946, Martin Beck Theater
A Moon for the Misbegotten	Feb. 20, 1947, Hartman Theater, Columbus, Ohio (v)

MAJOR PLAYS POSTHUMOUSLY PRODUCED IN NEW YORK

Long Day's Journey Into Night	Nov. 7, 1956, Helen Hayes Theater
A Touch of the Poet	Oct. 2, 1958, Helen Hayes Theater
Hughie	Dec. 22, 1964, Royale Theater
More Stately Mansions (Unfinished)	Oct. 31, 1967, Broadhurst Theater (vi)

(i)   First produced July 28, 1916, Wharf Theater, Provincetown, Mass.
(ii) Produced as *Chris* and closed out of town.
(iii) No script exists.
(iv) Not produced in New York.
(v)   Closed out of town; first produced in New York posthumously, May 2, 1957, Bijou Theater.
(vi) Play O'Neill believed he had destroyed; it was posthumously "finished" by others and presented as "by O'Neill" Oct. 31, 1967, Broadhurst Theater.

"Homage to Eugene O'Neill," an oil painting by Tennessee Williams, acquired after his death by Columbia University's Rare Book and Manuscript Library.

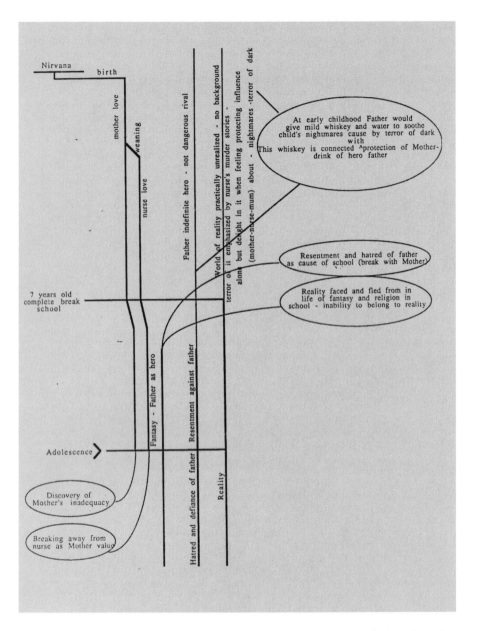

Transcription of diagram made by O'Neill, describing his family dynamics, probably dating from 1927, when he underwent a brief psychoanalysis.

ILLUSTRATIONS

James O'Neill with Brandon Tynan
COURTESY BRANDON TYNAN

EMERGING PLAYWRIGHT   *(section following page 494)*

Charles Ellis painting
COURTESY ELIZABETH BARNETT, LITERARY EXECUTOR, EDNA ST. VINCINT MILLAY
    SOCIETY, PHOTO BY CHARLES KALISCHER

John Reed with O'Neill in Provincetown
HUTCHINS HAPGOOD COLLECTION

Emma Goldman
THE NEW YORK TIMES PHOTO ARCHIVES

Terry Carlin
LOUIS SHEAFFER COLLECTION, CONNECTICUT COLLEGE

Clarence Darrow and James B. McNamara
BROWN BROS.

Wharf Theater, Provincetown
THEODORE MANN/CIRCLE IN THE SQUARE COLLECTION

Painting of Provincetown by Bror Nordfeldt
COLLECTION OF ALLEN AND SALLY McDANIEL, PHOTO COURTESY OF RICHARD
    YORK GALLERY, N.Y.

George Cram Cook and Susan Glaspell
AUTHORS' COLLECTION

Provincetown Players list of charter members
AUTHORS' COLLECTION

O'Neill in Provincetown, 1916
HARVARD UNIVERSITY, HOUGHTON LIBRARY

Louise Bryant
HARVARD UNIVERSITY, HOUGHTON LIBRARY

Hapgood family and friends
HUTCHINS HAPGOOD COLLECTION

GALLERY OF O'NEILL FRIENDS:

Mabel Dodge, BEINECKE RARE BOOK & MANUSCRIPT LIBRARY, YALE UNIVERSITY;
Neith Boyce, ADELE HELLER COLLECTION;
The Zorachs, ADELE HELLER COLLECTION;
Harry Kemp, UNITED NEWS PICTURES;
H. L. Mencken & George Jean Nathan, BROWN BROS.;
Eastman & Ida Rauh, MAX EASTMAN COLLECTION;
Edward Goodman, LAWRENCE LANGNER COLLECTION;
Floyd Dell, MAX EASTMAN COLLECTION

Scene from *Thirst*

Nude photo of Louise Bryant

First New York production of *Bound East for Cardiff*

James O'Neill in *The Wanderer*

PAGES 723 & 724:

"Homage to Eugene O'Neill" by Tennessee Williams

O'Neill diagram of family dynamics

JACKET PHOTO

INDEX

and Provincetown Players, 546,
551–577, 591, 594
and Reed, John, 545–546, 552, 562–563,
565, 566, 567–568, 570–571, 577,
578–580, 586–588, 589–591, 599,
614–616, 619–620
as reporter, 599, 615–616, 619
and *Strange Interlude*, 579
and *Thirst*, 571–572
and Trullinger, Paul, 564–565, 579
unpublished material, xvii
Bryer, Jackson, xv
Buenos Aires, 282–288
Buenos Aires *Herald*, 288
Buffalo, New York, xvi, 40–43, 44
Bull, John, xiii, 504
Burgess, Florence R., 384
Burke, Edmund, 94
Burns, Robert, 344
Burns, William J., 511–513
Burt, Frederic, 557, 569
Byrant, Sheridan, 564
Byron, George Gordon Noel, 142, 523
Byth, James. *see* Findlater-Byth, James
By Way of Obit, 532

C

Cadillac Hotel. *see* Barrett House (NY)
Cahill, Dr., 42
Cahill, Holger, 629–630
Caldwell, Zoe, xix
California house, xvii, 3–5, 7
California Theater, 85
Call, The (magazine), 414–415, 619
"Call, The" (poem), 291–292, 365
Call of the Wild, The, 407
Calms of Capricorn, The, 198
Calvary Cemetery, 102
Camblos, Henry Shaw, 252
Campbell, Alexander, 212, 437
Campbell, Mrs. Pat, 247, 553
Candida, 597–598
Canfield's (NY), 316–317
Cape Cod, 493
Cape Cod School of Art, 494
Caplan, David, 512–514
Carb, David, 576

Carlin, Terry, 514–527, 528, 567
and *An Anarchist Woman*, 518
background of, 517–518
and brother Jim, 518–520
and Catholicism, 520
and Eugene, 521, 522, 524–527, 528,
534, 547, 554–555, 556–557, 562,
571, 574, 615, 620, 621
and The Hell Hole, 516–517, 521,
524–526
homeless with Eugene, 524–525
and *The Iceman Cometh*, 514–517,
520–521
and Marie, 518, 519, 522–523
and peyote party, 517
"Carmagnole" (song), 539
Carmelite Nuns, 425–426, 428
Carpenter, Bruce, 465–466, 468, 470, 471
Carruthers, Robert (Capt.), 289
Castle Richmond, 38–39
Cataline, 171
Cather, Willa, 494
cattle ship (Buenos Aires-Durban),
285–286
Cecilia (Liverpool friend), 302–303, 305
Celebrated Case, A, 86, 90
Century Girl, The, 584
Century Theater (NY), 373
Cerf, Bennett, xi, 14–17
Cerf, Phyllis, xi
Chambermaid's Diary, A, 217
Change Your Style, 497, 552, 571
Chappell Family (New London, Conn.),
208–209
Charles Racine (ship), 267–270, 273–281,
285, 336
Charlier Institute, 164
Chasm, The, 491
Chateau d'If (France), 104
Checkhov, Anton, 470
Chicago *Daily Times*, 56
Chicago *Evening Post*, 491, 526
Chicago *Journal*, 237
Chicago *Record Herald*, 237–241
Chicago *Tribune*, 55
Chieftain (ship), 300
Childe Harold, 523
children in Eugene's plays, 407–408, 633
Children of the Sea. see Bound East for

E

F

M

S

Sailor's Opera Saloon (Buenos Aires), 283, 284, 288
Salomé, 187
Salsbury, Nate, 80, 84, 124
Saltus, Edgar, 184
Salvation Nell, 265, 431–433
Salvini, Tommaso, 57–58, 91
Samovar (NY), 586, 625
Samuels, Maurice V., 595
Sanborn, Ralph, 373
Sandburg, Carl, 487, 489
Sandy, Sarah Jane Bucknell, 125–128, 129, 133, 134, 135, 136
San Francisco, 3–5, 7–8, 61–62, 79–85, 178
San Francisco *Chronicle*, 65
San Francisco *Evening Post*, 68
San Francisco *News Letter*, 85, 94–95
Sanger, Margaret, 486
Saratoga, 81
Saratoga Club, 185
Saturday Evening Post, 539
Schleip, Hans, 186
Schmidt, Matthew A., 512–514
Schopenhauer, Arthur, 199, 243, 359
Schubert, Franz (Peter), 198
Scott, Adam, 349–350
Scott, John, 354
Scott, Maibelle, 353–362, 367, 370–371, 379, 391–392, 395, 419, 434–435, 436, 440, 559, 560
Scott, Mrs. John, 357
Scott, Sir Walter, 142
Scott, Thomas A. (Capt.), 354
Sea Fever, 291
Seaman, Alfred (Pop) Hamilton, 76–78
Sea-Mother's Son, The, 72, 275
Second Engineer, The. see Personal Equation, The
Second Story Club (New London), 199, 209, 212, 242, 350, 351, 437, 617
Selected Letters of Eugene O'Neill, xv
self-analysis, xiv, 43, 71–73, 74, 81, 82, 99, 100–101, 102, 106, 111, 116, 119, 123, 125, 127, 134, 136–137
self-analysis diagram, 124–125, 126, 135, 174

Sells Circus, 532
Sergeant, Elizabeth Shepley, 135, 142, 170, 174, 224, 503
Service, Robert W., 344
Servitude, 264, 315, 397, 443–444
Seven Arts (magazine), 607–609
Shakespeare, William, 33, 45, 50, 51, 52, 60, 144–145, 399
Sharkey's Athletic Club, Tom's (NY), 243
Shaw, George Bernard, 86, 152, 191, 208, 214–215, 229, 432, 433, 490, 541, 543, 567, 584, 597
Shay, Frank, 582, 594, 609
Shay, Jim, 209–210
Sheffield, Edith Chappell, 209
Sheldon, Edward, 265, 431–433, 476, 639
Shelton Sanatorium. *see* Fairfield County State Tuberculosis Sanatorium
"Shenandoah" (song), 278
Sheridan, Bessie, 206
Sheridan, Phil, 213, 394, 425
Sheridan, Richard Brinsley, 50
Sherman, Claire Brennan, 111, 121–122
Sherwin, Louis, 623
Sherwood, Robert, 287
"She's the Sunshine of Paradise Valley" (song), 539
Shrine of Our Lady of Lourdes, 141–142
"Shut-eye Candidate, The" (poem), 348
Sigval Bergensen Line, 269
"Silence" (poem), 555
Sinclair, Arthur, 313
Sinclair, Catherine, 48
Sinclair, Upton, 485, 487
Singer Sewing Machine Company, 284, 286
Sisk, Robert, 413
Sisters of Charity, 135, 137, 164
Sitting Bull, Chief, 124
"Six Poems" (Louise Bryant), 568
Sixty Cafe, The, 501, 502
Skjoerestad, Rolf, 276
Slade, Howard, 634–635
Slevin, James, 187
Slim. *see* Martin, James Joseph (Slim)
Sloan, John, 502
Smart Set (magazine), 610–611, 625, 628
Smith, Joseph, 348
"Smitty" (Buenos Aires friend), 284

ABOUT THE AUTHORS

ARTHUR GELB is the former managing editor of The New York Times. In the 1950's, he was assistant drama critic under Brooks Atkinson, then served as the newspaper's chief cultural correspondent, cultural editor and later as metropolitan editor. He is co-editor of *Great Lives of the Twentieth Century*, among other books. He now directs The New York Times College Scholarship Program.

BARBARA GELB is the author of *So Short a Time*, a biography of John Reed and Louise Bryant, and the one-character play, *My Gene*, based on O'Neill's widow, Carlotta Monterey, in which Colleen Dewhurst starred. She is also the author of two studies of the New York Police Department, *On the Track of Murder* and *Varnished Brass*. She has lectured extensively and has written numerous articles about the theater.